lonely

Berlin

"All you've got to do is decide to go
and the hardest part is over.

So go!"

Contents

Plan Your Trip · 4

Explore Berlin · 76

Understand Berlin · 245

Survival Guide · 287

Berlin Maps · 315

(left) **Potsdamer Platz p120** A postmodern take on an historic area

(above) **Holocaust Memorial p85** A maze of 2711 concrete plinths

(right) **Fernsehturm p110** Germany's tallest structure

Welcome to Berlin

Berlin's glamour and grit are bound to mesmerise anyone keen to explore its vibrant culture, cutting-edge architecture, fabulous food, intense parties and tangible history.

High on History

Bismarck and Marx, Einstein and Hitler, JFK and Bowie, they've all shaped – and been shaped by – Berlin, whose richly textured history stares you in the face at every turn. This is a city that staged a revolution, was headquartered by Nazis, bombed to bits, divided in two and finally reunited – and that was just in the 20th century! Walk along remnants of the Berlin Wall, marvel at the splendour of a Prussian palace, visit Checkpoint Charlie or stand in the very room where the Holocaust was planned. Berlin is like an endlessly fascinating 3D textbook where the past is very much present wherever you go.

Party Paradise

Forget about New York – Berlin is the city that truly never sleeps. Sometimes it seems as though Berliners are the lotus eaters of Germany, people who love nothing more than a good time. The city's vast party spectrum caters for every taste, budget and age group. From tiny basement clubs to industrial techno temples, chestnut-canopied beer gardens to fancy cocktail caverns, saucy cabarets to ear-pleasing symphonies – Berlin delivers hot-stepping odysseys, and not just after dark and on weekends but pretty much 24/7. Pack your stamina!

Cultural Trendsetter

When it comes to creativity, the sky's the limit in Berlin. Since the fall of the Berlin Wall, the city has become a giant lab of cultural experimentation thanks to an abundance of space, cheap rent and a free-wheeling spirit that nurtures and encourages new ideas. Top international performers grace its theatre, concert and opera stages; international art world stars like Olafur Eliasson and Jonathan Meese make their home here; and Clooney and Hanks shoot blockbusters in the German capital. High-brow, low-brow and everything in between – there's plenty of room for the full arc of expression.

Laidback Lifestyle

Berlin is a big multicultural metropolis but deep down it maintains the unpretentious charm of an international village. Locals follow the credo 'live and let live' and put greater emphasis on personal freedom and a creative lifestyle than on material wealth and status symbols. Cafes are jammed at all hours, drinking is a religious rite and clubs keep going until the wee hours or beyond. Sizewise, Berlin is pretty big but its key areas are wonderfully compact and easily navigated on foot, by bike or by using public transport.

Why I Love Berlin

By Andrea Schulte-Peevers, Author

Berlin is a bon vivant, passionately feasting on the smorgasbord of life, never taking things – or itself – too seriously. To me, this city is nothing short of addictive. It embraces me, inspires me, accepts me and makes me feel good about myself, the world and other people. I enjoy its iconic sights, its vast swaths of green, its sky bars and chic restaurants, but I love its gritty sides more. There's nothing static about Berlin: it's unpredictable, unpretentious and irresistible. And it loves you back – if you let it in.

For more about our authors, see p344.

Above: A streetside cafe-bar

Berlin's
Top 10

1

Brandenburger Tor (p84)

1 Prussian emperors, Napoleon and Hitler have marched through this neoclassical royal city gate that was once trapped east of the Berlin Wall. Since 1989 it has gone from a symbol of division and oppression to the symbol of a united Germany. The powerful landmark, which overlooks the stately Pariser Platz with its embassies and banks, is at its most atmospheric – and photogenic – at night when light bathes its stately columns and proud Goddess of Victory sculpture in a mesmerising golden glow.

⊙ *Historic Mitte*

Reichstag (p82)

2 This famous Berlin landmark has been set on fire, bombed, left to crumble, and wrapped in fabric before emerging as the home of the German parliament (the Bundestag) and focal point of the reunited country's government quarter. The plenary hall can only be seen on guided tours but, with advance booking, you're free to catch the lift to the dazzling glass dome designed by Lord Norman Foster. Enjoy not only the fabulous views, but learn about the building and surrounding landmarks on a free audio tour.

⊙ *Historic Mitte*

Berlin Wall *(p35)*

3 Few events in history have the power to move the entire world. The Kennedy assassination. The moon landing. The events of 9/11. And, of course, the fall of the Berlin Wall in 1989. If you were alive and old enough back then, you will probably remember the crowds of euphoric revellers cheering and dancing at the Brandenburg Gate. Although little is left of the physical barrier, its legacy lives on in the imagination, and in such places as Checkpoint Charlie, the Gedenkstätte Berliner Mauer and the East Side Gallery with its colourful murals. TOP LEFT: EAST SIDE GALLERY (P173)

⊙ *Berlin Wall*

Museumsinsel *(p100)*

4 Berlin's 'Louvre on the Spree', this imposing ensemble of five treasure houses is the undisputed highlight of the city's museum landscape. Declared a Unesco World Heritage site, Museum Island represents 6000 years of art and cultural history, from the Stone Age to the 19th century. Feast your eyes on majestic antiquities at the Pergamonmuseum and Altes Museum, report for an audience with Egyptian queen Nefertiti at the Neues Museum, take in 19th-century art at the Alte Nationalgalerie and marvel at medieval sculptures at the Bodemuseum. ABOVE: NEUES MUSEUM (P105)

⊙ *Museumsinsel & Alexanderplatz*

Nightlife *(p56)*

5 Berlin is your oyster when the moon's high in the sky. Cosy pubs, riverside beach bars, beer gardens, underground dives, DJ bars, snazzy hotel lounges, designer cocktail temples – with such variety, finding a party location to match your mood is not exactly a tall order. If you're not into hobnobbing with hipsters at hot-stepping bars or clubs, you could always relive the roaring twenties in a high-kicking cabaret, indulge your ears with symphonic strains in iconic concert halls or point your highbrow compass towards the opera.

🍷 *Drinking & Nightlife*

Potsdamer Platz *(p120)*

6 No other area around town better reflects the 'New Berlin' than this quarter forged from the death-strip that separated East and West Berlin for 28 years. The world's biggest construction site through much of the 1990s, Potsdamer Platz 2.0 is a postmodern take on the historic area that until WWII was Berlin's equivalent of Times Square. A cluster of plazas, offices, museums, cinemas, theatres, hotels and flats, it shows off the talents of seminal architects of our times, including Helmut Jahn and Renzo Piano.

⊙ *Potsdamer Platz & Tiergarten*

Holocaust Memorial *(p85)*

7 Listen to the sound of your footsteps and feel the presence of uncounted souls as you make your way through the massive warped labyrinth that is Germany's central memorial to the Jewish victims of the Nazi-orchestrated genocide. New York architect Peter Eisenman poignantly captures this unspeakable horror with a maze of 2711 tomblike concrete plinths of varying heights that rise from an unsettlingly wavy ground. The memorial's abstract design contrasts with the graphic and emotional exhibits in the subterranean information centre.

⊙ *Historic Mitte*

THOMAS WINZ/GETTY IMAGES

7

8

Street Art & Alternative Living *(p44)*

8 Berlin has world-class art, cultural events galore and increasingly sophisticated dining – but so do most other capital cities. What makes this metropolis different is the legendary climate of openness and tolerance that fosters experimentation, a DIY ethos and a thriving subculture. Hip and funky Kreuzberg, Friedrichshain and the northern reaches of Neukölln are hotbeds of diversity and creativity where tomorrow's trends take shape. No surprise, then, that some of the city's finest street art is brightening facades and house entrances around here.

☆ *The Berlin Art Scene*

Schloss Charlottenburg *(p201)*

9 We can pretty much guarantee that your camera will have a love affair with Berlin's largest and loveliest remaining royal palace. A late-baroque jewel inspired by Versailles, it backs up against an idyllic park, complete with carp pond, rhododendron-lined paths, two smaller palaces and a mausoleum. The palace itself is clad in a subtle yellow typical of the royal Hohenzollern family and wonderfully adorned with slender columns and geometrically arranged windows. An ornate copper-domed tower overlooks the forecourt and the imposing equestrian statue of the Great Elector Friedrich Wilhelm.

◉ *City West & Charlottenburg*

GAVIN HELLIER/GETTY IMAGES ©

Kulturforum *(p126)*

10 Conceived in the 1950s, the Kulturforum was West Berlin's answer to Museumsinsel and is an equally enthralling cluster of museums and concert halls, albeit in modern buildings. The most stunning are the Neue Nationalgalerie (New National Gallery) in a glass temple stunner by Ludwig Mies van der Rohe and Hans Scharoun's honey-coloured freeform Berliner Philharmonie. The depth and breadth of the art collections here is mind-blowing. Rembrandt to Picasso, fragile Dürer prints to a flute played by a Prussian king, famous medieval masters to German 1920s expressionists – it's all here in one neat package. ABOVE: NEUE NATIONALGALERIE (P127)

◉ *Potsdamer Platz & Tiergarten*

What's New

Museum Openings & Closures

The north wing and the Pergamonaltar at the Pergamonmuseum (p101) are closed for an extensive facelift until 2019. The Neue Nationalgalerie (p127) will also remain closed for renovation until at least 2018. New on the scene is the free Museum in der Kulturbrauerei (p188), which paints a vivid picture of daily life in East Germany. The Kunstgewerbemuseum (Museum of Decorative Arts; p126) should have re-opened by the time you're reading this.

Comeback of the City West

West Berlin's commercial and entertainment centre around Zoo Station is finally on an upswing after several high-profile openings, including the Bikini Berlin (p214) concept mall, designer hotels such as the 25hours (p242) and the Hotel am Steinplatz (p244), and restaurants and bars such as Neni (p208), Monkey Bar (p211) and Brasserie Lamazere (p211).

Unter den Linden

The grand boulevard has been turned into a giant construction zone as Berlin builds a new U-Bahn line and the Berlin City Palace over the coming years. At least the restoration of the Staatsoper Unter den Linden (State Opera House; p91) should be completed by 2015.

Berliner Stadtschloss (Berlin City Palace)

In June 2013 construction commenced on one of Europe's biggest cultural projects, the reconstruction of the Prussian royal city palace opposite Museum Island in the historic city centre. Upon completion, possibly in 2019, the so-called Humboldt-Forum will contain museums, a library and university collections. For a preview, visit the Humboldt-Box (p115).

Park am Gleisdreieck

Berlin is no slouch when it comes to city parks and in 2013 it added another huge swath of open space to its green credentials with the opening of the Park am Gleisdreieck (p155) on a former railway junction south of Potsdamer Platz.

Gedenkstätte Berliner Mauer

A work in progress since 1998, the central memorial site of German division (p186) was due to be completed in November 2014, on the 25th anniversary of the fall of the Berlin Wall. Exhibits illustrate what the Wall looked like and how it impacted on the lives of people on both sides.

Museumsinsel Masterplan

Construction has begun on the central entrance building called James-Simon-Galerie (p101). Upon completion of the masterplan, projected for 2025, the Pergamonmuseum will gain a fourth wing, and the Archaeological Promenade will connect the buildings underground.

LP12 Mall of Berlin

At press time, the opening date of Berlin's sleek and chic mega-mall (p133) with 270 stores right on Leipziger Platz was scheduled for September 2014.

Hotel Tax

A 5% city tax (p231) on hotel stays went into effect on 1 January 2014.

For more recommendations and reviews, see **lonelyplanet. com/berlin**

Need to Know

For more information, see Survival Guide (p287)

Currency
Euro (€)

Language
German

Visas
Generally not required for tourist stays of up to 90 days (or at all for EU nationals); some nationalities need a Schengen visa.

Money
ATMs widespread. Cash is king; credit cards are not widely used.

Mobile Phones
Mobile phones operate on GSM900/1800. Local SIM cards can be used in unlocked European and Australian phones. Most US multiband phones also work in Germany.

Time
Central European Time (GMT/ UTC plus one hour). Daylight savings: last Sunday in March to last Sunday in October.

Tourist Information
Visit Berlin (www.visitberlin.de) has branches at the airports, the main train station, the Brandenburg Gate, the TV Tower and on Kurfürstendamm, and a **call centre** (☑2500 2333) for information/bookings.

Daily Costs

Budget:
Less than €80

➡ Dorm bed or peer-to-peer rental €10–30

➡ Doner kebab €2–3

➡ Club cover €5–12

➡ Public transport day pass €6.70

Midrange:
€80–€200

➡ Private apartment or double room €80–120

➡ Two-course dinner with wine €25–40

➡ Guided tour €10–15

➡ Museum admission €20

Top end:
More than €200

➡ Upmarket apartment or double in top-end hotel from €150

➡ Gourmet two-course dinner with wine €70

➡ Cab ride €20

➡ Cabaret ticket €50–80

Advance Planning

Two to three months Book tickets for the Berliner Philharmonie, the Staatsoper, Sammlung Boros and top-flight events.

Up to one month Book online tickets for the Reichstag dome, the Neues Museum and the Pergamonmuseum.

Up to two weeks Reserve a table at trendy restaurants, especially for weekend dinners.

Useful Websites

Lonely Planet (www.lonelyplanet.com) Destination information, hotel bookings, traveller forum and more.

Visit Berlin (www.visitberlin.de) Official tourist authority info.

Museumsportal (www.museums portal-berlin.de) Gateway to the city's museums.

Resident Advisor (www. residentadvisor.net) Guide to parties and clubbing.

Exberliner (www.exberliner. com) Expat-geared monthly English-language Berlin culture magazine.

WHEN TO GO

July and August are warm but often rainy. May, June, September and October offer plenty of festivals and cooler weather. Winters are cold and quiet.

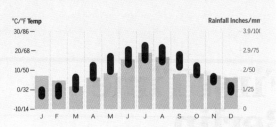

°C/°F Temp

30/86 —		3.9/100
20/68 —		2.9/75
10/50 —		2/50
0/32 —		1/25
-10/14 —	J F M A M J J A S O N D	0

Rainfall Inches/mm

Arriving in Berlin

Tegel Airport TXL express bus to Alexanderplatz (40 minutes) and bus X9 for City West (eg Kurfürstendamm 20 minutes) €2.60; taxi €20–25.

Schönefeld Airport Airport-Express trains (RB14 or RE7) to central Berlin twice hourly (20 to 30 minutes) and S9 train every 20 minutes for Friedrichshain and Prenzlauer Berg €3.20; taxi €40.

Hauptbahnhof Main train station in the city centre and served by S-Bahn, U-Bahn, tram, bus and taxi.

Zentraler Omnibus Bahnhof (ZOB) The central bus station is on the western city edge. U-Bahn U2 to city centre (eg Bahnhof Zoo 8 minutes, Alexanderplatz 28 minutes) €2.60; taxi €18.

For much more on **arrival** see p288

Getting Around

➡ **U-Bahn** Most efficient way to travel; operates 4am to 12.30am and all night Friday, Saturday and public holidays. From Sunday to Thursday, half-hourly night buses take over in the interim.

➡ **S-Bahn** Not as frequent as U-Bahn trains but fewer stops and thus useful for longer distances. Same operating hours as the U-Bahn.

➡ **Bus** Slow but useful for sightseeing on the cheap. Run frequently 4.30am to 12.30am; half-hourly night buses in the interim; MetroBuses (M1, M19) operate 24/7.

➡ **Tram** Only operate in the eastern districts; MetroTrams (M1, M2) run 24/7.

➡ **Cycling** Designated bike lanes and rental stations abound; bikes are fine in designated U-Bahn and S-Bahn carriages.

➡ **Taxi** Can be hailed and are fairly inexpensive; avoid during daytime rush hour.

➡ For information and trip planning see www.bvg.de.

For much more on **getting around** see p290

Sleeping

There are over 135,000 hotel rooms but the most desirable properties book up quickly, especially in summer and around major holidays, festivals and trade shows; prices soar and reservations are essential during these periods. Otherwise, rates are mercifully low by Western capital standards. Options range from luxurious ports of call to ho-hum international chains, trendy designer boutique hotels to Old Berlin-style B&Bs, happening hostels to handy self-catering apartments.

Useful Websites

➡ **Visit Berlin** (www.visitberlin. de) Official tourist office books rooms at partner hotels.

➡ **Hostelworld** (www. hostelworld.com) Hostel and budget hotel bookings.

➡ **HRS** (www.hrs.com) Good for last-minute bargains.

➡ **Booking.com** (www. booking.com) General site with community reviews.

➡ **Lonely Planet** (www. lonelyplanet.com/hotels) Reviews of Lonely Planet's top choices.

For much more on **sleeping** see p229

First Time Berlin

For more information, see Survival Guide (p287)

Checklist

➡ Make sure your passport is valid for at least four months after your arrival date

➡ Check the airline baggage restrictions

➡ Inform your debit-/credit-card company of your upcoming trip

➡ Organise travel insurance

➡ Check if your mobile/cell phone will work in Germany and the cost of roaming

➡ If you're taking prescription medicine, bring enough for your entire trip and put it in your carry-on

What to Pack

➡ Good walking shoes – Berlin is best appreciated on foot

➡ Umbrella or rain jacket – rain is possible any time of year

➡ Small day pack

➡ Travel adapter plug

Top Tips for Your Trip

➡ Plan on doing most of your sightseeing by foot. Only by walking will you truly experience Berlin at eye level. For covering larger areas quickly, rent a bicycle. Otherwise, public transportation is the best way of getting around.

➡ Don't pack too much sightseeing into a day – Berlin's spirit reveals itself to those walking around a neighbourhood, people-watching in a park or lounging in a cafe.

➡ There is no curfew, making it easy to pace your alcohol intake on bar-hops and in clubs to keep your stamina.

➡ When picking a place to stay, consider which type of experience you're most keen on – shopping, clubbing, museums, outdoors, urban cool, partying, history – then choose a neighbourhood to match. For ideas, check our Where to Stay table on p232.

What to Wear

The short answer is: whatever you want. Berlin is an extremely casual city when it comes to fashion. Basically anything goes, including jeans at the opera or a little black dress in a beer garden. Individuality trumps conformity and expensive labels at any time. In fact, flaunting your own style – any style – is often the ticket for making it past a picky club bouncer. Venues or restaurants with official dress codes are extremely rare.

Berlin weather is immensely changeable, even in summer, so make sure you bring layers of clothing. A waterproof coat and sturdy shoes are a good idea for all-weather sightseeing. Winters can get fiercely cold, so be sure you bring your favourite gloves, hat, boots and heavy coat.

Be Forewarned

➡ Credit card use is not common. Expect to pay in cash, especially in bars and at restaurants.

➡ After a long club night, save some money for the cab home.

➡ Don't travel without a valid public transportation ticket – getting caught results in a painful €40 fine.

Money

Germany is still largely a cash-based society. International hotel chains, high-end restaurants, department stores and fancy boutiques usually accept credit cards, but make it a habit to enquire first. MasterCard and Visa are more widely accepted, American Express rarely and Diner's Club almost never.

ATMs are ubiquitous in all neighbourhoods. Be wary of those not affiliated with major banks as they may charge exorbitant transaction fees. ATMs do not recognise pins with more than four digits.

Debit cards featuring the MasterCard or Visa logos are fairly widely used. Chip-and-pin is the norm for card transactions – few places accept signatures as an alternative.

For more information, see p295.

Taxes & Refunds

Value-added tax (VAT; *Mehrwertsteuer*) is a 19% sales tax levied on most goods. The rate for services is usually 7% and is always included in the price. If your permanent residence is outside the EU, you may be able to partially claim back the VAT you paid on purchased goods.
See p297 for details.

Tipping

➔ **Hotels** Porters €1 to €2 per bag, room cleaners €2 per day
➔ **Pubs, bars and beer gardens** If self-service none, for bartenders and servers 10%
➔ **Restaurants** 5% to 10%

Also see p296 for details.

Language

You can easily have a great time in Berlin without speaking a word of German. In fact, some bars and restaurants in expat-heavy Kreuzberg and Neukölln have entirely English- (and sometimes Spanish-) speaking staff. Restaurant and cafe menus are usually in German only. See Language (p299) for more information.

 Do you accept credit cards?
Nehmen Sie Kreditkarten?
nay·men zee kre·deet·kar·ten

Cash is still king in Germany, so don't assume you'll be able to pay by credit card – it's best to enquire first.

 Which beer would you recommend?
Welches Bier empfehlen Sie?
vel·khes beer emp·fay·len zee

Who better to ask for advice on beer than the Germans, whether at a beer garden, hall, cellar or on a brewery tour?

 Can I get this without meat?
Kann ich das ohne Fleisch bekommen?
kan ikh das aw·ne flaish be·ko·men

In the land of *Wurst* and *Schnitzel* it may be difficult to find a variety of vegetarian meals, especially in smaller towns.

 A (non)smoking table, please.
Einen (Nicht)rauchertisch, bitte.
ai·nen (nikht·)row·kher·tish bi·te

Germany and Austria have only partial smoking bans, so you may want to choose where to sit in cafes, bars and restaurants.

5 **Do you run original versions?**
Spielen auch Originalversionen?
shpee·len owkh o·ri·gi·nahl·fer·zi·aw·nen

German cinemas usually run movies dubbed into German – look for a cinema that runs subtitled original versions.

Etiquette

Although Berlin is fairly informal, there are a few general rules worth keeping in mind when meeting strangers.

➔ **Greetings** Shake hands and say 'Guten Morgen' (before noon), 'Guten Tag' (between noon and 6pm) or 'Guten Abend' (after 6pm). Use the formal 'Sie' (you) with strangers and only switch to the informal 'du' and first names if invited to do so. With friends and children, use first names and 'du'.

➔ **Asking for help** Germans use the same word – *Entschuldigung* – to say 'excuse me' (to attract attention) and 'sorry' (to apologise).

➔ **Eating and drinking** At table, say 'Guten Appetit' before digging in. Germans hold the fork in the left hand and the knife in the right hand. To signal that you have finished eating, lay your knife and fork parallel across your plate. If drinking wine, the proper toast is 'Zum Wohl', with beer it's 'Prost'.

Top Itineraries

Day One

Historic Mitte (p80)

 One day in Berlin? Follow this whirlwind itinerary to take in all the key sights. Book ahead for an early lift ride up to the dome of the **Reichstag**, then snap a picture of the **Brandenburg Gate** before exploring the maze of the **Holocaust Memorial** and admiring the contemporary architecture of **Potsdamer Platz**. View the **Berlin Wall remnants**, then head to **Checkpoint Charlie** to ponder the full extent of the Cold War madness.

> **Lunch** Renew your energies at Augustiner am Gendarmenmarkt (p94).

Historic Mitte (p80)

After lunch, soak up the glory of **Gendarmenmarkt**, drop by **Fassbender & Rausch** for a chocolate treat and get a dose of retail therapy at the **Friedrichstadtpassagen**. Follow Unter den Linden east to **Museumsinsel** and spend at least an hour marvelling at the antiquities in the **Pergamonmuseum**. Beer-o'clock! Head over to **Strandbar Mitte** in the Scheunenviertel.

> **Dinner** There are many enticing dinner spots in the Scheunenviertel (p141).

Scheunenviertel (p134)

After dinner, stroll over to the all-ages **Clärchens Ballhaus** for a spin on the dance floor or process the day's impressions over night-cap drinks at **Butcher's** or wine at **Maxim**.

Day Two

Prenzlauer Berg (p184)

 Spend a couple of hours coming to grips with what life in Berlin was like when the Wall still stood by exploring the **Gedenkstätte Berliner Mauer**. Take a quick spin around **Mauerpark**, then grab a coffee at **Bonanza Coffee Heroes** and poke around the boutiques on Kastanienallee.

> **Lunch** W - der Imbiss (p194) or District Môt (p141) are buzzy pit stops.

Museumsinsel & Alexanderplatz (p98)

Start the afternoon by budgeting at least an hour for your audience with Queen Nefertiti and other treasures at the stunning **Neues Museum**, then relax while letting the sights drift by on a one-hour **river cruise** around Museumsinsel. Pop into the nearby **Humboldt-Box** to find out about the giant construction site next to the museums (hint: it's the reconstruction of the Prussian royal city palace) and enjoy the views over a coffee or cocktail from the top-floor cafe.

> **Dinner** Head to Kreuzberg and dine riverside at Spindler & Klatt (p164).

Kreuzberg & Neukölln (p151)

 After dinner, find your favourite libation station along Schlesische Strasse, or shake your booty at **Chalet** or the hipster waterfront **Club der Visionäre**.

Day Three

City West & Charlottenburg (p199)

 Day three starts at **Schloss Charlottenburg**, where the Neuer Flügel (New Wing) and the palace garden are essential stops. Take the bus to Zoologischer Garten and meditate upon the futility of war at the **Kaiser-Wilhelm-Gedächtniskirche**, then – assuming it's not Sunday – satisfy your shopping cravings along **Kurfürstendamm** and its side streets. Keep your wallet handy and drop by shopping malls **Bikini Berlin** and **KaDeWe**.

 Lunch Enjoy a casual lunch in the KaDeWe (p213) food hall.

Kreuzberg & Neukölln (p151)

Spend an hour or two at the amazing Daniel Libeskind–designed **Jüdisches Museum**, then go local on a stroll down Bergmannstrasse, building in a cafe stop for a pick-me-up. Follow your nostrils to the **Marheineke Markthalle**, perhaps picking up some gourmet treats. Then either amble east along the Landwehrkanal or take the U-Bahn to Schönleinstrasse.

Dinner Make reservations at eins44 (p163), Neukölln's new hot spot.

Kreuzberg & Neukölln (p151)

You're already in party central, so hit the bars in Neukölln (**Das TiER** is recommended), then grab a cab to **Prince Charles** if you want to extend your evening.

Day Four

Potsdam (p216)

 There's plenty more to do in Berlin proper, but we recommend you spend the better part of the day exploring the parks and royal palaces in Potsdam, a mere 40-minute S-Bahn ride away. Buy online tickets for your favourite time slot to see **Schloss Sanssouci**, a rococo jewel of a palace. Afterwards, explore the surrounding park and its many smaller palaces at leisure. The **Chinesisches Haus** is a must-see.

Lunch Have lunch at the exotic Drachenhaus (p218) in the park.

Potsdam (p216)

Continue your park explorations or head to Potsdam's old town for a spin around the **Holländisches Viertel** (Dutch Quarter). If you've still got room, have a *Flammkuche* (French pizza) at **Maison Charlotte**, otherwise head back to Berlin and enjoy a well-deserved drink at **Prater** beer garden.

Dinner Pull up a stool at Prenzlauer Berg's lovely Umami (p194).

Prenzlauer Berg (p184)

After dinner, enjoy a stroll around beautiful Kollwitzplatz. Still got stamina? Turn your evening into a bar-hop, perhaps stopping at buzzy **August Fengler** or classy **Becketts Kopf**.

If You Like...

Museums

Pergamonmuseum A treasure trove of monumental architecture from ancient civilisations. (p101)

Neues Museum Pay your respects to Queen Nefertiti, star of the Egyptian collection, then explore other priceless artefacts from ancient Troy and elsewhere. (p105)

Jüdisches Museum Comprehensive exhibits going beyond the Holocaust in tracing the rich history of Jews in Germany. (p153)

Museum für Naturkunde Meet giant dinos in Berlin's own 'Jurassic Park', then learn about the universe, evolution and even the anatomy of a housefly. (p140)

Deutsches Technikmuseum Plenty of planes, trains, boats and automobiles plus the world's first computer and other techno gems. (p155)

Clubbing

Prince Charles Stylish sounds and cocktails in a former swimming pool. (p165)

Ritter Butzke Labyrinthine party house for extended electro-house dance-a-thons. (p165)

://about blank Wild, trashy, unpredictable and with a great garden for daytime chilling. (p181)

Clärchens Ballhaus Salsa, tango, ballroom, disco and swing's the thing in this grand retro ballroom. (p145)

House of Weekend Views and barbecue on rooftop terrace, top DJs and grown-up eye candy on main floor. (p117)

MICHAEL TAYLOR/GETTY IMAGES ©

Display at Flohmarkt am Mauerpark (p197)

Berghain/Panorama Bar Big, bad Berghain is still Berlin's dancing den of iniquity. (p181)

Views

Fernsehturm Check off the landmarks from the needle-like TV Tower, Germany's tallest building. (p110)

Reichstag Dome Book ahead for the lift to the landmark glass dome atop German's historic parliament building. (p82)

Panoramapunkt Catch Europe's fastest lift at Potsdamer Platz for top views of the eastern city. (p121)

Weltballon Berlin Soar above Berlin in this tethered hot-air balloon near Checkpoint Charlie. (p96)

Berliner Dom Climb into Berlin's largest church dome for gobsmacking views of Museum Island and construction of the Berlin City Palace. (p115)

Monkey Bar Exotic cocktails with a view of the Berlin Zoo from the 10th floor of the 25hours Hotel. (p211)

Cold War History

Gedenkstätte Berliner Mauer Everything you wanted to know about the Berlin Wall in a 1.4km-long indoor-outdoor exhibit. (p186)

Stasimuseum Learn about the machinations of East Germany's secret police in its historic headquarters. (p176)

Stasi Prison Take a tour for a behind-the-scenes look at East Berlin's most notorious prison. (p176)

East Side Gallery The longest remaining stretch of Berlin Wall, turned art canvas by more than 100 artists. (p173)

Tränenpalast Connect with the emotional impact of the Berlin Wall at this 'Palace of Tears' border-crossing pavilion. (p92)

WWII Sites

Topographie des Terrors Peels away the layers of brutality of the Nazi regime on the site of the SS and Gestapo command centres. (p89)

Gedenkstätte Deutscher Widerstand Tells the stories of the brave German Nazi resistance, including Stauffenberg's failed 'Operation Valkyrie'. (p123)

Haus der Wannsee-Konferenz Get shivers while standing in the very room where Nazi leaders discussed the 'Final Solution'. (p226)

Sachsenhausen A visit to one of Nazi Germany's first concentration camps, in Oranienburg just north of Berlin, will leave no one untouched. (p222)

Deutsch-Russisches Museum Berlin-Karlshorst The signing of the Wehrmacht's unconditional surrender, ending WWII, took place here. (p225)

Bold Architecture

Jüdisches Museum Daniel Libeskind's astonishing zigzag-shaped architectural metaphor for Jewish history. (p153)

Neues Museum David Chipperfield's reconstructed New Museum ingeniously blends old and new into something bold and beautiful. (p105)

Sony Center Helmut Jahn's svelte glass-and-steel complex is the most striking piece of architecture on Potsdamer Platz. (p120)

IM Pei Bau Relentlessly geometrical, glass-spiral-fronted

For more top Berlin spots, see the following:
➡ Eating (p50)
➡ Drinking & Nightlife (p56)
➡ Gay & Lesbian Berlin (p64)
➡ Entertainment (p68)
➡ Shopping (p73)

PLAN YOUR TRIP IF YOU LIKE...

museum annexe by the 'Mandarin of Modernism'. (p86)

Quirky Experiences

Monsterkabinett Descend into a dark and bizarre underworld inhabited by a small army of endearingly spooky mechanical monsters. (p140)

Madame Claude Reality is literally flipped on its head in this kooky bar and concert space where the furniture hangs from the ceiling. (p167)

Badeschiff Cool off in summer or heat up in winter in this river barge turned swimming pool. (p155)

Roses The wildest, wackiest and campest bar in Kreuzberg (hint: pink fur on the walls). (p161)

Monster Ronson's Ichiban Karaoke Loosen your throat and your inhibitions to hang with the crowd. (p182)

Art Collections

Gemäldegalerie An Aladdin's cave of Old Masters has heads turning in its expansive Kulturforum space. (p123)

Sammlung Boros World-class private collection of contemporaries in a rambling WWII bunker. (p138)

Hamburger Bahnhof Sweeping survey of post-1950 global art in a spectacularly converted train station. (p136)

Museum Berggruen Priceless Picassos plus works by Klee and Giacometti in a newly expanded building. (p205)

Brücke-Museum Groundbreaking canvases by 'the Bridge', Germany's first modern-artist group (1905–13). (p225)

Bauhaus Archiv Showcase of works by key teachers of the school that was the midwife of modern architecture and design. (p129)

Royal Encounters

Schloss Charlottenburg Inspired by Versailles, this pretty Prussian power display delivers a glimpse into the sumptuous lifestyles of the rich and royal. (p201)

Schloss Sanssouci This most famous palace in Park Sanssouci drips in opulence and overlooks vine-draped terraces and a big fountain. (p228)

Berliner Dom The royal court church has impressive dimensions, a palatial design and elaborately carved sarcophagi for the remains of kings and queens. (p115)

Humboldt-Box Get a preview of how the replica Berlin City Palace, currently under construction, will fit within the historic centre. (p115)

Music

Berliner Philharmonie Berlin's most iconic classical concert venue and home of the world-famous Berliner Philharmoniker. (p133)

Konzerthaus This Schinkel-built jewel graces Gendarmenmarkt

and is a fabulous concert venue. (p96)

Sonntagskonzerte Enjoy intimate concerts amid the faded glamour of a century-old mirror-clad ballroom. (p147)

Astra Kulturhaus This mid-size concert hall with commie-era decor draws big rock, pop and electro names. (p182)

Magnet Club Good chance to see tomorrow's headliners today, plus dance parties till dawn. (p169)

Markets

Flohmarkt am Mauerpark Gets deluged with visitors in summer but still offers a primo urban archaeology experience. (p197)

Nowkoelln Flowmarkt Less crowded hipster market with lots of handmade treasures and impromptu concerts. (p170)

Türkenmarkt Berlin meets Bosphorus at this bustling canalside farmers market with budget-priced produce. (p169)

Kollwitzplatzmarkt Discerning gourmets can source the finest morsels for that ultimate picnic. (p197)

Flohmarkt am Boxhagener Platz Treasure-hunting grounds with plenty of entertainment, cafes and people-watching. (p182)

Tours

Fat Tire Bike Tours An eclectic roster including English-language tours for foodies, history buffs and urban explorers. (p292)

Trabi Safari Turn the clock back while driving yourself around the city in an original East German Trabant car. (p293)

Berliner Unterwelten Get a look at Berlin from below as you explore a dark and dank WWII bunker. (p293)

Berlin Music Tours Find out what Bowie, U2, Depeche Mode and other seminal musicians were up to in Berlin. (p293)

Walking Tours Discover Berlin in a nutshell on a general walk – or opt for a themed tour for a more in-depth experience. (p292)

Parks & Gardens

Tiergarten Take pleasure in getting lost amid the lawns, trees and paths of one of the world's largest city parks. (p129)

Schlossgarten Charlottenburg Stake out a picnic spot near the carp and ponder royal splendours. (p201)

Park Sanssouci Find your favourite corner away from the crowds for a little time 'without cares'. (p216)

Volkspark Friedrichshain Rambling 'people's park' offering plenty of diversions and covering two 'mountains' made from WWII debris. (p174)

Viktoriapark Pint-sized park atop Berlin's highest 'peak', the 66m-high Kreuzberg; with beer garden and playground. (p155)

A Touch of Luxury

Dinner at a Michelin restaurant There's over a dozen to choose from, including Reinstoff, (p143) Tim Raue (p95) and Facil (p132).

Customised shopping at Galeries Lafayette Let the personal shopper put together the perfect outfit just for you. (p97)

Private lifestyle tour with Berlinagenten Feel like a Berlin insider as your guide takes you

MICHAEL TAYLOR/GETTY IMAGES ©

Above: Original East German Trabant car

Below: Cyclist in Tiergarten (p129)

JOHN FREEMAN/GETTY IMAGES ©

to the city's culinary, cultural, party and shopping hot spots. (p293)

Naughty Berlin

KitKatClub Dive in and be as nice or nasty as you desire – but do follow the dress code. (p168)

Insomnia Worship at the altar of hedonism at this sassy, sexy dance club with performances and playrooms. (p168)

Schwarzer Reiter Classy purveyor of anything boys and girls with imagination might need for a fun encounter. (p150)

Lab.oratory *The* place for gays to live out their most frisky, completely uncensored, fantasies. (p182)

1920s & Cabaret

Chamäleon Varieté Intimate former ballroom delivering an alchemy of acrobatics, artistry and sex appeal. (p147)

Bar Jeder Vernunft Gorgeous mirrored tent that makes you feel as if you're on the set of *Cabaret*. (p213)

Friedrichstadtpalast Europe's largest revue theatre has long-legged beauties putting on sparkly Old Vegas–style shows. (p148)

1. Absinth Depot Berlin Make a date with the 'green fairy' at this eccentric libation station. (p150)

Hotel Askanischer Hof Channel 1920s glamour by bedding down in chintz-laden rooms filled with frills and antiques. (p242)

Month by Month

January

New Year's Eve may be wrapped up, but nighttime hot spots show no signs of slowing down, especially during Fashion Week. Cold weather invites extended museum visits and foraging at the International Grüne Woche ('Green Week') food fair.

🔒 Berlin Fashion Week

Twice a year (again in July), international fashion folk book up all the trendy hotels (and restaurants) while here to present or assess next season's threads. See www.fashion-week-berlin.com for public events.

✗ Internationale Grüne Woche

Find out about the latest food trends and gorge on global morsels at this nine-day fair (www.gruenewoche.de) for food, agriculture and gardening.

February

Days are still dark but Berlin perks up when glamour comes to town during the famous film festival. A full theatre, opera, concert and party schedule also tempts people out of the house.

🎬 Berlinale

Berlin's international film festival (www.berlinale.de) draws stars, starlets, directors, critics and the world's A-to-Z-list celebrities for two weeks of screenings and parties around town. The lucky ones go home with a Golden or Silver Bear.

March

Could there be spring in the air? This is still a good time to see the sights without the crowds, but hotel rooms fill to capacity during the big tourism fair.

🎬 Internationale Tourismus Börse

Take a virtual trip around the globe at the world's largest international travel expo (www.itb-berlin.de); it's trade-only during the week but open to the public at the weekend.

☆ MaerzMusik

'Music' or 'soundscapes'? You decide after a day at this contemporary music festival (www.berlinerfestspiele.de) that explores and celebrates a boundary-pushing palette of sounds – from orchestral symphonies to experimental recitals.

April

Life starts moving outdoors as cafe tables appear on pavements and you start seeing budding trees on walks in the park. Hotels get busy over the Easter holidays.

🎬 Achtung Berlin

Flicks about Berlin, and at least partially produced in the city, compete for the New Berlin Film Award at this festival (achtungberlin.de). Screenings are often attended by writers, directors, producers and actors.

☆ Festtage

Daniel Barenboim, music director of Berlin's internationally renowned Staatsoper opera house, brings the world's finest conductors, soloists and orchestras together for this 10-day highbrow hoedown of gala concerts and operas (www.staatsoper-berlin.de).

✯ Gallery Weekend

Join collectors, critics and other fellow art-aficionados in keeping tabs on the Berlin art scene on a free hop around 40 of the city's best galleries (www.galleryweekend-berlin.de) held over a three-day weekend.

May

Spring is in, making this a fabulous month to visit Berlin. Time for beer gardens, picnics and walks among blossoming trees. White asparagus appears in markets and on menus. Don't forget your sunglasses!

✯ Lange Nacht der Museen

Culture meets entertainment during the Long Night of the Museums (www.lange-nacht-dermuseen.de) when around 80 museums welcome visitors between 6pm and 2am. Tickets are also good the following day.

✯ Karneval der Kulturen

Every Whitsuntide (Pentecost) weekend, the Carnival of Cultures (www.karnevalberlin.de) celebrates Berlin's multicultural tapestry with four days of music, dance, art and culture, culminating in a raucous

parade of flamboyantly dressed performers shimmying through the streets of Kreuzberg.

☆ Theatertreffen

The Berlin Theatre Meeting is a three-week showcase of new productions by emerging and established German-language ensembles from Germany, Austria and Switzerland (www.theatertreffen-berlin.de).

🍺 Berlin Craft Bier Fest

Since 2013 this free festival (www.braufest-berlin.de) has celebrated Berlin's growing craft-beer scene with two days of tastings, entertainment and an after-show party. The same organisers bring an international cast of craft brewers to town for Braufest Berlin in September.

June

Festival season kicks into high gear around the summer solstice with plenty of alfresco

events, thanks to a rising temperature gauge.

✯ Berlin Biennale

This biennial curated forum for contemporary art explores international trends and invites newcomers to showcase their work around town for about eight weeks (www.berlinbiennale.de). Next in 2016.

☆ Fête de la Musique

Summer starts with good vibrations thanks to hundreds of free concerts during this global music festival (www.fetedelamusique.de) that first came online in Paris in 1982. Held each year on 21 June.

✯ Christopher Street Day

No matter what your sexual persuasion, come out and paint the town pink at this huge pride parade (www.csd-berlin.de/en) featuring floats, often decorated with queer political statements and filled with naked torsos writhing to loud techno music.

MAY DAY/MYFEST

May Day demonstrations in Berlin used to be riotous affairs with heavily armed police and leftist groups facing off against each other in the district of Kreuzberg, complete with flying stones and burning cars. Although an official 'Revolutionary May Day' demonstration still draws as many as 15,000 people of an anti-capitalist, anti-fascist persuasion, the event has been considerably more peaceful in recent years. This is partly due to an enormous police presence and partly because of an alternative, largely unpolitical festival called Myfest that's been held in Kreuzberg since 2003. It runs all day from noon to midnight. The actual Revolutionary May Day demonstration starts at 6pm at Lausitzer Platz. RevolutionaryBerlin Tours (www.revolutionaeresberlin.wordpress.com) runs English-language walking tours about the history of the May Day Riots.

🎎 48 Hours Neukölln

For one long weekend Neukölln's multicultural denizens transform stores, courtyards, parks, sidewalks, galleries, bars and other spaces into an offbeat art and cultural showcase (www.48-stunden-neukoelln.de).

July

Hot summer days send Berliners scurrying to the lakes in town or the surrounding countryside. Gourmets rejoice in the bounty of fresh local produce in the markets. Expect long lines at main attractions.

☆ Classic Open Air Gendarmenmarkt

Six nights, six alfresco concerts – from opera to pop – delight an adoring crowd hunkered on bleachers before the palatial backdrop of the Konzerthaus (www.classicopenair.de).

☆ Wassermusik

The Haus der Kulturen der Welt makes waves with this popular series of water-themed concerts (www.hkw.de/wassermusik) held on its roof terrace and combined with related events like markets and movies.

August

More outdoor fun than anyone can handle with concerts in parks, daytime clubbing, languid boat rides, beach-bar partying, lake swimming and a huge beer festival.

Top: Christmas market at Gendarmenmarkt (p87)
Bottom: Karneval der Kulturen (p25)

Berliner Bierfestival

Who needs Oktoberfest when you can have the 'world's longest beer garden' (www.bierfestival-berlin.de)? As the bands play on, pick your poison from some 340 breweries representing 90 countries with over 2000 beers along 2.2km of Karl-Marx-Allee.

☆ Tanz im August

Step out gracefully to this two-week dance festival (www.tanzimaugust.de) that attracts loose-limbed talent and highly experimental choreography from around the globe.

September

Kids are back in school but there's still plenty of partying to be done and often fine weather to enjoy it. As days get shorter, the new theatre, concert and opera season begins.

☆ Berlin Music Week

This festival-conference combo (www.berlin-music-week.de) brings together the music trade and global performers over four days. Old hands and tomorrow's headliners take over the city's best clubs in Friedrichshain and Kreuzberg. The party culminates with the weekend-long Berlin Music Festival at Tempelhof Airport.

☆ Berlin Art Week

Inaugurated in 2012 this contemporary art fair (www.berlinartweek.de) brings together galleries and artists with the hotshots of the international scene.

Berlin Marathon

Sweat it out with the other 40,000 runners or just cheer 'em on during Germany's biggest street race (www.berlin-marathon.com), which has seen nine world records set since 1977.

☆ Musikfest Berlin

World-renowned orchestras, choirs, conductors and soloists come together for 21 days of concerts (www.berlinerfestspiele.de) at the Philharmonie and other venues.

October

It's getting nippy again and trees start shedding their summer coats, but Berlin keeps a bright disposition and not only during the Festival of Lights.

☆ Festival of Lights

For two weeks Berlin is all about 'lightseeing' during this shimmering festival (www.festival-of-lights.de) when historic landmarks such as the TV Tower, the Berliner Dom and the Brandenburg Gate sparkle with illuminations, projections and fireworks.

☆ Porn Film Festival

Vintage porn, Japanese porn, indie porn, sci-fi porn – the 'Berlinale' of sex (www.pornfilmfestivalberlin.de) brings alternative skin flicks out of the smut corner and onto the big screen.

November

A great time to visit if you don't like crowds but are keen on snapping up hotel bargains. Weatherwise it's not the prettiest of months.

☆ BerMuDa

A celebration of electronic dance music, BerMuDa (Berlin Music Days) brings the world's best DJs to Berlin's top clubs for sweaty dance-a-thons (www.bermuda-berlin.de).

☆ JazzFest Berlin

This top-rated jazz festival (www.berlinerfestspiele.de) has doo-wopped in Berlin since 1964 and presents fresh and big-time talent in dozens of performances all over town.

December

Days are short and cold but the mood is festive, thanks to dressed-up shop windows, illuminated streets and facades, and Christmas markets redolent with the aroma of roast almonds and mulled wine.

☆ Christmas Markets

Pick up shimmering ornaments or indulge in mulled wine at dozens of yuletide markets held throughout the city.

☆ Silvester

New Year's Eve is the time to hug strangers, coo at fireworks, guzzle bubbly straight from the bottle and generally misbehave. The biggest party is at the Brandenburg Gate.

With Kids

Travelling to Berlin with kids can be child's play, especially if you keep a light schedule and involve them in day-to-day planning. There's plenty to keep youngsters occupied, from zoos to kid-oriented museums. Parks and imaginative playgrounds abound in all neighbourhoods, as do public pools.

Legoland Discovery Centre (p121)

Museums

Museum für Naturkunde (Museum of Natural History)

Meet giant dinosaurs, travel through space back to the beginning of time and find out why zebras are striped in this wonderful museum (p140).

Science Center Spectrum

Toddlers to teens get to play, experience and learn about such concepts as balance, weight, water, air and electricity while pushing buttons, pulling levers and otherwise engaging in dozens of hands-on science experiments (p155).

Deutsches Technikmuseum (German Museum of Technology)

Next to the Science Center Spectrum, the collection here is so vast, it is best to concentrate time and energy on two or three sections that interest your tech-loving kids the most. The one-hour kid-geared audioguide tour provides a good introduction (p155).

Madame Tussauds

Kids of any age are all smiles when posing with the waxen likeness of their favourite pop star or celluloid celebrity (p90).

Legoland Discovery Centre

The milk-tooth set delights in this Lego wonderland with rides, entertainment and interactive stations (p121).

Computerspielemuseum (Computer Games Museum)

Teens can get their kicks in this universe of computer games – from Pac-Man to World of Warcraft (p175).

Mauermuseum (Wall Museum)

Teenagers with an interest in history and a decent attention span may enjoy the ingenious homemade contraptions used to escape from East Germany (p92).

Loxx am Alex Miniatur Welten Berlin

Berlin in miniature built around a huge model railway (p112).

Labyrinth Kindermuseum

Slip into a fantasy world while learning about tolerance, working together and just having fun. See www.kindermuseum-labyrinth.de.

Parks, Pools & Playgrounds

Park am Gleisdreieck

This brand-new family-friendly park (p155) is packed with fun zones including adventure playgrounds, basketball courts, a huge skate park and a nature garden.

Kollwitzplatz

This square (p188) sports three playgrounds for different age groups, including one with giant wooden toys. All get busy in the afternoon and on weekends. Cafes and ice-cream parlours are just a hop, skip and jump away.

Kinderbad Monbijou

Keep cool on hot days splashing about this family-friendly public pool in the Scheunenviertel. See www.berliner baederbetriebe.de.

Volkspark Friedrichshain

Play in the 'Indian Village', gather your pirate mateys on the boat in the 'harbour' or find your favourite fairy-tale characters at the enchanting Märchenbrunnen in this park (p174).

Animals

Berlin Zoo & Aquarium

If the 20,000 furry, feathered and finned friends fail to enchant the little ones, there's also always the enormous adventure playground (p206).

Tierpark Berlin

Expect plenty of ooh and aah moments when kids watch baby elephants at play or see lions and tigers being fed at this vast animal **park** (☎030-515 310; www.tierpark-berlin.de; adult/child/student €11/5.50/8; ⏰9am-7pm; [S]Tierpark).

NEED TO KNOW

Child Minding Services Find an English-speaking babysitter at Babysitter Express (www.babysitter-express.de) or Welcome Kids (www.welcome-kids.de).

Public Transport Children under six travel free and those between six and 14 pay the reduced fare.

Entrance Fees Many museums, monuments and attractions are free to anyone under age 18, but the cut-off might also be age 12 or 14.

SeaLife Berlin

Little ones get to press their noses against dozens of fish-filled tanks, solve puzzles and even touch starfish and sea anemones – ever so gently, of course (p111).

Domäne Dahlem

Kids can interact with their favourite barnyard animals, help collect eggs, harvest potatoes or just generally watch daily farm life unfold at this fun working farm (www.domaene-dahlem.de).

Eating Out with Kids

It's fine to eat out as a family any time of the day, especially in cafes, bistros and pizzerias. Many offer a limited *Kindermenü* (children's menu) or *Kinderteller* (children's dishes) to meet small appetite requirements. If they don't, most will be happy to serve half-size portions or prepare a simple meal. Popular dishes include *schnitzel, Pommes mit Ketchup or Mayonnaise* (fries with ketchup or mayo), *Nudeln mit Tomatensosse* (noodles with tomato sauce) and *Fischstäbchen* (fish sticks).

Large malls have food courts while larger department stores feature self-service cafeterias. Farmers markets also have food stalls. Bakeries selling scrumptious cakes or sandwiches are plentiful. The most popular snacks-on-the-run are bratwurst in a bun or doner kebab (sliced meat tucked into a pita pocket with salad and sauce).

Baby food, infant formula, soy and cow's milk, disposable nappies (diapers) and the like are widely available in supermarkets and chemists (drugstores).

Like a Local

Local life in Berlin is not as settled upon as in other cities but is defined to some extent by the enormous influx of neo-Berliners from abroad and other parts of Germany. As such, it's comparatively easy to mingle with locals and to partake in their customs.

ANTENNA/GETTY IMAGES ©

Fresh bread at a local bakery

Dining Like a Local

Berliners love to dine out and, taking advantage of the many reasonably priced cafes and restaurants, do so quite frequently. This can mean scarfing down a quick doner at the local kebab joint or indulging in a four-course meal in a foodie hot spot. Eating out is rarely just about getting fed but is also a social experience. Meeting friends or family over a meal is considered a great way to catch up, engage in heated discussions or exchange the latest gossip.

Going out for breakfast has been a beloved pastime for years, although the trend seems to have peaked. Going out to lunch is no longer the domain of desk jockeys and business people on expense accounts as many restaurants (including Michelin-starred ones) now offer lunch menus at reduced prices. The traditional German afternoon-coffee-and-cake ritual is not practised widely in Berlin, and is pretty much the realm of more mature generations. The main going-out meal is dinner, with restaurant tables usually filled at 7.30pm or 8pm. Since it's customary to stretch meals to two hours and then linger over a last glass of wine, restaurants only count on one seating per table per night. Servers will not present you with the bill until you ask for it.

Partying Like a Local

Most Berliners will start the night around 9pm or 10pm in a pub or bar, although it's also common to meet at someone's home for a few cheap drinks in a ritual called 'Vorglühen' (literally 'pre-glowing'). Once out on the town, people either stay for a few drinks at the same place or pop into several before moving on to a club around 1am or 2am at the earliest.

In most pubs and bars, it's common practice to place orders with a server rather than pick up your own drinks at the bar. Only do the latter if that's what everyone does or if you see a sign saying 'Selbstbedienung' (self-service). In pubs, the number of drinks is sometimes tallied on round cardboard coasters sporting a brewery logo and paid for when you're ready to leave, rather than with each round. It is not expected (nor customary) to buy entire rounds for everyone at the table.

Once in the club, how long one stays depends on individual stamina and alcohol and drug consumption. Hardy types stagger out into the morning sunshine, although the most hardcore may last even longer. Don't feel bad if you want to go home before 5am. Partying in Berlin takes some practice...

NEED TO KNOW

For many Berliners, the preferred way of getting around town is by bicycle, so why not join them and rent your own two-wheeler? Alternatively, and especially in bad weather, take advantage of Berlin's excellent public transportation system. For sightseeing on the cheap, hop aboard bus 100 or 200.

Shopping Like a Local

Berliners pretty much fulfil all their shopping needs in their local *Kiez* (neighbourhood). There will usually be three or four supermarkets within walking distance, and grocery shopping is not done in one fell swoop but, rather, in several smaller trips spread over the course of the week. The local farmers market is the preferred source of fresh produce and speciality products like handmade noodles, artisanal cheese or Middle Eastern cheese spreads. Days start with fresh *Brötchen* (rolls) bought from the bakery around the corner. Nonfood needs are also met locally where possible, be it stationery, gifts, flowers, books, hardware, wine and so on.

Clothing will come from a mix of places that may include the high-street chains, upmarket boutiques, vintage stores and flea markets. When Berliners venture out of their neighbourhoods to shop, it's usually to buy big-ticket items like furniture or vehicles or speciality items not available locally. Malls are comparatively rare in Berlin and frequented as much for recreational purposes as for large-scale shopping.

Living Like a Local

The typical Berlin dwelling is a spacious rented 1½-bedroom flat on at least the 1st floor of a large early-20th-century apartment building (no one wants to live at street level), probably facing onto a *Hinterhof* (back courtyard) full of bicycles and coloured recycling bins. The apartment itself has very high ceilings, large windows and, as often as not, stripped

wooden plank floors. The kitchen will almost invariably be the smallest room in the house and used mainly for stacking crates of beer and mineral water. A few flats still have the traditional tiled heating stoves in place, though no one actually uses them.

Berlin flats are usually nicely turnedout, whatever the style favoured by the occupant, and a lot of attention is paid to design, though comfort is also considered. At least one item of furniture will come from a certain Swedish furniture chain. Depending on income, the rest may come from the Stilwerk design centre, Polish crafters, a flea market or eBay – or any combination thereof.

Relaxing Like a Local

Although they are passionate about their city, Berliners also love to get out of town, especially in summer. If they're not jetting off to Mallorca or Madagascar, they will at least try to make it out to a local lake on a sunny day. There are dozens right in town, including the vast Müggelsee in Köpenick and the Wannsee in Zehlendorf, and hundreds more a quick car or train ride away in the surrounding countryside of Brandenburg. Everyone's got their favourite body of water and, having staked out the perfect spot, tends to return there time and again.

With equally easy access to some fabulous parks, Berliners love heading for the greenery to work on their tan, relax in the shade, play Frisbee or catch up on their reading. Some parks have sections where barbecuing is permitted, and this is a popular thing to do with friends.

DAVID PEEVERS/GETTY IMAGES ©

Cafe life on Bergmannstrasse in Kreuzberg (p151)

Sightseeing Like a Local

Most locals – especially more recent arrivals – are very appreciative of Berlin's cultural offerings and keep tabs on the latest museum and gallery openings, theatre productions and construction projects. It's quite common to discuss the merits of the latest blockbuster show or exhibit at dinner tables.

Although they love being a tourist in their own city, Berliners stay away from the big-ticket sights in summer when the world comes to town. More likely they will bide their time until the cold and dark winter months or visit on late-opening nights for smaller crowds. The annual *Lange Nacht der Museen* (Long Night of the Museums), when dozens of museums stay open past midnight, brings out culture vultures by the tens of thousands.

Local Obsessions

Soccer

Many Berliners live and die by the fortunes of the local soccer team, Hertha BSC, which has seen its shares of ups and downs in recent years. After a brief stint in *2. Fussball-Bundesliga* (Second Soccer League), the team returned to the top-level Bundesliga in the 2013–14 season – much to the relief of locals. Still, true fans don't quit the team when it's down and, during the season, many will inevitably don their blue-and-white fan gear to make the trek out to the Olympic Stadium (p210) for home games.

Berlin's other major team, 1. FC Union, plays in the second league and has an especially passionate following in the eastern parts of the city.

The Weather

Many locals are hobby meteorologists who will never pass up a chance to express their opinion on tomorrow's weather or on whether it's been a good summer so far, whether the last winter was mild or brutal, what to expect from the next one, and so on... So if you run out of things to say to a local, get the conversation going again by mentioning the weather. Other popular topics are rising rents, the perceived ineptitude of the local government or the much delayed opening of the Berlin Brandenburg Airport.

For Free

It's no secret that you can get more bang for your euro in Berlin than in any other Western European capital. Better still, there are plenty of ways to stretch your budget even further by cashing in on some tip-top freebies, including such sights as the Reichstag dome and Checkpoint Charlie.

DAVID CLAPP/GETTY IMAGES ©

Dome of the Reichstag (p82)

Free History Exhibits

Given that Germany has played a disproportionate role in 20th-century history, it's only natural that there are plenty of memorial sites and exhibits shedding light on various (mostly grim) milestones. Best of all, they're all free.

World War II

Study up on the SS, Gestapo and other organisations of the Nazi power apparatus at the Topographie des Terrors (p89) exhibit, then see the desk where WWII ended with the signing of Germany's unconditional surrender at the Deutsch-Russisches Museum Berlin-Karlshorst (p228). You can stand in the very room where the 'Final Solution' was planned at the Haus der Wannsee-Konferenz (p226), get shivers while walking around the Sachsenhausen (p222) concentration camp, then pay your respects to Jewish Nazi victims at the Holocaust Memorial (p85). German resistance against the Nazis is the focus of the Gedenkstätte Deutscher Widerstand (p127).

Cold War

The East Side Gallery (p173) may be the longest surviving section of the Berlin Wall, but also swing by the Gedenkstätte Berliner Mauer (p186) to get the full picture of what the Wall looked like, and by the Tränenpalast (p92) to learn about the personal hardships of living in a divided city. For an eyeful of what daily life was like behind the Iron Curtain, drop by the new Museum in der Kulturbrauerei (p188). At Checkpoint Charlie, an outdoor exhibit chronicles milestones in Cold War history, while the nearby Stasi Ausstellung (p92) peels away the layers on East Germany's sinister secret service. For the Cold War years from the point of view of the Allies, swing by the AlliiertenMuseum (p225).

Free Museums & Galleries

State Museums

Admission to the permanent exhibits at Berlin's state museums (including the Pergamonmuseum, Neues Museum, Gemäldegalerie and Hamburger Bahnhof) is free for anyone under 18.

NEED TO KNOW

Websites

Search for free stuff by date at www.gratis-in-berlin.de or www.berlin.eintritt-frei.org.

Discount Cards

The Museumpass Berlin (p294) is a steal for culture lovers. The Berlin Welcome Card (p294) or CityTourCard (p294) may also be a good investment.

Wi-Fi

Many cafes let their customers get online for free.

Niche Museums

Although the blockbuster state museums do charge admission to adults, a few niche museums don't. Learn about the history of German democracy at the Deutscher Dom (p87), life during the Biedermeier at the Knoblauchhaus (p113), and Berlin's equivalent of Oskar Schindler at the Museum Blindenwerkstatt Otto Weidt (p141). Free art can be enjoyed at the Daimler Contemporary (p122). Military and airplane buffs will want to make the trip to the city outskirts for the Militärhistorisches Museum (p224).

Sometimes Free

Museums offering free admission at certain times include the Akademie der Künste (p129; 3pm to 7pm Tuesday), Kunsthalle Deutsche Bank (p90; all day Monday) and Museum für Film und Fernsehen (p121; 4pm to 8pm Thursday); and the Bröhan Museum (p205), Märkisches Museum (p113) and Nikolaikirche (p112) – all first Wednesday of the month.

Free Guided Tours

Many museums and galleries include free multilingual audioguides in the admission price; some also offer free guided tours, although these are usually in German.

Alternative Berlin Tours (p292), New Berlin Tours (p292) and Brewer's Berlin Tours (p292) are English-language walking tour companies that advertise 'free' guided tours, although the guides actually depend on tips.

Free Music

Free gigs and music events take place all the time, in pubs, bars, parks and churches. See the listings magazines for what's on during your stay.

Summer Concerts

In summer, many of Berlin's parks and gardens ring out with the free sound of jazz, pop, samba and classical music. Case in point: the lovely Teehaus im Englischen Garten (p132) presents two Sunday concerts (at 4pm and 7pm) in July and August.

Karaoke

The Mauerpark is a zoo-and-a-half on hot summer Sundays, thanks largely to the massively entertaining outdoor **Bearpit Karaoke** (www.bearpitkaraoke.de), which has thousands of spectators cramming onto the stone bleachers to cheer and applaud crooners of various talent levels.

Classical

At 1pm on Tuesdays from September to mid-June, the foyer of the Berliner Philharmonie (p133) fills with music lovers for free lunchtime chamber music concerts. Students of the prestigious Hochschule für Musik Hanns Eisler (p96) also show off their skills at several free recitals weekly. At 12.30pm from Tuesday to Sunday, you can also enjoy free organ recitals at the Matthäuskirche (p127) in the Kulturforum. The Französischer Dom (p87) on Gendarmenmarkt has free organ concerts at 12.30pm from Tuesday to Friday.

Rock & Jazz

For one-off free concerts, check the listings magazines. Jazz fans can bop gratis at A Trane (p210) on Mondays and at the late-night jam session after 12.30am on Saturday. On Wednesdays, b-flat (p148) and Quasimodo (p213) have their own free jam sessions. Kunstfabrik Schlot (p148) is the go-to freebie on most Mondays and Thursdays.

Sections of the Berlin Wall in Potsdamer Platz (p120)

◉ The Berlin Wall

It's more than a tad ironic that Berlin's most popular tourist attraction is one that no longer exists. For 28 years the Berlin Wall, the most potent symbol of the Cold War, divided not only a city but the world.

The Beginning

Shortly after midnight on 13 August 1961, East German soldiers and police began rolling out miles of barbed wire that would soon be replaced with prefab concrete slabs. All of a sudden, streets were cut in two, transportation between the city halves was halted and East Germans, including commuters, were no longer allowed to travel to West Berlin.

The Berlin Wall was a desperate measure launched by the German Democratic Republic (GDR; East Germany) government to stop the sustained brain-and-brawn drain the country had experienced since its 1949 founding. Some 3.6 million people had already headed to western Germany, putting the GDR on the brink of economic and political collapse. The actual construction of the Wall, however, came as a shock to many: only a couple of months before that fateful August day, GDR head of state Walter Ulbricht had declared at a press conference: 'No one has the intention of constructing a wall.'

The Physical Border

Euphemistically called the 'Anti-Fascist Protection Barrier', the Berlin Wall was an instrument of oppression that turned West Berlin into an island of democracy within a sea of socialism. It consisted of a 43km-long inner-city barrier separating West from East Berlin and a 112km border between West Berlin and East Germany. Each reinforced concrete segment was 3.6m high, 1.2m wide and weighed 2.6 tonnes.

Continually reinforced and refined over time, the Berlin Wall eventually grew into a complex border-security system consisting of not one, but two, walls: the main wall abutting the border with West Berlin and the so-called hinterland security wall, with the 'death strip' in between. A would-be escapee who managed to scale the hinterland wall was first confronted with an electrified fence that triggered an alarm. After this, he or she would have to contend with guard dogs, spiked fences, trenches and other obstacles. Other elements included a patrol path with lampposts that flooded the death strip with glaring light at night. Set up at regular intervals along the entire border were 300 watchtowers staffed by guards with shoot-to-kill orders. Only nine towers remain, including the one at Erna-Berger-Strasse (p121) near Potsdamer Platz.

In West Berlin, the Wall came right up to residential areas. Artists tried to humanise the grey concrete scar by covering it in colourful graffiti. The West Berlin government erected viewing platforms, which people could climb to peek across into East Berlin.

Escapes

There are no exact numbers, but it is believed that of the nearly 100,000 GDR citizens who tried to escape, hundreds died in the process, many by drowning, suffering fatal accidents or committing suicide when caught. More than 100 were shot and killed by border guards – the first only a few days after 13 August 1961. Guards who prevented an escape were rewarded with commendations, promotions and bonuses.

The first person to be shot at the Wall was 24-year-old trained tailor Günter Litfin. The Wall had been in existence for only 11 days when a hailstorm of bullets ripped through his body as he tried to swim to freedom across a 40m-wide canal on 24 August 1961, a Sunday. Since 2003, his brother Jürgen Litfin has kept Günter's legacy alive with a **memorial exhibit** (☏030-2362 6183; www.gedenkstaetteguenterlitfin.de; Kieler Strasse 2; ☉tours half-hourly 11.30am-1.30pm Sun-Thu Mar-Oct; 🚌120, Ⓢ Naturkundemuseum) FREE in a GDR watchtower near where he was killed. It's a bit off the beaten path but well worth swinging by not only to see the inside of this rare border relic but mainly for a chance to meet this outspoken eyewitness to history.

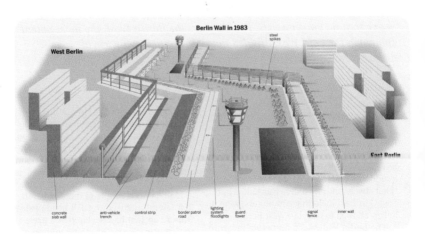

Berlin Wall in 1983

West Berlin

steel spikes

East Berlin

concrete slab wall | anti-vehicle trench | control strip | border patrol road | lighting system floodlights | guard tower | signal fence | inner wall

Another famous incident illustrating the barbarity of the shoot-to-kill order occurred on 17 August 1962 when 18-year-old would-be escapee Peter Fechter was shot and wounded and then left to bleed to death as East German guards looked on. There's a **memorial** in his honour on Zimmerstrasse, near Checkpoint Charlie. Behind the Reichstag, on the southern bank of the Spree River, the Gedenkort Weisse Kreuze (White Crosses Memorial; p88) also commemorates the Wall victims, as does the emotional 'Window of Remembrance' at the Gedenkstätte Berliner Mauer (Berlin Wall Memorial; p186). It features the names and photographs of all the people who were shot or died in an accident while attempting to escape.

The Wall Memorial runs along 1.4km of Bernauer Strasse which was literally split in two by the Berlin Wall, with one side of apartment buildings on the western side and the other in the east. As the barrier was erected, many residents on the eastern side decided to flee spontaneously by jumping into rescue nets or sliding down ropes, risking severe injury and death. Bernauer Strasse was also where several escape tunnels were dug, most famously Tunnel 29 in 1962, so named because 29 people managed to flee to the West before border guards took notice.

The fact that there was no limit to the ingenuity of would-be escapees is engagingly documented at the Mauermuseum (p92) near Checkpoint Charlie. On display are several original contraptions used to flee East Germany, including a hot air balloon, a hollow surfboard, a specially rigged car and even a homemade mini-submarine.

The End

The Wall's demise came as unexpectedly as its creation. Once again the GDR was losing its people in droves, this time via Hungary, which had opened its borders with Austria. Thus emboldened, East Germans took to the streets by the hundreds of thousands, demanding improved human rights and an end to the dictatorship of the SED (Sozialistische Einheitspartei Deutschland), the single party in East Germany. A series of demonstrations culminated in a gathering of half a million people on Alexanderplatz on 4 November 1989, vociferously demanding political reform. Something had to give.

It did, on 9 November, when government spokesperson Günter Schabowski announced during a press conference on live TV that all travel restrictions to the West would be lifted. When asked by a reporter when this regulation would come into effect, he nervously shuffled his papers looking for the answer, then responded with the historic words: 'As far as I know, immediately.' In fact, the ruling was not supposed to take effect until the following day, but no one had informed Schabowski.

The news spread through East Berlin like wildfire, with hundreds of thousands heading towards the Wall. Border guards had no choice but to stand back. Amid scenes of wild partying and mile-long parades of GDR-made Trabant cars, the two Berlins came together again.

Today

The dismantling of the hated border fortifications began almost immediately and by now the city halves have visually merged so perfectly that it takes a keen eye to tell East from West. Fortunately, there's help in the form of a **double row of cobblestones** that guides you along 5.7km of the Wall's course. Also keep an eye out for the **Berlin Wall History Mile**, which consists of 30 information panels set up along the course of the Wall. They draw attention, in four languages, to specific events that took place at each location. For details, see www.berlin.de/mauer/geschichtsmeile.

Only about 2km of the actual concrete barrier are still standing today, most famously the 1.3km stretch that is now the **East Side Gallery**. But there are plenty of other traces scattered throughout the city, including lamps, patrol paths, fences, perimeter defences, switchboxes and so on. Most are so perfectly integrated they're only discernible to the practised eye. A brilliant source for tracking down these fragments is the **Memorial Landscape Berlin Wall** (www.berlin-wall-map.com), an interactive Geographic Information System (GIS) that documents all remaining bits and pieces, no matter how small.

The Berlin Wall

The construction of the Berlin Wall was a unique event in human history, not only for physically bisecting a city but by becoming a dividing line between competing ideologies and political systems. It's this global impact and universal legacy that continue to fascinate people more than a quarter century after its triumphant tear-down. Fortunately, plenty of original Wall segments and other vestiges remain, along with museums and memorials, to help fathom the realities and challenges of daily life in Berlin during the Cold War.

Our illustration points out the top highlights you can visit to learn about different aspects of these often tense decades. The best place to start is at the **Gedenkstätte Berliner Mauer ❶** for an excellent introduction to what the inner-city border actually looked liked and what it meant to live in its shadow. Reflect upon what you've learned while relaxing on the former death strip that is now the **Mauerpark ❷** before heading to the emotionally charged exhibit at the **Tränenpalast ❸**, an actual border crossing

Brandenburg Gate

People around the world cheered as East and West Berliners partied together atop the Berlin Wall in front of the iconic city gate which today is a photogenic symbol of united Germany.

GERARD MALIE/AFP/GETTY IMAGES ©

Tränenpalast

This modernist 1962 glass-and-steel border pavilion was dubbed 'Palace of Tears' because of the many tearful farewells that took place outside the building as East Germans and their western visitors had to say goodbye.

IMAGEBROKER/ROBERT HARDING ©

Potsdamer Platz

Nowhere was the death strip as wide as on the former no-man's-land around Potsdamer Platz from which sprouted a new postmodern city quarter in the 1990s. A tiny section of the Berlin Wall serves as a reminder.

JOHN FREEMAN/GETTY IMAGES ©

Checkpoint Charlie

Only diplomats and foreigners were allowed to use this border crossing. Weeks after the Wall was built, US and Soviet tanks faced off here in one of the hottest moments of the Cold War.

LONELY PLANET/GETTY IMAGES ©

Bernauer Strasse

Chausseestr

Unter den Linden

Leipziger Str

pavilion. Relive the euphoria of the Wall's demise at the **Brandenburg Gate** ❹, then marvel at the revival of **Potsdamer Platz** ❺ that was nothing but death strip wasteland until the 1990s. The Wall's geopolitical significance is the focus at **Checkpoint Charlie** ❻, which saw some of the tensest moments of the Cold War. Wrap up with finding your favourite mural motif at the **East Side Gallery** ❼.

It's possible to explore these sights by using a combination of walking and public transport, although a bike ride is actually the best method for getting a sense of the former Wall's erratic flow through the central city.

FAST FACTS

» **Beginning of construction:** 13 August 1961
» **Total length:** 155km
» **Height:** 3.6m
» **Weight of each segment:** 2.6 tonnes
» **Number of watchtowers:** 300

Mauerpark
Famous for its flea market and karaoke, this popular park actually occupies a converted section of death strip. A 30m segment of surviving Wall is now an official practice ground for budding graffiti artists.

remnants of the Wall →

Gedenkstätte Berliner Mauer
Germany's central memorial to the Berlin Wall and its victims exposes the complexity and barbaric nature of the border installation along a 1.4km stretch of the barrier's course.

Alexanderplatz

Alexander Str

East Side Gallery
Paralleling the Spree for 1.3km, this is the longest Wall vestige. After its collapse, more than a hundred international artists expressed their feelings about this historic moment in a series of colourful murals.

Engelbecken

❼

Tours

Fat Tire Bike Tours (p292) and Berlin on Bike (p292) offer guided trips along the course of the Wall. If you're feeling ambitious, follow all or part of the 160km-long **Berliner Mauerweg** (Berlin Wall Trail), a signposted walking and cycling path that runs along the former border fortifications, with 40 multilingual information stations posted along the way. For a description and route maps in English, search online for 'Berlin Wall Trail'.

A high-tech way to walk the Wall is with the **Mauerguide** (☑030-8871 3624; www.mauerguide.com; adult/concession per 4hr €8/5, per 24hr €10/7), a hand-held GPS-guided mini-computer that provides intelligent commentary and historic audio and video. Hire stations are at Checkpoint Charlie, in the U-Bahn station Brandenburger Tor and at the Documentation Centre of the Berlin Wall Memorial.

Berlin Wall by Neighbourhood

These original Wall remnants, museums and memorials keep the legacy of the Berlin Wall alive.

➡ **Historic Mitte** Checkpoint Charlie, Mauermuseum, Peter Fechter Memorial, Mauer Panorama, BlackBox Kalter Krieg, Brandenburg Gate, Parlament der Bäume (Parliament of Trees), Wall segments at Marie-Elisabeth-Lüders-Haus, Tränenpalast, Gedenkort Weisse Kreuze (White Crosses Memorial). (p84)

➡ **Potsdamer Platz & Tiergarten** Wall remnants at Potsdamer Platz, Watchtower Erna-Berger-Strasse, Wall section at Niederkirchner Strasse (next to Topographie des Terrors). (p120)

➡ **Friedrichshain** East Side Gallery. (p173)

➡ **Prenzlauer Berg** Gedenkstätte Berliner Mauer, Mauerpark. (p186)

Entrance to Gedenkstätte und Museum Sachsenhausen (p222)

Historical Museums & Memorials

From its humble medieval beginnings, Berlin's history – and especially its key role in major events of the 20th century – is a rich and endlessly fascinating tapestry. It's also extremely well documented in numerous museums, memorial sites and monuments, many of them in original historic locations.

The Evolution of Berlin & Germany

Trace Berlin's evolution from its medieval birth to today's modern metropolis at the Märkisches Museum (p113), which brims with original objects arranged like a city stroll through the ages. Across town, the Story of Berlin (p207) uses a more experiential multimedia approach to provide insight into Berlin's various epochs.

For a comprehensive survey of German history from the early Middle Ages to the present, visit the Deutsches Historisches Museum (p86). Berlin's Jewish history gets the spotlight at the Jüdisches Museum (p153).

The Third Reich

Few periods shaped the fate of Berlin as much as its 12-year stint as capital of Nazi Germany. Numerous museums and memorial sites, all of them free, keep the memory alive. For insight into the sinister machinations of the Nazi state, visit the Topographie des Terrors (p89). Nazi leaders decided on

NEED TO KNOW

Tickets

Admission to many museums and memorial sites is free. Major museums that do charge admission include the Jüdisches Museum, Deutsches Historisches Museum, Mauermuseum, Story of Berlin and Schloss Cecilienhof.

Opening Hours

➡ Core museum hours are 10am to 6pm, with a number of major venues open until at least 8pm.

➡ Closed Monday; Märkisches Museum, Ort der Information, Schloss Cecilienhof, Deutsch-Russisches Museum Berlin-Karlshorst, Tränenpalast.

➡ Closed Wednesday: AlliertenMuseum.

➡ Although the Sachsenhausen camp grounds are open on Mondays, most exhibits are closed.

Tours

➡ Schloss Cecilienhof and the Stasi Prison can only be seen on guided tours (no need to prebook). Call or check the websites for timings of English tours.

the implementation of the so-called 'Final Solution' in a lakeside villa that is now the Gedenkstätte Haus der Wannsee-Konferenz (p226).

The unfathomable impact of Nazi terror is emotionally documented at the Ort der Information (p85) and at the Sachsenhausen (p222) concentration camp. The brave locals who tried to stand up against the Nazis are commemorated at the Gedenkstätte Deutscher Widerstand (p127), the Gedenkstätte Stille Helden (p141) and the Museum Blindenwerkstatt Otto Weidt (p141).

When WWII finally came to an end, the German surrender was signed at what is now the Deutsch-Russisches Museum Berlin-Karlshorst (p229), whose exhibits present WWII from the point of view of the Soviet Union. Two giant monuments honour the vast number of Russian soldiers who died in the Battle of Berlin: the Sowjetisches Ehrenmal Treptow (p159) and the Sowjetisches Ehrenmal Tiergarten (p89). To see where the victorious Allies hammered out Germany's postwar fate, visit Schloss Cecilienhof (p221).

The Cold War

After World War II, Berlin was caught in the cross-hairs of the Cold War superpowers – the US and the USSR – as epitomised in the city's division and the construction of the Berlin Wall. The longest surviving vestige of this barrier is the East Side Gallery (p173), but to deepen your understanding of what the border fortifications looked like and their impact, the Gedenkstätte Berliner Mauer (p186) and the Tränenpalast (p92) are essential stops. Daily life behind the Iron Curtain is documented in interactive fashion at the DDR Museum (p112), while the free new Museum in der Kulturbrauerei (p188) follows a comparatively traditional approach on the same subject. Both exhibits also address the role of East Germany's Ministry of State Security (Stasi) in shoring up the power base of the country's regime. Learn more at the Stasimuseum Berlin (p176) and on a tour of the Stasi Prison (p176). For a quick overview on the subject, there's also the Stasi Ausstellung (p92) near Checkpoint Charlie (p93). This is also where you'll find the Mauermuseum (p92), which uncovers the daring escape attempts of East Germans to the West. For a take on the Cold War in Berlin from the perspective of the occupying Western allies, visit the AlliiertenMuseum (p225).

Historical Museums & Memorials by Neighbourhood

➡ **Historic Mitte** Ort der Information, Topographie des Terrors, Deutsches Historisches Museum, Tränenpalast, Mauermuseum, Stasi Ausstellung, Sowjetisches Ehrenmal Tiergarten. (p85)

➡ **Museumsinsel & Alexanderplatz** Märkisches Museum, DDR Museum. (p112)

➡ **Potsdamer Platz & Tiergarten** Gedenkstätte Deutscher Widerstand. (p127)

➡ **Scheunenviertel** Museum Blindenwerkstatt Otto Weidt, Gedenkstätte Stille Helden. (p141)

➡ **City West & Charlottenburg** Story of Berlin. (p207)

➡ **Kreuzberg & Northern Neukölln** Jüdisches Museum. (p153)

➡ **Prenzlauer Berg** Gedenkstätte Berliner Mauer, Museum in der Kulturbrauerei. (p186)

➡ **Outer Berlin** Haus der Wannsee-Konferenz, Sachsenhausen, Deutsch-Russisches Museum Berlin-Karlshorst, Stasimuseum Berlin, Stasi Prison, AlliiertenMuseum, Sowjetisches Ehrenmal Treptow. (p222)

➡ **Potsdam** Schloss Cecilienhof. (p221)

Lonely Planet's Top Choices

Deutsches Historisches Museum (p86) Charts German history in the European context from the Middle Ages to the present in a former Prussian armoury.

Jüdisches Museum (p153) Daniel Libeskind's contorted building is a striking backdrop for this thorough survey of the history and cultural heritage of Jews in Germany.

Topographie des Terrors (p89) Gripping examination of the origins of Nazism, its perpetrators and its victims on the site of the SS and Gestapo headquarters.

Gedenkstätte Berliner Mauer (p186) Indoor-outdoor multi-media exhibit vividly illustrates the history, physical appearance and impact of the Berlin Wall.

Sachsenhausen Memorial and Museum (p222) No book or movie comes close to the emotional impact of actually standing in a concentration camp.

Best in Historic Locations

Stasi Prison (p176) Former inmates lead tours of this infamous jail that had a starring role in the Academy Award–winning *The Lives of Others*.

Stasimuseum Berlin (p176) The headquarters of East Germany's feared and loathed Ministry of State Security are now a museum.

Tränenpalast (p92) Exhibit explains why tears of goodbye once flowed in this Friedrichstrasse border pavillion.

Sachsenhausen Memorial and Museum (p222) North of Berlin, this early concentration camp served as a model for many others.

Best for Jewish Remembrance

Jüdisches Museum (p153) Engagingly laid out chronicle and celebration of nearly 2000 years of Jewish life in Germany.

Ort der Information (p85) Chilling exhibit below the Holocaust Memorial examines personal aspects of this unfathomable chapter in human history.

Museum Blindenwerkstatt Otto Weidt (p141) Learn how one heroic man saved untold Jewish lives.

Best for Kids

Story of Berlin (p207) Plenty of engaging visuals and a tour of an atomic bunker make this one a winner with teens.

DDR Museum (p112) Highly experiential and hands-on journey into daily life behind the Iron Curtain.

Mauermuseum (p92) Outdated exhibit, but fascinating collection of ingenious original contraptions used by East Germans to escape their country.

Best for Momentous Moments

Haus der Wannsee-Konferenz (p226) Get shivers while standing in the very room where Nazi leaders planned the systematic annihilation of European Jews on 20 January 1942.

Deutsch-Russisches Museum Berlin-Karlshorst (p228) With the stroke of a pen WWII ended on 8 May 1945 with the signing of the German surrender at this former seat of the Soviet Military Administration.

Schloss Cecilienhof (p221) The Potsdam Conference brought Stalin, Truman and Attlee to this pretty palace to divvy Germany up into four occupation zones between 17 July and 2 August 1945.

Best for Architecture

Märkisches Museum (p113) This imposing red-brick pile is a clever mashup of actual historic buildings from the surrounding state of Brandenburg.

Deutsches Historisches Museum (p86) Highlights of this ex-armoury are the baroque dying-warrior sculptures in the courtyard and the modern annexe by IM Pei.

Jüdisches Museum (p153) Daniel Libeskind's structures are never just buildings, they're also moving metaphors, as beautifully illustrated by Berlin's Jewish Museum.

PLAN YOUR TRIP HISTORICAL MUSEUMS & MEMORIALS

Strollers pass by street art by JR

◉ The Berlin Art Scene

Art aficionados will find their compass on perpetual spin in Berlin. Home to 440 galleries, scores of world-class collections and some 10,000 international artists, it has assumed pole position on the global artistic circuit. Adolescent energy, restlessness and experimental spirit combined and infused with an undercurrent of grit are what give this 'eternally unfinished' city its street cred.

Sammlung Boros (p138)

Major Art Museums

Berlin's most famous art museums are administered by the Staatliche Museen Berlin (Berlin State Museums; www.smb. museum). Masterpieces are showcased by period in five locations:

Alte Nationalgalerie (p108) Neoclassical, romantic, impressionist and early modernist art, including Caspar David Friedrich, Adolf Menzel and Monet; on Museumsinsel.

Neue Nationalgalerie (p127) Early-20th-century art, especially German expressionists such as Grosz and Kirchner, as well as Max Beckmann; part of the Kulturforum (note: set to close for renovation in 2015).

Museum Berggruen (p205) Classical Modernist, mostly Picasso and Klee; near Schloss Charlottenburg.

Sammlung Scharf-Gerstenberg (p204) Surrealist art by Goya, Magritte, Jean Dubuffet, Max Ernst and more; near Schloss Charlottenburg.

Hamburger Bahnhof (p136) International contemporary art, Warhol to Rauschenberg to Beuys; east of the Hauptbahnhof.

Aside from these heavy hitters, Berlin teems with smaller museums specialising in a particular artist or genre. You can admire the colourful canvasses of artist group Die Brücke in a lovely museum (p225) on the eastern edge of the Grunewald forest; see the paintings of Max Liebermann while standing in the studio in the Liebermann-Villa am Wannsee (p227) where he painted them; or take a survey of a century of Berlin-made art in the Berlinische Galerie (p155).

Two museums train the spotlight on women: the Käthe-Kollwitz-Museum (p207), which is dedicated to one of the finest and most outspoken early-20th-century German artists, and the Das Verborgene Museum (p207), which champions lesser-known German female artists from the same period.

NEED TO KNOW

Tickets

➡ Generally, buy tickets at the gallery or museum. Blockbuster visiting shows often sell out so it's best to prepurchase tickets online.

➡ Most private collections require advance registration; reserve months ahead for the Sammlung Boros.

➡ Commercial galleries do not charge admission. Most hold *vernissage* (opening) and *finissage* (closing) parties.

➡ The Berlin Museum Pass buys admission to about 50 museums and galleries for a three-day period. Available at participating museums and the tourist offices.

Opening Hours

➡ The big museums and galleries are typically open from 10am to 6pm, with extended viewing one day a week, usually Thursday. Many are closed on Mondays.

➡ Commercial galleries tend to be open from noon to 6pm Tuesday to Saturday and by appointment.

Tours

GoArt! Berlin (www.goart-berlin.de) runs customised tours that demystify Berlin's art scene by opening doors to private collections, artist studios and galleries or by taking you to exciting street-art locations. Also does art consulting.

Websites

➡ **Museumsportal** (www.museumsportal.de) Gateway to the city's museums and galleries.

➡ Search online for 'Berliner Kunstfaltplan' for a comprehensive overview of the latest commercial gallery shows.

Above: Berlinische Galerie (p155)
Left: Street art by Alias in Kreuzberg

There are also corporate collections like the Kunsthalle Deutsche Bank (p90) and private ones such as the Sammlung Boros (p138).

Art Galleries

The **Galleries Association of Berlin** (www.berliner-galerien.de) counts some 440 galleries within the city, but there are at least 200 noncommercial showrooms and off-spaces that regularly show new exhibitions. Although the orientation is global, it's well worth keeping an eye out for the latest works by major contemporary artists living and working in Berlin, including Thomas Demand, Jonathan Meese, Via Lewandowsky, Isa Genzken, Tino Seghal, Esra Ersen, John Bock and the artist duo Ingar Dragset and Michael Elmgreen.

Galleries cluster in five main areas:

Scheunenviertel (Mitte) Auguststrasse and Linienstrasse were the birthplaces of Berlin's post-Wall contemporary art scene. Some pioneers have since moved on to bigger digs but key players like Eigen + Art, neugerriemschneider and Kicken remain. Other spaces to keep an eye on include KOW, Galerie Neu and Mehdi Chouakri.

Checkpoint Charlie area (northern Kreuzberg) A number of key galleries hold forth on Zimmerstrasse, Charlottenstrasse, Rudi-Dutschke-Strasse and Markgrafenstrasse, including Galerie Krone, Galerie Thomas Schulte and Galerie Barbara Thumm.

Lindenstrasse (northern Kreuzberg) Of late, another Kreuzberg hub is developing, along Lindenstrasse near the Berlinische Galerie and the Jewish Museum, where you'll find Galerie Konrad Fischer, Galerie Nordenhake and Galerija Gregor Podnar.

Potsdamer Strasse (Schöneberg) In recent years, the gritty area around Potsdamer Strasse and Kurfürstenstrasse has emerged as one of Berlin's most dynamic art quarters with a great mix of established galleries and newcomers. Heavy hitters include Galerie Arndt, Galerie Isabella Bortolozzi, Galerie Thomas Fischer and Galerie Klosterfelde.

Around Savignyplatz (Charlottenburg) In the traditional gallery district in the western city centre, standouts include Galerie Max Hetzler, Galerie Buchholz and Galerie Brockstedt.

Street Art & Where to Find It

Berlin is sometimes called the world's street art capital and, indeed, some of the hottest players have left their mark on local walls. This includes international artists like Blu, JR, Os Gemeos, Romero, Swoon, Flix, Pure Evil and Miss Van alongside local talent like Bonk, Bimer and El Bocho.

There's street art pretty much everywhere, but the area around U-Bahn station Schlesisches Tor in Kreuzberg has some house-wall-size classics, including pieces by Blu and the Brazilian twins Os Gemeos. Skalitzer Strasse is also a fertile hunting ground with Victor Ash's *Astronaut* and ROA's *Nature Morte* being highlights (look for them on the north side of the tracks when riding the above-ground U1).

Across the Spree River in Friedrichshain, the RAW Gelände has plenty of great stuff, especially at the Urban Spree Bar & Gallery. Around Boxhagener Platz you'll find works by Boxi, Alias and El Bocho. In Mitte, there's plenty of art underneath the S-Bahn arches although the undisputed hub is the courtyard of Haus Schwarzenberg. Prenzlauer Berg has the Mauerpark, where budding artists may legally polish their skills along a section of the Berlin Wall. In the entryway of the Tuntenhaus at Kastanienallee 86 are nice works by Alias and El Bocho.

In Schöneberg, **ATM Gallery Berlin** (☎0176 3416 4222; www.atmberlin.de; Eylauerstrasse 13; ⏲3-8pm Thu-Sat & by appointment; [S]Platz der Luftbrücke) keeps its finger on the pulse of the scene. Alternative Berlin Tours (p292) runs a four-hour street-art workshop and walking tour (€15). **Hidden Path** (www.thehiddenpath.de) also does customised tours for small groups. A good book on the subject is *Urban Illustration Berlin: Street Art City Guide,* by Benjamin Wolbergs.

PUBLIC ART

Free installations, sculptures and paintings? Absolutely. Public art is big in Berlin, which happens to be home to the world's longest outdoor mural, the 1.3km-long East Side Gallery (p173). No matter which neighbourhood you walk in, you're going to encounter public art on a grand scale. The Potsdamer Platz area offers especially rich pickings. See our DaimlerCity public sculpture tour on p126.

TOP FIVE BERLIN ART BLOGS

Berlin Art Link (www.berlinartlink. com) Online magazine delving into the contemporary art scene via studio visits and artist interviews, reviews and event listings.

Street Art Berlin (www.streetartbln. com) Keeps tabs on new works, profiles Berlin artists and posts about events.

Art News (www.artnews.org) Lists new exhibitions by opening date, closing date and venue.

Art Berlin (www.artberlin.de) Excellent site opening the door to the city's art scene by portraying artists, galleries, collections, exhibits and fairs; in German only.

Berlin Art Parasites (www.artparasites. com) Navigates through the Berlin art jungle with reviews, artist profiles and offbeat opinion pieces.

Here's a roundup of our street-art faves:

Astronaut (Mariannenstrasse; S Kottbusser Tor) Kreuzberg; stencilling by Victor Ash.

Nature Morte (Skalitzer Strasse 27; S Görlitzer Bahnhof) Kreuzberg; large-scale black and white painting by ROA.

Rounded Heads (S Schlesisches Tor) Kreuzberg; pictogram by Nomad.

Yellow Man (Oppelner Strasse; S Schlesisches Tor) Kreuzberg; painting by Os Gemeos.

Take off That Mask & Shackled by Time (cnr Cuvrystrasse & Schlesische Strasse; S Schlesisches Tor) Kreuzberg; two side-by-side paintings by Blu and JR.

Leviathan (Falckensteinstrasse 48; S Schlesisches Tor) Kreuzberg; by Blu.

Fish (Modersohnstrasse near Revaler Strasse; R Warschauer Strasse) Friedrichshain; by Ema.

Sad Girl with Rabbit Ears (Gabriel-Max-Strasse; R Warschauer Strasse) Friedrichshain; by Boxi.

Berlin Art Scene by Neighbourhood

➡ **Historic Mitte** Galleries around Checkpoint Charlie; Kunsthalle Deutsche Bank; Akademie der Künste. (p84)

➡ **Museumsinsel & Alexanderplatz** Alte Nationalgalerie. (p108)

➡ **Potsdamer Platz & Tiergarten** Neue Nationalgalerie, Gemäldegalerie, Bauhaus Archiv, Martin-Gropius-Bau. (p123)

➡ **City West & Charlottenburg** High-end galleries, eg on Fasanenstrasse, Mommsenstrasse and Kurfürstendamm; art museums near Schloss Charlottenburg. (p201)

➡ **Scheunenviertel** Top-notch galleries around Auguststrasse; street art; Sammlung Boros; Hamburger Bahnhof. (p136)

➡ **Kreuzberg & Neukölln** Best for street art; Berlinische Galerie. (p155)

➡ **Friedrichshain** East Side Gallery and more good street art. (p173)

Lonely Planet's Top Choices

Gemäldegalerie (p123)
Sweeping survey of Old Masters from Germany, Italy, France, Spain and the Netherlands from the 13th to the 18th centuries.

Hamburger Bahnhof (p136)
Warhol, Beuys and Twombly are among the many legends aboard the contemporary-art express at this former train station.

Sammlung Boros (p138)
Book ahead for tickets to see this stunning cutting-edge private collection housed in a WWII bunker.

Martin-Gropius-Bau (p126)
First-rate travelling exhibits take up residence in this gorgeous Renaissance-style building.

Best Single-Artist Galleries

Käthe-Kollwitz-Museum (p207) Representative collection of works by Germany's greatest woman artist, famous for her haunting depictions of war and human loss and suffering.

Liebermann-Villa am Wannsee (p227) Charming exhibit set up in the lakeside summer home of the great German impressionist and leading Berlin Secession founder Max Liebermann.

Dalí – Die Ausstellung (p126) Private collection showcasing lesser-known drawings, illustrated books and sculptures by the famous Catalán surrealist.

Best Artistic Genre Galleries

Classical Modernism at Museum Berggruen (p205) Picasso, Klee and Giacometti form the heart of this stunning collection donated to the city by Heinz Berggruen.

Surrealism at Sammlung Scharf-Gerstenberg (p204) Across from Museum Berggruen, this space delves into the fantastical worlds conjured up by Goya, Max Ernst, Magritte and other giants of the genre.

Romanticism at Alte Nationalgalerie (p108) The 3rd floor of this venerable art temple is packed with period masterpieces by such genre practitioners as Caspar David Friedrich, Karl Friedrich Schinkel and Carl Blechen.

German Expressionism at the Brücke-Museum (p225) Forest-framed gem focusing on works by Karl Schmidt-Rottluff, Ernst Ludwig Kirchner and other members of the Bridge, Germany's first modern-artist group.

Bauhaus Archiv (p129) Offers comprehensive insight into the pioneering modernist school and its main teachers and practitioners.

Best Private Collections

Sammlung Boros (p138) The latest works by established and emerging artists displayed in a labyrinthine WWII bunker.

Sammlung Hoffmann (p139) Every Saturday, artficionados

can join a tour of long-time collector Erika Hoffmann's private loft.

Best Art Museum Architecture

Bauhaus Archiv (p129)
Walter Gropius himself drew up the blueprints of this complex, distinguished by its curved shed-roof silhouette.

Hamburger Bahnhof (p136)
Flanked by two towers and centred on a cathedral-like hall, this 19th-century train station is home to one of Germany's finest contemporary art collections.

Neue Nationalgalerie (p127)
Ludwig Mies van der Rohe's temple-like final masterpiece is as edgy today as it was at its 1967 opening.

Best Art-Exhibition Halls

Martin-Gropius-Bau (p126)
Top of the heap with headline-making travelling art exhibits from all fields of creative endeavour.

Akademie der Künste (p84)
Berlin's oldest arts institution (founded in 1699) presents genre-hopping exhibits drawn from its archives in two locations.

Kunsthalle Deutsche Bank (p90) Shines the spotlight on the art scene in emerging countries and examines the effects of globalisation on the art world.

Haus der Kulturen der Welt (p88) Mounts shows with a special focus on non-European cultures and societies.

Pfannkuchen (p53)

Eating

If you crave traditional German comfort food, you'll certainly find plenty of places to indulge in pork knuckles, smoked pork chops and calf's liver in Berlin. These days, though, 'typical' local fare is lighter, healthier, more creative, and more likely to come from an organic eatery, an ethnic restaurant or a gourmet kitchen (including 13 flaunting Michelin stars).

Food Trends

Just like with art and fashion, Berliners love discovering something new when it comes to food. Following are some of the current food obsessions in the capital.

MODERN GERMAN CUISINE

The organic, slow-food and locavore movements have inspired a new generation of Berlin chefs to let the ingredients trifecta of seasonal, regional and organic steer their menus. This has added pizzazz to classic, time-tested recipes by making them lighter, healthier and more creative. Many chefs now travel to Brandenburg, the rural region surrounding Berlin, to source apple-fed pork from the Havelland, fish from the Müritz Lake District or wild boar from the Schorfheide. Menus increasingly champion traditional (and long underrated) ingredients such as heirloom vegetables, old-fashioned grains like barley and buckwheat, and game and other meats like *Blutwurst* (blood sausage), *Zickleinleber* (baby goat liver) or *Ochsenbäckchen* (ox cheeks).

FOOD TRUCKS & STREET FOOD

The food-truck phenomenon finally started making a splash in Berlin in 2013. The colourful mobile kitchens can be spotted throughout the city, usually at parties, events or open-air markets, with exact dates and locations posted on their Facebook pages.

There are also a growing number of roving food-truck gatherings staged by local culinary entrepreneurs. Established in 2013, **Bite Club** (www.biteclub.de) has regular gigs next to Badeschiff on the Spree River and also behind the Platoon Kunsthalle in Mitte. Every two months, it is grill and grind at **Burgers & Hip Hop** (www.facebook.com/burgersandhiphop), which has a residency at Prince Charles club on Moritzplatz. **Beer&Beef** (www.facebook.com/BeerBeefFestival), a wild party combining street food, beer, a gourmet market featuring local products, and live bands, made its debut at Urban Spree in Friedrichshain in 2014. Check the website for dates.

If there's no event while you're in town, you can still sample top bites at the weekly Street Food Thursday at Markthalle Neun, a historic market hall in Kreuzberg. See p162 for the low-down.

GOURMET BURGERS

Carnivores rejoice: once a humble fast-food staple, burgers have of late been elevated into the pantheon of culinary greats. Hardly a day seems to pass without the opening of yet another pattie temple, further fuelling locals' obsession with the hunt for the perfect burger. What constitutes perfection is also the subject of much debate, although there seems to be a general consensus that the use of premium cuts of freshly ground meat – preferably hormone- and antibiotic-free, locally raised, grass-fed and organic – is a main criterion. Any twist on the familiar is cheered, be it yak or wild-boar burgers, unusual homemade sauces like chipotle beetroot mayo or red wine barbecue sauce, or out-there toppings like caramelised kimchi, ramen noodles, foie gras or rice crackers.

VEGETARIANS & VEGANS

Slow in coming, Berlin is now embracing animal-free fare with the fervour of a religious convert. Vegetarian and vegan cafes and restaurants have been sprouting faster than alfafa and serve up inspired menus that leave the staple vegie or tofu burger

NEED TO KNOW

Price Ranges

The following prices are per main course.

€	less than €8
€€	€8 to €18
€€€	more than €18

Opening Hours

Cafes 8am to 8pm

Restaurants 11am to 11pm

Fast-food joints 11am to midnight or later

Bills & Tipping

➡ It's customary to add between 5% and 10% for good service.

➡ Tip as you hand over the money, rather than leaving it on the table (as this is considered rude). For example, if your bill comes to €28 and you want to give a €2 tip, say €30. If you have the exact amount and don't need change, just say 'Stimmt so' (that's fine).

Reservations

Reservations are essential at the top eateries and are recommended for midrange restaurants – especially for dinner and at weekends. Many restaurant websites now offer an online booking function. Berliners tend to linger at the table, so if a place is full at 8pm it's likely that it will stay that way for a couple of hours.

Late-Night & Sunday Shopping

➡ One handy feature of Berlin culture is the Spätkauf (Späti in local vernacular), which are small neighbourhood stores stocked with the basics and open from early evening until 2am or later.

➡ Some supermarkets stay open until midnight; a few are even 24 hours.

➡ Shops and supermarkets in major train stations (Hauptbahnhof, Ostbahnhof, Friedrichstrasse) are open late and on Sundays.

in the dust. With dishes like sweet potato saltimbocca, tandoori seitan, pearl barley strudel with chanterelles, or parmesan dumplings, chefs strive to push the creative envelope. Even many nonvegetarian restaurants now offer more than the token vegie

Eating by Neighbourhood

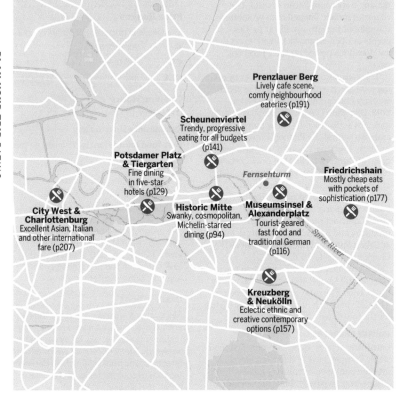

Prenzlauer Berg
Lively cafe scene,
comfy neighbourhood
eateries (p191)

Scheunenviertel
Trendy, progressive
eating for all budgets
(p141)

**Potsdamer Platz
& Tiergarten**
Fine dining
in five-star
hotels (p129)

Fernsehturm

Friedrichshain
Mostly cheap eats
with pockets of
sophistication (p177)

**City West &
Charlottenburg**
Excellent Asian, Italian
and other international
fare (p207)

Historic Mitte
Swanky, cosmopolitan,
Michelin-starred
dining (p94)

**Museumsinsel &
Alexanderplatz**
Tourist-geared
fast food and
traditional German
(p116)

Spree River

**Kreuzberg
& Neukölln**
Eclectic ethnic and
creative contemporary
options (p157)

lasagne. Berlin also premiered Germany's first all-vegan supermarket, Veganz, in 2011, which is now expanding fast throughout Germany, Austria and the Czech Republic. For a comprehensive list of vegetarian and vegan restaurants in Berlin, search on www.happycow.net.

SUPPER CLUBS
The supper-club trend seems to be fading, but for now there are still quite a few Berlin locals (usually transplants from other countries) that throw open their homes to turn perfect strangers into friends over home-cooked meals. Recommending a supper club can be tricky, since these below-the-radar restaurants are rarely permanent. The best we can suggest is to Google 'Berlin supper clubs' and see what pops up. The **Ghetto Gourmet** (www.theghet.com) keeps a finger on the pulse of the scene. Meanwhile, the folks of Thyme Supper Club have

opened Muse (p194) in Prenzlauer Berg, a regular bistro during the week that still keeps the supper-club tradition alive on Saturdays.

Eating Like a Local
Restaurants are often formal places with full menus, crisp white linen and high prices. Some restaurants are open for lunch and dinner only, but more casual places tend to be open all day. Same goes for cafes, which usually serve both coffee and alcohol, as well as light meals, although ordering food is not obligatory. Many cafes and restaurants offer inexpensive weekday 'business lunches' that usually include a starter, main course and drink for under €10.

English menus are now quite common, and some places (especially those owned by neo-Berliners from the US, UK or around Europe) don't even bother with German menus at all. When it comes to paying, sometimes the person who invites pays, but very often Germans go Dutch and split the bill. This might mean everyone chipping in at the end of a meal or asking the server if you can pay separately *(getrennte Rechnung)*. Handy speed-feed shops, called *Imbiss,* serve all sorts of savoury fodder, from sausage-in-a-bun to *Döner* and pizza. Many bakeries serve sandwiches alongside pastries.

Locals love to shop at farmers markets and nearly every *Kiez* (neighbourhood) runs at least one or two weekly. For a list of our favourites, see p75. For more tips on local dining habits, see Dining Like a Local on p30.

LOCAL SPECIALITIES YOU SHOULD TRY – AT LEAST ONCE

Pfannkuchen Known as 'Berliner' in other parts of Germany, these doughnut-like pastries are made from a yeasty dough, stuffed with a dollop of jam, deep-fried and tossed in granulated sugar.

Currywurst This classic cult snack, allegedly invented in Berlin in 1949, is a smallish fried or grilled wiener sliced into bite-sized ringlets, swimming in a spicy tomato sauce and dusted with curry powder. It's available *'mit'* or *'ohne'* (ie with or without) its crunchy epidermis and traditionally served on a flimsy plate with a plastic toothpick for stabbing.

Döner Spit-roasted meat may have been around forever, but the idea of serving it in a lightly toasted bread pocket with copious amounts of fresh salad and a healthy drizzle of yoghurt-based *Kräuter* (herb), *scharf* (spicy) or *Knoblauch* (garlic) sauce is a Berlin tradition conceived by Mehmed Ayguen, owner of the Hasir minichain of local Turkish restaurants.

Boulette Called *Frikadelle* in other parts of Germany, this cross between a meatball and a hamburger is eaten with a little mustard and perhaps a dry roll. The name is French for 'little ball' and might have originated during Napoleon's occupation of Berlin in the early 19th century.

Eisbein or Grillhaxe Boiled or grilled pork hock typically paired with sauerkraut and boiled potatoes.

Königsberger Klopse This classic dish may have its origin in Königsberg in eastern Prussia (today's Kaliningrad in Russia), but it has of late made a huge comeback on Berlin menus. It's a simple but elegant plate of golf-ball-sized veal meatballs in a caper-laced white sauce served with a side of boiled potatoes and beetroot.

Berliner Weisse This cloudy, slightly sour and very light wheat beer sweetened with a shot of woodruff or raspberry syrup is a refreshing drink on a hot summer's day.

TOP FIVE BERLIN FOOD BLOGS

It's no secret that Berlin is a fast-changing city and so it's only natural that the food scene also develops at lightning speed. Fortunately there are a number of passionate foodies keeping an eye on new openings and developments. As well as the following blogs, other recommended online sources (not necessarily only about food) include **Slow Travel Berlin** (www.slowtravelberlin.com), **CeeCee** (www.ceecee.cc) and **Sugar High** (www.sugarhigh.de).

Berlin Food Stories (www.berlinfoodstories.com) Excellent up-to-the-minute site by a dedicated food lover who keeps tabs on new restaurants and visits each one several times before writing honest, mouthwatering reviews.

Berlin on a Platter (www.thewednesdaychef.com/berlin_on_a_platter) Former New Yorker and cookbook editor Luisa Weiss (aka 'The Wednesday Chef') helps you get under the skin of Berlin's foodie scene by blogging about her favourite hidden gems and culinary discoveries.

Good Food in Berlin (www.goodfoodinberlin.de) On a quest to ferret out the best restaurants in Berlin, this blog can be a little dated, but still full of interesting nuggets.

Berlin Reified (www.reified.typepad.com) Not only about food, this is an inspirational blog about all those places that make Berlin special, written by expat Sylee Gore.

Stil in Berlin (www.stilinberlin.de) One of the longest-running city blogs (since 2006), Mary Sherpe's 'baby' keeps track of developments in food, fashion, style and art.

Lonely Planet's Top Choices

Reinstoff (p143) Double-Michelin temple puts your taste receptors on overtime with exotically reimagined German flavours.

Cafe Jacques (p158) Empty tables are as rare as hens' teeth in this candlelit cocoon with top Mediterranean food and wine.

Habba Habba (p191) This hole in the wall stuffs Middle Eastern wraps with unexpected meatless ingredients.

La Soupe Populaire (p194) Star chef Tim Raue takes German classics to new levels in an industrial-strength ex-brewery.

eins44 (p163) Neukölln fine-dining pioneer whips up clever but unfussy French-leaning food in a pimped-up old distillery.

Best by Budget

€

Berlin Burger International (p163) Gets our vote for Berlin's 'burger king'.

Bier's Kudamm 195 (p207) Our current currywurst favourite. There, we said it.

W – der Imbiss (p194) Perfect yin and yang of Italian-Indian cooking amid tiki decor.

District Mot (p141) Vietnamese comfort food in a setting inspired by the streets of Saigon.

€€

Frau Mittenmang (p193) Neighbourhood charmer puts unexpected riffs on traditional German cuisine.

Umami (p194) Sharp Indochine nosh for fans of the classics and the innovative amid sensuous lounge decor.

Bar Raval (p163) Fresh and vivid tapas for demanding grazers in an actor-owned Kreuzberg lair.

Der Hahn ist tot! (p194) Succulent coq au vin and more French faves at wallet-friendly prices.

Ishin (p94) Sushi may be the star of the show, but this unassuming cafeteria also rocks the rice bowls.

€€€

Restaurant Tim Raue (p95) Eponymous gourmet kitchen of bad-boy-turned-double-Michelin-star chef.

Katz Orange (p144) This stylish 'cat' fancies anything that's regional, seasonal and creative amid chic country decor.

Volt (p162) Seduces diners with contemporary spins of German classics starring regional bounty.

Pauly Saal (p144) Time-honoured regional dishes reinterpreted in modern Michelin-decorated fashion.

Best by Cuisine

Berlin Classics

Weinbar Rutz (p145) Fabulous wine complements the soulful goodness of Michelin-chef-interpreted local fare.

Zur Letzten Instanz (p116) Has done a roaring trade with local rib-stickers since 1621.

Max und Moritz (p161) Industrial-weight platters and local brews in charmingly decorated centenarian pub.

Modern German

Lokal (p144) True to its name, only top-notch local products are rendered into feisty flavour bombs.

Restaurant am Steinplatz (p211) Diverse and sometimes surprising array of ingredients find their destination in superb creations.

Oderquelle (p193) Consistent and inspired port of call for flawlessly executed favourites.

Traditional German

Augustiner am Gendarmenmarkt (p94) Go the whole hog at this famous Munich beer hall transplant.

Henne (p159) No misty-eyed nostalgia, just the ultimate roast chicken, and that since 1907.

Schwarzwaldstuben (p143) Oldies but goodies from Germany's south amid delightfully irreverent decor.

Asian

Cocolo Ramenbar (p158) Oodles of noodles in romantic canalside spot.

Umami (p194) Vietnamese food so perky it may get you off your Prozac.

Good Friends (p208) Berlin's best Chinese restaurant delivers a taste-bud tingling culinary journey.

Chèn Chè (p143) *Pho*-nomenal Vietnamese soups and more at courtyard-cloistered hideaway.

Italian

Osteria Centrale (p211) Serves a pan-Italian pastiche as comfortable as a hug from an old friend.

Lavanderia Vecchia (p163) Palate-pleasing and waist-expanding 13-course indulgence in a converted industrial laundry.

Muret La Barba (p143) Wine shop–cum-restaurant where meals have all the flavours of Italy locked inside them.

Vegetarian

Lucky Leek (p194) Richly satisfying meat-free dishes in stylish-minimalist Prenzlauer Berg haunt.

Mio Matto (p179) Pizza, pasta and other Italian tastebud teasers with a gourmet vegan twist.

Cookies Cream (p94) Clandestine meat-free kitchen tiptoes between hip and haute.

Turkish/Arabic

Hasir Kreuzberg (p161) Original outpost of classic local chain that invented the Berlin-style doner sandwich.

Maroush (p158) Finger-lickin' felafel makes an excellent stop on a bar hop.

City Chicken (p163) Perfect roasted birds and hummus at no-frills Neukölln shack.

Defne (p159) Turkish delights beyond the doner kebab, on the terrace in summer.

Best for Breakfast

Chipps (p94) Get the day in gear with a 'Sugar Daddy' or a 'Greek Goddess' at this vegetarian city slicker.

Anna Blume (p196) The three-tiered 'Anna Blume Special' on the sidewalk terrace of this floral charmer is the perfect greet-the-day choice.

Tomasa (p158) Rambling old villa with garden serves breakfast bonanza with homemade specialities until a hangover-friendly 4pm.

Cabslam – California Breakfast Slam (p162) Bloodshot party eyes disappear quickly with huevos rancheros, eggs Benedict and other West Coast faves.

Café am Neuen See (p132) Sleepyheads love the quiet Tiergarten park setting for leisurely alfresco breakfast served until 4pm.

Best for Burgers

Burgermeister (p163) Patty-and-bun joint in a historic toilet is a hugely popular pit stop on a budget.

Bird (p191) Expat favourite makes cooked-to-order burgers, now in two locations.

White Trash Fast Food (p169) New location, same habit-forming two-fisted burgers in circus-like ambience.

Best for Romance

Spindler & Klatt (p164) If your date doesn't make you swoon, the riverside setting should still make for an unforgettable evening.

Reinstoff (p143) Gourmet emporium is proof positive that the way to the heart is through the stomach.

Volt (p162) Modern German fare in a converted transformer station makes the sparks fly.

Cafe Jacques (p158) Fine wine, caring staff, candlelight and, above all, mouthwatering fare are the hallmarks of a romantic night out.

Cookies Cream (p94) Herbivore haven where you'll get kudos and kisses merely for finding the entrance.

Best for Celebrity-Spotting

Borchardt (p95) The extended dining room of a carousel of celebrities from film, fashion and politics.

Grill Royal (p144) Scan the crowd for Clooney or Damon while tucking into aged steaks and oysters at this riverside hang out.

Pauly Saal (p144) The fab and famous have adopted this Michelin haunt for off-the-radar noshing.

JÜRGEN HENKELMANN PHOTOGRAPHY/ALAMY ©

Beer garden at Clärchens Ballhaus (p145)

Drinking & Nightlife

With its well-deserved reputation as one of Europe's primo party capitals, Berlin offers a thousand and one scenarios for getting your cocktails and kicks (or wine or beer, for that matter).

Vodka martinis

Bars & Pubs

Berlin is a notoriously late city: bars stay packed from dusk to dawn and beyond, and some clubs don't hit their stride until 4am. The lack of a curfew never created a tradition of binge drinking, which is why many party folk prefer to pace their alcohol consumption and thus manage to keep going until the wee hours. Of course there's no denying that illegal drugs also play their part...

Edgier, more underground venues cluster in Kreuzberg, Friedrichshain, Neukölln and up-and-coming outer boroughs like Wedding (north of Mitte) and Lichtenberg (past Friedrichshain). Places in Charlottenburg, Mitte and Prenzlauer Berg tend to be quieter, close earlier and are thus more suited for date nights than dedicated drinking. Generally, the emphasis is on style and atmosphere and some proprietors have gone to extraordinary lengths to come up with special design concepts.

The line between cafe and bar is often blurred, with many changing stripes as the hands move around the clock. Alcohol, however, is served (and consumed) pretty much all day. Some bars have happy hours that usually run from 6pm to 9pm.

Cocktail bars are booming in Berlin and several new arrivals have measurably elevated the 'liquid art' scene. Dedicated drinking dens tend to be elegant cocoons with mellow lighting and low sound levels, helmed by mix-meisters capable of applying their classic training to boundary-pushing experimental riffs. A good cocktail will set you back between €10 and €15.

NEED TO KNOW

Opening Hours

➡ Many pubs also serve food and tend to be open from noon.

➡ Regular bars start up around 6pm and close at 1pm or 2pm the next day, later on weekends.

➡ Trendy places and cocktail bars don't open until 8pm or 9pm and stay open until the last tippler leaves.

➡ Clubs open at 11pm or midnight but don't fill up until 1am or 2am, reaching their peak between 4am and 6am. Many open only Friday and Saturday nights.

Costs

Big clubs like Berghain/Panorama Bar or Watergate will set you back €12 to €15 admission, but there are plenty of others that charge between €5 and €10. Places that open a bit earlier don't charge admission until a certain hour, usually 11pm or midnight. Student discounts are virtually unheard of, but some of the more mainstream clubs run 'Ladies Nights' when women get in free.

Dress Code

Berlin's clubs are very relaxed. In general, individual style almost always beats high heels and Armani. Cocktail bars and some clubs like Felix and Pearl may prefer a more glam look, but in pubs anything goes.

What's On?

For the latest scoop, scan the listings magazines *Zitty* (www.zitty.de), *Tip* (www.tip-berlin.de) or *030;* sift through flyers in shops, cafes, clubs and bars; and check internet platforms such as **Resident Advisor** (www.residentadvisor.net).

Most bars and pubs serve cocktails too, but of the Sex on the Beach and Cosmopolitan variety. Prices are lower (between €7 and €9) and quality can be hit-or-miss due to mediocre mixing talents and/or inferior spirits.

Although still lower than in other major capital cities, drinks prices have crept up over the last couple of years. To cater to the truly cash-strapped, some of Berlin's late-night convenience stores (called *Spätkauf* or

Above: Berghain/Panorama Bar (p181)
Left: Strandbar Mitte (p145)

Späti for short) have started to put out tables on the sidewalks for patrons to gather and consume their store-bought beverages.

BEER GARDENS, BEACH & ROOFTOP BARS

Berliners are sun cravers and as soon as the first rays spray their way into spring, outdoor tables show up faster than you can pour a pint of beer. The most traditional places for outdoor chilling are of course the beer gardens with long wooden benches set up beneath leafy old chestnuts and with cold beer and bratwurst on the menu.

In 2002, Berlin also jumped on the 'sandwagon' with the opening of its first beach bar, Strandbar Mitte, in a prime location on the Spree River. Many that followed have since been displaced by development, which has partly fuelled the latest trend: rooftop bars. Some of the best are in hotels, eg Amano (p146), Hotel de Rome (p233) and 25hours (p242), but also on the top decks of shopping malls, such as Deck 5 (p195) and Klunkerkranich (p166), and office buildings, such as House of Weekend (p117).

Outdoor boozing grounds tend to open from May to October, weather permitting.

ETIQUETTE

Table service is common, and you shouldn't order at the bar unless you intend to hang out there or there's a sign saying *Selbstbedienung* (self-service). It's customary to keep a tab instead of paying for each round separately. In bars with DJs €1 or €2 is usually added to the cost of your first drink. Tip bartenders about 5%, servers 10%. Drinking in public is legal and widely practised, especially around party zones. Try to be civilised about it, though. No puking on the U-Bahn, please!

Clubbing

Over the past 25 years, Berlin's club culture has put the city firmly on the map of hedonists. With more than 200 venues, finding one to match your mood shouldn't be a tall order. Electronic music in its infinite varieties continues to define Berlin's afterdark action but other sounds like hip hop, dancehall, rock, swing and funk have also made inroads. The edgiest clubs have taken up residence in power plants, transformer stations, abandoned apartment buildings and other repurposed locations.

The scene is in constant flux as experienced club owners look for new challenges and a younger generation of promoters enters the scene with new ideas and impetus. Overall, though, rising costs, development and noise complaints have shifted the focus away from heavily gentrified Prenzlauer Berg and Mitte down to Kreuzberg, Neukölln and Friedrichshain. However, as these districts too become more and more hyped, the wildest parties are staged even further afield in such boroughs as Lichtenberg, Treptow and Wedding.

WHEN TO GO

Whatever club or party you're heading for, don't bother showing up before 1am unless you want to have a deep conversation with a bored bartender. And don't worry about closing times – Berlin's famously long nights have gotten even later of late and, thanks to a growing number of after parties and daytime clubs, not going home at all is definitely an option at weekends. In fact, many folks put in a good night's sleep, then hit the dance floor when other people head for Sunday church.

AT THE DOOR

Doors are tough at some clubs such as Watergate (p167), Berghain/Panorama Bar (p181), Salon zur Wilden Renate (p181), Felix (p95) or Pearl (p211) but, overall, making it past the bouncer is still easier in Berlin than in other European capitals. There's generally no need to dress up, and sometimes flaunting fancy labels and glam cocktail dresses can get in the way of your getting in. And if your attitude is right, age rarely matters. If you have to queue, be respectful, don't drink and don't talk too loudly. Don't arrive wasted. As elsewhere, large groups (even mixed ones) have a lower chance of getting in, so split up if you can. If you do get turned away, don't argue. And don't worry, there's always another party somewhere...

Drinks

Predictably, beer is big in Berlin and served – and consumed – almost everywhere all day long. Most places pour a variety of local, national and imported brews, including at least one draught beer *(vom Fass)* served in 300mL or 500mL glasses. In summer, drinking your lager as an Alster, Radler or Diesel (mixed with Fanta, Sprite or Coke, respectively) is a popular thirst quencher.

Beer has been brewed in Berlin since the Middle Ages, reaching its peak in the 19th century when there used to be hundreds of breweries, especially in Prenzlauer Berg. Today, the only commercial one left is the **Berliner Kindl-Schultheiss Brauerei** (www.schultheiss.de; Indira-Gandhi-Strasse 66-69; tours €5, with beer tasting €7; ☉10am, 2pm & 5.30pm Mon-Thu; 🚊M13 to Betriebshof Indira-Gandhi-Strasse), which produces the Berliner Pilsner, Schultheiss, Berliner Kindl and Berliner Bürgerbräu brands. For a behind-the-scenes look, book a guided tour (in German) – preferably followed by a beer tasting – via its website.

In recent years the craft-beer trend finally reached a tipping point in Berlin, with numerous boutique brewers now in business and craft-beer festivals luring thousands to quaff homemade IPA (Indian pale ale), pilsner, wheat beer and other classic and novel varieties. Local brands to look for include Rollberger, Heidenpeters, Vagabund, Flessa Bräu and Bierfabrik. Brewpubs include Pfefferbräu (p196) in Prenzlauer Berg, Hops & Barley (p179) and Schalander (p177) in Friedrichshain and Brauhaus Georgbräu (p117) near Museum Island.

Other German and imported beers are widely available. There's plenty of Beck's and Heineken around but for more flavour look for Jever Pilsener from northern Germany, Rothaus Tannenzäpfle from the Black Forest, Zywiec from Poland, and Krušovice and Budweiser from the Czech Republic. American Budweiser is practically nonexistent here.

For a selection of other Berlin-made beverages, see p166.

BEER VARIETIES

The most common brews include the following:

Pils (pilsner) Bottom-fermented beer with a pronounced hop flavour and a creamy head.

Weizenbier/Weissbier (wheat beer) Top-fermented wheat beer that's fruity and refreshing. Comes bottled either as *Hefeweizen*, which has a stronger shot of yeast, or the filtered and fizzier *Kristallweizen*.

Berliner Weisse This cloudy, slightly sour wheat beer is typically sweetened with a *Schuss* (shot) of woodruff or raspberry syrup. It's quite refreshing on a hot day but few locals drink it.

Wheat beer

Schwarzbier (black beer, like porter) This full-bodied dark beer is fermented using roasted malt.

Bockbier Strong beer with around 7% alcohol; brewed seasonally. Maibock shows up in May, Weihnachtsbock around Christmas.

WINE

Oenophiles rejoice! If the recent crop of newcomers is any indication, wine bars seem to be approaching their zenith in Berlin. Many are bar/shop hybrids and some also serve food. Run by wine enthusiasts, they have an egalitarian rather than elitist mood, with wines for all budgets. Some specialise in *vin naturel* ('natural wine', ie organically grown and handled with minimal chemical interference), which often looks cloudy and tastes a bit tart at first. But then,,,,

In regular pubs and bars the quality of wine ranges from drinkable to abysmal, which is probably why so many Germans drink it with fizzy water, called a *Weinschorle*. Wine is usually served in 200mL glasses. However, in better bars, as well as in a growing number of restaurants, better-quality wine is now served in mere 100mL glasses.

Sparkling wine comes in 100mL flutes. Depending on where a place sees itself on the trendiness scale, it will offer German *Sekt,* Italian Prosecco or French *cremant.* In clubs it's often served *Sekt auf Eis* (on the rocks). Champagne is trendy among the monied set.

Party Miles
SCHEUNENVIERTEL

Torstrasse This noisy strip is where Berlin demonstrates that it too can grow up. A globe-spanning roster of monied creatives populates the chic drinking dens with their well-thought-out bar concepts, sleek decor and drinks made with top-shelf spirits.

Oranienburger Strasse Tourist zone where you have to hopscotch around sex workers and pub crawlers to find the few remaining thirst parlours worth your money.

KREUZBERG & NORTHERN NEUKÖLLN

Weserstrasse The main party drag in hyped Neukölln hood is packed with an eclectic mix of pubs and bars, from trashy to stylish.

Kottbusser Tor & Oranienstrasse Grunge-tastic area perfect for dedicated drink-a-thons with a punky-funky flair.

Schlesische Strasse Freestyle strip where you could kick off with cocktails at Badeschiff, catch a band at Magnet Club, heat up the dance floor at Watergate, then chill in the morning sun at Club der Visionäre.

Köpenicker Strasse Industrial-flavoured riverside patch where nights might start with supper and drinks at chic Spindler & Klatt, then move on to first-hour techno temple Tresor or the libidinous KitKatClub.

Skalitzer Strasse Eclectic, more local-flavoured street with some quality cocktail bars just off it (Schwarze Traube, Locke Müller)

FRIEDRICHSHAIN

Revaler Strasse The skinny-jeanster set invades the gritty clubs and bars along this 'techno strip' set up in a former train-repair station. Live concerts at Astra Kulturhaus, techno-electro at Suicide Circus, a potpourri of sounds at Cassiopeia and various off-kilter bars in between.

PLAN YOUR TRIP DRINKING & NIGHTLIFE

Cafe life in Kreuzberg (p164)

Drinking & Nightlife by Neighbourhood

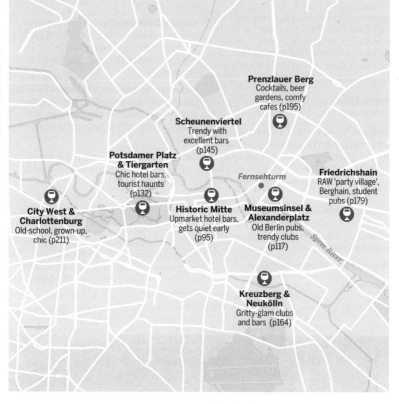

Prenzlauer Berg
Cocktails, beer gardens, comfy cafes (p195)

Scheunenviertel
Trendy with excellent bars (p145)

Potsdamer Platz & Tiergarten
Chic hotel bars, tourist haunts (p132)

Fernsehturm

Friedrichshain
RAW 'party village', Berghain, student pubs (p179)

City West & Charlottenburg
Old-school, grown-up, chic (p211)

Historic Mitte
Upmarket hotel bars, gets quiet early (p95)

Museumsinsel & Alexanderplatz
Old Berlin pubs, trendy clubs (p117)

Spree River

Kreuzberg & Neukölln
Gritty-glam clubs and bars (p164)

Ostkreuz Draw a bead on this cool party zone by staggering through the dark trying to find the entrance to Salon zur Wilden Renate or ://about blank.

Ostbahnhof Hardcore partying at Berghain/ Panorama Bar and mellow chilling at Yaam.

Simon-Dach-Strasse If you need a cheap buzz, head to this well-trodden booze strip popular with field-tripping school groups and stag parties. Locals? More towards the lower end (towards Revaler Strasse).

Lonely Planet's Top Choices

Berghain/Panorama Bar (p181) Hyped but still happening Holy Grail of techno clubs with DJ royalty every weekend.

Clärchens Ballhaus (p145) Hipsters mix it up with grannies for tango and jitterbug in a kitsch-glam 1913 ballroom.

Club der Visionäre (p167) Summers wouldn't be the same without chilling and dancing in this historic canalside boat shed.

Prater (p196) Berlin's oldest beer garden still rocks beneath the chestnuts after 175 years in business.

Würgeengel (p160) Fun crowd keeps the cocktails and conversation flowing in a genuine '50s setting.

Best Clubs

Prince Charles (p165) Bar-club combo spinning fine electro in a former swimming pool.

://about blank (p181) Trashy techno hot spot with enchanting garden chill zone.

Sisyphos (p180) Summer-only party village in retired dog-food factory.

Salon zur wilden Renate (p181) Psychedelic home of flashy-trashy electro parties in an abandoned apartment building.

Suicide Circus (p180) Top techno line-ups on indoor/outdoor floors in former warehouse.

Best Brewpubs

Hops & Barley (p179) Fabulous unfiltered pilsner, dark and wheat beer made in a former butcher's shop.

Schalander (p177) Off-the-tourist-radar gastro-pub named for the breakroom used by brewery workers.

Pfefferbräu (p196) Recent reincarnation of 19th-century brewery with small beer garden.

Hopfenreich (p167) Doesn't brew its own but gets our nod for being Berlin's first craft-beer bar.

Best Cocktail Bars

Schwarze Traube (p165) Pint-size drinking parlour with bespoke cocktails.

Locke Müller (p165) Chilled Kreuzberg dispensary of some of the finest cocktails in town.

Becketts Kopf (p195) Wait for Godot while sipping supreme classics and seasonal inspirations.

Le Croco Bleu (p196) Artful potions in an industrial magical forest at an ex-brewery.

Bar Marques (p167) Cocktail classics for grown-ups in a colonial-style basement bar.

Best Wine Bars

Maxim (p146) Minimalist-chic emporium for top-flight natural wines and gooey cheeses.

Vin Aqua Vin (p165) Eliminates wine-bar trepidation with casual vibe and wallet-friendly vintages.

Weinerei (p196) Works on the honour system: drink, then decide how much to pay.

Otto Rink (p160) For relaxed oenophiles with a penchant for German vintages.

Best Rooftop Bars

Klunkerkranich (p166) Hipster spot with garden atop Neukölln shopping centre.

Deck 5 (p195) Beach vibe with a view from the top parking deck of a Prenzlauer Berg shopping mall.

House of Weekend (p117) Cocktails and barbecue at eye level with the TV Tower.

Monkey Bar (p211) Exotic tiki drinks with view of the baboons of the Berlin Zoo.

Amano Bar (p146) Bird's-eye views of the Scheunenviertel at the summer edition of the fine Amano hotel bar.

Best for Final Drinks

Mein Haus am See (p146) Any time is a good time to stumble into this 24/7 bar at Rosenthaler Platz.

Roses (p161) This 'Queen of Camp' is the ultimate on Kreuzberg's roster of eccentric trash dive bars.

August Fengler (p196) When the party shuts down in Prenzlauer Berg, Fengler keeps going...and going...

Revellers at Christopher Street Day (p66)

Gay & Lesbian Berlin

Berlin's legendary liberalism has spawned one of the world's biggest, most divine and diverse GLBT playgrounds. Anything goes in 'Homopolis' (and we do mean anything!), from the highbrow to the hands-on, the bourgeois to the bizarre, the mainstream to the flamboyant. Except for the most hardcore places, gay spots get their share of opposite-sex and straight patrons.

Gay in Berlin

Generally speaking, Berlin's gayscape runs the entire spectrum from mellow cafes, campy bars and cinemas to saunas, cruising areas, clubs with darkrooms and all-out sex venues. In fact, sex and sexuality are entirely everyday matters to the unshockable city folks and there are very few, if any, itches that can't be quite openly and legally scratched. As elsewhere, gay men have more options for having fun, but grrrrls – from lipstick lesbians to hippie chicks to bad-ass dykes – won't feel left out either.

History

Berlin's emergence as a gay capital has roots in 1897 when sexual scientist Magnus Hirschfeld founded the Scientific Humanitarian Committee, the world's first homosexual advocacy group. Gay life thrived in the wild and wacky 1920s, driven by a demimonde that drew and inspired writers like Christopher Isherwood, until the Nazis put an end to the fun in 1933. Postwar recovery came slowly, but by the 1970s the scene was firmly re-established, at least in the western city. Since 2001, Berlin has been governed by an openly gay mayor, Klaus Wowereit. To learn more about Berlin's queer history, visit the Schwules Museum (p129).

Clubbing

Berlin's scene is especially fickle and venues and dates may change at the drop of a hat, so make sure you always check the websites or the listings magazines for the latest scoop. Unless noted, these parties are geared towards men.

Cafe Fatal All comers descend on SO36 (p165) for the ultimate rainbow tea dance that goes from 'strictly ballroom' to 'dirty dancing' in a flash. If you can't tell a waltz from a foxtrot, come at 7pm for free lessons. Sundays.

Chantals House of Shame Trash diva Chantal's louche lair at Bassy (p196) is a beloved institution, not so much for the glam factor as for the over-the-top transvestite shows and the hotties who love 'em. Thursdays.

Girls Town (www.girlstown-berlin.de) Suse and Zoe's buzzy girl-fest takes over Gretchen (p165) in Kreuzberg with down-and-dirty pop, electro, indie and rock. Second Saturday of every other month, September to May.

Gayhane Geared towards gay and lesbian Muslims, but everyone's welcome to rock the kasbah when this 'homoriental' party takes over SO36 (p165) with Middle Eastern beats and belly dancing. Last Saturday of the month.

GMF (www.gmf-berlin.de) Berlin's premier Sunday club, currently at Club Avenue (p117), is known for excessive SM (standing and modelling) with lots of smooth surfaces – and that goes for both the crowd and the setting. Predominantly boyz, but girls OK.

L-Tunes (www.l-tunes.com) Lesbians get their groove on in the dancing pit of SchwuZ (p167). With speed-dating lounge and darkroom. Last Saturday of the month.

Homopatik Get lost on the multiple dark dance floors and in the idyllic garden when this hipster party for gays and friends takes over ://about blank (p181) in Friedrichshain. Third Friday of the month.

Horse Meat Disco This London import now has a queer free-for-all monthly residency in Berlin with electro-house beats raining down on a burly crowd at Prince Charles (p165). Every second Saturday of the month.

Irrenhaus (www.ninaqueer.com) The name means 'insane asylum' and that's no joke. Party hostess with the mostest, trash queen Nina Queer puts on nutty, naughty shows at Kreuzberg's **Comet Club** (Falckensteinstrasse 48; [S]Schlesische Strasse) that are not for the faint-of-heart. Expect the best. Fear the worst. Third Saturday of the month.

NEED TO KNOW

Magazines

Blu (www.blu.fm) Print and online magazine with searchable, up-to-the-minute location and event listings.

L-Mag (www.l-mag.de) Bimonthly magazine for lesbians.

Out in Berlin (www.out-in-berlin.com) Up-to-date free English/German booklet and website, often found at tourist offices.

Siegessäule (www.siegessaeule.de) Free weekly lesbigay 'bible'.

Websites

Gay Berlin4u (www.gayberlin4u.com)

GayCities Berlin (www.berlin.gay cities.com)

Discodamaged (www.discodamaged.net)

Patroc Gay Guide (www.patroc.de/ berlin)

Tours

Berlinagenten (p293) Customised gay-lifestyle tours (nightlife, shopping, luxury, history, culinary).

Lügentour (www.luegentour.de) Interactive and humorous walking tour takes you back to the lesbigay scene in 1920s Schöneberg; alas in German only.

Schröder Reisen Comedy Bus (www. comedy-im-bus.de) Outrageous comedy bus tours led by trash drag royalty and self-styled 'VIP housewife on the dole' Edith Schröder and friends.

Help

Mann-O-Meter (www.mann-o-meter.de) Gay men's information centre.

Maneo (www.maneo.de) Gay victim support centre and gay-attack hotline.

Lesbenberatung (www.lesbenbera tung-berlin.de) Lesbian resource centre.

Mermaids (www.mermaids-party.de) This steamy summer-only party draws lesbians and their queer and straight friends. Check the website for dates and location. Usually third Saturday of the month, May to September.

Klub International (www.klub-international. com) Up to 1500 boyz-to-men come out to the glamorous Kino International (p183) to work three sizzling dance floors presided over by trash queens like Biggy van Blond, Nina Queer and Ades Zabel. First Saturday of the month.

Pet Shop Bears (www.petshopbears.com) This party attracts a *Butt* magazine type international crowd of lean but hairy 30- and 40-somethings who come for kicking electropop. At Kantine am Berghain (p183). Last Friday of the month.

Pork A down-at-heel sex club during the week, **Ficken 3000** (www.ficken3000.com; Urbanstrasse 70; ⏰10pm Sun; SHermannplatz) truly hits its stride on Sundays for this polysexual artytrash party. Dancing upstairs, orgy downstairs.

Propaganda (www.propaganda-party.de) Currently at the **Imperial Club** (Friedrichstrasse 101) in Mitte, this New York–style house and electro party-and-a-half draws fashionable see-and-be-scenesters with its big sound and buff and bronzed go-go dancers. First Saturday of the month.

Rose Kennedy (www.ninaqueer.de) Another Nina Queer production, this one lures revellers down into the catacombs of **Brunnen 70** (www.brunnen70.de; Brunnenstrasse 70; SVoltastrasse) in Wedding for a night of pop and house. Every fourth Saturday of the month.

WednesGay New party series at the **Sophienclub** (www.sophienclub.de; Sophienstrasse 6) with pop, dance and electro on two floors. First and third Wednesday of the month.

Festivals & Events

Leather & Fetish Week (www.blf.de) Europe's biggest fetish fest whips the leather, rubber, skin and military sets out of the dungeons and into the clubs over the long Easter weekend. It culminates with the crowning of the 'German Mr Leather'.

Lesbisch-Schwules Stadtfest (www.regenbogenfonds.de) The Lesbigay Street Festival takes over the Schöneberg rainbow village in June, with bands, food, info booths and partying.

Christopher Street Day (www.csd-berlin.de) Later in June, hundreds of thousands of people of various sexual persuasions paint the town pink with a huge parade and more queens than at a royal wedding.

Transgenialer CSD (www.transgenialercsd.wordpress.com) Also in June, Kreuzberg celebrates this alternative version of CSD.

Lesbischwules Parkfest (www.parkfest-friedrichshain.de) The gay community takes over the Volkspark Friedrichshain for this delightfully noncommercial festival in August.

Folsom Europe (www.folsomeurope.info) The leather crowd returns in early September for another weekend of kinky partying.

Hustlaball (www.hustlaball.de) The party year wraps up in October with a weekend of debauched fun in the company of porn stars, go-gos, trash queens, stripping hunks and about 3000 other men who love 'em.

Gay & Lesbian by Neighbourhood

➡ **Museumsinsel & Alexanderplatz** GMF, the best gay Sunday party, currently has a residency at the retro Club Avenue on Karl-Marx-Allee. (p117)

➡ **Scheunenviertel** Gets a mixed crowd, but its stylish and trendy bars and cafes also draw a sizeable contingent of queer customers. (p145)

➡ **Kreuzberg & Neukölln** Hipster central. Things are still comparatively subdued in the bars and cafes along main-strip Mehringdamm. Around Kottbusser Tor and along Oranienstrasse the crowd skews younger, wilder and more alternative, and key venues stay open till sunrise and beyond. For a DIY subcultural vibe, head across the canal to northern Neukölln, which also has a couple of outrageously offbeat theatres. (p164)

➡ **Friedrichshain** This area is thin on gay bars but is still a de rigueur stop on the gay nightlife circuit thanks to clubs like Berghain and the hands-on Lab.oratory, and monthly parties at Kino International. (p179)

➡ **Prenzlauer Berg** East Berlin's pink hub before the fall of the Wall has a few surviving relics as well as a couple of popular cruising dens and fun stations for the fetish set. (p195)

➡ **Schöneberg** The area around Nollendorfplatz (Motzstrasse and Fuggerstrasse especially) has been a gay mecca since the 1920s. Institutions like Tom's, Connection and Hafen pull in the punters night after night, and there's also plenty of action for the leather and fetish set. (p211)

Lonely Planet's Top Choices

GMF (p117) Glamtastic Sunday club with pretty people in stylish East Berlin retro location.

Roses (p161) Plush, pink, campy madhouse – an essential stop on a lesbigay bar hop.

Möbel Olfe (p160) This old furniture store recast as busy drinking den is standing room only on (unofficial) gay Thursdays.

Chantals House of Shame (p197) Eponymous trash-drag diva's parties run wild and wicked.

Horse Meat Disco (p165) Monthly residency brings manly men to Prince Charles for electro-house beats.

Best Venues by Day of the Week

Monday
Monster Ronson's Ichiban Karaoke (p182) Loosen those lungs and get louche.

Tuesday
Himmelreich (p179) Smart cocktails and 'ladies' only.

Möbel Olfe (p160) Comfortably cheerful femme fave.

Wednesday
Marietta (p196) Meet, sip and chat.

Thursday
Möbel Olfe (p160) Boys' get-together.

Chantals House of Shame (p197) Over-the-top drag queen party.

Friday
SchwuZ (p167) Weekend warm-up.

Lab.oratory (p182) Two-4-one drinks, no dress code.

Saturday
SchwuZ (p167) Good for newbies.

Berghain (p181) Advanced partying.

Sunday
GMF (p117) Hot-stepping weekend wrap-up.

Cafe Fatal @ SO36 (p165) All-ages tea dance.

Best Gay Bars & Cafes

Möbel Olfe (p160) Relaxed Kreuzberg joint goes into gay turbodrive on Thursdays, femmes dominate at Tuesday's Mädchendisko.

Himmelreich (p179) This '50s retro lounge is a lesbigay-scene stalwart in Friedrichshain.

Zum Schmutzigen Hobby (p181) Cheap drinks and campy fun in Friedrichshain.

Best for Camp

Roses (p161) This pink-fur-walled kitsch institution is an unmissable late-night fuelling stop.

Best for Women

Himmelreich (p179) Women's Lounge on Tuesdays brings cool chicks to this comfy Friedrichshain bar.

Möbel Olfe (p160) Pop, disco and rock music get lesbians and their friends into party mood at Mädchendisko on Tuesdays.

Best Sex Clubs/ Darkrooms

Lab.oratory (p182) Fetish-oriented experimental play zone in industrial setting below Berghain.

Greifbar (p196) Friendly cruising bar in Prenzlauer Berg with video, darkroom and private areas.

Connection Club (p213) Legendary dance club in Schöneberg with Berlin's largest cruising labyrinth.

FRANZISKA KRUG/GETTY IMAGES ©

Performance by Friedrichstadtpalast (p148) dancers

⭐ Entertainment

Berlin's cultural scene is lively, edgy and the richest and most varied in the German-speaking world. With three state-supported opera houses, five major orchestras – including the world-class Berliner Philharmoniker – scores of theatres, cinemas, cabarets and concert venues, you've got enough entertainment options to last you a lifetime.

Classical Music

Classical-music fans are truly spoilt in Berlin. Not only is there a phenomenal range of concerts throughout the year, but most of the major concert halls are architectural and acoustic gems of the highest order. A trip to the Philharmonie or the Konzerthaus is a particular treat, and regular concerts are also organised in many churches and palaces such as Schloss Charlottenburg and Schloss Köpenick.

Top of the pops is, of course, the world-famous Berliner Philharmoniker, which was founded in 1882 and counts Hans Bülow, Wilhelm Furtwängler and Herbert von Karajan among its music directors. Since 2002, Sir Simon Rattle has continued the tradition.

Though not in the same league, the other orchestras are no musical slouches either. Look for concerts by the Berliner Symphoniker, the Deutsches Symphonie-Orchester, the Konzerthausorchester and the Rundfunk-Sinfonieorchester Berlin. Note that most venues take a summer hiatus (usually July and August).

A special treat are the Sunday concerts (p147) in a historic mirror hall above Clärchens Ballhaus in the Scheunenviertel.

Opera

Not many cities afford themselves the luxury of three state-funded opera houses, but then opera has been popular in Berlin ever since the first fat lady loosened her lungs. Today, fans can catch some of Germany's biggest and best performances here. Leading the pack in the prestige department is the **Staatsoper Unter den Linden** (Unter den Linden 7; 🚌100, 200, TXL, [S]Bahn Französische Strasse), the oldest among the three, founded by Frederick the Great in 1743. The hallowed hall hosted many world premieres, including Carl Maria von Weber's *Der Freischütz* and Alban Berg's *Wozzeck*. Giacomo Meyerbeer, Richard Strauss and Herbert von Karajan were among its music directors. Since reunification, Daniel Barenboim has swung the baton.

The Komische Oper (Comic Opera; p96) opened in 1947 with *Die Fledermaus* by Johann Strauss and still champions light opera, operettas and dance theatre. Across town in Charlottenburg, the Deutsche Oper Berlin (p213) entered the scene in 1912 with Beethoven's *Fidelio*. It was founded by local citizens keen on creating a counterpoint to the royal Staatsoper.

Film

Berliners keep a wide array of cinemas in business, from indie art houses and tiny neighbourhood screens to stadium-style megaplexes. Mainstream Hollywood movies are dubbed into German, but numerous theatres also show flicks in their original language, denoted in listings by the acronym 'OF' *(Originalfassung)* or 'OV' *(Originalversion)*; those with German subtitles are marked 'OmU' *(Original mit Untertiteln)*. The Cinestar Original (p133) at the Sony Center in Potsdamer Platz only screens films in the original English.

Food and drink may be taken inside the auditoriums, although you are of course expected to purchase your beer and popcorn (usually at inflated prices) at the theatre. Almost all cinemas also add a sneaky *Überlängezuschlag* (overrun supplement) of €0.50 to €1.50 for films longer than 90 minutes. There's also a surcharge for 3D

NEED TO KNOW

Tickets

➡ It's always advisable to buy tickets in advance, but essential in the case of the Berliner Philharmoniker, the Staatsoper and big-name concerts.

➡ Credit-card bookings by telephone, or online through a venue's box office, are fairly common but usually come with a small service charge. Some places only take reservations, requiring you to pick up tickets before the show.

➡ *Theaterkasse* (ticket agencies) may still have tickets when the theatre's own contingent is sold out. These are commonly found in shopping malls. Service fees can be hefty. The main online agency is **Eventim** (www.eventim.de).

➡ **Hekticket** (www.hekticket.de) sells left-over tickets for same-day performances at half price between 2pm and 7pm online, by phone and in person at its outlets near Zoo Station (Hardenbergstrasse 29d) and Alexanderplatz (Karl-Liebknecht-Strasse 13; cash only).

➡ Some theatres sell unsold tickets at a discount 30 minutes or an hour before curtain. Some restrict this to students.

➡ It's fine to buy spare tickets from other theatregoers, but you might want to make sure they're legit (eg by showing them to an usher or the box-office clerk) before forking over any cash.

➡ For indie concerts and events, the best agency is **Koka 36** (www.koka36.de; Oranienstrasse 29) in Kreuzberg. Takes orders from out-of-country.

➡ Classical-music aficionados under 30 can get cheaper tickets by buying the **ClassicCard** (www.classiccard.de).

Print & Online Resources

Tip (www.tip.de) Biweekly listings magazine (in German).

Zitty (www.zitty.de) Biweekly listings magazine, more alternative than *Tip* (in German).

Ex-Berliner (www.ex-berliner.de) Expat-oriented English-language monthly.

Gratis in Berlin (www.gratis-in-berlin.de) Free events (in German).

movies plus a €1 rental fee if you don't have your own glasses. Seeing a flick on a *Kinotag* (film day, usually Monday or Tuesday) can save you a couple of euros.

From May to September, alfresco screenings are a popular tradition, with classic and contemporary flicks spooling off in *Freiluftkinos* (open-air cinemas). Come early to stake out a good spot, and bring pillows, blankets and snacks. Films are usually screened in their original language with German subtitles, or in German with English subtitles. Here are some of our favourites:

Freiluftkino Friedrichshain (p174) In the open-air amphitheatre at Volkspark Friedrichshain.

Freiluftkino Insel im Cassiopeia (☎030-694 1147; www.freiluftkino-insel.de; Revaler Strasse 99; tickets €6.50; [S]Warschauer Strasse, 🚇Warschauer Strasse) Free blankets; Friedrichshain.

Freiluftkino Kreuzberg (☎030-2936 1628; www.freiluftkino-kreuzberg.de; Mariannenplatz; tickets €7; ⏰daily May-Aug) In the courtyard of Kunstquartier Bethanien.

Open Air Kino Mitte (☎030-2859 9973; Rosenthaler Strasse 39; tickets €6; 🚋M1, 🚇Hackescher Markt) In the courtyard of Haus Schwarzenberg.

Berlin also plays host to most German and international movie premieres and, in February, stages the single most important event on Germany's film calendar, the Berlin International Film Festival. Better known as the **Berlinale** (www.berlinale.de), it was founded in 1951 on the initiative of the Western Allies. Around 400 films are screened in theatres around town, with some of them competing for the Golden and Silver Bear trophies.

Dozens of other film festivals take place throughout the year, including 'Achtung Berlin', featuring movies made in Berlin and, yes, the 'Porn Film Festival'. For the entire schedule, see http://berliner-film festivals.de.

Live Rock, Pop, Jazz & Blues

Berlin's live-music scene is as diverse as the city itself. There's no Berlin sound as such, but many simultaneous trends, from punk rock to hardcore rap and hip hop, reggae to sugary pop and downtempo jazz. With three top clubs – Magnet (p169), Bii Nuu (p169) and Lido (p169) – the area around Schlesisches Tor U-Bahn station in Kreuzberg is sound central. Another prime venue, the Astra Kulturhaus (p182), is just across the river in Friedrichshain. Some venues turn into dance clubs after the concerts. With scores of pubs and bars also hosting concerts, you're never far from a musical good time.

International top artists perform at various venues around town:

C-Halle (☎030-698 0980; www.c-halle.de; Columbiadamm 13-21; [S]Platz der Luftbrücke) Started out as a US air-force gym and now hosts up to 3500 fans, primarily for rock and pop concerts.

Kindl-Bühne Wuhlheide (www.kindl-buehne-wuhlheide.de; An der Wuhlheide 187; ⏰May-Sep; 🚇Wuhlheide) This 17,000-seat outdoor amphitheatre in the deep east was built in the early 1950s from war debris and is much beloved for its vibe and variety.

O2 World (☎tickets 030-206 070 8899; www.o2world.de; Mühlenstrasse 12-30; [S]Warschauer Strasse, 🚇Ostbahnhof, Warschauer Strasse) The jewel among Berlin's multiuse venues, this 17,000-seat arena has welcomed entertainment royalty (Tina Turner, Lady Gaga) and is also home turf for the city's professional ice-hockey team, the Eisbären Berlin, and basketball team, Alba Berlin.

Olympiastadion (p210) With 74,400 seats, the historic Olympic stadium is Berlin's biggest venue and also home to soccer team Hertha BSC.

Tempodrom (☎tickets 01806 554 111; www.tempodrom.de; Möckernstrasse 10; 🚇Anhalter Bahnhof) The white, tent-shaped Tempodrom has supereclectic programming that may feature a salsa congress, a Steve Winwood concert and the German snooker masters all in the same month.

Waldbühne Berlin (☎01806 570 070; www.waldbuehne-berlin.de; Glockenturmstrasse 1; ⏰May-Sep; 🚇Pichelsberg) The 22,000-seat open-air amphitheatre in the woods has been around since 1936 and has exceptional acoustics.

Theatre

Get ready to smell the greasepaint and hear the roar of the crowd; with more than 100 stages around town, theatre is a mainstay of Berlin's cultural scene. Add in a particularly active collection of roaming companies and experimental outfits and you'll find there are more than enough offerings to satisfy all possible tastes. Kurfürstendamm in

Charlottenburg and the area around Friedrichstrasse in Mitte (the 'East End'), are Berlin's main drama drags.

Most plays are performed in German, naturally, but of late several of the major stages – including Schaubühne (p213), Volksbühne (p148) and Maxim Gorki (p96) – have started using English surtitles in some of their productions. There's also the English Theatre Berlin (p167), which has some pretty innovative productions often dealing with sociopolitical themes, including racism, identity and expat-related issues.

Many theatres are closed on Mondays and from mid-July to late August.

The **Berliner Theatertreffen** (Berlin Theatre Meeting; www.theatertreffen-berlin.de), in May, is a three-week-long celebration of new plays and productions that brings together top ensembles from Germany, Austria and Switzerland.

Cabaret

The light, lively and lavish variety shows of the Golden Twenties have been undergoing a sweeping revival in Berlin. Get ready for an evening of dancing and singing, jugglers, acrobats and other entertainers. A popular venue is the Bar Jeder Vernunft (p213) and its larger sister Tipi am Kanzleramt (p96) whose occasional reprise of the musical *Cabaret* plays to sell-out audiences. In the heart of the 'East End' Theatre District, Friedrichstadtpalast (p148) is Europe's largest revue theatre and the realm of leggy, feather-clad dancers and Vegas-worthy technology. The nearby Chamäleon Varieté (p147) is considerably more intimate. Travelling shows camp out at the lovely **Wintergarten Varieté** (☑030-2500 8888; www.wintergarten-variete.de; Potsdamer Strasse 96; tickets €22-67; ⓤKurfürstenstrasse).

These 'cabarets' should not be confused with *Kabarett,* which are political and satirical shows with monologues and skits.

Dance

With independent choreographers and youthful companies consistently promoting experimental choreography, Berlin's independent dance scene is thriving as never before. The biggest name in choreography is Sasha Waltz, whose company Sasha Waltz & Guests has a residency at the cutting-edge Radialsystem V (p183). Other indie venues include Dock 11 (p197) and Hebbel am Ufer (p168). The latter, in cooperation with Tanzwerkstatt Berlin, organises **Tanz im August** (www.tanzimaugust. de), Germany's largest contemporary-dance festival, which attracts loose-limbed talent and highly experimental choreography from around the globe.

In the mainstream, the Staatsballett Berlin (Berlin State Ballet) performs both at the Staatsoper Unter den Linden and at the Deutsche Oper Berlin.

Live Comedy

Berlin's vast expat community fuels a lively English-language comedy scene with everything from stand-up to sketch and musical comedy being performed around town. Upcoming events are posted on www.comedyinenglish.de. One of the better-known regular shows is the biweekly Fish Bowl Comedy Showcase. The Kookaburra (p197) comedy club does English-language shows on Tuesdays nights.

Entertainment by Neighbourhood

- ➡ **Historic Mitte** Tops for classical music and opera. (p96)
- ➡ **Potsdamer Platz & Tiergarten** State-of-the-art multiplexes, casino. (p133)
- ➡ **Scheunenviertel** Cabaret, comedy, cinema and the 'East End' theatre district. (p147)
- ➡ **Kreuzberg & Neukölln** Live music, off-theatre, art-house cinemas. (p167)
- ➡ **Friedrichshain** Live music, outdoor cinema. (p182)
- ➡ **Prenzlauer Berg** Live music. (p197)
- ➡ **City West & Charlottenburg** Theatre, opera, jazz and indie screens. (p213)

Lonely Planet's Top Choices

Berliner Philharmonie (p133) One of the world's top orchestras within its own 'cathedral of sound'.

Staatsoper im Schiller Theater (p213) Top-ranked opera house.

Babylon (p147) Diverse and intelligent film programming in a 1920s building.

Lido (p169) Head-bobbing platform for indie bands, big names included.

Best for Classical Music

Philharmonie (p133) The one and only. Enough said.

Konzerthaus Berlin (p96) Schinkel-designed concert hall festooned with fine sculpture; a festive backdrop for fine symphonies.

Sonntagskonzerte (p147) Intimate concerts amid charmingly faded 1920s grandeur.

Best for Theatre

English Theatre Berlin (p167) Innovative and often provocative productions by Berlin's English-language theatre.

Volksbühne am Rosa-Luxemburg-Platz (p148) Cutting-edge and nonmainstream interpretations of the classics and new plays, with English surtitles.

Schaubühne (p213) Thought-provoking contemporary plays in repurposed 1920s Streamline Moderne cinema, with English surtitles.

Maxim Gorki (p96) 'Postmigrant' theatre with multicultural cast picks up on works that address upheavals and transitions in society; with English surtitles.

Best Live-Music Venues

Magnet Club (p169) Essential indie-rock venue and new-artist incubator.

Lido (p169) Great for catching tomorrow's headliners of the rock-indie-electro-pop persuasions.

Astra Kulturhaus (p182) Clued-in bookers fill this rambling space with everything from big-name artists to electro swing parties.

Waldbühne (p70) Berliner Philharmoniker to the Rolling Stones: they've all rocked this enchanting outdoor amphitheatre near the Olympic Stadium.

Best for Jazz & Blues

Kunstfabrik Schlot (p148) This cellar club delights an appreciative audience with quality jazz and does improv and cabaret on other nights.

A-Trane (p213) Occasionally hosts jazz A-listers and has a rollicking Saturday-night jam session.

Yorckschlösschen (p168) Easygoing and long-running, this knick-knack-filled club draws a no-nonsense, all-comers crowd.

b-Flat (p148) Intimate jazz joint mixing it up with Balkan beats and a through-the-roof jam session on Wednesdays.

Best Cabaret

Chamäleon Varieté (p147) Historic variety theatre in the Hackesche Hoefe presenting mesmerising contemporary spins on acrobatics, dance, theatre, magic and music.

Bar Jeder Vernunft (p213) An art nouveau mirrored tent provides a suitably glam backdrop for high-quality entertainment.

Tipi am Kanzleramt (p96) There's not a bad seat in the house at this festive dinner theatre in a tent on the edge of the Tiergarten park.

Best Cinemas

Babylon (p147) Art-house cinema in protected 1920s Bauhaus building with restored theatre organ.

Cinestar Original (p133) The best place to see English-language blockbusters in the original language.

Arsenal (p133) Presents arty fare from around the world in the original language, often with English subtitles.

Freiluftkino Kreuzberg (p70) Classics, indies, documentaries and blockbusters under the stars in the courtyard of a 19th-century hospital.

Kino Central (p148) At the funky Haus Schwarzenberg, this small indie house plays new and classic art-house fare, also outdoors in summer.

Best for Experimental Performance

Radialsystem V (p183) Gets bragging rights for its cutting edge, genre-defying productions, especially in dance.

Hebbel am Ufer (p168) Boundary-pushing and polygenre productions that challenge preconceptions.

Flohmarkt am Mauerpark (p197)

Shopping

Berlin is a great place to shop, and we're definitely not talking malls and chains. The city's appetite for the individual manifests in small neighbourhood boutiques and buzzing markets that are a pleasure to explore. Shopping here is as much about visual stimulus as it is about actually spending your cash, no matter whether you're ultrafrugal or a power-shopper.

Where to Shop

Berlin's main shopping boulevard is Kurfürstendamm (Ku'damm) in the City West and Charlottenburg, which is largely the home of mainstream retailers (from H&M to Prada). Its extension, Tauentzienstrasse, is anchored by KaDeWe, continental Europe's largest department store. Standouts among the city's dozens of other shopping centres are the concept mall Bikini Berlin and the vast new Mall of Berlin at Leipziger Platz.

Getting the most out of shopping in Berlin, though, means venturing off the high street and into the *Kieze* (neighbourhoods). This is where you'll discover a cosmopolitan cocktail of indie boutiques stirred by the city's zest for life, envelope-pushing energy and entrepreneurial spirit.

Local Designers

Michael Michalsky may be Berlin's best-known fashion export, but hot on his heels are plenty of other fashion-forward

NEED TO KNOW

Opening Hours

➡ Shopkeepers may set their opening hours from Monday to Saturday. In practice, only department stores, supermarkets, shops in major commercial districts (such as the Kurfürstendamm) and those in malls take full advantage of this. These stores usually open around 9.30am and close at 8pm or 9pm.

➡ Boutiques and other smaller shops keep flexible hours, opening some time midmorning and generally closing at 7pm, often earlier on Saturday.

➡ Stores are closed on Sunday, except for some bakeries, flower shops, souvenir shops and supermarkets in major train stations, including Hauptbahnhof, Friedrichstrasse and Ostbahnhof. Shops may also open from 1pm to 8pm on two December Sundays before Christmas and on a further six Sundays throughout the year, the latter being determined by local government.

➡ Some supermarkets are open 24 hours (though they're closed from midnight Saturday to Monday morning).

Taxes & Refunds

If your permanent residence is outside the EU, you may be able to partially claim back the 19% value-added tax (VAT, *Mehrwertsteuer*) you have paid on purchased goods. The rebate applies only to items purchased in stores displaying the 'Tax-Free for Tourists' sign. Obtain a tax-free form from the sales clerk, then show this form, your unused goods and the receipt to a customs official at the airport before checking your luggage. The customs official will stamp the form, which you can then take straight to the cash-refund office at the airport.

local designers such as C.Neeon, Firma Berlin, C'est Tout, Claudia Skoda, Kostas Murkudis, Kaviar Gauche, Potipoti and LalaBerlin. In typical Berlin style, they walk the line between originality and contemporary trends in a way that more mainstream labels do not. Key streetwear

labels include Irie Daily, Hasipop and Butterflysoulfire. Fishbelly is an internationally renowned local underwear label. Trend-pushers also include Umasan's vegan fashion, schmidttakahashi's take on upcycling and Christine Mayer's 'spiritual' fashion. When it comes to accessories, look for eyewear by ic! Berlin and Mykita, bags by Ta(u)sche and hats by Fiona Bennett.

Flea Markets

Flea markets are like urban archaeology: you'll need plenty of patience and luck when sifting through other people's cast-offs, but oh, the thrill, when finally unearthing a piece of treasure! Berlin's numerous hunting grounds set up on weekends (usually Sundays) year-round – rain or shine – and are also the purview of fledgling local fashion designers and jewelry makers. The most famous market is the weekly Flohmarkt am Mauerpark (p197) in Prenzlauer Berg, which is easily combined with nearby Flohmarkt am Arkonaplatz (p197).

Shopping by Neighbourhood

➡ **Historic Mitte** Along Friedrichstrasse and Unter den Linden souvenir shops rub shoulders with top-flight retailers and galleries. (p97)

➡ **Museumsinsel & Alexanderplatz** Eastern Berlin's mainstream shopping hub, plus a weekend collectables market. (p117)

➡ **Potsdamer Platz & Tiergarten** Two big malls and little else. (p133)

➡ **Scheunenviertel** Edgy international labels alongside local fashions and accessories in chic boutiques. (p148)

➡ **Kreuzberg & Neukölln** Vintage fashion and streetwear along with music and accessories, all in indie boutiques. (p169)

➡ **Friedrichshain** Up-and-coming area centred around Boxhagener Platz, site of a Sunday flea market; antiques market at Ostbahnhof. (p183)

➡ **Prenzlauer Berg** Berlin-made fashions, nicho boutiques, anything for children and a fabulous flea market. (p197)

➡ **City West & Charlottenburg** Mainstream on Kurfürstendamm, indie boutiques in the side streets, concept stores at Bikini Berlin, homewares on Kantstrasse. (p213)

Lonely Planet's Top Choices

KaDeWe (p213) The ultimate consumer temple seemingly has everything every heart desires.

Bikini Berlin (p214) Edgy shopping in revitalised 1950s landmark building near Zoo Station.

Galeries Lafayette (p97) French je ne sais quoi in uber-stylish building by Jean Nouvel.

Dussmann – Das Kulturkaufhaus (p97) The mother lode of books and music with high-profile author readings and signings.

Fassbender & Rausch (p97) Palace of pralines and chocolate, plus ingenious model-size replicas of famous Berlin landmarks – made of chocolate, of course.

Hard Wax (p170) Key music stop for electro heads.

Best Bookshops

Another Country (p169) Quirkily run English-language bookstore/library/community living room.

Pro Qm (p150) Floor-to-ceiling shelves crammed with tomes on art, architecture and design.

Hundt Hammer Stein (p150) Capably curated literary bookshop run by well-read staff.

Best Quirky Stores

1. Absinth Depot Berlin (p150) Make your acquaintance with the Green Fairy at this quaint Old Berlin–style shop.

Käthe Wohlfahrt (p214) Where it's Christmas 365 days

of the year so you can stock up on things that shine and glitter in July.

Ampelmann Galerie (p150) The little traffic-light guy that helps you across the street now has his own franchise.

Best Gastro Delights

KaDeWe Food Hall (p213) Mindboggling bonanza of gourmet treats from around the world.

Markthalle Neun (p162) Revitalised historic market hall serves up global bites during Street Food Thursday.

Bonbonmacherei (p150) Willy Wonka would feel right at home in this old-fashioned candy kitchen.

Best Malls & Department Stores

Bikini Berlin (p214) The city's first concept mall with hip stores and views of the monkeys at Berlin Zoo.

LP12 Mall of Berlin (p133) Huge new high-end shopping quarter with 270 stores alongside apartments, a hotel and offices.

Alexa (p117) Vast all-purpose mall with all the usual high-street chains and an exhibit of Berlin in miniature.

KaDeWe (p213) The largest department store in continental Europe.

Best Flea Markets

Flohmarkt am Mauerpark (p197) The mother of all markets is overrun but still a good show.

Nowkoelln Flowmarkt (p170) This internationally flavoured hipster market is also a showcase of local creativity.

RAW Flohmarkt (p182) True bargains still abound at this little market on the grounds of a railway-repair station turned party zone.

Best Berlin Fashion & Accessories

Umasan (p149) Vegan designer has you looking good in fabrics made from wood pulp, soy and seaweed.

Butterflysoulfire (p149) Avant-garde fashion label gets minimalist elegance right.

Trippen (p149) Handmade designer footwear that's sustainable, ergonomic and stylish.

Yackfou (p183) Eye-catching graphics beautify this local outfit's T-shirts, hoodies and sweaters.

ausberlin (p117) Witty, irreverent and stylish music, clothing, jewellery, books and knick-knacks.

Best Farmers Markets

Türkenmarkt (p169) Bazaar-like canalside market with bargain-priced produce and Mediterranean deli fare.

Kollwitzplatzmarkt (p197) Posh player with top-quality produce, artisanal cheeses and pasta, homemade pesto and other exquisite morsels.

Wochenmarkt am Boxhagener Platz (p183) Lively and colourful neighbourhood meet-up with great selection of unusual foods and snack stands.

Explore Berlin

BERLIN'S
TOP SIGHTS

Neighbourhoods at a Glance

❶ Historic Mitte p80

With the mother lode of sights clustered within a walkable area, this part of the city should be your first port of call. Book ahead for access to the Reichstag dome, then check off the Brandenburger Tor, Holocaust Memorial, Unter den Linden boulevard and splendid Gendarmenmarkt on an easy stroll. Head to Friedrichstrasse for upmarket shopping and entertainment.

❷ Museumsinsel & Alexanderplatz p98

Museum lovers hit the jackpot on this little Spree island with its five world-class museums, including the unmissable Pergamonmuseum. The majestic Berliner Dom watches over it all and across the street to the Berlin City Palace reconstruction. Catch the lift up the Fernsehturm on socialist-style Alexan-

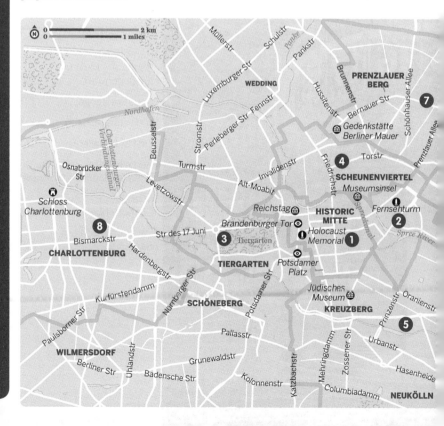

derplatz, discover Berlin's birthplace in the Nikolaiviertel and learn about life under socialism at the DDR Museum.

[3] Potsdamer Platz & Tiergarten p118

This new quarter, forged from ground once bisected by the Berlin Wall, is a showcase of fabulous contemporary architecture. Art lovers should not skip the Kulturforum museums, especially the Gemäldegalerie, which sits right next to the world-class Berliner Philharmonie. The leafy Tiergarten, with its rambling paths and hidden beer gardens, makes for a perfect sightseeing break.

[4] Scheunenviertel p134

With its boutique-lined lanes and charming courtyards like the Hackesche Höfe, the Scheunenviertel is fashionista central and teems with hip bars and restaurants. Come face to face with the quarter's Jewish roots on a visit of the Neue Synagoge, then check out the galleries along Auguststrasse and Linienstrasse.

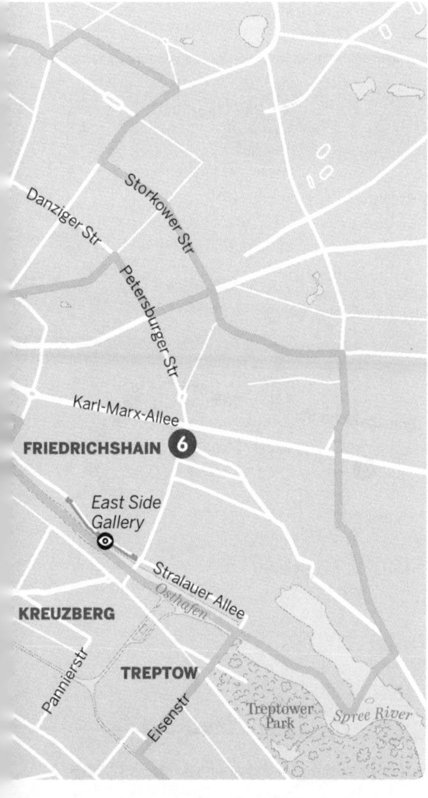

[5] Kreuzberg & Neukölln p151

Kreuzberg and northern Neukölln are epicentres of free-wheeling, multicultural and alternative Berlin. Spend the day hunting down vintage threads and street art, chill in a cafe or an airport-turned-public-park, then plunge headlong into the city's most vibrant nightlife. A more grown-up vibe rules around Bergmannstrasse in no less charismatic western Kreuzberg, home to the district's main sight, the Jüdisches Museum.

[6] Friedrichshain p171

Student-flavoured Friedrichshain is tailor-made for soaking up Berlin's relaxed vibe and is great for nightlife explorations and chilling in understated bars along Revaler Strasse and around Boxhagener Platz. Fun ways to connect with the district's past are walks along the East Side Gallery, the largest surviving section of the Berlin Wall, and along monumental Karl-Marx-Allee, a showcase of socialist architecture.

[7] Prenzlauer Berg p184

Prenzlauer Berg is one of Berlin's most pleasant residential neighbourhoods and a joy to explore on foot. On Sundays, the world descends on its Mauerpark for flea marketeering, outdoor karaoke and chilling in the sun. A visit to the Gedenkstätte Berliner Mauer is essential to understanding how the Berlin Wall shaped the city.

[8] City West & Charlottenburg p199

Charlottenburg's main artery, Kurfürstendamm, is nirvana for shopaholics and spills into leafy side streets teeming with boutiques, galleries, cafes and restaurants. Witness the revitalisation of the area around the landmark Kaiser-Wilhelm-Gedächtniskirche, a church ruin turned antiwar memorial, then head out to must-see Schloss Charlottenburg for a glimpse of royal life.

Historic Mitte

GOVERNMENT QUARTER | PARISER PLATZ | UNTER DEN LINDEN | GENDARMENMARKT |
FRIEDRICHSTRASSE | CHECKPOINT CHARLIE

Neighbourhood Top Five

1 Standing in awe of history at the **Reichstag** (p82), then taking in the views from its landmark dome.

2 Soaking in the stillness and presence of uncounted souls at the **Holocaust Memorial** (p85).

3 Indulging in a gourmet meal at one of the stellar restaurants surrounding **Gendarmenmarkt** (p87).

4 Confronting the horrors of Nazi Germany at the haunting **Topographie des Terrors** (p89) exhibit.

5 Catching cabaret, comedy, musicals or concerts at the historic **Admiralspalast** (p96).

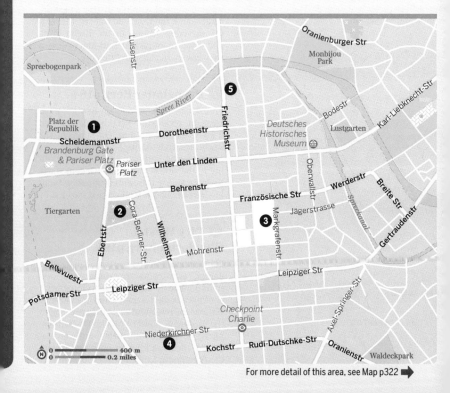

For more detail of this area, see Map p322 ➡

Explore: Historic Mitte

A cocktail of culture, commerce and history, Mitte packs it in when it comes to blockbuster sights: the Reichstag, the Brandenburg Gate, the Holocaust Memorial and Checkpoint Charlie are all within its confines. Cutting through it all is Unter den Linden, a chic boulevard stretching from Pariser Platz to Museum Island, past a phalanx of imposing structures built under various Prussian kings and reflecting the one-time grandeur of the royal family.

These days, though, the grand boulevard is one giant construction zone, thus upholding Berlin's reputation as the 'eternally unfinished city'. A ballet of cranes swings above sites where the U-Bahn is being extended, the Berlin City Palace is resurfacing and the State Opera House is getting a facelift. It'll be years before all is finished.

Unaffected by the temporary turmoil is Friedrichstrasse, which bisects Unter den Linden and runs north into the 'East End' theatre district and south to Checkpoint Charlie. Gendarmenmarkt, Berlin's most beautiful square, is just one block east and surrounded by ritzy restaurants and fancy shops. It too is expected to get a makeover starting in 2015.

Local Life

→**Glamour shopping** Brand-name bunnies flock to Friedrichstrasse to give their credit cards a serious workout. Aside from boutiques, the Friedrichstadtpassagen, led by the stunningly designed Galeries Lafayette (p97), beckon with top-flight Berlin and international designers.

→**High-brow culture** Music and theatre fans are drawn to this part of town to take in concerts at the Konzerthaus Berlin (p96), theatre at the Maxim Gorki (p96) and opera at the Komische Oper (p96).

→**Power of words** What's better than a night off in front of the TV? Browsing a bookstore, of course. Open until 11pm, Dussmann (p97), the self-titled 'cultural department store', is an eldorado for bookworms and also has a huge music selection.

Getting There & Away

→**Bus** Buses 100 and 200 run along most of Unter den Linden from Alexanderplatz.

→**S-Bahn** S1 and S2/25 stop at Brandenburger Tor and Friedrichstrasse.

→**Tram** The M1 travels from Museumsinsel to Prenzlauer Berg via Friedrichstrasse.

→**U-Bahn** Stadtmitte (U2, U6), Französische Strasse (U6) and Hausvogteiplatz (U2) are all convenient for Gendarmenmarkt. For Unter den Linden, get off at Brandenburger Tor (U55), Friedrichstrasse (U6) or Französische Strasse (U6).

Lonely Planet's Top Tip

For an engaging overview of the Berlin Wall and related key Cold War sites scattered around the city, visit the Mauerinformation exhibit in the Brandenburger Tor U-Bahn station. Aside from photographs and an aerial map, it presents a film about the border installations and an opportunity to rent a Berlin Wall audioguide for a more in-depth experience.

✖ Best Places to Eat

→ Restaurant Tim Raue (p95)

→ Augustiner am Gendarmenmarkt (p94)

→ Chipps (p94)

→ Ishin (p94)

For reviews, see p94 →

☐ Best Places to Drink

→ Drayton Bar (p95)

→ Tausend (p96)

→ Berliner Republik (p96)

For reviews, see p95 →

◉ Best Landmarks

→ Brandenburger Tor (p84)

→ Reichstag (p82)

→ Holocaust Memorial (p85)

→ Gendarmenmarkt (p87)

For reviews, see p82 →

 TOP SIGHT
REICHSTAG

It's been burned, bombed, rebuilt, buttressed by the Berlin Wall, wrapped in fabric and finally turned into the modern home of the German parliament: the Reichstag is one of Berlin's most iconic buildings. Its most eye-catching feature is the glistening glass dome, which draws more than three million visitors each year. The grand old structure was designed by Paul Wallot and completed in 1894 when Germany was still a constitutional monarchy known as the Deutsches Reich (German Empire), hence the building's name.

Home of the Bundestag

Today, the Reichstag is the historic anchor of the new federal government quarter built after reunification. The Bundestag, Germany's parliament, has hammered out its policies here since moving from the former German capital of Bonn to Berlin in 1999. The parliament's arrival followed a complete architectural revamp masterminded by Lord Norman Foster, who preserved only the building's 19th-century shell and added the landmark glass dome.

Dome

Resembling a giant glass beehive, the sparkling cupola is open at the top and bottom and sits right above the plenary chamber as a visual metaphor for transparency and openness in politics. A lift whisks you to the rooftop terrace from where you can easily pinpoint such sights as the curvaceous House of World Cultures and the majestic Berliner Dom (Berlin Cathedral) or marvel at the enormous dimensions of Tiergarten park. To learn more about these and other landmarks, the Reichstag building and the workings of parliament, pick up a free multilingual audioguide as you exit the lift. The commentary starts automatically as you mosey up

DON'T MISS...

➜ The dome
➜ The facade
➜ The free audioguide

PRACTICALITIES

➜ Map p322
➜ www.bundestag.de
➜ Platz der Republik 1, Service Center: Scheidemannstrasse
➜ ⊙lift ride 8am-midnight, last entry 11pm, Service Center 8am-8pm Apr-Oct, 8am-6pm Nov-Mar
➜ 🚌100, 🅂Bundestag, 🚆Hauptbahnhof, Brandenburger Tor

the dome's 230m-long ramp, which spirals around a mirror-clad cone that deflects daylight down into the plenary chamber.

Main Facade

Stylistically, the monumental west-facing main facade borrows heavily from the Italian Renaissance, with a few neo-baroque elements thrown into the mix. A massive staircase leads up to a portico curtained by six Corinthian columns and topped by the dedication 'Dem Deutschen Volke' (To the German People), which wasn't added until 1916. The bronze letters were designed by Peter Behrens, one of the fathers of modern architecture, and cast from two French cannons captured during the Napoleonic Wars of 1813–15. The original dome, made of steel and glass and considered a high-tech marvel at the time, was destroyed during the Reichstag fire in 1933.

Historic Milestones

Home of the German parliament from 1894 to 1933 and again from 1999, the hulking Reichstag will likely give you more flashbacks to high-school history than any other Berlin landmark. On 9 November 1919, parliament member Philipp Scheidemann proclaimed the German republic from one of its windows. In 1933, the Nazis used a mysterious fire as a pretext to seize dictatorial powers. A dozen years later, victorious Red Army troops raised the Soviet flag on the bombed-out building, which stood damaged and empty on the western side of the Berlin Wall throughout the Cold War. In the late 1980s, megastars including David Bowie, Pink Floyd and Michael Jackson performed concerts on the lawn in front of the building.

The Wall collapsed soon thereafter, paving the way to German reunification, which was enacted here in 1990. Five years later the Reichstag made headlines once again when the artist couple Christo and Jeanne-Claude wrapped the massive structure in silvery fabric. It had taken an act of the German parliament to approve the project, which was intended to mark the end of the Cold War and the beginning of a new era. For two weeks starting in late June 1995, visitors from around the world flocked to Berlin to admire this unique sight. Shortly after the fabric came down, Lord Norman Foster set to work.

An extensive photographic exhibit at the bottom of the dome captures many of these historic moments.

VISITING THE DOME

Free reservations for visiting the Reichstag dome must be made at www.bundestag.de. Book early, especially in summer, and prepare to show ID, pass through a metal detector and have your belongings X-rayed. If you haven't prebooked, swing by the **Visitors' Service** (Map p322; Scheidemannstrasse, next to Berlin Pavillon; ⊙8am-8pm Apr-Oct, 8am-6pm Nov-Mar) near the Reichstag to inquire about remaining tickets for that day and the next two. You can also reach the rooftop by making reservations at the **Dachgartenrestaurant Käfer** (Map p322; ☑030-2262 9933; Platz der Republik 1; mains €10-30; ⊙9am-4.30pm & 6.30pm-midnight).

It was the night of 27 February 1933: the Reichstag was ablaze. In the aftermath, a Dutch anarchist named Marinus van der Lubbe was arrested for arson without conclusive proof. Historians regard the incident as a pivotal moment in Hitler's power grab. Claiming that the fire was part of a large-scale Communist conspiracy, the Nazis pushed through the 'Reichstag Fire Decree', quashing civil rights and triggering the persecution of political opponents.

 TOP SIGHT
BRANDENBURGER TOR & PARISER PLATZ

A symbol of division during the Cold War, the landmark Brandenburger Tor (Brandenburg Gate) now epitomises German reunification and often serves as a photogenic backdrop for festivals, concerts and New Year's Eve parties. Carl Gotthard Langhans found inspiration in Athens' Acropolis for the elegant triumphal arch, completed in 1791 as the royal city gate. It stands sentinel over Pariser Platz, a harmoniously proportioned square once again framed by banks as well as the US, British and French embassies, just as it was during its 19th-century heyday.

Crowning the Brandenburger Tor is the **Quadriga**, Johann Gottfried Schadow's sculpture of the winged goddess of victory piloting a chariot drawn by four horses. After trouncing Prussia in 1806, Napoleon kidnapped the lady and held her hostage in Paris until she was freed by a gallant Prussian general in 1815.

The first building to be reconstructed on Pariser Platz was a near-replica of the 1907 Hotel Adlon, Berlin's poshest caravanserai, which allegedly inspired the 1932 movie *Grand Hotel*, starring Greta Garbo. Now called Hotel Adlon Kempinski (p233), it's still a celebrity favourite. Remember Michael Jackson dangling his baby over a hotel balcony? It happened at the Adlon.

If the doors are open, pop into the Frank Gehry–designed **DZ Bank** (Pariser Platz 3) on the square's south side to catch a glimpse of the glass-roofed atrium with its bizarre free-form sculpture that's actually a conference room.

The only building on Pariser Platz with a glass facade is the **Akademie der Künste** (Academy of Arts; ☑200 571 000; www.adk.de; Pariser Platz 4; admission varies, free 3-7pm Tue; ⊘exhibits 11am-7pm Tue-Sun), designed by Günter Behnisch. This is one of Berlin's oldest cultural institutions, founded by King Friedrich I in 1696 as the Prussian Academy of Arts. Come here for readings, lectures, workshops and exhibits, many of them free.

DON'T MISS...

➤ Quadriga

➤ Hotel Adlon Kempinski

PRACTICALITIES

➤ Map p322

➤ Pariser Platz

➤ ⊘24hr

➤ Ⓢ Brandenburger Tor, Ⓡ Brandenburger Tor

TOP SIGHT
HOLOCAUST MEMORIAL

It took 17 years of discussion, planning and construction, but on 10 May 2005 the Denkmal für die ermordeten Juden Europas (Memorial to the Murdered Jews of Europe) was officially dedicated. Colloquially known as Holocaust Memorial, it's Germany's central memorial to the Nazi-planned genocide during the Third Reich. For the football-field-size space, New York architect Peter Eisenman created 2711 sarcophagi-like concrete stelae (slabs) of equal size but various heights, rising in sombre silence from undulating ground.

You're free to access this massive concrete maze at any point and make your individual journey through it. At first it may seem austere, even unemotional. But take time to feel the coolness of the stone and contemplate the interplay of light and shadow, then stumble aimlessly among the narrow passageways, and you'll soon connect with a metaphorical sense of disorientation, confusion and claustrophobia. Guided tours run at 3pm on Saturday in English and at 3pm on Sunday in German.

For context, visit the subterranean **Ort der Information** (information centre), which movingly lifts the veil of anonymity from the six million Holocaust victims. A graphic timeline of Jewish persecution during the Third Reich is followed by a series of rooms documenting the fates of individuals and families. The most visceral is the darkened Room of Names, where the names and years of birth and death of Jewish victims are projected onto all four walls while a solemn voice reads their short biographies. Poignant and heart-wrenching, these exhibits will leave no one untouched.

DON'T MISS...

→ Field of Stelae
→ Ort der Information
→ Room of Names

PRACTICALITIES

→ Memorial to the Murdered European Jews
→ Map p322
→ ☏ 030-2639 4336
→ www.stiftung-denkmal.de
→ Cora-Berliner-Strasse 1
→ audioguide adult/concession €4/2
→ ⊘ field 24hr, information centre 10am-8pm Tue-Sun Apr-Sep, to 7pm Oct-Mar, last entry 45min before closing
→ Ⓢ Brandenburger Tor, Ⓡ Brandenburger Tor

TOP SIGHT
DEUTSCHES HISTORISCHES MUSEUM

If you're wondering what the Germans have been up to for the past two millennia, take a spin around this engaging museum in the baroque Zeughaus, formerly the Prussian arsenal and now home of the German Historical Museum. Upstairs, displays concentrate on the period from the 1st century AD to the end of WWI in 1918, while the ground floor tracks the 20th century all the way through to German reunification.

DON'T MISS...

➡ Nazi globe
➡ Schlüter's sculptures in the courtyard
➡ IM Pei Exhibition Hall

PRACTICALITIES

➡ Map p322
➡ ☎030-203 040
➡ www.dhm.de
➡ Unter den Linden 2
➡ adult/concession/under 18 €8/4/free
➡ ⏱10am-6pm
➡ 🚌100, 200, 🚇Alexanderplatz, Hackescher Markt

Permanent Exhibit

All the major milestones in German history are dealt with in a European context. The timeline begins with the Roman occupation and moves on to the coronation of Charlemagne, the founding of the Holy Roman Empire and everyday life in the Middle Ages. It then jumps ahead to Martin Luther and the Reformation and the bloody Thirty Years' War and its aftermath, addresses Napoleon and the collapse of the Holy Roman Empire in 1806 and the founding of the German Empire in 1871. WWI, which brought the end of the monarchy and led to the Weimar Republic, is a major theme, as are of course the Nazi era and the Cold War. The exhibit ends in 1994 with the withdrawal of Allied troops from German territory.

Displays are a potpourri of documents, paintings, books, dishes, textiles, weapons, furniture, machines and other objects ranging from the sublime to the trivial. One of the oldest objects is a 3rd-century Roman milestone. There's also splendid medieval body armour for horse and rider and a felt hat once worn by Napoleon I. Among the more unusual objects is a pulpit hourglass, which was introduced after the Reformation to limit the length of sermons to one hour. A startling highlight is a big globe that originally stood in the Nazi Foreign Office, with a bullet hole where Germany should be. Among the newer objects is a 1985 Robotron, the first PC made in East Germany.

The Building

The rose-coloured Zeughaus, which was used as a weapons depot until 1876, was a collaboration of four architects: Johann Arnold Nering, Martin Grünberg, Andreas Schlüter and Jean de Bodt. Completed in 1730, it is the oldest building along Unter den Linden and a beautiful example of secular baroque architecture. This is in no small part thanks to Schlüter's magnificent sculptures, especially those in the glass-covered courtyard whose facades are festooned with heads of dying soldiers, their faces contorted in agony. Although intended to represent vanquished Prussian enemies, they actually make more of a pacifist statement for modern viewers.

IM Pei Exhibition Hall

High-calibre temporary exhibits take up a spectacular contemporary **annexe** (IM Pei Exhibition Hall; Map p322; Hinter dem Giesshaus 3) designed by Chinese-American architect IM Pei. Fronted by a glass spiral, it's an uncompromisingly geometrical space, made entirely from triangles, rectangles and circles, yet imbued with a sense of lightness achieved through an airy atrium and generous use of glass.

JOHN FREEMAN/GETTY IMAGES ©

TOP SIGHT GENDARMENMARKT

The Gendarmenmarkt area is Berlin at its ritziest, dappled with luxury hotels, fancy restaurants and bars. The graceful square was named after the Gens d'Armes, an 18th-century Prussian regiment of French Huguenots who settled here after being expelled from France in 1685.

Completed in 1705, the **Französischer Dom** (French Cathedral; ☎030-229 1760, 030-229 1760; www.franzoesischer-dom.de; Gendarmenmarkt; church free, museum adult/concession €2/1, tower adult/child €3/1; 🕐church & museum noon-5pm Tue-Sun, tower 10am-7pm Apr-Oct, to 6pm Nov-Mar) consists of two buildings: the French Church, a copy of the Huguenots' mother church in Charenton, and the domed tower, which was added by Carl von Gontard in 1785. There's a small Huguenot museum on the ground floor of the tower whose viewing platform is reached via 284 steps. The church hosts concerts and free organ recitals at 12.30pm Tuesday to Friday.

The **Deutscher Dom** (German Cathedral; ☎030-2273 0431; Gendarmenmarkt 1; 🕐10am-6pm Tue-Sun May-Sep, to 6pm Oct-Apr) [FREE] wasn't much of a looker until it was topped by Gontard's dazzling galleried dome in 1785. Built between 1702 and 1708 for German-speaking congregants, it is now home to a recently updated, interactive exhibit charting Germany's path to parliamentary democracy. English audioguides and tours are available.

One of Karl Friedrich Schinkel's finest buildings, the Konzerthaus (p96) rose from the ashes of Carl Gotthard Langhans' Schauspielhaus (National Theatre). Schinkel kept the surviving walls and columns and added a grand staircase leading to a raised columned portico. The building is fronted by an elaborate sculpture of 18th-century poet and playwright Friedrich Schiller. For an inside look at this beacon of Berlin high-brow culture, catch a concert or take a guided tour (€3; in German) at 1pm on Saturdays.

DON'T MISS...

- Free organ recital in the French Church
- Climbing the tower of the Französischer Dom
- Concert at the Konzerthaus

PRACTICALITIES

- Map p322
- 🕐24hr
- [S]Französische Strasse, Stadtmitte

SIGHTS

Government Quarter

REICHSTAG HISTORIC BUILDING

See p82.

BUNDESKANZLERAMT BUILDING

Map p322 (Federal Chancellery; Willy-Brandt-Strasse 1; ⏰closed to public; 🚌100, [S]Bundestag) Germany's 'White House', the Federal Chancellery is a sparkling, modern compound designed by Axel Schultes and Charlotte Frank and consisting of two parallel office blocks flanking a central white cube. Eduardo Chillida's rusted-steel *Berlin* sculpture graces the eastern forecourt. The best views of the entire building are from the Moltkebrücke (bridge) or the northern Spree River promenade.

PAUL-LÖBE-HAUS BUILDING

Map p322 (Konrad-Adenauer-Strasse; 🚌100, [S]Bundestag, 🚆Hauptbahnhof) The glass-and-concrete Paul-Löbe-Haus houses offices for the Bundestag's parliamentary committees. It's filled with modern art that can be viewed during guided tours (in German) at 2pm on Saturday and Sunday. Advance online registration (www.bundestag.de) is required.

MARIE-ELISABETH-LÜDERS-HAUS BUILDING

Map p322 (www.bundestag.de; Schiffbauerdamm; ⏰galleries 11am-5pm Tue-Sun; [S]Bundestag, 🚆Hauptbahnhof) [FREE] Home to the parliamentary library, this recently expanded, extravagant structure has a massive tapered stairway, a flat roofline jutting out like a springboard and giant circular windows. In the basement is an art installation by Ben Wagin featuring original segments of the Wall. Accessible from the Luisenstrasse entrance is the Kunst-Raum, which presents politically infused contemporary art.

WALL MEMORIAL 'PARLAMENT DER BÄUME' MEMORIAL

Map p322 (Parliament of Trees; cnr Schiffbauerdamm & Adele-Schreiber-Krieger-Strasse; ⏰24hr; [S]Bundestag) [FREE] Started by Ben Wagin in 1990, this art installation commemorates those who died at the Berlin Wall. Standing near the original border strip, it consists not only of trees but also of pieces of the border fortification, memorial stones, pictures and text. The names of 258 victims are inscribed on slabs of granite.

GEDENKORT WEISSE KREUZE MEMORIAL

Map p322 (White Crosses Memorial; Reichstagufer; [S]Bundestag) [FREE] The Berlin Wall ran right behind the Reichstag. The southern bank of the Spree River still belonged to West Berlin, while the water itself was already East Berlin territory. In 1971, a group of citizens established this memorial consisting of seven white crosses to commemorate East Berliners who died in their attempt to escape to the west.

HAUS DER KULTUREN DER WELT BUILDING

Map p322 (House of World Cultures; ☎030-397 870; www.hkw.de; John-Foster-Dulles-Allee 10; cost varies; ⏰exhibits 11am-7pm Wed-Mon; 🚌100, [S]Bundestag, 🚆Hauptbahnhof) This highly respected cultural centre showcases contemporary non-European art, music, dance, literature, films and theatre, and also serves as a discussion forum on Zeitgeist-reflecting issues. The gravity-defying parabolic roof of Hugh Stubbins' extravagant building, designed as the American contribution to a 1957 architectural exhibition, is echoed by Henry Moore's sculpture *Butterfly* in the reflecting pool. Computerised chime concerts ring out at noon and 6pm daily from the nearby 68-bell carillon, and live concerts take place Sundays at 3pm from May to September (also at 2pm in December).

STRASSE DES 17 JUNI STREET

Map p322 ([S]Brandenburger Tor, 🚆Brandenburger Tor) The broad boulevard bisecting Tiergarten was named Street of 17 June in honour of the victims of the bloodily quashed 1953

VIEWS WITH A THRILL

Drift up but not away for about 15 minutes with the helium-filled **Weltballon Berlin** (Map p322; ☎030-5321 5321, for wind conditions 030-226 678 811; www.air-service-berlin.de; cnr Wilhelmstrasse & Zimmerstrasse; adult/concession/child 3 10 €20/15/5, ⏰10am-10pm Apr-Oct, 11am-6pm Nov-Mar; [S]Kochstrasse, Mohrenstrasse), which remains tethered to the ground as it lifts you 150m into the air for panoramas of the historic city centre. Your pilot will help you pinpoint all the key sights. Confirm ahead as there are no flights in windy conditions.

TOP SIGHT
TOPOGRAPHIE DES TERRORS

In the same spot where once stood the most feared institutions of Nazi Germany (including the Gestapo headquarters and the SS central command), this compelling exhibit dissects the anatomy of the Nazi state. By chronicling the stages of terror and persecution, it puts a face on the perpetrators and details the impact these brutal institutions had on all of Europe. From their desks, top Nazi commanders like Himmler and Heydrich hatched Holocaust plans and organised the systematic persecution of political opponents, many of whom suffered torture and death in the Gestapo prison.

From spring to autumn, another exhibit called 'Berlin 1933–1945: Between Propaganda & Terror' opens in a trench against glassed-in foundations of the Gestapo prison cells. It zeroes in on the role of Berlin during the Third Reich and how life changed for local residents after the city had become the nexus of the Nazi leadership's political power. To complement the exhibits,a self-guided tour of the historic grounds takes you past 15 information stations with photos, documents and 3D graphics as well as a 200m stretch of the Berlin Wall along Niederkirchner Strasse.

DON'T MISS...

- Model of the grounds
- Diagram of the concentration camp system

PRACTICALITIES

- Topography of Terror
- Map p322
- ☎030-2548 0950
- www.topographie.de
- Niederkirchner Strasse 8
- 🕒10am-8pm, grounds until dusk or 8pm latest
- [S]Potsdamer Platz, [U]Potsdamer Platz

workers' uprising in East Berlin. It originally linked two royal palaces and was turned into a triumphal road under Hitler. The section between the Brandenburger Tor and the Siegessäule (Victory Column; 1km west of Brandenburg Gate) turns into a mega-party zone on New Year's Eve and for such festivals as Christopher Street Day.

SOWJETISCHES EHRENMAL TIERGARTEN MEMORIAL

Map p322 (Soviet War Memorial; Strasse des 17 Juni; [S]Brandenburger Tor, [U]Brandenburger Tor) The imposing Soviet War Memorial is flanked by two Russian T-34 tanks said to have been the first to enter the city in 1945. It was built by German workers on order of the Soviets and completed just months after the end of the war. More than 2000 Red Army soldiers are buried behind the colonnade.

DENKMAL FÜR DIE IM NATIONALSOZIALISMUS ERMORDETEN SINTI UND ROMA EUROPAS MEMORIAL

Map p322 (Memorial to the Sinti and Roma of Europe Murdered under the Nazi Regime; www.stiftung-denkmal.de; Scheidemannstrasse; 🕒24hr; 🚌100, [S]Brandenburger Tor, [U]Brandenburger Tor) Inaugurated in 2012, this memorial commemorates the Sinti and Roma victims of the Holocaust and consists of a fountain with a submersed stone decorated daily with a fresh flower. It was designed by Israeli sculptor Dani Karavan.

DENKMAL FÜR DIE IM NATIONALSOZIALISMUS VERFOLGTEN HOMOSEXUELLEN MEMORIAL

Map p322 (Memorial to the Homosexuals Persecuted under the Nazi Regime; www.stiftung-denkmal.de; Ebertstrasse; 🕒24hr; [S]Brandenburger Tor, Potsdamer Platz, [U]Brandenburger Tor, Potsdamer Platz) Since 2008 this memorial has trained the spotlight on the tremendous suffering of Europe's gay community under the Nazis. The freestanding, 4m-high, off-kilter concrete cube was designed by Danish-Norwegian artists Michael Elmgreen and Ingar Dragset. A looped video plays through a warped, narrow window.

Pariser Platz & Unter den Linden

BRANDENBURGER TOR & PARISER PLATZ LANDMARK

See p84.

HOLOCAUST MEMORIAL MEMORIAL

See p85.

DEUTSCHES HISTORISCHES MUSEUM MUSEUM

See p86.

HITLER'S BUNKER HISTORIC SITE

Map p322 (cnr In den Ministergärten & Gertrud-Kolmar-Strasse; ⏲24hr; [S]Brandenburger Tor, [U]Brandenburger Tor) Berlin was burning and Soviet tanks advancing relentlessly when Adolf Hitler committed suicide on 30 April 1945, alongside Eva Braun, his long-time female companion, hours after their marriage. Today, a parking lot covers the site, revealing its dark history only via an information panel with a diagram of the vast bunker network, construction data and the site's post-WWII history. The interior was blown up and sealed off by the Soviets in 1947.

MADAME TUSSAUDS MUSEUM

Map p322 (☎01806-545 800; www.madametussauds.com/berlin; Unter den Linden 74; adult/child 3-14 €21/16; ⏲10am-7pm Sep-Jul, 10am-8pm Aug, last admission 1hr before closing; 🚌100, [S]Brandenburger Tor, [U]Brandenburger Tor) No celebrity in town to snare your stare? Don't fret: at this legendary wax museum the world's biggest pop stars, Hollywood legends, sports heroes and historical icons stand still – very still – for you to snap a picture. Sure, it's an expensive haven of kitsch and camp but where else can you have a candle-light dinner with George Clooney, play piano with Beethoven or test your IQ against Albert Einstein? Avoid wait times and save money by buying tickets online.

KUNSTHALLE DEUTSCHE BANK GALLERY

Map p322 (☎030-202 0930; www.deutsche-bank-kunsthalle.de; Unter den Linden 13-15; adult/concession/child €4/3/free, free Mon; ⏲10am-8pm; 🚌100, 200, [S]Französische Strasse) This small exhibition hall is a platform for contemporary art, especially from emerging art centres in Africa, China, India and South America. The three to four exhibits per year (often in cooperation with international museums like the Tate Modern) seek to push artistic boundaries and examine the effects of a globalised society.

HUMBOLDT UNIVERSITÄT BUILDING

Map p322 (☎030-2093 2951; Unter den Linden 6; 🚌100, 200, TXL) Marx and Engels studied here and the Brothers Grimm and Albert Einstein taught here, at Berlin's oldest university, founded in 1810 and housed in a palace built by Frederick the Great for his brother Heinrich. Statues of the uni's founder, philosopher Wilhelm von Humboldt, and his explorer brother Alexander flank the main entrance.

Until the 1950s it produced plenty of Nobel Prize winners, including Max Planck (physics, 1918) and Albert Einstein (physics, 1921). The last prize went to Werner Forssmann for medicine in 1956. These days, some 33,500 students try to pick up on this illustrious legacy.

REITERDENKMAL FRIEDRICH DER GROSSE MONUMENT

Map p322 (Unter den Linden 6; 🚌100, 200, TXL) Seemingly surveying his domain, Frederick the Great cuts a commanding figure on horseback in this famous 1850 monument that kept sculptor Christian Daniel Rauch busy for a dozen years. The plinth is decorated with a parade of German military men, scientists, artists and thinkers.

BEBELPLATZ MEMORIAL

Map p322 (Bebelplatz; ⏲24hr; 🚌100, 200, TXL, [S]Hausvogteiplatz) In 1933, books by Brecht, Mann, Marx and other 'subversives' went up in flames on this treeless square during the first full-blown public book burning, staged by the Nazi German Student League. Named for August Bebel, the cofounder of Germany's Social Democratic Party (SPD), it was first laid out in the 18th century under Frederick the Great.

Then called Opernplatz (Opera Square), it was intended to be the hub of the Forum Fridericianium, a cultural centre envisioned by the king. Money woes meant that only some of the buildings could be realised: the Staatsoper Unter den Linden (State Opera House), the Alte Königliche Bibliothek (Old Royal Library), a palace for the king's brother Heinrich (now the Humboldt University) and the copper-domed St-Hedwigs-Kathedrale.

ALTE KÖNIGLICHE
BIBLIOTHEK
HISTORIC BUILDING

Map p322 (Bebelplatz; 🚇100, 200, TXL, Ⓢ Hausvogteiplatz) Thanks to its curvaceous facade, this handsome baroque building is nicknamed *Kommode* (chest of drawers). Built under Frederick the Great to shelter the royal book collection, it has been part of the Humboldt University since 1914. It now houses the university's law school. Lenin used to hit the books in the Reading Room behind the central columns.

STAATSOPER UNTER
DEN LINDEN
HISTORIC BUILDING

Map p322 (Bebelplatz; 🚇100, 200, TXL, Ⓢ Hausvogteiplatz) Berlin's opulent state opera was commissioned as the royal opera house by Frederick the Great and designed by his friend and master architect Georg Wenzelslaus von Knobelsdorff. It has graced Bebelplatz since 1742 and risen from the ashes three times. Again in need of an overhaul, the famous song palace will remain closed until at least 2015. Since 1992 Argentine-Israeli conductor Daniel Barenboim has swung the lead baton as music director.

ST-HEDWIGS-KATHEDRALE
BERLIN
CHURCH

Map p322 (☎030-203 4810; www.hedwigs-kathedrale.de; Hinter der Katholischen Kirche 3; ⊙10am-5pm Mon-Sat, 1-5pm Sun; 🚇100, 200, Ⓢ Hausvogteiplatz) This copper-domed church (1773) was commissioned by Frederick the Great, designed by Knobelsdorff, modelled after the Pantheon in Rome and named for the patron saint of Silesia. It was restored after WWII, and its circular, modern interior is lidded by a ribbed dome and accented with Gothic sculpture and an altar cross made of gilded and enamel-decorated ivory.

It was Berlin's only Catholic house of worship until 1854. During WWII St Hedwig was a centre of Catholic resistance led by Bernard Lichtenberg, who died en route to the Dachau concentration camp in 1943 and is buried in the crypt.

KRONPRINZENPALAIS
PALACE

Map p322 (Crown Prince's Palace; Unter den Linden 3; ⊙closed to the public; 🚇100, 200, TXL) This froufrou baroque palace was blue-printed by Johann Arnold Nering and was the residence of young Frederick before he became 'the Great'. In the 1920s, the National Gallery showcased top contemporary artists here until the Nazis deemed them 'degenerate' and closed down the exhibit. In 1990 the formal German reunification agreement was signed here on 31 August.

NEUE WACHE
MEMORIAL

Map p322 (Unter den Linden 4; ⊙10am-6pm; 🚇100, 200, TXL) **FREE** This columned, templelike neoclassical structure (1818) was Karl Friedrich Schinkel's first Berlin commission. Originally a Prussian royal guardhouse, it is now an antiwar memorial whose austere interior is dominated by Käthe Kollwitz's heart-wrenching sculpture of a mother cradling her dead soldier son.

Buried beneath are the remains of an unknown soldier, a Nazi resistance fighter and soil from nine European battlefields and concentration camps.

FRIEDRICHSWERDERSCHE
KIRCHE
CHURCH

Map p322 (Werderscher Markt; 🚇100, 200, Ⓢ Hausvogteiplatz) This perkily turreted church is a rare neo-Gothic design by Schinkel (1830) and cuts a commanding presence on the Werderscher Markt. Normally housing a museum of 19th-century German sculpture, the building was closed in 2014 for structural damage and will remain closed until further notice. The postmodern hulk next to the church is the German Foreign Office.

SCHLOSSBRÜCKE
BRIDGE

Map p322 (Unter den Linden; 🚇100, 200, TXL) Marking the transition from Unter den Linden to Museum Island, the Palace Bridge is considered among Berlin's prettiest. Designed by Karl Friedrich Schinkel in the 1820s, it is decorated with eight marble sculptures depicting the life and death of a warrior. Alas, empty royal coffers kept them from being chiselled until the late 1840s, a few years after the master's death.

⊙ Gendarmenmarkt

GENDARMENMARKT
SQUARE

See p87.

MENDELSSOHN EXHIBIT
MUSEUM

Map p322 (☎030-8170 4726; www.jaegerstrasse.de; Jägerstrasse 51; donations welcome; ⊙noon-6pm; Ⓢ Hausvogteiplatz, Französische Strasse) **FREE** The Mendelssohns are one of the great German family dynasties, starting with the *pater familias,* Jewish Enlightenment philosopher Moses Mendelssohn (1729–86). The bank founded by his son Joseph in 1795 grew into Berlin's largest private banking house and moved into the city's 'Wall Street' on Jägerstrasse in 1890. An exhibit in its former counter hall traces the fate and history of this influential family, who was forced into bankruptcy by the Nazis, prompting many members to flee Germany.

◉ Friedrichstrasse & Checkpoint Charlie

TRÄNENPALAST   MUSEUM
Map p322 (☑030-4677 7790; www.hdg.de; Reichstagufer 17; ☺9am-7pm Tue-Fri, 10am-6pm Sat & Sun; ⓢFriedrichstrasse, ⓡFriedrichstrasse) **FREE** During the Cold War, tears flowed copiously in this glass-and-steel border-crossing pavilion where East Berliners had to bid adieu to family visiting from West Germany – hence its moniker 'Palace of Tears'. The exhibit uses original objects (including the claustrophobic passport control booths and a border auto-firing system), photographs and historical footage to document the division's social impact on the daily lives of Germans on both sides of the border.

FRIEDRICHSTADTPASSAGEN   ARCHITECTURE
Map p322 (Friedrichstrasse btwn Französische Strasse & Mohrenstrasse; ☺10am-8pm Mon-Sat; ⓢFranzösische Strasse, Stadtmitte) Even if you're not part of the Gucci and Prada brigade, the architectural wow factor of this trio of shopping complexes (called Quartiere) linked by a subterranean passageway is undeniable. Highlights are Jean Nouvel's shimmering glass funnel inside the Galeries Lafayette, the dazzlingly patterned art deco–style Quartier 206 and John Chamberlain's tower made from crushed automobiles in Quartier 205.

MAUERMUSEUM   MUSEUM
Map p322 (Haus am Checkpoint Charlie; ☑030-253 7250; www.mauermuseum.de; Friedrichstrasse 43-45; adult/concession €12.50/9.50; ☺9am-10pm; ⓢKochstrasse) The Cold War years, especially the history and horror of the Berlin Wall, are engagingly, if haphazardly, documented in this privately run tourist magnet. Open since 1961, the ageing exhibit is still strong when it comes to telling the stories of escape attempts to the West.

Original devices used in the process, including a hot-air balloon, a one-person submarine and a BMW Isetta, are crowd favourites. Other galleries (all are multilingual) address NATO and its involvement in world conflicts and global human rights struggles.

MAUER PANORAMA   GALLERY
Map p322 (☑030-355 5340; www.asisi.de; Friedrichstrasse 205; adult/concession/child €10/8/4; ☺10am-6pm Oct-Jul, 10am-7pm Aug & Sep; ⓢKochstrasse) Artist Yadegar Asisi is famous for creating bafflingly detailed monumental photographic panoramas. At 15m high and 60m wide, his latest creation depicts the bleakness of everyday life along the Berlin Wall on a random day in the 1980s. Standing on a scaffold in the West, visitors get to look across the death strip and contemplate what it was like to live in the shadow of barbed wire and guard towers. The exhibit will run until at least spring 2015, possibly longer. Call or check the website.

BLACKBOX KALTER KRIEG   MUSEUM
Map p322 (☑030-216 3571; www.bfgg.de; Friedrichstrasse 47; adult/concession €5/3.50; ☺10am-6pm; ⓜKochstrasse) This small pop-up museum chronicles the history of the Cold War. Using photographs, maps, original footage and recordings and various memorabilia, it seeks to explain how the Berlin Wall fit into the conflict and how surrogate conflicts in Korea and Vietnam fuelled the rivalry between the US and the Soviet Union. Organisers hope to eventually put up a permanent Cold War Museum on the site.

STASI AUSSTELLUNG   MUSEUM
Map p322 (☑030-2324 7951; www.bstu.bund.de; Zimmerstrasse 90; ☺10am-6pm; ⓢKochstrasse) **FREE** How was East Germany's Ministry for State Security (Stasi) structured? How were people spied on and by whom? How did the Stasi affect people's daily lives? Using case studies, original artefacts and documents, this compact exhibit seeks to answer these questions and to reveal the all-out zeal of the Stasi when it came to controlling, manipulating and repressing its own people. Free English audioguide available.

TRABI MUSEUM   MUSEUM
Map p322 (☑030-201 030; www.trabi-museum.com; Zimmerstrasse 14; adult/concession €5/3; ☺10am-6pm; ⓢKochstrasse) If you were

TOP SIGHT
CHECKPOINT CHARLIE

Checkpoint Charlie was the principal gateway for foreigners and diplomats between the two Berlins from 1961 to 1990. Since it was the third Allied checkpoint to open, it was named 'Charlie' in reference to the third letter in the NATO phonetic alphabet (alfa, bravo, charlie…). The only direct Cold War–era confrontation between the US and the Soviet Union took place in this very spot, when tanks faced off shortly after the Wall went up, nearly triggering a third world war. A simple plaque affixed to a pile of sandbags in front of a replica army guardhouse commemorates this tense moment.

Alas, little else indicates Checkpoint Charlie's historical importance as the site has, in recent years, degenerated into a tacky tourist trap. Souvenir shops and fast-food restaurants line the street, students dressed as soldiers pose with tourists for tips, and school kids crowd into the 'Freedom Park' beach bar. A rare redeeming aspect is the free open-air gallery that uses photos and documents to illustrate milestones in Cold War history as does the Blackbox Kalter Krieg (p92). Although a bit pricey, Yadegar Asisi's Mauer Panorama (p92) also adds an element of authenticity.

DON'T MISS…
➜ Open-air gallery

PRACTICALITIES
➜ Map p322
➜ cnr Zimmerstrasse & Friedrichstrasse
➜ ⊘24hr
➜ Ⓢ Kochstrasse, Stadtmitte

lucky enough to own a car in East Germany, it would most likely have been a Trabant (Trabi in short), a tinny two-stroker whose name ('satellite' in German) was inspired by the launch of the Soviet Sputnik in 1956. The small exhibit displays the entire production line of Trabis, including rare wooden and racing versions.

MUSEUM FÜR KOMMUNIKATION BERLIN MUSEUM
Map p322 (☑030-202 940; www.mfk-berlin.de; Leipziger Strasse 16; adult/concession/under 17 €4/2/free; ⊘9am-8pm Tue, 9am-5pm Wed-Fri, 10am-6pm Sat & Sun; Ⓢ Mohrenstrasse, Stadtmitte) Three cheeky robots welcome you to this elegant, neo-baroque museum, which takes you on an entertaining romp through the evolution of communication, from smoke signals to computers. Admire such rare items as a Blue Mauritius stamp, test time-honoured communication techniques or ponder the impact of information technology on our daily lives.

A multimedia iPod touch guide (€1.50) provides the full low-down.

DEUTSCHES CURRYWURST MUSEUM MUSEUM
Map p322 (☑030-8871 8647; www.currywurst-museum.com; Schützenstrasse 70; adult/concession/child 6-13 €11/8.50/7; ⊘10am-8pm; Ⓢ Stadtmitte, Kochstrasse) Bright, fun and interactive, this museum is entirely dedicated to the *Currywurst*, Berlin's beloved cult snack. Sniff out curry secrets in the Spice Chamber, find out what kind of curry type you are, learn about the wurst's history and watch a movie about one woman's quest for the best *Currywurst*. Tickets include a wurst-tasting in the snack bar.

FORMER REICHSLUFTFAHRT-MINISTERIUM HISTORIC BUILDING
Map p322 (Reich Aviation Ministry; Leipziger Strasse 5-7; ⊘closed to the public; Ⓢ Kochstrasse) Designed by Ernst Sagebiel in 1935 and '36, this behemoth was not only Hermann Göring's power centre but also where the resistance group 'Red Orchestra' conspired until being caught and executed in 1942. There's a memorial to them in the foyer of what is today the Federal Finance Ministry. Facing Leipziger Strasse is Max Lingner's monumental GDR-era mural made of Meissen porcelain tiles.

🍴 EATING

Mitte is awash with swanky restaurants where the decor is fabulous, the crowds cosmopolitan and the menus stylish. Sure, some places may be more sizzle than substance, but the see-and-be-seen punters don't seem to mind. The area also has several Michelin-starred restaurants.

🍴 Government Quarter

BERLIN PAVILLON — INTERNATIONAL €

Map p322 (☎030-2065 4737; www.berlin-pavillon.de; Scheidemannstrasse 1; mains €3-9; 🚌100, [S]Bundestag, Brandenburger Tor, 🚆Brandenburger Tor) For quick feeds this tourist-geared, self-service cafeteria on the edge of Tiergarten comes in rather handy for breakfast, cakes and simple hot dishes. In summer, the beer garden offers shaded respite.

🍴 Pariser Platz & Unter den Linden

ISHIN – MITTELSTRASSE — JAPANESE €€

Map p322 (www.ishin.de; Mittelstrasse 24; sushi platter €8-19.50, bowl €5-13; 🕐11am-10pm Mon-Sat; [S]Friedrichstrasse, 🚆Friedrichstrasse) Look beyond the cafeteria-style get-up to sushi glory for minimal prices. Combination platters are ample and affordable, especially during happy hour (which is all day Wednesday and Saturday, and until 4pm on other days). If you're not in the mood for raw fish, tuck into a steaming rice bowl topped with meat and/or veg. Nice touch: the unlimited free green tea. There's another **branch** (Map p322; Charlottenstrasse 16; [S]Kochstrasse) near Checkpoint Charlie.

COOKIES CREAM — VEGETARIAN €€€

Map p322 (☎030-2749 2940; www.cookiescream.com; Behrenstrasse 55; mains €22, 3-course menu €39; 🕐from 7pm Tue-Sat; ✎; [S]Französische Strasse) Kudos if you can locate this chic herbivore haven right away. Hint: it's upstairs past a giant chandelier in the service alley of the Westin Grand Hotel. Ring the bell to enter an elegantly industrial loft for flesh-free, flavour-packed dishes from current-harvest ingredients.

🍴 Gendarmenmarkt

SOYA COSPLAY — ASIAN €€

Map p322 (☎030-2062 9093; www.soyacosplay.com; Jägerstrasse 59-60; plates €6-22; 🕐noon-midnight Mon-Sat, 5pm-midnight Sun; [S]Französische Strasse) At this stylish contender, colourful lanterns and nifty lamps create cosiness without kitsch, and dishes on the menu are veritable aroma explosions. The pork belly beautifully plays off pungent Asian herbs, shrimp balls are perked up with wasabi mayonnaise, and even the jellyfish carpaccio is delicate rather than slimy.

AUGUSTINER AM GENDARMENMARKT — GERMAN €€

Map p322 (☎030-2045 4020; www.augustiner-braeu-berlin.de; Charlottenstrasse 55; mains €6-19; 🕐10am-2am; [S]Französische Strasse) Tourists, concert-goers and hearty-food lovers rub shoulders at rustic tables in this surprisingly authentic Bavarian beer hall. Soak up the down-to-earth vibe right along with a mug of full-bodied Augustiner brew. Sausages, roast pork and pretzels provide rib-sticking sustenance, but there's also plenty of lighter (even meat-free) fare as well as good-value lunch specials.

CHIPPS — VEGETARIAN €€

Map p322 (☎030-3644 4588; www.chipps.eu; Jägerstrasse 35; mains €11-17; 🕐9am-11pm Mon-Sat, 9am-5pm Sun; ✎; [S]Hausvogteiplatz) Well worth a little detour, this crisp corner spot with show kitchen and panorama windows turns heads with yummy cooked breakfasts (served all day on Sundays), build-your-own salads and creative hot specials that spin regional, seasonal ingredients into taste-bud magic. Most dishes are vegetarian, some are vegan.

GOODTIME — THAI €€

Map p322 (☎030-2007 4870; www.goodtime-berlin.de; Hausvogteiplatz 11; mains €11-22; 🕐noon-midnight; ✎; [S]Hausvogteiplatz) Sweep on down to this busy dining room with a garden courtyard for fragrant Thai and Indonesian dishes. Creamy curries, succulent shrimp, roast duck or an entire *rijstafel* spread (an elaborate buffet-style meal) all taste flavourful and fresh, if a bit easy on the heat to accommodate German stomachs.

BORCHARDT FRENCH €€€

Map p322 (☎030-8188 6262; Französische Strasse 47; 3-course business lunch €15, dinner mains €20-40; ⏰11.30am-1am; [S]Französische Strasse) Jagger, Clooney and Redford are among the celebs who have tucked into dry-aged steaks and plump oysters in the marble-pillared dining hall of this Berlin institution, established in 1853 by a caterer to the Kaiser. No dish, however, moves as fast as the *Wiener Schnitzel*, a wafer-thin slice of breaded veal fried to crisp perfection.

🍴 Friedrichstrasse & Checkpoint Charlie

TAZ.CAFE CAFE €

Map p322 (☎030-2590 2164; www.taz.de; Rudi-Dutschke-Strasse 23; mains €6.50-8; ⏰8am-8pm Mon-Fri; 📶; [S]Kochstrasse) Join *taz* newspaper staffers at fire-engine-red tables for daily-changing lunches (noon to 3pm) with global pizzazz and prepared with seasonal vegetables and free-range meats. Afternoons bring cakes, snacks and fair-trade 'tazpresso'.

CHA CHÃ THAI €€

Map p322 (☎030-206 259 613; www.eatcha-cha.com; Friedrichstrasse 63; mains €8-11; ⏰11.30am-10pm Mon-Fri, noon-10pm Sat, 12.30-9pm Sun; 🥕; [S]Stadtmitte) Feeling worn out from sightseeing or power-shopping? No problem: a helping of massaman curry should quickly return you to top form for, according to the menu of this Thai nosh spot, the dish has an 'activating' effect. In fact, all menu items are described as having a 'positive eating' benefit, be it vitalising, soothing or stimulating. Gimmicky? Perhaps, but darn tasty too.

RESTAURANT TIM RAUE ASIAN €€€

Map p322 (☎030-2593 7930; www.tim-raue.com; Rudi-Dutschke-Strasse 26; 3-/4-course lunch €38/48, 4-/6-course dinner €118/158; ⏰noon-3pm & 7pm-midnight Tue-Sat; [S]Kochstrasse) Now here's a twin-Michelin-starred restaurant we can get our mind around. Unstuffy ambience and subtly sophisticated design pair perfectly with Raue's briliant Asian-inspired plates that each shine the spotlight on a few choice ingredients. Various taste sensations – sweet and salty, mild and hot – play off each other in perfect harmony. The Peking duck is a perennial bestseller. Popular at lunchtime, too.

🍷 DRINKING & NIGHTLIFE

🍷 Pariser Platz & Unter den Linden

DRAYTON BAR BAR

Map p322 (☎030-680 730 473; www.draytonberlin.com; Behrenstrasse 55; ⏰from 7pm Tue-Sat; [S]Französische Strasse) This glamour vixen of a bar oozes speakeasy sophistication from every dimly lit corner. Gilded peacock lamps guard the bar, whose focus is on creatively updated classic drinks inspired by the season. Enter via Cookies Cream restaurant through the alleyway behind the Westin Grand Hotel.

BEBEL BAR BAR

Map p322 (☎030-460 6090; www.hotelderome.com; Behrenstrasse 37; ⏰9am-1am; 🚌100, 200, TXL, [S]Hausvogteiplatz) Plush luxury is the mojo of the Bebel Bar at the Hotel Rome, where the *Mad Men* crew would fit right in. Try a Roccos Mule, a mix of brandy, plum, fresh raspberries, lemon and spicy ginger. On balmy nights, the action moves to the rooftop terrace. It has great views of the Berlin Cathedral and the ballet of construction cranes currently hovering over historic Mitte.

FELIX CLUB

Map p322 (☎030-301 117 152; www.felix-clubrestaurant.de; Behrenstrasse 72; ⏰from 11pm Mon, Fri & Sat, from 7pm Thu; [S]Brandenburger Tor, 🚆Brandenburger Tor) Once past the velvet rope of this swanky club, you too can shake your booty to high-octane hip-hop, dance and disco beats, sip Champagne cocktails, watch the crowd from the gallery and flirt up a storm. Women get free entry and a glass of Prosecco until midnight on Mondays, while the worker-bee brigade kicks loose on after-work Thursdays.

🍷 Gendarmenmarkt

ASPHALT CLUB

Map p322 (☎030-2200 2396; www.asphalt-berlin.com; Mohrenstrasse 30; ⏰11pm-7am Thu-Sat; [S]Stadtmitte) This Hilton-based party boîte lures cashed-up, dressed-up weekend warriors (and the occasional celebrity) to its extravagantly minimalist space with an impressive 400-speaker sound ceiling.

Musically, it's whatever makes the dance floor hum, mostly hip-hop, house and r 'n' b.

🍷 Friedrichstrasse & Checkpoint Charlie

BERLINER REPUBLIK   PUB
Map p322 (🖱030-3087 2293; www.die-berliner-republik.de; Schiffbauerdamm 8; ⊙10am-6am; 🚇Friedrichstrasse, 🚉Friedrichstrasse) Just as in a mini–stock exchange, the cost of drinks fluctuates with demand at this raucous riverside pub. Everyone goes Pavlovian when a heavy brass bell rings, signalling rock-bottom prices. You won't be hoisting mugs with many Berliners here, but it's a fun spot nonetheless.

TAUSEND   BAR
Map p322 (www.tausendberlin.com; Schiffbauerdamm 11; ⊙from 7.30pm Tue-Sat; 🚇Friedrichstrasse, 🚉Friedrichstrasse) No sign, no light, no bell, just an anonymous steel door tucked under a railway bridge leads to one of Berlin's chicest bars. Behind it, flirty frocks sip raspberry mojitos alongside London Mule–cradling three-day stubbles. The eye-catching decor channels '80s glam while DJs and bands fuel the vibe.

⭐ ENTERTAINMENT

KONZERTHAUS BERLIN   CLASSICAL MUSIC
Map p322 (🖱tickets 030-203 092 101; www.konzerthaus.de; Gendarmenmarkt 2; 🚇Stadtmitte, Französische Strasse) This top-ranked concert hall – a Schinkel design from 1821 – counts the Konzerthaus-Orchester as its 'house band' but also hosts international soloists, thematic concert cycles, children's events and concerts by the Rundfunk-Sinfonieorchester Berlin. Guided tours (€3; in German) at 1pm on Saturdays.

ADMIRALSPALAST   PERFORMING ARTS
Map p322 (🖱tickets 030-2250 7000; www.admiralspalast.de; Friedrichstrasse 101; 🚇Friedrichstrasse, 🚉Friedrichstrasse) This beautifully restored 1920s 'palace' stages crowd-pleasing plays, concerts and comedy shows in its glamorous historic main hall. More intimate programs are presented on the smaller studio stage on the 4th floor. Most performances are suitable for non-German speakers, but do check ahead.

TIPI AM KANZLERAMT   CABARET
Map p322 (🖱tickets 030-3906 6550; www.tipi-am-kanzleramt.de; Grosse Queralle; 🚇100, 🚉Bundestag, 🚉Hauptbahnhof) Tipi stages a year-round program of high-calibre cabaret, dance, acrobatics, musical comedy and magic shows starring German and international artists. It's all staged in a huge and festively decorated permanent tent stationed between the Federal Chancellery and the House of World Cultures on the edge of Tiergarten park. Pre-show dinner is available.

KOMISCHE OPER   OPERA
Map p322 (Comic Opera; 🖱tickets 030-4799 7400; www.komische-oper-berlin.de; Behrenstrasse 55-57; ⊙box office 11am-7pm Mon-Sat, 1-4pm Sun; 🚇100, 200, 🚉Französische Strasse) Musical theatre, light opera, operetta and dance theatre from many periods are the bread and butter of the high-profile Comic Opera venue with its opulent neo-baroque auditorium. Seats feature an ingenious subtitling system that gives you the option of reading along in German, English, French or Turkish. The **box office** (Map p322; 🖱030-4799 7400; Unter den Linden 41; ⊙11am-7pm Mon-Sat, 1-4pm Sun; 🚇100, 200, 🚉Französische Strasse, Friedrichstrasse) is located at Unter den Linden.

MAXIM GORKI THEATER   THEATRE
Map p322 (🖱030-2022 1115; www.gorki.de; Am Festungsgraben 2; 🚇100, 200, 🚉Friedrichstrasse, 🚉Friedrichstrasse) Since the 2013/14 season, new artistic director Shermin Langhoff has made the smallest of Berlin's four state-funded theatres the dedicated home of the so-called 'post-migrant theatre'. Productions look at the lives of second- and third-generation Germans and examine such issues as integration, identity, transition and discrimination. All performances have English surtitles.

HOCHSCHULE FÜR MUSIK HANNS EISLER   CLASSICAL MUSIC
Map p322 (🖱tickets 030-203 092 101; www.hfm-berlin.de; Charlottenstrasse 55; 🚇Stadtmitte, Französische Strasse) The gifted students at Berlin's top-rated music academy populate several orchestras, a choir and a big band, which collectively stage as many as 400 performances annually, most of them in the Neuer Marstall (p115) on Schlossplatz, where the Prussian royals once kept their coaches and horses. Many concerts are free or low-cost.

SHOPPING

There are some souvenir shops along Unter den Linden and around Checkpoint Charlie, but for fancy fashion and accessories, make a beeline to Friedrichstrasse with its dazzling Friedrichstadtpassagen and Galeries Lafayette.

DUSSMANN – DAS KULTURKAUFHAUS — BOOKS, MUSIC

Map p322 (☎030-2025 1111; www.kulturkaufhaus.de; Friedrichstrasse 90; 🕒9am-midnight Mon-Fri, to 11.30pm Sat; [S]Friedrichstrasse, 🚆Friedrichstrasse) It's easy to lose track of time in this cultural playground with wall-to-wall books, DVDs and CDs, leaving no genre unaccounted for. Bonus points for the free reading-glass rentals, downstairs cafe and performance space used for concerts, political discussions and high-profile book readings and signings.

GALERIES LAFAYETTE — DEPARTMENT STORE

Map p322 (☎030-209 480; www.galerieslafayette.de; Friedrichstrasse 76-78; 🕒10am-8pm Mon-Sat; [S]Französische Strasse) Stop by the Berlin branch of the exquisite French fashion emporium if only to check out the show-stealing interior (designed by Jean Nouvel, no less), centred on a huge glass cone shimmering with kaleidoscopic intensity. Around it wrap three circular floors filled with fancy fashions, fragrances and accessories, while glorious gourmet treats await downstairs in the food hall.

FASSBENDER & RAUSCH — FOOD

Map p322 (☎030-2045 8443; www.fassbender-rausch.com; Charlottenstrasse 60; 🕒10am-8pm Mon-Sat, 11am-8pm Sun; [S]Stadtmitte) If the Aztecs thought of chocolate as the elixir of the gods, then this emporium of truffles and pralines must be heaven. Bonus: the chocolate volcano and giant replicas of Berlin landmarks. The upstairs cafe-restaurant has views of Gendarmenmarkt and serves sinful drinking chocolates and cakes as well as dishes prepared and seasoned with cocoa.

KREATIVKAUFHAUS VIELFACH — DEPARTMENT STORE

Map p322 (☎030-9148 4678; www.fachmiete.de; Zimmerstrasse 11; [S]Kochstrasse) Pick up unique gifts or souvenirs handmade in Germany at this new store where artists and craftspeople can rent shelf space to display beauty products, stuffed animals, bags, ceramics, photographs and lots of other pretty things. The all-white store occupies a beautifully renovated listed building near Checkpoint Charlie.

BERLIN STORY — BOOKS

Map p322 (☎030-2045 3842; www.berlinstory.de; Unter den Linden 40; 🕒10am-7pm Mon-Sat, to 6pm Sun; 🚌100, 200, [S]Friedrichstrasse, Französische Strasse, 🚆Friedrichstrasse) Never mind the souvenirs, this store's ammo is its broad selection of Berlin-related books, maps, DVDs, CDs and magazines, in English and a dozen other languages, some published in-house. For a primer on Berlin's vivid history, visit the in-store museum (admission €5).

ANTIK- UND BUCHMARKT AM BODEMUSEUM — ANTIQUES

Map p322 (www.antikbuchmarkt.de; Am Kupfergraben; 🕒11am-5pm Sat & Sun; [S]Hackescher Markt, 🚋M1, 🚆Hackescher Markt) This arts and collectible market has a gorgeous setting with Museum Island as a backdrop. Book collectors have plenty of boxes to sift through alongside a smattering of furniture, toys, coins, bric-a-brac and old photographs.

FRAU TONIS PARFUM — BEAUTY

Map p322 (☎030-2021 5310; www.frau-tonis-parfum.com; Zimmerstrasse 13; 🕒10am-6pm Mon-Sat; [S]Kochstrasse) Follow your nose to this scent-sational made-in-Berlin perfume boutique and pick up a custom blend to match your type – classic, extravagant or modern. Bestsellers include Marlene Dietrich's favourite, 'Pure Violet'.

RITTER SPORT BUNTE SCHOKOWELT — FOOD

Map p322 (☎030-2009 5080; www.ritter-sport.de; Französische Strasse 24; 🕒10am-7pm Mon-Wed, to 8pm Thu-Sat, to 6pm Sun; 👪; [S]Französische Strasse) Fans of Ritter Sport's colourful square chocolate bars can pick up limited edition, organic and diet varieties in addition to all the classics at this flagship store. Upstairs, a free exhibit explains the journey from cocoa bean to finished product, but we're especially fond of the chocolate station where you can create your personalised bars.

Museumsinsel & Alexanderplatz

ALEXANDERPLATZ | NIKOLAIVIERTEL | SCHLOSSPLATZ

Neighbourhood Top Five

❶ Time-travelling through ancient Greece and Babylon to the Middle East at the glorious **Pergamonmuseum** (p101).

❷ Making a date with Nefertiti and her royal entourage at the stunningly rebuilt **Neues Museum** (p105).

❸ Letting the sights drift by while enjoying cold drinks on the deck of a **Spree River tour boat** (p111).

❹ Dipping behind the 'iron curtain' at the interactive **DDR Museum** (p112).

❺ Getting high on the knockout views from the top of the **Fernsehturm** (p110), Germany's tallest structure.

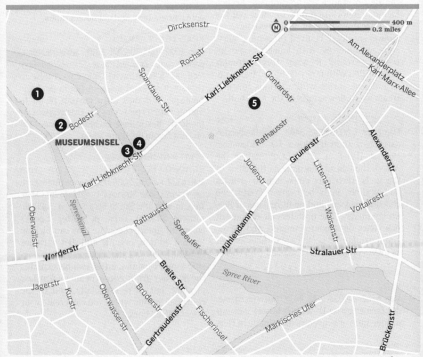

For more detail of this area, see Map p320 ➡

Explore: Museumsinsel & Alexanderplatz

Noisy and hectic, Alexanderplatz (Alex for short) is the transport and commercial hub of the eastern city centre but not really the kind of square that invites lingering. Despite post-reunification attempts to temper the 1960s socialist look, it remains an oddly cluttered, soulless jumble that's all concrete, no trees. Confusingly bifurcated by roads, train and tram tracks, its main redeeming feature is the soaring TV Tower, which sticks out of the city skyline like the tall kid in your school picture. It delivers great views from the top and is handy for orientation from below.

Fans of antique treasures and fine art, meanwhile, will feel as though they've hit the jackpot at nearby Museumsinsel (Museum Island), the main attraction in these parts. Opposite the museums, construction of the historic Berlin City Palace has been under way since mid-2013. The adjacent Humboldt-Box provides a preview of the massive building that will house a cultural centre called Humboldt-Forum. They're big on reconstruction in this part of town and another example is the nearby Nikolaiviertel, a medieval-looking quarter built in 1987 atop Berlin's original settlement. Nearby, the U-Bahn extension has created another big construction site.

Local Life

→**Late-night openings** Clued-in locals know that the best time to see the Museumsinsel collections without the crowds is on Thursday evening when all five of them stay open until 8pm.

→**Shopping** Big shopping centres are scarce in central Berlin, which probably explains the enormous local popularity of the Alexa (p117) mega-mall, which harbours practically every franchise under the sun and stays open until 9pm.

→**Drinks with a view** There are few better places for summertime sunset cocktails than the rooftop terrace of the House of Weekend (p117) club, with the entire glittering city at your feet.

Getting There & Away

→**Bus** M48 links Alexanderplatz with Potsdamer Platz; bus 248 goes to Märkisches Museum and Nikolaiviertel.
→**S-Bahn** S5, S7/75 and S9 all converge at Alexanderplatz.
→**Tram** M4, M5 and M6 connect Alexanderplatz with Marienkirche.
→**U-Bahn** U2, U5 and U8 stop at Alexanderplatz. Other main stops are Klosterstrasse and Märkisches Museum (U2) and Jannowitzbrücke (U8).

Lonely Planet's Top Tip

It would take superhuman stamina to visit all five museums on Museumsinsel in one day, so don't even try; concentrate your energy on those that interest you most. Skip the worst crowds by arriving first thing in the morning, late in the afternoon or on Thursdays, when all museums stay open until 8pm.

✗ Best Places to Eat

→ Dolores (p116)
→ Zur Letzten Instanz (p116)

For reviews, see p116 →

☕ Best Places to Drink

→ House of Weekend (p117)
→ Club Avenue @ Café Moskau (p117)
→ Brauhaus Georgbräu (p117)

For reviews, see p117 →

⊙ Best Non-Museum Sights

→ Berliner Dom (p115)
→ Fernsehturm (p110)
→ Humboldt-Box (p115)
→ Marienkirche (p111)
→ Nikolaiviertel (p114)

For reviews, see p110 →

MUSEUMSINSEL & ALEXANDERPLATZ

TOP SIGHT
MUSEUMSINSEL

Walk through ancient Babylon, meet an Egyptian queen, clamber up a Greek altar or be mesmerised by Monet's ethereal landscapes. Welcome to Museumsinsel (Museum Island), Berlin's most important treasure trove, spanning 6000 years' worth of art, artefacts, sculpture and architecture from Europe and beyond. Spread across five grand museums built between 1830 and 1930, the complex takes up the entire northern half of the little Spree Island where Berlin's settlement began in the 13th century.

Berlin's 'Louvre'

The first repository to open was the **Altes Museum** (Old Museum), completed in 1830 next to the Berlin Cathedral and the Lustgarten park. Today it presents Greek, Etruscan and Roman antiquities. Behind it, the **Neues Museum** (New Museum) showcases the Egyptian collection, most famously the bust of Queen Nefertiti, and also houses the Museum of Pre- and Early History. The temple-like **Alte Nationalgalerie** (Old National Gallery) trains the focus on 19th-century European art. The island's top draw is the **Pergamonmuseum**, with its monumental architecture from ancient worlds, including the namesake Pergamonaltar. The **Bodemuseum**, at the island's northern tip, is famous for its medieval sculptures.

Museumsinsel Masterplan

In 1999 the Museumsinsel repositories collectively became a Unesco World Heritage site. The distinction was at least partly achieved because of a master plan for the renovation and modernisation of the complex, which is expected to be completed in 2025 under the

DON'T MISS...

➡ Ishtar Gate
➡ Bust of Nefertiti
➡ Berlin Goldhut
➡ *Praying Boy*
➡ Sculptures by Tilman Riemenschneider

PRACTICALITIES

➡ Map p320
➡ 🎧 all museums
030-266 424 242
➡ www.smb.museum
➡ price varies by museum, combined day ticket for all museums adult/concession €18/9
➡ 🚌 100, 200,
🚉 Hackescher Markt, Friedrichstrasse

aegis of British architect David Chipperfield. Except for the Pergamon, whose exhibits are currently being reorganised, the restoration of the museums themselves has been completed. Construction has also begun on the **James-Simon-Galerie**, a colonnaded modern foyer named for an early-20th-century German-Jewish philanthropist. It will serve as the central entrance to four of the five museums and also harbour a cafe and other service facilities. Another master plan key feature is the subterranean 'Archaeological Promenade' that will eventually link the four archaeological museums. For more details see www.museumsinsel-berlin.de.

Pergamonmuseum

Berlin's top museum attraction, the **Pergamon-museum** (Map p320; ☑030-266 424 242; www.smb.museum; Bodestrasse 1-3; adult/concession €12/6; ☺10am-6pm Fri-Wed, to 8pm Thu; ☑100, ☒Hackescher Markt, Friedrichstrasse) opens a fascinating window onto the ancient world. Completed in 1930, the palatial three-wing complex presents a rich feast of classical sculpture and monumental architecture from Greece, Rome, Babylon and the Middle East in three collections: the Collection of Antiquities, the Museum of Near Eastern Antiquities and the Museum of Islamic Art. Most of the pieces were excavated and spirited to Berlin by German archaeologists around the turn of the 20th century.

The Pergamonmuseum is the fourth treasure chest on Museum Island to undergo extensive gradual restoration work that will leave some sections closed for years. The north wing and the hall containing the namesake Pergamon Altar will be off limits until 2019. This will be followed by the closure of the south wing, presumably until 2025. A fourth wing facing the Spree River will also be added so that in future all parts of the museum can be experienced on a continuous walk. During the restoration, the museum entrance is off Bodestrasse, behind the Neues Museum.

Antikensammlung

The Antikensammlung (Collection of Antiquities) presents artworks from ancient Greece and Rome here and at the Altes Museum. Since the Pergamon Altar is currently closed to the public, the main sight is now the 2nd-century AD **Market Gate of Miletus**. Merchants and customers once flooded through the splendid 17m-high gate into the bustling market square of this wealthy Roman trading town in modern-day Turkey. A strong earthquake levelled much of the town in the early Middle Ages, but German archaeologists dug up the site between 1903

> MUSEUMSINSEL & ALEXANDERPLATZ MUSEUMSINSEL

TOP TIP

Arrive early or late on weekdays or skip the queues by purchasing your ticket online, which also nets a small discount. An excellent multilanguage audioguide is included in the admission price.

Museumsinsel is the product of a late-19th-century fad among European royalty to open their private collections to the public. The Louvre in Paris, the British Museum in London, the Prado in Madrid and the Glyptothek in Munich all date back to this period. In Berlin, King Friedrich Wilhelm III and his successors followed suit.

A ROYAL CAPITAL

Pergamon was the capital of the Kingdom of Pergamon, which reigned over vast stretches of the eastern Mediterranean in the 3rd and 2nd centuries BC. Inspired by Athens, its rulers, the Attalids, turned their royal residence into a major cultural and intellectual centre. Draped over a 330m-high ridge were grand palaces, a library, a theatre and glorious temples dedicated to Trajan, Dionysus and Athena.

Museumsinsel

Navigating around this five-museum treasure repository can be a little daunting, so we've put together this itinerary to help you find the must-see highlights while maximising your time and energy. You'll need a minimum of four hours and an 'area ticket' for entry to all museums.

Start in the Altes Museum by admiring the roll call of antique gods guarded by a perky bronze statue called the **Praying Boy** ❶, the poster child of a prized collection of antiquities. Next up, head to the Neues Museum for your audience with **Queen Nefertiti** ❷, the star of the Egyptian collection atop the grand central staircase. One more floor up, don't miss the dazzling Bronze Age **Berliner Goldhut** ❸ (room 305). Leaving the Neues Museum, turn left for the Pergamonmuseum. With the namesake altar off limits until 2019, the first major sight you'll see is the **Ishtar Gate** ❹. Upstairs, pick your way through the Islamic collection, past carpets, prayer niches and a caliph's palace to the intricately painted **Aleppo Room** ❺. Jump ahead to the 19th century at the Alte Nationalgalerie to zero in on paintings by **Caspar David Friedrich** ❻ on the 3rd floor and precious sculptures such as Schadow's **Statue of Two Princesses** ❼ on the ground floor. Wrap up your explorations at the Bodemuseum, reached in a five-minute walk. Admire the foyer with its equestrian statue of Friedrich Wilhelm, then feast your eyes on European sculpture without missing masterpieces by **Tilman Riemenschneider** ❽ in room 212.

FAST FACTS

» **Oldest object:** 700,000-year-old Paleolithic hand axe at Neues Museum
» **Newest object:** piece of barbed wire from Berlin Wall at Neues Museum
» **Oldest museum:** Altes Museum, 1830
» **Most popular museum in Germany:** Pergamonmuseum (1.26 million visitors)
» **Total Museumsinsel visitors (2013):** 2.92 million

Sculptures by Tilman Riemenschneider
(Room 212, Bodemuseum)

Dazzling detail and great emotional expressiveness characterise the wooden sculptures by late-Gothic master carver Tilman Riemenschneider as in this portrayal of *St Anne and Her Three Husbands* from around 1510.

Bust of Queen Nefertiti
(Room 210, Neues Museum)

In the north dome, fall in love with Berlin's most beautiful woman, the 3330-year-old Egyptian queen Nefertiti, she of the long graceful neck and timeless good looks – despite the odd wrinkle and missing eye.

Aleppo Room
(Room 16, Pergamonmuseum)

A highlight of the Museum of Islamic Art, this richly painted, wood-panelled reception room from a Christian merchant's home in 17th-century Aleppo, Syria, combines Islamic floral and geometric motifs with courtly scenes and Christian themes.

Ishtar Gate
(Room 9, Pergamonmuseum)

Draw breath as you enter the 2600-year-old city gate to Babylon with soaring walls sheathed in radiant blue glazed bricks and adorned with ochre reliefs of strutting lions, bulls and dragons representing Babylonian gods.

Pergamonmuseum

Spree

5 **6**

Alte Nationalgalerie

4

7

2

Entrance

Entrance

Entrance

Neues Museum

Bodestraße

3

1

Altes Museum

Entrance

Berliner Dom

Lustgarten

Paintings by Caspar David Friedrich
(Top Floor, Alte Nationalgalerie)

A key artist of the romantic period, Caspar David Friedrich put his own stamp on landscape painting with his dark, moody and subtly dramatic meditations on the boundaries of human life vs the infinity of nature.

Statue of Two Princesses
(Ground Floor, Alte Nationalgalerie)

Johann Gottfried Schadow captures Prussian princesses (and sisters) Luise and Friederike in a moment of intimacy and thoughtfulness in this double marble statue created in 1795 at the height of the neoclassical period.

Berliner Goldhut
(Room 305, Neues Museum)

Marvel at the Bronze Age artistry of the Berlin Gold Hat, a ceremonial gold cone embossed with ornamental bands believed to have been used in predicting the best times for planting and harvesting.

Praying Boy
(Room 5, Altes Museum)

The top draw at the Old Museum is the *Praying Boy*, ancient Greece's 'Next Top Model'. The life-size bronze statue of a young male nude is the epitome of physical perfection and was cast around 300 BC in Rhodes.

and 1905 and managed to put the puzzle back together. The richly decorated marble gate blends Greek and Roman design features and is the world's single largest monument ever to be reassembled in a museum.

Also from Miletus is a beautifully restored **floor mosaic** starring Orpheus, a gifted musician from ancient Greek mythology whose lyre-playing charmed even the beasts surrounding him. It originally graced the dining room of a 2nd-century Roman villa.

Vorderasiatisches Museum

Step through the Gate of Miletus and travel back 800 years to yet another culture and civilisation: Babylon during the reign of King Nebuchadnezzar II (604–562 BC). You're now in the Museum of the Ancient Near East, where it's impossible not to be awed by the magnificence of the **Ishtar Gate**, the **Processional Way** leading to it and the facade of the **king's throne hall**. All are sheathed in radiant blue glazed bricks and adorned with ochre reliefs of strutting lions, bulls and dragons representing Babylonian gods. They're so striking, you can almost imagine hearing the roaring and fanfare as the procession rolled into town.

Other treasures from the collection include the colossal statue of the weather god Hadad (775 BC; room 2) from Syria and the nearly 5000-year-old cone mosaic temple facade from Uruk (room 5).

Museum für Islamische Kunst

Top billing in the Museum of Islamic Art upstairs belongs to the facade from the **caliph's palace of Mshatta** (8th century; room 9) in today's Jordan, which was a gift to Kaiser Wilhelm II from Ottoman Sultan Abdul Hamid II. A masterpiece of early Islamic art, it depicts animals and mythical creatures frolicking peacefully amid a riot of floral motifs in an allusion to the Garden of Eden.

PERGAMONMUSEUM

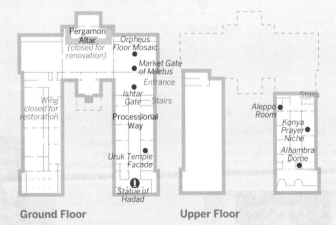

Ground Floor   Upper Floor

Altes Museum (p106)

TAKE A BREAK

The nearest cafe is Alegretto at the Neues Museum, which serves regional and international fare, plus coffee and cakes. A short walk away, **Zwölf Apostel** (Map p322; www.12-apostel.de; Georgenstrasse 2; mains €8-16; ⓜM1, ⓇFriedrichstrasse, Ⓢ Friedrichstrasse) does breakfast and also has lunchtime pizza specials at heavenly prices.

The Pergamon-museum was purpose-built between 1910 and 1930 to house the massive amounts of ancient art and archaeological treasures excavated by German scientists at such sites as Babylon, Assur, Uruk and Miletus. Designed by Alfred Messel, the building was constructed after his death by his close friend Ludwig Hoffmann and badly pummelled in WWII. Lots of objects were whisked away to the Soviet Union as war booty but most were returned in 1958.

Other rooms feature fabulous ceramics, carvings, glasses and other artistic objects as well as the brightly turquoise 11th-century **prayer niche** from a mosque in Konya, Turkey and an intricately patterned cedar-and-poplar **ceiling dome** from the Alhambra in Spain's Granada. Capping a tour of the museum is the **Aleppo Room** (room 16). Guests arriving in this richly painted, wood-panelled reception room would have had no doubt as to the wealth and power of its owner, a Christian merchant in 17th-century Aleppo, Syria.

Neues Museum

David Chipperfield's reconstruction of the bombed-out **Neues Museum** (New Museum; Map p320; ☑030-266 424 242; www.smb.museum; Bodestrasse 1-3; adult/concession €12/6; ⊙10am-6pm Fri-Wed, 10am-8pm Thu; ⓜ100, 200, ⓇHackescher Markt) is the residence of Queen Nefertiti, the show-stopper of the **Ägyptisches Museum** (Egyptian Museum), and the equally enthralling **Museum für Vor- und Frühgeschichte** (Museum of Pre- and Early History). Like working on a giant jigsaw puzzle, the British architect incorporated every original shard, scrap and brick he could find into the new building. This brilliant blend of the historic and modern creates a dynamic space that beautifully juxtaposes massive stairwells, domed rooms, muralled halls and high ceilings. Museum tickets are only valid for admission during a designated half-hour time slot. Skip the queue by buying advance tickets online.

Ägyptisches Museum

Most visitors come to the Neues Museum for an audience with the eternally gorgeous Egyptian queen **Nefertiti**. Her bust was created around 1340 BC by the court sculptor Thutmose. Extremely well preserved, the sculpture was part of the treasure trove unearthed around 1912 by a Berlin expedition of archaeologists who were sifting through the sands of Armana, the royal city built by Nefertiti's husband, King Akhenaten (r 1353–1336 BC).

Another famous work is the so-called **Berlin Green Head** – the bald head of a priest carved from smooth green stone. Created around 400 BC in the Late Egyptian Period, it shows Greek influence and is unusual in that it is not an actual portrait of a specific person but an idealised figure meant to exude universal wisdom and experience.

Museum für Vor- und Frühgeschichte

Within this collection, pride of place goes to the **Trojan antiquities** discovered by archaeologist Heinrich Schliemann in 1870 near Hisarlik in modern-day Turkey. However, most of the elaborate jewellery, ornate weapons and gold mugs on display are replicas because the originals became Soviet war booty after WWII and remain in Moscow. Exceptions are the three humble-looking 4500-year-old silver jars proudly displayed in their own glass case.

One floor up the grand staircase, just past Nefertiti and the precious **papyrus collection** (room 211), is another head turner: the bronze **Xanten Youth** (room 202), which served as a dumb waiter in a Roman villa. The massive sculpture of the **sun god Helios** in the south dome (room 203) also has its admirers.

The recently revamped permanent exhibit on the top floor travels back even further to the stone, bronze and iron ages. Highlights include the 45,000-year-old **fossilised skull** of an 11-year-old Neanderthal boy found in 1909 in Le Moustier, as well as a newly added reconstruction of his face. The biggest crowds of all gather around the 3000-year-old **Berliner Goldhut** (Berlin Gold Hat; room 305). Resembling a wizard's hat, it is covered in elaborate bands of astronomical symbols and must indeed have struck the Bronze Age people as something magical. It's one of only four of its kind unearthed worldwide.

Altes Museum

Karl Friedrich Schinkel pulled out all the stops for the grand neoclassical **Altes Museum** (Old Museum; Map p320; ☎030-266 424 242; www.smb.museum; Am Lustgarten; adult/concession €10/5; ☺10am-6pm Tue, Wed & Fri-Sun, 10am-8pm Thu; ☐100, 200, ⓇFriedrichstrasse, Hackescher Markt), which was the first exhibition space to open on Museumsinsel in 1830. A curtain of fluted columns gives way to a Pantheon-inspired rotunda that's the focal point of a prized antiquities collection. In the downstairs galleries, sculptures, vases, tomb reliefs and jewellery shed light on various facets of life in ancient Greece, while upstairs the focus is on the Etruscans and Romans. Top draws include the *Praying Boy* bronze sculpture, Roman silver vessels and portraits of Caesar and Cleopatra.

Greeks

This chronologically arranged exhibit spans all periods in ancient Greek art from the 10th to the 1st centuries BC. Among the oldest items is a collection of bronze helmets, but it's the statues and elaborate vases that show the greatest artistry.

Among the first eye-catchers is the strapping **Kouros** (room 2), a nude male with a Mona Lisa smile and a great mop of hair. In the next gallery, all eyes are on the **Berlin Goddess**, a beautifully preserved funerary statue of a wealthy young woman in a fancy red dress. The finely carved **Seated Goddess of Tarent** (room 9) is another highlight.

The biggest crowd-pleaser is the **Praying Boy** (room 5), an idealised young male nude sculpted in Rhodes around 300 BC and brought to Berlin by Frederick the Great in 1747. Both Napoleon and Stalin took a fancy to the pretty boy and temporarily abducted him as war booty to Paris and Moscow, respectively. Today, his serene smile once again radiates over the museum's soaring **rotunda** that's lidded by a grand coffered and frescoed ceiling. Light filters through a central skylight illuminating 20 large-scale statues representing a who's who among antique gods, including Nike, Zeus and Fortuna.

Etruscans & Romans

The museum's Etruscan collection is one of the largest outside Italy and contains some stunning pieces. Admire a circular shield from the grave of a warrior alongside amphorae, jewellery, coins and other items from daily life dating back as far as the 8th century BC. Learn about Etruscan language by studying the **tablet from Capua** and about funerary rites by examining the highly decorated **cinerary urns** and **sarcophagi**. Ensuing rooms are dedicated to the Romans. There's fantastic sculpture, a superb 70-piece silver table service called the **Hildesheim Treasure** and busts of Roman leaders, including Caesar and Cleopatra. An adults-only **erotic cabinet** (behind a closed door, no less) brims with not-so-subtle depictions of satyrs, hermaphrodites and giant phalli.

Bodemuseum

Mighty and majestic, the **Bodemuseum** (Map p320; ☑030-266 424 242; www.smb.museum; Am Kupfergraben/Monbijoubrücke; adult/concession €10/5; ◷10am-6pm Tue, Wed & Fri-Sun, 10am-8pm Thu; ⑧Hackescher Markt) has pushed against the northern tip of Museumsinsel like a proud ship's bow since 1904. The gloriously restored neo-baroque beauty presents several collections in mostly naturally lit galleries.

The building, designed by Ernst von Ihne, was originally named Kaiser-Friedrich-Museum before being renamed for its first director, Wilhelm von Bode, in 1956. It's a beautifully proportioned architectural composition built around a central axis. Sweeping staircases, interior courtyards, frescoed ceilings and marble floors give the museum the grandeur of a palace.

The tone is set in the grand domed entrance hall where visitors are greeted by Andreas Schlüter's monumental sculpture of Great Elector Friedrich Wilhelm on horseback. From here head straight to the central Italian Renaissance–style basilica, where all eyes are on colourfully glazed terracotta sculpture by Luca della Robbia. This leads to a smaller

MUSEUMSINSEL & ALEXANDERPLATZ MUSEUMSINSEL

OPEN-AIR CONCERTS

In July and August, classical open-air concerts take place at 8.30pm on Sundays outside the Bodemuseum between Monbijoustrasse and Am Kupfergraben. Admission is free but show up early to admire the scenic surrounds and stake out a good spot. Check www.sonntagskonzerte.de for the schedule. There's also nightly outdoor tango, salsa and swing dancing at riverside **Strandbad Mitte** (Map p326; ☑030-2462 8963; www.strandbad-mitte. de; Kleine Hamburger Strasse 16; ◷9am-2am; ☏; ⑧Oranienburger Strasse) across from the museum.

The massive granite basin outside the Altes Museum was designed by Karl Friedrich Schinkel and carved from a single slab by Christian Gottlieb Cantian. It was considered an artistic and technical feat back in the 1820s. The original plan to install it in the museum's rotunda had to be ditched when the bowl ended up being too massive to fit its dimensions. Almost 7m in diameter, it was carved in situ from a massive boulder in Brandenburg.

domed, rococo-style hall with marble statues of Frederick the Great and his generals. The galleries radiate from both sides of this axis and continue upstairs.

Skulpturensammlung

The majority of rooms showcase the Bode's Sculpture Collection, which British Museum director Neil MacGregor hailed as 'the most comprehensive display of European sculpture anywhere'. The works span the arc of artistic creativity from the early Middle Ages to the late 18th century, with a special focus on the Italian Renaissance. There are priceless masterpieces like Donatello's **Pazzi Madonna**, Giovanni Pisano's **Man of Sorrows** relief, and the portrait busts of Desiderio da Settignano. Staying on the ground floor, you can cruise from the Italians to the Germans by admiring the 12th-century **Gröninger Empore**, a church gallery from a former monastery that is considered a major work of the Romanesque period.

Most of the German sculptures are upstairs, with an entire room dedicated to late-Gothic master carver Tilman Riemenschneider. Highlights include the exquisite **St Anne and Her Three Husbands** as well as the **Four Evangelists**. In the next room, you can compare Riemenschneider's emotiveness to that of his contemporaries Hans Multscher and Nicolaus Gerhaert van Leyden. The monumental **knight-saints** from the period of the Thirty Years' War are another impressive standout on this floor.

Museum für Byzantische Kunst

Before breaking for coffee at the elegant cafe, pop back down to the ground floor where the Museum of Byzantine Art takes up just a few rooms off the grand domed foyer. It presents mainly western Roman and Byzantine art from the 3rd to the 15th centuries. The elaborate Roman sarcophagi, the ivory carvings and the mosaic icons point to the high level of artistry in these early days of Christianity.

Münzsammlung

Coin collectors will get a kick out of the Numismatic Collection on the 2nd floor. With half a million coins – and counting – it's one of the largest of its kind in the world, even if only a small fraction can be displayed at one time. The oldest farthing is from the 7th century BC and displayed in a special case alongside the smallest, largest, fattest and thinnest coins.

Alte Nationalgalerie

The Greek temple-style **Alte Nationalgalerie** (Old National Gallery; Map p320; ☎030-266 424 242; www.smb.museum; Bodestrasse 1-3; adult/concession €10/5; ⊙10am-6pm Tue, Wed & Fri-Sun, 10am-8pm Thu; ☐100, 200, ☒Hackescher Markt), open since 1876, is a three-

---

THE MYSTERY OF PRIAM'S TREASURE

Heinrich Schliemann (1822–90) was not a particularly careful or skilled archaeologist, but he was certainly one of the luckiest. Obsessed with the idea of uncovering Homer's Troy, he hit the mother lode in 1873 near Hisarlik in today's Turkey, putting paid to the belief that the town mentioned in the *Iliad* was mere myth. He also famously unearthed a hoard of gold and silver vessels, vases and jewellery, which he believed had once belonged to King Priam. The fact that it later turned out to be a good thousand years older than Homer's Troy doesn't make the find any less spectacular.

Schliemann illegally smuggled the cache to Berlin, had to pay a fine to the Ottoman Empire and eventually donated it to Berlin's ethnological museum. In a strange twist of fate, the treasure was carted off as WWII war booty by the Soviets, who remained mum about its whereabouts until 1993. It remains at the Pushkin Museum in Moscow to this day, leaving only replicas in Berlin.

Alte Nationalgalerie

LUSTGARTEN

The patch of green fronting the Altes Museum has seen almost as many makeovers as Madonna. It started as a royal kitchen garden and became a military exercise ground before being turned into a pleasure garden by Schinkel. The Nazis held mass rallies here, the East Germans ignored it. Restored to its Schinkel-era appearance, it's now a favourite resting spot for foot-weary tourists.

storey showcase of first-rate 19th-century European art. It was a tumultuous century, characterised by revolutions and industrialisation that brought about profound changes in society. Artists reacted to the new realities in different ways. While German romantics like Caspar David Friedrich sought solace in nature and the Nazarenes like Anselm Feuerbach turned to religious subjects, the epic canvases of Adolf Menzel and Franz Krüger glorified moments in Prussian history, and the impressionists focused on nature and aesthetics.

Johann Gottfried Schadow's **Statue of Two Princesses** and a bust of Johann Wolfgang von Goethe are standout sculptures on the ground floor. In the next galleries, Adolf Menzel gets the star treatment – look for his famous **A Flute Concert of Frederick the Great at Sanssouci**, showing the king playing the flute at his Potsdam palace.

The 2nd floor shows impressionist paintings by such famous French artists as Monet, Degas, Cezanne, Renoir and Manet, whose **In the Conservatory** is considered a masterpiece. Among the Germans, there's Arnold Böcklin's **Isle of Death** and several canvases by Max Liebermann.

Romantics rule the top floor where all eyes are on Caspar David Friedrich's mystical landscapes and the Gothic fantasies of Karl Friedrich Schinkel. Also look for key works by Carl Blechen and portraits by Philip Otto Runge and Carl Spitzweg.

The banker JHW Wagener was an avid collector of art and a generous man who, in 1861, bequeathed his entire collection of 262 paintings to the Prussian state to form the basis of a national gallery. Just one year later, William I commissioned Friedrich August Stüler to design a suitable museum. He came up with the Alte Nationalgalerie, an imposing temple-like structure perched on a pedestal and fronted by a curtain of Corinthian columns. The entrance is reached via a sweeping double staircase crowned by a statue of King Friedrich Wilhelm IV on horseback.

TOP SIGHT
FERNSEHTURM

No matter where you are in Berlin, simply look up and chances are that you will see the Fernsehturm (TV Tower). Germany's tallest structure, which is as iconic to the city as the Eiffel Tower is to Paris, has been soaring 368m high (including the antenna) since 1969. Views are stunning on clear days from the panorama platform at 203m. Pinpoint city landmarks from there or from the upstairs Restaurant Sphere (mains €14 to €28), which makes one revolution per hour.

Ordered by East German government leader Walter Ulbricht in the 1950s, the tower was built not only as a transmitter for radio and TV programs but also as a demonstration of the GDR's strength and technological prowess. However, it ended up becoming a bit of a laughing stock when it turned out that, when struck by the sun, the steel sphere below the antenna produces the reflection of a giant cross. This inspired a popular joke (not appreciated by the GDR leadership) that the phenomenon was the 'Pope's revenge' on the secular socialist state for having removed crucifixes from churches.

The tower's rocket-like shape was inspired by the space race of the 1960s and in particular the launch of the first satellite, the Soviet Sputnik. The tower is made up of the base, a 250m high shaft, the 4800-tonne sphere and the 118m-high antenna. Its original location was supposed to be the Müggelberg hills on the city's southeastern edge. Construction had already begun when the authorities realised that the tower would be in the flight path of the planned airport at nearby Schönefeld. Ulbricht then decided on its current location.

Holders of Fast View, VIP, Early Bird and Late Night tickets, which must be pre-purchased online and printed, can jump the queue.

DON'T MISS...

➡ Sunset cocktails at the cafe in the sky

PRACTICALITIES

➡ Map p320

➡ ☏030-247 575 875

➡ www.tv-turm.de

➡ Panoramastrasse 1a

➡ adult/child €13/8.50, Fast View ticket €19.50/11.50

➡ ⊙9am-midnight Mar-Oct, 10am-midnight Nov-Feb

➡ Ⓢ Alexanderplatz, Ⓡ Alexanderplatz

⊙ SIGHTS

A lovely way to experience Berlin from April to October – and a great break from museum-hopping – is from the open-air deck of a river cruiser. Several companies run relaxing Spree spins through the city centre from landing docks on the eastern side of Museumsinsel (eg outside the DDR Museum). Sip refreshments while a guide showers you with titbits (in English and German) as you glide past grand old buildings and museums, beer gardens and the government quarter. The one-hour tour costs about €11.

MUSEUMSINSEL   MUSEUM
See p100.

⊙ Alexanderplatz

FERNSEHTURM   LANDMARK
See p110.

MARIENKIRCHE   CHURCH
Map p320 (www.marienkirche-berlin.de; Karl-Liebknecht-Strasse 8; ◷10am-6pm; ⬛100, 200, ⓡHackescher Markt, Alexanderplatz) This Gothic brick gem has welcomed worshippers since the 13th century, making it one of Berlin's oldest surviving churches. A faded *Dance of Death* fresco in the vestibule inspired by a 15th-century plague leads to a relatively plain interior enlivened by elaborate epitaphs and a baroque alabaster pulpit by Andreas Schlüter (1703). Check the schedule for organ concerts and English-language services.

NEPTUNBRUNNEN   FOUNTAIN
Map p320 (ⓢAlexanderplatz, ⓡAlexanderplatz) This elaborate fountain was designed by Reinhold Begas in 1891 and depicts Neptune holding court over a quartet of buxom beauties symbolising the rivers Rhine, Elbe, Oder and Vistula. Kids get a kick out of the water-squirting turtle, seal, crocodile and snake.

ROTES RATHAUS   HISTORIC BUILDING
Map p320 (Rathausstrasse 15; ◷closed to the public; ⓢAlexanderplatz, Klosterstrasse, ⓡAlexanderplatz) The Rotes Rathaus is the office of Berlin's Senate and governing mayor. The structure blends Italian Renaissance elements with northern German brick architecture and is framed by a terracotta frieze that illustrates milestones in Berlin history until 1871.

SEALIFE BERLIN   AQUARIUM
Map p320 (☏0180-666 690 101; www.visitsealife.com; Spandauer Strasse 3; adult/child €18/13; ◷10am-7pm (last admission 6pm); ⬛100, 200, ⓡHackescher Markt, Alexanderplatz) Sharks dart, moray eels lurk and spider crabs scuttle in this rambling aquarium; other crowd favourites include sea horses, jellyfish and Ophira the Octopus. Visits conclude with a slow lift ride through the **Aquadom**, a 25m-high cylindrical tropical fish tank (get a free preview in the lobby of the Radisson Blu Hotel). Check the website for online savings.

BERLIN DUNGEON   AMUSEMENT PARK
Map p320 (☏0180-625 5544; www.thedungeons.com/berlin; Spandauer Strasse 2; adult/child 10-14 €20/16; ◷10am-6pm Mar-Oct, 10am-5pm Nov-Feb; ⬛100, 200, ⓡHackescher Markt) This is a tour

MUSEUMSINSEL & ALEXANDERPLATZ SIGHTS

THE BRAVE WOMEN OF ROSENSTRASSE

Rosenstrasse is a small, quiet, nondescript street where one of the most courageous acts of civilian defiance against the Nazis took place. It was at Nos 2–4, outside a Jewish welfare office, where hundreds of local women gathered in freezing rain in the middle of the winter of 1943. They all had one thing in common: they were Christians whose Jewish husbands had been locked inside for deportation to Auschwitz. Until that time, Jews married to non-Jewish Germans had enjoyed a certain degree of protection – but no more. 'Give us our husbands back', the women shouted – unarmed, unorganised and leaderless but with one voice. When the police threatened to shoot them, they shouted even louder. It took several weeks, but eventually they were heard. Propaganda minister Joseph Goebbels personally ordered the release of every single prisoner.

Today a pale-pink sandstone memorial called **Block der Frauen** (Map p320; Rosenstrasse; ⓢAlexanderplatz, ⓡHackescher Markt, Alexanderplatz), by the late Jewish-German artist Inge Hunzinger, marks the site of the building while information pillars provide further background. The incident was movingly recounted in Margarethe von Trotta's 2003 feature film *Rosenstrasse*.

TOP SIGHT
DDR MUSEUM

How did regular East German Joes and Janes spend their day-to-day lives? The 'touchy-feely' DDR Museum does an entertaining job of pulling back the iron curtain on an extinct society. In hands-on fashion you'll learn how, under socialism, kids were put through collective potty training, engineers earned little more than farmers, and everyone, it seems, went on nudist holidays. You get to rummage through schoolbags, open drawers and cupboards or watch TV in a 1970s living room. And it's not only kids who love squeezing behind the wheel of a Trabant (Trabi) car for a virtual drive through a concrete-slab housing estate.

The more sinister sides of life in the GDR are also addressed, including chronic supply shortages, surveillance by the Stasi (secret police) and the SED party power monopoly. You can stand in a recreated prison cell or imagine what it was like to be in the cross hairs of a Stasi officer by sitting on the victim's chair in a tiny, windowless interrogation room.

For a taste of the GDR, drop by the museum restaurant to try a *Grilletta*, *Ketwurst* or *Broiler*, as burgers, hot dogs and grilled chicken were called in East Germany.

DON'T MISS...

➜ Trabi ride
➜ Stasi interrogation room

PRACTICALITIES

➜ GDR Museum
➜ Map p320
➜ ☎030-847 123 731
➜ www.ddr-museum.de
➜ Karl-Liebknecht-Strasse 1
➜ adult/concession €6/4
➜ ⊙10am-8pm Sun-Fri, 10am-10pm Sat
➜ ☐100, 200, ☒Hackescher Markt

through a camped-up chamber of horrors that's brought to life by actors in nine shows with such spine-tingling names as 'Elevator of Doom' and the 'Butcher of Berlin'. Lucky ones get to escape the plague on a river raft ride across the Spree River. Check timings for English-language tours and the website for steep ticket discounts.

LOXX AM ALEX MINIATUR WELTEN BERLIN MUSEUM
Map p320 (☎030-4472 3022; www.loxx-berlin.de; Grunerstrasse 20, 3rd fl, Alexa shopping mall; adult/concession/child €13/12/8; ⊙10am-8pm; ⓢAlexanderplatz, ☒Alexanderplatz) If you want to see Dad turn into a little kid, take him to this huge model railway where digitally controlled trains zip around central Berlin in miniature. All has been recreated on a scale of 1:87 and more scenes are added all the time.

⊙ Nikolaiviertel

NIKOLAIKIRCHE MUSEUM
Map p320 (☎030-2400 2162; www.stadtmuseum.de; Nikolaikirchplatz; adult/concession/under 18 €5/3/free; ⊙10am-6pm; ☐M48, ⓢKloster-

strasse) The late-Gothic Church of St Nicholas (1230) is Berlin's oldest surviving building and is now a museum documenting the architecture and history of the church. Grab the free audioguide for the scoop on the octagonal baptismal font and the triumphal cross or find out why the building is nicknamed 'pantheon of prominent Berliners'. Getting buried here cost a noble 80 thalers and an 'old person' 50 thalers. There's an organ concert on Fridays at 5pm (€3/2). Head up to the gallery for close-ups of the organ, a sweeping view of the interior and a chance to listen to recorded church hymns.

EPHRAIM-PALAIS MUSEUM
Map p320 (☎030-2400 2162; www.stadtmuseum.de; Poststrasse 16; adult/concession €5/3; ⊙10am-6pm Tue & Thu-Sun, noon-8pm Wed; ⓢKlosterstrasse) Once the home of Veitel Heine Ephraim – court jeweller and coin minter to Frederick the Great – this pretty, pint-size 1766 town palace hosts exhibits focusing on aspects of Berlin's artistic and cultural legacy. The original building was levelled in 1935 during the construction of the Mühlendamm bridge. Only the curved rococo facade with its gilded ironwork

balconies and sculptural ornamentation was saved and stored in what later became West Berlin. In 1984, it was returned to East Berlin and incorporated in the Palais' reconstruction.

KNOBLAUCHHAUS MUSEUM

Map p320 (☎030-2400 2162; www.stadtmuseum.de; Poststrasse 23; donation requested; ⏲10am-6pm Tue-Sun; [S]Klosterstrasse) [FREE] This private rococo home features a series of painstakingly restored period rooms that impart a sense of how the well-to-do lived, dressed and spent their days during the Biedermeier. The structure once belonged to the prominent Knoblauch family, which included politicians, architects and patrons of the arts who enjoyed tea and talk with Schinkel, Schadow and other luminaries of the day.

ZILLE MUSEUM MUSEUM

Map p320 (☎030-2463 2500; www.heinrich-zille-museum.de; Propststrasse 11; adult/concession €6/5; ⏲11am-7pm Apr-Oct, to 6pm Nov-Mar; [S]Klosterstrasse) Like no other artist of his time, Heinrich Zille (1859–1929) managed to capture the hardships of working-class life in the Industrial Age with empathy and humour. This small private museum in the Nikolaiviertel preserves his legacy with a selection of drawings, photographs and graphic art. There's also an interesting video on his life (in German only). Afterwards, you can channel Zille's ghost over a beer at the nearby **Zum Nussbaum** (Map p320) pub, his rather authentically re-created favourite watering hole.

HANF MUSEUM MUSEUM

Map p320 (Hemp Museum; ☎030-242 4827; www.hanfmuseum.de; Mühlendamm 5; adult/concession €4.50/3; ⏲10am-8pm Tue-Fri, noon-8pm Sat & Sun; [S]Klosterstrasse) One of only four in the world devoted to the subject of hemp, this small museum introduces the many uses of the versatile plant as well as its cultural, medicinal and religious significance in various cultures. Another gallery deals with the debate about the legalisation of marijuana.

MÄRKISCHES MUSEUM MUSEUM

Map p320 (☎030-2400 2162; www.stadtmuseum.de; Köllnischer Park 5; adult/concession/under 18 €5/3/free; ⏲10am-6pm Tue-Sun; [S]Märkisches Museum) This old-school history museum is a rewarding stop for anyone keen on learning how the medieval trading village of Berlin-Cölln evolved into today's metropolis. The exhibits take you on a virtual walk through the city's streets and quarters, from the medieval Klosterviertel to the socialist Stalinallee boulevard. Paintings and sculpture, artefacts, furniture and objects from daily life illustrate the urban evolution, while scale models help visually demonstrate the city's physical growth.

HISTORISCHER HAFEN BERLIN HARBOUR

Map p320 (Historical Harbour Berlin; ☎030-2147 3257; www.historischer-hafen-berlin.de; Märkisches Ufer; adult/concession €2/1.50; ⏲11am-6pm Sat & Sun; [S]Märkisches Museum) Laced by rivers, canals and lakes, it's not surprising that Berlin has a long history in inland navigation and even that it had the busiest river port in Germany until WWII. This outdoor museum showcases more than 20 vessels,

LOCAL KNOWLEDGE

EYE-POPPING VIEWS ON A BUDGET

Heading up the TV Tower may give you bragging rights for having been atop Germany's tallest building, but those wonderful vistas come at a price. Here are a couple of nearby alternatives that will leave less of a dent in your wallet.

Park Inn Panorama Terrasse (Map p320; ☎030-23 890; Alexanderplatz 7; admission €3; ⏲3-10pm Mon-Thu, noon-10pm Fri-Sun, weather permitting) At 150m above ground, the Panorama Terrasse atop the Park Inn Hotel may put you 53m lower than the viewing platform of the TV Tower, but it does give you splendid views not only of the surrounds but of the photogenic tower itself. Relax with a cold drink while draped into a sun lounger or marvel at gutsy baseflyers leaping off the edge of the building (Friday to Sunday only). Attached to a special winch rappel system usually used by stunt performers, these daredevils plunge towards the ground in a controlled fall, reaching near free-fall speeds.

House of Weekend (p117) On a hot summer night, the absolute high point for party people is the rooftop garden of the rejuvenated former Weekend club atop the GDR-era Haus des Reisens (House of Travel). Aside from picture-postcard views, there's a glamorous crowd, delicious barbecue and cool drinks.

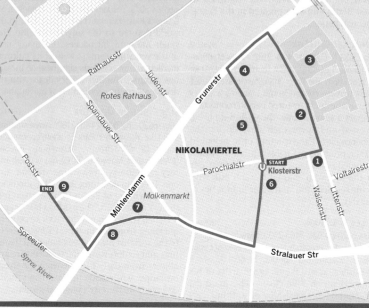

🏃 Neighbourhood Walk
Back to the Roots

START KLOSTERSTRASSE U-BAHN
END NIKOLAIVIERTEL
LENGTH 1.3KM

This walk charts Berlin history from its medieval beginnings to the early 20th century. From U-Bahn station Klosterstrasse, walk east on Parochialstrasse. Note the historic restaurant **1 Zur Letzten Instanz** (p116), then turn left on Littenstrasse and stop at a crude 8m-long pile of boulders and bricks. It's what's left of **2 Stadtmauer**, the city wall built around 1250 to protect the first settlers from marauders. Looming above is the monumental **3 Justizgebäude Littenstrasse**, a 1912 courthouse with a grand art nouveau foyer – feel free to pop in and take a look.

On your left, the Gothic **4 Franziskaner Klosterkirche** (Franciscan Monastery Church) was once a school for such luminaries as Schinkel and Bismarck and is now used for outdoor art exhibits and concerts. Follow Littenstrasse north, turn left on Grunerstrasse and left again on Klosterstrasse. The

building on your right is **5 Altes Stadthaus** (Old City Hall), whose distinctive 87m-high domed tower is crowned by the goddess Fortuna. Keep going on Klosterstrasse to the 17th-century **6 Parochialkirche**, which manages to be at once graceful and monumental. Designed by the same architect as Schloss Charlottenburg, it was burnt out in WWII and, though restored, deliberately still reveals the scars of war.

Turn right on Stralauer Strasse, which leads to **7 Molkenmarkt**, Berlin's oldest square and one-time thriving marketplace. The ornate building at No 2 is the historic **8 Alte Münze**, the old mint turned event location. Reichsmark, GDR Mark, Deutsche Mark and even euro coins were all minted here until 2006. Note the frieze depicting the evolution of metallurgy and coin minting.

Across the street, the **9 Nikolaiviertel** may look medieval, but don't be fooled: it's a product of the 1980s, built by the East German government to celebrate Berlin's 750th birthday. The 1230 Nikolaikirche and a handful of small museums are worth a gander.

BERLIN CITY PALACE: BACK TO THE FUTURE

After two decades of debate and bickering, construction of the Humboldt-Forum in the historic heart of Berlin finally got under way in July 2013. The large-scale project will look like a replica of the baroque Berliner Stadtschloss (Berlin City Palace) but with a modern interior. Although barely damaged in WWII, the grand residence where the Prussian rulers had made their home since 1443 was blown up by East Germany's government in 1950 and replaced 26 years later with the Palast der Republik (Palace of the Republic). It housed the GDR parliament and a cultural venue but, riddled with asbestos, it too had its date with the wrecking ball in 2006.

The Stadtschloss 2.0 comes with a projected price tag of €590 million, with most of the bill footed by the federal government. The design by Italian architect Franco Stella has three sides of the facade looking like a baroque blast from the past and thus visually completing the historic ensemble of Museum Island, Berlin Cathedral and New Royal Stables. The modern interior will be a forum for science, education and intercultural dialogue and shelter the Museum of Ethnology and the Museum of Asian Art – both currently in the outer suburb of Dahlem – as well as the Central State Library and university collections. It will be named Humboldt-Forum after philosopher and university founder Wilhelm von Humboldt and his explorer brother Alexander.

The building shell should be completed in 2015, the entire project in 2019. In the meantime, the eccentrically shaped and advertising-clad **Humboldt-Box** (Map p320; ☎0180-503 0707; www.humboldt-box.com; Schlossplatz; admission €2; 🕒10am-7pm; 🚌100, 200, [S]Hausvogteiplatz) opens a window onto the ambitious project by displaying interactive teaser exhibits from each future resident.

barges and tugboats, many still operational. One boat doubles as a cafe in summer while another contains a small exhibit documenting 250 years of river shipping.

BUCHSTABENMUSEUM MUSEUM

Map p320 (☎0177 420 1587; www.buchstabenmuseum.de; Holzmarktstrasse 66; adult/concession €6.50/3.50; 🕒1-5pm Thu-Sun; [S]Jannowitzbrücke) A must for fans of quirky museums, this nonprofit collection in a former supermarket is entirely dedicated to letters of the alphabet. There's the 'U' from the U-Bahn station Frankfurter Tor, an 'E' from the filming of *Inglorious Basterds* and an 'R' from the factory of light-bulb maker Osram.

Schlossplatz

BERLINER DOM CHURCH

Map p320 (Berlin Cathedral; ☎030-2026 9136; www.berlinerdom.de; Am Lustgarten; adult/concession/under 18 €7/4/free; 🕒9am-8pm Sun Apr-Sep, to 7pm Oct-Mar; 🚌100, 200, [R]Hackescher Markt) Pompous yet majestic, the Italian Renaissance-style former royal court church (1905) does triple duty as house of worship, museum and concert hall. Inside it's gilt to the hilt and outfitted with a lavish marble-and-onyx altar, a 7269-pipe Sauer organ and elaborate royal sarcophagi. Climb up the 267 steps to the gallery for glorious city views. For more dead royals, albeit in less extravagant coffins, drop below to the crypt. Skip the cathedral museum unless you're interested in the building's construction.

STAATSRATSGEBÄUDE HISTORIC BUILDING

Map p320 (Schlossplatz 1; 🚌100, 200, [S]Hausvogteiplatz) The hulking 1960 State Council Building is the only remaining Schlossplatz structure from the GDR era. It integrates the arched portal from the demolished original Berlin City Palace from where Karl Liebknecht proclaimed a socialist republic on 9 November 1918. The colourful window in the foyer is by the artist Walter Womacka and depicts scenes from the German workers' movement. Somewhat ironically, the building is now used by a private international business school financed by blue-chip corporations.

NEUER MARSTALL HISTORIC BUILDING

Map p320 (New Royal Stables; Schlossplatz 7; 🚌100, 200, TXL, [S]Hausvogteiplatz) This 1901 neo-baroque building once sheltered royal horses and carriages. In 1918, revolutionaries hatched plans to topple the Prussian monarchy here; a GDR-era bronze relief on the (north) facade facing Schlossplatz shows Karl Liebknecht proclaiming a German socialist republic from the Berlin City Palace that same year. The building now hosts concerts of the Hochschule für Musik Hanns Eisler.

EATING

With its abundant fast-food outlets, Alexanderplatz itself is not exactly a foodie haven, although there is a respectable self-service cafeteria in the Galeria Kaufhof. Otherwise, try the food court in the Alexa mall, the traditional German restaurants in the Nikolaiviertel or head to the Scheunenviertel for better options.

Alexanderplatz

DOLORES
CALIFORNIAN €

Map p320 (☑030-2809 9597; www.dolores-online.de; Rosa-Luxemburg-Strasse 7; burrito €4-6; ☻11.30am-10pm Mon-Fri, 1-10pm Sun; 🛜🍴; 🚇100, 200, Ⓢ Alexanderplatz, Ⓡ Alexanderplatz) Dolores is a bastion of California-style burritos – fresh, authentic and priced to help you stay on budget. The 'Calimex' menu is organised module-style with you selecting your favourite combo of marinated meats, or tofu, rice, beans, veggies, cheese and salsa, and the cheerful staff will build it on the spot.

RESTAURANT WANDEL
INTERNATIONAL €

Map p320 (☑030-2404 7230; www.wandel-berlin.de; Bernhard-Weiss-Strasse 6; ☻7am-7pm Mon-Fri; Ⓢ Alexanderplatz, Ⓡ Alexanderplatz) Prices are hard to beat in this stylish cafeteria where German-French-Asian-peppered mains top out at €4.90. It drowns in office drones at lunchtime, but is a relaxed spot just before and after. Waist-watchers will welcome the salad buffet. Respectable coffee to boot.

ZUR LETZTEN INSTANZ
GERMAN €€

Map p320 (☑030-242 5528; www.zurletzten-instanz.de; Waisenstrasse 14-16; mains €9-18; ☻noon-1am Mon-Sat, noon-11pm Sun; Ⓢ Kloster-strasse) Oozing folksy Old Berlin charm, this rustic eatery has been an enduring hit since 1621 and has fed everyone from Napoleon to Beethoven to Angela Merkel. Although now tourist-geared, the food quality is still pretty high when it comes to such local rib-stickers as *Grillhaxe* (grilled pork knuckle) and *Bouletten* (meat patties).

HOFBRÄUHAUS BERLIN
GERMAN €€

Map p320 (☑030-679 665 520; www.hofbraeu-haus-berlin.de; Karl-Liebknecht-Strasse 30; mains €4-18; ☻10am-1am Sun-Thu, 10am-2am Fri & Sat; 🚇100, 200, Ⓢ Alexanderplatz, Ⓡ Alexanderplatz) Popular with coach tourists and field-tripping teens, this giant beer hall with 2km of wooden benches serves the same litre-size mugs of beer and big plates of German fare as the Munich original.

BROOKLYN BEEF CLUB
AMERICAN €€€

Map p320 (☑030-2021 5820; www.thebrook-lyn.de; Köpenicker Strasse 92; mains €28-58; ☻6pm-1am Mon-Sat; Ⓢ Märkisches Museum) You'll have a fine time giving your credit card a workout with the flavour-packed Angus-certified meats served in this former Stasi hang-out turned classic American steakhouse. Blood-red walls, vaulted ceilings, historic black-and-white photographs and a bar stocked with 150 whiskies give the place a noir vibe.

THE NEW U5
....

Over 110 years after the first U-Bahn train embarked on its maiden journey, Berlin's subway network is getting an extension – of the U5 line from Alexanderplatz to the Brandenburg Gate. There, it will link with the already completed U55 and continue to the Hauptbahnhof (main train station), thus closing a major east–west gap.

The ground-breaking ceremony for the 2.2km-long stretch was held in 2010 but construction had to be halted after archaeological remnants were discovered near the Berliner Rathaus (Berlin Town Hall). It resumed in 2012 and, if all goes according to plan (and that's a big IF in Berlin), the line will be completed in 2019.

Three new stations are being built: Unter den Linden (at the intersection of Unter den Linden and Friedrichstrasse), Museumsinsel and Berliner Rathaus (next to the Nikolaiviertel). The tunnel is being carved 12m below ground by a custom-built 75m-long steel mole nicknamed Bärlinde that manages to advance an average of 8m per day. How this works is explained in a five-minute film (in German) in the **U5-Infowaggon** (Map p320; cnr Rathausstrasse & Poststrasse; ☻10am-6pm Tue-Sun) ⓕⓡⒺⒺ near the Nikolaiviertel. There are also two bright yellow viewing platforms stationed outside the **town hall** (Map p320) and in **Rathausstrasse** (Map p320) from where you can sneak a peek down at the construction sites.

✖ Nikolaiviertel

BRAUHAUS GEORGBRÄU
GERMAN €€

Map p320 (✆030-242 4244; www.georgbraeu.
de; Spreeufer 4; mains €10-14; ⊗noon-midnight;
ⓈKlosterstrasse) Tourist-geared but cosy,
this brewpub is the only place where you
can guzzle the local St Georg pilsner. In
winter the woodsy beer hall is perfect for
tucking into hearty Berlin-style goulash
or *Eisbein* (boiled pork knuckle), while in
summer the riverside beer garden beckons.

STEELSHARK
JAPANESE €€

Map p320 (✆030-2576 2461; www.steelshark.
de; Propststrasse 1; nigiri €3.20-4.70, platters
€3.50-15; ⊗11.30am-10pm Mon-Sat, 3-10pm Sun;
ⓈAlexanderplatz, ⓇAlexanderplatz) At this
hole in the wall, all morsels are carefully assembled and feature thick cuts of fresh fish
and perfectly cooked rice. The selection is
mostly classic, but there's also 'Italian-style
sushi' featuring rolls filled with such things
as marinated artichokes, mozzarella, rucola
and figs. Best of all, it delivers: order by
phone or online.

🍷 DRINKING & NIGHTLIFE

HOUSE OF WEEKEND
CLUB

Map p320 (✆reservations 0152 2429 3140; www.
week-end-berlin.de; Am Alexanderplatz 5; ⊗roof
garden from 7pm (weather permitting), studio
fl 11pm; ⓈAlexanderplatz, ⓇAlexanderplatz)
After a facelift, the former Weekend reopened in summer 2014 with the same sophisticated summertime rooftop terrace
for cocktails and barbecue with stunning
views. After 11pm, the cadre of shiny happy
people moves down to the 15th floor for
sweet dance sounds, mostly electro from
local DJs, with the occasional excursion
into hip hop and dubstep.

CLUB AVENUE @ CAFÉ MOSKAU
CLUB

(✆0174 600 3000, 0174 600 3000; www.avenue-
berlin.com; Karl-Marx-Allee 34; ⊗from 10pm Thu,
from 11pm Fri & Sat; ⓈSchillingstrasse) This
high-octane club has taken over the cellar
of Café Moskau, a protected East Berlin
landmark. Dress to impress the doormen
in order to gyrate on the dance floor to
hip-hop, house and disco. The classy retro
interior is the work of the decorating team
behind Berghain/Panoramabar. It's also the
new home of the GMF gay Sunday party.

GOLDEN GATE
CLUB

Map p320 (www.goldengate-berlin.de; Schickler-
strasse 4; ⊗from midnight Thu-Sat; ⓈJannowitz-
brücke) If you yearn for the rough sound and
aesthetics of '90s Berlin, you'll break into a
sweaty flashback at this small club beneath
the Jannowitzbrücke train tracks. Dedicated
hedonists, dressed down for business, slam
the dance floor for extended technofests
fuelled by (mostly) local DJs. Scary toilets,
nice garden. Best time: Friday in the am.

☆ ENTERTAINMENT

THEATERDISCOUNTER
THEATRE

Map p320 (✆030-2809 3062; www.theaterdis-
counter.de; Klosterstrasse 44; ⓈKlosterstrasse)
This indie troupe is a lab for contemporary
plays that often push the thespian envelope.
Plays have minimal rehearsal times, a rapid
turnover and tickets are cheap. Quality can
be from 'what the...?' to 'awesome'.

🛍 SHOPPING

GALERIA KAUFHOF
DEPARTMENT STORE

Map p320 (✆030-247 430; www.galeria-kaufhof.
de; Alexanderplatz 9; ⊗9.30am-8pm Mon-Wed,
to 10pm Thu-Sat; ⓈAlexanderplatz, ⓇAlexander-
platz) A total renovation by the late John P
Kleihues turned this former GDR-era department store into a retail cube fit for the
21st century, complete with a glass-domed
light court and a sleek travertine skin that
glows green at night. There's little you won't
find on the five football-field-size floors.

AUSBERLIN
GIFTS, SOUVENIRS

Map p320 (✆030-4199 7896; www.ausberlin.de;
Karl-Liebknecht-Strasse 17; ⊗10am-8pm Mon-
Sat; 🚌100, 200, ⓈAlexanderplatz, ⓇAlexander-
platz) 'Made in Berlin' is the motto of this hip
store where you can source the latest BPitch
or Ostgut CD, eccentric ubo jewellery, wit-
tily printed linen bags and all sorts of other
knickknacks (anti-monster spray anyone?)
designed right here in this fair city.

ALEXA
SHOPPING MALL

Map p320 (✆030-269 3400; www.alexacentre.
com; Grunerstrasse 20; ⊗10am-9pm Mon-Sat;
ⓈAlexanderplatz, ⓇAlexanderplatz) Power shoppers love this XXL mall that cuts a rose-
hued presence near Alexanderplatz. The
predictable range of high street retailers
is here, plus a few more upmarket stores.
Good food court for a bite on the run.

Potsdamer Platz & Tiergarten

POTSDAMER PLATZ | KULTURFORUM | TIERGARTEN | DIPLOMATENVIERTEL

Neighbourhood Top Five

1 Feeling your spirit soar while perusing an Aladdin's cave of Old Masters at the magnificent **Gemälde-galerie** (p123).

2 Getting lost amid the lawns, trees and leafy paths of the **Tiergarten** (p129) park, then guzzling a cold one at **Café am Neuen See** (p132).

3 Stopping for coffee and people-watching beneath the magnificent canopy of the svelte glass-and-steel **Sony Center** (p120).

4 Admiring the brave people who stood up to the Nazis and often paid the ultimate price at the **Gedenkstätte Deutscher Widerstand** (p127).

5 Catching Europe's fastest lift to the **Pano-ramapunkt** (p121) to take in Berlin's impressive cityscape.

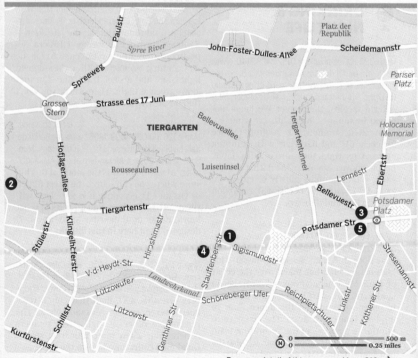

For more detail of this area, see Map p318 ➡

Explore: Potsdamer Platz & Tiergarten

Despite the name, Potsdamer Platz is not really a square but Berlin's newest quarter, forged in the '90s from terrain once bifurcated by the Berlin Wall. A collaborative effort by the world's finest architects, it is a vibrant showcase of urban renewal. The area itself is rather compact and quickly explored – unless you choose to linger in the shopping mall, have a restorative coffee in the Sony Center plaza, see Berlin from above from the Panoramapunkt or dive into German film history at the Museum für Film und Fernsehen.

At the nearby Kulturforum complex, you can mingle with masters old and modern in several museums, then head south to the up-and-coming gallery strip on Potsdamer Strasse. Further west, black limousines are a common sight in the Diplomatenviertel (Diplomatic Quarter), which doubles as a showcase of contemporary architecture, while a bit east Leipziger Platz has sprouted the huge and fancy LP12 Mall of Berlin. If your head is spinning after all that stimuli, the leafy paths of the vast Tiergarten, Berlin's equivalent of New York's Central Park, should provide a restorative antidote.

Local Life

→**Concerts** Empty seats are a rare sight at the Berliner Philharmonie (p133), especially when Sir Simon Rattle swings the baton. The free Tuesday lunchtime concerts lure the gamut of music fans, from students to tourists and desk-jockeys.

→**Tiergarten** When the sun is out, Berliners just want to get outdoors to the sweeping lawns, shady paths and romantic corners of the Tiergarten (p129) park, followed by a cold beer and pizza at the beer garden of Café am Neuen See (p132).

→**Traffic light** The clock-tower-shaped replica of Europe's first traffic light, from 1924, at the corner of Potsdamer Platz and Stresemannstrasse is a popular meeting point.

Getting There & Away

→**Bus** No 200 comes through from Zoologischer Garten and Alexanderplatz, M41 links the Hauptbahnhof with Kreuzberg and Neukölln via Potsdamer Platz, and the M29 comes in from Checkpoint Charlie.

→**S-Bahn** S1 and S2 link Potsdamer Platz with Unter den Linden and the Scheunenviertel.

→**U-Bahn** U2 stops at Potsdamer Platz and Mendelssohn-Bartholdy-Platz.

Lonely Planet's Top Tip

From July to September, the lovely Teehaus im Englischen Garten (p132) presents free concerts in its beer garden at 4pm and 7pm every Saturday and Sunday.

Best Places to Eat

→ Facil (p132)
→ Vapiano (p131)
→ Joseph-Roth-Diele (p131)
→ Restaurant Gropius (p131)

For reviews, see p131 →

Best Places to Drink

→ Solar (p132)
→ Kumpelnest 3000 (p133)
→ Stue Bar (p133)
→ Victoria Bar (p132)

For reviews, see p132 →

Best for Architecture

→ Philharmonie (p126)
→ Bauhaus Archiv (p129)
→ Sony Center (p120)

For reviews, see p120 →

ALDO PAVAN/GETTY IMAGES ©

TOP SIGHT
POTSDAMER PLATZ

Potsdamer Platz 2.0 was built from scratch in the 1990s on terrain once bifurcated by the Berlin Wall. After 1989, developers quickly swooped on the real estate on the former 'death strip' and pretty soon an international cast of star architects, including Helmut Jahn, Renzo Piano and Rafael Moneo, got to work. Their goal: to create a modern reinterpretation of the once historic Potsdamer Platz, which was Berlin's central traffic, entertainment and commercial hub until WWII sucked all life out of the area.

Today there are three sections, of which the Sony Center is the flashiest and most visitor-friendly, with a central plaza canopied by a glass roof that erupts in a light show of changing colours after dark. Segments from the Berlin Wall stand in the corner of Potsdamer Strasse and Ebertstrasse. Across Potsdamer Strasse, DaimlerCity has big hotels, a shopping mall, sprinkles of public art and entertainment venues that host movie premieres and galas during the Berlinale film festival in February. The Beisheim Center, with the Ritz-Carlton Hotel, is modelled after classic American skyscrapers.

DON'T MISS...

- Panoramapunkt
- Sony Center
- Berlin Wall remnants

PRACTICALITIES

- Map p318
- 🚌200, [S]Potsdamer Platz, 🚇Potsdamer Platz

Sony Center

Designed by Helmut Jahn, the visually dramatic **Sony Center** (Potsdamer Strasse) is fronted by a 26-floor, glass-and-steel tower that's the highest building on Potsdamer Platz. It integrates rare relics from Potsdamer Platz's prewar era, such as a section of the facade of the **Hotel Esplanade** (visible from Bellevuestrasse) and the opulent **Kaisersaal**, whose 75m move to its current location required some wizardly technology. The heart of the Sony Center is a central plaza canopied by a tentlike glass roof with supporting beams radiating like bicycle spokes. The plaza and its many cafes lend themselves to hanging out and people-watching.

Museum für Film und Fernsehen

From silent movies to sci-fi, Germany's long and illustrious film history gets the star treatment at the engaging **Museum für Film und Fernsehen** (⊘030-300 9030; www.deutsche-kinemathek.de; Potsdamer Strasse 2; adult/concession €7/4.50; ⊘10am-6pm Tue, Wed & Fri-Sun, to 8pm Thu). The tour kicks off with an appropriate sense of drama as it sends you through a dizzying mirrored walkway that conjures visions of *The Cabinet of Dr Caligari*. Major themes include pioneers and early divas, silent-era classics such as Fritz Lang's *Metropolis*, Leni Riefenstahl's groundbreaking Nazi-era documentary *Olympia*, German exiles in Hollywood and post-WWII movies. Stealing the show, as she did in real life, is femme fatale Marlene Dietrich, whose glamour lives on through her original costumes, personal finery, photographs and documents. The **TV exhibit** upstairs has more niche appeal but is still fun if you always wanted to know what *Star Trek* sounds like in German.

Be sure to make use of the excellent free audioguide as you work your way through various themed galleries. Admission is free from 4pm to 8pm Thursdays. The museum is part of the Filmhaus, which also harbours a film school, the Arsenal cinemas, a library, museum shop and bistro.

Legoland Discovery Centre

The **Legoland Discovery Centre** (⊘01806 6669 0110; www.legolanddiscoverycentre.de/berlin; Potsdamer Strasse 4; admission €14-18.50; ⊘10am-7pm, last admission 5pm) is an indoor amusement park made entirely of those little coloured plastic building blocks that many of us grew up with. Cute but low-tech, it's best suited for kids aged three to eight. Skip the promotional introductory film and head straight to such adventure stations as Ninjago, where kids can battle snakes and brave a laser labyrinth, or Merlin's Magic Library, where they become a wizard apprentice and 'fly' through a magical potion room. Other 'thrills' include the 4D cinema (with tactile special effects), a ride through the Dragon's Castle (top speed: 10km/h), and a 'torture-tickle chamber'. Grown-ups will have fun marvelling at a Berlin in miniature at Miniland, which uses more than two million Lego bricks to recreate major landmarks.

The website has ticket deals and combination tickets with other attractions.

Weinhaus Huth & Daimler Contemporary

Looking a bit lost amid all the postmodern skyscrapers, the 1912 **Weinhaus Huth** (Alte Potsdamer Strasse 5) was one of the first steel-frame buildings

VIEW FROM THE TOP

Europe's fastest lift, **Panoramapunkt** (⊘030-2593 7080; www.panoramapunkt.de; Potsdamer Platz 1; adult/concession €6.50/5, without wait €10.50/8; ⊘10am-8pm, last ride 7.30pm, reduced hours in winter), yo-yos up and down the Kollhof Tower. From the bi-level viewing platform at a lofty 100m, you can pinpoint the sights, make a java stop in the 1930s-style cafe, enjoy the sunset from the terrace and check out the exhibit that peels back the layers of the quarter's history.

In WWII Potsdamer Platz suffered 80% destruction and plunged into a coma before being bisected by the Berlin Wall in 1961. Today, a double row of cobblestones follows the course of the Wall, and a few Berlin Wall segments outside the Potsdamer Platz train station entrance feature explanatory texts about other memorial sites and future Wall-related projects. An original Berlin Wall Watchtower is just a short walk away on Erna-Berger-Strasse (off Stresemannstrasse).

POTSDAMER PLATZ & TIERGARTEN POTSDAMER PLATZ

Potsdamer Platz

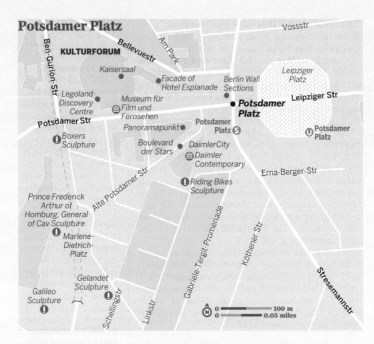

in town and the only Potsdamer Platz structure that survived WWII intact. On the top floor is the free **Daimler Contemporary** (☎030-2594 1420; www.sammlung. daimler.com; 4th fl, Weinhaus Huth, Alte Potsdamer Strasse 5; ⊙11am-6pm) FREE, a loft-style gallery showcasing first-rate international abstract, conceptual and minimalist art. Andy Warhol, Jonathan Monk – you never know who will be on view. Ring the bell to be buzzed in.

Boulevard der Stars

Berlin's own Walk of Fame, the **Boulevard der Stars** (Boulevard of the Stars; www. boulevard-der-stars-berlin.de; Potsdamer Strasse; ⊙24hr) FREE features dozens of German TV and film actors (including Marlene Dietrich, Werner Herzog and Romy Schneider) with brass stars embedded in a red-asphalt 'carpet' along Potsdamer Strasse. A cute gimmick is the Pepper's Ghost Cameras, which create a holographic image of the celebrity hovering above their brass star. Best of all: you can step next to and take a photo with your favorite celeb.

TOP SIGHT
GEMÄLDEGALERIE

The **Gemäldegalerie** ranks among the world's finest and most comprehensive collections of European art from the 13th to the 18th centuries. Its opening in a custom-built Kulturforum space in 1998 marked the happy reunion of a collection separated by the Cold War for half a century. Some works had remained at the Bodemuseum in East Berlin, the rest went on display in the West Berlin suburb of Dahlem. Today, about 1500 works span the arc of artistic vision over five centuries. Dutch and Flemish painters, including Rembrandt, are especially well represented, as are exponents of the Italian Renaissance. Another focus is on German artists from the late Middle Ages, and there's also a sprinkling of British, French and Spanish masters. Expect to feast your eyes on masterpieces by Titian, Goya, Botticelli, Holbein, Gainsborough, Canaletto, Hals, Rubens, Vermeer and other heavy hitters.

Rooms radiate from the football-field-size central foyer. The following highlights some of the key canvases, but you'll likely find your own favourites as you explore the dozens of galleries, many of them beautifully lit by muted daylight.

East Wing: German, Dutch & Flemish Masters

The exhibit kicks off with religious paintings from the Middle Ages but moves quickly to the Renaissance and works by two of the era's most famous artists: Albrecht Dürer and Lucas Cranach the Elder. A standout in Room II is Dürer's **Portrait of Hieronymus Holzschuher** (1526), a Nuremberg

DON'T MISS...

→ Rembrandt Room (Room X)
→ *Amor Victorius* (Room XIV)
→ *Dutch Proverbs* (Room VII)
→ *Fountain of Youth* (Room III)

PRACTICALITIES

→ Gallery of Paintings
→ Map p318
→ ☏030-266 424 242
→ www.smb.museum/gg
→ Matthäikirchplatz 8
→ adult/concession €10/5
→ ⏱10am-6pm Tue, Wed & Fri-Sun, 10am-8pm Thu
→ ◻M29, M41, 200, Ⓢ Potsdamer Platz, Ⓡ Potsdamer Platz

FURTHER INFORMATION

Be sure to pick up a free map from the ticket counter and also take advantage of the excellent free audioguide to get the low-down on selected works. The room numbering system is quite confusing as both Latin (I, II, III) and Arabic numbers (1, 2, 3) are used. A tour of all 72 rooms covers almost 2km, so budget at least a couple of hours if you want to see it all. Admission is free to anyone under 18.

Three small rooms in the gallery's northwest corner present a smattering of English and French works, including Thomas Gainsborough's Portrait of John Wilkinson. Works by Gainsborough are rarely seen outside the UK, which is what makes this portrait of the British industrialist so special. Nicknamed 'Iron Mad Wilkinson' for pioneering the making and use of cast iron, he is – somewhat ironically – shown in a nature setting and practically blends in with his surroundings.

patrician, career politician and strong supporter of the Reformation. Note how the artist brilliantly lasers in on his friend's features with utmost precision, down to the furrows, wrinkles and thinning hair.

One of Cranach's finest works is **Fountain of Youth** (1546) in Room III, which illustrates humankind's yearning for eternal youth. Old crones plunge into a pool of water and emerge as dashing hotties – no need for plastic surgeons! The transition is also reflected in the landscape, which is stark and craggy on the left and lush and fertile on the right.

A main exponent of the Dutch Renaissance was Peter Bruegel the Elder who here is represented with the dazzling **Dutch Proverbs** (1559) in Room VII. The moralistic yet humorous painting crams more than 100 proverbs and idioms into a single seaside village scene. While some point up the absurdity of human behaviour, others unmask its imprudence and sinfulness. Some sayings are still in use today, among them 'swimming against the tide' and 'armed to the teeth'.

North Wing: Dutch 17th-Century Paintings

The first galleries in the north wing feature some exceptional portraits, most notably Frans Hals' **Malle Babbe** (1633) in Room XIII. Note how Hals ingeniously captures the character and vitality of his subject 'Crazy Barbara' with free-wielding brushstrokes. Hals met the woman with the near-demonic laugh in the workhouse for the mentally ill where his son Pieter was also a resident. The tin mug and owl are symbols of Babbe's fondness for a tipple.

Another eye-catcher is **Woman with a Pearl Necklace** (1662) in Room XVIII, one of the most famous paintings by Dutch realist Jan Vermeer. It depicts a young woman studying herself in the mirror while fastening a pearl necklace around her neck, an intimate moment beautifully captured with characteristic soft brushstrokes.

The real highlight of the north wing awaits in the octagonal Room X, which is dedicated to Rembrandt and dominated by the large-scale **Mennonite Minister Cornelius Claesz Anslo** (1641), which shows the preacher in conversation with his wife. The huge open Bible and his gesturing hand sticking out in almost 3D-style from the centre of the painting are meant to emphasise the strength of his religious convictions. Also note Rembrandt's small self-portrait next to it.

West Wing: Italian Masterpieces

The first galleries in the west wing stay in the 17th and 18th centuries. Crowds often form before Canaletto's **Il Campo di Rialto** (1758–63) in Room XII,

GEMÄLDEGALERIE

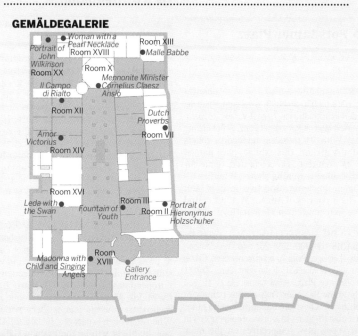

which depicts the arcaded main market square of the artist's hometown Venice with stunning precision and perspective. Note the goldsmith shops on the left, the wig-wearing merchants in the centre and the stores selling paintings and furniture on the right.

Older by 150 years is Caravaggio's delightful **Amor Victorius** (1602/3) in Room XIV. Wearing nothing but a mischievous grin, a pair of black angel wings and a fistful of arrows, this cheeky Amor means business. Note the near-photographic realism achieved by the dramatic use of light and shadow.

The next galleries travel back to the Renaissance when Raphael, Titian and Correggio dominated Italian art. The latter's **Leda with the Swan** (1532) in Room XVI is worth a closer look. Judging by her blissed-out expression, Leda is having a fine time with that swan who, according to Greek mythology, is none other than Zeus himself. The erotically charged nature of this painting apparently so incensed its one-time owner Louis of Orleans that he cut off Leda's head with a knife. It was later restored.

Lest you think that all west wing paintings have a naughty subtext, let us draw your attention to Sandro Botticelli's **Madonna with Child and Singing Angels** (1477) in Room XVIII. This circular painting (a format called a *tondo*) shows Mary flanked by two sets of four wingless angels. It's an intimate moment that shows the Virgin tenderly embracing – perhaps even about to breastfeed – her child. The white lilies are symbols of her purity.

SIGHTS

Potsdamer Platz

POTSDAMER PLATZ NEIGHBOURHOOD
See p120.

MARTIN-GROPIUS-BAU GALLERY
Map p318 (☎030-254 860; www.gropiusbau.de; Niederkirchner Strasse 7; cost varies; ⏰10am-7pm Wed-Mon; [S]Potsdamer Platz, 🚇Potsdamer Platz) With its mosaics, terracotta reliefs and airy atrium, this exhibit space named for its architect is a celebrated venue for high-calibre travelling shows. Whether it's a David Bowie retrospective or an exhibit on the mysteries of Angkor Wat, it's bound to be well curated and fascinating.

DALÍ – DIE AUSSTELLUNG GALLERY
Map p318 (☎0700 3254 237 546; www.daliberlin.de; Leipziger Platz 7; adult/concession €11/9; ⏰noon-8pm Mon-Sat, 10am-8pm Sun; 🚌200, [S]Potsdamer Platz, 🚇Potsdamer Platz) If you only know Salvador Dalí as the painter of melting watches, burning giraffes and other surrealist imagery, this private collection will likely open new perspectives on the man. Here, the focus is on his graphics, illustrations, sculptures, drawings and films.

Kulturforum

GEMÄLDEGALERIE GALLERY
See p123.

PHILHARMONIE ARCHITECTURE
Map p318 (☎030-2548 8156; www.berliner-philharmoniker.de; Herbert-von-Karajan-Strasse 1; tour adult/concession €3/2; ⏰tour 1.30pm; 🚌200, [S]Potsdamer Platz, 🚇Potsdamer Platz) A masterpiece of organic architecture, Hans Scharoun's 1963 honey-coloured concert venue is the home base of the prestigious Berliner Philharmoniker. The auditorium feels like the inside of a finely crafted instrument and boasts supreme acoustics and excellent sightlines from every seat.

KUNSTGEWERBEMUSEUM MUSEUM
Map p318 (Museum of Decorative Arts; ☎030-266 424 242; www.smb.museum; Matthäikirchplatz; 🚌200, [S]Potsdamer Platz, 🚇Potsdamer Platz) At press time this prestigious museum was still reorganising its prized collection of European design and decorative arts from the Middle Ages, Renaissance, baroque and rococo, art nouveau and art deco periods. When it reopens (perhaps in late 2014), a new highlight will be the Fashion Gallery, with outfits and accessories from the past three centuries.

DAIMLERCITY PUBLIC SCULPTURE TOUR

DaimlerCity is not only a postmodern urban landscape but also an exquisite outdoor gallery. Large-scale abstract sculptures by blue-chip artists like Keith Haring and Robert Rauschenberg explore the relationship between art and urban space and inject much-needed visual appeal into what would otherwise be a fairly austere environment.

A self-guided tour might start with Haring's **Boxers** (Map p318), which shows two cut-steel stick figures – one blue, one red – seemingly punching each other out. Or are they embracing each other? You decide, then walk south to ponder Frank Stella's otherworldly **Prince Frederick Arthur of Homburg, General of Cav** (Map p318; Marlene-Dietrich-Platz; 🚌200, [S]Potsdamer Platz, 🚇Potsdamer Platz) [FREE]. Made of white-silver aluminium, carbon and fibreglass, it explores the relationships of space, colour and form in a three-dimensional setting. Just beyond, in the middle of a pond, is Mark Di Suvero's **Galileo** (Map p318; 🚌200, [S]Mendelssohn-Bartholdy-Platz, Potsdamer Platz, 🚇Potsdamer Platz) [FREE], an abstract jumble of rusted steel T-beams assembled into a gravity-defying sculpture.

You need to crane your neck to spot Auke de Vries's **Gelandet** (Landed; Map p318; Schellingstrasse; ⏰24hr; 🚌200, [S]Mendelssohn-Bartholdy-Platz, Potsdamer Platz, 🚇Potsdamer Platz) [FREE] teetering on the edge of the roof of the DaimlerServices building (look for the square tower with the green top). North of here, Robert Rauschenberg's **Riding Bikes** (Map p318; Fontaneplatz; ⏰24hr; 🚌M41, 200, [S]Potsdamer Platz, 🚇Potsdamer Platz) [FREE] consists of two recycled bicycles illuminated by multicoloured neon tubes. It's an excellent example of his approach to turning reality into art while creating as little wastage as possible.

TOP SIGHT
GEDENKSTÄTTE DEUTSCHER WIDERSTAND

If you've seen the movie *Valkyrie* you know the story of Claus von Stauffenberg, the poster boy of the German resistance against Hitler and the Third Reich. The very rooms where senior army officers led by Stauffenberg plotted their bold but ill-fated assassination attempt on the Führer on 20 July 1944 now form part of the German Resistance Memorial Centre. The building itself, the historic Bendlerblock, harboured the Wehrmacht high command from 1935 to 1945 and today is the secondary seat of the German defence ministry (the primary is still in Bonn).

The centre also documents the efforts of many other Germans who risked their lives opposing the Third Reich for ideological, religious or military reasons. Most were just regular folks, such as the students Hans and Sophie Scholl or the craftmaker Georg Elser; others were prominent citizens like the artist Käthe Kollwitz and the theologian Dietrich Bonhoeffer.

In the yard, a sculpture marks the spot where Stauffenberg and three of his co-conspirators were executed right after the failed coup.

DON'T MISS...

➡ Stauffenberg exhibit
➡ Stauffenberg memorial statue

PRACTICALITIES

➡ Map p318
➡ ☎030-2699 5000
➡ www.gdw-berlin.de
➡ Stauffenbergstrasse 13-14
➡ ⊙9am-6pm Mon-Wed & Fri, 9am-8pm Thu, 10am-6pm Sat & Sun
➡ 🚌M29, Ⓢ Potsdamer Platz, Kurfürstenstrasse, Ⓡ Potsdamer Platz

POTSDAMER PLATZ & TIERGARTEN SIGHTS

MUSIKINSTRUMENTEN-MUSEUM
MUSEUM

Map p318 (Musical Instruments Museum; ☎030-254 810; www.mim-berlin.de; Tiergartenstrasse 1, enter via Ben-Gurion-Strasse; adult/concession €6/3; ⊙9am-5pm Tue, Wed & Fri, 9am-8pm Thu, 10am-5pm Sat & Sun; 🚌200, Ⓢ Potsdamer Platz, Ⓡ Potsdamer Platz) This darling museum is packed with fun, precious and rare sound machines, including the glass harmonica invented by Ben Franklin, a flute played by Frederick the Great, and Johann Sebastian Bach's harpsichord. Stop at the listening stations to hear what some of the more obscure instruments sound like.

KUPFERSTICHKABINETT
GALLERY

Map p318 (Gallery of Prints and Drawings; ☎030-266 424 242; www.smb.museum/kk; Matthäikirchplatz; adult/concession €6/3; ⊙10am-6pm Tue-Fri, 11am-6pm Sat & Sun; 🚌200, Ⓢ Potsdamer Platz, Ⓡ Potsdamer Platz) One of the world's largest and finest collections of art on paper, this gallery shelters a bonanza of hand-illustrated books, illuminated manuscripts, drawings and prints produced mostly in Europe from the 14th century onward – Dürer to Rembrandt to Schinkel, Picasso to Giacometti to Warhol.

MATTHÄUSKIRCHE
CHURCH

Map p318 (Church of St Matthew; ☎030-262 1202; www.stiftung-stmatthaeus.de; Matthäikirchplatz; ⊙noon-6pm Tue-Sun; 🚌200, Ⓢ Potsdamer Platz, Ⓡ Potsdamer Platz) FREE Standing a bit lost and forlorn within the Kulturforum, the Stüler-designed Matthäuskirche (1846) is a beautiful neo-Romanesque confection with alternating bands of red and ochre brick and a light-flooded, modern sanctuary that doubles as a gallery. Climb the tower for good views of the Kulturforum and Potsdamer Platz. A nice time to visit is for the free 20-minute organ recitals at 12.30pm Tuesday to Sunday.

NEUE NATIONALGALERIE
GALLERY

Map p318 (www.neue-nationalgalerie.de; Potsdamer Strasse 50; ⊙closed for renovation; Ⓢ Potsdamer Platz, Ⓡ Potsdamer Platz) This fabulous collection of early-20th-century art will not be on view during renovations, being undertaken by David Chipperfield and expected to last until 2018 or 2019. The building itself is a late masterpiece by Ludwig Mies van der Rohe. All glass and steel and squatting on a raised platform, it echoes a postmodern Buddhist temple.

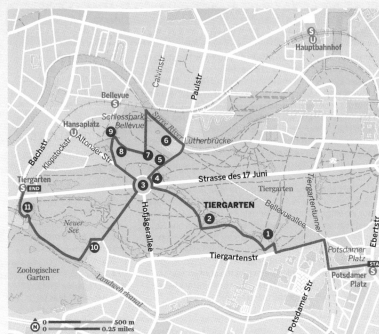

Neighbourhood Walk
A Leisurely Tiergarten Meander

START POTSDAMER PLATZ
END TIERGARTEN S-BAHN STATION
LENGTH 5KM

A ramble around Tiergarten delivers a relaxing respite from the sightseeing track. From Potsdamer Platz, make your way to ❶**Luiseninsel**, an enchanting gated garden dotted with statues and flower beds. Not far away is ❷**Rousseauinsel**, a memorial to 18th-century French philosopher Jean-Jacques Rousseau. It was modelled after his actual burial site near Paris and placed on a teensy island in a sweet little pond.

At the heart of the park, the imposing ❸**Siegessäule** (Victory Column; p129) commemorates Prussian military triumphs enforced by Iron Chancellor Otto von Bismarck. Nearby, the colossal ❹**Bismarck Denkmal**, a monument to the man, shows him flanked by statues of Atlas (with the world on his back), Siegfried (wielding a sword) and Germania (stomping a panther).

Following Spreeweg north takes you past the oval ❺**Bundespräsidialamt**, the offices of the German president, to his residence in ❻**Schloss Bellevue** (p129), a former royal palace. Follow the path along the Spree, then turn left into the ❼**Englischer Garten** (English Garden) created in the '50s in commemoration of the 1948 Berlin Airlift. At its heart, overlooking a pretty pond, the thatched-roof ❽**Teehaus im Englischen Garten** (p132) hosts free summer concerts in its beer garden. Afterwards, check out the latest exhibit at the nearby ❾**Akademie der Künste** (p129), on the edge of the Hansaviertel, a modernist quarter borne from a 1957 international building exhibition.

Walk south back through the park, crossing Altonaer Strasse and Strasse des 17 Juni, to arrive at the Neuer See with ❿**Café am Neuen See** (p132) at its south end. Stroll north along the Landwehrkanal via the ⓫**Gaslaternenmuseum**, an open-air collection of 90 historic gas lanterns, and wrap up your tour at Tiergarten S-Bahn station.

◉ Tiergarten & Diplomatenviertel

TIERGARTEN PARK

(🚌100, 200, [S]Brandenburger Tor, 🚆Potsdamer Platz, Brandenburger Tor) [FREE] Berlin's rulers used to hunt boar and pheasants in the rambling Tiergarten until garden architect Peter Lenné landscaped the grounds in the 18th century. Today, one of the world's largest urban parks is popular for strolling, jogging, picnicking, Frisbee tossing and, yes, nude sunbathing and gay cruising (especially around the Löwenbrücke). It is bisected by a major artery, the Strasse des 17 Juni.

SIEGESSÄULE MONUMENT

Map p318 (Victory Column; Grosser Stern; adult/concession €3/2.50; 🕘9.30am-6.30pm Mon-Fri, to 7pm Sat & Sun Apr-Oct, 10am-5pm Mon-Fri, to 5.30pm Sat & Sun Nov-Mar; 🚌100, 200) Like arms of a starfish, five roads merge into the Grosser Stern roundabout at the heart of the Tiergarten. The Victory Column at its centre was built to celebrate 19th-century Prussian military triumphs and is now a symbol of Berlin's gay community.

SCHLOSS BELLEVUE HISTORIC BUILDING

Map p318 (Spreeweg 1; 🕘closed to public; 🚆Bellevue) The home of the German president is snowy white Schloss Bellevue. The neoclassical palace was built in 1785 by Philipp Daniel Boumann for the youngest brother of Frederick the Great, then became a school under Kaiser Wilhelm II and a museum of ethnology under the Nazis.

AKADEMIE DER KÜNSTE GALLERY

Map p318 (Academy of Arts; ☎030-200 572 000; www.adk.de; Hanseatenweg 10; cost varies by exhibit, free 3-7pm Tue; 🕘exhibits 11am-7pm Tue-Sun; [S]Hansaplatz, 🚆Bellevue) The Academy of Arts has a pedigree going back to 1696 but its programming is solidly rooted in the here and now. It covers all forms of artistic expression, from architecture to literature to music, theatre and digital media, and also stages high-profile exhibits.

DIPLOMATENVIERTEL NEIGHBOURHOOD

Map p318 (Diplomatic Quarter; 🚌200, [S]Potsdamer Platz, 🚆Potsdamer Platz) The Brothers Grimm were among the 19th-century intellectuals living in the villa-studded colony south of the Tiergarten, which evolved into the capital's embassy quarter in the 1920s. After WWII the obliterated area remained in a state of decay while the embassies all set up in the West German capital of Bonn. After reunification, many countries rebuilt on their historic lots, accounting for some of Berlin's boldest new architecture.

> **ⓘ BARGAIN BOX**
>
> A Kulturforum area ticket *(Bereichskarte)* costs €12 (concession €6) and includes same-day admission to the Gemäldegalerie, the permanent collection of the Neue Nationalgalerie and the Musikinstrumenten-Museum. Special exhibits cost extra but buying tickets online saves €1. Admission is free to anyone under 18.

BAUHAUS ARCHIV MUSEUM

Map p318 (☎030-254 0020; www.bauhaus.de; Klingelhöferstrasse 14; adult/concession incl audioguide Sat-Mon €7/4, Wed-Fri €6/3; 🕘10am-5pm Wed-Mon; 🚌100, [S]Nollendorfplatz) Founded in 1919, the Bauhaus was a seminal school of architecture, design and art in the 20th century. This building presents paintings, drawings, sculptures, models and other objects and documents by its famous teachers, including Klee, Feininger and Kandinsky. There's a nice cafe and cool shop stocked with Bauhaus-inspired baubles.

SCHWULES MUSEUM MUSEUM

(Gay Museum; ☎030-6959 9050; www.schwulesmuseum.de; Lützowstrasse 73; adult/concession €6/4; 🕘2-6pm Wed-Fri & Sun-Mon, 2-7pm Sat; 🚌M29, [S]Nollendorfplatz, Kurfürstenstrasse) In a new and larger location in a former print shop near Schöneberg, this nonprofit museum is one of the largest and most important cultural institutions documenting GLBT culture around the world, albeit with a special focus on Berlin and Germany. Until the permanent exhibit is completed, changing ones on gay icons, artists, gender issues or historical themes keep the space dynamic.

🍴 EATING

The best restaurants on Potsdamer Platz are in the hotels. For a quick nibble, head to the food court in the Potsdamer Platz Arkaden (p133) mall. LP12 Mall of Berlin (p133) also has plenty of food options, while Tiergarten park beckons with its share of beer gardens.

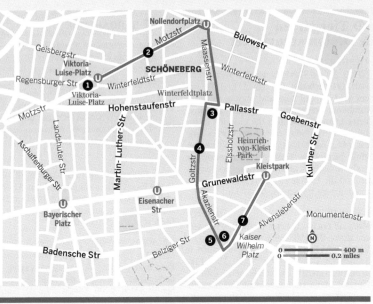

🏃 Local Life
Saunter Around Schöneberg

Schöneberg flaunts a mellow middle-class identity but has a radical pedigree rooted in the squatter days of the '80s. Stroll from bourgeois Viktoria-Luise-Platz through Berlin's original gay quarter and along streets squeezed tight with boho cafes and smartly curated indie boutiques to ethnically flavoured Hauptstrasse.

❶ Viktoria-Luise-Platz
Soak up the laid-back vibe of Schöneberg's prettiest square, a classic symphony of flower beds, big old trees, a lusty fountain and benches where locals swap gossip or watch kids at play. The square is framed by several inviting cafes and ornate historic facades at numbers 7, 12 and 12a.

❷ Nollendorfplatz & the 'Gay Village'
In the early 20th century, Nollendorfplatz was a bustling urban square filled with cafes, theatres and people on parade. Then as now, it was also the gateway to Berlin's historic gay quarter, where British writer Christopher Isherwood penned *Berlin Stories* (the inspiration for *Cabaret*) while living at Nollendorfstrasse 17. Rainbow flags still fly proudly, especially along Motzstrasse and Fuggerstrasse. A memorial plaque at Nollendorfplatz U-Bahn station commemorates Nazi-era GLBT victims.

❸ Chocophile Alert
Winterfeldt Schokoladen (☎030-2362 3256; www.winterfeldt-schokoladen.de; Goltzstrasse 23; ⊘9am-8pm Mon-Fri, 9am-6pm Sat, noon-7pm Sun; Ⓢ Nollendorfplatz) stocks a vast range of international handmade gourmet chocolates, all displayed in the original oak fixtures of a 19th-century pharmacy that doubles as a cafe. Kosher, raw and gluten-free chocolates are among the more unusual choices.

❹ Boutique Hopping
Goltzstrasse and its extension Akazienstrasse teem with indie boutiques selling everything from vintage clothing to slinky underwear, antique books to handmade jewellery, exotic teas to cooking supplies. No high-street chain in sight! Wedged in between are comfy cafes.

Memorial plaque at Nollendorfplatz commemorating Nazi-era GLBT victims

5 Double Eye

Local coffee lovers are addicted to the award-winning espresso of **Double Eye** (Akazienstrasse 22; 🕒9am-6.30pm Mon-Fri, 9am-6pm Sat; [S]Eisenacher Strasse), which is why no one seems to mind the inevitable out-the-door queue. Prices are fair, smiles big and the quality tops.

6 Möve im Felsenkeller

An artist hang-out since the '20s, woodsy **Möve im Felsenkeller** (☎030-781 3447; Akazienstrasse 2; 🕒4pm-1am; [S]Eisenacher Strasse) was where Jeffery Eugenides penned his 2002 bestseller *Middlesex* (upstairs, at the round table in the corner). A stuffed seagull dangling from the ceiling keeps an eye on patrons seeking inspiration from the eight beers on tap.

7 Hauptstrasse

Chic boutiques give way to grocers and doner kebab shops along main artery Hauptstrasse. The Turkish supermarket **Öz-Gida** (www.ozgida.de; Hauptstrasse 16; [S]Kleistpark, Eisenacher Strasse) is known citywide for its olive selection, cheese spreads and quality meats. In the '70s, David Bowie and Iggy Pop shared a pad at Hauptstrasse 155.

🍴 Potsdamer Platz

JOSEPH-ROTH-DIELE — GERMAN €

Map p318 (☎030-2636 9884; www.joseph-roth-diele.de; Potsdamer Strasse 75; dishes €4-10; 🕒10am-midnight Mon-Fri; [S]Kurfürstenstrasse) Named for an Austrian Jewish writer, this saloon time-warps you back to the 1920s, when Roth used to live next door. Walls decorated with bookshelves and quotations from his works draw a literary, chatty crowd, especially at lunchtime. There's only four or five German home-cooking classics on the daily-changing menu. Pay at the counter.

VAPIANO — ITALIAN €

Map p318 (☎030-2300 5005; www.vapiano.de; Potsdamer Platz 5; mains €5.50-10; 🕒10am-1am Mon-Sat, 10am-midnight Sun; 🚌200, [S]Potsdamer Platz, 🚆Potsdamer Platz) Matteo Thun's jazzy decor is a great foil for the tasty Italian fare at this successful German self-service chain. Mix-and-match pastas, creative salads and crusty pizzas are all prepared right before your eyes. Your order is recorded on a chip card and paid for upon leaving. There's another branch in **Charlottenburg** (Map p338; ☎030-8871 4195; www.vapiano.de; Augsburger Strasse 43; €5.50-9; 🕒10am-1am Mon-Sat, 10am-midnight Sun; [S]Kurfürstendamm).

CAFFE E GELATO — ICE CREAM €

Map p318 (☎030-2529 7832; www.caffe-e-gelato.de; Alte Potsdamer Strasse 7; 🕒10am-10.30pm Mon-Thu, to 11pm Fri, to midnight Sat, 10.30am-10pm Sun; [S]Potsdamer Platz, 🚆Potsdamer Platz) Traditional Italian-style ice cream gets a 21st-century twist at this space on the upper floor of the Potsdamer Arkaden Mall.

QIU — INTERNATIONAL €€

Map p318 (☎030-590 051 230; www.qiu.de; Mandala Hotel, Potsdamer Strasse 3; 2-course lunch €14; 🕒business lunch noon-3pm Mon-Fri; 🚌200, [S]Potsdamer Platz, 🚆Potsdamer Platz) The two-course business lunch at this stylish lounge also includes soup or salad, a nonalcoholic beverage and coffee or tea.

RESTAURANT GROPIUS — INTERNATIONAL €€

Map p318 (☎030-2548 6406; www.mosaik-berlin.de/restaurant-gropius; Martin-Gropius-Bau, Niederkirchner Strasse 7; mains €7-11; 🕒10am-7pm Wed-Mon; 🚌M41, 200, [S]Potsdamer Platz, 🚆Potsdamer Platz) Even without seeing an exhibit, it's well worth stopping by the restaurant of the Martin-Gropius-Bau for delicious dishes inspired by the current shows.

HANSA STUDIOS: BOWIE'S 'HALL BY THE WALL'

Complete this analogy: London is to Abbey Road what Berlin is to...

Well? **Hansa Studios** (Map p318; www.meistersaal-berlin.de; Köthener Strasse 38; 🚆Potsdamer Platz, [S]Potsdamer Platz), of course, that seminal recording studio that has exerted a gravitational pull on top international artists since the Cold War. The 'Big Hall by the Wall' was how David Bowie fittingly dubbed its glorious Studio 2, better known as the **Meistersaal** (Masters' Hall), through whose arched windows one could look across the concrete barrier and wave at the gun-toting guards in their watchtowers. In the late '70s the White Duke recorded his tortured visions in the seminal album *Heroes* after completing *Low*, both part of his Berlin Trilogy. Bowie also co-produced *The Idiot* and *Lust for Life* with his buddy Iggy Pop.

There's a long list of other music legends who have taken advantage of Studio 2's special sound quality, including Nina Hagen, Nick Cave, David Byrne, Einstürzende Neubauten, Die Ärzte, Snow Patrol, Green Day, REM and The Hives. Depeche Mode produced three albums here – *Construction Time Again, Some Great Reward* and *Black Celebration* – between 1983 and 1986.

The only way to get inside this hallowed hall is with the highly recommended Berlin Music Tours (p293).

FACIL INTERNATIONAL €€€

Map p318 (☎030-590 051 234; www.facil.de; 5th fl, Mandala Hotel, Potsdamer Strasse 3; 1-/2-/3-course lunch €19/32/42, 4-/8-course dinner €92/152; ⏰noon-3pm & 7-11pm Mon-Fri; 🚌200, [S]Potsdamer Platz, 🚆Potsdamer Platz) With two Michelin stars to his name, Michael Kempf's fare is hugely innovative yet deliciously devoid of unnecessary flights of fancy. Enjoy it while draped in a sleek Donghia chair and surrounded by a bamboo garden. The glass ceiling can be retracted for alfresco dining in fine weather. Budget-minded gourmets take advantage of the lunchtime menu.

🍴 Tiergarten

CAFÉ AM NEUEN SEE INTERNATIONAL €€

(☎030-254 4930; www.cafeamneuensee.de; Lichtensteinallee 2; mains €9-20; ⏰9am-11pm, beer garden from 11am Mon-Fri, from 10am Sat & Sun; 🚌100, 200) Next to an idyllic pond in the southwestern section of Tiergarten, this restaurant is jammed year-round for its sumptuous breakfast, pizza and seasonal fare, but really comes into its own during beer garden season. Enjoy a microvacation from the city bustle over a cold one or take your sweetie on a spin in a row boat (per half hour €5).

TEEHAUS IM ENGLISCHEN GARTEN INTERNATIONAL €€

Map p318 (☎030-3948 0400; www.teehaus-tiergarten.com; Altonaer Strasse 2; mains €7.50-16.50; ⏰10am-11pm; 🚌100, 🚆Bellevue) Not even many Berliners know about this enchanting reed-thatched teahouse tucked into the northwestern corner of Tiergarten park. It's best in summer, when the beer garden overlooking an idyllic pond seats up to 500 people for cold beers and a global roster of simple but tasty dishes. On Sundays in July and August it hosts a hugely popular concert series (www.konzertsommer-berlin.de) with concerts at 4pm and 7pm.

🍷 DRINKING & NIGHTLIFE

🍷 Potsdamer Platz

SOLAR BAR

Map p318 (☎0163 765 2700; www.solar-berlin.de; Stresemannstrasse 76; ⏰6pm-2am Sun-Thu, to 4am Fri & Sat; 🚆Anhalter Bahnhof) Watch the city light up from this 17th-floor glass-walled sky lounge above a posh restaurant (mains €18 to €29). With its dim lighting, soft black leather couches and breathtaking views, it's a great spot for a date or sunset drinks. Enter via the chunky high-rise behind the Pit Stop auto shop.

VICTORIA BAR BAR

(☎030-2575 9977; www.victoriabar.de; Potsdamer Strasse 102; ⏰6.30pm-3am Sun-Thu, to 4am Fri & Sat; [S]Kurfürstenstrasse) Original art decorates this discreet cocktail lounge favoured by a grown-up crowd that's like a two-inch heel – chic but sensible. 'The Pleasure of Serious Drinking' is the motto of this communicative space teeming with arty regulars.

CURTAIN CLUB BAR

Map p318 (☎030-337 776 196; www.ritzcarlton.de; Ritz-Carlton Berlin, Potsdamer Strasse 3; ⏰from 6pm; 🚌200, [S]Potsdamer Platz, [U]Potsdamer Platz) Every night at 6pm sharp, it's showtime at the Ritz-Carlton Berlin: a uniformed former beefeater (Tower of London guard) ceremoniously pulls back the heavy curtains on this elegant, wood-panelled bar presided over by cocktail-meister Arnd Heissen, who has created his own range of perfume-inspired cocktails, each served in a unique glass.

KUMPELNEST 3000 BAR

Map p318 (Lützowstrasse 23; [S]Kurfürstenstrasse) A former brothel, this lurid bat cave would be sensuous, kooky and kitsch enough to feature in a 1940s Shanghai noir thriller. A classic dive, famous for its wild, debauched all-nighters, it attracts a hugely varied public, although there can be a preponderance of butch boys. Watch out for pickpockets.

EX'N'POP PUB

(☎030-2199 7470; www.exnpop.de; Potsdamer Strasse 157; ⏰from 10pm Tue-Sun; [S]Bülowstrasse) The ghosts of Einstürzende Neubauten and other Berlin bands still may be partying at this rough-house with a pedigree going back to the 1980s punk era. Though it has moved to a new location, it's still a good place to down the last drink of the night.

🍷 Tiergarten

STUE BAR BAR

Map p318 (☎030-311 7220; www.das-stue-com; Drakestrasse 1; ⏰noon-1am Sun-Thu, to 2am Fri & Sat; 🚌100, 106, 200) In the Stue Hotel, light installations and animal sculptures pave the way to the bar where serious mixologists give classic cocktails from the 1920s and '30s a contemporary makeover.

☆ ENTERTAINMENT

BERLINER PHILHARMONIE CLASSICAL MUSIC

Map p318 (☎tickets 030-2548 8301; www.berliner-philharmoniker.de; Herbert-von-Karajan-Strasse 1; 🚌200, [S]Potsdamer Platz, [U]Potsdamer Platz) This world-famous concert hall has supreme acoustics and, thanks to Hans Scharoun's terraced vineyard design, not a bad seat in the house. It's the home turf of the Berliner Philharmoniker, which will be led by Sir Simon Rattle until 2018. Chamber music concerts take place at the adjacent Kammermusiksaal.

CINESTAR ORIGINAL CINEMA

Map p318 (☎030-2606 6400; www.cinestar.de; Potsdamer Strasse 4, Sony Center; [S]Potsdamer Platz, [U]Potsdamer Platz) A favourite among English-speaking expats and Anglophile Germans, this state-of-the-art cinema with big screens, comfy seats and ear-popping surround-sound shows the latest Hollywood blockbusters, all in English, all the time.

ARSENAL CINEMA

Map p318 (☎030-2695 5100; www.arsenal-berlin.de; Sony Center, Potsdamer Strasse 2; [S]Potsdamer Platz, [U]Potsdamer Platz, bus 200) This artsy twin-screen cinema features a bold global flick schedule that hopscotches from Japanese satire to Brazilian comedy and German road movies. Many films have English subtitles.

BLUE MAN GROUP THEATRE

Map p318 (☎01805 4444; www.bluemangroup.de; Marlene-Dietrich-Platz 4; tickets from €70; [U]Potsdamer Platz) This musical and visual extravaganza, starring slightly nutty and energetic guys dipped in Smurf-blue latex suits, performs at its own permanent theatre, a converted IMAX now called Bluemax. Shows are suitable for non-German speakers.

THEATER AM POTSDAMER PLATZ MUSICALS

Map p318 (☎tickets 01805 4444; www.stage-entertainment.de; Marlene-Dietrich-Platz 1; ticket price varies; [S]Potsdamer Platz, [U]Potsdamer Platz) Big-name musicals (in German) are showcased at this up-in-lights location designed by Renzo Piano.

🛍 SHOPPING

POTSDAMER PLATZ ARKADEN SHOPPING MALL

Map p318 (☎030-255 9270; www.potsdamer-platz-arkaden.de; Alte Potsdamer Strasse 7; ⏰10am-9pm Mon-Sat; [S]Potsdamer Platz, [U]Potsdamer Platz) All your basic shopping cravings will be met at this attractive indoor mall. The basement has a Rewe supermarket, a dm drugstore and numerous fast-food outlets.

LP12 MALL OF BERLIN SHOPPING MALL

Map p318 (www.mallofberlin.de; Leipziger Platz 12; 🚌200, [S]Potsdamer Platz, [U]Potsdamer Platz) This new retail quarter is tailor-made for black-belt mall rats. More than 270 stores vie for your shopping euros, including flagship stores by Karl Lagerfeld, Hugo Boss, Liebeskind, Muji and other high-end brands.

Scheunenviertel

HACKESCHER MARKT AREA | HAUPTBAHNHOF | ORANIENBURGER TOR | TORSTRASSE

Neighbourhood Top Five

1 Exploring idiosyncratic shops, galleries and cafes in the charismatic maze of the **Hackesche Höfe** (p139).

2 Glimpsing high drama, abstract mind-benders and glowing colour among the contemporary artworks at **Sammlung Boros** (p138).

3 Sizing yourself up next to giant dinos at Berlin's mini *Jurassic Park* in the **Museum für Naturkunde** (p140).

4 Strutting your stuff to salsa, tango, ballroom, waltz and swing at the grand retro ballroom **Clärchens Ballhaus** (p145).

5 Studying up on the quarter's Jewish history at the **Neue Synagoge** (p137).

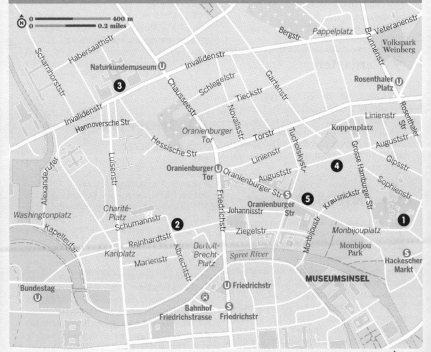

For more detail of this area, see Map p326 and p328 ➡

Explore: Scheunenviertel

Scheunenviertel, or Barn Quarter, packs bunches of charisma into its relatively compact frame. Its greatest charms reveal themselves in the labyrinth of quiet lanes fanning out from its main drags, Oranienburger Strasse and Rosenthaler Strasse. Embark on an aimless wander and you'll constantly stumble upon the unexpected here, an idyllic courtyard or bleeding-edge art gallery, a fashion-forward boutique, a shabby-chic bar or a glam belle époque ballroom. A distinctive feature of the quarter is its *Höfe* – interlinked courtyards filled with cafes, stores and party venues.

Since reunification, the Scheunenviertel has also reprised its historic role as Berlin's main Jewish quarter, with the Neue Synagoge as its shining beacon. Gritty Torstrasse, meanwhile, delivers a roll call of trendy restaurants and bars that lure a cashed-up creative crowd of locals, expats and visitors.

This chapter also covers the area between the Hauptbahnhof and Friedrichstrasse, which harbours two of Berlin's contemporary arts highlights, the Hamburger Bahnhof and the Sammlung Boros. North of the Hauptbahnhof itself, a new city quarter called Europa-City is slowly getting off the drawing board.

Local Life

➡ **Shopping** Find out what keeps Berlin designers' sewing machines humming by prowling the backstreets for fashion-forward local-label stores.

➡ **Bar-hopping** Play it cool when joining hotties and hopefuls for a classy buzz in Torstrasse's doorstaff-guarded booze burrows.

➡ **Monbijoupark** Set out a picnic, sip a beer in Strandbar Mitte (p145; Berlin's first beach bar), or catch an alfresco concert or play at the Monbijoutheater (p148) in this riverfront park.

Getting There & Away

➡ **Bus** No 142 runs along Torstrasse.

➡ **S-Bahn** Hackescher Markt (S5, S7 and S9) and Oranienburger Strasse (S2) stations are both good jumping-off points.

➡ **Tram** M1 runs from Museumsinsel (Museum Island) to Prenzlauer Berg and makes key stops throughout the Scheunenviertel.

➡ **U-Bahn** Weinmeisterstrasse (U8) is the most central station. Rosenthaler Platz (U8), Rosa-Luxemburg-Platz (U2) and Oranienburger Tor (U6) are closer to Torstrasse and the northern Scheunenviertel.

Lonely Planet's Top Tip

To get a better understanding of the Scheunenviertel's role in Berlin's Jewish history, rent a multimedia iGuide from the Anne Frank Zentrum (p141) for €5 (concession €2.50). Available in English and German, it takes you to key sites around the Scheunenviertel and uses photographs and interviews to add dimension and depth.

Best Places to Eat

➡ Pauly Saal (p144)
➡ Chèn Chè (p143)
➡ Katz Orange (p144)
➡ Muret La Barba (p143)

For reviews, see p141 ➡

Best Places to Drink

➡ G&T Bar (p146)
➡ Strandbar Mitte (p145)
➡ Butcher's (p146)
➡ Clärchens Ballhaus (p145)

For reviews, see p145 ➡

Best Jewish History Sites

➡ Neue Synagoge (p137)
➡ Gedenkstätte Stille Helden (p141)
➡ Alter Jüdischer Friedhof (p142)
➡ Museum Blindenwerkstatt Otto Weidt (p141)

For reviews, see p137 ➡

SCHEUNENVIERTEL

TOP SIGHT
HAMBURGER BAHNHOF – MUSEUM FÜR GEGENWART

Berlin's contemporary art showcase opened in 1996 in the former Hamburger Bahnhof railway station, whose loft and grandeur are the perfect foil for this Aladdin's cave of paintings, sculptures and installations.

The museum's inventory is based on permanent loans from three collectors – Erich Marx, Friedrich Christian Flick and Egidio Marzona – and spans the entire arc of post-1950 artistic movements from conceptual art and pop art to minimal art, Arte Povera and Fluxus. Seminal works by such major players as Andy Warhol, Cy Twombly and Bruce Nauman are presented in changing configurations in both the main museum and the adjacent 300m-long Rieckhallen (Rieck Halls). Anselm Kiefer and Cy Twombly get quite a bit of play, but not as much as the ultimate artistic boundary-pusher Joseph Beuys, whose works fill the entire ground floor of the west wing. Pride of place goes to the sculpture *The End of the Twentieth Century*.

Trains first rolled through the Hamburger Bahnhof in 1874, but after only 32 years the station had become too small and was turned into a traffic museum. After WWII, the building stood empty until the late Josef Paul Kleihues was hired in 1989 to create an exhibition space. He kept the elegant exterior, which at night is bathed in the light of a Dan Flavin installation. The interior, though, was gutted and turned into modern minimalist galleries that orbit the central hall with its exposed iron girders.

Free guided **English tours** run at noon on Saturday and Sunday (German tours run daily). Wrap up your visit with a browse around the museum bookshop and a bite in the smart on-site restaurant (p144).

DON'T MISS...

➡ Andy Warhol's *Chairman Mao* (1975)
➡ Anselm Kiefer's *Volkszählung* (Census; 1991)
➡ Joseph Beuys' *The End of the Twentieth Century* (1983)
➡ Robert Rauschenberg's *Pink Door* (1954)

PRACTICALITIES

➡ Map p328
➡ ☏030-266 424 242
➡ www.hamburger bahnhof.de
➡ Invalidenstrasse 50-51
➡ adult/concession €10/5
➡ ⊙10am-6pm Tue, Wed & Fri, to 8pm Thu, 11am-6pm Sat & Sun
➡ Ⓢ Hauptbahnhof, Ⓡ Hauptbahnhof

KARL JOHAENTGES/GETTY IMAGES ©

TOP SIGHT
NEUE SYNAGOGE

The gleaming gold dome of the Neue Synagoge is the most visible symbol of Berlin's revitalised Jewish community. Architect Eduard Knoblauch looked to the Alhambra in Granada for inspiration, which explains the exotic Moorish-Byzantine design elements, including the elaborate facade and the shiny dome. The building was consecrated on Rosh Hashanah in 1866 in the presence of Otto von Bismarck and other Prussian dignitaries. Seating 3200 people, it was Germany's largest synagogue.

During the 1938 Kristallnacht (Night of the Broken Glass) pogroms, a local police chief prevented a gang of SA (*Sturmabteilung;* a militia of the Nazi party) from setting it on fire, an act of courage commemorated by a plaque. The synagogue was eventually desecrated anyway, although not destroyed until hit by bombs in 1943. After the war, the ruin lingered until reconstruction began in 1988 on the 50th anniversary of Kristallnacht.

Rededicated in 1995, today's Neue Synagoge is not so much a house of worship (although prayer services do take place), but a museum and place of remembrance called **Centrum Judaicum**. In addition to temporary presentations, a permanent exhibit features architectural fragments and objects recovered from the ruins of the building before its reconstruction. They include a Torah scroll and an eternal lamp, and help tell the history of the building and the lives of the people associated with it. A multilingual audioguide (€3) also helps bring the past to life. On guided tours (call for times) you can also see the glass-and-steel mantle propping up the ruins of the original sanctuary in back. The dome can be climbed.

DON'T MISS...

- The facade
- The dome

PRACTICALITIES

- Map p326
- ☎030-8802 8300
- www.centrumjudaicum.de
- Oranienburger Strasse 28-30
- adult/concession €3.50/3, dome €2/1.50
- 🕒10am-8pm Sun & Mon (to 6pm Nov-Feb), to 6pm Tue-Thu, to 5pm Fri (to 2pm Oct-Mar)
- [S]Oranienburger Tor, 🚋Oranienburger Strasse

SIGHTS

⊙ Hackescher Markt Area

NEUE SYNAGOGE
SYNAGOGUE

See p137.

HECKMANNHÖFE
HISTORIC SITE

Map p326 (Oranienburger Strasse 32; 🚊M1, 🚈Oranienburger Strasse) For a retreat from the urban frenzy, skip on over to this idyllic courtyard complex linking Oranienburger Strasse with Auguststrasse. Kick back with cake and cappuccino in one of the cafes or browse around some unique shops like the Bonbonmacherei (p150), an old-fashioned candy kitchen.

JÜDISCHE MÄDCHENSCHULE
HISTORIC BUILDING

Map p326 (www.maedchenschule.org; August-strasse 11-13; ⊘hours vary; 🚇Oranienburger Tor, 🚊M1, 🚈Oranienburger Strasse) FREE A 1920s former Jewish Girls' School reopened in 2012 as a cultural and culinary centre in a sensitively restored New Objectivity struc-ture by Alexander Beer. Three renowned Berlin galleries – **Eigen+Art Lab**, **CWC** and **Michael Fuchs** – and the **Museum The Kennedys** have set up shop in the former classrooms, while the ground floor has the Jewish deli Mogg & Melzer (p143) and the Michelin-starred Pauly Saal (p144). Plenty of original design features have survived, including the tiles in the entrance and the classroom lights.

MUSEUM THE KENNEDYS
MUSEUM

Map p326 (📞030-2065 3570; www.thekenne-dys.de; Auguststrasse 11-13; adult/concession €5/2.50; ⊘11am-7pm; 🚇Oranienburger Tor, 🚊M1, 🚈Oranienburger Strasse) US president John F Kennedy has held a special place in German hearts since his defiant *'Ich bin ein Berlin-er!'* solidarity speech in 1963. This private exhibit addresses the president's continued mystique as such topics as the Berlin visit and his assassination in Dallas through photographs, documents and relics. Among the stand-out relics are JFK's reading glasses and a crocodile-leather briefcase, Jackie's Persian-lamb pillbox hat and a hilarious Superman comic book edition starring the president.

BUNKER ART

The vibes of war, vegetables and whips still hangs over the 80-room labyrinth of the **Sammlung Boros** (Boros Collection; Map p328; 📞030-2759 4065; www.sammlung-boros. de; Reinhardtstrasse 20; adult/concession €12/6; ⊘tours 3-8pm Thu, 10am-8pm Fri, 10am-6pm Sat & Sun; 🚇Oranienburger Tor, Friedrichstrasse, 🚊M1, 🚈Friedrichstrasse), a Nazi-era bunker turned shining beacon of art thanks to Christian Boros, advertising guru and collector of art by practitioners currently writing history. Boros purchased the concrete behemoth in 2003 and, after years of painstaking renovation, began shar-ing selections from his private stash in 2008 with an enthusiastic public. Many years later, a spot on a **guided tour** (also in English) is still one of the hottest tickets in town and should be booked weeks, if not months, ahead.

Since 2012, the second hanging has kicked off with Boros favourite (and Berlin resi-dent) Olafur Eliason, whose brass-and-mirror *Orientation Star* is cleverly juxtaposed with *Colour Experiment No 10*. Wolfgang Tillmann is represented with around three dozen photographs, including portraits of techno DJ Richie Hawtin and Kate Moss posing with broccoli. A major eye-catcher is Ai Weiwei's 6m-tall *Tree* whose installation required cutting out ceilings and walls. Boros is also big on championing new artists, which is why not-yet-household names like Alicja Kwade, Lidén, Thea Djordjadze, Michael Sailstorfer and Danh Vo are also featured quite prominently.

During the tour you'll also be peppered with fascinating nuggets about the history of the war-scarred shelter with its preserved original fittings, pipes, steel doors and vents. Built for 2000 people, its dank rooms crammed in twice as many during the heaviest air raids towards the end of WWII. After the shooting stopped, the Soviets briefly used it as a POW prison before it assumed a more benign role as a fruit and vegetable storeroom in East Berlin, a phase that spawned the nickname 'Banana Bun-ker'. In the 1990s, the claustrophobic warren saw some of Berlin's naughtiest techno raves and fetish parties.

TOP SIGHT
HACKESCHE HÖFE

The Hackesche Höfe is the largest and most famous of the courtyard ensembles peppered throughout the Scheunenviertel. Built in 1907 it links Rosenthaler Strasse with Sophienstrasse, and lingered through the city's division until being acquired by West German investors in 1994. After a total makeover, the complex of eight interlinked courtyards reopened to great fanfare in 1996 with a congenial mix of cafes, galleries, boutiques and entertainment venues.

The main entrance off Rosenthaler Strasse leads you to **Court I**, prettily festooned with ceramic tiles by art nouveau architect August Endell. One of Berlin's best cabarets, the Chamäleon Varieté (p147), is located here, as is an art-house cinema. Shoppers can look forward to plenty of flagship stores by Berlin designers. If you're a fan of the little characters on Berlin traffic lights, stock up on souvenirs in the Ampelmann Galerie (p150). Court VII leads off to the **Rosenhöfe**, a frilly art nouveau–inspired courtyard with a sunken rose garden and tendril-like balustrades.

DON'T MISS...

➜ Endell's art nouveau facade in Court I

➜ Berlin designer boutiques

PRACTICALITIES

➜ Map p326

➜ ☏030-2809 8010

➜ www.hackesche-hoefe.com

➜ Rosenthaler Strasse 40/41, Sophienstrasse 6

➜ ⬛M1, ⬛Hackescher Markt

SCHEUNENVIERTEL SIGHTS

KW INSTITUTE FOR CONTEMPORARY ART
GALLERY

Map p326 (☏030-243 4590; www.kw-berlin.de; Auguststrasse 69; adult/concession €6/4; ⊙noon-7pm Tue, Wed & Fri-Sun, to 9pm Thu; ⓈOranienburger Strasse, ⬛M1, ⬛Oranienburger Tor) In an old margarine factory, nonprofit KW helped chart the fate of the Scheunenviertel as Berlin's original post-Wall art district. It still stages ground-breaking shows reflecting the latest – and often radical – trends in contemporary art. Free tours (with reduced admission) run Thursday at 7pm. KW's founders also inaugurated the **Berlin Biennale** (www.berlinbiennale.de) in 1998.

ME COLLECTORS ROOM
GALLERY

Map p326 (☏030-8600 8510; www.me-berlin.com; Auguststrasse 68; adult/concession €7/4; ⊙noon-6pm Tue-Sun; ☎; ⬛M1, ⬛Oranienburger Strasse) Created by private collector Thomas Olbricht, this modern space showcases not only his own art collection from the 16th century to today, but also serves as a platform for other collectors to present their works in themed group shows. The only permanent feature is the *Wunderkammer,* a global 'cabinet of curiosities' that includes rare postage stamps, art-nouveau objects and toys. The on-site Me Cafe is a pleasant spot to reflect upon it all.

SAMMLUNG HOFFMANN
GALLERY

Map p326 (☏030-2849 9120; www.sammlung-hoffmann.de; Sophienstrasse 21; tours €10; ⊙11am-4pm Sat Sep-Jul; ⓈWeinmeisterstrasse) Blink and you'll miss the doorway leading to the Sophie-Gips-Höfe, a trio of courtyards linking Sophienstrasse and Gipsstrasse. The former sewing-machine factory now harbours stores, offices and flats as well as this stellar contemporary art collection in a private home, which is open for guided 90-minute tours every Saturday (registration required).

RAMONES MUSEUM
MUSEUM

Map p326 (☏030-7552 8889; www.ramones-museum.com; Krausnickstrasse 23; admission €3.50; ⊙noon-8pm Sun-Thu, to 10pm Fri & Sat; ☎; ⬛Oranienburger Strasse) They sang 'Born to Die in Berlin', but the legacy of punk pioneers the Ramones is kept very much alive in the German capital, thanks to this eclectic collection of memorabilia. Look for Marky Ramone's drumsticks and Johnny Ramone's jeans amid signed album covers, posters, flyers, photographs and other flotsam and jetsam. The on-site cafe also hosts the occasional concert.

TOP SIGHT
MUSEUM FÜR NATURKUNDE

Fossils and minerals don't quicken your pulse? Well, how about a 12m-high brachiosaurus, the Guinness Book–certified world's largest mounted dino? Nicknamed Oskar, the gentle giant is joined by a dozen Jurassic buddies including the ferocious allosaurus and a spiny-backed kentrosaurus, all about 150 million years old and from Tanzania. Clever 'Juraskopes' bring half a dozen of them back to virtual flesh-and-bone life. The same hall also houses an ultrarare fossilised archaeopteryx.

Beyond the dinosaurs you can journey deep into space or clear up such age-old mysteries as why zebras are striped and why peacocks have such beautiful feathers. Surprises include massively magnified insect models – wait until you see the mind-boggling anatomy of an ordinary house fly! A newish highlight is the wet collection: 276,000 glass jars containing over one million ethanol-preserved animals displayed in a huge glowing glass cube in its own darkened hall.

A crowd favourite among the taxidermied animals is Bobby, the gorilla, although he may soon be eclipsed by the late polar bear celebrity Knut.

DON'T MISS...

- Brachiosaurus
- Archaeopteryx
- Insect models

PRACTICALITIES

- Museum of Natural History
- Map p328
- ☎030-2093 8591
- www.naturkunde-museum-berlin.de
- Invalidenstrasse 43
- adult/concession incl audioguide €5/3
- 🕒9.30am-6pm Tue-Sun
- [S]Naturkunde-museum

MONSTERKABINETT ART INSTALLATION

Map p326 (☎0178 806 0202; www.monsterkabinett.de; Rosenthaler Strasse 39, 2nd courtyard; tours adult/concession €8/5; 🕒tours 6-10pm Thu, 4-10pm Fri & Sat; 🚋M1, 🚆Hackescher Markt) If you want to meet 'Püppi' the techno-loving go-go dancer or 'Orangina' the twirling six-legged doll, you need to descend a steep spiral staircase into Hannes Heiner's surrealist underground world. Inspired by his dreams, the artist has fashioned a menagerie of mechanical robot-monsters and assembled them in a computer-controlled art and sound installation that will entertain, astound and perhaps even frighten you just a little bit.

⊙ Hauptbahnhof & Oranienburger Tor

HAMBURGER BAHNHOF MUSEUM FÜR GEGENWART MUSEUM

See p136.

BERLINER MEDIZINHISTORISCHES MUSEUM MUSEUM

Map p328 (☎030-450 536 156; www.bmm-charite.de; Charitéplatz 1; adult/concession €7/3.50; 🕒10am-5pm Tue, Thu, Fri & Sun, to 7pm Wed & Sat; [S]Hauptbahnhof, 🚆Hauptbahnhof) This Charité Hospital–run museum chronicles 300 years of medical history in an anatomical theatre, a pathologist's dissection room, a laboratory and a historical patients' ward. The heart of the exhibit, though, is a grisly pathology collection that's essentially a 3D medical textbook on human disease and deformities. Those under 16 must be accompanied by an adult.

BRECHT-WEIGEL GEDENKSTÄTTE MEMORIAL

Map p328 (☎030-200 571 844; www.adk.de/de/archiv/gedenkstaetten; Chausseestrasse 125; tours adult/concession €5/2.50; 🕒tours half-hourly 10-11.30am Tue-Fri & 2-3.30pm Tue, 5-6.30pm Thu, 10am-3.30pm Sat, hourly 11am-6pm Sun; [S]Oranienburger Tor, Naturkundemuseum) Playwright Bertolt Brecht lived in this house from 1953 until his death in 1956. Guides take you inside his office, a large library and the tiny bedroom where he died. Decorated with Chinese artwork, it's been left as though he'd briefly stepped out, leaving his hat and woollen cap hanging on the door. Downstairs are the cluttered quarters of his actress wife, Helene Weigel.

DOROTHEENSTÄDTISCHER FRIEDHOF
CEMETERY

Map p328 (Chausseestrasse 126; ⊘8am-dusk, closes 8pm May-Aug; ⓢOranienburger Tor, Naturkundemuseum) FREE Being close to the Humboldt University, this compact 18th-century cemetery is the place of perpetual slumber for a veritable roll call of famous Germans and dotted with artistic tombstones. Karl Friedrich Schinkel, in fact, designed his own. Brecht, who lived next door, chose to be buried here, allegedly to be close to his idols, the philosophers Hegel and Fichte. A map by the entrance shows grave locations.

EATING

Hackescher Markt Area

SUSURU
JAPANESE €

Map p326 (✆030-211 1182; www.susuru.de; Rosa-Luxemburg-Strasse 17; mains €6.50-9; ⊘11.30am-11.30pm; 🖥✎; ⓢRosa-Luxemburg-Platz) Go ye forth and slurp! *Susuru* is Japanese for slurping and, quite frankly, that's the best way to deal with the oodles of noodles at this soup parlour, which looks as neat and stylish as a bento box.

DISTRICT MÔT
VIETNAMESE €

Map p326 (✆030-2008 9284; www.districtmot.com; Rosenthaler Strasse 62; dishes €4-19; ⊘noon-1am Sun-Thu, to 2am Fri & Sat; ⓢRosenthaler Platz, 🚋M1) At this mock-Saigon street-food parlour, patrons squat on tiny plastic stools around wooden tables where rolls of toilet paper stand in for paper napkins. The menu mixes the familiar (steamy *pho* noodle soup, papaya salad) with the adventurous (stewed eel, deep-fried silk worms).

BARCOMI'S DELI
CAFE €

Map p326 (www.barcomis.de; 2nd courtyard, Sophie-Gips-Höfe, Sophienstrasse 21; dishes €2.30-11; ⊘9am-9pm Mon-Sat, 10am-9pm Sun; ⓢWeinmeisterstrasse) Join latte-rati, families and expats at this New-York-meets-Berlin deli for custom-roasted coffee, wraps, bagels with smoked salmon, creative sandwiches

---

HAUS SCHWARZENBERG

In contrast to its luxe neighbours, **Haus Schwarzenberg** (Map p326; www.haus-schwarzenberg.org; Rosenthaler Strasse 39; 🚋M1, 🚉Hackescher Markt) is a final holdout in the heavily gentrified area around the Hackescher Markt. Run by a nonprofit organisation, it's an unpretentious, authentic space where art and creativity are allowed to flourish beyond mainstream and commerce. Festooned with street art and bizarre metal sculptures, the courtyards lead to studios, offices, an underground 'amusement park', the edgy-arty Eschloraque Rümschrümp (p145) bar, an art-house cinema (p148), and a trio of exhibits dealing with Jewish persecution during the Third Reich.

Museum Blindenwerkstatt Otto Weidt (✆030-2859 9407; www.museum-blindenwerkstatt.de; 1st courtyard left; ⊘10am-8pm) Otto Weidt was a broom and brush maker who risked his life protecting his blind and deaf Jewish workers from the Nazis. The exhibit is inside the very workshop where he hid an entire family in a room behind a cabinet, provided food and false papers and bribed Gestapo officials into releasing Jews scheduled for deportation. A highlight is an emotional video in which survivors recall Weidt's efforts to save their lives.

Anne Frank Zentrum (✆030-288 865 600; www.annefrank.de; adult/concession €5/2.50; ⊘10am-6pm Tue-Sun) This exhibit uses artefacts and photographs to tell the extraordinary story of a girl who needs no introduction. Who hasn't read the diary of Anne Frank, penned while in hiding from the Nazis in Amsterdam? Frank perished from typhus at Bergen-Belsen concentration camp just days before her 16th birthday. An entire room is devoted to her diary and its profound impact on postwar generations.

Gedenkstätte Stille Helden ('Silent Heroes' Memorial Exhibit; ✆030-2345 7919; www.gedenkstaette-stille-helden.de; ⊘10am-8pm) The 'Silent Heroes' Memorial Exhibit is dedicated to ordinary Germans who found the courage to hide and help their persecuted Jewish neighbours, just as Otto Weidt had done. Interactive media tables provide themed background information, while upstairs multimedia information pillars document the fate of individuals, both from the point of view of the helpers and of the persecuted.

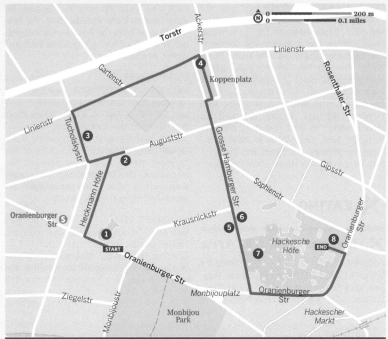

Neighbourhood Walk
Traces of Jewish Life in the Scheunenviertel

START NEUE SYNAGOGE
END HAUS SCHWARZENBERG
LENGTH 1.5KM; ONE TO THREE HOURS

This easy walk takes you past vestiges, memorials and revitalised sites of Jewish life throughout the Scheunenviertel. It starts at the imposing ❶ **Neue Synagoge** (p137), inaugurated in 1866 as Germany's largest Jewish house of worship and now a museum and community centre. Enter the Heckmann Höfe, which exits on Auguststrasse. Turn right to find yourself at the ❷ **Jüdische Mädchenschule** (p138), a Bauhaus-style Jewish Girls' School turned gallery and restaurant space.

Head back down Auguststrasse, then follow Tucholskystrasse north, perhaps stopping for a bite at the kosher ❸ **Beth Cafe** at No 40, then follow Linienstrasse east to ❹ **Der Verlassene Raum** (The Deserted Room). Karl Biedermann's art installation consists of a table and two chairs, one knocked over as a symbol of Jewish residents being forced to flee suddenly from their homes.

Head south on Grosse Hamburger Strasse and look for the ❺ **Missing House**, Christian Boltanski's 1990 memorial installation on the site of a bombed-out apartment building. Signs bearing the names of its former residents are affixed to the facades of the adjacent buildings. The structure opposite, at No 27, was a ❻ **Jewish Boys' School** founded in 1788. The Nazis closed it down, but it survived the war intact. Since 1993, both boys and girls – Jewish and not – have once again hit the books here. A few steps south, the ❼ **Alter Jüdischer Friedhof** was Berlin's first Jewish cemetery. Some 12,000 people were buried here between 1672 and 1827, including Enlightenment philosopher Moses Mendelssohn.

The tour concludes at street-art decorated ❽ **Haus Schwarzenberg** (p141), which harbours three small museums dealing with the fate of Jews under the Nazis.

BEYOND THE SCHEUNENVIERTEL: LESSER-KNOWN JEWISH SITES

The Holocaust Memorial, the Neue Synagoge and the Jüdisches Museum are Berlin's flagship Jewish sites, but there are plenty of other important places of remembrance. Here's a top five:

➡ Gleis 17 (p225) Trains departed for the concentration camp from these tracks.

➡ Gedenkstätte Haus der Wannsee-Konferenz (p226) The villa where Nazi leaders planned the 'Final Solution'.

➡ Mendelssohn Exhibit (p91) A homage to one of Berlin's most prominent Jewish families.

➡ Jüdischer Friedhof Schönhauser Allee (p188) Final resting place for famous Jewish Berliners.

➡ Block der Frauen (p111) Memorial to a successful act of Nazi resistance.

and possibly the best brownies and cheesecake this side of the Hudson River. Bonus points for the charming and quiet setting in a classic Scheunenviertel courtyard.

MONSIEUR VUONG
VIETNAMESE €

Map p326 (☑030-9929 6924, 030-9929 6924; www.monsieurvuong.de; Alte Schönhauser Strasse 46; mains €5-10; ⊗noon-11pm Mon-Thu, to midnight Fri & Sat; ⓈWeinmeisterstrasse, Rosa-Luxemburg-Platz) Berlin's 'godfather' of upbeat Indochina nosh-stops, Monsieur has been copied many times – the concept is just that good. They don't take reservations, so come in the afternoon to avoid the feeding frenzy and to enjoy the flavour-packed soups and fresh fragrant mains at leisure. The compact menu changes every other day.

MURET LA BARBA
ITALIAN €€

Map p326 (☑030-2809 7212; www.muretlabarba.de; Rosenthaler Strasse 61; mains €9-19; ⊗10am-midnight Mon-Fri, noon-midnight Sat & Sun; ⓈRosenthaler Platz) This wine shop–bar-restaurant combo oozes the kind of rustic authenticity that instantly transports cognoscenti to the Boot. The food is hearty, inventive and made with top ingredients imported from the motherland. All wine is available by the glass or by the bottle (corkage fee €9.50).

CHÈN CHÈ
VIETNAMESE €€

Map p326 (www.chenche-berlin.de; Rosenthaler Strasse 13; dishes €7-11; ⊗noon-midnight; ☑; ⓈRosenthaler Platz, ⓂM1) Settle down in the charming Zen garden or beneath the hexagonal chandelier of this exotic Vietnamese teahouse and pick from the small menu of steaming *pho* (soups), curries and noodle dishes served in traditional clay pots. Exquisite tea selection and small store.

SCHWARZWALDSTUBEN
GERMAN €€

Map p326 (☑030-2809 8084; Tucholskystrasse 48; mains €7-14; ⊗9am-midnight; ⓂM1, ⓇOranienburger Strasse) In the mood for a Hansel and Gretel moment? Then join the other 'lost kids' for satisfying southern German food amid tongue-in-cheek forest decor. Thumbs up for the *Spätzle* (mac 'n' cheese) and *Maultaschen* (ravioli-like pasta), best washed down with a crisp Rothaus Tannenzäpfle beer, straight from the Black Forest.

MOGG & MELZER
DELI €€

Map p326 (☑030-330 060 770; www.moggandmelzer.com; Auguststrasse 11-13; mains €7-15; ⊗8am-late Mon-Fri, 10am-late Sat & Sun; ⓂM1, ⓇOranienburger Strasse) At Berlin's first New York–style Jewish deli, pastrami, barbecued brisket, matzo ball soup and grilled sandwiches feed tummy and soul in an arty 1930s-inspired setting with purple-topped benches and Finnish designer chairs.

KOPPS
VEGAN €€

Map p326 (☑030-4320 9775; www.kopps-berlin.de; Linienstrasse 94; 2-/3-course lunch €8.50/10.50, dinner mains €16-19; ⊗noon-11pm Mon-Fri, 9.30am-11pm Sat & Sun; ☑; ⓈRosenthaler Platz, ⓂM1) 'German vegan' has not been an oxymoron since Kopps opened as Berlin's first high-end animal-product-free restaurant. The menu follows the seasons and might bring barbecued buckwheat burgers, smoked tomato soup or chanterelle risotto. The space is sparse but stylish. Note the lunch specials, full cocktail menu and opulent weekend brunch.

★REINSTOFF
INTERNATIONAL €€€

Map p328 (☑030-3088 1214; www.reinstoff.eu; Schlegelstrasse 26c; 5-course menu €100, additional courses €20; ⊗7pm-late Tue-Sat;

Ⓢ Naturkundemuseum, Ⓡ Nordbahnhof) With two Michelin stars to this name, Daniel Achilles creates poetry on a plate and pairs it punctiliously with wines from Germany and Spain. Clear lines and a glass bubble canopy give the space an elegant, unhurried ambience. Choose from the 'quite near' menu with its regional focus or the 'far away' menu, which draws upon cosmopolitan influences.

★ PAULY SAAL   GERMAN €€€

Map p326 (☑030-3300 6070; www.paulysaal. com; Auguststrasse 11-13; mains lunch €15-20, dinner €29-40; ⊙noon-3pm & 8pm-3am Mon-Sat; Ⓢ Oranienburger Tor, ⍟M1, Ⓡ Oranienburger Strasse) Regionally hunted and gathered ingredients steer the seasonal menu of Michael Hoepfl, who needed only one year to coax a star from the Michelin testers for his earthy gourmet cuisine. Try the Pomeranian entrecôte amid 1920s inspired decor spiced up with provocative art work.

✖ Hauptbahnhof & Oranienburger Tor

SARAH WIENER IM HAMBURGER BAHNHOF   AUSTRIAN €€€

Map p328 (☑030-7071 3650, 030-7071 3650; www.sarahwiener.de; Invalidenstrasse 50-51; mains €18-25; ⊙10am-6pm Tue & Wed, to 8pm Thu, to 11pm Fri, 11am-6pm Sat & Sun; Ⓢ Hauptbahnhof, Ⓡ Hauptbahnhof) Berlin's smartest museum cafe is a great spot for discussing the latest exhibit over a sumptuous breakfast, gooey homemade cakes or star-chef Sarah's famous veal schnitzel and inspired seasonal mains.

STUMBLING UPON HISTORY

If you lower your gaze, you'll see them everywhere, but especially in the Scheunenviertel: small brass paving stones engraved with names and placed in front of house entrances. Called *Stolpersteine* (stumbling blocks), they are part of a nationwide project by Berlin-born artist Gunter Demnig and are essentially mini-memorials honouring the people (usually Jews) who lived in the respective house before being killed by the Nazis.

GRILL ROYAL   STEAKHOUSE €€€

Map p328 (☑030-2887 9288; www.grillroyal. com; Friedrichstrasse 105b; mains €15-44, steaks €24-110; ⊙10am-late Mon-Fri, noon-late Sat & Sun; Ⓢ Friedrichstrasse, Ⓡ Friedrichstrasse) A platinum card is a handy accessory at this 'look-at-me' temple where A-listers, power politicians, pouty models and 'trust-a-farians' can be seen slurping oysters and tucking into their aged organic prime cuts. For an extra €24, you can get a lobster with your steak. Riverside tables beckon in fine weather.

✖ Torstrasse

LOKAL   MODERN GERMAN €€

Map p326 (☑030-2844 9500; www.lokal-berlin. blogspot.de; Linienstrasse 160; mains €14-22; ⊙noon-4pm & 6-10pm; Ⓢ Rosenthaler Platz, Ⓡ Oranienburger Strasse) If you think the stark and basic interior (white walls, wooden tables, white candles) is a bit ho-hum, perhaps the inspired, fresh and colourful takes on German fare will make you a fan of Lokal after all. Mellow at lunch, things get trendier at dinner time, when reservations are a must.

HARTWEIZEN   ITALIAN €€

Map p326 (☑030-2849 3877, 030-2849 3877; www.hartweizen.com; Torstrasse 96; mains €11-23; ⊙6-11.30pm; Ⓢ Rosenthaler Platz) With its simple wooden tables and panorama windows Hartweizen is hipster haven, thankfully with plenty of substance on the southern-Italian-leaning menu. The most creativity goes into appetisers such as caramelised goat cheese or salmon tartare with orange slices and kohlrabi, but fish and meat are also first rate, the pasta homemade and the wine fairly priced.

★ KATZ ORANGE   INTERNATIONAL €€€

Map p326 (☑030-983 208 430; www.katz orange.com; Bergstrasse 22; mains €18-26; ⊙6-11pm; Ⓢ Rosenthaler Platz, ⍟M8) With its gourmet organic farm-to-table menu, feel-good country styling and swift and smiling servers, the 'Orange Cat' hits a gastro grand slam. It will have you purring for Duroc pork that's been slow-roasted for 12 hours, giving extra-rich flavour. The setting in a castle-like former brewery is stunning, especially in summer when the patio opens.

LOCAL KNOWLEDGE

ROSENTHALER PLATZ: SNACK CENTRAL

For feeding hunger pangs on the quick and cheap, choices could not be greater than the area around Rosenthaler Platz. Here's our personal hit list:

Côcô (Map p326; ☎030-2463 0595; www.co-co.net; Rosenthaler Strasse 2; sandwiches €4.20-5.50; ⏲11am-10pm Mon-Thu, to 11pm Fri & Sat, noon-10pm Sun; [S]Rosenthaler Platz) This hip little joint was the first to introduce *bánh mì* (Vietnamese sandwiches) to Berlin. A relic from French-colonial times, it combines marinated meats, pâtés, spicy sauces and fresh herbs into a firework of aromas stuffed into a toasted baguette.

Rosenburger (Map p326; ☎030-2408 3037; Brunnenstrasse 196; burgers €3-6; ⏲11am-3am Sun-Thu, to 5am Fri & Sat; [S]Rosenthaler Platz) This burger joint is especially busy from the early evening onwards when prospective night owls stop by to fortify themselves with handmade burgers and piles of handcut fries. Organic meats cost a bit more.

Rosenthaler Grill und Schlemmerbuffet (Map p326; ☎030-283 2153; Torstrasse 125; dishes €2.80-7; ⏲24hr; [S]Rosenthaler Platz) Oscar-worthy doner kebabs. Enough said.

WEINBAR RUTZ — GERMAN €€€

Map p328 (☎030-2462 8760; www.rutz-weinbar.de; Chausseestrasse 8; bar mains €16-25, 3-/4-course menu €44/54; ⏲4-11pm Tue-Sat; [S]Oranienburger Tor) Below his high-concept gourmet temple, Michelin-starred Marco Müller operates a more down-to-earth wine bar where the menu has a distinct earthy and carnivorous bent. Many of the meats and sausages are sourced from Berlin and surrounds. Finish up with a Berlin cheesecake with walnuts and elderberry ice cream.

MANI — FUSION €€€

Map p326 (☎0163 635 9464; www.amanogroup.de; Torstrasse 136; small plates €6-10.50, mains €21-25, business lunch €10.50; ⏲11.30am-2.30pm Mon-Fri & 7pm-late Tue-Sat; [S]Rosenthaler Platz, 🚋M1) Perched at a shiny black table, perhaps near the fireplace, you can watch the kitchen staff churn out dishes that sound deceptively simple on the menu but turn out to be meals with complex textures and flavour pairings. Case in point: sweet potato teamed with pistachio, tahini yoghurt and black cumin. Good-value business lunches.

🍷 DRINKING & NIGHTLIFE

🍷 Hackescher Markt Area

★STRANDBAR MITTE — BAR

Map p326 (☎030-2838 5588; www.strandbar-mitte.de; Monbijoustrasse 3; ⏲10am-late May-Sep; 🚋M1, [R]Oranienburger Strasse) With a full-on view of the Bodemuseum, palm trees and a relaxed ambience, Germany's first beach bar (since 2002) is great for balancing a surfeit of sightseeing stimulus with a revivifying drink. At night, there's dancing under the stars with tango, cha cha, swing and salsa. Lessons (€6) run from 7pm to 8pm.

CLÄRCHENS BALLHAUS — CLUB

Map p326 (☎030-282 9295; www.ballhaus.de; Auguststrasse 24; ⏲11am-late, dancing from 9pm or 9.30pm; 🚋M1, [R]Oranienburger Strasse) Yesteryear is right now at this late, great 19th-century dance hall where groovers and grannies hoof it across the parquet without even a touch of irony. There's different sounds nightly – salsa to swing, tango to disco – and a live band on Saturday. Pizza and German staples provide sustenance all day long (in summer in the pretty garden; pizza €5.50 to €11.50, mains €6.50 to €18). Dance classes, dinners and classical Sunday concerts (p147) are held upstairs amid the stylishly faded grandeur of the Spiegelsaal (Mirror Hall).

ESCHLORAQUE RÜMSCHRÜMP — BAR

Map p326 (www.eschloraque.de; Rosenthaler Strasse 39; ⏲from 2pm; 🚋M1, [R]Hackescher Markt) This brilliant bar is a delightful retreat tucked into the street art–festooned courtyard of Haus Schwarzenberg, the last ungentrified house around Hackescher Markt. Run by the artist collective Dead Chicken, it's filled with metal monster sculptures and hosts wacky parties and eclectic shows – from dada burlesque to Balkan post-punk concerts. Beer garden in summer.

TACHELES IS DEAD! LONG LIVE TACHELES!

The graffiti-slathered empty hulk on Oranienburger Strasse is all that's left of the **Kunsthaus Tacheles** (Map p328; Oranienburger Strasse 54-56; S Oranienburger Tor, R Oranienburger Strasse), which for over 20 years was one of Berlin's most beloved alternative art and cultural spaces. Shortly after the fall of the Wall, in early 1990, an artist collective occupied the crumbling wartime ruin of a 1909 shopping arcade, creating a utopian parallel world and luring locals and tourists to its anti-mainstream venues, bizarre sculptures and trashy-cool beer garden. Although the anarchic vibe eventually faded, the building remained the lodestar of alternative culture in heavily gentrified Mitte until falling victim to Berlin's burgeoning real estate craze in 2012. The last of the artists were evicted in September, leaving behind a forlorn and neglected landmark. Many found refuge in the eastern suburb of Marzahn, where they've turned the stables of a former stockyard and police barracks into studios and living spaces. The complex, which is called **Alte Börse Marzahn**, also encompasses a concert hall, a movie theatre and even a brewery that produces – what else? – a beer called 'Marzahner'.

SCHEUNENVIERTEL DRINKING & NIGHTLIFE

AMANO BAR
BAR

Map p326 (030-809 4150; www.bar.hotel-amano.com; Auguststrasse 43; 5pm-late; S Rosenthaler Platz, M1) This glamour vixen at the budget-hip Hotel Amano, with its marble bar, cubistic furnishings and warm chocolate hues, attracts chatty sophisticates with original libations that verge on cocktail alchemy. In summer, the action expands to the rooftop terrace.

CORDOBAR
WINE BAR

Map p326 (030-2758 1215; www.cordobar.net; Grosse Hamburger Strasse 32; 6pm-2am Tue-Sat; M1, R Hackescher Markt, Oranienburger Strasse) At this joint effort of a music producer, a movie director and two sommeliers, characterful German and Austrian vintages dominate the well-curated wines-by-the-glass list, which is kept in a frequent state of flux, as is the globally inspired small-plate menu (€6 to €15).

☕ Torstrasse

★ G&T BAR
BAR

Map p328 (www.amanogroup.de; Friedrichstrasse 113; 8pm-late; S Oranienburger Tor, M1) In classic Berlin style, Germany's first drinking salon devoted to gin-based libations is appropriately dressed in Tanqueray green and tucked into the back of a courtyard off busy Friedrichstrasse. Here, even a basic gin and tonic is elevated to complex cocktail concoction thanks to richly nuanced tea infusions that turn it into a so-called GT&T.

BUTCHER'S
BAR

Map p326 (www.butcher-berlin.de; Torstrasse 116; 8.30pm-late Tue-Sat; S Rosenthaler Platz, M1) Channelling PDT in New York, cocktail whisperer David Wiedemann has created a furtive libation station in a former butcher-shop entered via a red British phone booth tucked into a sausage parlour called Fleischerei. Drinks are expertly mixed and the ambience is refined, even if meat hooks, a leather bar and blood-red light play upon the place's early incarnation.

MAXIM
WINE BAR

Map p326 (030-6583 3962; Gormannstrasse 25; 6pm-1am; S Rosa-Luxemburg-Platz, Rosenthaler Platz) Amid sleek Zeitgeist-capturing aesthetics, Maxime Boillat serves only prime natural wines – organic, unfiltered and additive-free. Most hail from Italy, Spain and France and are on equal footing with the imaginatively curated fusion menu (signature dish: pulpo with tarragon syrup and smoked tea sausage) and the exquisitely gooey cheeses.

KAFFEE BURGER
CLUB

Map p326 (030-2804 6495; www.kaffeeburger.de; Torstrasse 60; S Rosa-Luxemburg-Platz) Nothing to do with either coffee or meat patties, this sweaty cult club with lovingly faded Commie-era decor is a fun-for-all concert and party pen with a sound policy that swings from indie and electro to klezmer punk without missing a beat.

MEIN HAUS AM SEE
CAFE, BAR

Map p326 (030-2759 0873; www.mein-haus-am-see.blogspot.de; Brunnenstrasse 197/198; 24hr;

[S]Rosenthaler Platz, 🚋M1) The 'House by the Lake' is nowhere near anything liquid, unless you count the massive amount of beverages consumed at this multitasking all-hours cafe-bar, gallery, performance space and club. Plop down onto grandma's sofa for intimate chats or grab a seat on the staircase for stadium-style hipster watching.

COSMIC KASPAR CLUB

Map p326 (☎030-2759 0873; www.cosmic-kaspar.com; Brunnenstrasse 197/198; ⏰10pm-late; [S]Rosenthaler Platz, 🚋M1) Cosmic Kaspar is the 'baby' of the popular cafe-bar Mein Haus am See. Live acts, dance bashes and quirky events such as 'Porno Karaoke' draw punters downstairs for full-on electro-beat partying amid surreal, spacey decor.

BONBON BAR BAR

Map p326 (☎030-2462 8718; www.bonbonbar.de; Torstrasse 133; ⏰7pm-3am Sun-Wed, to 5am Thu-Sat; [S]Rosenthaler Platz, 🚋M1) This new haunt is a seductively lit and expensively decorated retreat whose eye-catching design accents and cheeky soundtrack in the bathrooms are likely to fuel any conversation. When big-name DJs hit the decks, the place gets delightfully dancy.

BUCK AND BRECK BAR

Map p326 (☎0176 3231 5507; www.buckandbreck.com; Brunnenstrasse 177; ⏰7pm-late; [S]Rosenthaler Platz) Berlin barmeister Gonçalo de Sousa Monteiro treats clued-in patrons to his libational flights of fancy in an intimate cocktail salon behind a nameless door. Historical concoctions are his strength, including the eponymous Buck and Breck, a potent blend of cognac, bitters, absinthe and champagne. Call ahead as space is limited.

KING SIZE BAR BAR

Map p328 (www.kingsizebar.de; Friedrichstrasse 112b; ⏰9pm-7am Wed-Sat; [S]Oranienburger Tor) Good things come in small packages at this ironically named and well-stocked hole in the wall. A local favourite of boho-bourgeois elite, it's at its raucous best after 1am when the space before the toilet turns into an impromptu dance floor. Join in or watch the action sipping a signature Moscow mule, served – as are all drinks – in cut-crystal whisky tumblers. Smoking is allowed.

☆ ENTERTAINMENT

CHAMÄLEON VARIETÉ CABARET

Map p326 (☎030-400 0590; www.chamaeleonberlin.com; Rosenthaler Strasse 40/41; 🚋M1, 🚆Hackescher Markt) A marriage of art nouveau charms and high-tech theatre trappings, this intimate 1920s-style cabaret in an old ballroom presents classy variety shows – comedy, juggling acts and singing – often in sassy, sexy and unconventional fashion.

BABYLON CINEMA

Map p326 (☎030-242 5969; www.babylonberlin.de; Rosa-Luxemburg-Strasse 30; tickets €7-9; [S]Rosa-Luxemburg-Platz) This top-rated indie screens a well-curated potpourri of new German films, international art-house flicks, themed retrospectives and other

LOCAL KNOWLEDGE

SUNDAY CONCERTS

Wind down the weekend by taking in one of the classical **Sonntagskonzerte** (Map p326; ☎030-5268 0256; www.sonntagskonzerte.de; Auguststrasse 24; adult/concession €10/7; ⏰Sep-Jun; [S]Oranienburger Tor, 🚋M1, 🚆Oranienburger Strasse) held in one of the most unusual spaces in Berlin: the Spiegelsaal (Mirror Hall) upstairs at Clärchens Ballhaus (p145), a 19th-century ballroom right in the heart of the Scheunenviertel. From roughly September to June, a small crowd of clued-in fans gathers at 7pm on Sundays amid the faded elegance of this historic room to listen to piano concerts, opera recitals, string quartets and other musical offerings.

With its cracked and blinded mirrors, elaborate chandeliers and old-timey wallpaper, the hall recalls the decadence of past eras when it was the domain of the city's elite, while the common folks hit the planks in the ballroom downstairs.

For upcoming concerts, check the website or call ahead. It's possible to make reservations, but there are no assigned seats, so come early. In July and August performances are free and held outdoors against the glorious backdrop of the Bodemuseum on Museumsinsel (8.30pm, weather permitting).

LOCAL KNOWLEDGE

TRENDY TORSTRASSE

Though loud and heavily trafficked, Torstrasse is booming, and not just since Brangelina were rumoured to have bought a flat nearby. With surprising speed, this main thoroughfare has turned into a hip strip where trendy eats pop up with the frequency of fruit-fly births, gritty-glam bars pack in night crawlers, and indie boutiques lure the fashion-savvy.

stuff you'd never catch at the multiplex. For the silent movies, the original theatre organ is put through its paces. It's in a fantastic protected 1920s building by New Objectivity wizard Hans Poelzig.

B-FLAT LIVE MUSIC

Map p326 (☎030-283 3123; www.b-flat-berlin.de; Rosenthaler Strasse 13; 🕒8pm-late Sun-Thu, 9pm-late Fri & Sat; [S]Rosenthaler Platz, 🚋M1) Cool cats of all ages come out to this intimate jazz venue, where the audience sits within spitting distance of the performers. Mal Waldron, Randy Brecker and even Mikis Theodorakis have graced its stage. Wednesday's free jam session often brings down the house.

MONBIJOUTHEATER THEATRE

Map p326 (www.amphitheater-berlin.de; Monbijouplatz 1-3; 🕒May-Sep; 🚋M1, 🚆Oranienburger Strasse) Every summer, the Theater Hexenkessel presents crowd-pleasing classics from Shakespeare to Molière in a lovely outdoor amphitheatre near Museum Island.

KINO CENTRAL CINEMA

Map p326 (☎030-2859 9973; www.kino-central.de; Rosenthaler Strasse 39; tickets €6-8; 🚋M1, 🚆Hackescher Markt) This art-house cinema screens international films, usually in the original with German subtitles. In summer, the screenings move into the courtyard.

VOLKSBÜHNE AM ROSA-LUXEMBURG-PLATZ THEATRE

Map p326 (☎030-2406 5777; www.volksbuehne-berlin.de; Rosa-Luxemburg-Platz; [S]Rosa-Luxemburg-Platz) Nonconformist, radical and provocative: performances at the 'People's Stage' are not for the squeamish. Since 1992, the theatre has been led by enfant terrible Frank Castorf who regularly tears down the confines of the proscenium stage with Zeitgeist-critical productions that manage to be both populist and elitist at once.

FRIEDRICHSTADTPALAST CABARET

Map p328 (☎030-2326 2326; www.palast-berlin.eu; Friedrichstrasse 107; [S]Oranienburger Tor, 🚋M1) Europe's largest revue theatre has a tradition going back to the 1920s and is famous for glitzy-glam Vegas-style productions with leggy showgirls, a high-tech stage, mind-boggling special effects and plenty of artistry.

KUNSTFABRIK SCHLOT LIVE MUSIC

Map p328 (☎030-448 2160; www.kunstfabrik-schlot.de; Invalidenstrasse 117, Schlegelstrasse 26; 🕒daily; [S]Naturkundemuseum, 🚆Nordbahnhof) Hidden in the Edison-Höfe, a stylishly renovated light-bulb factory, this long-time cellar venue hosts high-quality jazz concerts, many of them free (usually on Mondays and Thursdays), as well as free readings on Sundays from 1pm to 3pm. Enter from Schlegelstrasse or Invalidenstrasse.

🛍 SHOPPING

Label hounds addicted to staying ahead of the fashion curve and seekers of the latest Berlin fashions should concentrate their browsing along and around Alte Schönhauser Strasse, Neue Schönhauser Strasse, Münzstrasse, Mulackstrasse and inside the Hackesche Höfe. Cutting-edge galleries line Linienstrasse and Auguststrasse and their side streets.

KONK FASHION

Map p326 (☎030-2809 7839; www.konk-berlin.de; Kleine Hamburger Strasse 15; 🕒noon-7pm Mon-Fri, to 6pm Sat; 🚋M1, 🚆Oranienburger Strasse) Get that hip 'just back from Berlin' look by stocking up on Berlin-made threads at Edda Mann's style emporium. She has championed local designers like Anntian, Rita in Palma and Tiedeken since 2003 at prices above sportswear but below couture.

KAUF DICH GLÜCKLICH FASHION

Map p326 (☎030-2887 8817; www.kaufdich-gluecklich-shop.de; Rosenthaler Strasse 17; 🕒11am-8pm Mon-Sat; [S]Weinmeisterstrasse, Rosenthaler Platz) What began as a waffle cafe and vintage shop has turned into a small emporium of indie fashion boutiques with this branch being the new flagship. It's a prettily arranged and eclectic mix of reasonably priced accessories, music and clothing for him and her from its own collection and a number of other hand-picked labels.

TRIPPEN FLAGSHIP STORE SHOES

Map p326 (☑030-2839 1337; www.trippen.com; Courts IV & VI, Hackesche Höfe, Rosenthaler Strasse 40/41; ☺11am-8pm Mon-Fri, 10am-8pm Sat; 🚇M1, 🚈Hackescher Markt) Forget about 10cm heels! Berlin-based Trippen's shoes are designed with the human anatomy in mind, yet are light years ahead in style compared to the loafers grandma used to buy in the orthopaedic store. The award-winning brand prides itself on its 'socially responsible' manufacturing and love of unusual shapes. The stores themselves are gorgeous.

UMASAN FASHION

Map p326 (☑030-2408 5534; www.umasanworld.com; Linienstrasse 40; ☑; 🚈Rosa-Luxemburg-Platz) With an outfit from Umasan you can look good knowing that no sheep had to surrender its wool for your dress, skirt or top. Although Germany's first vegan label uses only plant-based materials, the look is hardly hippie, but decidedly high fashion, relying on asymmetric cuts, subtle prints and muted colours.

BUTTERFLYSOULFIRE FASHION

Map p326 (www.butterflysoulfire.com; Mulackstrasse 11; ☺noon-8pm Mon-Sat; 🚈Rosa-Luxemburg-Platz, Weinmeisterstrasse) Only at the flagship store of Maria Thomas and Thoas Lindner's avant-garde Berlin fashion label can you get the latest cuts of cleverly geometric and asymmetric shirts, pants, jackets and basics. The store also has deals and steals from last season, plus bags by Garnet, jewellery by Bjorg and other hipster items from small fashion-forward labels.

NO 74 BERLIN FASHION

Map p326 (☑030-5306 2513; www.no74-berlin.com; Torstrasse 74; ☺noon-8pm Mon-Sat; 🚈Rosenthaler Platz) Sleek, minimalist and gallery-style, No 74 is the holy grail for kool kids in search of the latest threads, shoes and accessories by adidas brands Y-3, SLVR and adidas by Stella McCartney along with limited sneaker editions by adidas Originals.

LALA BERLIN FASHION

Map p326 (☑030-2576 2924; www.lalaberlin.com; Mulackstrasse 7; ☺noon-8pm Mon-Sat; 🚈Rosa-Luxemburg-Platz) Ex-MTV editor Leyla Pie-

dayesh makes top-flight women's fashion that flatters both the twig-thin and the well upholstered. Originally known for her knitwear, you can now drop by her flagship boutique to pick up boldly patterned tunics, silk dresses or a sassy Lala Girl T-shirt.

HAPPY SHOP FASHION, ACCESSORIES

Map p326 (☑030-2900 9502; www.happyshop-berlin.com; Torstrasse 67; ☺11am-7pm Tue-Sat; 🚈Rosa-Luxemburg-Platz) Fashion outside the mainstream is the mojo of Happy Shop, in an artsy wooden pavilion with striped facade and pink doors. Aside from owner-designer Micha Woeste's own Smeilinener label, the global line-up includes 'Scandinasian' fashions by the Inoue Brothers and Japanese wunderkind Mihara Yasuhiro's Puma Black Label line. Ring the bell to enter.

IC! BERLIN ACCESSORIES

Map p326 (☑030-2472 7200; www.ic-berlin.de; Max-Beer-Strasse 17; ☺11am-8pm Mon-Sat; 🚈Weinmeisterstrasse) What looks like a bachelor pad, with worn sofas, wacky art and turntables, is the flagship store of this internationally famous eyewear maker. The feather-light frames with their klutz-proof, screwless hinges are stored in retro airline serving trolleys and have added 'spec appeal' to celebs from Madonna to the king of Morocco.

LOCAL KNOWLEDGE

THE SCHEUNENVIERTEL: FROM HAY TO HIP

The Scheunenviertel's odd name, Barn Quarter, hearkens back centuries to the days of wooden houses, frequent fires and poor fire-fighting techniques, which is why the Prussian king ordered all barns containing flammable crops to be stored outside the city walls. In the early 20th century, the quarter absorbed huge numbers of poor Eastern European Jewish immigrants, many of whom were later killed by the Nazis. After the war, the Scheunenviertel gradually deteriorated into a down-at-heel East Berlin barrio but has catapulted from drab to fab since reunification. Now a creative-class darling, its cafes and bars brim with iPad-toters, sassy fashionistas and bearded hipsters.

ROTATION RECORDS
MUSIC

Map p326 (☑030-2532 9116; www.rotation-records.de; Weinbergsweg 3; ⊘noon-7pm; Ṣ Rosenthaler Platz, 🚇 M1) Click, click, click…is the sound of electro-heads flipping through the vinyl selection in what many consider Berlin's best store for electronic dance music, mainly house and techno, both new and used. Also stocks hand-picked street fashion, some by Berlin designers or DJs like Ellen Allien, along with useful and clever gadgets and accessories.

GROBER UNFUG
BOOKS

Map p326 (☑030-281 7331; www.groberunfug. de; Torstrasse 75; ⊘11am-7pm Mon-Wed, 11am-6pm Sat; Ṣ Rosenthaler Platz) Fans of international comics and graphic novels can easily lose a few hours in this very cool repository of books, DVDs, soundtracks and knick-knacks. There's a mega-selection of indie and mainstream imports from the US, Japan and elsewhere. Exhibits, auctions, signings and performances take over the adjacent gallery space. There's a smaller branch in **Kreuzberg** (Map p336; ☑030-6940 1490; www. groberunfug.de; Zossener Strasse 33; ⊘11am-7pm Mon-Fri, to 6pm Sat; Ṣ Gneisenaustrasse).

HUNDT HAMMER STEIN
BOOKS

Map p326 (☑030-2345 7669; www.hundthammerstein.de; Alte Schönhauser Strasse 23/24; ⊘11am-7.30pm Mon-Sat; Ṣ Weinmeisterstrasse) Kurt Hammerstein has a nose for good books beyond the bestseller lists. Feel free to browse through this tidy and well-curated lit lair with word candy from around the world or ask the affable owner to match a tome to your taste. There's a sizeable English selection, quality books for tots and a sprinkling of travel guides as well.

PRO QM
BOOKS

Map p326 (☑030-2472 8520; www.pro-qm.de; Almstadtstrasse 48-50; ⊘11am-8pm Mon-Sat; Ṣ Rosa-Luxemburg-Platz) This treasure trove of the printed word is squarely focused on design, art, architecture, pop and photography with a sprinkling of political and philosophical tomes (many in English) and a broad selection of obscure mags from around the world. With floor-to-ceiling shelves and stacks of books throughout, it's a browser's paradise.

BONBONMACHEREI
FOOD

Map p326 (☑030-4405 5243; www.bonbonmacherei.de; Oranienburger Strasse 32, Heckmann Höfe; ⊘noon-8pm Wed-Sat Sep-Jun; 🚇 M1, 🚊 Oranienburger Strasse) The aroma of peppermint and liquorice wafts through this old-fashioned basement candy kitchen whose owners use antique equipment and time-tested recipes to churn out such tasty treats as their signature leaf-shaped Berliner Maiblätter.

1. ABSINTH DEPOT BERLIN
FOOD, DRINK

Map p326 (☑030-281 6789; www.erstesabsinthdepotberlin.de; Weinmeisterstrasse 4; ⊘2pm-midnight Mon-Fri, 1pm-midnight Sat; Ṣ Weinmeisterstrasse) Van Gogh, Toulouse-Lautrec and Oscar Wilde were among the *fin-de-siècle* artists who drew inspiration from the 'green fairy', as absinthe is also known. This quaint little shop has over 100 varieties of the potent stuff and an expert owner who'll happily help you pick out the perfect bottle for your own mind-altering rendezvous.

AMPELMANN GALERIE
SOUVENIRS

Map p326 (☑030-4472 6438; www.ampelmann. de; Court V, Hackesche Höfe, Rosenthaler Strasse 40/41; ⊘9.30am-10pm Mon-Sat, 10am-7pm Sun; 🚇 M1, 🚊 Hackescher Markt) It took a vociferous grassroots campaign to save the little Ampelmann, the endearing fellow on East German pedestrian traffic lights. Now the beloved cult figure and global brand graces an entire store worth of T-shirts, fridge magnets, pasta, onesies, umbrellas and other knick-knacks. There are a number of other Ampelmann branches across the city.

AESOP MITTE
BEAUTY

Map p326 (☑030-2809 6560; www.aesop. com; Alte Schönhauser Strasse 48; ⊘11am-7pm Mon-Sat; Ṣ Rosa-Luxemburg-Platz, Weinmeisterstrasse) The first German branch of this coveted Australian beauty label occupies stunning digs tiled in emerald-green and accented with a vintage washbasin salvaged from an old farm. The high-end skin, hair and body products are displayed apothecary-style on oak and steel shelves.

SCHWARZER REITER
EROTICA

Map p326 (☑030-4503 4438; www.schwarzer-reiter.de; Torstrasse 3; ⊘noon-8pm Mon-Sat, Ṣ Rosa-Luxemburg-Platz) If you worship at the altar of hedonism, you'll find a wide range of luxe erotica in this classy store decked out in sensuous black and purple. Beginner and advanced pleasure needs can be fulfilled, from rubber duckie vibrators, feather teasers and furry blindfolds to unmentionable hardcore stuff.

Kreuzberg & Neukölln

BERGMANNKIEZ | KOTTBUSSER TOR | THE LANDWEHRKANAL | NEUKÖLLN | SCHLESISCHES TOR | THE SPREE

Neighbourhood Top Five

❶ Challenging your party stamina by catching tomorrow's headliners at **Magnet Club** (p169), then dancing till breakfast at **Watergate** (p167) and wrapping up with a chill session at **Club der Visionäre** (p167).

❷ Stepping back into the long, tumultuous and fascinating history of Jews in Germany at the **Jüdisches Museum** (p153).

❸ Soaking up the punky-funky alt feel of eastern Kreuzberg or northern Neukölln in search of your favourite **drinking den** (p160) around Kottbusser Tor.

❹ Foraging for unusual gifts for you and yours in the charming boutiques along **Bergmannstrasse** (p169).

❺ Immersing yourself in multicultural bounty on a crawl through the bustling **Türkenmarkt** (p169).

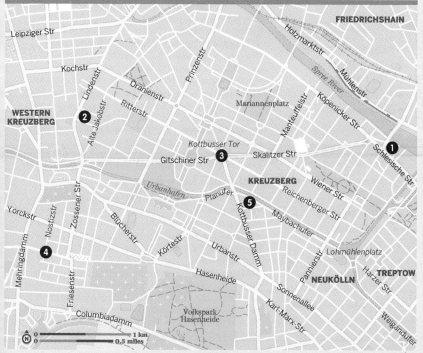

For more detail of this area, see Map p332 and p336 ➡

Lonely Planet's Top Tip

For the ultimate 'Turkish Delight', head for **Sultan Hamam** (☎030-2175 3375; www.sultanhamamberlin.de; Bülowstrasse 57; 3/5hr session €16/21; ⏰noon-11pm; [S]Yorckstrasse, 🚆Yorckstrasse), where a traditional Turkish bath house meets modern spa culture. Relax in the richly tiled sauna and steam room, then treat yourself to a soapy scrub and *kese* (full body peeling with silken gloves). It's mostly for women, although men are welcome on Sundays and Mondays.

🍴 Best Places to Eat

- ➡ Cafe Jacques (p158)
- ➡ Defne (p159)
- ➡ Volt (p162)
- ➡ Henne (p159)

For reviews, see p157 ➡

🍷 Best Places to Drink

- ➡ Schwarze Traube (p165)
- ➡ Club der Visionäre (p167)
- ➡ Locke Müller (p165)
- ➡ Möbel Olfe (p160)
- ➡ Otto Rink (p160)

For reviews, see p164 ➡

🍷 Best Places to Dance

- ➡ Watergate (p167)
- ➡ Prince Charles (p165)
- ➡ Chalet (p167)
- ➡ Fuchs & Elster (p166)

For reviews, see p164 ➡

Explore: Kreuzberg & Neukölln

Kreuzberg gets its street cred from being delightfully edgy, bipolar, wacky and, most of all, unpredictable. While the western half, around Bergmannstrasse, has an upmarket, genteel air, eastern Kreuzberg (still nicknamed SO36, after its prereunification postal code) is a multicultural mosaic, a bubbly hodgepodge of tousled students, aspiring creatives, *shisha*-smoking Turks and Arabs, and international life artists. Spend a day tracking down fabulous street art, scarfing a *shawarma*, browsing vintage stores and hanging by the canal, then find out why Kreuzberg is also known as a night-crawler's paradise.

All that hipness has spilled across the Landwehrkanal to the northern part of Neukölln, sometimes also called Kreuzkölln. Once making headlines for its crime and poor schools, the district has catapulted from ghetto-gritty to funkytown-hip in no time. At least partly thanks to an influx of young, creative neo-Berliners (including many from Italy, Spain and Australia), the quarter sees trash-trendy bars, performance spaces and galleries coming online almost daily. If you need a break from all that hipness, head over to the vast Tempelhofer Park.

Local Life

➡**Bar-hopping** Kreuzberg and Kreuzkölln deliver some of the city's most happening night-time action, especially around Kottbusser Tor, along Schlesische Strasse and on Weserstrasse.

➡**Shopping** Delightfully devoid of high-street chains, shopping in Kreuzberg is all about individual style. Join locals in putting together that inimitable outfit from vintage shops, local designers and streetwear boutiques.

➡**Chilling** The locals don't live to work. Heck, they may not work at all, which is why they have plenty of time to chill in green oases like Tempelhofer Park, Viktoriapark or Görlitzer Park or to count the boats floating by on the Landwehrkanal or Spree River.

Getting There & Away

➡**Bus** M29 links Potsdamer Platz with Oranienstrasse via Checkpoint Charlie; the M41 hits the Bergmannkiez before trudging down to Neukölln via Hermannplatz.

➡**S-Bahn** The Ringbahn (Circle Line) S41/S42 stops at Treptower Park, Sonnenallee, Neukölln and Hermannstrasse.

➡**U-Bahn** Getting off at Kottbusser Tor puts you in the thick of eastern Kreuzberg, although Görlitzer Bahnhof and Schlesisches Tor are also handy. For northern Neukölln, Schönleinstrasse, Hermannplatz and Rathaus Neukölln are key stops. For the Bergmannkiez area, head to Mehringdamm or Gneisenaustrasse.

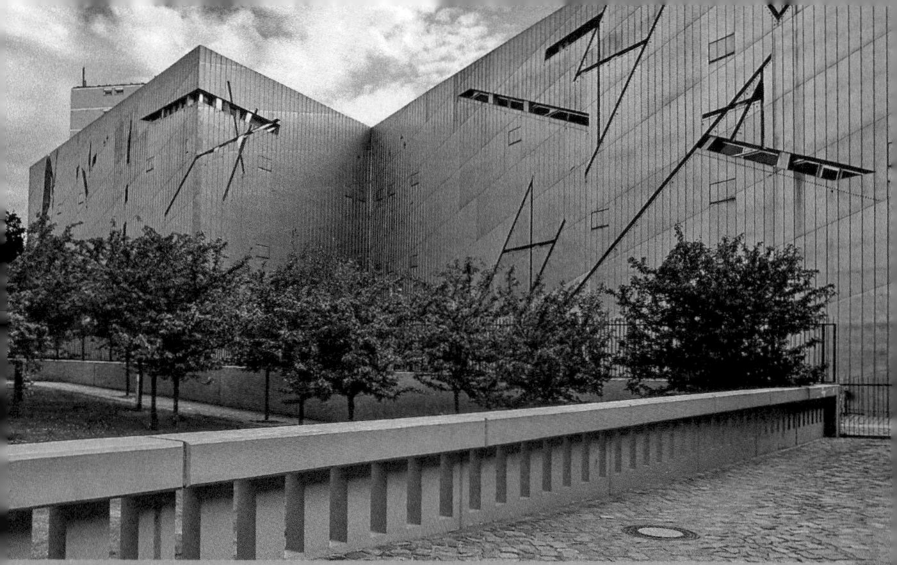

TOP SIGHT
JÜDISCHES MUSEUM

In a landmark building by Daniel Libeskind, Berlin's Jewish Museum offers a chronicle of the trials and triumphs from 2000 years of German history seen through the eyes of the Jewish minority. The exhibit smoothly navigates all major periods, from the Middle Ages via the Enlightenment to the community's current renaissance. Find out about Jewish cultural contributions, holiday traditions, the difficult road to emancipation, outstanding individuals (eg Moses Mendelssohn, Levi Strauss) and the fates of ordinary people and families.

The Building

Libeskind's architectural masterpiece (which he titled *Between the Lines*) is essentially a 3D metaphor for the tortured history of the Jewish people. Its zigzag outline symbolises a broken Star of David; its silvery titanium-zinc walls are sharply angled, and instead of windows there are only small gashes piercing the building's gleaming facade.

The Axes

The building's visual allegory continues on the inside. Exhibits are accessed through an adjoining baroque structure that once housed the Prussian supreme court. A steep staircase descends to the museum basement where three intersecting walkways – called 'axes' – represent the fates of Jews during the Nazi years. The **Axis of Emigration** leads to a disorienting 'garden' of 49 tilted concrete columns; oleaster, a symbol of hope, sprouts from each. The **Axis of the Holocaust** ends in the tomblike 'void' that stands for the loss of Jewish life, culture and humanity in Europe. Only the **Axis of Continuity**, which represents

DON'T MISS...

- Axis of the Holocaust
- *Shalechet – Fallen Leaves* installation
- Moses Mendelssohn exhibit
- Art Vending Machine

PRACTICALITIES

- Jewish Museum
- Map p336
- ☎030-2599 3300
- www.jmberlin.de
- Lindenstrasse 9-14
- adult/concession €8/3
- 🕗10am-10pm Mon, to 8pm Tue-Sun, last admission 1hr before closing
- [S]Hallesches Tor, Kochstrasse

FURTHER INFORMATION

Budget at least two hours to visit the museum, plus extra time to go through the airport-style entrance security checks. For a more in-depth experience, rent an audioguide for €3. Several themed tours (€3) take place on Saturdays and Sundays, in German only.

Tickets to the Jewish Museum are also good for reduced admission on the same day and the following two days to the Berlinische Galerie (p155), located just 500m away.

TAKE A BREAK

For a refuelling stop, pop by the museum's **Cafe Schmus** (Map p336; ☑030-2579 6751; www.koflerkompanie.com; Lindenstrasse 9-14; dishes €5.50-8; ☺10am-10pm Mon, to 8pm Tue-Sun; ⓢKochstrasse, Hallesches Tor) for modern takes on traditional Jewish cuisine. Dishes are not kosher but don't feature pork or shellfish. On sunny days, the glass courtyard or the garden are pleasant relaxation spots.

the present and the future, leads to the actual exhibits, but it too is a cumbersome journey up a sloping walkway and several steep flights of stairs.

The Exhibit

The permanent exhibit portrays facets and milestones of German-Jewish life and culture through art, daily objects, photographs and letters, media stations and interactive displays. An entire section is dedicated to the philosopher Moses Mendelssohn (1729–86), who paved the way for the Emancipation Edict of 1812 that made Jews full citizens with equal rights and duties. Elsewhere you can learn about holiday traditions, what it means to live kosher, or how people such as composer Arnold Schönberg, writer Walter Benjamin or artist Max Liebermann influenced global culture from their Berlin base. The subject of anti-Semitism pops up throughout, culminating in the 'National Socialism' section. The final section deals with the revival of Jewish life in Germany and features an ingenious **'Art Vending Machine'** stocked with artworks by seven Jewish artists which reflect their interpretation of life in contemporary Berlin.

Art Installations

The Jewish Museum is peppered with art installations, of which Menashe Kadishman's **Shalechet – Fallen Leaves** is among the most poignant. More than 10,000 open-mouthed faces cut from rusty iron plates lie arbitrarily scattered on the floor in an ocean of silent screams. The haunting effect is exacerbated by the space itself, another cold and claustrophobic 'void'. Also note Dresden-born artist Via Lewandowsky's **Gallery of the Missing**, which consists of black glass sculptures erected near three of these voids. Each contains acoustic descriptions of missing or destroyed objects relating to German-Jewish culture, such as the *Encyclopaedia Judaica,* the completion of which came to a sudden halt in 1934.

Academy of the Jewish Museum

The academy across from the main museum, open since November 2012, houses the museum's archive, library and education department, but for general visitors is mostly of interest for its architecture. Another Libeskind design, the house-in-house concept consists of three inclined cubes with the first forming the entrance and leading to a central hall. From here two more wood-panelled cubes – tilted towards one another and intended to evoke Noah's Ark – house the auditorium and a library. The inner courtyard called 'Diaspora Garden' is a quiet place of reflection.

⊙ SIGHTS

⊙ Bergmannkiez

One of Berlin's most charismatic neighbourhoods, the Bergmannkiez in western Kreuzberg is bisected by the Bergmannstrasse, which is filled with cafes and quirky shops. Above it all 'soars' the Kreuzberg hill, Berlin's highest natural elevation and a wonderful summertime play zone.

JÜDISCHES MUSEUM   MUSEUM
See p153.

BERLINISCHE GALERIE   GALLERY
Map p336 (☑030-7890 2600; www.berlinischegalerie.de; Alte Jakobstrasse 124-128; adult/child/concession €8/free/5; ☉10am-6pm Wed-Mon; ⓈKochstrasse, Hallesches Tor) The Berlin Gallery, in a converted glass warehouse, is a superb spot for taking stock of what the local scene has been up to since 1870. Two intersecting floating stairways lead to the permanent collection, which is especially strong when it comes to Dada, New Objectivity, Eastern Europe avant-garde and art created during the city's division. Jüdisches Museum ticket-holders qualify for reduced admission on the same day and the following two days, and vice versa.

DEUTSCHES TECHNIKMUSEUM   MUSEUM
Map p336 (German Museum of Technology; ☑030-902 540; www.sdtb.de; Trebbiner Strasse 9; adult/concession €6/3, after 3pm under 18 free, audioguide €2/1; ☉9am-5.30pm Tue-Fri, 10am-6pm Sat & Sun; ♿; ⓈGleisdreieck) A roof-mounted 'candy bomber' (the plane used in the 1948 Berlin Airlift) is merely the overture to the hugely engaging German Museum of Technology. Fantastic for kids, this giant shrine to technology counts the world's first computer, an entire hall of vintage locomotives and extensive exhibits on aviation and navigation among its top attractions. At the adjacent **Science Center Spectrum** (Map p336; www.sdtb.de; Möckernstrasse 26; same ticket as Deutsches Technikmuseum; ☉9am-5.30pm Tue-Fri, 10am-6pm Sat & Sun; ⓈMöckernbrücke, Gleisdreieck) kids can participate in hands-on experiments.

PARK AM GLEISDREIECK   PARK
Map p336 (entrances incl cnr Obentrautstrasse & Möckernstrasse; ☉24hr; ⓈMöckernbrücke) FREE Berliners crave green open spaces, and this vast new park on a former railway junction is only the latest in a string of urban oases. A railway line still separates the sprawling grounds into the wide-open Westpark, with expansive lawns and play zones for kids, and the Ostpark, with a nature discovery area, a half-pipe, a little maple and oak forest and even an outdoor dance floor. Historic relics like tracks, signals and ramps are smoothly integrated throughout.

LUFTBRÜCKENDENKMAL   MEMORIAL
Map p336 (Berlin Airlift Memorial; Platz der Luftbrücke; ⓈPlatz der Luftbrücke) Nicknamed *Hungerharke* (Hunger Rake), the Berlin Airlift Memorial honours those who participated in keeping the city fed and free during the 1948 Berlin Blockade. A trio of spikes represents the three air corridors used by the Western Allies, while a plinth bears the names of the 79 people who died in this colossal effort.

VIKTORIAPARK   PARK
Map p336 (btwn Kreuzbergstrasse, Methfesselstrasse, Dudenstrasse & Katzbachstrasse; ⓈPlatz der Luftbrücke) Take a break in this unruly, rambling park draped over the 66m-high Kreuzberg hill, Berlin's highest natural elevation. It's home to a vineyard, a waterfall and – at the top – a pompous 19th-century Karl Friedrich Schinkel memorial commemorating Napoleon's 1815 defeat. In summer, locals arrive to chill, tan or have a beer at the Golgatha (p164) beer garden.

ALL ABOARD THE BADESCHIFF

Take an old river barge, fill it with water, moor it in the Spree and voila: **Badeschiff** (Map p332; ☑030-533 2030; www.arena-berlin.de; Eichenstrasse 4; summer adult/concession €5/3; ☉8am-midnight May-Sep, shorter hours in winter; ☐265, ⓈSchlesische Strasse, ⓇTreptower Park) – an artist-designed urban lifestyle pool that is the preferred swim-and-tan spot for Berlin cool kids. With music blaring, a sandy beach, wooden decks, lots of hot bods and a bar to fuel the fun, the vibe is distinctly 'Ibiza on the Spree'. Come early on scorching days as it's often filled to capacity by noon. Or show up for sunset and night-time parties or concerts. In winter, an eerily glowing plastic membrane covers the pool and a deliciously toasty chill zone is set up, including sauna and bar.

KREUZBERG & NEUKÖLLN SIGHTS

AN AVIATION LEGEND: TEMPELHOF AIRPORT

In Berlin history, Tempelhof Airport is a site of legend. British architect Norman Foster even called it 'the mother of all airports'. It was here in 1909 that aviation pioneer Orville Wright ran his first flight experiments, managing to keep his homemade flying machine in the air for a full minute. The first Zeppelin landed the same year and in 1926 Lufthansa's first scheduled flight left here for Zurich. The Nazis held massive rallies on the airfield and enlarged the smallish terminal into a massive semicircular compound that measures 1.23km from one end to the other. Designed by Ernst Sagebiel, it was constructed in only two years and is still one of the world's largest freestanding buildings. Despite its monumentalism, Sagebiel managed to inject some pleasing design features, especially in the grand art-deco-style departure hall.

After the war, the US Armed Forces took over the airport and expanded its facilities, installing a power plant, bowling alley and basketball court. In 1948–49 the airport saw its finest hours during the Berlin Airlift (p260). After Tegel Airport opened in 1975, passenger volume declined, and flight operations stopped in 2008 after much brouhaha and (initially) against the wishes of many Berliners. That sentiment changed dramatically when the airfield opened as a public **park** (Map p336; ☎030-2801 8162; www.tempelhoferfreiheit.de; enter via Oderstrasse, Tempelhofer Damm or Columbiadamm; 🕒sunrise to sunset; [S]Paradestrasse, Boddinstrasse, Leinestrasse), a wonderfully noncommercial, creative open-sky space where cyclists, bladers and kitesurfers whisk along the tarmac. Fun zones include the Luftgarten beer garden near Columbiadamm, barbecue areas, dog parks, an artsy minigolf course, art installations, abandoned aeroplanes and an urban gardening project.

In fact, this vast, untamed urban playground has by now become so intensely beloved by Berliners that plans by the city to build thousands of apartments, offices and a central library along its perimeter were thwarted in a referendum held in May 2014. The airport building hosts special events such as music festivals and trade fairs like the Bread & Butter fashion show. Two-hour **tours** (Map p336; ☎030-200 037 441; www.tempelhoferfreiheit.de; Platz der Luftbrücke; tours adult/concession €13/9; 🕒4pm Mon-Fri, 1pm Fri, 11am & 2pm Sat & Sun; [S]Platz der Luftbrücke) of both airport and airfield are available.

CHAMISSOPLATZ SQUARE

Map p336 ([S]Platz der Luftbrücke) On Saturday mornings, the entire neighbourhood turns out for Berlin's longest-running **organic farmers market** held on this pretty square framed by stately 19th-century townhouses. With cobbled streets, old-timey lanterns and even an octagonal pissoir, the entire square looks virtually unchanged a century on.

Kottbusser Tor & the Landwehrkanal

KÜNSTLERHAUS BETHANIEN GALLERY

Map p332 (☎030-616 9030; www.bethanien.de; Kottbusser Strasse 10; 🕒2-7pm Tue-Sun; [S]Kottbusser Tor, Schönleinstrasse) [FREE] Founded in 1975, this is an artistic sanctuary and creative cauldron for emerging artists from around the globe. In 2010 it moved into this former light-fixture factory where it maintains one of Germany's largest artist-in-residence programs. Exhibits showcase their work, as well as that of former residents and other artists.

KUNSTQUARTIER BETHANIEN ARTS CENTRE

Map p332 (www.kunstquartier-bethanien.de; Mariannenplatz 2; [S]Kottbusser Tor) This grand old hospital was designed by three students of Karl Friedrich Schinkel. The original pharmacy where poet Theodor Fontane worked in 1848–49 can be admired through a glass door (ground floor, turn right). Today, the complex harbours nearly three dozen art and cultural institutions, including the **Kunstraum Kreuzberg** gallery, as well as the 3 Schwestern restaurant.

FHXB FRIEDRICHSHAIN-KREUZBERG MUSEUM MUSEUM

Map p332 (☎030-5058 5233; www.kreuzberg-museum.de; Adalbertstrasse 95a; 🕒noon-6pm Wed-Sun; [S]Kottbusser Tor) [FREE] The ups and downs of one of Berlin's most colourful districts are chronicled in this converted red-brick factory. The permanent exhibit zeros in on such themes as Kreuzberg's radical legacy and how immigrants have shaped the area.

AUFBAU HAUS
BUILDING

Map p332 (www.aufbauhaus.de; Prinzenstrasse 85; S Moritzplatz) Injecting life into once drab and neglected Moritzplatz since 2011, the Aufbau Haus harbours a bright bouquet of creative and cultural ventures, led by the venerable namesake publishing house Aufbau Verlag, which also operates a non-mainstream theatre. The eclectic offerings include a bookshop, a gallery representing Roma and Sinti art, the Parker Bowles deli and the nightclub Prince Charles.

MUSEUM DER DINGE
MUSEUM

Map p332 (Museum of Things; ☑030-9210 6311; www.museumderdinge.de; Oranienstrasse 25; adult/concession €5/3; ☺noon-7pm Thu-Mon; S Kottbusser Tor) With its extensive assemblage of everyday items, this museum ostensibly traces German design history from the early 20th century to today but actually feels more like a cross between a cabinet of curiosities and a flea market. Alongside detergent boxes and cigarette cases are plenty of bizarre items, like a spherical washing machine, inflation money from 1923 and a swastika-adorned mug. The collection is based on the archive of the Deutscher Werkbund (German Work Federation), an association of artists, architects, designers and industrialists formed in 1907 to integrate traditional crafts and industrial mass-production techniques.

GRENZWACHTURM SCHLESISCHER BUSCH
HISTORIC SITE

Map p332 (☑030-5321 9658; www.flutgraben.org; Am Flutgraben 3; ☺1-5pm Sat & Sun May-Oct; S Schlesisches Tor, ℝ Treptower Park) East German guards, machine guns at the ready, used to keep an eye on the inner-city border and the infamous 'death strip' from the top of this grey concrete watchtower. The non-profit organisation Kunstfabrik uses the protected building as a project space.

◉ Neukölln

PUPPENTHEATER-MUSEUM BERLIN
MUSEUM

Map p332 (Puppet Theatre Museum; ☑030-687 8132; www.puppentheater-museum.de; Karl-Marx-Strasse 135, rear bldg; adult/child €3/2.50, shows €5; ☺9am-3pm Mon-Fri, 11am-4pm Sun; S Karl-Marx-Strasse) At this little museum, you'll enter a fantasy world inhabited by adorable hand puppets, marionettes, shadow puppets, stick figures and all manner of dolls, dragons and devils from around the world.

Many of them hit the stage singing and dancing during shows that enthral both the young and the young at heart.

RIXDORF
NEIGHBOURHOOD

Map p332 (Richardplatz; S Karl-Marx-Strasse, Neukölln) The contrast between the cacophonous Karl-Marx-Strasse and quiet Rixdorf, a tiny historic village centred on Richardplatz, seems almost surreal given that they're only steps apart. Weavers from Bohemia first settled here in the early 18th century and some of the original buildings still survive, including a **blacksmith** (Map p332; Richardplatz 24), a **farmhouse** (Map p332; Richardplatz 3a) and the 15th-century **Bethlehemskirche** (Map p332; Richardplatz 22). From U-Bahn station Karl-Marx-Strasse, go south on Karl-Marx-Strasse for about 300m, then turn left on Karl-Marx-Platz and continue for another 300m to Richardplatz.

KÖRNERPARK
GARDENS

(Schierker Strasse; ☺park 24hr, gallery noon-8pm Tue-Sun; S Neukölln, ℝ Neukölln) FREE This elegant sunken baroque garden comes with a secret: strolling past the flower beds and cascading fountain, you are actually standing in a reclaimed gravel pit! Ponder this as you sip a cuppa in the cafe, then check out the latest exhibit in the adjacent gallery. In summer you can join locals for free alfresco classical, jazz and world-music concerts. From U-/S-Bahn station Neukölln, follow Karl-Marx-Strasse north for 250m, turn left on Schierker Strasse and continue 125m to the park.

SCHLOSS BRITZ
PALACE

(☑030-6097 9230; www.schlossbritz.de; Alt-Britz 73; adult/concession €3/2; ☺11am-6pm Tue-Sun; S Parchimer Allee, then bus M46 to Fulhamer Allee) This 18th-century country estate, with its frilly neo-Renaissance facade and surrounding park, once served as the residence of Prussian ministers and high-ranking court officials. Today it's a nice place for strolls, picnics or summer concerts in the park.

✗ EATING

Kreuzberg has become one of Berlin's most exciting foodie districts, with some of the best eating done in neighbourhood restos, ethnic eateries and canalside cafes. Northern Neukölln is still more of a drinking and partying zone but with new eateries opening all the time that's changing fast.

🍴 Bergmannkiez

CURRY 36 GERMAN €

Map p336 (☎030-251 7368; www.curry36.de; Mehringdamm 36; snacks €2-6; 🕘9am-5am; [S]Mehringdamm) Day after day, night after night, a motley crowd – cops, cabbies, queens, office jockeys, savvy tourists etc – wait their turn at this top-ranked Currywurst purveyor that's been frying 'em up since 1981.

SEEROSE VEGETARIAN €

Map p332 (☎030-6981 5927; www.seerose-berlin.de; Körtestrasse 38; meals under €10; 🕘10am-midnight Mon-Sat, noon-11pm Sun; 🖉; [S]Südstern) Long before vegan and vegetarian became hip, there was Seerose. Though in a new location, it serves the same fresh, creative and completely animal-free nosh against a backdrop of classical music.

MASELLI ITALIAN €€

Map p336 (☎030-6900 4363; www.maselliristorante.de; Nostitzstrasse 49; 🕘5pm-midnight Tue-Sun; [S]Gneisenaustrasse) Modern and stylish without going overboard, Maselli showcases Pugliese cuisine from the heel of Italy. Flavours are rustic but complex and best sampled by ordering a parade of small plates such as *caciocavallo alla griglia* (grilled cheese) or *polipetti in umido* (stewed octopus).

TOMASA INTERNATIONAL €€

Map p336 (☎030-8100 9885; www.tomasa.de; Kreuzbergstrasse 62; lunch specials €5.50, mains €7-19; 🕘9am-1am Sun-Thu, to 2am Fri & Sat; 🖉👪; [S]Mehringdamm) It's not only breakfast that is a joy at this enchanting late-19th-century villa at the foot of the Viktoriapark. The menu also features inspired salads and vegetarian mains, *Flammekuche* (Alsatian pizza) and grilled meats. Kids can make new friends in the play room or the adjacent petting zoo.

VAN LOON INTERNATIONAL €€

Map p332 (☎030-692 6293; www.vanloon.de; Carl-Herz-Ufer 5; mains €10-23; 🕘9am-11pm; 🖉; [S]Prinzenstrasse) This retired Dutch cargo ship moored on the Landwehrkanal is perhaps best known for its fresh and smoked fish but is also a delightful greet-the-day spot, with sumptuous breakfast served on the wooden deck until 3pm. At night, candles and a crackling fire are conducive to romantic dinners. The menu changes daily and includes vegan options.

AUSTRIA AUSTRIAN €€

Map p336 (☎030-694 4440; www.austria-berlin.de; Bergmannstrasse 30; mains €13-19; 🕘6-11pm; [S]Gneisenaustrasse) Deer antlers and Romy Schneider preside over this hunting-lodge-style restaurant perfect for camping out with a baseball-glove-size veal schnitzel and a cold Kapsreiter beer. The rest of the menu will also be prized by carnivores with a big appetite. Thursday's suckling-pig special brings out local devotees in droves.

🍴 Kottbusser Tor & the Landwehrkanal

COCOLO RAMENBAR JAPANESE €

Map p332 (☎030-9833 9073; Paul-Lincke-Ufer 39-40; soups €7.50-9.50; 🕘noon-11pm Mon-Sat, 6-11pm Sun; [S]Kottbusser Tor) For the best noodle bar in Berlin, follow locals to this lantern-lit canalside charmer. Its hearty soups based on richly flavoured pork broth teem with homemade noodles and fresh vegetables. In fine weather, the terrace tables are most coveted.

MAROUSH LEBANESE €

Map p332 (☎030-6953 6171; www.maroush-berlin.de; Adalbertstrasse 93; sandwiches €2-2.50, platters €5-8; 🕘11am-2am; [S]Kottbusser Tor) This warm and woodsy hole in the wall is tailor-made for restoring balance to the brain with soulful felafel or *shawarma* paired with a glass of date juice or fresh mint tea.

TA'CABRÓN TAQUERÍA MEXICAN €

Map p332 (☎030-3266 2439; Skalitzer Strasse 60; dishes €3.50-7; 🕘1-11pm; [S]Schlesisches Tor) Joaquín Robredo's tiny outpost feeds fans with the kind of homemade food his mother used to make back home in Culiacán. Tacos, burritos and quesadillas bulge with such finger-lickin' fillings as *cochinita pibil* (spicy pulled pork) and chicken mole (chicken in chocolate-based sauce), while the salsa packs a respectable punch and the guacamole is silky smooth.

★**CAFE JACQUES** INTERNATIONAL €€

Map p332 (☎030 694 1048; Maybachufer 14; mains €12-20; 🕘6pm-late; [S]Schönleinstrasse) A favourite with off-duty chefs and local foodies, Jacques infallibly charms with flattering candlelight, arty-elegant decor, fantastic wine and uberfriendly staff. It's the perfect date spot but, quite frankly, you only have to be in love with good food to appreciate the French- and North African–

TREPTOW PARK & THE SOVIET WAR MEMORIAL

Southeast of Kreuzberg, the former East Berlin district of Treptow gets its character from the Spree River and two parks, the Treptower Park and the Plänterwald. Both are vast sweeps of expansive lawns, shady woods and tranquil riverfront and have been popular for chilling, tanning, picnicking, jogging or just strolling around for well over a century. In summer, Stern und Kreisschiffahrt (p293) operate cruises from landing docks just south of the Treptower Park S-Bahn station. A bit further south, you can scarf a sausage or swill a beer at **Zenner-Eierschale** (☑030-533 7370; www. eierschale-zenner.com; Alt-Treptow 14-17; mains €6-12; ☺10am-midnight; ⓡTreptower Park, ⓡPlänterwald), a historic restaurant and beer garden with an integrated Burger King. From the terrace, you'll have a lovely view of the **Insel der Jugend** (www.inselberlin.de; Alt-Treptow 6; ⓡPlänterwald, Treptower Park), a pint-sized island reached via a 1915 steel bridge that was the first of its kind in Germany. In summer there's a cafe, boat rentals, movie screenings, concerts and parties.

Nearby awaits Treptower Park's main sight: the gargantuan **Sowjetisches Ehrenmal Treptow** (Soviet War Memorial; Treptower Park; ☺24hr; ⓡTreptower Park) FREE, which stands above the graves of 5000 Soviet soldiers killed in the 1945 Battle of Berlin. Inaugurated in 1949, it's a bombastic and sobering testament to the immensity of Russia's wartime losses. Coming from the S-Bahn station, you'll first be greeted by a **statue of Mother Russia** grieving for her dead children. Beyond, two mighty walls fronted by soldiers kneeling in sorrow flank the gateway to the memorial itself; the red marble used here was supposedly scavenged from Hitler's ruined chancellery. Views open up to an enormous sunken lawn lined by **sarcophagi** representing the then 16 Soviet republics, each decorated with war scenes and Stalin quotations. The epic dramaturgy reaches a crescendo at the **mausoleum**, topped by a 13m statue of a Russian soldier clutching a child, his sword resting melodramatically on a shattered swastika. The socialist-realism mosaic within the plinth shows grateful Soviets honouring the fallen.

South of here, near the *Karpfenteich* (carp pond), is the **Archenhold Sternwarte** (☑030-536 063 719; www.sdtb.de; Alt-Treptow 1; exhibit adult/concession €2.50/2, tours €4/3; ☺exhibit 2-4.30pm Wed-Sun, tours 8pm Thu, 3pm Sat & Sun; ⓡPlänterwald), Germany's oldest astronomical observatory. It was here in 1915 that Albert Einstein gave his first public speech in Berlin about the theory of relativity. The observatory's pride and joy is its 21m-long refracting telescope, the longest in the world, built in 1896 by astronomer Friedrich Simon Archenhold. Demonstrations of this giant of the optical arts usually take place at 3pm Sunday. Exhibits in the foyer are a bit ho-hum but still impart fascinating nuggets about the planetary system, astronomy in general and the history of the observatory. Kids love having their picture taken next to a huge meteorite chunk.

Speaking of kids... Generations of East Germans still have fond memories of the Kulturpark Plänterwald, a small state-run amusement park created in 1969 and privatised and renamed **Spreepark Berlin** in 1990. Dwindling visitor numbers forced it into bankruptcy in 2001, leaving the Ferris wheel and other carousels standing still ever since. The grounds became off limits, which didn't stop urban adventurers from trespassing and frolicking among the abandoned dinos and dragons. Legal tours were eventually available until the city of Berlin purchased the lease for the land in March 2014, with plans to reanimate it as an amusement park. Stay tuned.

inspired blackboard menu. The cold appetiser platter is big enough for sharing, fish and meat are always tops and the pasta is homemade. Reservations essential.

★ **DEFNE**   TURKISH €€

Map p332 (☑030-8179 7111; www.defne-restaurant. de; Planufer 92c; mains €8-20; ☺4pm-1am Apr-Sep, 5pm-1am Oct-Mar; ⓢKottbusser Tor, Schönleinstrasse) If you thought Turkish cuisine stopped at the doner kebab, canalside Defne

will teach you otherwise. The appetiser platter alone elicits intense cravings, but inventive mains such as *ali nacik* (sliced lamb with puréed eggplant and yoghurt) also warrant repeat visits. Lovely summer terrace.

★ **HENNE**   GERMAN €€

Map p332 (☑030-614 7730; www.henne-berlin. de; Leuschnerdamm 25; half chicken €7.90; ☺6pm-midnight Tue-Sat, 5pm-midnight Sun; ⓢMoritzplatz) This Old Berlin institution

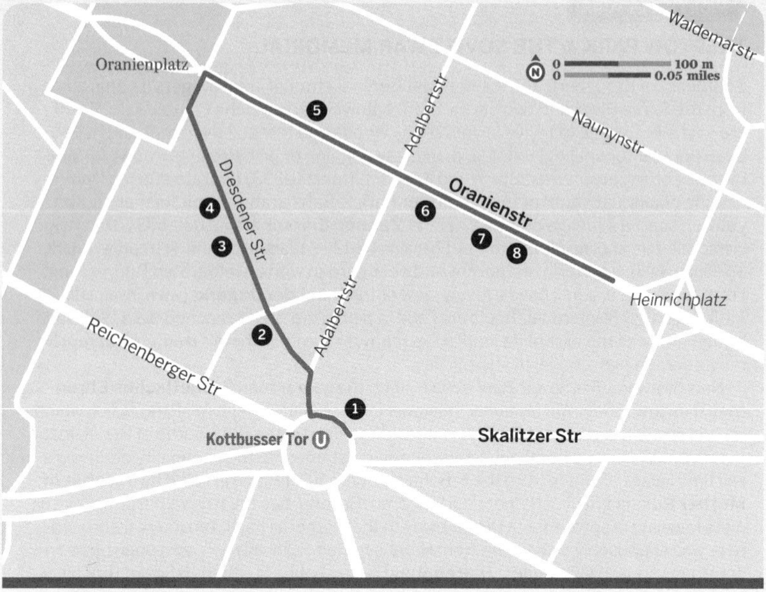

Local Life
Kotti Bar-Hop

Noisy, chaotic and sleepless, the area around Kottbusser Tor U-Bahn station (Kotti, for short) defiantly retains the alt feel that's defined it since the 1970s. More gritty than pretty, this beehive of snack shops, cafes, pubs and bars delivers some of the city's most hot-stepping night-time action and is tailor-made for bar-hopping.

1 Elevated Speakeasy

Behind a long steamed-up window front, eye level with the elevated U-Bahn tracks, **Monarch Bar** (Map p332; www.kottimonarch.de; Skalitzer Strasse 134; 🕒from 9pm Tue-Sat; [S]Kottbusser Tor) has an ingenious blend of trashy sophistication, an international crowd and danceable tunes beyond the mainstream. Enter via the signless steel door adjacent to the doner kebab shop east of the Kaiser's supermarket. Smoking OK.

2 Funky Salon

An old furniture store, **Möbel Olfe** (Map p332; www.moebel-olfe.de; Reichenberger Strasse 177; 🕒Tue-Sun; [S]Kottbusser Tor) has been recast as an always-busy drinking den with cheap libations and a friendly mixed crowd that goes predominantly gay on Thursdays. Watch out: the skeletons above the bar get downright trippy after a few Polish beers or vodkas. Enter via Dresdener Strasse. Smoking OK.

3 Grape Delights

Cosy **Otto Rink** (Map p332; www.ottorink.de; Dresdener Strasse 124; 🕒6pm-3am Mon-Sat; [S]Kottbusser Tor) is a favourite among local oenophiles who appreciate the casually intimate ambience and reasonable prices. The slate-covered bar hints at the owner's penchant for whites from the slate-rich soils of the Moselle region, although other German wines are also well represented, as are reds from France, Spain and South America.

4 '50s Cocktail Cave

Swish **Würgeengel** (Map p332; www.wuergeengel.de; Dresdener Strasse 122; 🕒from 7pm; [S]Kottbusser Tor) is a stylish art-deco-style bar with chandeliers and shiny black surfaces. It's always busy but especially so after the final credits roll at the adjacent Babylon cinema. The name pays homage to the surreal 1962 Buñuel movie *Exterminating Angel.* Smoking allowed.

❺ Luscious Lair

Tarted up nicely with vintage furniture, baroque wallpaper and whimsical wall art by Chin Chin, **Luzia** (Map p332; ☎030-8179 9958; Oranienstrasse 34; 🕓from noon till late; [S]Kottbusser Tor) draws eastern Kreuzberg's more sophisticated urban dwellers. Some punters have derided it as Mitte-goes-Kreuzberg but it's still a comfy spot with lighting that gives even pasty-faced hipsters a glow. Smokers' lounge.

❻ Burlesque Boite

The sassy glamour of the Golden Twenties gets a classy reboot at **Prinzipal** (Map p332; ☎030-6162 7326; www.prinzipal-kreuzberg.com; Oranienstrasse 178; 🕓8pm-5am Mon-Sat; [S]Kottbusser Tor), an apothecary-style burlesque bar right on funky Oranienstrasse. The menu features all the classics along with 10 signature cocktails named for famous booty-shakers (Date with Dita, Monroe's Kiss). On some nights, burlesque performers swing from the ceiling and a make-up artist turns patrons into vamps.

❼ Beer Heaven

A hetero-friendly gay hang-out, **Bierhimmel** (Map p332; ☎030-615 3122; www.bierhimmel-kreuzberg.de; Oranienstrasse 183; 🕓9am-1am Sun-Thu, to 3am Fri & Sat; 🚌Kottbusser Tor) draws the coffee-and-cake crowd but is also a relaxed place to get the evening into gear before moving on to saucier places like Roses.

❽ Den of Debauchery

A palace of camp and kitsch with pink furry walls Barbie would love, **Roses** (Map p332; ☎030-615 6570; Oranienstrasse 187; 🕓9pm-late; [S]Kottbusser Tor) is a glittery fixture on the lesbigay Kreuzberg booze circuit. Drinks are cheap and the bartenders pour with a generous elbow, making this a packed – and polysexual – pit stop during hard-party nights. Smoking OK.

operates on the KISS (keep it simple, stupid!) principle: milk-fed chicken spun on the rotisserie for moist yet crispy perfection. That's all it's been serving for over a century, alongside tangy potato and white cabbage salads. Eat in the garden or in the cosy 1907 dining room that's resisted the tides of time. Reservations essential.

MAX UND MORITZ GERMAN €€

Map p332 (☎030-6951 5911; www.maxundmoritz-berlin.de; Oranienstrasse 162; mains €9.50-17; 🕓5pm-midnight; [S]Moritzplatz) The patina of yesteryear hangs over this ode-to-old-school brewpub named for the Wilhelm Busch cartoon characters. Since 1902 it has packed hungry diners and drinkers into its rustic rooms for sudsy home brews and granny-style Berlin fare. A menu favourite is the *Kutschergulasch* (goulash cooked with beer).

3 SCHWESTERN INTERNATIONAL €€

Map p332 (☎030-600 318 600; www.3schwestern-berlin.de; Mariannenplatz 2; lunch specials €7.50, dinner mains €10-22; 🕓11am-11pm; [S]Kottbusser Tor) In a beautiful spot at the Kunstquartier Bethanien, a hospital turned art centre, the 'Three Sisters' is a dependable pit stop for fresh regional fare with Mediterranean and sometimes Middle Eastern touches. Weekday lunch specials, weekend breakfast and occasional postdining concerts.

HASIR KREUZBERG TURKISH €€

Map p332 (☎030-614 2373; www.hasir.de; Adalbertstrasse 10; mains €8-13; 🕓24hr; [S]Kottbusser Tor) Mehmed Aygün, the founder of this local minichain, is said to have invented the Berlin-style doner kebab back in 1971. Since 1984, this original branch has been packed at all hours with patrons lusting after grilled meats, velvety hummus, lentil soup and other tasty morsels. The adjacent branch specialises in grilled meats.

PARKER BOWLES INTERNATIONAL €€

Map p332 (☎030-5527 9099; www.parker-bowles.com; Prinzenstrasse 85d; mains lunch €7.50-9.50, dinner €12.50-23.50; 🕓9am-8pm Mon-Wed, to 4am Thu-Sat; [S]Moritzplatz) This smartly seductive neighbourhood bistro is usually packed to capacity. The draw is the sophisticated and creative fare, variously denoted 'vegan' or 'low carb' and also available in small portions perfect for grazers. Dinner stars are beef that's been smoked for 48 hours, Thai-basil-infused scampi and kohlrabi ravioli. Lunch options change daily.

KIMCHI PRINCESS
KOREAN €€

Map p332 (☎0163 458 0203; www.kimchiprincess.com; Skalitzer Strasse 36; mains lunch €7.50-9, dinner €11-24; ⏲noon-11.30pm; [S]Görlitzer Bahnhof) This Korean kitchen delivers legit classics like *bibimbap* (hot pot rice dish) and *kimchi jigae* (spicy pork and tofu stew) in a buzzy and trendy ambience. Carnivores should go for the barbecue, grilled at your table.

★VOLT
MODERN GERMAN €€€

Map p332 (☎030-338 402 320; www.restaurant-volt.de; Paul-Lincke-Ufer 21; mains €22-32, 4-course dinner €64; ⏲6pm-midnight Mon-Sat; [S]Görlitzer Bahnhof, Schönleinstrasse) The setting in a 1928 transformer station would be enough to seek out this culinary outpost of Matthias Geiss, crowned Berlin's most promising new chef in 2011. More drama awaits on the plates, where smartly combined regional meats, fish and vegetables put on an artful show in innovative yet honest-to-goodness ways.

HORVÁTH
AUSTRIAN €€€

Map p332 (☎030-6128 9992; www.restaurant-horvath.de; Paul-Lincke-Ufer 44a; 4-/8-/10-course menus €58/98/119; ⏲6-11pm Wed-Sun; [S]Kottbusser Tor) At his canalside restaurant, Michelin-starred Sebastian Frank performs culinary alchemy with Austrian classics, fearlessly combining textures, flavours and ingredients. To truly test his talents, order the 10-course small-plate dinner. Despite the fanciful cuisine, the ambience in the dining room remains relaxed; service is top-notch.

LA RACLETTE
FRENCH €€€

Map p332 (☎030-6128 7121; www.la-raclette.de; Lausitzer Strasse 34; mains €14-22; ⏲5-11pm Wed-Sun; [S]Görlitzer Bahnhof) With red-brick walls, a fireplace, good wine and delicious gooey raclette, this cosy hole in the wall owned by German soap actor Peer Kusmagk is so fantastically French you half expect to see the Eiffel Tower through the window.

🍴 Neukölln

HAMY CAFE
VIETNAMESE €

Map p332 (☎030-6162 5959; www.hamycafe.com; Hasenheide 10; mains €4.90; ⏲noon-11.30pm; [S]Hermannplatz) If you're in the mood for a quick *pho* (soup), glass noodle salad or fragrant curry, follow the locals to this low-key landmark. Clever spicing and mountains of fresh herbs give dishes a special kick, and even during busy times you can be in and out in half an hour or less.

CABSLAM - CALIFORNIA BREAKFAST SLAM
AMERICAN, VEGETARIAN €

Map p332 (☎030-686 9624; www.cabslam.com; Innstrasse 47; mains €6-9; ⏲10am-midnight; 📝; 🚌104, 167, [S]Rathaus Neukölln) It serves lunch and dinner too, but it's the breakfast that has 'slam' groupies in a headlock. If the prospect of fluffy maple-syrup-drenched pancakes, eggs Benedict with homemade hollandaise, or big fat huevos rancheros doesn't get you

LOCAL KNOWLEDGE

IN GASTRO HEAVEN: MARKTHALLE NEUN

As the name implies, **Markthalle Neun** (Map p332; ☎030-577 094 661; www.markthalle-neun.de; Eisenbahnstrasse 42/43; ⏲5-10pm Thu, 10am-6pm Fri & Sat; [S]Görlitzer Bahnhof) was the ninth (of a total of 14) market hall built in Berlin in the late 19th century. It did a roaring trade for decades but over time succumbed to competition from supermarkets, eventually becoming the haunt of tacky discount stores. In 2009 a group of dedicated locals banded together to revive the grand iron-beam-supported hall and turn it into an international food temple for local and regional producers. On market days (Friday and Saturday 10am to 6pm) you can stock up on apples from Brandenburg, baked goods from Neukölln and vegetables from a local urban garden collective. A few permanent kitchens provide sustenance such as sandwiches from the much-lauded Big Stuff Smoked BBQ and smoked fish from Glut & Späne.

The best time to visit is during **Street Food Thursday**, when the historic market hall gets mobbed by hungry hipsters keen on a first-class culinary journey at economy prices. From 5pm to 10pm, a changing cast of 20 or so amateur or semipro chefs set up their food stalls to serve delicious street food from all corners of the world. It's an exotic smorgasbord that might feature New Zealand meat pies, Taiwanese burgers, Argentine pulled pork sandwiches, Korean tacos or Vietnamese steamed pork buns. Pick your favourite, grab a seat at a communal table and chow down with a glass of wine or pint of Heidenpeters' Thirsty Lady pale ale, a yummy craft beer brewed right on the premises.

out of bed, what will? The coffee comes from local top microroastery Five Elephant.

MASANIELLO ITALIAN €

Map p332 (☎030-692 6657; www.masaniello.de; Hasenheide 20; pizzas €6-9.50; ⏰noon-midnight; [S]Hermannplatz) Tables are almost too small for the wagon-wheel-size certified Neapolitan pizzas tickled by wood fire at this low-key pizzeria, whose large and flowery terrace transports you to the Boot on a balmy summer night. A vegan fave is the Pizza Contadina with eggplant, peppers, zucchini, mushrooms and artichokes.

CITY CHICKEN MIDDLE EASTERN €

Map p332 (☎030-624 8600; Sonnenallee 59; chicken plates €5.50; ⏰11am-2am; [S]Rathaus Neukölln) There's chicken and then there's City Chicken, an absolute cult destination when it comes to juicy birds sent through the rotisserie for the perfect tan. Well worth ordering with the full complement of sides – especially the wicked garlic sauce and the creamy hummus.

BERLIN BURGER INTERNATIONAL AMERICAN €

Map p332 (☎0178 540 7409; www.berlinburgerinternational.com; Pannierstrasse 5; burgers €4.90-7.50; ⏰noon-midnight Mon-Thu, to 1am Fri, noon-10pm Sun; 🌿; [S]Hermannplatz) The guys at BBI know that size matters. At least when it comes to burgers: handmade, two-fisted, bulging and sloppy contenders. Get 'em with a side of chilli cheese fries and you'll be in fast-food heaven. Paper towel supplied. You'll need it.

SAUVAGE PALEOTHEK PALEO €€

Map p332 (☎030-5316 7547; www.sauvageberlin.com; Pflügerstrasse 25; small plates €4-9; ⏰6-11pm Tue-Sun; [S]Hermannplatz) You'll have a 'wild' time at Berlin's first paleo restaurant, which opened in 2011 in a former brothel and has since spawned a fancier cousin in Prenzlauer Berg (p195). The original branch is now a gastrobar where you can sample such paleo tapas as Cajun frog legs or halibut ceviche. It also doubles as a meeting place for the paleo community and offers a library and cooking courses (in English).

★EINS44 FRENCH €€€

Map p332 (☎030-6298 1212; www.eins44.com; Elbestrasse 28/29; mains lunch €6-8, dinner €22-25, 3-/4-/5-course meals €36/46/56; ⏰11am-4pm Mon-Fri, 7pm-midnight Wed-Sat; 🚌M41, 104, 167, [S]Hermannplatz) This fine-dining outpost in a late-19th-century distillery became a foodie favourite shortly after opening. It specialises in Franco-German cuisine that ranges beautifully from old-fashioned to postmodern. Metal lamps, tiles and heavy wooden tables create industrial charm enhanced by large black-and-white photos. Lunches are mellow, dinners trendy.

LAVANDERIA VECCHIA ITALIAN €€€

Map p332 (☎030-6272 2152; www.lavanderiavecchia.de; Flughafenstrasse 46; lunch mains from €5.50, 3 courses from €10, 13-course dinner menu €58; ⏰noon-2.30pm Tue-Fri, dinner Tue-Sat; [S]Boddinstrasse) For a first-class culinary journey around Italy, book a table amid the rustic-industrial charm of this historic laundry. Cooked-to-order antipasti courses are followed by pasta or risotto, a fishy or meaty main, and dessert. Dinner starts at 7.30pm and includes half a bottle of wine, plus water, coffee and digestif. Reservations essential. The entrance is from the courtyard. The restaurant has been so successful that the owners have opened a smaller a la carte restaurant called Lava in the front building.

🍴 Schlesisches Tor & the Spree

BURGERMEISTER AMERICAN €

Map p332 (www.burger-meister.de; Oberbaumstrasse 8; burgers €3-4.50; ⏰11am-3am Sun-Thu, to 4am Fri & Sat; [S]Schlesisches Tor) It's green, ornate, a century old and...it used to be a toilet. Now it's a burger joint beneath the elevated U-Bahn tracks. Don't fret, don't shudder: the plump all-beef patties are tops and great with fries and homemade dips such as peanut and mango curry.

FRÄULEIN FROST ICE CREAM €

Map p332 (Friedelstrasse 39; ⏰from 1pm Mon-Fri, from noon Sat & Sun; [S]Schönleinstrasse) Sure, it's got vanilla, strawberry and chocolate but ordering these would be missing the point of this popular parlour in northern Neukölln. Fräulein Frost is all about experimentation, as reflected in such courageous – and delectable – concoctions as GuZiMi, which stands for Gurke-Zitrone-Minze (cucumber-lemon-mint), or Graceland (peanut butter and banana).

BAR RAVAL SPANISH €€

Map p332 (☎030-5316 7954; www.barraval.de; Lübbener Strasse 1; tapas from €5; ⏰noon-midnight Apr-Sep, 6pm-midnight Oct-Mar; 📶; [S]Görlitzer Bahnhof) Forget folklore kitsch.

A 'ROYAL' GARDEN FOR THE PEOPLE

Urban gardening is taking root all over the world, and in Berlin a site on Moritzplatz that sat abandoned in the shadow of the Berlin Wall for over 60 years has been transformed into one of these delightful oases, the **Prinzessinnengarten** (Princess Gardens; Map p332; www.prinzessinnengarten.net; Prinzenstrasse 35-38, Moritzplatz; ☉11am-6pm Apr-Oct; ⑤Moritzplatz) FREE. In 2009, founders Robert Shaw and Marco Clausen inspired a small army of volunteers to help turn wasteland into an urban farm. It's become a bright and thriving space where volunteers get their hands dirty planting and tending more than 400 varieties of organic herbs, vegetables and flowers grown in raised compost beds without pesticides or fertilisers. If you want to help, simply show up between 3pm and 6pm on Thursdays or 11am and 2pm on Saturdays. Meals prepared with the crops are served in the **Gartencafe** (Map p332; mains €5-8; ☉lunch noon-3pm, dinner 6-10pm Apr-Oct, weather permitting; ⑤Moritzplatz). There are also workshops on gardening, beekeeping and sustainable living, and activities for kids. A flea market takes place every second Sunday of the month.

Although the gardens' long-term future is by no means certain, a 2012 attempt to sell the grounds to developers was thwarted thanks to the support of more than 30,000 people. Negotiations with the district government over a long-term lease were underway at the time of writing.

Owned by actor Daniel Brühl, this tapas bar is fit for the 21st century. The delish homemade Iberian morsels pack comfort and complexity, as do the seasonal specials and hand-picked wines. Great *patatas bravas* (spicy potatoes) and *sobrasada* (a pâté-style sausage from Mallorca).

FREISCHWIMMER
CAFE €€

Map p332 (☏030-6107 4309; www.freischwimmer-berlin.de; Vor dem Schlesischen Tor 2a; mains €8-17; ☉from noon Mon-Fri, from 10am Sat & Sun; ⑤Schlesisches Tor) In summertime, few places are more idyllic than this rustic 1930s boathouse turned canalside chill zone. The kitchen has of late stepped up its game and now offers meat and fish cooked to perfection on a lava rock grill, in addition to crisp salads and *Flammekuche*. It's also a popular Sunday brunch spot. Kayak and boat rentals available.

RESTAURANT RICHARD
FRENCH €€€

Map p332 (☏030-4920 7242; www.restaurant-richard.de; Köpenicker Strasse 174; 4-/5-course dinner €54/66, additional courses €10; ☉7pm-midnight Tue-Sat; ⑤Schlesische Strasse) Fine food solidly rooted in the French tradition is what's cooking in this extravagant space where oriental carpets meet concrete floors, bubble chandeliers dangle from a coffered ceiling and avant-garde artwork graces the walls. The arty concept transitions smoothly into such exquisitely orchestrated dishes as duck breast with caramelised sesame or trout with oyster Béarnaise.

SPINDLER & KLATT
FUSION €€€

Map p332 (☏030-319 881 860; www.spindlerklatt.com; Köpenicker Strasse 16-17; mains €14.50-29; ☉from 6pm Sun-Thu, from 8pm Fri & Sat; ⑤Schlesisches Tor) It's not the hot spot it once was, but summer nights on the riverside terrace are magical in this Prussian bread factory turned stylish nosh and party spot. Sit at a long table or lounge on a platform bed while tucking into seasonal fusion fare. The equally dazzling interior morphs into a dance club after 11pm on Friday and Saturday.

🍷 DRINKING & NIGHTLIFE

🍷 Bergmannkiez

GOLGATHA
BEER GARDEN

Map p336 (☏030-785 2453; www.golgatha-berlin.de; Dudenstrasse 48-64; ☉from 9am Apr-Sep; ⑤Platz der Luftbrücke; ⓡYorckstrasse) This classic beer garden right in Viktoriapark gets a changing cast of characters depending on where the hand of the clock points. Families invade in the daytime, lured by the adjacent adventure playground. Laid-back locals catch the day's final rays on the rooftop terrace, and wrinkle-free party folk arrive after 10pm when a DJ hits the decks.

LIMONADIER BAR
Map p336 (📞0170 601 2020; www.limonadier-barkultur.de; Nostitzstrasse 12; ⏰7pm-2am Mon-Thu, to 3am Fri & Sat, to 1am Sun; Ⓢ Mehringdamm) A portrait of Harry Johnson, whose 1882 bartenders' manual is still the profession's 'bible', keeps an eye on imbibers at this neighbourhood-adored cocktail cavern. The drinks menu shows tiki, apothecary and classic influences. Worth trying: locally inspired modern drinks like Berlin at Night or Kreuzberg Spritz. Happy hour: 7pm to 9pm.

GRETCHEN CLUB
Map p336 (📞030-2592 2702; www.gretchen-club.de; Obentrautstrasse 19-21; ⏰hours vary, always Fri & Sat; Ⓢ Mehringdamm, Hallesches Tor) Berlin's drum-and-bass temple has set up in the brick-vaulted stables of a former Prussian regiment, but Gretchen is no one-trick pony – other musical styles, from electro to indie and jazz, get plenty of play as well. Pleasant door, unpretentious crowd.

📍 Kottbusser Tor & the Landwehrkanal

⭐ SCHWARZE TRAUBE BAR
Map p332 (📞030-2313 5569; www.facebook.com/schwarzetraube1; Wrangelstrasse 24; ⏰7pm-5am; Ⓢ Görlitzer Bahnhof) Mixologist Atalay Aktas was Germany's Best Bartender of 2013 and this pint-sized drinking parlor is where he and his staff create their magic potions. Since there's no menu, each drink is calibrated to the taste and mood of each patron using premium spirits, expertise and a dash of psychology.

⭐ LOCKE MÜLLER BAR
Map p332 (📞0176 2430 2393; Spreewaldplatz 14; ⏰from 8pm; Ⓢ Görlitzer Bahnhof) This pretense-free, retro-chic bar is named for a fictitious local boxer whose image graces a wall along with dozens of old parking tickets. Dedicated bartenders are not shy about applying their classic training to boundary-pushing experimental riffs. Cocktails aren't the cheapest in Kreuzberg (€8) but are certainly among the best.

PRINCE CHARLES CLUB
Map p332 (📞030-200 950 933; www.princecharlesberlin.com; Prinzenstrasse 85f; ⏰from 7pm Wed-Sat; Ⓢ Moritzplatz) Prince Charles is a stylish mix of club and bar ensconced in a former pool and overlooked by a kitschy-cute fish mural. Electro, techno and house rule the turntables on weekends. The venue also hosts concerts, gay parties and the 'Burgers & Hip Hop' street food party. In summer the action spills into the courtyard.

SO36 CLUB
Map p332 (www.so36.de; Oranienstrasse 190; ⏰open most nights; Ⓢ Kottbusser Tor) This club began as an artist squat in the early 1970s and soon evolved into Berlin's seminal punk venue, known for wild concerts by the Dead Kennedys, Die Ärzte and Einstürzende Neubauten. The crowd depends on the night's program: electro party, punk concert, lesbigay tea dance, night flea market – anything goes at this long-time epicentre of Kreuzberg cool.

LERCHEN & EULEN BAR
Map p332 (www.lerchenundeulen.de; Pücklerstrasse 33; 📷; Ⓢ Kottbusser Tor) One of the friendliest bars in town, 'Larks & Owls' tantalises an international crowd with get-real fairtrade java, kick-ass cocktails and other beverages, all budget-priced amid cosy granny-style furnishings. Smoking allowed.

ANKERKLAUSE PUB
Map p332 (📞030-693 5649; www.ankerklause.de; Kottbusser Damm 104; ⏰from 4pm Mon, from 10am Tue-Sun; Ⓢ Schönleinstrasse) Ahoy there! This nautical kitsch tavern with an arse-kicking jukebox is anchored in an old harbour-master's shack; it's great for quaffing and waving to the boats puttering along the canal. Breakfast, burgers and snacks provide sustenance.

RITTER BUTZKE CLUB
Map p332 (www.ritterbutzke.de; Ritterstrasse 24; ⏰Fri & Sat; Ⓢ Moritzplatz) Although it cut its illegal underground roots long ago, Ritter Butzke has hardly gone mainstream. This labyrinthine fixture on the Berlin house and electro party circuit has three floors and lots of dark nooks and crannies inside a former lamp factory, which mostly wrinkle-free hotties invade for extended dance-floor jams.

📍 Neukölln

VIN AQUA VIN WINE BAR
Map p332 (📞030-9405 2886; www.vinaquavin.de; Weserstrasse 204; ⏰from 3pm; 🚌171, M29, Ⓢ Hermannplatz) Vin Aqua Vin does triple duty as a wine shop, bar and eatery amid a homey, anti-snob vibe that takes out the intimidation factor and means even hipsters drop by for a sip. Instead of expensive

LOCAL KNOWLEDGE

A TASTE OF BERLIN

In recent years a flurry of indie boutique-beverage purveyors has cropped up in Berlin. Look for them at kiosks, cool bars and pubs and even supermarkets. Here are our favourites:

Berliner Brandstifter Berliner Vincent Honrodt is the man behind the Brandstifter Korn, a premium schnapps that gets extraordinary smoothness from a seven-stage filtering process. It also makes a mean gin.

Fountain of Youth OK, this one is not really 'made' in Berlin but it comes courtesy of the ever-innovative Michelberger Hotel (p240) crew who teamed up with a coconut farm in Thailand to bring us this 100% fresh coconut water in jazzily retro cans. Health nuts drink it pure, the rest with a shot of vodka, rum or gin.

Original Berlin Cidre OBC is made from 100% German apples by two Berliners, Urs Breitenstein and Thomas Godel. There are three varieties: the dry OBC Strong, the sweet OBC Classic and the fruity OBC Rose.

Our/Berlin Made with Berlin water and German wheat, this smooth vodka is distilled in small batches at Flutgraben 2 on the Kreuzberg-Treptow border and sold in stylish bottles right there and in select shops.

Rixdorfer Fassbrause The name translates as 'keg brew' but the Fassbrause is actually a beer-coloured nonalcoholic drink made from fruit, spice and malt extract. It's produced by the Berliner Kindl Brauerei.

Wostok This Kreuzberg-made lemonade flavoured with eucalyptus and ginseng was inspired by a Soviet drink called Baikal.

trophy wines, owner Jan Kreuzinger pours and sells a shifting set of affordable boutique favorites, many from small German producers with a willingness to experiment.

KLUNKERKRANICH BAR

Map p332 (www.klunkerkranich.de; Karl-Marx-Strasse 66; 🕒10am-midnight Mon-Sat, noon-midnight Sun, weather permitting; [S]Rathaus Neukölln) Open only in the warmer months, Klunkerkranich (German for 'wattled crane') is a club-garden-beach-bar combo that 'roosts' amid potted plants on the rooftop parking deck of the Neukölln Arcaden shopping mall. It's a great place for sundowners while chilling to local DJs or bands.

DAS TIER BAR

Map p332 (Weserstrasse 42; 🕒7pm-2am; 🚌M41, [S]Rathaus Neukölln) Neukölln barflys with a hankering for finely crafted cocktails flock to this softly lit laid-back lair. With its top-shelf spirits, smartly clad pro bar staff and small-groups-only policy, the vibe feels grown-up for the area. Try its inspired take on the Old Fashioned, a smoky Blood and Sand or the Mescal Sour.

FUCHS & ELSTER CLUB

Map p332 (www.fuchsundelster.com; Weserstrasse 207; 🚌M41, M29, [S]Hermannplatz) The basement club Fuchs und Elster takes its name from two characters out of an East German children's TV show. DJs (and the occasional band) rock the comfy, low-ceilinged cellar with a broad musical spectrum ranging from soul, swing and funk to jazz and Eastern European pop-rock.

FREUDENREICH BAR, CLUB

Map p332 (Sonnenallee 67; 🕒from 7pm Tue-Sat; 🚌M41, [S]Rathaus Neukölln) Past the upstairs bar, a narrow spiral staircase descends to two small rooms and a heavy door beyond which electro dominates the musical spectrum, with occasional field trips to jazz, funk and rock. 'Pong Club' on Tuesdays and Thursdays brings table-tennis competitions and movie screenings.

LOFTUS HALL CLUB

Map p332 (www.loftushall.de; Maybachufer 48; 🕒Fri & Sat; 🚌M29, 171, [S]Hermannplatz) This '70s retro paradise in a former factory cafeteria takes its name from a haunted mansion in Ireland – you half expect a resident ghost to lurk behind the wood-panelled walls and heavy curtains. The sound system and music, however, are very up-to-the-minute, with next-gen DJ royalty helming the decks most nights.

BAR MARQUES
COCKTAIL BAR

Map p332 (⚡030-6162 5906; Graefestrasse 92; ⏱from 6pm; ⓢSchönleinstrasse) Maverick mixer Marcus Wolff presides over this tiny shrine to spirits tucked beneath the eponymous Spanish restaurant. Amid velvet sofas, antique tables and, in winter, a lustily roaring fireplace, the emphasis is on drinks that have written cocktail history – Martini to Negroni – served in stylish cut-glass tumblers.

SILVERFUTURE
BAR

Map p332 (⚡030-7563 4987; www.silverfuture. net; Weserstrasse 206; ⏱5pm-2am Sun-Thu, to 3am Fri & Sat; ⓢHermannplatz) Dressed in rich purple, burgundy and silver, this kitschy-campy queer pub collective is as charmingly over-the-top as a playful grope from your favourite drag queen. There's disco on the jukebox, Polish and Czech beer in the fridge and enough smiling faces for a dependably good time. Check the website for concerts or art shows.

SCHWUZ
CLUB

Map p332 (⚡030-5770 2270; www.schwuz. de; Rollbergstrasse 26; ⏱Wed-Sun; 🚌104,167, ⓢRathaus Neukölln) Despite its new location at the former Kindl brewery, this queer party institution is still the go-to spot for high-energy flirting and dancing. Different nightly parties draw different punters, so check what's on before heading out. Good for easing into the gay party scene.

📍 Schlesisches Tor & the Spree

⭐CLUB DER VISIONÄRE
CLUB

Map p332 (⚡030-6951 8942; www.clubdervision aere.com; Am Flutgraben 1; ⏱from 2pm Mon-Fri, from noon Sat & Sun; ⓢSchlesisches Tor, 🚆Trep-tower Park) It's cold beer, crispy pizza and fine electro at this summertime chill and party playground in an old canalside boat-shed. Park yourself beneath the weeping willows, stake out some turf on the upstairs deck or hit the teensy dance floor. At weekends party people invade. The toilets suck.

CHALET
CLUB

Map p332 (Vor dem Schlesischen Tor 3; ⓢSchle-sisches Tor, 🚆Treptower Park) This electro club in a handsome red-brick 19th-century customs house attracts a somewhat grown-up crowd. Open almost nightly, the venue is warmly decked out in vintage furnishings, patterned wallpaper and a coffered ceiling.

The enchanting garden with its lanterns, lily pond and old trees is perfect for taking a break from the beats.

HOPFENREICH
PUB

Map p332 (⚡030-8806 1080; Sorauer Strasse 31; ⏱from 4pm Tue-Sun; ⓢSchlesisches Tor) Berlin's first dedicated craft-beer bar pours up to 14 brews from Germany and the rest of the world. Its initial line-up included several IPAs, Belgian beer and a southern German pilsner, all served in a cosy pub near the Schlesische Strasse party mile.

WATERGATE
CLUB

Map p332 (⚡030-6128 0394; www.water-gate. de; Falckensteinstrasse 49a; ⏱from midnight Wed, Fri & Sat; ⓢSchlesisches Tor) For a short night's journey into day, check into this high-octane riverside club with two floors, panoramic windows and a floating terrace overlooking the Oberbaumbrücke and Universal Music. Top DJs keep electro-hungry hipsters hot and sweaty till way past sunrise. Long queues, tight door.

MADAME CLAUDE
PUB

Map p332 (⚡030-8411 0859; www.madame-claude.de; Lübbener Strasse 19; ⏱from 7pm; ⓢSchlesisches Tor, Görlitzer Bahnhof) Gravity is literally upended at this David Lynchian booze burrow where the furniture dangles from the ceiling and the moulding is on the floor. There are concerts, DJs and events every night, including eXperimondays, Wednesday's music quiz night and open-mike Sundays. The name honours a famous French prostitute – *très* apropos given the place's bordello pedigree.

SAN REMO UPFLAMÖR
PUB

Map p332 (⚡030-7407 3088; Falckensteinstrasse 46; ⏱from 10am; ⓢSchlesisches Tor) Gather your posse at this laid-back hang-out before heading a few doors down to the area's celebrated clubs and concert venues. The odd name, by the way, is a mash up of San Remo in Italy and Upflamör in southern Germany. Coffee and cake in the daytime, preferably while catching some rays on the footpath.

⭐ ENTERTAINMENT

ENGLISH THEATRE BERLIN
THEATRE

Map p336 (⚡030-691 1211; www.etberlin.de; Fidicinstrasse 40; ⓢPlatz der Luftbrücke) Berlin's oldest English-language theatre puts on a well-respected potpourri of in-house

SEX & THE CITY

The decadence of the Weimar years is alive and kicking in this city long known for its libertine leanings. While full-on sex clubs are most common in the gay scene (eg Lab.Oratory, p182), places such as Insomnia and the KitKatClub allow straights, gays, lesbians, the bi-curious and polysexuals to live out their fantasies in a safe if public setting. Surprisingly, there's nothing seedy about this, but you do need to check your inhibitions – and much of your clothing – at the door. If fetish gear doesn't do it for you, wear something sexy or glamorous; men can usually get away with tight pants and an open (or no) shirt. No normal street clothes, no tighty-whities. As elsewhere, couples and girl groups get in more easily than all-guy crews. And don't forget Mum's 'safe sex only' speech (condoms are usually provided).

Insomnia (www.insomnia-berlin.de; Alt-Tempelhof 17-19; 🕒Tue-Sun; [S]Alt-Tempelhof) A late-19th-century ballroom has been reincarnated as a classy playground of passion. Besides the dance floor and big-screen Andrew Blake porn, there are performances and various pleasure pits, including a whirlpool, a gynaecological chair and a bondage room. Saturday's Circus Bizarre is good for first-timers. The dress code is sexy, fetish or elegant black. During the week, more advanced players invade for special-themed sex and swinger parties that often require preregistration. Check the website for full details. The club is right outside U-Bahn station Alt-Tempelhof.

KitKatClub (Map p332; www.kitkatclub.de; Köpenicker Strasse 76, enter via Brückenstrasse; 🕒Fri-Sun; [S]Heinrich-Heine-Strasse) This 'kitty' is naughty and sexy, raucous and decadent, listens to techno and house, and fancies leather and lace, vinyl and whips. It hides out at Sage with its four dance floors, shimmering pools and fire-breathing dragon. On weekends, the party never stops, starting with the classic Carneball Bizarre on Saturday and continuing to midmorning Monday. The dress code varies; usually a combination of fetish, leather, uniforms, latex, costumes, Goth, evening dresses, glamour, or an extravagant outfit of any type. No dress code on Sunday.

Club Culture Houze (Map p332; ☎030-6170 9669; www.club-culture-houze.de; Görlitzer Strasse 71; 🕒from 7pm Mon, from 8pm Wed-Sat; [S]Görlitzer Bahnhof) Fetishistas of all sexual persuasions are welcome to get in on the action at this playground for advanced sexual experimentation. Gay only on Monday and Friday, polysexual on Wednesdays, Thursdays and Sundays. High kink factor.

productions, plays by international visiting troupes, concerts, comedy, dance and cabaret by local performers. It's located in a former-brewery-turned-artist-complex and shares space with Theater Thikwa, featuring actors with and without disabilities.

YORCKSCHLÖSSCHEN — LIVE MUSIC

Map p336 (☎030-215 8070; www.yorckschloesschen.de; Yorckstrasse 15; 🕒5pm-3am Mon-Sat, from 10am Sun; [S]Mehringdamm) Cosy and knick-knack-laden, this Kreuzberg institution has plied an all-ages, all-comers crowd of jazz and blues lovers with tunes and booze for over 30 years. Toe-tapping bands invade several times a week, but there's also a pool table, a beer garden for chilling, local beer on tap and European soul food served till 1am. Jazz brunch on Sundays.

HEBBEL AM UFER — THEATRE

Map p336 (HAU; ☎030-2590 0427; www.hebbel-am-ufer.de) A pack of pit bulls mills about the seats while the audience gathers on the stage. An upside-down world? No, just another performance at Hebbel am Ufer, one of Germany's most avant-garde, groundbreaking and adventurous theatres. Performances are held in three venues: **Hau 1** (Map p336; Stresemannstrasse 29; [S]Möckernbrücke, [S]Hallesches Tor), **Hau 2** (Map p336; Hallesches Ufer 32; [S]Möckernbrücke, [S]Hallesches Tor) and **Hau 3** (Map p336; Tempelhofer Ufer 10; [S]Möckernbrücke, [S]Hallesches Tor).

BALLHAUS NAUNYNSTRASSE — THEATRE

Map p332 (☎030-7545 3725; www.ballhausnaunynstrasse.de; Naunynstrasse 27; [S]Kottbusser Tor) This fringe theatre in a repurposed 19th-century ballroom presents cutting-edge and often provocative intercultural plays around the issues of migration and integration.

NEUKÖLLNER OPER — PERFORMING ARTS

Map p332 (☎tickets 030-6889 0777; www.neukoellneroper.de; Karl-Marx-Strasse 131-133;

[S]Karl-Marx-Strasse) Neukölln's refurbished prewar ballroom has an actively anti-elitist repertoire ranging from intelligent musical theatre to original productions and experimental interpretations of classics. Many pick up on contemporary themes or topics relevant to Berlin and some are suitable for non-German speakers.

MAGNET CLUB LIVE MUSIC

Map p332 (www.magnet-club.de; Falckensteinstrasse 48; [S]Schlesisches Tor) This indie and alt-sound bastion is known for bookers with an astronomer's ability to detect stars in the making. After the last riff, the mostly student-age crowd hits the dance floor to – depending on the night – Britpop, indietronics, neodisco, rock or punk.

LIDO LIVE MUSIC

Map p332 (☎030-6956 6840; www.lido-berlin.de; Cuvrystrasse 7; [S]Schlesisches Tor) A 1950s cinema has been recycled into a rock-indie-electro-pop mecca with mosh-pit electricity and a crowd that cares more about the music than about looking good. Global DJs and talented upwardly mobile live noise-makers pull in the punters. Holds legendary Balkanbeats parties every few weeks.

WHITE TRASH FAST FOOD LIVE MUSIC

Map p332 (☎030-5034 8668; www.whitetrash-fastfood.com; Flutgraben 2; [S]Schlesische Strasse, 🚆Treptower Park) Displaced by skyrocketing rent, this heavily ironic den of burgers, booze and bands has decamped from posh Prenzlauer Berg to friendlier Kreuzberg pastures. Owner Wally has imported not only his greatest hits menu but also the vaunted tattoo parlour and a booking policy that favours off-the-radar artists. New: the apocalyptic beer garden with barbecue pit.

AUSTER CLUB LIVE MUSIC

Map p332 (☎030-611 3302; www.auster-club.com; Pücklerstrasse 34; 🕐hours vary, usually Fri & Sat; [S]Görlitzer Bahnhof) With its L-shaped bar and leather sofas, this dimly lit, living-room-size cellar club exudes sensuous noir flair vaguely reminiscent of 1940s American jazz clubs. The music too takes punters on an eclectic journey through past decades – '20s jazz to '60s psychedelic soul, '70s punk and '80s pop. Live concerts are followed by DJ parties.

BII NUU LIVE MUSIC

Map p332 (☎030-6956 6840; www.bi-nuu.de; Im Schlesischen Tor; [S]Schlesisches Tor) This smallish, frill-free venue, in the catacombs below the U-Bahn station Schlesisches Tor, presents gigs by below-the-radar musicians, rap competitions and '90s flashback parties.

WILD AT HEART LIVE MUSIC

Map p332 (☎030-611 9231; www.wildatheartberlin.de; Wiener Strasse 20; 🕐from 8pm; [S]Görlitzer Bahnhof) Named after a David Lynch road movie, this kitsch-cool dive with blood-red walls, tiki gods and Elvis paraphernalia hammers home punk, ska, surf-rock and rockabilly. Touring bands, including acts such as Girlschool and Dick Dale, bring in the tattooed set nightly. It's really, REALLY loud, so if your ears need a break, head to the tiki-themed restaurant-bar next door.

🛍 SHOPPING

★ANOTHER COUNTRY BOOKS

Map p336 (☎030-6940 1160; www.anothercountry.de; Riemannstrasse 7; 🕐2-8pm Mon, 11am-8pm Tue-Fri, noon-6pm Sat; [S]Gneisenaustrasse) Run by the eccentric Sophie Raphaeline, this nonprofit boho outfit is really more a library and (countercultural) salon than a bookshop. Pick a tome from around 20,000 used English-language books – classic lit to science fiction – and, if you want, sell it back, minus a €1.50 borrowing fee. Also hosts an English Filmclub (9pm Tuesday) and dinners (8pm Friday).

★VOOSTORE FASHION, ACCESSORIES

Map p332 (☎030-6165 1119; www.vooberlin.com; Oranienstrasse 24; 🕐11am-8pm Mon-Sat; [S]Kottbusser Tor) Kreuzberg's first concept store opened in an old backyard locksmith shop off gritty Oranienstrasse, stocking style-forward designer threads and accessories by such crave-worthy labels as Acne, Soulland, Kenzo and Carven and dozens more along with tightly curated books, gadgets, mags and spirits.

★TÜRKENMARKT MARKET

Map p332 (Turkish Market; www.tuerkenmarkt.de; Maybachufer; 🕐11am-6.30pm Tue & Fri; [S]Schönleinstrasse, Kottbusser Tor) Berlin goes Bosphorus at this lively canalside market where thrifty hipsters mix it up with Turkish-Germans and pram-pushing mothers. Stock up on fragrant olives, creamy cheese spreads, crusty flatbreads and mountains of fruit and vegetables, all at bargain prices. In good weather, a small crowd gathers for impromptu concerts towards the eastern end of the strip.

MARHEINEKE MARKTHALLE FOOD

Map p336 (www.meine-markthalle.de; Marheinekeplatz; ⏲8am-8pm Mon-Fri, to 6pm Sat; [S]Gneisenaustrasse) After substantial renovations, this historic market hall has traded its grungy 19th-century charm for bright modern digs. It's like a giant deli, where vendors ply everything from organic sausage to handmade cheese, artisanal honey and other delicious bounty, both local and international. Snack stands feed tummy pangs.

COLOURS VINTAGE

Map p336 (☎030-694 3348; www.kleidermarkt.de; Bergmannstrasse 102, 1st fl; ⏲11am-7pm Mon-Fri, noon-7pm Sat; [S]Mehringdamm) This huge, light-filled loft has great used clothes going back to the 1960s for both men and women, plus a smaller selection of new street- and club-wear threads. Items are clean, in good condition and priced by the kilo (€18, 30% discount during happy hour, 11am to 3pm Tuesdays). The entrance is via the courtyard.

SPACE HALL MUSIC

Map p336 (☎030-694 7664; www.spacehall.de; Zossener Strasse 33; ⏲11am-8pm Mon-Wed & Sat, to 10pm Thu & Fri; [S]Gneisenaustrasse) This galaxy for electronic-music gurus has four floors filled with everything from acid to techno by way of drum and bass, neotrance, dubstep and whatever other genres take your fancy, both back stock and new stuff. Alas, it's not terribly well organised but pack a little patience and you'll be fine.

UVR CONNECTED FASHION

Map p332 (☎030-6981 4350; www.uvr-connected.de; Oranienstrasse 36; ⏲11am-8pm Mon-Sat; [S]Kottbusser Tor, Moritzplatz) This huge space is the flagship store of this Berlin label but also stocks the gamut of other 'it' brands like Bench, Ben Sherman, Minimum and Selected. Plenty of accessories too. There are two more branches in **Schöneberg** (☎030-2196 2284; Goltzstrasse 40a; [S]Eisenacher Strasse) and **Friedrichshain** (Map p330; ☎030-2757 1498; Gärtnerstrasse 5; ⏲11am-8pm Mon-Sat; [S]Samariterstrasse).

HARD WAX MUSIC

Map p332 (☎030-6113 0111; www.hardwax.com; Paul-Lincke-Ufer 44a, 3rd fl, door A, 2nd courtyard; ⏲noon-8pm Mon-Sat; [S]Kottbusser Tor) This well-hidden outpost has been on the cutting edge of electronic music for about two decades and is a must-stop for fans of techno, house, minimal, dubstep and whatever permutation comes along next.

UKO FASHION FASHION

Map p332 (☎030-693 8116; www.uko-fashion.de; Oranienstrasse 201; ⏲11am-8pm Mon-Fri, to 4pm Sat; [S]Görlitzer Bahnhof) High quality at low prices is the magic formula that has garnered this uncluttered clothing store a loyal clientele.

NOWKOELLN FLOWMARKT MARKET

Map p332 (www.nowkoelln.de; Maybachufer; ⏲10am-6pm 2nd & 4th Sun of month; [S]Kottbusser Tor, Schönleinstrasse) Less overrun than many other Berlin flea markets, the hipster-heavy Flowmarkt sets up twice monthly along the scenic Landwehrkanal and delivers second-hand bargains galore along with handmade threads and jewellery. It's seasonal, so check the website for dates.

SAMEHEADS FASHION

Map p332 (☎030-7012 1060; www.sameheads.com; Richardstrasse 10; ⏲2pm-late Tue-Sat; [S]Karl-Marx-Strasse) The living room of Neukölln hipsters, Sameheads is all over the place: it's a shop/gallery/bar/party space as well as soapbox for budding talent of all stripes. Aside from stocking out-there fashion, art and music, it hosts live shows at 8pm on Friday and Saturday and also operates Radio Rixdorf, which streams live during opening hours.

SING BLACKBIRD VINTAGE

Map p332 (☎030-5484 5051; Sanderstrasse 11; ⏲noon-7pm Mon-Sat; 📶; [S]Schönleinstrasse) Is it a store? Or a cafe? In fact, this blackbird sings its song for lovers of vintage clothing *and* fabulous homemade cakes and locally roasted java. Browse racks of neatly colour-sorted clothing (including designer labels) from the '70s to the '90s, then revel in your purchases over a steamy cuppa and homemade cakes.

KILLERBEAST FASHION

Map p332 (☎030-9926 0319; www.killerbeast.de; Schlesische Strasse 31; ⏲3-8pm Mon, 1-8pm Tue-Fri, 1-5pm Sat; [S]Schlesisches Tor) 'Kill uniformity' is the motto of this boutique where Claudia and her colleagues have made new clothes from old ones long before 'up-cycling' entered the urban dictionary. No two pieces are alike and prices are very reasonable. There's even a line for kids.

Friedrichshain

BOXHAGENER PLATZ | NORTH KIEZ | REVALER STRASSE | OSTKREUZ | WESTERN FRIEDRICHSHAIN

Neighbourhood Top Five

❶ Confronting the ghosts of the Cold War at the world's longest outdoor artwork, the **East Side Gallery** (p173).

❷ Partying till sunrise at Suicide Circus or one of the many other rough-around-the-edges bars and clubs of the **RAW Gelände** (p174).

❸ Shuddering at the brutality and arbitrariness of East Germany's judicial system on a tour of the **Stasi Prison** (p176).

❹ Marvelling at the bombastic socialist architecture of **Karl-Marx-Allee** (p174), then learning the story behind it at **Café Sybille** (p175).

❺ Shopping at the Sunday **flea market** (p182) on Boxhagener Platz, followed by brunch in a nearby cafe.

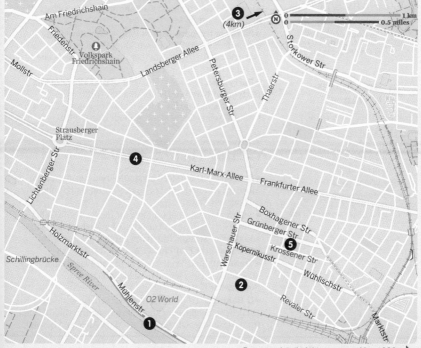

For more detail of this area, see Map p330 ➡

Lonely Planet's Top Tip

Enjoy bird's-eye views of Karl-Marx-Allee from the rooftop above Café Sibylle (p175), then ask staff about renting the audio tour by **Stadt im Ohr** (www.stadt-im -ohr.de; €9) to peel away the layers of Friedrichshain on a self-guided 2.5km walk culminating at Kaufbar (p179).

✗ Best Places to Eat

➡ Schneeweiss (p178)
➡ Spätzle & Knödel (p177)
➡ Lisboa Bar (p178)
➡ Mio Matto (p179)

For reviews, see p177 ➡

☕ Best Places to Drink

➡ Antlered Bunny (p179)
➡ Hops & Barley (p179)
➡ Chapel Bar (p181)
➡ Place Clichy (p181)

For reviews, see p179 ➡

☕ Best Places to Dance

➡ Suicide Circus (p180)
➡ Berghain/Panorama Bar (p181)
➡ Salon zur Wilden Renate (p181)
➡ Sisyphos (p180)
➡ ://about blank (p181)

For reviews, see p179 ➡

Explore: Friedrichshain

Rents may be rising, gentrification unstoppable and families multiplying but, for now, Friedrichshain, once in the former East Berlin, is still largely the domain of the young and free-spirited, students, artists and eccentrics. There are few standout sights, but the web of boutique- and cafe-lined streets will repay those happy to simply wander and soak up the district's multilayered character. Daytime diversions include taking in the socialist vibe on Karl-Marx-Allee, revelling in postreunification euphoria at the East Side Gallery or blowing your budget in sassy urban boutiques. Relax in sprawling Volkspark Friedrichshain or enjoy a lazy lunch at a comfy cafe.

At night Friedrichshain truly comes into its own. The district still celebrates its underground-punk-squatter roots in the industrial bars and clubs along Revaler Strasse and around the Ostkreuz S-Bahn station. Steps away, Simon-Dach-Strasse is a bar-stumbling zone where the young and the restless drink and dance with all the mad exuberance of a stag party. In the small hours, many will move on and hit a dance floor or, by the grace of the door staff, drift off into the utopia of Berghain/Panorama Bar.

Local Life

➡**Marketeering** Forage for vintage finds at flea markets on Boxhagener Platz (p182), at the RAW Flohmarkt (p182) and at Ostbahnhof (p182) – urban archaeology at its finest.

➡**Picnic in the park** Berlin's long summer evenings are perfect for chilling in rambling Volkspark Friedrichshain (p174), whether it involves a barbecue or sunset with a six-pack.

➡**Partytown** Become the master of the lost weekend, partying at Berghain/Panorama Bar (p181) or less hyped – though no less fun – clubs like Suicide Circus (p180), Cassiopeia (p181) or ://about blank (p181).

Getting There & Away

➡**Bus** Take bus 200 for Volkspark Friedrichshain from Mitte (eg Alexanderplatz); bus 240 from Ostbahnhof to Boxhagener Platz.

➡**S-Bahn** Ostbahnhof is handy for the East Side Gallery; Warschauer Strasse and Ostkreuz for Boxhagener Platz and Revaler Strasse. Ringbahn (circle line) trains S41 and S42 stop at Frankfurter Allee and Ostkreuz.

➡**Tram** M10 links Prenzlauer Berg and Warschauer Strasse; M13 runs from Warschauer Strasse to Boxhagener Platz.

➡**U-Bahn** The U1 links Warschauer Strasse with Kreuzberg, Schöneberg and Charlottenburg; the U5 runs from Alexanderplatz down Karl-Marx-Allee and beyond.

TOP SIGHT
EAST SIDE GALLERY

The year was 1989. After 28 years, the Berlin Wall, that grim divider of humanity, finally met its maker. Most of it was quickly dismantled, but along Mühlenstrasse, paralleling the Spree, a 1.3km stretch between Oberbaumbrücke and Ostbahnhof became the East Side Gallery, the world's largest open-air mural collection. In more than 100 paintings, dozens of artists from 20 countries translated the era's global euphoria and optimism into a mix of political statements, drug-induced musings and truly artistic visions.

Time, taggers and tourists getting a kick out of signing their favourite picture took their toll over the years. In 2009 the entire thing got a makeover, a process accompanied by controversy since some artists considered the €3000 honorarium too low. In the end, all but six agreed to redo their work.

Alas, the East Side Gallery is once again under threat, this time from property developers. It has already lost ground: in 2006 a 45m section was taken down to create a plaza and boat landing docks for the O2 World arena. The planned removal of another section, to create direct access to the Spree for the future residents of a 63m-high residential tower being constructed by a former Stasi informer, led to large-scale protests in 2013 that even inspired David Hasselhoff to join the fight. In the end, a 6m section was removed.

Check out our list of Top Five murals on p175.

DON'T MISS...

➡ Taking a picture in front of your favourite mural

➡ Sunset drinks on the riverside lawn

PRACTICALITIES

➡ Map p330

➡ www.eastside gallery-berlin.de

➡ Mühlenstrasse btwn Oberbaumbrücke & Ostbahnhof

➡ ⏲24hr

➡ Ⓢ Warschauer Strasse, Ⓡ Ostbahnhof, Warschauer Strasse

◉ SIGHTS

EAST SIDE GALLERY   HISTORIC SITE
See p173.

BOXHAGENER PLATZ   SQUARE
Map p330 (⬚240, Ⓢ Samariterstrasse, Warschauer Strasse, Ⓡ Warschauer Strasse) The heart of Friedrichshain, Boxhagener Platz is a lovely, leafy square with benches and a playground. It's framed by restored 19th-century buildings harbouring boho cafes and shabby-chic boutiques. The area is busiest during the Saturday farmers market and on Sundays when a flea market (p182) brings in folks from all over town.

RAW GELÄNDE   ARTS CENTRE
Map p330 (along Revaler Strasse; Ⓢ Warschauer Strasse, Ⓡ Warschauer Strasse, Ostkreuz) The postindustrial jumble of derelict buildings along Revaler Strasse is one of the last alternative compounds in central Berlin. In its earlier life it was a train-repair station, founded in 1867 as the 'Reichsbahn-Ausbesserungs-Werk' (RAW for short) and in operation until 1994. Since 1999, the graffiti-slathered grounds have been

a thriving off-beat sociocultural centre offering workspace for artists and creatives of all stripes along with clubs and bars, an indoor skate park and – in summer – a bunker-turned-climbing-wall with attached beer garden and outdoor cinema. Flea market (p182) on Sundays.

URBAN SPREE   ARTS CENTRE
Map p330 (www.urbanspree.com; Revaler Strasse 99; Ⓢ Warschauer Strasse, Ⓡ Warschauer Strasse) This artistic collective and grassroots gallery for street art, photography and urban art is a top stop on the RAW compound along Revaler Strasse. Its main facade is a changing canvas of top street artists, including Nunca, Os Gemeos and M-City. Beer garden, food truck and lots of events (parties, markets, workshops), especially in summer.

KARL-MARX-ALLEE   STREET
Map p330 (Ⓢ Strausberger Platz, Weberwiese, Frankfurter Tor) It's easy to feel like Gulliver in the Land of Brobdingnag when walking down monumental Karl-Marx-Allee (KMA), one of Berlin's most impressive GDR-era relics. Built between 1952 and 1960, the

---

◉ TOP SIGHT
VOLKSPARK FRIEDRICHSHAIN

Berlin's oldest public park has provided relief from urbanity since 1840, but has been hilly only since the late 1940s when wartime debris was piled here to create two 'mountains' – **Mont Klamott** is the taller, at 78m. Diversions include lawns, tennis courts, beer gardens and outdoor cinema **Freiluftkino Friedrichshain** (☎030-2936 1629; www.freiluftkino-berlin.de; Volkspark Friedrichshain; tickets €6.50; ⏱ daily mid-May–mid-Sep). Kids in tow? Head for the themed playgrounds and enchanting 1913 **Märchenbrunnen**, where frogs and turtles are flanked by Cinderella, Snow White and other Brothers Grimm stars.

Or visit communist-era memorials: along Friedenstrasse, the **Denkmal der Spanienkämpfer** pays respect to the German members of the International Brigades who died in the Spanish Civil War. The **Friedhof der Märzgefallenen** (☎030-2147 2723; www.friedhof-der-maerzgefallenen.de; cnr Ernst-Zinna-Weg & Landsberger Allee; ⏱ exhibit 10am-6pm; ⬚240, Ⓡ M5, M6, M8) is a cemetery for the victims of the revolutionary riots in March 1848, and the **Denkmal des Polnischen Soldaten und des deutschen Antifaschisten** (cnr Virchowstrasse & Margarete-Sommer-Strasse) memorial honours the joint fight of Polish soldiers and German resistance against the Nazis.

DON'T MISS...
➡ Märchenbrunnen
➡ Picnic on Mont Klamott
➡ Refreshments at Cafe Schönbrunn (p178)
➡ Alfresco movies

PRACTICALITIES
➡ Map p330
➡ bounded by Am Friedrichshain, Friedenstrasse, Danziger Strasse & Landsberger Allee
➡ ⬚200, Ⓢ Schillingstrasse, Ⓡ M5, M6, M8 & M10

TOP FIVE EAST SIDE GALLERY MURALS

You'll most likely find your own favourite among the 100 or so murals, but here's our take:

It Happened in November (Kani Alavi) A wave of people being squeezed through a breached Wall in a metaphorical rebirth reflects Alavi's recollection of the events of 9 November 1989. Note the different expressions on the faces, ranging from hope, joy and euphoria to disbelief and fear.

Test the Rest (Birgit Kinder) Another shutterbug favourite is Kinder's painting of a GDR-era Trabant car (known as a Trabi) bursting through the Wall with the licence plate reading 'November 9, 1989'. Originally called 'Test the Best', the artist renamed her work after the image's 2009 restoration.

Hommage to the Young Generation (Thierry Noir) This Berlin-based French artist has done work for Wim Wenders and U2, but he's most famous for these cartoon-like heads. Naive, simple and boldly coloured, they symbolise the new-found freedom following the Wall's collapse.

Detour to the Japanese Sector (Thomas Klingenstein) Born in East Berlin, Klingenstein spent time in a Stasi prison for dissent before being extradited to West Germany in 1980. This mural was inspired by his childhood love for Japan, where he ended up living from 1984 to the mid-'90s.

My God, Help Me Survive amid This Deadly Love (Dmitry Vrubel) The gallery's best-known painting – showing Soviet and GDR leaders Leonid Breshnev and Erich Honecker locking lips with eyes closed – is based on an actual photograph taken by French journalist Remy Bossu during Breshnev's 1979 Berlin visit. This kind of kiss was an expression of great respect in socialist countries.

90m-wide boulevard runs for 2.3km between Alexanderplatz and Frankfurter Tor and is a fabulous showcase of East German architecture. A considerable source of national pride back then, it provided modern flats for comrades and served as a backdrop for military parades. Some of the finest East German architects of the day (Hartmann, Henselmann, Hopp, Leucht, Paulick and Souradny) collaborated on KMA's construction, looking to Moscow for inspiration. There, Stalin favoured a style that was essentially a socialist reinterpretation of good old-fashioned neoclassicism. In East Berlin, Prussian building master Karl Friedrich Schinkel would be the stylistic godfather, rather than Walter Gropius and the boxy modernist aesthetic embraced in the West.

Living here was a privilege; in fact, for a long time there was no better standard of living in East Germany. Flats featured such luxuries as central heating, lifts (elevators), tiled baths and built-in kitchens; facades were swathed in Meissen tiles.

CAFÉ SIBYLLE   HISTORIC SITE

Map p330 (☏030-2935 2203; www.cafe-sibylle-berlin.de; Karl-Marx-Allee 72; exhibit free, rooftop 1-5 people €15, extra person €3; ⊗10am-8pm Mon-Wed, 10am-10pm Thu & Fri, noon-10pm Sat & Sun, rooftop 1-5pm Mon, Wed & Fri; ⓢWeberwiese, Strausberger Platz) FREE Open since 1953, this was once one of East Berlin's most popular cafes and still makes for a delightfully retro coffee break. It also features a small exhibit charting the milestones of Karl-Marx-Allee from its inception to today and Instagram-worthy views of the boulevard from the rooftop terrace. The exhibit features portraits and biographies of the architects of KMA, alongside posters, toys and other items from socialist times. There's even a piece of Stalin's moustache scavenged from the nearby statue that was torn down in 1961. The cafe operates two-hour **tours** (in German) of KMA at 3pm on Thursdays and noon on Sundays (€8.50, three-person minimum).

COMPUTERSPIELEMUSEUM   MUSEUM

Map p330 (☏030-6098 8577; www.computer-spielemuseum.de; Karl-Marx-Allee 93a; adult/concession €8/5; ⊗10am-8pm Wed-Mon; ⓢWeberwiese) No matter if you grew up with PacMan, World of Warcraft or no games at all, this well-curated museum takes you on a fascinating trip down computer-game memory lane while putting the industry's evolution into historical and cultural context. Colourful and engaging, it features interactive stations amid hundreds of original

WORTH A DETOUR

STASI SIGHTS IN EAST BERLIN

In the German Democratic Republic (GDR; East Germany), the walls had ears. Modelled after the Soviet KGB, the GDR's Ministerium für Staatssicherheit (Ministry of State Security, 'Stasi' for short) was founded in 1950. It was secret police, central intelligence agency and bureau of criminal investigation all rolled into one. Called the 'shield and sword' of the SED, the sole East German party, it put millions of GDR citizens under surveillance in order to suppress internal opposition. The Stasi grew steadily in power and size and, by the end, had 91,000 official full-time employees and 189,000 IMs (*inoffizielle Mitarbeiter;* unofficial informants). The latter were regular folks recruited to spy on their coworkers, friends, family and neighbours. There were also 3000 IMs based in West Germany.

When the Wall fell, the Stasi fell with it. Thousands of citizens stormed the organisation's headquarters in January 1990, thus preventing the shredding of documents that reveal the full extent of institutionalised surveillance and repression through wire-tapping, videotape observation, opening private mail and other methods. The often cunningly low-tech surveillance devices (hidden in watering cans, rocks, even neckties) are among the more intriguing exhibits in the **Stasimuseum** (☎030-553 6854; www.stasimuseum.de; Haus 1, Ruschestrasse 103; adult/concession €5/4; ⏲10am-6pm Mon-Fri, noon-6pm Sat & Sun; [S]Magdalenenstrasse), which occupies several floors of the former fortress-like ministry. At its peak, more than 8000 people worked in this compound alone; the scale model in the entrance foyer will help you grasp its vast dimensions. Another museum highlight is the 'lion's den' itself, the stuffy offices, private quarters and conference rooms of Erich Mielke, head of the Stasi for an incredible 32 years, from 1957 until the bitter end. Other rooms introduce the ideology, rituals and institutions of East German society. There's also background on the SED party and on the role of the youth organisation *Junge Pioneere* (Young Pioneers). Panelling is partly in English.

No words are needed to understand the purpose of the van in the foyer. Outfitted with five teensy, lightless cells, it was used to transport suspects to the **Stasi prison** (☎030-9860 8230; http://en.stiftung-hsh.de; Genslerstrasse 66; adult/concession €5/2.50; ⏲German tours hourly 11am-3pm Mon-Fri Mar-Oct, 11am, 1pm & 3pm Mon-Fri Nov-Feb, hourly 10am-4pm year-round Sat & Sun, English tours 2.30pm Wed, Sat & Sun; 🚋M5 to Freienwalder Strasse), a few kilometres from the ministry. It too is a memorial site today – called Gedenkstätte Hohenschönhausen – and is, if anything, even more creepy than the Stasi Museum.

Tours, sometimes led by former prisoners, reveal the full extent of the terror and cruelty perpetrated upon thousands of suspected political opponents, many utterly innocent. If you've seen the Academy Award–winning film *The Lives of Others,* you may recognise many of the original settings. Since October 2013, a permanent exhibit has documented the history of the prison and explained the system of political persecution in the GDR.

Old maps of East Berlin show a blank spot where the prison was: officially, it did not exist. In reality, the compound had three incarnations. Right after WWII, the Soviets used it to process prisoners (mostly Nazis, or those suspected to be) destined for the gulag. More than 3000 detainees died here because of atrocious conditions – usually by freezing in their unheated cells – until the Western Allies intervened in October 1946.

The Soviets then made it a regular prison, dreaded especially for its 'U-Boat', an underground tract of damp, windowless cells outfitted only with a wooden bench and a bucket. Prisoners were subjected to endless interrogations, beatings, sleep deprivation and water torture. Everybody signed a confession sooner or later.

In 1951 the Soviets handed over the prison to the Stasi, who ended up adopting its mentors' methods. Prisoners were locked up in the U-Boat until a new, much bigger cell block was built, with prison labour, in the late '50s. Psycho-terror now replaced physical torture: inmates had no idea of their whereabouts and suffered total isolation and sensory deprivation. Only the collapse of the GDR in 1989 put an end to the horror.

exhibits, including an ultra-rare 1972 Pong arcade machine and its twisted modern cousin, the 'PainStation' (must be over 18 to play...). Other features include the Wall of Hardware, a gallery-like presentation of 50 consoles and computers from 1971 to 2001. Games Milestones provides high-tech background on dozens of seminal games such as SimCity and Tomb Raider. Other parts of the exhibit explain how games are designed or how they transport players into virtual worlds through sound, music and 3D effects. And, lest you thought it was all fun and games, one section also examines the medium's more sinister aspects, such as violence and addiction.

OBERBAUMBRÜCKE BRIDGE

Map p330 (Oberbaumstrasse; [S]Schlesisches Tor, Warschauer Strasse, 🚇Warschauer Strasse) With its jaunty towers and turrets, crenellated walls and arched walkways, the Oberbaumbrücke (1896) gets our nod for being Berlin's prettiest bridge. Linking Kreuzberg and Friedrichshain across the Spree, it smoothly integrates a steel middle section by Spanish bridgemeister Santiago Calatrava. In summer, street musicians and artists often turn the bridge into an impromptu party zone.

Added bonus: the fabulous views. Looking south you'll spot the Universal Music HQ, MTV Europe and the extravagantly designed nHow hotel. On the Kreuzberg side is the Watergate club, the Badeschiff and, in the distance, a giant aluminium sculpture called **Molecule Man** (Map p332) by American artist Jonathan Borofsky. Right in the river, it shows three bodies embracing and is meant as a symbol of the joining of the three districts of Kreuzberg, Friedrichshain and Treptow across the former watery border.

🍴 EATING

🍴 Boxhagener Platz & North Kiez

LEMON LEAF ASIAN €

Map p330 (☎030-2900 9428; www.lemonleaf.de; Grünberger Strasse 69; mains €6-9; 🕒noon-midnight; 🌿; [S]Frankfurter Tor) Cheap and cheerful, this place is always swarmed by loyal local hipsters and for good reason: light, inventive and fresh, the Vietnamese menu has few false notes. Intriguing choice: the sweet-sour Indochine Salad with banana blossoms. The menu is supplemented by daily specials, and the homemade mango lassi is rave-worthy.

★**SCHNEEWEISS** GERMAN €€

Map p330 (☎030-2904 9704; www.schneeweiss-berlin.de; Simplonstrasse 16; mains €10-24; 🕒6pm-1am Mon-Fri, 10am-1am Sat & Sun; [S]Warschauer Strasse, 🚇Warschauer Strasse) The chilly-chic all-white decor with the eye-catching 'ice' chandelier is only the first thing to tip you off that 'Snow White' is no student nosh spot. The menu is inspired by the Alps, from classics like schnitzel or *Spätzle* to more innovative territory like braised ox cheeks or duck breast with bramble berries. Reservations essential for weekend brunch.

★**SPÄTZLE & KNÖDEL** GERMAN €€

Map p330 (☎030-2757 1151; www.spaetzlek-noedel.de; Wühlischstrasse 20; mains €7-14; 🕒5-11pm; [S]Samariterstrasse) This elbows-on-the-table gastropub is a great place to get your southern German comfort food fix, from waist-expanding portions of roast pork, goulash and of course the eponymous *Spätzle* (German mac 'n' cheese) and *Knödel* (dumplings). Check the blackboard for seasonal specials like venison goulash or wild boar stew. Bonus: Bavarian Riegele, Maisel and Weihenstephan beers on tap.

★**LISBOA BAR** PORTUGUESE €€

Map p330 (☎030-9362 1978; www.lisboa-bar-berlin.de; Krossener Strasse 20; tapas €3-10; 🕒from 5pm Mon, from 3pm Tue-Fri, from 11am Sat & Sun; [S]Warschauer Strasse, Samariterstrasse, 🚋M13, 🚇Warschauer Strasse) Thanks to an expansion, getting a table at this beloved Portuguese outpost is no longer as tall an order. The hearty tapas are an excellent base for a dedicated neighbourhood pub crawl. Try the *pasteis de bacalhau* (fish dumplings), brandy shrimp or chicken in hot piri-piri sauce or any of the weekly specials.

SCHALANDER GERMAN €€

Map p330 (☎030-8961 7073; www.schalander-berlin.de; Bänschstrasse 91; snacks €3.50-10, mains €8-14; 🕒4pm-1am Mon-Fri, noon-1am Sat & Sun; 📶; [S]Samariterstrasse, 🚇Frankfurter Allee) See the pub action reflected in the very shiny steel vats that churn out the full-bodied pilsner, *Dunkel* and *Weizen* at this old-school gastropub far off the tourist track. The menu is big on beer-hall-type

HERE'S THE SCOOP!

There's ice cream and then there's **Caramello** (Map p330; ☑030-6095 5226; Wühlischstrasse 31; ☺from 11am; ⓈFrankfurter Tor, Warschauer Strasse, ⓂM13, ⒭Warschauer Strasse). Join the inevitable queue for more than 40 varieties of tastebud-teasers ranging from pistachio to bitter orange, all organic and homemade. There are soy-based concoctions for vegans and the lactose-intolerant, plus strong coffees and other tempting sweets.

meaty mains along with *Flammkuche* (Alsatian pizza). For an unusual finish, order the wheat beer crème brûlée.

VINERIA DEL ESTE
SPANISH €€

Map p330 (☑030-4202 4943; www.vineriay-tapas.de; Bänschstrasse 41; tapas €2.90-7.90, mains €12-17; ☺3pm-midnight; ⓈSamariter-strasse) Off the tourist track, this low-key Iberian jumps with local foodies hungry for a piñata of flavours. The tapas menu covers all the classics (bacon-wrapped dates, fried shrimp, garlic mushrooms etc), while the weekly changing mains can bring grilled roast beef or blood-sausage-stuffed squid. Savour it all with a glass of tasty Spanish or Uruguayan wine.

KATER MIKESCH
BOHEMIAN €€

Map p330 (☑030-2804 1950; www.kater-mikesch.com; Proskauer Strasse 13; mains €6-14; ☺5pm-midnight Tue-Fri, 11.30am-midnight Sat & Sun; ⓈSamariterstrasse) Although the Czech Republic is pretty close, there's a dearth of decent Bohemian food in Berlin, so Kater Mikesch fills a big void. And well. And generously. In fact, the plates of feisty goulash and chicken paprikash are so huge, you may find it hard to leave room for the sweet dumplings with vanilla sauce. Bonus points for the folklore-free setting.

SCHWARZER HAHN
GERMAN €€€

Map p330 (☑030-2197 0371; Seumestrasse 23; mains €14-21; ☺noon-3pm Mon-Fri, 6-11pm Mon-Sat; ⓈSamariterstrasse, ⓂM13, ⒭Ostkreuz, Warschauer Strasse) The menu at this slow-food bistro shines the spotlight on regionally sourced German soul food, elegantly updated for the 21st century. At dinnertime, it's best to reserve ahead for seats.

✕ Revaler Strasse & Ostkreuz

TRANSIT
ASIAN €

Map p330 (☑030-2694 8415; www.transit-restaurants.com; Sonntagstrasse 28; small/large dishes €3/8; ☺noon-midnight; ✐; ⒭Ostkreuz) Sit beneath the colourful birdcages at this Thai and Indonesian tapas joint and order by ticking cheekily named dishes on a tear-off menu pad. There's great variety – papaya salad to spicy salmon soup – but quality can be hit-or-miss. Expect to order three or four small dishes to get fed. There's another **branch** (Rosenthaler Strasse 68; ☺11am-1am) in Mitte.

VÖNER
VEGAN €

Map p330 (☑030-9926 5423; www.voener.de; Boxhagener Strasse 56; dishes €3-4; ☺noon-11pm; ✐; ⒭Ostkreuz) Owner Holger used to live in a so-called *Wagenburg*, a counter-cultural commune made up of old vans, buses and caravans. The alt-spirit lives on in this funky joint, the speciality of which is the eponymous 'Vöner', an anti-doner made from seitan and vegetables drizzled with garlic sauce. Yummy fries, to boot.

MILJA & SCHÄFA
CAFE €€

Map p330 (☑0176 6266 8459; www.miljaundschaefa.com; Sonntagstrasse 1; mains €6-11; ☺8am-midnight Mon-Thu, to 2am Fri & Sat; ⒭Ostkreuz) Stylishly dressed in natural woods, this mellow cafe is a fabulous eye-opener with strong coffee and mouthwatering breakfast options listed on a black-slate board behind the counter with cases full of homemade cakes. Much creativity goes into the pasta dishes as well. Bonus: sunny footpath seating.

FISCHSCHUPPEN
SEAFOOD €€

Map p330 (☑030-2243 5039; Boxhagener Strasse 68; mains €5-17; ☺10am-10.30pm Mon-Sat, noon-8pm Sun; ⒭Ostkreuz) This shop-restaurant combo gets salty flair not only from its big selection of sustainably caught, fresh fish but also from its ship-cabin-like wooden walls, big aquarium and fishy mural.

✕ Western Friedrichshain

CAFE SCHÖNBRUNN
AUSTRIAN, MEDITERRANEAN €€

Map p330 (☑030-453 056 525; www.schoen-brunn.net; Am Schwanenteich im Volkspark Friedrichshain; mains €9-20, pizzas €6.50-9.60;

⊘10am-midnight daily Apr-Sep, 10am-6pm Sat & Sun Nov-Mar; 🚇200) Watch snow-white swans drift around their pond at this fairytale setting in the middle of Volkspark Friedrichshain. If you're not in the mood for the formal restaurant, report to the beer garden for a cold one with pizza or sausage. Breakfast is served until 2pm.

PAVILLON IM VOLKSPARK
FRIEDRICHSHAIN   INTERNATIONAL €€
Map p330 (📞030-4208 0990, 0172 750 4724; www.pavillon-berlin.de; Friedenstrasse 101; mains €8-11; ⊘beer garden 11am-midnight Apr-Oct; 🛜; 🚇200) An East Berlin institution since 1973, Pavillon serves breakfast until 4pm and is best on sunny days, when you can dig into schnitzel, burgers or salads in the sprawling beer garden.

★**MIO MATTO**   VEGAN €€€
Map p330 (📞030-364 281 040; www.mio-matto.de; Warschauer Strasse 33; mains €15-19, 3-/4-course dinner from €23/27; ⊘noon-10pm; 📆; Ⓢ Warschauer Strasse, 🚋M10, 🚈Warschauer Strasse) Chandeliers meet red-and-white-checkered tablecloths. Love meets Hate in the signature drink. And vegan meets Italian on the menu. At his new outpost, Björn Moschinkski likes to orchestrate opposites, often making plate-fellows out of surprising ingredients, usually with great success. The well-stocked bar, weekend brunch and daily lunch specials have their devotees.

🍷 DRINKING & NIGHTLIFE

🍷 Boxhagener Platz & North Kiez

★**HOPS & BARLEY**   PUB
Map p330 (📞030-2936 7534; Wühlischstrasse 40; ⊘from 5pm Mon-Fri, from 3pm Sat & Sun; Ⓢ Warschauer Strasse, 🚈Warschauer Strasse) Conversation flows as freely as the unfiltered pilsner, malty *Dunkel* (dark), fruity *Weizen* (wheat) and potent cider produced right at this congenial microbrewery inside a former butcher's shop. For variety, the brewmasters produce seasonal blackboard specials such as a malty Bernstein or a robust Indian pale ale. Also try the delicious

homemade *Treberbrot,* a hearty bread made from spent grain collected during brewing.

★**ANTLERED BUNNY**   BAR
Map p330 (Oderstrasse 7; ⊘6pm-2am Tue-Fri, 1pm-2am Sat & Sun; Ⓢ Frankfurter Allee, 🚈Frankfurter Allee) At this pocket-size neighbourhood bar only a dozen or so lucky barflys can get their groove on with Tony Galea's intriguing seasonally changing cocktails. A perennial fave seems to be the gin-based 'Jack the Ripper' with a slice of fried bacon balancing atop the glass. There's local craft beer on tap and plenty of whiskies to keep connoisseurs happy.

SÜSS WAR GESTERN   BAR
Map p330 (📞0176 2441 2940; Wühlischstrasse 43; Ⓢ Warschauer Strasse, Samariterstrasse, 🚈Warschauer Strasse, Ostkreuz) Chilled electro and well-mixed cocktails fuel the party spirit and the low light makes everyone look good. Beware of the ubercomfy retro sofas – it may be too hard to get up to order that next drink, even if it's the eponymous house cocktail made with real root ginger, ginger ale and whisky. Smoking OK.

KAUFBAR   BAR
Map p330 (📞030-2877 8825; www.kaufbar-berlin.de; Gärtnerstrasse 4; breakfast €5.50-7.50; ⊘10am-midnight; Ⓢ Samariterstrasse, 🚈Warschauer Strasse) The name is the concept at this sweet, unhurried cafe where everything is *'kaufbar'* (for sale): the sofa you're sitting on, the cup you're drinking from, the vases decorating the table. Tousled students, young mums and local artists invade for breakfast (until 4pm), locally roasted coffee, homemade cakes, drinks and light snacks. Nice garden, too.

HIMMELREICH   GAY
Map p330 (📞030-2936 9292; www.himmelreich-berlin.de; Simon-Dach-Strasse 36; ⊘6pm-2am Mon-Thu, to 4am Fri, 2pm-4am Sat, 2pm-2am Sun; Ⓢ Warschauer Strasse, 🚈Warschauer Strasse) Confirming all those stereotypes about gays having good taste, this smart red-hued cocktail bar cum retro-style lounge makes most of the competition look like a straight guy's bedsit. Tuesdays are women-only and on Wednesdays drinks are two-for-one.

GROSSE FREIHEIT 114   BAR
Map p330 (www.grosse-freiheit-114.de; Boxhagener Strasse 114; ⊘from 10pm Tue-Sun; Ⓢ Frankfurter Tor, Warschauer Strasse) Named for a

LOCAL KNOWLEDGE

MORE FUN FURTHER AFIELD

With plenty of beloved locations being displaced by apartment and office developments, some of the coolest venues have retreated to outer suburbs like Lichtenberg, east of Friedrichshain.

Sisyphos (☑030-9836 6839; www.sisyphos-berlin.net; Hauptstrasse 15; ⊘hrs vary, usually Fri & Sat Jun-Aug, weather permitting; 🚊21, 🚉Ostkreuz) On summer weekends, an old dog food factory turns into a hedonistic party village that proves that Berlin can still 'do underground'. Climb to the viewing platform to take in the space which includes a pond and a fire truck. Electro dominates the turntables on the main floor with its great sound system. Relaxed door. It's 2km southeast of Ostkreuz S-Bahn station; for tram 21, use exit Gustav-Holzmann-Strasse.

Hafenküche (☑030-4221 9926; www.hafenkueche.de; Zur Alten Flussbadeanstalt 5; lunch €5-5.50, dinner mains €12-22; ⊘10am-midnight ; 🚊21) What began as the staff restaurant of the adjacent bus operator has turned into a top address for clued-in fans of seasonal and regional cuisine. In a dream location on Rummelsburg Bay, it's a great lunch destination during riverside bike rides. Dinners are more elaborate and best enjoyed on the romantically lit terrace. It's about 2.5km southeast of Ostkreuz. Take tram 21 to Gustav-Holzmann-Strasse, then follow that to the river and turn left.

Subland (Map p330; www.sub-land.com; Wiesenweg 5; ⊘Fri & Sat; 🚉Ostkreuz) This rough-and-ready drum 'n' bass club has carved out a spot in a former transformer station in an industrial wasteland between Ostkreuz train station and Frankfurter Allee. Decorated with old machines, circuit boards and graffiti, and sporting a tricked-out sound system from Bulgaria (nicknamed the 'Beast from the East'), it often gets a respectable DJ lineup. It's about 1km from S-Bahn station Ostkreuz. Follow Neue Bahnhofstrasse north, then turn right on Wiesenweg. The club is two long blocks down on your right.

lane in Hamburg's red-light district where the Beatles cut their teeth, Grosse Freiheit is a popular men-only cruising joint (with darkroom) and also a harbour for just a drink and meet-up. The campy nautical decor looks the way most '80s films portrayed gay bars. Different mottoes nightly.

BOOZE BAR
BAR

Map p330 (☑030-9559 1145; Boxhagener Strasse 105; ⊘from 7pm; 🚉Samariterstrasse) The classy antidote to the happy-hour madness of the Simon-Dach-Strasse party drag. Sink into comfy lounge sofas, surrounded by warmly lit brick walls and a photograph of actor Terence Hill, a cigarette coolly stuck between his lips. The ambience is relaxed and the classic drinks finely crafted by a young team. DJs hit the decks on some nights.

ASTRO BAR
BAR

Map p330 (☑0173 768 2625; www.astro-bar.de; Simon-Dach-Strasse 40; ⓢWarschauer Strasse, Frankfurter Tor, 🚉Warschauer Strasse) At this Simon-Dach-Strasse staple, you can get 'beamed' into a cosmic lounge where sci-fi fiends from the hood and beyond drown in

cheap drinks and long conversations, often until the stars begin to fade. DJs kick into action after 10pm. One of the few respectable spots on this well-trodden party drag.

SANATORIUM 23
BAR

Map p330 (☑030-4202 1193; www.sanatorium23.de; Frankfurter Allee 23; ⊘from 6pm; 🛜; ⓢFrankfurter Tor) This Zen-meets-pop-art-in-hospital lounge is likely to cure whatever ails you. First, though, risk chemistry-class flashbacks when facing the drinks menu set up like a periodic table: ordering an *He* gets you a Hemingway sour, *Ps* a prosecco and *Mi* a mojito. From Thursday to Saturday DJs turn the place into an electro party zone after 9pm.

📍 Revaler Strasse & Ostkreuz

SUICIDE CIRCUS
CLUB

Map p330 (www.suicide-berlin.com; Revaler Strasse 99; ⊘usually Wed-Sun; 🚉Warschauer Strasse) Tousled hipsters hungry for an eclectic electro shower invade this gritty dancing den that at times can feel like a mini-Berghain – sweaty, industrial and with a top-notch sound system. In summer, watch the stars fade on the outdoor floor with chillier sounds and grilled bratwurst.

://ABOUT BLANK CLUB

Map p330 (www.aboutparty.net; Markgrafendamm 24c; ☻Fri & Sat; ⓡOstkreuz) This club collective also organises cultural and political events that often segue into long, intense club nights, when talented DJs feed a diverse bunch of revellers dance-worthy electronic gruel. Drinks are fairly priced, and if you get the spirit of openness and tolerance, you'll have a grand old time.

SALON ZUR WILDEN RENATE CLUB

(www.renate.cc; Alt Stralau 70; ☻Fri & Sat; ⓡOstkreuz) Yes, things can indeed get pretty wild at Renate, where stellar local spinners feed self-ironic freethinkers with sweat-inducing electro in the rambling rooms of an abandoned residential building. Sofas, a fireplace room and several bars provide suitable chill zones. The crowd skews young.

CASSIOPEIA CLUB

Map p330 (☎030-4738 5949; www.cassiopeia-berlin.de; Revaler Strasse 99, Gate 2; ☻Tue-Sun; ⓢWarschauer Strasse, ⓡWarschauer Strasse) The varied and down-to-earth crowd at this charmingly trashy party den defines the word eclectic and so does the music. Dive deep into a sound spectrum ranging from vintage hip-hop to hard funk, reggae and punk to electronic beats.

★CHAPEL BAR COCKTAIL BAR

Map p330 (☎030-6593 6574; www.chapelberlin.com; Sonntagstrasse 30; ☻from 6pm; ⓡOstkreuz) Another star on the Friedrichshain cocktail firmament is the Chapel Bar. Its 'altar' is helmed by meister mixer Michael Blair, whose repertory includes both classic and out-there drinks like the Jägermeister-based Hubertus & Jade. A giant chandelier bathes the otherwise rather simple room in a complexion-friendly glow.

★PLACE CLICHY BAR

Map p330 (☎030-2313 8703; Simon-Dach-Strasse 22; ☻Tue-Sat; ⓢWarschauer Strasse, ⓡWarschauer Strasse) *Chapeau!* Clichy brings a whiff of Paris to the lower end of Simon-Dach-Strasse. Candlelit, artist-designed and cosy, the postage-stamp-size *boîte* exudes an almost existentialist vibe, so

don your black turtleneck and join the chatty crowd for Bordeaux and sweaty cheeses.

BADEHAUS SZIMPLA MUSIKSALON BAR

Map p330 (www.badehaus-berlin.com; Revaler Strasse 99, RAW Gelände, enter near Simon-Dach-Strasse; ⓢWarschauer Strasse, ⓡWarschauer Strasse) The little sister of the famous Szimpla Kert ruin bar in Budapest is now making a splash in an old Berlin bathhouse. Head past the golden tub for eclectic bathhouse-themed decor, cheap drinks and a relaxed vibe. With various cultural events and a musical spectrum ranging from swing to soul, the place covers all the bases.

CRACK BELLMER BAR, CLUB

Map p330 (www.crackbellmer.de; RAW Gelände, enter near Simon-Dach-Strasse; ☻from 7pm; ⓢWarschauer Strasse, ⓡM13, ⓡWarschauer Strasse) Behind the requisite street-art-festooned facade awaits an industrial-chic space with vintage sofas, lofty ceilings and chandeliers. Popular for preparty warm-ups, postparty nightcaps and any time in between, including Sunday afternoon swing tea dance.

KPTN A MÜLLER PUB

Map p330 (www.kptn.de; Simon-Dach-Strasse 32; ☏; ⓢWarschauer Strasse, ⓡWarschauer Strasse) Arrgh, matey, the captain's in town, bringing much-needed relief from the strip's cookie-cutter cocktail-lounge circuit. Pretensions are checked at the door of this self-service joint where drinks are cheap and table football and wi-fi are free. The Matterhorn photo wallpaper in the DJ room out back makes for an easy conversation starter.

ZUM SCHMUTZIGEN HOBBY BAR

Map p330 (www.ninaqueer.com; Revaler Strasse 99, RAW Gelände, gate 2; ⓢWarschauer Strasse, ⓡWarschauer Strasse) Although founder and trash-drag deity Nina Queer has moved on to other pastures, her louche den of kitsch and glam is still swarmed night after night.

🍺 Western Friedrichshain

BERGHAIN/PANORAMA BAR CLUB

Map p330 (www.berghain.de; Wriezener Bahnhof; ☻midnight Fri-Mon morning; ⓡOstbahnhof) Only world-class spinmasters heat up this hedonistic bass-junkie hellhole inside a labyrinthine ex-power plant. Hard-edged

FRIEDRICHSHAIN DRINKING & NIGHTLIFE

MARKETS GALORE

If you're into marketeering, Sundays are a great time to swing by Friedrichshain.

Antikmarkt am Ostbahnhof (Map p330; www.oldthing.de; Erich-Steinfurth-Strasse; ◎9am-5pm Sun; ⓇOstbahnhof) If it's genuine antiques you're after, head straight to this sprawling market which starts right outside the Ostbahnhof station's north exit. The 'Grosser Antikmarkt' (large antiques market) is more professional and brims with genuine collectibles – old coins, Iron Curtain–era relics, gramophone records, books, stamps, jewellery etc. It segues neatly into the 'Kleiner Antikmarkt' (small antiques market), which has more bric-a-brac and lower prices.

Flohmarkt am Boxhagener Platz (Map p330; Boxhagener Platz; ◎10am-6pm Sun; ⓈWarschauer Strasse, Frankfurter Tor, ⓇWarschauer Strasse) The most popular market gets some pros along with regular folks unloading their spring-cleaning detritus for cheap. Best of all, stalls are just a java whiff away from Sunday brunch cafes.

RAW Flohmarkt (Map p330; www.raw-flohmarkt-berlin.de; Revaler Strasse 99, RAW Gelände; ◎9am-7pm Sun; ⓈWarschauer Strasse, ⓇWarschauer Strasse) The smallest of the bunch takes over the grounds of the RAW Gelände creative colony. It's wonderfully free of professional sellers, meaning you'll find everything from the proverbial kitchen sink to 1970s go-go boots. Bargains are plentiful.

minimal techno dominates the ex-turbine hall (Berghain) while house dominates at Panorama Bar one floor up. Strict door, no cameras. Check the website for midweek concerts and record-release parties at the main venue and the adjacent Kantine am Berghain.

YAAM
CLUB

Map p330 (⌨030-615 1354; www.yaam.de; An der Schillingsbrücke; ◎from 11am; ⓇOstbahnhof) This reggae and dancehall institution literally got a new (long-term rental) lease on life when it moved into the former Magdalena space in May 2014. A slice of the Caribbean on the Spree River, it attracts an all-ages, multicultural crowd to its live concerts, parties and plenty of outdoor sports, art, food and fun in the sand.

MONSTER RONSON'S
ICHIBAN KARAOKE
KARAOKE

Map p330 (⌨030-8975 1327; www.karaokemonster.com; Warschauer Strasse 34; ◎from 7pm; ⓈWarschauer Strasse, ⓇWarschauer Strasse) Knock back a couple of brewskis if you need to loosen your nerves before belting out your best Beyoncé or Lady Gaga at this mad, great karaoke joint. *Pop Idol* wannabes too shy to hit the stage can book a booth for music and mischief in private. Some nights are GLBT-geared, like Mondays' MultiSEXxual BOXhopping. Must be 21 to enter.

CSA
BAR

Map p330 (⌨030-2904 4741; www.csa-bar.de; Karl-Marx-Allee 96; ◎from 7pm; ⓈWeberwiese) This sophisticated bar has been carved out of the eponymous Czech national airline offices and emanates an understated 1960s vintage vibe. Dim lights and classic cocktails mean that a more grown-up set balances on the white leather bar stools.

LAB.ORATORY
CLUB

Map p330 (www.lab-oratory.de; Am Wriezener Bahnhof; ◎Thu-Mon; ⓇOstbahnhof) Part of the Berghain complex, this well-equipped 'lab' has plenty of toys and rooms for advanced sexual experimentation in what looks like the engine room of an aircraft carrier. Party names like Yellow Facts, Naked Sex Party and Fausthouse leave little to the imagination. Hedonism pure. Come before midnight and skip the aftershave.

☆ ENTERTAINMENT

ASTRA KULTURHAUS
LIVE MUSIC

Map p330 (⌨030-2005 6767; www.astra-berlin.de; Revaler Strasse 99; ⓈWarschauer Strasse, ⓇWarschauer Strasse) With space for 1500, Astra is one of the bigger indie venues in town, yet often fills up easily, and not just for such headliners as Melissa Etheridge, Kasabian or Paul van Dyk's Vandit Records label parties. Bonus: the sweet '50s GDR decor. Beer garden in summer.

RADIALSYSTEM V
PERFORMING ARTS

Map p330 (📞030-2887 8850; www.radialsystem.de; Holzmarktstrasse 33; 📷; 🚇Ostbahnhof) Contemporary dance meets medieval music, poetry meets pop tunes, painting meets digital. This progressive performance space in an old riverside pump station blurs the boundaries between the arts to nurture new forms of creative expression. Nice riverside cafe-bar from 10am.

KINO INTERNATIONAL
CINEMA

Map p330 (📞030-2475 6011; www.yorck.de; Karl-Marx-Allee 33; 🚇Schillingstrasse) The East German film elite once held its movie premieres in this 1960s cinema, whose potpourri of chandeliers and glitter curtains is a show in itself. Today it presents smartly curated international indie hit flicks, usually in the original language with German subtitles. Mondays are reserved for gay-themed movies and the first Saturday of the month for the gay megabash Klub International.

KANTINE AM BERGHAIN
LIVE MUSIC

Map p330 (📞030-2936 0210; www.berghain.de; Am Wriezener Bahnhof; ⏱hours vary; 🚇Ostbahnhof) Big bad Berghain's little sister has taken over the former staff cantina right next to the giant ex-power station. It puts on concerts and party nights beyond electro starting at a weekday-friendly 10pm. In summer, the attached beer garden with outdoor fireplace is an ideal chill zone.

K17
LIVE MUSIC, CLUB

Map p330 (📞030-4208 9300; www.k17-berlin.de; Pettenkoferstrasse 17a; ⏱Thu-Sat; 🚇Frankfurter Allee, 🚇Frankfurter Allee) K17 used to be the go-to club for all things Goth, industrial, metal and other dark music. Although bands like Icon of Coil, Debauchery and Whipstriker still hit the stage, softer sounds have made inroads as well, especially on weekend party nights when there's four floors feeding different musical appetites, from electropop and NuWave to hip-hop.

🛍 SHOPPING

Friedrichshain has come along in the shopping department, with increasingly chic indie clothing boutiques and speciality stores sprinkled around Boxhagener Platz, Sonntagstrasse and its side streets near Ostkreuz.

WOCHENMARKT AM BOXHAGENER PLATZ
MARKET

Map p330 (Boxhagener Platz; ⏱8am-2.30pm Sat; 🚇Samariterstrasse) This hugely popular farmers market brings out the entire neighbourhood for fresh fare along with homemade liqueurs, a global cheese selection, exotic spices, smoked fish, hemp muesli, purple potatoes and other unusual culinary delights. Plenty of snack stands, to boot.

YACKFOU
FASHION

Map p330 (📞030-8411 4534; Gabriel-Max-Strasse 21; ⏱noon-8pm Mon-Fri, 11am-7pm Sat; 🚇Warschauer Strasse, Samariterstrasse, 🚇Warschauer Strasse) We would love YackFou even without its cool anagram name. 'Function follows form' is the anti-Bauhaus motto of Tobias and Martin, who've applied their graphic-design background to a line of T-shirts, hoodies and sweaters that define the Berlin look. You can even create your own piece from a selection of 120 motifs.

PRACHTMÄDCHEN
FASHION

Map p330 (📞030-9700 2780; www.prachtmaedchen.de; Wühlischstrasse 28; ⏱11am-8pm Mon-Fri, to 4pm Sat; 🚇Frankfurter Tor, Warschauer Strasse, 🚇Warschauer Strasse) This store was a pioneer on Wühlischstrasse, aka Friedrichshain's 'fashion mile'. Low-key and friendly, it's great for kitting yourself out in grown-up streetwear by such labels as Blutsgeschwister, skunkfunk and Tokyo Jane. Also, chic undies by Pussy Deluxe and Vive Maria.

PERLEREI
JEWELLERY

Map p330 (📞030-9788 2028; www.perlerei.de; Lenbachstrasse 7; ⏱2-8pm Tue-Fri, noon-6pm Sat; 🚇Ostkreuz) Looking for a unique souvenir? Simply make it yourself. A piece of jewellery, that is, and don't worry if you don't know how. At Meike Köster's bead boutique, you select your baubles and then turn them into beautiful necklaces, earrings, brooches or bracelets.

ZIGARREN HERZOG AM HAFEN
CIGARS

(📞030-2904 7015; www.herzog-am-hafen.de; Stralauer Allee 9; ⏱11am-9pm Mon-Sat; 🚇Warschauer Strasse, 🚇Warschauer Strasse) If you're a friend of Belinda, Cohiba or Trinidad, you can indulge your passion in this upmarket cigar boutique, in a 1909 riverside warehouse with a riverfront terrace for lighting up a smooth one. All cigars come straight from Havana and can be purchased by the date they were boxed or even by wrapping colour.

Prenzlauer Berg

MAUERPARK | THE NORTH KIEZ | KOLLWITZPLATZ | THE SOUTH KIEZ

Neighbourhood Top Five

1 Coming to grips with the absurdity of a divided city at the **Gedenkstätte Berliner Mauer** (p186), Germany's central memorial to the victims of the Berlin Wall.

2 Spending a sunny Sunday foraging for flea-market treasures and cheering on karaoke crooners in the **Mauerpark** (p188).

3 Taking a leisurely ramble around the leafy **Kollwitzplatz** (p188) neighbourhood with its beautiful townhouses, convivial cafes and upmarket indie boutiques.

4 Coming face to face with Berlin's subterranean mysteries on a WWII bunker tour with **Berliner Unterwelten** (p293).

5 Catching a concert or other cultural event at the **Kulturbrauerei** (p188).

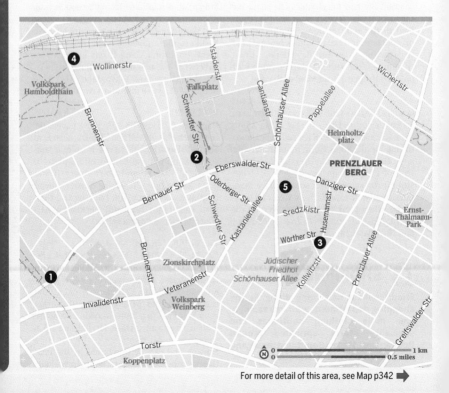

For more detail of this area, see Map p342 ➡

Explore: Prenzlauer Berg

Once a neglected backwater, Prenzlauer Berg went from rags to riches after reunification to emerge as one of Berlin's most desirable and expensive neighbourhoods. There are no must-see sights, but the ample charms reveal themselves in subtler, often unexpected ways and are best experienced on a leisurely meander. Look up at restored townhouses that not long ago bore the scars of war. Push open a carved doorway to stumble upon quiet courtyards. Source Berlin-made fashions on boho-trendy Kastanienallee or comb quiet side streets for indie boutiques selling handmade jewellery or organic baby clothes. Prenzlauer Berg also has one of the city's best cafe scenes. Carve out a spot in a cafe on Kollwitzplatz or Helmholtzplatz, or bask in the sun with views of Berlin's oldest water tower. On Sundays, the Mauerpark draws tens of thousands to the city's best flea market, outdoor karaoke, pick-up basketball, and other fun and games.

This is one of the most family-friendly districts in town: safe, quiet, and with plenty of playgrounds, toy stores and child-oriented cafes.

Local Life

➡ **Outdoor quaffing** Days get long, temperatures climb and spirits soar. Time to celebrate summer beneath the chestnut trees of the Prater (p196) beer garden, on the rooftop terrace of Deck 5 (p195) or at a sunny sidewalk table at Cafe Chagall (p196). Alternatively, score a bottle of beer at a local market and stake out some turf in the Mauerpark.

➡ **Shopping** Prenzlauer Berg's side streets are nirvana for indie shoppers. Browse for chic bags at Ta(u)sche (p198), Berlin designers at Flagshipstore (p198) or retro threads at the Flohmarkt am Mauerpark (p197).

➡ **Eating out** Favourites for foodies on the run include Habba Habba (p191) for Middle Eastern wraps, Zia Maria (p192) for pizza, and Konnopke's Imbiss (p194) for *Currywurst*. On Saturdays, join locals for gourmet snacks and a glass of bubbly at the bountiful farmers market (p197) on Kollwitzplatz.

Getting There & Away

➡ **U-Bahn** The U2 stops at Senefelderplatz, Eberswalder Strasse and Schönhauser Allee.

➡ **Tram** The M1 links Museumsinsel and Prenzlauer Berg via the Scheunenviertel, Kastanienallee and Schönhauser Allee.

➡ **S-Bahn** Ringbahn (Circle Line) trains S41 and S42 stop at Schönhauser Allee.

Lonely Planet's Top Tip

Stop by the local **tourist info center** (Map p342; ☎030-4435 2170; www.tic-berlin.de; Schönhauser Allee 36; ⏲11am-7pm; [S]Eberswalder Strasse) in the Kulturbrauerei, which has maps, flyers and booklets to help you plug into the Prenzlauer Berg neighbourhood. It also sells tickets to events around town.

🍴 Best Places to Eat

➡ Frau Mittenmang (p193)

➡ La Soupe Populaire (p194)

➡ Habba Habba (p191)

➡ Muse (p194)

➡ Umami (p194)

For reviews, see p191 ➡

🍷 Best Places to Drink

➡ Prater (p196)

➡ Becketts Kopf (p195)

➡ Le Croco Bleu (p196)

➡ Weinerei (p196)

➡ Deck 5 (p195)

For reviews, see p195 ➡

🛍 Best Places to Shop

➡ Flagshipstore (p198)

➡ Flohmarkt am Mauerpark (p197)

➡ Luxus International (p198)

➡ Ta(u)sche (p198)

For reviews, see p197 ➡

Few streets have played such a pivotal role in Cold War history as Bernauer Strasse. The Berlin Wall ran along its entire length, with one side of the street located in West Berlin and the other trapped in East Berlin. Today, the Berlin Wall Memorial seeks to explain how all the elements of the Wall and the death strip fit together, how the border fortifications were enlarged and perfected over time and what impact they had on the daily lives of people on both sides of the Wall.

The outdoor exhibit extends for 1.4km along Bernauer Strasse and is divided into four sections with overarching themes. Integrated within are an original section of Wall, vestiges of the border installations and escape tunnels, a chapel and a monument. Multimedia stations, 'archaeological windows' and markers provide context and details about events that took place along here.

Gartenstrasse to Ackerstrasse

This key segment explains how the Berlin Wall restricted citizens' freedom of movement and secured the East German government's power. An emotional highlight is the **Window of Remembrance**, where photographic portraits give identity to would-be escapees who lost their lives at the Berlin Wall, one of them only six years young. The park-like area surrounding the installation was once part of the adjacent cemetery.

Near Ackerstrasse, the **National Monument to German Division** consists of a 70m section of original Berlin Wall bounded by two rusted steel flanks and embedded in an artistic representation of the border complex. Walk down Ackerstrasse to enter the monument from the back. Through gaps in a wall, you can espy a reconstructed death strip

DON'T MISS...

➡ View from the Documentation Centre viewing platform

➡ Remembrance service at the Chapel of Reconciliation

➡ Ghost Station exhibit

PRACTICALITIES

➡ Berlin Wall Memorial

➡ ☎030-467 986 666

➡ www.berliner-mauer-gedenkstaette.de

➡ Bernauer Strasse btwn Schwedter Strasse & Gartenstrasse

➡ ⊙visitor center 9.30am-7pm Apr-Oct, to 6pm Nov-Mar, open-air exhibit 8am-10pm

➡ Ⓡ Nordbahnhof, Bernauer Strasse, Eberswalder Strasse

complete with a guard tower, a security patrol path and the lamps that bathed it in fierce light at night.

Ackerstrasse to Brunnenstrasse

Here the linear memorial focuses on the division's human toll and especially on the daring and desperate escapes that took place along Bernauer Strasse. Just past Ackerstrasse, the modern **Chapel of Reconciliation** stands in the spot of an 1894 brick church detonated in 1985 to make room for a widening of the border strip. A 15-minute remembrance service for Wall victims is held at noon Tuesday to Friday. Other information stations deal with the physical construction of the Wall and the continuous expansion of the border complex.

Brunnenstrasse to Schwedter Strasse

In the final section, info stations and exhibits must skirt private property and new apartment buildings and are mostly restricted to a narrow strip along the former border patrol path. Information stations address such topics as West Germany's take on the Berlin Wall, what daily life was like for an East German border guard and the eventual fall of the Wall in 1989. A highlight is the dramatic story of the world-famous **Tunnel 29**, which ran for 135m below Bernauer Strasse and helped 29 people escape from East Berlin in September 1962.

VIEW FROM DOCUMENTATION CENTRE

For a sweeping view of the memorial, climb the viewing tower of the Berlin Wall Documentation Centre at the corner of Ackerstrasse. Inside, an exhibit provides a historical overview of events from the period before the Wall was built up to the present day.

The visitors centre at the corner of Gartenstrasse and Bernauer Strasse has free maps and screens a short introductory documentary on the construcution, implications and history of the Berlin Wall.

GHOST STATIONS

The Berlin Wall divided the city's transport system. Three lines (today's U6, U8 and the north–south S-Bahn rails) that originated in West Berlin had to travel along tracks that happened to run beneath the eastern sector before returning to stations on the western side. Trains slowed down but did not stop at these 'ghost stations', which were closed and patrolled by heavily armed GDR border guards. An exhibit inside the Nordbahnhof S-Bahn station describes underground escape attempts and the measures taken by the East German government to prevent them.

SIGHTS

MAUERPARK PARK

Map p342 (www.mauerpark.info; btwn Bernauer Strasse, Schwedter Strasse & Gleimstrasse; [S]Eberswalder Strasse, 🚋M1) With its wimpy trees and anaemic lawn, Mauerpark is hardly your typical leafy oasis, especially given that it was forged from a section of Cold War–era death strip (a short stretch of Berlin Wall survives). It's this mystique combined with an unassuming vibe and a hugely popular Sunday flea market and karaoke show that has endeared the place to locals and visitors alike.

Behind the Wall segment – now an officially sanctioned practise ground for graffiti artists – loom the floodlights of the **Friedrich-Ludwig-Jahn-Sportpark** (☎030-4430 3730; Cantianstrasse 24; [S]Eberswalder Strasse), the stadium where Stasi chief Erich Mielke used to cheer on his beloved Dynamo Berlin football (soccer) team. Just north of here is the **Max-Schmeling-Halle** (☎030-4430 4430; www.max-schmeling-halle.de; Falkplatz 1; [S]Eberswalder Strasse), a venue for concerts, competitions and sports events.

KOLLWITZPLATZ SQUARE

Map p342 (👪; [S]Senefelderplatz) Triangular Kollwitzplatz is the epicentre of Prenzlauer Berg poshification. To pick up on the local vibe, linger with macchiato mamas and media daddies in a street cafe or join them at the organic farmers market (p197). The park in the square's centre is tot heaven with three playgrounds plus a bronze sculpture of the artist Käthe Kollwitz for clambering on.

JÜDISCHER FRIEDHOF SCHÖNHAUSER ALLEE CEMETERY

Map p342 (☎030-441 9824; Schönhauser Allee 23-25; ⏲8am-4pm Mon-Thu, 7.30am-2.30pm Fri; [S]Senefelderplatz) Berlin's second Jewish cemetery opened in 1827 and hosts many well-known dearly departed, such as the artist Max Liebermann and the composer Giacomo Meyerbeer. It's a pretty place with dappled light filtering through big old trees and a sense of melancholy emanating from overgrown graves and toppled tombstones.

The nicest and oldest have been moved to the Lapidarium by the main entrance. Liebermann's tomb is next to his family's crypt roughly in the centre along the back wall. Men must cover their heads; pick up a free skullcap by the entrance.

KULTURBRAUEREI HISTORIC BUILDING

Map p342 (☎030-4431 5152; www.kulturbrauerei.de; Schönhauser Allee 36; [S]Eberswalder Strasse, 🚋M1) The fanciful red-and-yellow brick buildings of this 19th-century brewery have been recycled into a cultural powerhouse with a small village's worth of venues, from concert and theatre halls to restaurants, nightclubs, shops and a multiscreen cinema. In December, the old buildings make a lovely backdrop for a Swedish-style Lucia Christmas market.

MUSEUM IN DER KULTURBRAUEREI MUSEUM

Map p342 (☎030-467 777 911; Knaackstrasse 97; ⏲10am-6pm Tue, Wed & Fri-Sun, to 8pm Thu; [S]Eberswalder Strasse, 🚋M1, 12) [FREE] This new exhibit at the Kulturbrauerei uses original documents and objects (including a camper-style Trabi car) to teach the rest of us about daily life in East Germany. Four themed sections juxtapose the lofty aspirations of the socialist state with the sobering realities of material shortages, surveillance and oppression. Case studies show the different paths individuals took to deal – and cope – with their situation.

PFEFFERBERG CULTURAL BUILDING

Map p342 (Schönhauser Allee 176; [S]Senefelderplatz) This rambling listed ex-brewery complex harbours several culture and gastro venues as well as a hostel and the Bassy

WWII BUNKER TOURS

After you've checked off the Brandenburg Gate and the TV Tower, why not explore Berlin's dark and dank underbelly? Join Berliner Unterwelten (p293) on their 'Dark Worlds' tour of a WWII underground bunker and pick your way through a warren of claustrophobic rooms, past heavy steel doors, hospital beds, helmets, guns, boots and lots of other wartime artefacts. Listen on in horror and fascination as guides bring alive the stories of the thousands of ordinary Berliners cooped up here, crammed and scared, as the bombs rained down on Berlin. Other tours explore a WWII anti-aircraft tower, a Cold War nuclear-bomb shelter and Berlin Wall escape tunnels. Buy tickets at the kiosk outside the south exit of Gesundbrunnen U-Bahn station (in front of Kaufland).

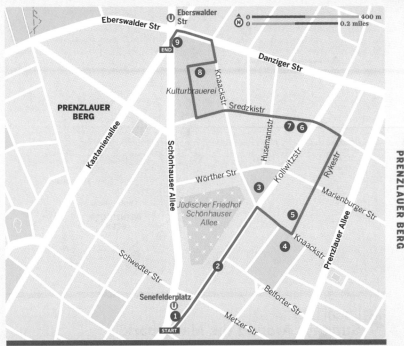

Neighbourhood Walk
Poking Around Prenzlauer Berg

START SENEFELDER PLATZ
END KONNOPKE'S IMBISS
LENGTH 1.2KM; 90 MINUTES

Start out at **1 Senefelder Platz**, a patch of green named for Alois Senefelder, an Austro-German actor who invented lithography. Note the marble statue with his name chiselled into the pedestal in mirror-writing, just as it would be using his printing technique. Head northeast on **2 Kollwitzstrasse**, where the huge LPG organic supermarket and the ultra-deluxe Palais KolleBelle apartment complex are solid indicators of the neighbourhood's upmarket demographics. You'll soon arrive at **3 Kollwitzplatz**, a square named for the artist Käthe Kollwitz, who lived here with her husband for over 40 years while tending to the destitute. A bronze statue in the square's centre park and a plaque on the blue building at Kollwitz-strasse 58 honour her legacy.

Follow Knaackstrasse to Rykestrasse, past a row of popular cafes, and note the circular **4 Wasserturm**, Berlin's oldest water tower (1877), which is now honey-combed with pie-sliced flats. In Nazi Germany, its machine room went through a sinister stint as an improvised prison and torture centre. Follow Rykestrasse, noting the handsome facades of its restored townhouses. At No 53 is the **5 Synagoge Rykestrasse**, which survived WWII and again hosts Shabbat services.

Continue on Rykestrasse to Sredzkis-trasse, perhaps stopping for a cuppa at **6 Anna Blume** (p196) and a browse at the kooky **7 Bücher Tauschbaum**, a free book exchange made from tree trunks. Further up on the right looms the sprawling **8 Kulturbrauerei** (p188). Admire the gorgeous architecture of this brewery-turned-cultural-complex, then head inside and get an eyeful of life in East Germany at the new Museum in der Kulturbrauerei. Exit the Kulturbrauerei onto Knaackstrasse and turn left on Danziger Strasse to wrap up your walk with a *Currywurst* from cult-kitchen **9 Konnopke's Imbiss** (p194).

PRENZLAUER BERG

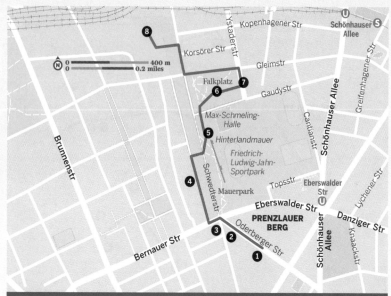

⁂ Local Life
Sundays Around the Mauerpark

Locals, neo-Berliners and tourists – everyone flocks to the Mauerpark on Sundays. It's an energetic urban tapestry where a flea market, karaoke and bands provide entertainment, and people gather for barbecues, basketball and boules. A graffiti-covered section of the Berlin Wall quietly looms above it all.

❶ Bright Beginnings
Start your day on Oderberger Strasse, with breakfast at **Hüftengold** (Map p342; ☏030-4171 4500; Oderberger Strasse 27) or waffles at **Kauf Dich Glücklich** (Map p342; Oderberger Strasse 44) and admire the facades of the restored 19th-century townhouses that were saved from demolition in the late '70s.

❷ Coffee Deluxe
The pioneers of third-wave coffee in Berlin, Yumi and Kiduk make a mean cuppa java from beans roasted freshly right in their tiny cafe, **Bonanza Coffee Heroes** (Map p342; www.bonanzacoffee.de, Oderberger Strasse 35; ☺8.30am-7pm Mon-Fri, 10am-7pm Sat & Sun). Lines can be long, so bring some patience.

❸ Confronting Cold War History
During the Cold War, East met West at Bernauer Strasse, now paralleled by a linear multimedia memorial (p186) that illustrates the realities of life with the Berlin Wall. It

starts at Schwedter Strasse and follows the former border-patrol path. Even walking just a short stretch is an eye-opening experience.

❹ Urban Archaeology
After a dose of history, hit the Flohmarkt am Mauerpark (p197) for some quality hunting and gathering, then drag your loot to a market beer garden for chilling in the sun.

❺ Bearpit Karaoke
On most summer Sundays, Berlin's best free entertainment kicks off around 3pm when Joe Hatchiban sets up his custom-made mobile karaoke unit in the Mauerpark's amphitheatre. As many as 2000 people cram onto the stone bleachers to cheer and clap for eager crooners ranging from giggling 11-year-olds to Broadway-calibre belters.

❻ Falkplatz
Flashback to 1825 and picture Prussian soldiers parading around what is now a leafy

Musicians performing at the Mauerpark

park studded with ancient chestnut, oak, birch, ash and poplar trees. Relax on the grass and watch kids frolicking around the sea-lion fountain, then search for other animal sculptures tucked among the shrubs.

7 Burgermania

New York meets Berlin at the **Bird** (Map p342; ☎030-5105 3283; www.thebirdinberlin.com; Am Falkplatz 5; burgers €9.50-14, steaks from €16; ⏲6pm-midnight Mon-Fri, noon-midnight Sat & Sun), a buzzy gastropub with steaks, burgers and hand-cut fries that might just justify the hype.

8 Northern Mauerpark

To escape the Mauerpark frenzy and see where the locals relax, head north of the Gleimstrasse tunnel. This is where you'll find an enchanting birch grove, the **Jugendfarm Moritzhof** (Map p342; ☎030-4402 4220; www.jugendfarm-moritzhof.de; Schwedter Strasse 90; ⏲11.30am-6pm Mon-Fri, 1-6pm Sat), a farm playground complete with barnyard animals, and daredevils scaling the **Schwedter Northface** (Map p342; www.alpinclub-berlin.de) climbing wall operated by the German Alpine Club.

(p196) nightclub. Beer production resumed in 2013 with the opening of the Pfefferbräu (p196) microbrewery. At the Christinenstrasse (northern) entrance, the **Museum für Architekturzeichnung** (Museum for Architectural Drawing; Map p342; ☎030-4373 9090; www.tchoban-foundation.de; Christinenstrasse 18; adult/concession €5/3; ⏲2-7pm Mon-Fri, 1-5pm Sat & Sun; [S]Senefelderplatz) is housed in a spectacular pile of relief-decorated sandstone cubes designed by Sergei Tchoban. Danish-Icelandic artist Olafur Eliasson has his studio next door.

GETHSEMANEKIRCHE CHURCH

Map p342 (www.gethsemanekirche.de; Stargarder Strasse 77; [S]Schönhauser Allee) This 1893 neo-Gothic church was a hotbed of dissent in the final days of the GDR and thus a thorn in the side of the Stasi, which, as late as October 1989, brutally quashed a peaceful gathering outside its portals. Ernst Barlach's *Geistkämpfer* (Ghost Fighter, 1928) sculpture stands outside the church, which is usually closed except for concerts and Sunday services.

ZEISS GROSSPLANETARIUM PLANETARIUM

Map p342 (☎030-421 8450; www.sdtb.de; Prenzlauer Allee 80; ⏲currently closed; [R]Prenzlauer Allee) The people of East Berlin were not allowed to see what was across the Wall, but at least they could gaze at the entire universe at this fine planetarium. It opened in 1987 as one of the largest star theatres in Europe, boasting a 'Cosmorama', back then the finest star projector ever built. Under restoration at the time of writing, the venue should reopen in 2015.

🍴 EATING

Being largely residential, Prenzlauer Berg has a high density of neighbourhood restaurants to cater for on-the-go locals with more money than time. Even without any Michelin shrines, there's still lots of good chowing down to be done.

🍴 Mauerpark & the North Kiez

★**HABBA HABBA** MIDDLE EASTERN €

Map p342 (☎030-3674 5726; www.habba-habba.de; Kastanienallee 15; dishes €4-8; ⏲10am-10pm; 🌿; [T]M1, 12, [R]Eberswalder Strasse) The best

WORTH A DETOUR

SCHLOSS SCHÖNHAUSEN

In Pankow, just north of Prenzlauer Berg, **Schloss Schönhausen** (☎030-3949 2625; www.spsg.de; Tschaikowskistrasse 1; adult/concession €6/5; ⌚10am-6pm Tue-Sun Apr-Oct, to 5pm Sat & Sun Nov-Mar; 🚋M1) is surrounded by a lovely park and packs a lot of German history into its pint-size frame. Originally a country estate of Prussian nobles, in 1740 it became the summer residence of Frederick II's estranged wife Elisabeth Christine, who had it enlarged and rendered in playful rococo. Taking a page from *Sleeping Beauty*, the palace fell into a long slumber after her death in 1797 until the Nazis used the dilapidated structure as a storeroom for 'degenerate' modern art. In 1949 the building was restored once more and became the seat of East Germany's first head of state, Wilhelm Pieck, before later becoming the country's state guesthouse.

After yet another mega-makeover, the palace sparkles in renewed splendour. The downstairs rooms, where the queen had her private quarters, reflect the 18th-century style with partly original furniture and wallpaper. More interesting – largely for their uniqueness – are the upstairs rooms where GDR fustiness is alive in the heavy furniture of Pieck's 1950s office and in the baby-blue bedspread in the Gentlemen's Bedroom where Castro, Ceauşescu, Gaddafi and other 'bad boys' slept. To get to the palace, catch tram M1 to the Tschaikowksistrasse stop, then walk about 300m east on Tschaikowksistrasse.

wraps in town for our money, especially the one stuffed with pomegranate-marinated chicken and nutty buckwheat dressed in a minty yoghurt sauce. One bite and you're hooked. Vegetarian loyalists swear by the sesame-coated halloumi. Take away or score a seat on the raised porch.

L'ANTICA DOGANA — ITALIAN €

(☎030-4737 6372; www.wbb-pankow.de/pizzeria; Berliner Strasse 80-82; pizzas €4.50-8.50; ⌚5-10pm; [S]Vinetastrasse, 🚋M1) In the frills-free surroundings of the former customs house of the defunct Willner Brewery, Lino di Napoli and Sebastiano Micieli crank out authentic thin-crust pies best consumed with a posse of friends and several carafes of cheap, tasty red wine. Some of the furniture is made from bric-a-brac scavenged from the brewery grounds.

VAN HOA — VIETNAMESE €

Map p342 (☎030-4057 4197; www.vanhoa-berlin.de; Stargarder Strasse 79; mains €4.90; ⌚noon-11pm; [S]Schönhauser Allee) Empty tables are a rare sight at this uncluttered cafe with its simply satisfying bowls of beef or chicken with rice or noodles and piled high with fresh veg and herbs. In winter, the *pho* soups go a long way towards staving off the chills.

A MAGICA — ITALIAN €

Map p342 (☎030-2280 8290; www.amagica.de; Greifenhagener Strasse 54; pizzas €5-10; ⌚noon-midnight Mon-Fri, 4pm-midnight Sat & Sun (to 10pm Oct-Mar); [S]Schönhauser Allee, 🚋M1, [R]Schönhauser Allee) This always-packed joint consistently delivers Neapolitan pizzas with pizazz straight from the wood-burning oven to the tables in the cosy, candlelit dining room. Pick a classic pie, build your own or try one of the *'magiche pizze'* like the Brunetto with hummus, shrimp and artichokes. Come by 8pm before local groupies have snapped up all the tables.

NALU DINER — AMERICAN €

Map p342 (☎030-8975 8633; www.nalu-diner.com; Dunckerstrasse 80a; mains €7-8.50; ⌚9am-10pm; [S]Eberswalder Strasse, 🚋M10, [R]Prenzlauer Allee) Kitsch-free Nalu is as authentic an American roadside diner as you'll find this side of the Atlantic. The no-nonsense ammo here is such good-old-fashioned cholesterol spikers as crispy hashbrowns, pancakes drenched in maple syrup, and fried eggs with bacon. Perks: iced tap water and free coffee refills.

ZIA MARIA — ITALIAN €

Map p342 (www.zia-maria.de; Pappelallee 32a; pizza slices €1.50-3.50; ⌚noon-11.30pm; [S]Schönhauser Allee, 🚋12, [R]Schönhauser Allee) This shoebox-sized pizza kitchen gets mobbed at all hours for its freshly made crispy-crust pies. Go classic or choose from such eclectic toppings as wafer-thin prosciutto, nutmeg-laced artichokes or pungent Italian sausage. Two slices are enough to fill up most. The grotto-like dining room doubles as a gallery.

★**FRAU MITTENMANG** INTERNATIONAL €€

Map p342 (☏030-444 5654; www.fraumitten-mang.de; Rodenbergstrasse 37; mains €9-17; ⊘6-11pm; Ⓢ Schönhauser Allee, ⓜ M1, Ⓡ Schönhauser Allee) This neighbourhood-adored restaurant with footpath bench seating delivers a daily changing roster of globally inspired dishes that sometimes push the culinary envelope, usually with delicious results. Reservations essential.

SI AN VIETNAMESE €€

Map p342 (☏030-4050 5775; www.sian-berlin.de; Rykestrasse 36; mains €7.80; ⊘noon-midnight; Ⓢ Eberswalder Strasse) This stylish nosh spot welcomes a steady stream of tousled hipsters, yoga mamas and even the occasional celeb (yes, Clooney was here). Everything is prepared freshly, seasonally, healthily and using traditional recipes from the ancient monasteries of Vietnam.

GUGELHOF FRENCH €€

Map p342 (☏030-442 9229; www.gugelhof.de; Knaackstrasse 37; mains €8-23; ⊘4pm-midnight Mon-Fri, from 10am-midnight Sat & Sun; Ⓢ Senefelderplatz) This country-French jewel made headlines when feeding Bill Clinton back in 2000, but thankfully it hasn't coasted on its fame since. Chefs still keep things real with robust *choucroute* (a sauerkraut-based stew), cheese fondue, *Flammkuche* (Alsatian pizza) and other Alsatian soul food, plus inventive daily specials. Fabulous wines and cheese and weekend breakfasts.

ODERQUELLE GERMAN €€

Map p342 (☏030-4400 8080; www.oderquelle.de; Oderberger Strasse 27; mains €8-20, 3-course dinner €23.50; ⊘6-11pm Mon-Sat, noon-11pm Sun; Ⓢ Eberswalder Strasse, ⓜ M1, 12) It's always fun to pop by this woodsy resto and see what's inspired the chef today. Most likely, it will be a well-crafted German meal, perhaps with a slight Mediterranean nuance. On the standard menu, the crispy *Flammkuche* is a reliable standby. Best seat: on the footpath so you can keep an eye on the parade of passers-by.

DER FISCHLADEN SEAFOOD €€

Map p342 (☏030-4000 5612; www.derfischladen.com; Schönhauser Allee 128; mains €3.50-15; ⊘10am-9pm Mon-Sat, 2-9pm Sun; Ⓢ Schönhauser Allee, ⓜ M1, Ⓡ Schönhauser Allee) Berlin may be landlocked, but Der Fischladen proves that this is no detriment to sourcing super-fresh fish and seafood. The shop-takeaway-snack-bar combo is especially proud of its English-style fish and chips, served with malt vinegar in a British newspaper. The spicy Sicilian shrimp or the grilled fish platter are other menu faves.

TAPITAS SPANISH €€

Map p342 (☏030-4673 6837; Gleimstrasse 23; tapas €3-7; ⊘4-11pm; Ⓢ Eberswalder Strasse, ⓜ M1) This darling teensy tapas bar is a top pick on the Gleimstrasse restaurant row. All the classics are there – *jamón serrano*, bacon-wrapped dates, tortillas etc – along with a changing roster of hot tapas like chicken in

PRENZLAUER BERG EATING

A CASE STUDY OF GENTRIFICATION

Badly pummelled but not destroyed during WWII, Prenzlauer Berg languished for decades, its grand but crumbling 19th-century townhouses becoming the domain of artists, creatives, intellectuals, gays and political dissidents. It was this community that stood up when the East German government came within a whisker of tearing down the old buildings in the late '80s. And it was they who fanned the flames of opposition that led to the Peaceful Revolution of 1989.

After the Wall collapsed, the district became party central, but was also among the first to show up in the crosshairs of developers. They snapped up the decrepit buildings for virtual pennies and scrubbed away decades of grime to reveal gorgeous facades and stucco-ornamented interiors. Nowadays, the sleekly renovated lofts are the haunts of worldly boho-bourgeois professionals, including many expats from France, Italy, the US and Britain.

These relatively recent arrivals have displaced nearly 80% of preunification residents, who could simply no longer afford the ever-rising rents or felt no cultural affinity for fancy coffee drinks. The demographic changes also account for the death of many long-standing party venues that had to cede to developers or noise-sensitive neighbours and have decamped to friendlier pastures, usually in Kreuzberg or Friedrichshain.

lime sauce. Fabulous aioli and robust Spanish wines to boot. Candelight and cosy inside, with a few sidewalk tables in summer.

🍴 Kollwitzplatz & the South Kiez

★MUSE INTERNATIONAL €
Map p342 (☎030-4005 6289; www.museberlin.de; Immanuelkirchstrasse 31; dishes €4.50-8.50; ⌚noon-4pm & 6-10pm Mon-Fri, 7.30pm-late Sat; 🚋M2) What began as a supper club in the home of owners Caroline and Tobias has grown into a rustic-chic neighbourhood bistro serving a small weekday menu of gourmet sandwiches, tasty casseroles and richly flavoured soups. On Saturdays, either they or guest chefs host multicourse meals in the supper-club tradition.

MARIA BONITA MEXICAN €
Map p342 (☎0176 7017 9461; www.mariabonitaberlin.wordpress.com; Danziger Strasse 33; mains €5.50-7.50; ⌚noon-11pm; [S]Eberswalder Strasse) Authentic Mexican food is still a rarity in Berlin, which is why we raise a cold Corona to this no-frills canteen where the tortillas are homemade, the salsas pack a pleasant punch and everything's prepared from scratch using seasonal produce. Menu highlights: the beef tacos and the chicken chipotle burritos.

KONNOPKE'S IMBISS GERMAN €
Map p342 (☎030-442 7765; www.konnopke-imbiss.de; Schönhauser Allee 44a; sausages €1.40-1.90; ⌚9am-8pm Mon-Fri, 11.30am-8pm Sat; [S]Eberswalder Strasse, 🚋M1, M10) Brave the inevitable queue at this famous sausage kitchen, ensconced in the same spot below the elevated U-Bahn track since 1930, but now equipped with a heated pavilion and an English menu. The 'secret' sauce topping its classic *Currywurst* comes in a four-part heat scale from mild to wild.

W - DER IMBISS FUSION €
Map p342 (☎030-4435 2206; www.w-derimbiss.de; Kastanienallee 49; dishes €4-12; ⌚noon-midnight; 🌿; [S]Rosenthaler Platz, 🚋M1) The love child of Italian and Indian cooking, W's signature naan pizza is freshly baked in the tandoor oven and decorated with such tasty meatless toppings as goats cheese, artichoke paste and guacamole. Enjoy it amid cheerful tiki decor alongside a healthy spirulina-laced apple juice. Or a beer from the fridge.

★LA SOUPE POPULAIRE GERMAN €€
Map p342 (☎030-4431 9680; www.lasoupepopulaire.de; Prenzlauer Allee 242; mains €14-21; ⌚noon-midnight Thu-Sat; [S]Rosa-Luxemburg-Strasse, 🚋M2) Local top toque Tim Raue's newest gastro destination embraces the soulful goodness of German home cooking, with a best seller being his riff on *Königsberger Klopse* (veal meatballs in caper sauce). It's all served in an industrial-chic space within a defunct 19th-century brewery where patrons sit at vintage tables overlooking a gallery space with changing contemporary art.

★UMAMI VIETNAMESE €€
Map p342 (☎030-2886 0626; www.umami-restaurant.de; Knaackstrasse 16; mains €7.50-14; ⌚noon-11.30pm; [S]Senefelderplatz, 🚋M2) This beautifully designed restaurant made an instant splash thanks to its mellow Asian lounge vibe and inspired menu of Indochine favourites. Solid menu choices include the Deep Gold Beef with fresh mango strips and the Mekong's Surf & Turf with king prawn and tenderloin. For a special kick, don't miss the Saigon mule.

DER HAHN IST TOT! FRENCH €€
Map p342 (☎030-6570 6756; www.der-hahn-ist-tot.de; Zionskirchstrasse 40; 4-course dinner €20; ⌚7-11pm Tue-Sun; [S]Eberswalder Strasse, 🚋M1) A French children's ditty inspired the curious name, which translates as 'The rooster is dead!' Here the deceased fowl is turned into coq au vin, the classic French country stew that's always on the menu at this pretension-free restaurant. Every night, staff dish up three four-course dinners, including a meat-free selection, at a truly unbeatable price.

LUCKY LEEK VEGAN €€
Map p342 (☎030-6640 8710; www.lucky-leek.de; Kollwitzstrasse 54; mains €12-18; ⌚6-11pm Wed-Sun; 🌿; [S]Senefelderplatz) Josita Hartanto not only knows how to coax maximum flavour out of the vegetable kingdom, but has a knack for combining them boldly and creatively. Even die-hard carnivores will likely swoon over such results as creamy wasabi-pea risotto, *seitan* dumplings and asparagus ravioli.

PAPALÓTL MEXICAN €€
Map p342 (☎030-4435 2184; www.papalotl-berlin.com; Belforter Strasse 22; mains €13-18; ⌚4pm-midnight Tue-Sun; 🚋M2, [U]Senefelderplatz) This Tex-Mex-free zone serves up authentic contemporary Mexican fare amid

an artsy vibe that's definitely more festive than fiesta. Everything's homemade, down to the complex moles, and prepared with quality meats and produce.

ZUM SCHUSTERJUNGEN GERMAN €€

Map p342 (☎030-442 7654; www.zumschusterjungen.com; Danziger Strasse 9; mains €5-13; ⏰11am-midnight; [S]Eberswalder Strasse) At this rustic corner pub, authentic Berlin charm is doled out with as much abandon as the delish home cooking. Big platters of goulash, roast pork and *Sauerbraten* feed both tummy and soul, as do the regionally brewed Berliner Schusterjunge pilsner and Märkischer Landmann black beer.

LA MUSE GUEULE FRENCH €€

Map p342 (☎030-4320 6596; Sredzkistrasse 14; mains €8-16; ⏰6pm-1am; [S]Eberswalder Strasse) It's the living room of Prenzlauer Berg's sizeable French community, but also popular for kicking back before or after attending an event at the Kulturbrauerei (p188). The country-style cuisine is as unpretentious as the chatty patrons, with blackboard specials showing especially imaginative flourishes.

SAUVAGE - THE RESTAURANT PALEO €€€

Map p342 (☎030-3810 0025; www.sauvageberlin.com; Winsstrasse 30; small plates €6.50-14, mains €21-33; ⏰11.30am-3.30pm Sat & Sun & 6pm-midnight Wed-Sun; 🚋M2, M10, 🚆Prenzlauer Allee) The Berlin outpost of the new paleo food trend, Sauvage is the grown-up cousin of the first branch that opened in Neukölln in 2011. Eating like Paleolithic cave dwellers means banishing dairy, grains and sugars and concentrating on organic, foraged, hunted, grass-fed and gluten-free ingredients. Dishes are hardly primitive, though, and feature carefully hunted and gathered ingredients. Reservations required.

DRINKING & NIGHTLIFE

Mauerpark & the North Kiez

★DECK 5 BAR

Map p342 (www.freiluftrebellen.de; Schönhauser Allee 80; ⏰10am-midnight Mon-Sat, noon-midnight Sun, in good summer weather only; [S]Schönhauser Allee, 🚋M1, 🚆Schönhauser Allee) Soak up the rays at this beach bar in the sky while sinking your toes into tonnes of sand lugged to the top parking deck of the Schönhauser Arkaden mall. Take the lift from within the mall or walk up a never-ending flight of stairs from Greifenhagener Strasse.

★BECKETTS KOPF COCKTAIL BAR

Map p342 (☎0162 237 9418; www.becketts-kopf.de; Pappelallee 64; ⏰8pm-2am Tue-Sun; [S]Schönhauser Allee, 🚋12, 🚆Schönhauser Allee) Past Samuel Beckett's portrait, the art of cocktail-making is taken very seriously. Settle into a heavy armchair in the warmly lit lounge and take your sweet time to peruse the extensive – and poetic – drinks menu. All the classics are accounted for, of course, as are such tempting specials as the mysterious gin- and bourbon-based Black Hawk.

EMILS BIERGARTEN BEER GARDEN

(www.wbb-pankow.de/biergarten; Berliner Strasse 80-82; ⏰3-10pm Mon-Fri, noon-10pm Sat & Sun Apr-Sep, weather permitting; [S]Vinetastrasse, 🚋M1) This simple, urban beer garden on the grounds of a former brewery has a pedigree going back to the early 20th century and, after a 20-year hiatus, was finally revived in 2013. The good beer selection, relaxed local crowd, pizza and bratwurst, all at down-to-earth prices, fill tables to capacity on balmy summer nights.

MAUERSEGLER BEER GARDEN

Map p342 (☎030-9788 0904; www.mauersegler-berlin.de; Bernauer Strasse 63; ⏰11am-2am daily May-Oct, 9am-7pm Sun year-round; 📶; [S]Eberswalder Strasse) Pram-pushing mummies, iPad toters and laid-back students all congregate at this funky-romantic beer garden for cold beers, cakes and barbecue. On the edge of the Mauerpark, it's busiest on Sundays as a rest stop for flea marketeers. Check the website for parties and concerts.

DUNCKER CLUB CLUB

Map p342 (☎030-445 9509; www.dunckerclub.de; Dunckerstrasse 64; ⏰9pm-late Wed-Sun; 🚋M10, 🚆Prenzlauer Allee) Way off the beaten track, Duncker is a rare club survivor in party-phobic Prenzlauer Berg in a building that's seen stints as a horse barn, a salt warehouse and a GDR-era youth club. Kool kids of all ages invade for an alchemy of (non-electronic) sounds, mostly indie rock, goth and '80s pop, plus free concerts on Thursdays. Chill-out garden in summer.

AUGUST FENGLER BAR, CLUB

Map p342 (www.augustfengler.de; Lychener Strasse 11; ⏱7pm-4am; [S]Eberswalder Strasse, 🚋M1) With its flirty vibe, teensy dance floor and foosball in the cellar, this local institution scores a trifecta on key ingredients for a good night out. Wallet-friendly drinks prices and a pretense-free crowd don't hurt either. Music-wise anything goes, from new wave, rock and Latin to soul, indie and ska.

MARIETTA CAFE, BAR

Map p342 (☎030-4372 0646; www.marietta-bar.de; Stargarder Strasse 13; ⏱10am-2am Sun-Thu, to 4am Fri & Sat; [S]Schönhauser Allee, 🚋M1, [R]Schönhauser Allee) Retro is right now at this neighbourly self-service retreat where you can check out passing eye candy through the big window or lug your beverage to the dimly lit back room for quiet bantering. On Wednesday nights it's a launch pad for the local gay party circuit.

GREIFBAR BAR

Map p342 (☎030-444 0828; www.greifbar.com; Wichertstrasse 10; ⏱10pm-6am; [S]Schönhauser Allee, [R]Schönhauser Allee) Men-Film-Cruising: Greifbar's motto says it all. This Prenzlauer Berg staple draws a mixed crowd of jeans, sneakers, leather and skin sniffing each other out below the big-screen video in the bar before retiring to the sweaty play zone in the back. Beers are two-for-one on Mondays.

🍷 Kollwitzplatz & the South Kiez

★PRATER BEER GARDEN

Map p342 (☎030-448 5688; www.pratergarten.de; Kastanienallee 7-9; ⏱noon-late Apr-Sep, weather permitting; [S]Eberswalder Strasse) This place has seen beer-soaked nights since 1837, making it Berlin's oldest beer garden. It's kept much of its traditional charm and is still perfect for guzzling a custom-brewed Prater pilsner beneath the ancient chestnut trees (self-service). Kids can romp around the small play area. In foul weather or winter, the adjacent beer hall is a fine place to sample classic Berlin dishes (mains €8 to €19).

★WEINEREI WINE BAR

Map p342 (☎030-440 6983; www.weinerei.com; Veteranenstrasse 14; ⏱8pm-late; 📶; [S]Rosenthaler Platz, 🚋M1) This living-room-style wine bar works on the honour principle: you 'rent' a wine glass for €2, then help yourself to as much vino as you like and in the end decide what you want to pay. Please be fair and do not take advantage of this fantastic concept.

★LE CROCO BLEU COCKTAIL BAR

Map p342 (☎0177 443 2359; www.lecrocobleu.com; Prenzlauer Allee 242; ⏱6pm-late Thu-Sat; [S]Rosa-Luxemburg-Strasse, 🚋M2) Berlin cocktail luminary Gregor Scholl's newest 'laboratory' occupies the machine room of a defunct 19th-century brewery. Amid stuffed animals, mushroom tables and other whimsical decor, you get to enjoy extravagant twists on time-tested classics. Fairy Floss – a Sazerac topped with absinthe-laced cotton candy – never fails to elicits oohs and aahs.

PFEFFERBRÄU BREWERY

Map p342 (☎030-473 773 640; www.pfefferbraeu.de; Schönhauser Allee 176; ⏱5.30-11pm Tue-Sat, 4-10pm Sun; [S]Senefelder Platz) On the same site where Joseph Pfeffer founded a brewery in 1841, the team from Pfefferbräu once again churn out delicious suds brewed in giant copper vats right on the premises. Sit in the woodsy beer hall or the leafy beer garden with a view of Senefelder Platz and enjoy a glass of hoppy Helles or the malty Dunkles.

ANNA BLUME CAFE

Map p342 (☎030-4404 8749; www.cafe-anna-blume.de; Kollwitzstrasse 83; ⏱8am-2am; [S]Eberswalder Strasse) Potent java, homemade cakes, and flowers from the attached shop perfume the art nouveau interior of this corner cafe named for a 1919 Dadaist poem by German artist Kurt Schwitters. In fine weather the footpath terrace is the best people-watching perch. Great for breakfast, especially the tiered tray for two.

CAFE CHAGALL CAFE, BAR

Map p342 (☎030-441 5881; Kollwitzstrasse 2; ⏱from 10am; [S]Senefelderplatz) Proof that the boho spirit is not dead in Prenzlauer Berg, Chagall gets flooded with a congenial mix of locals, expats and visitors who come for cold drinks and Russian treats, all served by smiling staff. Separate smoking room in back and big footpath terrace in summer.

BASSY CLUB

Map p342 (☎030-3744 8020; www.bassy-club.de; Schönhauser Allee 176a; ⏱9pm-late Wed, Fri & Sat; [S]Senefelderplatz) Most punters here have a post-Woodstock birth date, but happily ride the retro wave at this trashy-charming concert and party den dedicated 'strictly' to pre-1969 sounds – surf music, rockabilly, swing and country among them. Concerts, burlesque cabaret and the infamous **Chantals House of Shame** (Map p342; www.siteofshame.com; @Bassy Club, Schönhauser Allee 176a; ⏲from 11pm Thu; [S]Senefelderplatz) gay party on Thursdays beef up the schedule. Dress…creatively.

ROADRUNNER'S CLUB CLUB

Map p342 (www.roadrunners-paradise.de; 3rd courtyard, Saarbrücker Strasse 24; [S]Senefelderplatz) Rock-and-roll temple for rebels without a cause. From rockabilly parties to the monthly Mondo Klit lesbian fest, there's always some kick-ass party going on amid retro-Americana in the third backyard of a former brewery. Special treat: the heated Moroccan tent for chilling.

MORNING GLORY CAFE

Map p342 (☎030-4401 7512; Kastanienallee 75; ⏲8.30am-6pm Nov-Mar, 8am-8pm Apr-Oct; [S]Eberswalder Strasse, 🚋M1) This bright and low-key gem on the sunny side of Kastanienallee is the perfect place to banish hangovers with vitamin-packed smoothies, catch up on your reading over a top-shelf cappuccino or dig into an energy-restoring panino.

☆ ENTERTAINMENT

DOCK 11 DANCE

Map p342 (☎030-3512 0312; www.dock11-berlin.de; Kastanienallee 79; [S]Eberswalder Strasse, 🚋M1) For cutting-edge, experimental dance, there are few better places in town than this unpretentious space tucked into an old factory. Many productions are original works developed during courses and workshops held in-house.

LICHTBLICK KINO CINEMA

Map p342 (☎030-4405 8179; www.lichtblick-kino.org; Kastanienallee 77; [S]Eberswalder Strasse, 🚋M1) With space for only 32 cineastes, there's not a bad seat in Berlin's smallest cinema, run by a collective and known for its eclectic programming of fine retrospectives, political documentaries, shorts, Berlin-made movies and global avant-garde fare.

KOOKABURRA COMEDY

Map p342 (☎030-4862 3186; www.comedyclub.de; Schönhauser Allee 184; [S]Rosa-Luxemburg-Platz) This living-room-style comedy club delivers an assembly line of belly laughs in cosy digs at a former bank building. On Tuesday nights funny folk from English-speaking countries spin everyday material into comedy gold. Other treats: improv, open mike and the inimitable Fish & Whips burlesque shows.

🛍 SHOPPING

Kastanienallee and Oderberger Strasse are popular for Berlin-made fashions and streetwear. More indie stores hold forth along Stargarder Strasse and in the streets around Helmholtzplatz, especially lower Dunckerstrasse. Cool-hunters should also steer to the Mauerpark and Arkonaplatz to forage for flea-market treasure. For everyday needs stop by the Schönhauser Allee Arcaden mall right by the eponymous U-/S-Bahn station.

★**FLOHMARKT AM MAUERPARK** MARKET

Map p342 (www.mauerparkmarkt.de; Bernauer Strasse 63-64; ⏲10am-5pm Sun; [S]Eberwalder Strasse) Join the throngs of thrifty trinket hunters, bleary-eyed clubbers and excited tourists sifting for treasure at this always busy flea market right where the Berlin Wall once ran. Source new faves among retro threads, local-designer T-shirts, vintage vinyl and offbeat stuff. Ethnic food stands and beer gardens, including Mauersegler (p195), provide sustenance.

FLOHMARKT AM ARKONAPLATZ MARKET

Map p342 (www.mauerparkmarkt.de; Arkonaplatz; ⏲10am-4pm Sun; [S]Bernauer Strasse) Surrounded by cafes perfect for carbo-loading, this smallish flea market lets you ride the retro frenzy with plenty of groovy furniture, accessories, clothing, vinyl and books, including some GDR-era stuff. It's easily combined with a visit to the nearby Flohmarkt am Mauerpark.

KOLLWITZPLATZMARKT MARKET

Map p342 (Kollwitzstrasse; ⏲noon-7pm Thu, 9am-4pm Sat; [S]Senefelderplatz) Berlin's poshest farmers market has everything you need to put together a gourmet picnic or meal. Velvety gorgonzolas, juniper-berry smoked ham, crusty sourdough bread and homemade pesto are among the exquisite morsels scooped up by well-heeled locals. The Saturday edition also features handicrafts.

★ **FLAGSHIPSTORE** FASHION

Map p342 (☑030-4373 5327; www.flagshipstore-berlin.de; Oderberger Strasse 53; ⊙noon-8pm Mon-Sat; ⓢEberswalder Strasse, ☐M1) Beata and Johanna are geniuses when it comes to ferreting out the finest limited-edition streetwear from both up-and-coming Berlin designers and a few imports. There's unconventional but wearable fashion for him and her, plus plenty of cool accessories.

THATCHERS FASHION

Map p342 (☑030-2462 7751; www.thatchers.de; Kastanienallee 21; ⊙11am-7pm; ⓢEberswalder Strasse, ☐M1) Berlin fashion veterans Ralf Hensellek and Thomas Mrozek specialise in well-tailored clothing that's feminine and versatile. Their smart dresses, skirts and shirts look almost plain on the rack, but are transformed when worn as the sort of stylish garments that go from office to dinner to nightclub – but not hurriedly out of fashion. Also located at Court IV of the Hackesche Höfe (p139).

AWEAR FASHION

Map p342 (www.above-berlin.de; Kastanienallee 75; ⊙noon-8pm Mon-Fri, to 7pm Sat; ⓢEberswalder Strasse, ☐M1) This streetwear concept store feeds the urban-fashion craze with hats, hoodies, sneakers, tees and more by Dr Denim, Sixpack France, Just Female, dico Copenhagen and plenty of other cool-hunter faves.

★ **TA(U)SCHE** ACCESSORIES

Map p342 (☑030-4030 1770; www.tausche.de; Raumerstrasse 8; ⊙10am-8pm Mon-Fri, to 6pm Sat; ⓢEberswalder Strasse) Heike Braun and Antje Strubels now sell their messenger-style bags around the world, but this is the store where it all began. Bags come in 11 sizes with exchangeable flaps that zip off and on in seconds. There's a huge range of flaps to match your mood or outfit, plus various inserts, depending on whether you need to lug a laptop, a camera or nappies (diapers).

★ **LUXUS INTERNATIONAL** GIFTS, SOUVENIRS

Map p342 (☑030-8643 5500; www.luxus-international.de; Kastanienallee 84; ⊙11am-8pm Mon-Sat; ⓢEberswalder Strasse, ☐M1) There's no shortage of creative spirits in Berlin, but not many of them can afford their own store. In comes Luxus International, a unique concept store that rents them a shelf or two to display their original designs: T-shirts, tote bags, ashtrays, lamps, candles, mugs etc. You never know what you'll find, but you can bet it's a Berlin original.

VEB ORANGE GIFTS, SOUVENIRS

Map p342 (☑030-9788 6886; www.veborange.de; Oderberger Strasse 29; ⊙10am-8pm Mon-Sat; ⓢEberswalder Strasse) Viva vintage! With its selection of the most beautiful things from the '60s and '70s, this place is a tangible reminder of how colourful, campy and fun home decor used to be. True to its name, many of the furnishings, accessories, lamps and fashions are orange in colour.

SAINT GEORGES BOOKS

Map p342 (☑030-8179 8333; www.saintgeorgesbookshop.com; Wörther Strasse 27; ⊙11am-8pm Mon-Fri, to 7pm Sat; 🕾; ⓢSenefelderplatz) Laid-back and low-key, Saint Georges bookshop is a sterling spot to track down new and used Berlin-themed fiction and nonfiction. The selection includes plenty of rare and out-of-print books as well as literature by foreign authors translated into English.

GOLDHAHN UND SAMPSON FOOD

Map p342 (☑030-4119 8366; www.goldhahnundsampson.de; Dunckerstrasse 9; ⊙8am-8pm Mon-Fri, 10am-8pm Sat; ⓢEberswalder Strasse) Pink Himalaya salt, Moroccan argan oil and crusty German bread are among the global pantry stockers temptingly displayed at this stylish food gallery. Owners Sasha and Andreas hand-source all items, most of them rare, organic and from small suppliers.

RATZEKATZ TOYS

Map p342 (☑030-681 9564; www.ratzekatz.de; Raumerstrasse 7; ⊙10am-7pm Mon-Sat; ⓢEberswalder Strasse) Packed with quality playthings, this adorable store made headlines a few years ago when Angelina Jolie and son Maddox picked out a Jurassic Park's worth of dinosaurs. Even without the celeb glow, it's a fine place to source everything from Siku cars and trucks to Ravensburger jigsaws.

EISDIELER FASHION

Map p342 (☑030-2839 1291; www.eisdieler.de; Kastanienallee 12; ⊙noon-8pm Mon-Fri, 11am-7pm Sat; ⓢEberswalder Strasse) The urban streetwear designed by this co-op is as cool as the ice cream once sold in the store before it became a boutique. Find T-shirts, jeans and other clothes created under the Eisdieler label, plus fashion and shoes by Onitsuka Tiger, Palladium, Veja, Schmoove and Hummel along with bags by Qwstion and sunglasses by Le Specs and Spitfire.

City West & Charlottenburg

KURFÜRSTENDAMM | SCHLOSS CHARLOTTENBURG

Neighbourhood Top Five

1 Marvelling at the Prussian royal lifestyle at **Schloss Charlottenburg** (p201), then relaxing with a picnic by the carp pond in the palace park.

2 Tempting your taste buds in the fabulous food hall of the **KaDeWe** (p213) department store.

3 Meditating upon the futility of war at the majestically ruined **Kaiser-Wilhelm-Gedächtniskirche** (p208).

4 Communing with apes and zebras at **Berlin Zoo** (p206), the world's most species-rich animal park.

5 Giving your credit cards a workout on an extended shopping spree along Kurfürstendamm and at **Bikini Berlin** (p214).

For more detail of this area, see Map p338 ➡

Lonely Planet's Top Tip

Leaving from Zoo Station, buses 100 and 200 pass many blockbuster sights (including Potsdamer Platz and the Reichstag) on their route through the central city to Alexanderplatz. See p212 for details.

Best Places to Eat

➜ Osteria Centrale (p211)
➜ Good Friends (p208)
➜ Neni (p208)
➜ Restaurant am Steinplatz (p211)

For reviews, see p207 ➡

Best Places to Drink

➜ Monkey Bar (p211)
➜ Pearl (p211)
➜ Diener (p212)
➜ Universum Lounge (p212)

For reviews, see p211 ➡

Best Museums

➜ Museum Berggruen (p205)
➜ Käthe-Kollwitz-Museum (p207)
➜ Sammlung Scharf-Gerstenberg (p204)
➜ C/O Berlin (p209)

For reviews, see p204 ➡

Explore: City West & Charlottenburg

The glittering heart of West Berlin during the Cold War, Charlottenburg is nirvana for shopaholics, royal groupies and culture lovers. On its main artery – Kurfürstendamm – fashionable boutiques mix it up with high-street chains and department stores. The holy grail among the latter is the KaDeWe on nearby Tauentzienstrasse. There's more shopping in the leafy side streets, also home to relaxed cafes, neighbourhood-adored restaurants and both snazzy bars and Old Berlin–style pubs.

Eclipsed by historic Mitte and other eastern districts after reunification, Charlottenburg is finally reclaiming some of the limelight, especially in the city's west around Zoo Station. Recent developments include the 32-storey Zoo Fenster tower, with the Waldorf Astoria Hotel, which dramatically changed the western city skyline; the Bikini Berlin concept mall next door, delivering a dose of hipster cred; and the rejuvenated Zoopalast cinema, bringing a dose of retro glam. The prestigious C/O gallery space has also joined the westward migration.

About 3.5km northwest of here, Schloss Charlottenburg is not only the best-preserved royal palace in Berlin but is also surrounded by a lovely park and a trio of top museums.

Local Life

➜ **Shopping** Shop till you drop at high-street chains and high-fashion boutiques along Ku'damm and its side streets, at Bikini Berlin (p214) and the KaDeWe (p213) consumer temple.

➜ **The Asian mile** Find your favourite among the authentic Chinese eateries in Berlin's Little Asia along Kantstrasse.

➜ **Views** Enjoy sunset drinks with a view at the Monkey Bar (p211).

➜ **Cafe hang-outs** Spend an evening dolce vita–style with an alfresco dinner at Brel (p209) or another Savignyplatz restaurant.

Getting There & Away

➜ **Bus** Zoologischer Garten is the western terminus for buses 100 and 200, M19, M29 and X10 travel along Kurfürstendamm. Lines 309 and M45 go to Schloss Charlottenburg.

➜ **S-Bahn** Zoologischer Garten is the most central station.

➜ **U-Bahn** Uhlandstrasse, Kurfürstendamm and Wittenbergplatz stations put you right into shopping central.

TOP SIGHT
SCHLOSS CHARLOTTENBURG

Schloss Charlottenburg is an exquisite baroque palace and one of the few sites in Berlin that still reflects the one-time grandeur of the royal Hohenzollern clan. A visit is especially pleasant in summer when you can fold a stroll, sunbathing session or picnic by the carp pond into a day of peeking at royal treasures. And what treasures: lavishly furnished period rooms reflect royal tastes and lifestyles from the baroque period to the 20th century, as well as the largest collection of 18th-century French paintings outside of France.

The palace started out rather modestly, as a petite summer retreat built for Sophie-Charlotte, wife of Elector Friedrich III, and was expanded in the mode of Versailles after the elector's promotion to king in 1701. Subsequent royals dabbled with the compound, most notably Frederick the Great who added the spectacular Neuer Flügel. Reconstruction of the Schloss after its WWII drubbing became a priority and was completed in 1966.

The grand complex consists of the main building and three smaller structures scattered about the sprawling **Schlossgarten Charlottenburg** (palace park), which is part formal French baroque, part unruly English landscape and all idyllic playground. Hidden among the shady paths, flower beds, lawns, mature trees and carp pond are two smaller buildings, the sombre Mausoleum and the playful Belvedere. The palace exterior is undergoing phased renovations until 2016, but there should be no major disruptions to the visiting schedule.

DON'T MISS...

- Frederick the Great's apartments in the Neuer Flügel
- A stroll around the Schlossgarten
- Paintings by Watteau and other French masters
- Elaborate sarcophagi in the Mausoleum

PRACTICALITIES

- ☎030-320 910
- www.spsg.de
- Spandauer Damm 10-22
- day pass adult/concession €15/11
- 🕐hours vary by building
- 🚌M45, 109, 309, [S]Richard-Wagner-Platz, Sophie-Charlotte-Platz

TOP TIPS

Each Schloss building charges separate admission, but it's best to invest in the *Ticket charlottenburg+* (adult/concession €15/11) for one-day admission to every open building. Arrive early, especially on weekends and in summer when queues can be long.

The Schloss is at its most photogenic from outside the gate in front and from the carp pond in the Schlosspark. If you want to take photographs inside the palaces, you need to buy a photo permit (€3).

BAROQUE CONCERTS

Feel like a member of the Prussian court during the **Berliner Residenz Konzerte** (☑030-2581 0350; www. concerts-berlin.com; Grosse Orangerie, Schloss Charlottenburg, Spandauer Damm 22-24; ☺8.30pm Sat), a series of concerts held by candlelight with musicians dressed in powdered wigs and historical costumes who play works by baroque and early classical composers. Various packages are available, including one featuring a preconcert dinner.

Altes Schloss

Also known as the Nering-Eosander Building after its two architects, the **Altes Schloss** (☑030-320 911; adult/concession incl tour or audioguide €12/8; ☺10am-6pm Tue-Sun Apr-Oct, 10am-5pm Tue-Sun Nov-Mar) is the central, and oldest, section of the palace and fronted by Andreas Schlüter's grand **equestrian statue of the Great Elector** (1699). Inside, the baroque living quarters of Friedrich I and Sophie-Charlotte are an extravaganza in stucco, brocade and overall opulence. Highlights include the **Oak Gallery**, a wood-panelled festival hall draped in family portraits; the charming **Oval Hall** overlooking the park; Friedrich I's bedchamber, with the first-ever bathroom in a baroque palace; and the **Eosander Chapel**, with its trompe l'œil arches. The king's passion for precious china is reflected in the dazzling **Porcelain Chamber**, which boasts nearly 3000 pieces of Chinese and Japanese blueware.

Upstairs are paintings, vases, tapestries, weapons, porcelain, a 2600-piece silver table setting and other items essential to a royal lifestyle.

Neuer Flügel

The palace's most beautiful rooms are the private chambers of Frederick the Great in the **Neuer Flügel** (New Wing; check prices online; ☺10am-6pm), designed in 1746 by royal buddy and star architect of the period Georg Wenzeslaus von Knobelsdorff. The confection-like White Hall banquet room and the Golden Gallery, a rococo fantasy of mirrors and gilding, are both standouts. Other rooms display one of the largest collections of 18th-century French paintings by such masters as Watteau and Pesne. Also note the apartment of Luise (1776–1810; a popular queen and wife of King Friedrich Wilhelm III), with its lavish chandeliers, period furniture and hand-painted silk wall coverings.

Neuer Pavillon

Returning from a trip to Italy, Friedrich Wilhelm III (r 1797–1848) commissioned Karl Friedrich Schinkel to design the **Neuer Pavillon** (New Pavillon; adult/concession incl audioguide €4/3; ☺10am-6pm Tue-Sun Apr-Oct, 10am-5pm Tue-Sun Nov-Mar) as a summer refuge modelled on a villa in Naples. Today, the minipalace is filled with Biedermeier furniture and masterpieces by such Schinkel contemporaries as Caspar David Friedrich and Eduard Gaertner.

Belvedere

The late-rococo **Belvedere** (adult/concession €3/2.50; ☺10am-6pm Tue-Sun Apr-Oct) palace with the distinctive cupola got its start in 1788 as a tea house for

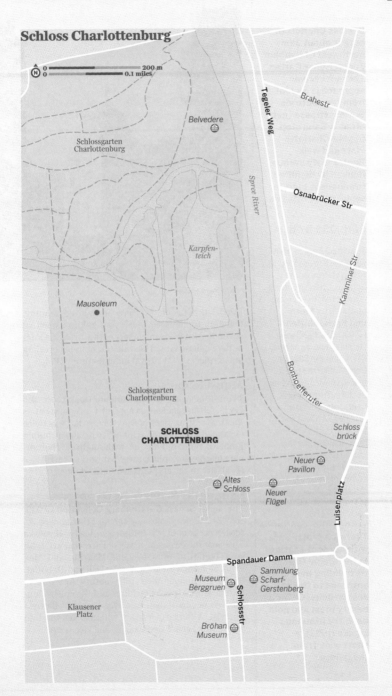

Schloss Charlottenburg

0 — 200 m
0 — 0.1 miles

Belvedere 🏛

Schlossgarten
Charlottenburg

Spree River

Brahestr

Tegeler Weg

Osnabrücker Str

Kammïner Str

Karpfen-
teich

Mausoleum ●

Bonhoefferufer

Schloss
brück

Schlossgarten
Charlottenburg

**SCHLOSS
CHARLOTTENBURG**

Neuer 🏛
Pavillon

Luïserplatz

Altes 🏛
Schloss

Neuer 🏛
Flügel

Neuer
Flügel

Spandauer Damm

Sammlung
Scharf-
Gerstenberg 🏛

Museum 🏛
Berggruen

Schlossstr

Klausener
Platz

Bröhan 🏛
Museum

Schloss Charlottenburg is about 3km northwest of Bahnhof Zoologischer Garten. The most scenic approach is on foot from the south via Schlossstrasse (get off at U-Bahn stop Sophie-Charlotte-Platz and walk 1km), a leafy avenue flanked by dignified townhouses built for senior court officials.

SCHLOSS BY BOAT

From mid-April to early October, a lovely way to travel to or from Schloss Charlottenburg is by Spree River cruise operated by **Stern und Kreisschiffahrt** (☏030-536 3600; www.sternundkreis.de; one way €15, round-trip €21.50). Boats make the trip twice daily from landing docks in Treptow (1¾ hours) and Jannowitz-brücke (1¼ hour) and go through Berlin's scenic historic centre to the palace boat landing just outside the northeast corner of the park. The return trip also drops off at Friedrichstrasse.

There's a pretty cafe with outdoor seating in the Kleine Orangerie building near the entrance to the palace gardens. Or for a hearty meal and cold beer, try Brauhaus Lemke (p211), a short walk from the palace.

Belvedere (p202)

Friedrich Wilhelm II. Here he enjoyed reading, listening to chamber music and holding spiritual sessions with fellow members of the mystical Order of the Rosicrucians. These days it houses porcelain masterpieces by the royal manufacturer KPM.

Mausoleum

The 1810 neoclassical **Mausoleum** (adult/concession €2/1; ⊙10am-6pm Tue-Sun Apr-Oct) was conceived as the final resting place of Queen Luise but was twice expanded to make room for other royals, including Emperor William I and his wife Augusta. Their ornate marble sarcophagi are great works of art. More royals are in the crypt (closed to the public).

Sammlung Scharf-Gerstenberg

The stellar **Scharf-Gerstenberg Collection** (☏030-266 424 242; www.smb.museum/ssg; Schlossstrasse 70; adult/concession €10/5; ⊙10am-6pm Tue-Fri, 11am-6pm Sat & Sun) showcases a survey of surrealist art, with large bodies of work by René Magritte and Max Ernst alongside dreamscapes by Dalí and Dubuffet. Standouts among their 18th-century forerunners include Goya's spooky etchings and the creepy dungeon scenes by Italian engraver Giovanni Battista Piranesi. A Berggruen ticket will also get you into Sammlung Scharf-Gerstenberg and vice versa.

Museum Berggruen

Fans of classical modern art will be in their element at the delightful **Museum Berggruen** (☑030-266 424 242; www.smb.museum/mb; Schlossstrasse 1; adult/concession €10/5; ☺10am-6pm Tue-Fri, 11am-6pm Sat & Sun). Picasso is especially well represented with paintings, drawings and sculptures from all major creative phases. Standouts include the *Seated Harlequin* from his early blue and rose periods and bold cubist canvases like his portrait of George Braque. Elsewhere it's off to Paul Klee's emotional world, Matisse's paper cut-outs, Giacometti's famous sculptures and a sprinkling of African art that inspired both Klee and Picasso.

A joint ticket (Bereichskarte Charlottenburg) for same-day visits to Museum Berggruen, Sammlung Scharf-Gerstenberg and the Museum für Fotografie (p206) costs €12 (concession €6). Buying tickets online nets a small discount.

Bröhan Museum

The **Bröhan Museum** (☑030-3269 0600; www.broehan-museum.de; Schlossstrasse 1a; adult/concession/under 18 €8/5/free; ☺10am-6pm Tue-Sun) trains the spotlight on art nouveau, art deco and functionalism, all decorative styles in vogue between 1889 and 1939 and considered the midwives of modern design. Highlights include fully furnished and decorated period rooms by Hector Guimard and Peter Behrens, a Berlin Secession picture gallery and a section dedicated to Henry van de Velde.

Abguss-Sammlung Antiker Plastik Berlin

If you are a fan of classical sculpture or simply enjoy studying naked guys with missing noses or other bodily protrusions, make the **Abguss-Sammlung An-tiker Plastik Berlin** (Antique Plaster-Cast Collection; ☑030-342 4054; www.abguss-sammlung-berlin.de; Schlossstrasse 69b; ☺2-5pm Thu-Sun) FREE a stopover. It has works spanning 3500 years, created by cultures as diverse as the Minoan, Roman or Byzantine, allowing you to trace the evolution of this ancient art form. The shop sells plaster-cast copies.

SIGHTS

The 3.5km Kurfürstendamm is a ribbon of commerce that began as a bridle path to the royal hunting lodge in the Grunewald forest. In the early 1870s, Otto von Bismarck, the Iron Chancellor, decided that the capital of the newly founded German Reich needed its own representative boulevard, which he envisioned as even bigger and better than the Champs-Élysées.

SCHLOSS CHARLOTTENBURG — PALACE

See p201.

EUROPA-CENTER — LANDMARK

Map p338 (www.europa-center-berlin.de; Breitscheidplatz; ⏰24hr; [S]Kurfürstendamm, Zoologischer Garte, 🚆Zoologischer Garten) The 103m-high Europa-Center was Berlin's first 'skyscraper' at its 1965 opening, with the giant Mercedes star spinning on its rooftop a symbol of capitalist West Germany's miraculous economic recovery. Today, the shopping centre exudes charming retro flair and is enlivened by such quirky sights as the Lotus Fountain and the psychedelic *Flow of Time Clock* by Bernard Gitton.

You can catch the lift to the 20th floor to enjoy the panorama or get an eyeful of pretty people and Berlin at the swish Puro Skylounge (p212). Europa-Center was built on the site of the Romanisches Cafe, a popular hang-out of 1920s artists and intellectuals.

ZOO PALAST — HISTORIC SITE

Map p338 (☎030-254 010; www.zoopalast-berlin.de; Hardenbergstrasse 29a; movies from €10.50; 🚌100, [S]Bahnhof Zoologischer Garten, 🚆Bahnhof Zoologischer Garten) International stars got the red carpet treatment during Berlin's International Film Festival (Berlinale) between 1957 and 1999 at West Berlin's most glamorous cinema. After a three-year renovation it returned to the spotlight in late 2013 and now screens blockbusters (dubbed into German) in seven fancily appointed theatres. Check out the cool 1950s foyer.

MUSEUM FÜR FOTOGRAFIE — MUSEUM

Map p338 (☎030-266 424 242; www.smb.museum/mf; Jebensstrasse 2; adult/concession €10/5; ⏰10am-6pm Tue, Wed & Fri-Sun, 10am-8pm Thu; [S]Zoologischer Garten, 🚆Zoologischer Garten) The artistic legacy of Helmut Newton (1920–2004), the Berlin-born enfant terrible of fashion and lifestyle photography, is

TOP SIGHT
BERLIN ZOO & AQUARIUM

Berlin's zoo holds a triple record as Germany's oldest, most species-rich and most popular. It was established in 1844 under King Friedrich Wilhelm IV, who donated the land plus animals from the royal family's private reserve. The menagerie includes orangutans, koalas, rhinos, giraffes and penguins. Animals are housed in open enclosures designed to resemble their habitat.

Especially popular are the **feeding sessions** that start at 10.30am with the polar bears. The California sea lions (3.15pm) usually elicit the biggest cheers.

The adjacent **Zoo-Aquarium** (Map p338; ☎030-254 010; www.aquarium-berlin.de; Budapester Strasse 32; adult/child €13/6.50, with zoo €20/10; ⏰9am-6pm; [S]Zoologischer Garten, 🚆Zoologischer Garten) presents three floors of exotic fish, amphibians and reptiles in old-fashioned darkened halls and glowing tanks. Its **Crocodile Hall** could be the stuff of nightmares, but jellyfish, iridescent poison frogs and a real-life 'Nemo' should bring smiles to most youngsters.

The zoo's architecture also deserves a special mention; a highlight is the exotic **Elephant Gate** (Map p338; Budapester Strasse). The main zoo entrance is from Hardenbergplatz via the **Lions' Gate**.

DON'T MISS...

- Elephant Gate
- Crocodile Hall

PRACTICALITIES

- Map p338
- ☎030-254 010
- www.zoo-berlin.de
- Hardenbergplatz 8
- adult/child €13/6.50, with aquarium €20/10
- ⏰9am-7pm mid Mar–Aug, 9am-6.30pm Sep & Oct, 9am-5pm Nov–mid-Mar
- 🚌100, 200, [S]Zoologischer Garten, 🚆Zoologischer Garten

given centre stage at Berlin's Photography Museum in a converted Prussian officers' casino behind Bahnhof Zoo. On the top floor, the gloriously restored barrel-vaulted **Kaisersaal** (Emperor's Hall) forms a grand backdrop for changing high-calibre photography exhibits drawn from the archive of the State Art Library. Shortly before his fatal car crash, Newton donated 1500 images along with personal effects to the city in which he was born. He had studied photography here with famed fashion photographer Yva before fleeing Nazi Germany in 1938. His work reflects a lifelong obsession with the female body.

KÄTHE-KOLLWITZ-MUSEUM MUSEUM

Map p338 (☎030-882 5210; www.kaethe-kollwitz.de; Fasanenstrasse 24; adult/concession €6/3, audioguide €3; 🕒11am-6pm; [S]Uhlandstrasse) This exquisite museum is devoted to the artist Käthe Kollwitz (1867–1945), whose social and political awareness lent a tortured power to her lithographs, graphics, woodcuts, sculptures and drawings. Highlights include the antihunger lithography *Brot!* (Bread!, 1924) and the woodcut series *Krieg* (War, 1922–23).

STORY OF BERLIN MUSEUM

Map p338 (☎030-8872 0100; www.story-of-berlin.de; Kurfürstendamm 207-208, enter via Ku'damm Karree mall; adult/concession €12/9; 🕒10am-8pm, last admission 6pm; [S]Uhlandstrasse) This multimedia museum breaks down 800 years of Berlin history into bite-size chunks that are easy to swallow but substantial enough to be satisfying. Each of the 23 rooms uses sound, light, technology and original objects to zero in on a specific theme or epoch in the city's history, from its founding in 1237 to the fall of the Berlin Wall. A creepily fascinating highlight is a tour (also in English) of a still functional atomic bunker beneath the building.

DAS VERBORGENE MUSEUM MUSEUM

Map p338 (Hidden Museum; ☎030-313 3656; www.dasverborgenemuseum.de; Schlüterstrasse 70; adult/concession €2/1; 🕒3-7pm Thu & Fri, noon-4pm Sat & Sun; [S]Ernst-Reuter-Platz, 🚆Savignyplatz) Founded by a pair of feminist artists and art historians, the nonprofit Hidden Museum has a unique focus: largely forgotten works by early-20th-century women artists, mostly from Germany. Past exhibits have trained the spotlight on expressionist artist Ilse Heller-Lazard and photographer Henriette Grindat. Curators mount about two exhibits annually, which run for three or four months each. At other times, the museum is closed.

LOCAL KNOWLEDGE

WATER 'MEATBALL' FOUNTAIN

Flanked by the Kaiser-Wilhelm-Gedächtniskirche and the Europa-Center, bustling Breitscheidplatz is where everyone from foot-sore tourists to buskers and skateboarding teens gather, in particular around its quirky **fountain** (World Fountain; Map p338; Breitscheidplatz; 🚌100, [S]Kurfürstendamm, Zoologischer Garten, 🚆Zoologischer Garten), a 1983 creation of local artist Joachim Schmettau. Nicknamed *Wasserklops* (water meatball), it's made from red granite and bronze, and festooned with sculptures of humans and animals.

🍴 EATING

The dining quality in Charlottenburg is dependably high. Savignyplatz exudes the relaxed and bustling vibe of an Italian piazza on balmy summer nights, while Kantstrasse is lined with many excellent Asian and Spanish eateries.

🍴 Kurfürstendamm

ALI BABA ITALIAN €

Map p338 (☎030-881 1350; www.alibaba-berlin.de; Bleibtreustrasse 45; dishes €3-10.50; 🕒11am-2am Sun-Thu, to 3am Fri & Sat; 🚆Savignyplatz) In business for more years than there are robbers in the eponymous fairy tale, Ali Baba is a bustling port of call beloved by shoppers, students, cabbies and party people for its delicious thin-crust pizza and generous portions of pasta served with crusty homemade bread.

BIER'S KUDAMM 195 GERMAN €

Map p338 (☎030-881 8942; Kurfürstendamm 195; Currywurst €2.50; 🕒11am-5am Mon-Thu, 11am-6am Fri & Sat, noon-5pm Sun; [S]Uhlandstrasse) This snazzy sausage parlour satisfies the proletarian hunger pangs of deep-pocketed locals, including – if the

TOP SIGHT
KAISER-WILHELM-GEDÄCHTNISKIRCHE

This ruin is one of Berlin's most photographed landmarks. The Allied bombing of 23 November 1943 left only the husk of the west tower standing, which now serves as an antiwar memorial. The original church was a magnificent neo-Romanesque pile designed by Franz Schwechten and completed in 1895. Historic photographs displayed in the **Gedenkhalle** (Hall of Remembrance) at the bottom of the tower should help you visualise its former grandeur. The hall also contains remnants of the elaborate **mosaics** that once swathed the entire church, depicting heroic moments from Kaiser Wilhelm I's life, among other scenes. Also note the marble reliefs, liturgical objects and two symbols of reconciliation: an icon cross donated by the Russian Orthodox church and a copy of the Cross of Nails from Coventry Cathedral.

In 1961 a modern bell tower and **octagonal new church** were completed next to the ruined tower; the latter is especially striking thanks to its mysteriously glowing midnight-blue glass walls. The huge golden statue of the resurrected Christ 'floating' above the altar is made of tombac, a type of brass with a high copper content, and weighs 300kg. Also note the 'Stalingrad Madonna' (a charcoal drawing) against the north wall.

DON'T MISS...

- Mosaics in the memorial hall in the ruined tower
- Blue glass walls

PRACTICALITIES

- Map p338
- www.gedaechtniskirche.com
- Breitscheidplatz
- 🕒church 9am-7pm, memorial hall 10am-6pm Mon-Fri, 10am-5.30pm Sat, noon-5.30pm Sun
- 🚌100, [S]Zoologischer Garten, Kurfürstendamm, 🚉Zoologischer Garten

photographs are anything to go by – the occasional celeb. The truly decadent wash down their *Currywurst* with a small bottle of Champagne (€23).

REPKE SPÄTZLEREI — GERMAN €

Map p338 (☎030-8871 8672; www.spaetzlerei.de; Bleibtreustrasse 46; lunches €2.90-5.90, dinner mains €6-13; 🕒11.30am-midnight; 🚉Savignyplatz) Rustic Repke is the neighborhood go-to place for big portions of such southern German faves as *Spätzle* (mac 'n' cheese), *Maultaschen* (ravioli) and *Flammekuche* (French pizza), all homemade of course. Budget-priced lunch specials drop 50% during the afternoon lull (4pm to 6pm).

★**GOOD FRIENDS** — CHINESE €€

Map p338 (☎030-313 2659; www.goodfriends-berlin.de; Kantstrasse 30; mains €7-20; 🕒noon-1am; 🚉Savignyplatz) Good Friends is widely considered Berlin's best and most authentic Chinese restaurant. The ducks dangling in the window are the overture to a menu long enough to confuse Confucius. If jellyfish with eggs or fried pork belly prove too challenging, you can always fall back on lemon chicken or king prawn curry.

★**NENI** — INTERNATIONAL €€

Map p338 (☎030-120 221 200; Budapester Strasse 40; mains €11-21; 🕒noon-10:30pm Sun-Thu, to 11:30pm Fri & Sat; 🚌100, 200, [S]Bahnhof Zoologischer Garten, 🚉Bahnhof Zoologischer Garten) Despite the hype, the food is actually quite good at this 10th-floor dining hall at the 25hours Hotel Bikini Berlin. Enjoy the view while picking from a menu influenced by the cuisines of Israel, Persia, Russia and Arabian and Mediterranean countries. The hummus is reported to be the best in town.

FRANKE BRASSERIE - ORGANIC EATERY — INTERNATIONAL €€

Map p338 (☎030-3155 1030; www.frankerestaurant.de; Excelsior Hotel, Hardenbergstrasse 14; 2-course weekday lunch €12, dinner mains €13-27; 🕒5.30-11pm Mon-Sat; [S]Zoologischer Garten, 🚉Zoologischer Garten) This is one stylish and sexy hotel restaurant, which has put its eggs into the organic basket right down to the beer and wine. Sit close to the open kitchen to watch the cooks do their magic in creating such palate teasers as the baby burger trio, tiger shrimp with mint and black pasta or the slow-cooked ribs teamed with pumpkin, spinach and pine nuts.

BREL FRENCH, BELGIAN €€

Map p338 (☏030-3180 0020; www.cafebrel.de; Savignyplatz 1; 3-course lunch €10.50, mains €10-23; ⊙9am-1am; ⊛Savignyplatz) Belgian cult crooner Jacques Brel is the namesake of this bistro in a former bordello that now draws bleary-eyed bohos for coffee and croissants, suits and tourists for lunch specials, and artsy types and stylish couples for oysters, rump steaks and crème brûlée at dinnertime.

MR HAI KABUKI JAPANESE €€

Map p338 (☏030-8862 8136; www.mrhai.de; Olivaer Platz 10; platters from €14; ⊙noon-midnight; ⬛M19, 109, ⓢAdenauerplatz, Uhlandstrasse) The menu features classic *nigiri* and maki but most regulars flock to Mr Hai for more unconventional sushi morsels, composed like little works of art. Some creations feature kimchi, pumpkin and cream cheese or are flambéed and deep-fried. Sounds bizarre but it works. From U-Bahn station Uhlandstrasse, take bus 109 or M19 two stops to Olivaer Platz.

CAFÉ-RESTAURANT WINTERGARTEN IM LITERATURHAUS INTERNATIONAL €€

Map p338 (☏030-882 5414; www.literaturhaus-berlin.de; Fasanenstrasse 23; mains €8-16; ⊙9am-midnight; ⓢUhlandstrasse) The hustle and bustle of Ku'damm is only a block away from this genteel art nouveau villa with attached literary salon and bookshop. Tuck into seasonal bistro cuisine amid elegant Old Berlin flair in the gracefully stucco-ornamented rooms or, if weather permits, in the idyllic garden. Breakfast is served until 2pm.

JULES VERNE INTERNATIONAL €€

Map p338 (☏030-3180 9410; www.jules-verne-berlin.de; Schlüterstrasse 61; breakfast €4.50-9.50, Sun brunch €14, 2-course lunch €7-9, dinner mains €11.50-28.50; ⊙9am-1am; ☏; ⊛Savignyplatz) Jules Verne was a well-travelled man, so it's only fitting that a cafe bearing his name would feature a globetrotting menu. French oysters, Moroccan couscous, Viennese schnitzel and Berlin *Currywurst* are all perennial best sellers. It's also a great 'greet-the-day' spot with substantial breakfasts named after Verne's books served until 3pm, and a big brunch buffet at weekends.

SCHLEUSENKRUG GERMAN €€

Map p338 (☏030-313 9909; www.schleusenkrug.de; Müller-Breslau-Strasse; mains €4-14.50; ⊙10am-midnight May-Sep, to 7pm Oct-Apr; ⓢZoologischer Garten, ⊛Zoologischer Garten) Sitting pretty on the edge of the Tiergarten, Schleusenkrug truly comes into its own during beer-garden season. People from all walks of life hunker over big mugs and comfort food – from grilled sausages to *Flammekuche* and weekly specials. Breakfast is served until 3pm.

DICKE WIRTIN GERMAN €€

Map p338 (☏030-312 4952; www.dicke-wirtin.de; Carmerstrasse 9; mains €6-16; ⊙from 11am-late; ⊛Savignyplatz) Old Berlin charm oozes from every nook and cranny of this been-here-forever pub which pours eight draught beers (including the superb Kloster Andechs) and nearly three dozen homemade schnapps varieties. Hearty local fare like roast pork, fried liver or breaded schnitzel keeps brains balanced. Bargain lunches.

CITY WEST & CHARLOTTENBURG EATING

LOCAL KNOWLEDGE

C/O RELOADED

Displaced from its last location in a grand old postal centre on Oranienburger Strasse in Mitte, the nonprofit **C/O Berlin** (Map p338; ☏030 2844 4160; www.co-berlin.org; Hardenbergstrasse 22-14; ⓢBahnhof Zoologischer Garten, ⊛Bahnhof Zoologischer Garten), Berlin's most exciting exhibition space for international photography, joined the westward migration and set up shop in the historic Amerika Haus near Zoo Station. The first exhibit in the new location was outdoors and presented historical photographs of the building. Previous exhibits have showcased the work of Annie Leibovitz, Martin Parr, Nan Goldin, Anton Corbijn and other members of the shutterbug elite.

The Amerika Haus was built in 1956–57 as part of the Interbau building exposition and served as a US culture and information centre with a library, cinema and exhibition spaces. After the building was pelted with eggs and rotten fruit during the anti–Vietnam War student protests of the 1960s and '70s, it became less and less accessible, turning into a virtual fortress after 9/11 and eventually closing down in September 2006. Plans to open a West Berlin museum here were ditched in favour of giving C/O a shiny new space.

WORTH A DETOUR

OLYMPIASTADION & AROUND

The main attraction in far western Berlin is the **Olympiastadion** (☎030-2500 2322; www.olympiastadion-berlin.de; Olympischer Platz 3; self-guided tour adult/concession €7/5, guided general tour €10/8, Hertha BSC tour €11/9; ☻9am-8pm Jun–mid-Sep, 9am-7pm mid-Sep–Oct & late Mar-May, 10am-4pm winter; ⓡOlympiastadion). Even though it was put through a total modernisation for the 2006 FIFA World Cup, it's hard to ignore the fact that this massive coliseum-like stadium was built by the Nazis for the 1936 Olympic Games. The bombastic bulk of the structure remains but has been softened by the addition of a spidery oval roof, snazzy VIP boxes and top-notch sound, lighting and projection systems. It seats up to 74,650 people for games played by the local Hertha BSC soccer team, concerts, the Pope or Madonna. On nonevent days, you can explore the stadium on your own, although renting a multilingual audioguide is recommended (€3). Several times daily, guided tours (some in English, phone ahead) take you into the locker rooms, warm-up areas and VIP areas that are otherwise off limits. Access the stadium from the Osttor (eastern gate).

To truly appreciate the grandeur of the stadium, head west past the Maifeld parade grounds to the outdoor viewing platform of the 77m-high **Glockenturm** (Bell Tower; ☎030-305 8123; www.glockenturm.de; Am Glockenturm; adult/concession €4/2; ☻9am-6pm Apr-Oct ; ⓡPichelsberg), which was also built for the 1936 Olympics. En route you'll pass a replica of the Olympic bell (the damaged original is displayed south of the stadium). In the foyer, an exhibit chronicles the ground's history, including the 1936 games, with panels in German and English. A documentary features rare original footage.

About 1.3km south of the stadium is the **Georg Kolbe Museum** (☎030-304 2144; www.georg-kolbe-museum.de; Sensburger Allee 25; adult/concession €5/3; ☻10am-6pm Tue-Sun; ⓡHeerstrasse), dedicated to one of Germany's most influential early-20th-century sculptors. A member of the Berlin Secession, Kolbe eschewed traditional sculpture and focused on depicting the idealised nude. His studio and home, built in the late 1920s and consisting of two rectangular brick buildings flanking a sculpture garden, now present works from all phases of his life alongside changing exhibits. The museum cafe, Cafe K, is one of the most charming in Berlin.

About 2km southeast of the stadium looms another Berlin landmark, the 147m-high **Funkturm** (Radio Tower; ☎030-3038 1905; www.funkturm-messeberlin.de; Messedamm 22; adult/concession €5/2.80; ☻platform 10am-8pm Mon, to 11pm Tue-Sun, weather permitting; ⓢKaiserdamm, ⓡMesse Nord/ICC). The filigree structure bears an uncanny resemblance to Paris' Eiffel Tower and looks especially attractive when lit up at night. It started transmitting signals in 1926; nine years later the world's first regular TV program was broadcast from here. From the viewing platform at 126m or the restaurant at 55m you can enjoy sweeping views of the Grunewald forest and the western city, as well as the **AVUS**, Germany's first car-racing track, which opened in 1921; AVUS stands for Automobil-, Verkehrs- und Übungsstrasse (auto, traffic and practice track). The Nazis made it part of the autobahn system, which it still is today.

★RESTAURANT
AM STEINPLATZ   GERMAN €€€
Map p338 (☎030-312 6589; www.marriott.de; Hardenbergstrasse 12; mains €16-26; ☻breakfast, lunch & dinner; ⓠM45, ⓢErnst-Reuter-Platz, Bahnhof Zoologischer Garten, ⓡBahnhof Zoologischer Garten) The 1920s get a 21st-century make-over here. The dining room is anchored by an open kitchen where veteran chef Marcus Zimmer uses mostly regional products to execute classic Berlin recipes. Even beer-hall dishes such as boiled pork knuckle are imaginatively reinterpreted and beautifully plated.

★OSTERIA CENTRALE   ITALIAN €€€
Map p338 (☎030-3101 3263; Bleibtreustrasse 51; mains €12-30; ☻6.30pm-midnight Mon-Sat; ⓡSavignyplatz) This neighbourhood Italian on the quiet end of Bleibtreustrasse fits like a well-worn shoe and lets you dip into a pool of pleasurable classics from around the Boot. Staples like octopus carpaccio, grilled calamari, truffle pasta or rosemary-scented beef stew are creatively perfected and keep regulars coming time and again. Reservations essential.

DUKE FRENCH €€€

Map p338 (☎030-683 154 000; www.duke-restaurant.com; Ellington Hotel, Nürnberger Strasse 50-55; 2-/3-course lunch €15/19.50, brunch €38, dinner mains €12.50-29; ⏰11.30am-midnight; ⓈAugsburger Strasse) Reservations are coveted for the Sunday jazz brunch in the very place where Louis Armstrong and Ella Fitzgerald once performed, but Florian Gauert's aroma-rich cuisine gets rave reviews at all other times as well. When the weather plays along, there's alfresco dining.

GROSZ CONTINENTAL €€€

Map p338 (☎030-652 142 199; www.grosz-berlin.de; Kurfürstendamm 193/194; lunch special €13.50, dinner mains €14-74; ⏰9am-11pm Sun-Thu, to 11.30pm Fri & Sat; ⓈUhlandstrasse) This high-ceilinged symphony of marble, brass, mirrors, glossy wood and stucco does a masterful job at re-creating the elegant aura of a Golden Twenties cafe. Drop by for coffee and a slice of Princess Victoria tart, a mouth-watering mash up of white chocolate and pistachios, or feast on fine crustaceans, meats and fish prepared in time-honoured continental fashion.

✖ Schloss Charlottenburg

BRASSERIE LAMAZERE FRENCH €€

(☎030-3180 0712; www.lamazere.de; Stuttgarter Platz 18; 2/3 courses €24/30; ⏰6pm-2am Tue-Sun; Ⓑ109, 309, ⒷCharlottenburg) At this down-to-earth brasserie the cooking is authentic, the wines hand-selected and the tables squeezed tight into a tunnel-shaped space. Each day the kitchen staff produce a new selection of tastebud tinglers, although thanks to popular demand *oeuf concotte* (coddled eggs), *confit de porc* (pork confit) and fragrant ratatouille reappear regularly.

BRAUHAUS LEMKE GERMAN €€

(☎030-3087 8979; www.brauhaus-lemke.com; Luisenplatz 1; mains €7.50-22; ⏰11am-midnight; ⒷM45, 109, 309, ⓈRichard-Wagner-Platz) This congenial tourist-geared beer hall serves soul-sustaining German fare alongside its homemade brews, including *Pils* (pilsner), wheat and seasonal specials.

ROGACKI GERMAN €€

Map p338 (☎030-343 8250; www.rogacki.de; Wilmersdorfer Strasse 145; meals €5-18; ⏰9am-6pm Mon-Wed, 9am-7pm Thu, 8am-7pm Fri, 8am-4pm Sat; ⓈBismarckstrasse) Family-run since 1928, Rogacki is chiefly a deli where glass display cases are piled high with cheeses, cold cuts, bread, game, salads, smoked fish (done in-house) and whatever else demanding palates desire. Put together a picnic to go, or stay put and join locals crowded around the stand-up tables for oysters and wine, a feisty stew or a plate of pasta.

🍷 DRINKING & NIGHTLIFE

★MONKEY BAR BAR

Map p338 (☎030-120 221 210; www.25hours-hotel.com; Budapester Strasse 40; ⏰3pm-1am Mon-Fri, to 2am Sat & Sun; 📶; Ⓑ100, 200, ⓈBahnhof Zoologischer Garten, ⒷBahnhof Zoologischer Garten) On the 10th floor of the 25hours Hotel Bikini Berlin, this 'urban jungle' hot spot delivers fabulous views of the city and the Berlin Zoo – in summer from a sweeping terrace. Drinks-wise, the list gives prominent nods to tiki concoctions and gin-based cocktail sorcery.

★PEARL CLUB

Map p338 (☎030-3151 8890; www.thepearl-berlin.com; Fasanenstrasse 81; ⏰from 6pm Thu, from 9pm Fri & Sat; ⒷM49, ⓈBahnhof Zoologischer Garten, ⒷBahnhof Zoologischer Garten) This new bauble in Berlin's necklace of party spots has injected some sass into the once fairly sleepy western city centre. Office jockeys invade on Thursdays for the after-work party, Fridays are big with wrinkle-free hip-hop hipsters while dolled-up weekend warriors bust a move beneath the feathery LED light installation on Saturdays.

BERLIN'S LITTLE ASIA

It's not quite Chinatown, but if you're in the mood for Asian food, simply head to Kantstrasse between Savignyplatz and Wilmersdorfer Strasse to find the city's densest concentration of authentic Chinese restaurants, including the perennially popular Good Friends (p208). At lunchtime, most offer value-priced specials perfect for filling up on the cheap. In between are Chinese furniture stores, massage parlours and Asian supermarkets as well as various Vietnamese and Thai eateries.

CITY WEST & CHARLOTTENBURG DRINKING & NIGHTLIFE

ℹ️ HAVE A BLAST ON THE BUS!

It's a poorly kept secret that one of Berlin's best bargains is a self-guided city tour aboard buses 100 or 200, the routes of which check off nearly every major sight in the city centre for the price of a public-transport ticket (tariff AB, €2.60). You can even get on and off within the two hours of its validity period as long as you continue in the same direction. If you plan to explore all day, a *Tageskarte* (day pass, €6.70) is your best bet.

Bus 100 travels from Bahnhof Zoo (Zoo Station) to Alexanderplatz, passing the Gedächtniskirche, the Siegessäule in the Tiergarten, the Reichstag, the Brandenburger Tor (Brandenburg Gate) and Unter den Linden. Bus 200 also starts at Bahnhof Zoo but follows a more southerly route via the Kulturforum museums and Potsdamer Platz before hooking up with Unter den Linden. Without traffic, trips take about 30 minutes. There's no commentary, of course, but it's still a great overview and useful for orientation and understanding the layout of the central city.

Buses run every few minutes but they do get crowded, so be wary of pickpockets. To snag a seat on the upper deck, it's best to board at either terminus, ie Bahnhof Zoo or Alexanderplatz.

★ DIENER   PUB
Map p338 (📞030-881 5329; www.diener-tatter saal.de; Grolmanstrasse 47; ⊗6pm-2am; 🚈Savignyplatz) In business for over a century, this Old Berlin haunt was taken over by German heavyweight champion Franz Diener in the 1950s and has since been one of West Berlin's preeminent artist pubs. From Billy Wilder to Harry Belafonte, they all came for beer and *Bulette* (meat patty) and left behind signed black-and-white photographs that grace Diener's walls to this day.

★ UNIVERSUM LOUNGE   BAR
Map p338 (📞030-8906 4995; www.universum lounge.com; Kurfürstendamm 153; ⊗6pm-3am; 🚇Adenauerplatz) This retro-glam libation station has daily happy-hour specials until 9pm, including an Aperitivo Italiano with free finger food on Wednesdays. After the final curtain at the theatre in the same building (a 1920s gem by the esteemed Erich Mendelsohn) you sometimes have to shoehorn your way inside. The bar is about 300m west of U-Bahn station Adenauerplatz.

BAR AM STEINPLATZ   BAR
Map p338 (📞030-554 4440; Steinplatz 4; 🚇Ernst-Reuter-Platz) The latest liquid playground of cocktail whisperer Christian Gentemann is at the art-deco jewel Hotel am Steinplatz. The classic and creative drinks (how about a porcini-infused martini?) often showcase regionally produced spirits, and even the draught beer is crafted by the Berlin-based Rollberg brewery. Bar bites complement the drinks.

ZWIEBELFISCH   PUB
Map p338 (📞030-312 7363; www.zwiebelfisch-berlin.de; Savignyplatz 7; ⊗noon-6am; 🚈Savignyplatz) With its clientele of grizzled and aspiring artists, actors and writers, this cosy pub has been Charlottenburg at its boho best since the patchouli-perfumed 1960s. Arrested in time, it's a fabulous sliver of pre-reunification West Berlin and ideal for guzzling that final drink while the suits are gearing up for the office grind.

GAINSBOURG À GAINSBARRE   BAR
Map p338 (📞030-313 7464; www.gainsbourg. de; Jeanne-Mammen-Bogen 576/577; ⊗from 5pm; 🚈Savignyplatz) The spirit of French crooner Serge Gainsbourg seems to waft through this seductively lit lair beneath the S-Bahn arches. Round tables, candlelight and chanson all exude a cosy Parisian vibe that speaks to a crowd that includes many old enough to have made out to 'Je t'aime', Serge's steamy 1969 duet with Jane Birkin. Classic cocktails.

PURO SKYLOUNGE   BAR, CLUB
Map p338 (📞030-2636 7875; www.puroberlin. de; Tauentzienstrasse 9-12; ⊗bar from 8pm Thu-Sat, club from 10pm Thu, from 11pm Sat; 🚇Kurfürstendamm) Puro has quite literally raised the bar in Charlottenburg – by moving it to the 20th floor of the Europa-Center, that is. Trade Berlin funky-trash for sleek decor, fabulous views and high-heeled hotties. Two dance floors flank a central bar with fireplaces, leather couches and dim lighting. The crowd skews young but moneyed. Dress nicely.

CONNECTION CLUB GAY

(www.connectionclub.de; Fuggerstrasse 33; ⊙from 9pm Wed, from 11pm Fri & Sat; ⓢWittenbergplatz) This legendary men-only party den with Berlin's largest darkroom was a techno pioneer way back in the '80s and still hasn't lost its grip on the scene. Its predecessor, run by drag-queen Romy Haag, was a favourite David Bowie hang-out.

⭐ ENTERTAINMENT

BAR JEDER VERNUNFT CABARET

Map p338 (☑030-883 1582; www.bar-jeder-vernunft.de; Schaperstrasse 24; ⓢSpichernstrasse) Life's still a cabaret at this intimate 1912 mirrored tent with playful art nouveau decor, which puts on sophisticated song-and-dance shows, comedy and chanson evenings nightly. Seating is in upholstered booths or at little tables. From the U-Bahn station, follow Meierottostrasse for 200m, turn right on Schaperstrasse and continue for another 100m. The entrance is behind the parking lot.

STAATSOPER IM
SCHILLER THEATER OPERA

Map p338 (☑information 030-2035 4438, tickets 030-2035 4555; www.staatsoper-berlin.de; Bismarckstrasse 110; ⓢErnst-Reuter-Platz) Point your highbrow compass towards the Daniel Barenboim–led Staatsoper, Berlin's top opera company. While its historic digs on Unter den Linden are getting a facelift, the high-calibre productions are staged at the Schiller Theater in Charlottenburg. All operas are sung in their original language.

A-TRANE JAZZ

Map p338 (☑030-313 2550; www.a-trane.de; Bleibtreustrasse 1; ⊙Sun-Thu 8pm-1am, Fri & Sat 8pm-open end; ⓡSavignyplatz) Herbie Hancock and Diana Krall have anointed the stage of this intimate jazz club, but mostly it's emerging talent bringing their A-game to the A-Trane. Entry is free on Monday when local boy Andreas Schmidt shows off his skills, and after midnight on Saturday for the late-night jam session.

SCHAUBÜHNE THEATRE

Map p338 (☑030-890 023; www.schaubuehne.de; Kurfürstendamm 153; ⓢAdenauerplatz) In a fabulous 1920s expressionist building by Erich Mendelsohn, this is western Berlin's main stage for experimental, contemporary theatre, often with a critical and analytical look at current social and political issues. The cast of dedicated actors is led by director Thomas Ostermeier. Some performances feature English surtitles.

QUASIMODO LIVE MUSIC

Map p338 (☑030-312 8086; www.quasimodo.de; Kantstrasse 12a; ⊙from 9pm, often Sep-Jun; ⓢZoologischer Garten, ⓡZoologischer Garten) One of Berlin's oldest jazz clubs has diversified its programming and now also pulls in fans of blues, rock, soul, funk and Motown to its intimate cellar space with a low ceiling and black walls. If that gets too claustrophobic, escape to the upstairs cafe, in summer with outside terrace.

DEUTSCHE OPER BERLIN OPERA

Map p338 (☑030-3438 4343; www.deutscheoperberlin.de; Bismarckstrasse 35; ⓢDeutsche Oper) The German Opera was founded by local citizens in 1912 as a counterpoint to the royal opera (today's Staatsoper) on Unter den Linden. The original building was destroyed in WWII and rebuilt by 1961 as a huge, modernist venue with seating for nearly 1900 people. It boasts a repertory of around 70 operas, all sung in their original language.

🔒 SHOPPING

Kurfürstendamm and Tauentzienstrasse are chock-a-block with multiple outlets of international chains flogging fashion and accessories. Further west on Ku'damm are the more high-end boutiques such as Hermès, Cartier and Bulgari. Kantstrasse is the go-to zone for home designs. Connecting side streets, such as Bleibtreustrasse and Schlüterstrasse, house upscale indie and designer boutiques, bookshops and galleries, while Bikini Berlin features cutting-edge concept and flagship stores.

KADEWE DEPARTMENT STORE

(☑030-212 10; www.kadewe.de; Tauentzienstrasse 21-24; ⊙10am-8pm Mon-Thu, 10am-9pm Fri, 9.30am-8pm Sat; ⓢWittenbergplatz) Just past the centennial mark, this venerable department store has an assortment so vast that a pirate-style campaign is the best way to plunder its bounty. If pushed for time, at least hurry up to the legendary 6th-floor gourmet food hall. The name, by the way, stands for *Kaufhaus des Westens* (department store of

BERLIN'S 'SEXY' NEW MALL

The opening of a new shopping centre usually elicits yawns but not **Bikini Berlin** (Map p338; www.bikiniberlin.de; Budapester Strasse 38-50; ⏰9am-9pm Mon-Sat; [S]Bahnhof Zoologischer Garten, [U]Bahnhof Zoologischer Garten), Germany's first concept mall. It opened in 2014 in a spectacularly rehabilitated 1950s architectural icon nicknamed 'Bikini' because of its design: a 200m-long upper and lower section separated by an open floor, now chastely covered by a glass facade.

The breezy mall occupying the lower three floors of the vast structure is primarily the domain of urban boutiques stocked with edgy fashion, design, tech gadgets and accessories, many made in Berlin. Look for fashion and accessories by Andreas Murkudis, eyewear by Mykita and vegan clothing by Umasan. On the ground floor, wooden pop-up stores can be rented for short periods and thus offer a platform for up-and-coming creatives to test new ideas, concepts and products.

Even if shopping leaves you cold, come for the spectacular interior, an industrial-flavored showstopper with exposed-steel girders, concrete walls and a huge panoramic window with front-row views of the Berlin Zoo's monkey enclosure. A wooden staircase leads to a huge rooftop terrace with sweeping views over the entire zoo and the Tiergarten.

the West). It's right outside U-Bahn station Wittenbergplatz.

SUPERMARKET — FASHION

Map p338 (http://supermarket.de; Budapester Strasse 38-50, 2nd floor Bikini Haus; ⏰10am-1am; 🚌100, [S]Bahnhof Zoologischer Garten, [U]Bahnhof Zoologischer Garten) Nope, you won't find cheese and toilet paper at this supermarket. Instead, it's all about design, fashion, snacks and drinks under one chic roof. This is only the third branch of this Belgrade-based concept store which stocks such choice labels as Muuto, Sigurd Larsen, Vladimir Karaleev and the local label llot lllov in spacious, industrial surroundings.

HAUTNAH — FASHION

Map p338 (☎030-882 3434; www.hautnahberlin.de; Uhlandstrasse 170; ⏰noon-8pm Mon-Fri, 11am-4pm Sat; [S]Uhlandstrasse) Being the sort of city Berlin is, sooner or later you may just need to update your fetish wardrobe, and Hautnah's three floors of erotic costuming should do the job naughtily. Expect a vast range of latex bodices, leather goods, themed get-ups, sex toys and vertiginous footwear, plus an interesting wine selection (Marquis de Sade Champagne anyone?).

KÄTHE WOHLFAHRT — HANDICRAFTS

Map p338 (☎www.wohlfahrt.com; Kurfürstendamm 225-226; ⏰10am-7pm Mon-Sat, 1-5pm Sun; [S]Kurfürstendamm) With its mind-boggling assortment of traditional German Yuletide decorations and ornaments, this shop lets you celebrate Christmas year-round. It's accessed via a ramp that spirals around an 8m-high Christmas tree.

STILWERK — HOMEWARES

Map p338 (☎030-315 150; www.stilwerk.de/berlin; Kantstrasse 17; ⏰10am-7pm Mon-Sat; [U]Savignyplatz) This four-storey temple of good taste will have devotees of the finer things itching to redecorate. Everything you could possibly want for home and hearth – from tactile key rings to glossy grand pianos and vintage lamps – is here, plus all the top brands (eg Bang & Olufsen, Ligne Roset, Niessing).

UNIQLO — FASHION

(☎030-2902 8260; www.uniqlo.com; Tauentzienstrasse 7; ⏰10am-8pm; [S]Wittenbergplatz) With its first flagship store in Germany, Uniqlo brings Japanese style to Berlin in a suitably futuristic setting complete with rotating mannequins and LED ticker tapes decorating the staircases. Clothes are displayed on Bauhaus-inspired furniture. Note that the sizes are a bit odd: if you're normally a 28, you'll probably need a 25 or 26 here.

BERLINER TRÖDELMARKT — MARKET

Map p338 (www.berliner-troedelmarkt.de; Strasse des 17 Juni; ⏰10am-5pm Sat & Sun; [U]Tiergarten) Vendors vie for your euros with yesteryear's fur coats, silverware, jewellery, lamps, dolls, hats and plenty of other stuff one might find in granny's attic. West of Tiergarten S-Bahn station, this is Berlin's oldest flea market (since 1973). The attached arts and crafts market sells mostly new stuff.

Day Trips from Berlin

Potsdam & Schloss Sanssouci p216

It's practically impossible to not be enchanted by this rambling park and palace ensemble starring Schloss Sanssouci.

Sachsenhausen Concentration Camp p222

The horrors of the Third Reich become all too real at what's left of one of Germany's oldest Nazi-built concentration camps.

Spandau p223

Anchored by a delightful Altstadt (old town), this northwestern Berlin district flaunts its historic pedigree.

Grunewald & Dahlem p224

Tree-lined streets with mansions and manicured lawns lace Berlin's poshest area, which also boasts plenty of culture cred.

Wannsee p226

Hemmed in by the Havel River, Berlin's southwestern-most district counts palaces, forests and historical sights among its assets.

Köpenick p227

Home to Berlin's largest lake, a sprawling forest, a handsome baroque castle and a medieval centre.

⊙ TOP SIGHT
POTSDAM & SCHLOSS SANSSOUCI

About 26km southwest of central Berlin and quickly reached by S-Bahn, Potsdam is the most popular day trip from Berlin. A former Prussian royal seat, it lures scores of visitors to its splendid gardens and palaces that garnered Unesco World Heritage status in 1990. Headlining the roll call of royal pads is Schloss Sanssouci, the private retreat of King Friedrich II (Frederick the Great), who was also the mastermind behind many of Potsdam's other fabulous parks and palaces, which miraculously survived WWII with nary a shrapnel wound.

When the shooting stopped, the Allies chose Schloss Cecilienhof for the Potsdam Conference of August 1945 to lay the groundwork for Germany's postwar fate.

Schloss & Park Sanssouci

This glorious park and palace ensemble is what happens when a king has good taste, plenty of cash and access to the finest architects and artists of the day. Sanssouci was dreamed up by Frederick the Great (1712–86) and is anchored by the eponymous palace, which was his favourite summer retreat, a place where he could be 'sans souci' (without cares). His grave is nearby. Frederick's great-great-nephew, King Friedrich Wilhelm IV (1795–1861), added a few more palaces and buildings that reflected his intense love for all things Italian.

The palaces are fairly well spaced – it's almost 2km between the Neues Palais (New Palace) and Schloss Sanssouci. Take your sweet time wandering along the park's meandering paths to discover your personal favourite spot.

DON'T MISS...

➡ Tour of Schloss Sanssouci
➡ Stroll around Park Sanssouci
➡ Chinesisches Haus
➡ View from Belvedere Pfingstberg

PRACTICALITIES

➡ ☎0331-969 4200
➡ www.spsg.de
➡ Maulbeerallee
➡ day pass to all palaces adult/concession €19/14
➡ ⊘varies by palace
➡ 🚌606, 695 from Potsdam Hauptbahnhof

Schloss Sanssouci

The biggest stunner, and what everyone comes to see, is Schloss Sanssouci, Frederick the Great's famous summer palace. Designed by Georg Wenzeslaus von Knobelsdorff in 1747, the rococo jewel sits daintily above vine-draped terraces with the king's grave nearby. Admission is limited and by timed ticket only; book online to avoid wait times and/or disappointment. Otherwise, only city tours booked through the Potsdam tourist office guarantee entry to the Schloss.

Standouts on the audioguided tours include the **Konzertsaal** (Concert Hall), whimsically decorated with vines, grapes, and even a cobweb where sculpted spiders frolic. The king himself gave flute recitals here. Also note the intimate **Bibliothek** (Library), lidded by a gilded sunburst ceiling, where the king would seek solace amid 2000 leather-bound tomes ranging from Greek poetry to the latest releases by his friend Voltaire. Another highlight is the **Marmorsaal** (Marble Room), an elegant white Carrara marble symphony modelled after the Pantheon in Rome.

As you exit the palace, don't be fooled by the **Ruinenberg**, a pile of classical 'ruins' looming in the distance: they're merely a folly conceived by Frederick the Great.

Bildergalerie

The **Bildergalerie** (Gallery of Paintings; Im Park Sanssouci 4; adult/concession €6/5; ⊙10am-6pm Tue-Sun May-Oct) is the oldest royal museum in Germany, rather plain on the outside but resplendent in yellow and white marble and gilded stuccowork on the inside. It shelters Frederick the Great's collection of Old Masters, including such pearls as Caravaggio's *Doubting Thomas*, Anthony van Dyck's *Pentecost* and several works by Peter Paul Rubens.

Neue Kammern

The **Neue Kammern** (New Chambers; Park Sanssouci; adult/concession incl tour or audioguide €4/3; ⊙10am-6pm Tue-Sun Apr-Oct) were built as an orangery and later converted into a guesthouse. The interior drips with rococo opulence, most notably in the Jasper Hall, which is drenched in precious stones and topped by a ceiling fresco starring Venus, and in the Ovidsaal, a grand ballroom with gilded wall reliefs depicting scenes from *Metamorphosis*.

Chinesisches Haus

The Far East was all the rage in the 18th century, as reflected in the adorable **Chinesisches Haus** (Chinese House; Am Grünen Gitter; admission €2; ⊙10am-6pm Tue-Sun May-Oct; 🚌605, 606 to Schloss Charlottenhof,

INFORMATION

There are two visitor centres in Park Sanssouci, the **Besucherzentrum an der Historischen Mühle** (An der Orangerie 1; ⊙8.30am-5.30pm Tue-Sun Apr-Oct, to 4.30pm Nov-Mar) and the **Besucherzentrum im Neuen Palais** (⊙10am-5.30pm Wed-Mon Apr-Oct, to 4.30pm Nov-Mar).

Regional trains leaving from Berlin-Hauptbahnhof and Zoologischer Garten take only 25 minutes to reach Potsdam Hauptbahnhof; some continue on to Potsdam-Charlottenhof and Potsdam-Park Sanssouci. The S7 from central Berlin makes the trip in about 40 minutes. You need a ticket covering zones ABC (€3.20) for either service.

(□91 to Schloss Charlottenhof). The clover-leaf-shaped pavilion is among the park's most photographed buildings, thanks to its enchanting exterior of exotically dressed gilded figures shown sipping tea, dancing and playing musical instruments. Inside is a precious collection of Chinese and Meissen porcelain.

Orangerieschloss

The 300m-long Mediterranean-styled 1864 **Orangerieschloss** (Orangery Palace; An der Orangerie 3-5; tour adult/concession €4/3, tower €2; ⊗10am-6pm Tue-Sun May-Oct, 10am-6pm Sat & Sun Apr) was Friedrich Wilhelm IV's favourite building project and was modelled after Italian villas. A tour highlight is the Raphaelsaal, which brims with 19th-century copies of the famous painter's masterpieces, while the tower delivers sweeping park views. The greenhouses are still used for storing potted plants in winter. Although under long-term restoration, the building remains open.

Belvedere auf dem Klausberg

Frederick the Great's final building project was this temple-like **Belvedere** (☑0331-969 4206; An der Orangerie 1; admission €2; ⊗10am-6pm Sat & Sun May-Oct), which delivers a sweeping panorama of the park, lakes and Potsdam itself. The upstairs hall has an impressive frescoed dome, oak parquet and fanciful stucco marble. En route, the **Drachenhaus** (Dragon House; 1770) is a fantastical Chinese mini-palace inspired by the Ta-Ho pagoda in Canton and now houses a cafe-restaurant.

Historische Mühle

The **Historische Mühle** (Historical Mill; ☑0331-550 6851; Maulbeerallee 5; adult/concession €3/2; ⊗10am-6pm daily Apr-Oct, 10am-4pm Sat & Sun Nov & Jan-Mar; □650, 695) is a functioning replica of the palace's original Dutch-style 18th-century windmill. Admission buys access to three floors of exhibits on mill technology, a close-up of the grinding mechanism and a top-floor viewing platform.

Neues Palais

The final palace commissioned by Frederick the Great, the **Neues Palais** (New Palace; Am Neuen Palais; adult/concession with audioguide €8/6; ⊗ 10am-6pm Wed-Mon Apr-Oct, to 5pm Nov-Mar; □605 or 606 to Neues Palais, □Potsdam Charlottenhof) has

EATING & DRINKING

Meierei im Neuen Garten (☑0331-704 3211; www.meierei-potsdam.de; Im Neuen Garten 10; snacks €2-7, mains €7-13; ⊗11am-10pm Tue-Sun; □603 to Höhenstrasse) The Berlin Wall once ran right past this brewpub that's especially lovely in summer when you can count the sailboats on the Jungfernsee from your beer-garden table. The hearty dishes are a perfect match for the delicious Helles and seasonal suds brewed on the premises. Service can be challenged on busy days. It's near Schloss Cecilienhof.

Drachenhaus (☑0331-505 3808; www.drachenhaus.de; Maulbeerallee 4; mains €7.50-23; ⊗11am-7pm or later Apr-Oct, to 6pm Tue-Sun Nov-Feb) Right in Park Sanssouci, the exotic Dragon House is now a pleasant cafe-restaurant serving gooey cakes, homemade bread and upmarket regional cuisine – in summer beneath a leafy canopy.

Maison Charlotte (☑0331-280 5450; www.maison-charlotte.de; Mittelstrasse 20; Flammkuche €8-13, mains €18-25; ⊗noon-11pm) There's a rustic lyricism to the French country cuisine in this darling Dutch Quarter bistro famous for its Breton fish soup and delectable *Flammkuche* (Alsatian pizza) with such creative toppings as crayfish or smoked salmon. Budget bon vivants come for the daily lunch special: €7.50, including a glass of wine.

Neues Palais

POTSDAM BY BOAT

Boats operated by **Schiffahrt in Potsdam** (📞0331-275 9210; www.schiffahrt-in-potsdam.de; Lange Brücke 6; ⊙10am-7pm Apr-Oct) depart throughout the day from the docks near Lange Brücke, below the towering Hotel Mercure. Choose from a 90-minute palace cruise (€13), a three-hour trip around several Havel lakes (€19) or the two-hour Lake Wannsee cruise (€14).

....

A one-day pass valid at all Potsdam palaces is €19 (concession €14) and is also available online (http://tickets.spsg. de) for an additional €2 per ticket fee. The family version (two adults and up to four children) costs €49. There's also a €3 day fee (*Fotoerlaubnis*) for taking noncommercial photographs inside the palaces.

made-to-impress dimensions, a central dome and a lavish exterior capped with a parade of sandstone figures. The interior attests to the high level of artistry and craftsmanship of the time. It's an opulent symphony of ceiling frescoes, gilded stucco ornamentation, ornately carved wainscoting and fanciful wall coverings alongside paintings (by Antoine Pesne, for example) and richly crafted furniture.

The palace was built in only six years, largely to demonstrate the undiminished power of the Prussian state following the bloody Seven Years War (1756–63). The king himself rarely camped out here, preferring the intimacy of Schloss Sanssouci and using it for representational purposes only. Only the last German Kaiser, Wilhelm II, used it as a residence until 1918.

The massive structure has been undergoing gradual restoration for years. Closed until at least late 2015 are two of its most memorable rooms, the rococo **Grottensaal** (Grotto Hall) and the **Marmorsaal** (Marble Hall). Already completed is the **Unteres Fürstenquartier** (Lower Royal Suite), which consists of a concert room, an oval-shaped chamber, an antechamber and, most impressively, a dining room with walls sheathed in red silk damask with gold-braided trim.

The pair of lavish buildings behind the Schloss is called the **Communs**. It originally housed the palace servants and kitchens and is now part of Potsdam University.

Potsdam

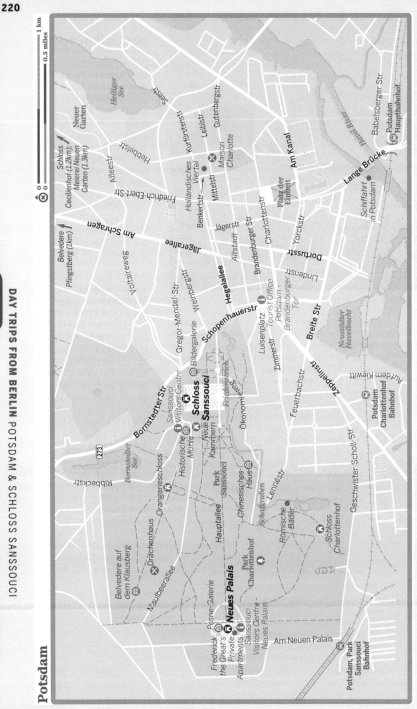

Park Charlottenhof

Laid out by Peter Lenné for Friedrich Wilhelm IV, this park segues imperceptibly from Park Sanssouci but gets far fewer visitors. Buildings in this quiet corner bear the stamp of Karl Friedrich Schinkel, most notably the small neoclassical **Schloss Charlottenhof** (Geschwister-Scholl-Strasse 34a; tour adult/concession €4/3; ⊙10am-6pm Tue-Sun May-Oct), which was modelled after a Roman villa and features a Doric portico and bronze fountain. Schinkel, aided by his student Ludwig Persius, also dreamed up the nearby **Römische Bäder** (Roman Baths; adult/concession €5/4; ⊙10am-6pm Tue-Sun mid-Apr–Oct), a picturesque ensemble of an Italian country villa. A same-day combination ticket is €5 (concession €4).

Other Potsdam Sights

East of Park Sanssouci, Potsdam's **Altstadt** makes for a pleasant stroll and also gives way to the **Holländisches Viertel** (Dutch Quarter), a picturesque cluster of 134 gabled red-brick houses built around 1730 for Dutch workers invited to Potsdam by Friedrich Wilhelm I. The entire district has been done up beautifully and brims with galleries, cafes and restaurants; Mittelstrasse is especially scenic.

North of the Altstadt, the key sight of the winding lakeside Neuer Garten (New Garden) is **Schloss Cecilienhof** (☎0331-969 4520; www.spsg.de; Im Neuen Garten 11; tours adult/concession €6/5; ⊙10am-6pm Tue-Sun Apr-Oct, to 5pm Nov-Mar; 🚌603), an English-style country palace famous for hosting the 1945 Potsdam Conference where Stalin, Truman and Churchill hammered out Germany's postwar fate. The conference room, with its giant round table, looks as though the delegates just left.

VIEWS

For splendid views over Potsdam and surrounds, ascend the spiraling wrought-iron staircases of the twin-towered **Belvedere Pfingstberg** (☎0331-2005 7930; www.pfingst-berg.de; adult/concession €4/3; ⊙10am-6pm Apr-Oct, 10am-4pm Sat & Sun Mar & Nov; 🚌92 or 96 from Hauptbahnhof), a palace commissioned by Friedrich Wilhelm IV and modelled on the Villa Medici in Naples.

The palaces all have different hours and admission prices. All are closed on Mondays. From November to April, some of the lesser sights are open on weekends and holidays only, while others are closed entirely.

Sachsenhausen Concentration Camp

Explore

Sachsenhausen was built by prisoners and opened in 1936 as a prototype for other concentration camps. By 1945 about 200,000 people had passed through its sinister gates, initially mostly political opponents, but later also gypsies, gays, Jews and, after 1939, POWs from eastern Europe, especially the Soviet Union. Tens of thousands died here from hunger, exhaustion, illness, exposure, medical experiments and executions. Thousands more succumbed during the death march of April 1945, when the Nazis evacuated the camp in advance of the Red Army. Note the memorial plaque to these victims as you walk towards the camp (at the corner of Strasse der Einheit and Strasse der Nationen). After the war, the Soviets held some 60,000 German POWs in what was now Speziallager No 7 (Special Camp No 7); about 12,000 died of malnutrition and disease before it was dissolved in 1950. Soviet and GDR military used the grounds for another decade until the camp became a memorial site in 1961.

Top Tip

Although the memorial site is open daily, it's best not to visit on a Monday when the indoor exhibits are closed.

Getting There & Away

➡ **Train** The S1 makes the trip thrice hourly from central Berlin (eg Friedrichstrasse) to Oranienburg (€3.20, 45 minutes).

Hourly regional RE5 and RB12 trains leaving from Hauptbahnhof are faster (€3.20, 25 minutes). The camp is about 2km from the Oranienburg train station. Turn right onto Stralsunder Strasse, right on Bernauer Strasse, left on Strasse der Einheit and right on Strasse der Nationen. Alternatively, bus 804 makes hourly trips.

Need to Know

➡ **Area Code** ☑03301
➡ **Location** About 35km north of central Berlin
➡ **Sachsenhausen Visitors Centre** (www.stiftung-bg.de; Strasse der Nationen 22; ⊙8.30am-6pm mid-Mar–mid-Oct, to 4.30pm mid-Oct–mid-Mar)

◉ SIGHTS

GEDENKSTÄTTE UND MUSEUM
SACHSENHAUSEN   MEMORIAL

(☑03301-200 200; www.stiftung-bg.de; Strasse der Nationen 22; ⊙8.30am-6pm mid-Mar–mid-Oct, to 4.30pm mid-Oct–mid-Mar, most exhibits closed Mon) FREE Unless you're on a guided tour, pick up a leaflet (€0.50) or, better yet, an audioguide (€3, including leaflet) at the visitors centre to get a better grasp of this huge site. The approach to the camp takes you past photographs taken during the death march and the camp's liberation. Just beyond the perimeter, the **Neues Museum** (New Museum) has exhibits on Sachsenhausen's precursor, the nearby Oranienburg concentration camp, and on the evolution of the memorial site from 1950 to 1990.

Proceed to **Tower A**, the entrance gate, cynically labelled, as at Auschwitz, *Arbeit Macht Frei* (Work Sets You Free). Beyond here is the roll-call area, with barracks and other buildings fanning out beyond. Off to the right, two restored barracks illustrate

---

GUIDED TOURS AT SACHSENHAUSEN

The nonprofit Mosaic Tours specialises in English-language Sachsenhausen tours lasting about six hours. Tours leave at 10am from below the TV Tower. Alternatively, the memorial-site-affiliated nonprofit Friends of Sachsenhausen Memorial operates four-hour tours from the historic traffic light at Potsdamer Platz. An ABC transport ticket is necessary for either tour, but reservations are not.

The English-language walking tour companies Berlin Walks (p292), Insider Tour Berlin (p292) and New Berlin Tours (p292) also operate guided tours of Sachsenhausen several times weekly.

the abysmal living conditions prisoners were subjected to. **Barrack 38** has an exhibit on Jewish inmates, while **Barrack 39** graphically portrays daily life at the camp. The **prison**, where famous inmates included Hitler-would-be-assassin Georg Elser and the minister Martin Niemöller, is next door. Exhibits in the **infirmary barracks** on the other side of the roll-call area illustrate the camp's poor medical care and the horrid medical experiments performed on prisoners. Moving towards the centre, the presentation in the **Prisoners' Kitchen** chronicles key moments in the camp's history. Exhibits include instruments of torture (such as a 'beating bench'), the original gallows that stood in the roll-call area and, in the cellar, heart-wrenching artwork scratched into the wall by prisoners.

The most sickening displays, though, are about the extermination area called **Station Z**, which was separated by a wall from the rest of the grounds and consisted of an execution trench, a crematorium and a gas chamber. The most notorious mass execution took place in autumn 1941 when over 10,000 Soviet POWs were executed here in the course of four weeks. In the far right corner, a new building and two original barracks house the **Soviet Special Camp** exhibit, which documents how Sachsenhausen was used by the Soviets between 1945 and 1950.

🍴 EATING & DRINKING

No food is available at the memorial site, although a vending machine in the Neues Museum dispenses hot drinks. There are cafes, bakeries and small markets outside Oranienburg train station.

Spandau

Explore

Spandau is a congenial mix of green expanses, rivers, industry and almost rural residential areas wrapped around a medieval core famous for its 16th-century bastion, the Zitadelle Spandau (Spandau Citadel). Older than Berlin by a few years, it sits at the confluence of Havel and Spree and thrived as an independent city for nearly eight centuries and only became part of Berlin in 1920. To this day, its people still talk about 'going to Berlin' when heading to any other city district. Nearly all sights handily cluster in and around the Altstadt.

The Best...

- **Sight** Zitadelle Spandau
- **Place to Eat** Restaurant Kolk (p224)
- **Place to Drink** satt und selig (p224)

Top Tip

In summer, big international acts like Billy Idol, Lana del Rey and Limp Bizkit gig to appreciative audiences alfresco during the **Citadel Music Festival** (www.citadel-music-festival.de). Year-round concerts take place in the Gothic Hall.

Getting There & Away

- **U-Bahn** The recommended route is via the U7, which travels to Spandau in 30 to 40 minutes and stops at the Zitadelle, the Altstadt and the Rathaus.
- **S-Bahn** The S5 makes the trip to central Spandau in about 30 to 40 minutes.

Need to Know

- **Area Code** ☎030
- **Location** About 13km northwest of central Berlin
- **Tourist Office** (☎030-333 9388; www.partner-fuer-spandau.de; Breite Strasse 32; ⏰10am-6pm Mon-Fri, to 3pm Sat; 🚆Spandau, [S]Altstadt Spandau) Hires out audioguides (€6.50) for self-guided tours of the historic centre.

👁 SIGHTS

ZITADELLE SPANDAU CASTLE

(☎030-354 9440; www.zitadelle-spandau.de; Am Juliusturm 64; adult/concession €4.50/2.50, audioguide €2; ⏰10am-5pm; [S]Zitadelle) The 16th-century Spandau Citadel, on a little island in the Havel River, is one of the world's best-preserved Renaissance fortresses. With its moat, drawbridge and arrowhead-shaped bastions, it is also a veritable textbook in military architecture and now multitasks as museum, cultural venue and wintering ground for thousands of bats. Climb the 30m-high **Juliusturm** for sweeping views.

WORTH A DETOUR

MILITARY AVIATION HISTORY ON THE RUNWAY

Operated by the Bundeswehr, the **Militärhistorisches Museum – Flugplatz Berlin-Gatow** (Museum of Military History – Airfield Berlin-Gatow; ☎030-3687 2601; www.mhm-gatow.de; Am Flugplatz Gatow 33; ⌚10am-6pm Tue-Sun; 🚌135) [FREE] is a fascinating destination for fans of aviation, technology, history and the military. It spreads its wings over a military airfield used both by the Nazis and the Royal Air Force. Exhibits in the control tower and two hangars focus on various aspects of aerial warfare, with plenty of old planes, air defense guns and engines on display. Over 100 fighter jets, bombers, helicopters and weapons systems litter the runway. The museum is about 9km south of central Spandau. Take bus 135 from S-/U-Bahn Rathaus Spandau to 'Kurpromenade', then walk for 1km.

NIKOLAIKIRCHE CHURCH

(Church of St Nicholas; ☎030-333 5639; www.nikolai-spandau.de; Reformationsplatz 6; tower €1; ⌚noon-4pm Mon-Fri, 11am-3pm Sat, 11am-4pm Sun, tower tours 12.30pm Sat, 2.30pm Sun Apr-Oct; [S]Altstadt Spandau) This red-brick Gothic pile is famous for hosting Brandenburg's first public Lutheran-style worship service in 1539 under Elector Joachim II, thereby bringing the Reformation to the region. Inside, important treasures include a 14th-century baptismal font, a baroque pulpit and a late-Renaissance altar. Tours up the 77m-high tower are available weekends only.

GOTISCHES HAUS HISTORIC BUILDING

(☎030-333 9388; Breite Strasse 32; ⌚10am-6pm Mon-Sat; [S]Altstadt Spandau) [FREE] This well-preserved late-Gothic gem sports ornate net-ribbed vaulting on the ground floor, which houses the local tourist office.

KOLK NEIGHBOURHOOD

([S]Altstadt Spandau) Separated from the Altstadt by the busy Strasse am Juliusturm, the Kolk quarter exudes medieval village flair with its narrow lanes, crooked, half-timbered houses and 78m-long section of town wall. Its key sight is the church of **St Marien am Behnitz** (☎030-353 9630; www.behnitz.de; Behnitz 9; ⌚ 2-5pm). A makeover of the 1848 brick pile saw the return of the hand-painted murals, decorative stucco and stained-glass windows that had been destroyed during a botched 1960s restoration job.

🍴 EATING & DRINKING

RESTAURANT KOLK GERMAN €€

(☎030-333 8879; www.kolk.im-netz.de; Hoher Steinweg 7; mains €9-15; ⌚11am-11pm; [S]Altstadt Spandau) Even after a quarter century, Kolk hasn't lost its grip on the crowd. The ambience of a converted 19th-century firehouse matches a menu headlined by such dishes as hearty goulash and boiled eel in dill sauce.

SATT UND SELIG INTERNATIONAL €€

(☎030-3675 3877; www.sattundselig.de; Carl-Schurz-Strasse 47; mains €8-18; ⌚9am-11pm; [S]Altstadt Spandau) In a baroque half-timbered house in the pedestrian zone (with outdoor tables in summer), this casual eatery is a good pit stop from morning to night.

Grunewald & Dahlem

Explore

Berlin's most upper-crust suburbs, Dahlem and Grunewald are packed with cultural and natural appeal. Set between their leafy streets and lavish villa colonies are gardens, parks, palaces and a sprinkling of museums, most notably the Museen Dahlem with its global ethnological collections. After WWII, the area was part of the American sector, a legacy reflected in such institutions as the AlliiertenMuseum (Allied Museum). A respite for Berliners and residents alike is the Grunewald forest, a vast fresh-air refuge crisscrossed by paths and dotted with lakes extending all the way west to the Havel River.

The Best...

- **Sight** Museen Dahlem
- **Place to Eat** Galileo (p226)
- **Place to Drink** Luise (p226)

Top Tip

The fragrant Botanischer Garten is the glorious backdrop for alfresco summer concerts – jazz to flamenco to classical – held every Friday from 6pm to 8pm in July and August. Tickets (€15) include garden access.

Getting There & Away

➡ **U-Bahn** The U3 meanders through this area, with key stops being Dahlem-Dorf for the museums and Krumme Lanke for easy access to the Grunewald forest.

➡ **S-Bahn** The S1 skirts southern Dahlem, while the S7 runs straight through the Grunewald forest.

Need to Know

➡ **Area Code** ☑030

➡ **Location** About 11km southwest of central Berlin

⊙ SIGHTS

MUSEEN DAHLEM   MUSEUM

(☑030-266 424 242; www.smb.museum; Lans-strasse 8; adult/concession/child €8/4/free; ⊙10am-5pm Tue-Fri, 11am-6pm Sat & Sun, Junior Museum 11am-6pm Sat & Sun; ⓢDahlem-Dorf) Unless some mad scientist invents a magic time-travel-teleporter machine, the three vast collections of art and objects from around the globe within the Museen Dahlem are your best bet for exploring the world in a single afternoon. Highlights of the **Museum of Ethnology** include masks and musical instruments in the Africa exhibit, and outriggers and traditional huts in the South Seas hall. Prime works in the **Museum of Asian Art** include the Japanese tearoom and a 16th-century Chinese imperial throne. At the **Museum of European Cultures**, exhibits range from Swedish armoires to a Venetian gondola. Small kids can have their horizons expanded at the Junior Museum.

BRÜCKE-MUSEUM   GALLERY

(☑030-831 2029; www.bruecke-museum.de; Bussardsteig 9; adult/concession €5/3; ⊙11am-5pm Wed-Mon; ⓢOskar-Helene-Heim, then bus 115 to Pücklerstrasse) In 1905 Karl Schmidt-Rottluff, Erich Heckel and Ernst Ludwig Kirchner founded Germany's first modern-artist group, called *Die Brücke* (The Bridge), thereby paving the way for German expressionism and modern art in general. Schmitt-Rottluff's personal collection forms the core of this superb presentation of expressionist art in a lovely bungalow in the Grunewald Forest. The gallery is about 2.5km north of U-Bahn station Oskar-Helene-Heim via Clayallee.

ALLIIERTENMUSEUM   MUSEUM

(Allied Museum; ☑030-818 1990; www.alliierten-museum.de; Clayallee 135; ⊙10am-6pm Tue-Sun; ⓢOskar-Helene-Heim) **FREE** The original Checkpoint Charlie guardhouse, a Berlin Airlift 'Candy Bomber' plane and a reconstructed spy tunnel are crowd favourites among the hundreds of objects that shed light on the daily life and challenges faced by the Western Allies in Berlin from 1945 to 1994. The museum is about 800m north of the U-Bahn station.

BOTANISCHER GARTEN   GARDENS

(☑030-8385 0100; www.bgbm.org; Königin-Luise-Strasse 6-8; adult/concession €6/3; ⊙garden 9am-dusk, museum 10am-6pm; ⓢDahlem-Dorf, ⓡBotanischer Garten) Berlin's vast botanical garden boasts 20,000 plant species and is a fragrant spot to reconnect with nature. Especially enchanting is the Grosse Tropenhaus greenhouse, the muggy home of an entire bamboo forest. Enter from Unter den Eichen or Königin-Luise-Platz.

DAY TRIPS FROM BERLIN GRUNEWALD & DAHLEM

TRACKS OF DEATH

The Holocaust Memorial in central Berlin may be more prominent and artistic, but there is another commemorative site that is at least as poignant: **Gleis 17** (Track 17; Am Bahnhof Grunewald), next to S-Bahn station Grunewald (S7). It was from these tracks that 186 trains left for Theresienstadt, Riga, Lodz and Auschwitz, carrying their Jewish cargo like cattle to the slaughter. More than 50,000 Berliners were deported between 1941 and 1945. Weathered iron plaques recording the number of people and destination by date along the platform edge honour their memory.

EATING & DRINKING

The Botanischer Garten and the Museen Dahlem both have nice cafes for a post-sightseeing pick-me-up.

LUISE INTERNATIONAL €€
(☎030-841 8880; www.luise-dahlem.de; Königin-Luise-Strasse 40-42; pizzas €6-12, mains €13-18; 🕐10am-1am; [S]Dahlem-Dorf) This is a cafe-restaurant-beer-garden combo with a long menu likely to please everyone.

GALILEO ITALIAN €€
(☎030-831 2377; www.ristorantegalileo.de; Otto-von-Simson-Strasse 26; mains €7-22; 🕐10am-10pm Mon-Fri; [S]Dahlem-Dorf) Overlooking the Free University campus, Galileo has plied students, faculty and locals with authentic southern Italian fare for around 25 years.

Wannsee

Explore

Leafy Wannsee, Berlin's southwestern-most suburb, is named for the enormous Wannsee lake. In fine weather, it's a fantastic place to leave the city bustle behind. You can cruise around the lake, walk in the forest, visit an enchanting island, tour a royal palace or work on your tan in the Strandbad Wannsee, a lakeside lido with a 1200m-long sandy beach. Famous Nazi and Cold War sites are among its more sinister attractions.

The Best...

- **Sight** Pfaueninsel
- **Place to Eat** Restaurant Seehaase
- **Place to Drink** Loretta am Wannsee

Top Tip

For cruising on the cheap, catch the ferry from Wannsee to Kladow using just a normal public-transport ticket (€2.60).

Getting There & Away

- **S-Bahn** S1 or S7 from central Berlin to Wannsee, then walk or bus depending on where you're headed.

Need to Know

- **Area Code** ☎030
- **Location** 25km southwest of central Berlin

IN & ON THE WANNSEE

Stern und Kreisschiffahrt (☎030-536 3600; www.sternundkreis.de; 🚌Treptower Park) Operates two-hour cruises around seven lakes from April to mid-October. Boats depart hourly from 10.30am to 5.30pm; the trip costs €11.

Strandbad Wannsee (www.strandbadwannsee.de; Wannseebadweg 25; adult/concession €5.50/3.50; 🕐Apr-Sep; 🚌Nikolassee) This lakeside public pool has delighted water rats for over a century. The Strandbad is located about 1.3km northwest of the S-Bahn station Nikolassee. Walk north on Borussenstrasse, then turn left onto Wannseebadweg.

SIGHTS

GEDENKSTÄTTE HAUS DER WANNSEE-KONFERENZ MEMORIAL
(☎030-805 0010; www.ghwk.de; Am Grossen Wannsee 56-58; 🕐10am-6pm; 🚌Wannsee, then bus 114) [FREE] In January 1942 a group of 15 high-ranking Nazi officials met in a stately villa near Lake Wannsee to hammer out the details of the 'Final Solution': the systematic deportation and murder of European Jews in Eastern Europe. Today, the same building houses a memorial exhibit and an education centre about this sinister meeting and its ramifications. You can stand in the room where discussions took place, study the minutes of the meeting (taken by Adolf Eichmann) and look at photographs of those involved, many of whom lived to ripe old age. The site is about 2.5km northwest of Wannsee S-Bahn station and served from there by bus 114 several times hourly.

PFAUENINSEL OUTDOORS
(☎030-8058 6830; www.spsg.de; Nikolskoer Weg; adult/concession ferry €3/2.50, palace €3/2.50, Meierei €2/1.50; 🕐ferry 9am-8pm May-Aug, shorter hours Sep-Apr, palace 10am-4.30pm Tue-Sun Apr-Oct, Meierei 10am-5.30pm Sat & Sun Apr-Oct; 🚌Wannsee, then bus 218) Back to nature was

the dictum in the 18th century, so Friedrich Wilhelm II had this little island turned into an idyllic playground, perfect for retreating from state affairs and for frolicking with his mistress in a snowy-white fairy-tale **palace**. To heighten the romance factor, he brought in a flock of peacocks that gave the island its name and that are still strutting their stuff to this day. The island is a nature preserve, so no smoking, cycling or swimming. Picnicking, though, remains legal. There are no cafes or restaurants. The island is about 4km northwest of S-Bahn station Wannsee, from where it's served several times hourly by bus 218.

SCHLOSS GLIENICKE   PALACE

(☏030-8058 6750; www.spsg.de; Königstrasse 36; palace tours adult/concession €5/4, casino €1; ⊙10am-6pm Tue-Sun Apr-Oct, 10am-5pm Sat & Sun Nov-Mar; ⌕Wannsee, then bus 316) Glienicke Palace is the result of a rich royal kid travelling to Italy and falling in love with the country. Prince Carl of Prussia (1801–83) was only 21 when he returned to Berlin giddy with dreams of building his own Italian villa, so he hired starchitect du jour Karl Friedrich Schinkel to turn an existing garden estate into an elegant, antique-looking compound. It's richly decorated with marble fireplaces, sparkling crystal chandeliers, gold-framed paintings and fine furniture. The palace is about 6km west of S-Bahn station Wannsee and served several times hourly by bus 316.

LIEBERMANN-VILLA
AM WANNSEE   MUSEUM

(☏030-8058 5900; www.liebermann-villa.de; Colomierstrasse 3; adult/concession €7/4, audioguide €3; ⊙10am-6pm Mon, Wed, Fri & Sat, to 7pm Thu & Sun Apr-Sep, 11am-5pm Wed-Mon Oct-Mar; ⌕Wannsee, then bus 114) This lovely villa was the summer home of Berlin Secession founder Max Liebermann from 1909 until his death in 1935. Bus 114 makes the trip to the villa several times hourly from the S-Bahn station Wannsee.

 **EATING & DRINKING**

RESTAURANT SEEHAASE   INTERNATIONAL €€

(☏030-8049 6474; www.restaurant-seehaase.de; Am Grossen Wannsee 58-60; mains €7-15; ⊙11am-10pm Mon-Fri, 10am-10pm Sat & Sun; ⌕Wannsee, then bus 114) Most of the waterfront lots are in private hands, so the Seehaase with its

THE STORY OF THE CAPTAIN OF KÖPENICK

Rathaus Köpenick (Town Hall; Alt-Köpenick 21; ⊙10am-5.30pm; ⌕62 to Rathaus Köpenick) FREE exudes a fairy-tale quality, but is actually more famous for an incident back in 1906. It involved an unemployed cobbler named Wilhelm Voigt, who managed to make a laughing stock of the Prussian authorities. Costumed as an army captain, he marched upon the town hall, arrested the mayor, confiscated the city coffers and disappeared with the loot. And no one questioned his authority! At least not initially. Although quickly caught and convicted, Voigt became quite a celebrity for his chutzpah. Today, his bronze statue guards the town hall.

lake views is justifiably popular. The menu is mostly classic German, but also features pasta, *Flammkuche* and an interesting array of Turkish appetisers.

LORETTA AM WANNSEE   GERMAN €€

(☏030-8010 5333; www.loretta-berlin.de; Kronprinzessinnenweg 260; mains €11-16; ⊙11am-11pm; ⌕Wannsee) Hearty Bavarian cooking is on the menu at this traditional restaurant with an enchanting beer garden overlooking Wannsee lake. The restaurant is about 350m south of Wannsee station.

Köpenick

Explore

A 20-minute S-Bahn ride away from central Berlin, Köpenick is famous for its baroque castle, a picturesque Altstadt and a trio of superlative natural assets: Berlin's largest lake (Müggelsee), biggest forest (Köpenicker Stadtforst) and highest natural elevation (Müggelberge, 115m).

The Best...

➡ **Sight** Schloss Köpenick (p228)
➡ **Place to Eat** Ratskeller Köpenick (p228)
➡ **Place to Drink** Krokodil (p228)

DAY TRIPS FROM BERLIN KÖPENICK

WORTH A DETOUR

DEUTSCH-RUSSISCHES MUSEUM BERLIN-KARLSHORST

On 8 May 1945, six years of madness ended with the unconditional surrender of the Wehrmacht in the headquarters of the Soviet army in what is today the **Deutsch-Russisches Museum Berlin-Karlshorst** (German-Russian Museum Berlin-Karlshorst; ✆030-5015 0810; www.museum-karlshorst.de; Zwieseler Strasse 4; ☺10am-6pm Tue-Sun; ⊠Karlshorst) FREE. Stand in the hall where the signing took place, then browse the exhibit commemorating this fateful day as well as the history of WWII from the Russian perspective. The museum is a 10- to 15-minute walk from the S-Bahn station; take the Treskowallee exit, then turn right onto Rheinsteinstrasse.

Top Tip

For a more in-depth understanding of Köpenick's history, take a self-guided tour with the help of a multimedia audioguide (€5) dispensed by the tourist office.

Getting There & Away

➡ **S-Bahn** For the Altstadt, take the S3 to S-Bahn station Köpenick, then walk 1.5km south along Bahnhofstrasse or take tram 62 to the Schloss Köpenick. For the Müggelsee get off at S-Bahn station Friedrichshagen and take tram 60 or walk 1.5km south on Bölschestrasse.

Need to Know

➡ **Area Code** ✆030

➡ **Location** About 16km southeast of central Berlin

➡ **Tourist Office** (www.tkt-berlin.de; Alt-Köpenick 31-33, Schlossplatz; ☺9am-6.30pm Mon-Fri year-round, 10am-4pm Sat May-Sep, 10am-1pm Sat Oct-Apr; ⊠Köpenick, ⊟62)

◉ SIGHTS

SCHLOSS KÖPENICK PALACE, MUSEUM
(✆030-266 424 242; www.smb.museum/kgm; Schlossinsel 1; adult/concession/child €6/3/free; ☺11am-6pm Tue-Sun; ⊟62, ⊠Köpenick) Berlin's only surviving baroque palace houses a branch of the **Kunstgewerbemuseum** (Museum of Decorative Arts). It's a rich and eclectic collection of furniture, tapestries, porcelain, silverware, glass and other frilly objects from the Renaissance, baroque and rococo periods. Tram 62 will take you there from S-Bahn station Köpenick.

GROSSER MÜGGELSEE LAKE
(⊟60, ⊠Friedrichshagen) Berlin's largest lake, the Müggelsee, is hemmed in by forest on two sides and is hugely popular for swimming

and boating on hot summer days. Taking tram 60 from S-Bahn to Friedrichshagen (or walking 1.5km south on Bölschestrasse) gets you to the Müggelpark. Besides restaurants and beer gardens, there's also the landing docks of **Reederei Kutzker** (✆03362-6251; www.reederei-kutzker.de; 1hr tour €7), which runs one-hour lake tours several times daily from mid-April to mid-October.

For a walk in the woods, head to the other side of the Spree via the nearby Spreetunnel. The closest public lake beach, with boat rental, **Seebad Friedrichshagen** (✆030-645 5756; www.seebad-friedrichshagen.de; Müggelseedamm 216; adult/concession €4/2.50; ☺10am-7pm May-Aug; ⊠Friedrichshagen, then tram 60) is about 300m east of the Müggelpark. On Sunday there's a **flea market** at S-Bahn station Friedrichshagen.

✖ EATING & DRINKING

RATSKELLER KÖPENICK GERMAN €€
(✆030-655 5178; www.ratskellerkoepenick.de; Alt-Köpenick 21; mains €7-20; ☺11am-11pm Mon-Sat, to 10pm Sun; ⊟62 or 68, ⊠Köpenick) The olde-worlde ambience at this cellar warren in the local town hall is fun, and the menu full of classic rib-stickers alongside healthier, seasonal and meatless selections. Reservations advised for the Friday and Saturday live-jazz nights.

KROKODIL MEDITERRANEAN €€
(✆030-6588 0094; www.der-coepenicker.de; Gartenstrasse 46-48; mains €7-15; ☺dinner daily, brunch Sun; ⊟62 or 68, ⊠Köpenick) The fare at this urban getaway is delish, but even more memorable is the setting on the Dahme river. There's a hostel attached in case you want to stay (dorm/double including breakfast €18/69). From S-Bahn station Köpenick take tram 62 or 68 to Schlossplatz, then walk east on Müggelheimer Strasse for 300m and turn south on Kietz for another 400m.

🛌 Sleeping

Berlin offers the gamut of places to unpack your suitcase. Just about every international chain now has a flagship in the German capital, but more interesting options that better reflect the city's verve and spirit abound. You can sleep in a former bank, boat or factory, in the home of a silent-movie diva, in a 'flying bed', or even in a coffin.

Hotels

With around 133,500 beds in 800 properties, Berlin has more beds than New York and more are scheduled to come online in the coming years. You'll find the entire range of hotels in Berlin, from no-frills cookie-cutter chains to all-out boutique hotels with top-notch amenities and fall-over-backwards service.

The best beds often sell out early, so make reservations, especially around major holidays, cultural events and trade shows. Most properties now have an internet booking function.

BUDGET, DESIGNER & ART HOTELS

Berlin being an art- and design-minded city, it's not surprising that there's a large number of smaller indie hotels catering to the needs of savvy urban nomads with at least a midrange budget. Properties often integrate distinguished architecture with a customised design concept that projects a sense of place and tends to appeal to creative spirits and travellers searching for an authentic experience.

There's usually great emphasis on the latest tech trends and on such lifestyle essentials as iPod docks, brand-name espresso machines and Bose sound systems. The antithesis of cookie-cutter chains, these types of abodes are sprinkled around the city but are especially prevalent in the Mitte district. Many have succeeded in cultivating the local community with hip rooftop lounges, cocktail bars, progressive restaurants, chic spas and one-off parties and events.

CHAIN HOTELS

In recent years, practically all international hotel chains have opened one or multiple properties in Berlin. Since most conform to certain standards of decor, service and facilities, they're great for people who enjoy predictability and privacy (or simply want to use up those frequent flyer points). Most have several categories of comfort, from cramped singles to high-roller suites, with rates reflecting size and amenities. Generally, prices fluctuate dramatically, with serious bargains a possibility when occupancy is low. Besides the international chains, there are also some Berlin-based contenders, including **Amano** (www.amanogroup.de) and **Meininger** (www.meininger-hotels.com).

Hostels

Berlin's hostel scene is as vibrant as ever and consists of both classic backpacker hostels with large dorms and a communal spirit, and modern 'flashpacker' crashpads catering to wallet-watching city-breakers. Also increasingly popular are hostel-hotel hybrids with hotel-like amenities. You'll find them in all districts, but especially in Kreuzberg and Friedrichshain, putting you within stumbling distance of bars and clubs. Dorm beds can be had for as little as €9, but spending a little more gets you a dorm with fewer beds, private quarters with attached bathroom, or self-catering apartments. Dorms tend to be mixed, although some hostels also offer women-only units with hairdryers and make-up mirrors. Indie hostels have no curfew and staff tend to be savvy, multilingual and keen to help with tips and advice. For bookings, try www.hostelworld.com, www.hostels.com or www.hostelbookers.com.

B&Bs

Nostalgic types seeking Old Berlin flavour should check into a charismatic B&B, called *Hotel-Pension* or simply *Pension*. They typically occupy one or several floors of a historic residential building and offer local colour and personal attention galore. Amenities, room size and decor vary, often within a single establishment. The cheapest rooms may have shared facilities or perhaps a sink and a shower cubicle in the room but no private toilet.

Travellers in need of buckets of privacy, high comfort levels or the latest tech amenities may not feel as comfortable, although wi-fi, cable TV and other mod cons are becoming increasingly available. Overall, though, *Pensions* are a dying breed in Berlin, where they're most prevalent in the western district of Charlottenburg, around Kurfürstendamm.

Short-Term Rentals

Furnished flats are a hugely popular – and economical – alternative to hotels in Berlin. The benefit of space, privacy and independence makes them especially attractive to families and small groups. Peer-to-peer rental communities like airbnb or its German competitors Wimdu and 9flats have also made enormous inroads. See the boxed text on p240 for more.

Both commercial and private rentals, however, are being perceived not only as a threat to the hotel industry but also to the availability of increasingly scarce affordable housing for permanent residents. In response, a new law went into effect in May 2014 requiring holiday-apartment owners to register with the local authorities in order to continue operating legally until at least April 2016. The issue will be revisited by the local government and at this point it remains unclear whether there will be a lasting impact on the availability or legality of short-term apartment rentals in the medium term.

Rates

Fierce competition has kept prices low compared to other capital cities in Europe. Prices spike during major trade shows, festivals and public holidays, when early reservations are essential. Business-geared hotels often have good deals at weekends. In winter, prices often plummet outside holidays, with five-star rooms costing as little as €100.

Amenities

Accommodation listings in this chapter are organised by neighbourhood and then by budget. We have aimed to feature well-situated, mostly independent hotels that offer good value, a warm welcome, charm and character, as well as a palpable sense of place. The bulk of our listings are mid-range options, which generally offer the best value for money. Expect clean, comfortable and decent-sized rooms with at least a modicum of style, a private bathroom, TV and wi-fi. Our selection is also sprinkled with a few top-end hotels with the full spectrum of international-standard amenities and perhaps a scenic location, designer decor or historical ambience. Budget places are generally hostels or other simple establishments where bathrooms may be shared.

Overall, rooms tend to be on the small side. You'll usually find that BBC and CNN are the only English-language channels on TV (nearly all foreign shows and films are dubbed into German) and that air-con is a rare commodity. Wi-fi is commonplace, although some hotels (especially international chains) still charge as much as €20 per day for access. In smaller hotels, access may be restricted to the lobby. Few hotels have their own parking lot or garage and even if they do, space will be limited and the cost as high as €25 per day. Public garages are widely available, but also cost a pretty penny.

Accommodation Websites

➜ **Berlin30** (www.berlin30.com) Specialises in accommodation costing less than €30 per person.

➜ **Lonely Planet** (lonelyplanet.com/germany/hotels) Lonely Planet's online booking service with insider low-down on the best places to stay.

➜ **Visit Berlin** (www.visitberlin.de) Official Berlin tourist office books rooms at partner hotels with a best-price guarantee.

Lonely Planet's Top Choices

Casa Camper (p238) Infectious irreverence paired with all the Zeitgeist essentials global nomads crave.

Michelberger Hotel (p240) Fun base with eccentric design, party pedigree and unpretentious attitude beautifully captures the Berlin vibe.

Das Stue (p235) Charismatic refuge from the urban bustle with understated grandeur and Tiergarten park as a front yard.

EastSeven Berlin Hostel (p241) Small, personable and spotless crash pad perfect for making new friends.

Hotel am Steinplatz (p244) Golden 1920s glamour still radiates from the listed walls of this recently revivified art deco jewel.

Hotel Askanischer Hof (p242) Ride the vintage wave at this frilly and lovingly kept old-school gem from the silent-movie era.

Best by Budget

€

Grand Hostel Berlin (p238) Connect to the magic of yesteryear at this historic lair imbued with both character and modern amenities.

Wombats City Hostel Berlin (p237) Fun seekers should thrive at this well-run hostel with hip in-house bar.

Hostel One80° (p234) Not for introverts, this central 700-bed hipster design hotel has an on-site restaurant and club.

€€

Circus Hotel (p237) Perennial pleaser thanks to being a perfect synthesis of style, comfort, location and value.

Hotel Amano (p237) Top value-for-money pick beloved by global nomads on a budget.

Adina Apartment Hotel Berlin Checkpoint Charlie (p233) Ideal base for budget-conscious space-craving self-caterers.

€€€

Mandala Hotel (p235) All-suite city slicker with uncluttered urban feel and top eats.

Louisa's Place (p244) Personal attention is key at this refined outpost with XL-sized suites.

Hotel de Rome (p233) Posh player in former bank building with rooftop bar and bank-vault spa.

Best Cool Factor

Soho House Berlin (p238) Members' only club with A-lister clientele meets posh boutique hotel in Bauhaus building.

25hours Hotel Bikini Berlin (p242) Inner-city playground with easy access to top shopping and rooms overlooking the Berlin Zoo.

Weinmeister (p238) Crash pad for creatives in the heart of Scheunenviertel hipsterville.

nhow (p241) Karim Rashid–designed shagadelic riverside hotel with own recording studio.

Best for Romance

Honigmond Garden Hotel (p237) Urban oasis with antique-filled rooms backed by dreamy 'Garden of Eden'.

Ackselhaus & Blue Home (p241) This cocoon of quiet and sophistication lets you match mood to room.

Das Stue (p235) Stylish boutique pad with luxe spa and park access for long walks.

NEED TO KNOW

Price Ranges

The following room-rate breakdown serves only as a guideline. Listed rates refer to one night in a standard double room with private bathroom during high season but outside of major events, holidays or trade-show periods. Many properties have pricier rooms in higher categories. Rates include 7% value-added tax (VAT). Breakfast is sometimes included, but more often than not is an optional extra – prices have been noted where applicable.

€	under €80
€€	€80 to €160
€€€	over €160

City Tax

VAT has long been included in room rates, but since 1 January 2014 an additional 5% 'City Tax' is payable on the net room rates, ie excluding VAT and fees for amenities and services such as minibar, sauna or spa. The tax is added to the hotel bill. Business travellers are exempt if they can prove the purpose of their trip (eg with a letter from the company or a bill issued to the employer). Rates quoted in this book do not include the tax.

Which Floor?

In Germany, 'ground floor' refers to the floor at street level. The 1st floor (what would be called the 2nd floor in the US) is the floor above that. The book follows local usage of the terms.

SLEEPING

Where to Stay

Neighbourhood	For	Against
Historic Mitte	Close to major sights like Reichstag and Brandenburg Gate; great transport links; mostly high-end hotels; Michelin-starred and other top restaurants; handy for the city's best theatre, opera and classical concert venues	Touristy, expensive, pretty dead at night
Museumsinsel & Alexanderplatz	Supercentral sightseeing quarter; easy transport access; close to blockbuster sights and mainstream shopping; large and new hotels	Noisy, busy, ugly and dusty thanks to lots of major construction; hardly any nightlife
Potsdamer Platz & Tiergarten	Urban flair in Berlin's newest quarter; cutting-edge architecture; high-end international hotels; top museums and Philharmonie; next to Tiergarten city park	Limited eating options; pricey; no street life at night
Scheunenviertel	Hipster quarter; trendy, historic, central; brims with boutique and designer hotels; superb indie shopping with lots of Berlin designer boutiques, international eats and strong cafe scene; top galleries and great street art	Pricey, busy, noisy, no parking
Kreuzberg & Neukölln	Vibrant arty, underground and multicultural party quarter; best for bar-hopping and clubbing; cheap; lots of hostels; great foodie scene	Gritty, noisy and busy; away from main sights
Friedrichshain	Student and young family quarter; bubbling nightlife; inexpensive; superb Cold War–era sights	Limited sleeping options; not so central for sightseeing; transport difficult in some areas
Prenzlauer Berg	Well-heeled, clean, charming residential area; lively cafe and restaurant scene; indie boutiques and Mauerpark flea market	Limited late-night action, no essential sights
City West & Charlottenburg	The former 'West Berlin'; great shopping at KaDeWe and on Kurfürstendamm; stylish lounges, 'Old Berlin' bars and top restaurants; best range of good-value lodging; historic B&Bs	Sedate; far from key sights and happening nightlife

🛏 Historic Mitte

ADINA APARTMENT HOTEL BERLIN
CHECKPOINT CHARLIE
APARTMENT €€

Map p322 (✆030-200 7670; www.adina.eu; Krausenstrasse 35-36; d from €125, 1-bedroom apt from €150; P ✳ @ 🛜 ⊠; S Stadtmitte, Spittelmarkt) Adina's contemporary one- and two-bedroom apartments with full kitchens are tailor-made for cost-conscious families, anyone in need of elbow room, and self-caterers (a supermarket is a minute away). Regular hotel rooms without kitchens are also available. Staff are accommodating and the pool and sauna are great for combating postflight fatigue. See the website for other Adina properties in town. Optional breakfast is €19.

ARTE LUISE
KUNSTHOTEL
BOUTIQUE HOTEL €€

Map p328 (✆030-284 480; www.luise-berlin. com; Luisenstrasse 19; d €99-169, with shared bathroom €59-84; ✳ @ 🛜; S Friedrichstrasse, ⊞Friedrichstrasse) At this 'gallery with rooms', each unit is designed by different artists who receive royalties whenever it's rented. They're all wonderfully imaginative, but we're especially fond of No 107 with its giant bed, and the boudoir-red 'Cabaret' (No 206). Cash-strapped art fans should enquire about the smaller, bathless rooms. Avoid those facing the train tracks. Optional breakfast is €11.

ARCOTEL JOHN F
HOTEL €€

Map p322 (✆030-405 0460; www.arcotelhotels. com; Werderscher Markt 11; r from €124; P ✳ @ 🛜; S Hausvogteiplatz) This lifestyle hotel pays homage to President John F Kennedy with plenty of whimsical detail, including hand-carved rocking chairs (an allusion to the president's back problem) and curvaceous lamps inspired by Jackie's ball gowns. Rooms are quiet and smartly outfitted with dark wooden furniture and beds backed by oversized tufted headboards. Optional breakfast is €22.

COSMO HOTEL BERLIN
HOTEL €€

Map p322 (✆030-5858 2222; www.cosmo-hotel. de; Spittelmarkt 13; d €100-210; P ✳ @ 🛜; S Spittelmarkt) Despite its ho-hum location on a busy street, this hotel scores high for comfort, design and a 'with-it' vibe. The lobby, with its extravagant lamps and armchairs, sets the tone for spacious rooms

decked out in shades of cinnamon and chocolate. All have floor-to-ceiling windows with blackout blinds. Free wi-fi in public areas only. The organic breakfast buffet is €18.

MERCURE HOTEL & RESIDENZ
CHECKPOINT CHARLIE
HOTEL €€

Map p322 (✆030-206 320; www.accorhotels. com; Schützenstrasse 11; r from €83; P ✳ @ 🛜; S Kochstrasse) In a handsome building by Aldo Rossi on a quiet side street, this modern hotel is a great sightseeing base of operation. Rooms are spacious and come in various configurations to cater to all needs, including suites with balconies and family rooms with two bedrooms. Perk: free massages on Tuesday afternoons. Optional breakfast is €18.

NOVOTEL BERLIN MITTE
HOTEL €€

Map p320 (✆030-206 740; www.novotel.com; Fischerinsel 12; r from €110; P ✳ @ 🛜; S Spittelmarkt, Märkisches Museum) At this dependable value-for-money pick, you'll retire to well-proportioned rooms that never threaten to become fussy or overdecorated, but are equipped with a good range of amenities, including soundproof windows and a desk in case you need to give your laptop a workout. The stylish lobby-bar is a welcome unwinding zone. Optional breakfast is €19 (free for two kids under 16).

HOTEL DE ROME
LUXURY HOTEL €€€

Map p322 (✆030-460 6090; www.hotelderome. com; Behrenstrasse 37; d from €345; P ◒ ✳ @ 🛜 ⊠; 🚍100, 200, S Hausvogteiplatz) A delightful alchemy of history and contemporary flair, this luxe contender in a 19th-century bank has richly furnished rooms with extra-high ceilings, marble baths and heated floors. Wind down in the former vault that is now the pool/spa area or over cocktails at the Bebel Bar (p95). In summer, drinks are also served on the rooftop terrace. Optional breakfast is €35.

HOTEL ADLON
KEMPINSKI
LUXURY HOTEL €€€

Map p322 (✆030-226 10; www.kempinski.com; Unter den Linden 77, Pariser Platz; r from €280; ✳ @ 🛜 ⊠; S Brandenburger Tor, ⊞Brandenburger Tor) The Adlon has been Berlin's most high-profile defender of the grand tradition since 1907. The striking lobby is a mere overture to the full symphony of luxury awaiting in spacious, amenity-laden rooms

SMOKING

Smoking rooms are a dying breed. Larger properties and chain hotels are most likely to have set aside floors with rooms where smoking is permitted. Smaller independent hotels and hostels usually don't allow smoking inside the rooms and may impose fines on those who light up anyway. By law, there's no smoking in indoor public areas.

and suites with timelessly regal decor. An ayurvedic spa, a double-Michelin-star restaurant and the Felix nightclub add 21st-century spice. Breakfast is €42.

SOFITEL BERLIN GENDARMENMARKT
HOTEL €€€

Map p322 (☎030-203 750; www.sofitel.com; Charlottenstrasse 50-52; d from €165; ⓟ✳@☎; ⓢ Französische Strasse) This cocoon of quiet sophistication has a killer location close to sights and shopping. Its 92 rooms and suites offer a flawless interplay of marble, glass and light; the nicest have a private balcony with views of Gendarmenmarkt. Perks include the top-floor sauna and gym and an upmarket Austro-German restaurant. Optional breakfast is €29.50.

📛 Museumsinsel & Alexanderplatz

MOTEL ONE BERLIN-ALEXANDERPLATZ
HOTEL €

Map p320 (☎030-2005 4080; www.motel-one. de; Dircksenstrasse 36; d from €73; ⓟ✳@☎; ⓢ Alexanderplatz, ⓡ Alexanderplatz) If you value location over luxury, this budget designer chain makes for an excellent crash pad. Smallish rooms come with up-to-the-minute touches (flat-screen TVs, granite counters, massage showerheads, air-con) that are normally the staples of posher players. Arne Jacobsen's turquoise egg chairs accent the hip lobby. Check the website for other Berlin locations. Optional breakfast is €7.50.

HOSTEL ONE80°
HOSTEL €

Map p320 (☎030-2804 4620; www.one80hostels.com; Otto-Braun-Strasse 65; dm €14-30; ⊝@☎; ⓢ Alexanderplatz, ⓡ Alexanderplatz) With its stylish designer sofas, cool music

and an industrial-chic dining area, One80° is a next-gen lifestyle hostel. There's space for over 700 people in dorms sleeping four to eight in comfy bunk beds. Assets include individual reading lamps, two electrical outlets and two lockers – per person, that is. Optional breakfast is €5.50.

PANGEA PEOPLE HOSTEL
HOSTEL €

Map p320 (☎030-886 695 810; www.pangeapeople.de; Karl-Liebknecht-Strasse 34; dm €13-22, d from €58; @☎; ⓢ Alexanderplatz, ⓡ Alexanderplatz) Before there were continents, there was Pangea, a single supercontinent that united the earth's landmass. At this central hostel, the name is the game, for the goal is to reunite people from all cultures, be it in airy dorms equipped with customised beds and lockers, or in the bar over beers, snacks and karaoke. Optional breakfast is €5.50.

RADISSON BLU HOTEL
HOTEL €€

Map p320 (☎030-238 280; www.radisson-blu.com/hotel-berlin; Karl-Liebknecht-Strasse 3; d from €140; ⓟ✳@☎✉; ⓡ Hackescher Markt) At this swish and supercentral contender, you quite literally 'sleep with the fishes', thanks to the lobby's 25m-high tropical aquarium. Streamlined design radiates urban poshness in the 427 rooms and throughout the two restaurants and various social nooks. Thoughtful perks include free wi-fi throughout and a 24/7 spa with pool and sauna. Optional breakfast is €25.

PARK INN BY RADISSON BERLIN ALEXANDERPLATZ
HOTEL €€

Map p320 (☎030-238 90; www.parkinn-berlin.de; Alexanderplatz 7; d €120-210; ⊝✳@☎; ⓢ Alexanderplatz, ⓡ Alexanderplatz) Views, views, views! Berlin's tallest hotel has got them. Right on Alexanderplatz, this sleek tower is honeycombed with 1012 rooms (some rather snug) sporting panoramic windows, soothing earth tones, flat-screen TVs and noiseless air-con. For superb sunsets, snag a room facing the Fernsehturm. Great rooftop panorama terrace with bar and lounge chairs. Optional breakfast is €19, wi-fi €9.90 for 24 hours.

HOTEL INDIGO ALEXANDERPLATZ
HOTEL €€

Map p320 (☎030-505 0860; www.hotelindigo berlin.com/alex; Bernhard-Weiss-Strasse 5; d €120-170; ⊝✳☎; ⓢ Alexanderplatz, ⓡ Alexanderplatz) Sophisticated, efficient and supercentral, this mod designer hotel spoils you with amenities normally reserved for pricier abodes (fluffy bathrobes, iPod docks, Tassimo coffee-makers, Aveda toiletries). Rooms, though rather small, are decorated in a minimal modern style and infused with local imagery. Free landline calls to 19 countries. Breakfast is €17.

ART'OTEL BERLIN MITTE HOTEL €€

Map p320 (☎030-240 620; www.artotels. de; Wallstrasse 70-73; d €110-180; P❋@☎; ⓢMärkisches Museum) This boutique hotel wears its 'art' moniker with a justified swagger: more than 400 works by renowned contemporary German artist Georg Baselitz decorate rooms and public areas. Suites have extra-cool bathrooms and those on the 6th floor even boast small balconies. The hotel is docked to the rococo Ermelerhaus, which harbours the restaurant with its glass-roofed courtyard. Optional breakfast is €17.50.

HOTEL ALEXANDER PLAZA HOTEL €€

Map p320 (☎030-240 010; www.classik-hotel-collection.com; Rosenstrasse 1; d from €115; P❋❋; ⓡHackescher Markt) This 94-room city hotel in a sensitively restored 19th-century merchant home retains such period details as a mosaic floor and a stucco-adorned floating stairway. After a recent revamp, rooms are dressed in soothing tan and carmine and get plenty of natural light filtering in through panoramic windows. Kick back in the sauna. Breakfast is €15.

🛏 Potsdamer Platz & Tiergarten

ABION SPREEBOGEN WATERSIDE HOTEL HOTEL €€

(☎030-3992 0990; www.abion-hotel.de; Alt-Moabit 99; d €85-220; P☎; ⓢTurmstrasse) In a converted dairy farm right on the Spree River, the Abion goes mostly for the suit brigade, but also comes with easy access to major sights, boat cruises and the Tiergarten park, though not to happening nightlife. Spend a bit extra on the newly renovated river-facing rooms. Optional breakfast is €19. The hotel is located about 1.6km west of the Hauptbahnhof via Invalidenstrasse and Alt-Moabit. From Turmstrasse U-Bahn station, walk 250m east on Alt-Moabit.

SCANDIC BERLIN POTSDAMER PLATZ HOTEL €€

Map p318 (☎030-700 7790; www.scandichotels.com; Gabriele-Tegit-Promenade 19; d €99-209; P❋@☎; ⓢMendelssohn-Bartholdy-Platz) 🌱 This Scandinavian import gets kudos for its central location and spacious blond-wood rooms with big bathrooms as well as for going the extra mile when it comes to being green. Distinctive features include the eighth-floor gym-with-a-view, the restaurant's Jamie Oliver–created kids menu and free bikes or walking sticks for spins around nearby Tiergarten park. Optional (partly organic) breakfast is €9.

MÖVENPICK HOTEL BERLIN HOTEL €€

Map p336 (☎030-230 060; www.moevenpick-berlin.com; Schöneberger Strasse 3; d €130-300; P❋@☎; ⓡAnhalter Bahnhof) This snazzy hotel smoothly marries contemporary boldness with the industrial flair of the protected Siemenshöfe factory. Rooms vamp it up with glass cube walls and sensuous olive wood furniture; some sport zany bath-tubs designed by Philippe Starck. The courtyard restaurant is lidded by a retractable glass roof for alfresco dining. Optional breakfast is €22.

★DAS STUE BOUTIQUE HOTEL €€€

Map p318 (☎030-311 7220; www.das-stue.com; Drakestrasse 1; r from €200; ❋☎🏊; 🚌100, 106, 200) Hugging the Tiergarten park, Das Stue is as warm and welcoming as its name (Danish for 'living room') suggests. At the trapezoidal bar locals and guests mingle over superb cocktails, the Michelin-starred restaurant serves a 24-course menu intended to stimulate all five senses, and the sleek spa comes with a pool, a small sauna and intuitive massages. Optional breakfast is €25.

MANDALA HOTEL LUXURY HOTEL €€€

Map p318 (☎030-590 050 000; www.themandala.de; Potsdamer Strasse 3; ste from €160; P❋@☎; ⓢPotsdamer Platz, ⓡPotsdamer Platz) How 'suite' it is to be staying at this swish cocoon of sophistication and unfussy ambience. Updated rooms come in six sizes (40 to 101 sq metres) and are equipped with a kitchenette, walk-in closets and spacious desks in case you're here to ink that deal. The spa is a gorgeous indulgence zone. Optional breakfast is €28.

QUIRKY SLEEPS

Propeller Island City Lodge (Map p338; ☑0163 256 5909, 030-891 9016; www.propeller-island.de; Albrecht-Achilles-Strasse 58; d €84-130; 🛜; Ⓢ Adenauerplatz) This hotel's name was inspired by a novel by the master of imagination, Jules Verne, and every room here is indeed a journey to a unique, surreal and slightly wicked world. To be stranded on Propeller Island may have you waking up on the ceiling, in a prison cell or inside a kaleidoscope. Artist-composer-owner Lars Stroschen crafted all the furniture and fixtures, creating sinks from metal beer barrels, faucets from heater valves and table bases from tree trunks. Don't expect TV, room service or pillow treats. Check-in is by prior arrangement. Located in the city's west; from U-Bahn station Adenauerplatz, walk 200m west on Kurfürstendamm, then 250m south on Albrecht-Achilles-Strasse.

Eastern Comfort Hostelboat (Map p330; ☑030-6676 3806; www.eastern-comfort.com; Mühlenstrasse 73-77; dm €16, d €50-78; ☺ reception 8am-midnight; @🛜; Ⓢ Warschauer Strasse, Ⓡ Warschauer Strasse) Let the Spree River murmur you to sleep while you're snugly ensconced in this two-boat floating hostel right by the East Side Gallery. Cabins are carpeted and trimmed in wood, but pretty snug (except for 'first-class'); all but the dorms have their own shower and toilet. The party zones of Kreuzberg and Friedrichshain are handily within staggering distance. Optional breakfast is €6. Linen is €5, or bring your own.

Hüttenpalast (Map p332; ☑030-3730 5806; www.huettenpalast.de; Hobrechtstrasse 66; d campervans & cabins/hotel €65/85; ☺ check-in 8am-6pm or by arrangement; 🛜; ⓈHermannplatz) Sure, it has hotel-style rooms with private bath, but who wants those when you can sleep in a romantic wooden hut with rooftop terrace or in a vintage caravan fitted with a homemade light sculpture? This indoor campground in an old vacuum-cleaner factory in Neukölln is an unusual place to hang your hat, even by Berlin standards. Wacky and welcoming, the compound also includes an idyllic garden and a communal cafe for socialising. Optional breakfast is €6.50.

Scube Park Berlin (Map p332; ☑030-6980 7841; www.scubepark.berlin; Columbiadamm 160; s/d €33/39; ☺ reception 8am-7pm; 🅿🛜; Ⓢ Boddinstrasse) An unsual place to hang your hat is a Scube, a cluster of 30 teensy (3m x 3m x 3m) wooden cabins with panoramic windows close to the grounds of a public summer pool and right next to the Tempelhofer Park. Simply furnished with wooden bunk beds, a table and electrical power, it's not quite glamping, especially since facilities are shared. Breakfast (€7) is a nice spread and the communal barbecue area a convivial spot. Cabins in back are quieter.

Das Andere Haus VIII (☑030-5544 0331; www.dasanderehaus8.de; Erich-Müller-Strasse 12; s/d €45/68; 🅿🚭🛜; Ⓡ Rummelsburg) At this converted 19th-century jailhouse overlooking scenic Rummelburger Bucht, anyone can stay in five 'cells' that are snug and sparsely, if comfortably, furnished. The waterfront walkway invites strolling or exploring by bike. Located in Lichtenberg, east of Friedrichshain; from S-Bahn station Rummelsburg, take tram 21 down Hauptstrasse to Kosanke-Siedlung and then walk 350m via Georg-Löwenstein-Strasse.

Yes Residenz (Map p342; www.yes-berlin.de; Fehrbelliner Strasse 84; s/d/tr/q €55/66/77/88; 🚭; Ⓢ Rosenthaler Platz, Senefelderplatz) Fancy sleeping on camping beds in a tent and taking showers from a watering can, all without roughing it in the woods? In this teensy yet undeniably unique mini-apartment, you can do just that. Architect Julian Marhold has created a charmingly unique space, complete with forest wallpaper, right in a regular Berlin building, so you can have your own Hansel and Gretel moment without leaving town. Rates include a welcome drink. Located in Prenzlauer Berg.

Alte Bäckerei Pankow (☑030-486 4669; www.alte-baeckerei-pankow.de; Wollankstrasse 130; d €80, 2-night minimum; 🚭; Ⓡ Wollankstrasse) Yesteryear is right now in this small rooftop apartment above a 19th-century bakery. Bedrooms and sitting rooms are furnished country-style and the bathroom has a deep wooden tub. The building also houses a local history museum, and fresh bread is still baked between 3pm and 6pm Tuesday, Wednesday and Friday. Located in Pankow, north of Prenzlauer Berg.

RITZ-CARLTON BERLIN LUXURY HOTEL €€€

Map p318 ([☎]030-337 777; www.ritzcarlton.com; Potsdamer Platz 3; d from €225; [P][✳][@][⁀][✉]; [S]Potsdamer Platz, [Ⓡ]Potsdamer Platz) Modelled on the Rockefeller Center in New York City, the Ritz-Carlton makes a grand statement with baronial rooms and suites that will make you feel as though you're staying at your rich uncle's country estate. Expect all the trappings of a big-league player, including a high-end restaurant, bar, spa and extensive Ritz Kids program. Optional breakfast is €38.

GRAND HYATT BERLIN HOTEL €€€

Map p318 ([☎]030-2553 1234; www.berlin.grand. hyatt.com; Marlene-Dietrich-Platz 2; d from €195; [P][✳][⁀][✉]; [S]Potsdamer Platz, [Ⓡ]Potsdamer Platz) The moment you step into the lavish, cedar-clad lobby of this designer temple, you sense that it's luxury all the way to the breathtaking rooftop pool. Rooms are dressed in drama and luxury, including Bang & Olufsen TVs and fancy coffee-makers. The snazzy bars and restaurants are great for winding down and planning tomorrow's sightseeing attack or spend-a-thon. Breakfast is €36.

[🛏] Scheunenviertel

CIRCUS HOSTEL HOSTEL €

Map p326 ([☎]030-2000 3939; www.circus-berlin.de; Weinbergsweg 1a; dm €23-31, s/d from €60/85; [@][⁀]; [S]Rosenthaler Platz) Clean, cheerfully painted rooms, abundant clean showers, helpful staff and a great location are among the factors that have kept Circus at the top of the hostel heap since 1997. The downstairs cafe serves inexpensive breakfasts, drinks and snacks, while the basement bar has different events and parties almost nightly.

WOMBATS CITY HOSTEL BERLIN HOSTEL €

Map p326 ([☎]030-8471 0820; www.wombats-hostels.com; Alte Schönhauser Strasse 2; dm/d €26/78; [@][⁀]; [S]Rosa-Luxemburg-Platz) Sociable and central, Wombats gets hostelling right. From backpack-sized in-room lockers to individual reading lamps and a guest kitchen with dishwasher, the attention to detail here is impressive. Spacious en-suite rooms are as much part of the deal as freebie linen and a welcome drink, best enjoyed with fellow party pilgrims at

the 7th-floor Wombar. Optional breakfast buffet €3.90.

[★]CIRCUS HOTEL HOTEL €

Map p326 ([☎]030-2000 3939; www.circus-berlin.de; Rosenthaler Strasse 1; d €85120; [@][⁀]; [S]Rosenthaler Platz) At our favourite budget boutique hotel, none of the mod rooms are alike, but all feature upbeat colours, thoughtful design details, sleek oak floors and quality beds. Baths have walk-in rain showers. Unexpected perks include a roof terrace with summertime yoga, bike rentals and a fabulous breakfast buffet (€9) served until 1pm. Simply good value all-around.

HOTEL AMANO HOTEL €€

Map p326 ([☎]030-809 4150; www.amanogroup. de; Auguststrasse 43; d €90-190; [P][✳][@][⁀]; [S]Rosenthaler Platz) This budget designer hotel have inviting public areas, dressed in brushed-copper walls and cocoa-hued banquettes, and efficiently styled rooms, where white furniture teams up with oak floors and natural-toned fabrics to create crisp cosiness. Space-cravers should book an apartment with kitchenette. There's a popular bar, which opens up a branch on the rooftop in summer. Breakfast is €15.

HONIGMOND GARDEN HOTEL HOTEL €€

Map p328 ([☎]030-2844 5577; www.honigmond-berlin.de; Invalidenstrasse 122; s & d incl breakfast from €121-186; [☻][@][⁀]; [S]Naturkundemuseum, [Ⓡ]Nordbahnhof) Never mind the busy thoroughfare: this well-managed 20-room guesthouse built in 1845 is an utterly sweet retreat. Reach your comfortable, classically styled rooms via an enchanting garden with koi pond, chirping birds, and rich foliage and flowers. Days start with a sumptuous breakfast in the winter garden. Avoid rooms facing the road.

MANI HOTEL BOUTIQUE HOTEL €€

Map p326 ([☎]030-5302 8080; www.hotel-mani.com; Torstrasse 136; d €90-180; [P][⁀]; [S]Rosenthaler Platz) Cocooned behind an elegant black facade on trendy Torstrasse, Mani flaunts an uncluttered urban feel and sleek rooms that pack plenty of creature comforts into a compact package. It's great value for the money, even if facilities are limited to the recommended restaurant that wows local cool-hunters with its French-Israeli fare. Optional breakfast is €15.

FLOWER'S
BOARDINGHOUSE MITTE   APARTMENT €€
Map p326 (☎030-2804 5306; www.flowersber
lin.de; Mulackstrasse 1; apt from €93; ☺recep-
tion 9am-6pm; 🛜; ⓈWeinmeisterstrasse, Rosa-
Luxemburg-Platz) Self-caterers won't miss
many comforts of home in these breezy
apartments with a heart-of-Scheunenviertel
location. Choose from three sizes: L, XL
and XXL, the latter being a split-level unit
with fabulous views over the rooftops.
Units come with full kitchens and TV/
DVD; rates include a small breakfast (rolls,
coffee, tea) you pick up at reception.

HOTEL I31   HOTEL €€
Map p328 (☎030-338 4000; www.hotel-i31.
de; Invalidenstrasse 31; r from €110; 🅿❄🛜;
ⓈNaturkundemuseum) New since May 2013,
this contemporary contender has a variety
of relaxation zones, including a sauna, a
sunny terrace and a small garden with sun
loungers. Nice touch: the minibar with free
soft drinks. For a little more space and luxury (Molton Brown amenties, for example)
book a 'comfort room' on the upper floors.
Optional breakfast is €16.50.

MONBIJOU HOTEL   HOTEL €€
Map p326 (☎030-6162 0300; www.monbijouho-
tel.com; Monbijouplatz 1; r/ste €110/149) A hop,
skip and jump from Hackescher Markt and
Museum Island, this newcomer couldn't
wish for a more central location. Rooms are
crisp and compact (except for the corner
suites) and contrast with the elegant public areas that ooze richly textured warmth
from wood, leather and a crackling fire.
The sleek bar will have you hankering for
high-balls. Breakfast is €15.

WEINMEISTER   HOTEL €€
Map p326 (☎030-755 6670; www.the-wein
meister.com; Weinmeisterstrasse 2; d €100-163;
🅿❄@🛜; ⓈWeinmeisterstrasse) Behind its
shiny facade, this slick glamour bastion un-
apologetically curries favour with creatives
from fashion, music and film. Heck, British
band Hurts and DJ Mousse T have designed
their own rooms (numbers 501 and 401, respectively). No need to run with this crowd
to appreciate the black-and-charcoal rooms
where iMacs replace the TV. Optional
breakfast is €18.

HOTEL HONIGMOND   HOTEL €€
Map p328 (☎030-284 4550; www.honigmond-
berlin.de; Tieckstrasse 12; d incl breakfast €132-

210; 🅿@🛜; ⓈOranienburger Tor) This delightful hotel scores a perfect 10 on our
'charm-o-meter', not for being particularly
lavish, but for its familiar yet elegant ambience. Rabbits frolic in the garden, the restaurant is a local favourite and rooms sparkle
in restored glory. The nicest are in the new
wing and flaunt their historic features –
ornate stucco ceilings, frescoes, parquet
floors – to maximum effect.

★CASA CAMPER   HOTEL €€€
Map p326 (☎030-2000 3410; www.casacamper.
com; Weinmeisterstrasse 1; r/ste incl breakfast
from €194/338; 🅿🛜; ⓈWeinmeisterstrasse)
Catalan shoemaker Camper has translated
its concept of chic yet sensible footwear into
this style-pit for trend-conscious travellers.
Rooms are mod if minimalist and come
with day-lit bathrooms and beds that in-
vite hitting the snooze button. Minibars are
eschewed for a top-floor lounge with stellar
views, free breakfast and 24/7 snacks and
drinks.

SOHO HOUSE BERLIN   BOUTIQUE HOTEL €€€
Map p326 (☎030-405 0440; www.sohohouse-
berlin.com; Torstrasse 1; d from €150; 🅿❄🛜🏊;
ⓈRosa-Luxemburg-Platz) This in-crowd darling packs plenty of design cachet into its
eclectic-mod rooms equipped with such
lifestyle essentials as Jamboxes, huge flat-
screen TVs and rain showers. Staying here
also buys access to members-only areas
such as the restaurant, the rooftop pool/
bar and a small movie theatre. It's all in a
Bauhaus building that's seen stints as a department store, Hitler Youth HQ and East
German party elite offices.

🛏 Kreuzberg & Neukölln

★GRAND HOSTEL BERLIN   HOSTEL €
Map p336 (☎030-2009 5450; www.grandhostel-
berlin.de; Tempelhofer Ufer 14; dm from €14,
d €58; @🛜; ⓈMöckernbrücke) Afternoon
tea in the library bar? Check. Rooms with
stucco-ornamented ceilings? Got 'em. Canal
views? Yup. OK, the Grand Hostel may be
no five-star hotel, but it is one of Berlin's
most supremely comfortable and atmospheric hostels. Ensconced in a fully renovated 1870s building are private rooms and
dorms with quality single beds (linen costs
€3.60) and large lockers. Optional buffet
breakfast is €6.20.

GAY SLEEPS

All Berlin hotels are, of course, open to gay visitors, but these places are especially geared to (male) scene crawlers.

Axel Hotel (☑030-2100 2893; www.axelhotels.com/berlin; Lietzenburger Strasse 13/15; d/ste from €110/170; P✳🛜; SWittenbergplatz) Close to Schöneberg's 'gay village', Axel cheekily bills itself as hetero-friendly, but is squarely aimed at the gay community. The soundproof rooms are stylish if on the small side, but come with king-sized beds, bathrobes and above-average amenities. Follow a workout in the rooftop gym with a massage or a soak in the outdoor jacuzzi. In summer, the Sky Bar is the perfect launch pad for a night out. Optional breakfast is €12.70. The hotel is about 200m south of U-Bahn station Wittenbergplatz via Bayreuther Strasse.

Gay Hostel (☑030-2100 5709; www.gay-hostel.de; Motzstrasse 28; dm €22-25, s/d €48/56; ➹🛜; SNollendorfplatz) It's a hostel, so you know the drill. Except that this one is in the heart of Queertown and open to gay men only. Rooms (all with shared bathrooms) are bright and contemporary and come with lockers; private rooms also have flat-screen TVs. The communal kitchen and lounge provide plenty of mingling opportunities. Check-in is at **Tom's Hotel** (☑030-2196 6604; www.toms-hotel.de; Motzstrasse 19; s/d from €79/99; SNollendorfplatz) from 10am to midnight.

Enjoy B&B (☑030-2362 3610; www.ebab.com; s/d from €20/40; SNollendorfplatz) This private-room referral service caters specifically for gays and lesbians. It's easiest to make your reservations online. See the website for details.

RIVERSIDE LODGE HOSTEL
HOSTEL €

Map p332 (☑0176 3112 9791; www.riverside-lodge.de; Hobrechtstrasse 43; dm/d incl breakfast €22/58; ⊙ check-in 11am-2pm & 7-9.30pm; @🛜; SSchönleinstrasse) This sweet little 12-bed hostel is as warm and welcoming as an old friend's hug thanks to its wonderful owners, Jutta and Liane. Both avid travellers, they have created a clean, cosy and communicative hang-out near the canal in booming Neukölln. In the six-bed dorm, beds can be curtained off for extra privacy. Linen is €3.

HOTEL SAROTTI-HÖFE
HOTEL €€

Map p336 (☑030-6003 1680; www.hotel-sarotti-hoefe.de; Mehringdamm 55; d €90-180; P@🛜; SMehringdamm) You'll have sweet dreams in this 19th-century ex-chocolate factory whose courtyard-cloistered rooms are quiet despite being smack-dab in the bustling Bergmannstrasse quarter. Rooms exude elegant yesteryear flair with earth-toned fabrics and dark-wood furniture. The nicest (deluxe category) even have a small private terrace. Check-in is at the on-site Cafe Sarotti-Höfe (great breakfast, €10).

HOTEL RIEHMERS HOFGARTEN
HOTEL €€

Map p336 (☑030-7809 8800; www.riehmers-hofgarten.de; Yorckstrasse 83; s/d from €98/131, apt €175; 🛜; SMehringdamm) Take a romantic 19th-century building, add contemporary art, stir in a few Zeitgeist touches such as iPod docks and you'll get one winning cocktail of a hotel. Riehmers' high-ceilinged rooms are modern but not stark; if you're noise-sensitive, get a (slightly pricier) courtyard-facing room. Assets include in-room tea and coffee facilities and a popular on-site gourmet restaurant. Optional breakfast €7.

HOTEL JOHANN
HOTEL €€

Map p336 (☑030-225 0740; www.hotel-johann-berlin.de; Johanniterstrasse 8; d incl breakfast €95-120; P@🛜; SPrinzenstrasse) This 33-room hotel consistently tops the popularity charts, thanks to its eager-to-please service and good-sized rooms where minimalist designer style contrasts with such historic flourishes as scalloped ceilings and exposed-brick walls. The small garden is perfect for summery breakfasts, while happening Bergmannstrasse and the Jüdisches Museum are within strolling distance.

🛏 Friedrichshain

PLUS BERLIN
HOSTEL, HOTEL €

Map p330 (☑030-2123 8501; www.plushostels.com/plusberlin; Warschauer Platz 6; dm/d from €14/26; @🛜🏊; SWarschauer Strasse, 🚆Warschauer Strasse) A hostel with an indoor pool, sauna and yoga classes? Yep. Within stumbling distance of Berlin's best nightlife, Plus

FURNISHED APARTMENTS

For self-caterers, independent types, families and anyone wanting extra privacy, a short-term furnished-apartment rental may well be the cat's pyjamas. Also check **airbnb** (www.airbnb.com), **Be My Guest** (www.be-my-guest.com), **HomeAway** (www.homeaway.com) or **OTA Berlin** (www.ota-berlin.de).

Miniloft Berlin (Map p328; ☑030-847 1090; www.miniloft.com; Hessische Strasse 5; apt €125-165; ⚃; Ⓢ Naturkundemuseum) Eight stunning lofts in an architect-converted building, some with south-facing panorama windows, others with cosy alcoves, all outfitted with modern designer furniture and kitchenettes. Near the Natural History Museum.

Brilliant Apartments (Map p342; ☑030-8061 4796; www.brilliant-apartments.de; Oderberger Strasse 38; apt from €93; ⚃; Ⓢ Eberswalder Strasse) These 11 stylish and modern units have full kitchens and neat historic touches such as exposed red-brick walls and parquet floors. Four have balconies, one a little garden. They're located on Oderberger Strasse, one of the hippest drags in Prenzlauer Berg, which puts you close to good eats, bars, boutiques and the Mauerpark. Apartments facing out back are quieter.

ÏMA Loft Apartments (Map p332; ☑030-6162 8913; www.imalofts.com; Ritterstrasse 12-14; apt €55-200; ⚃; Ⓢ Moritzplatz) These uncluttered, contemporary apartments are part of the ÏMA Design Village, an old factory shared by design studios and a dance and theatre academy. They sleep from one to four and are close to Kreuzberg's Moritzplatz, which is emerging as an edgy design hub.

T&C Apartments (Map p342; ☑030-405 046 612; www.tc-apartments-berlin.de; Kopenhagener Strasse 72; studio apt from €45; Ⓢ Schönhauser Allee) Huge selection of stylish, hand-picked, one- to four-room apartments in Mitte, Prenzlauer Berg, Tiergarten and Schöneberg; main office is in Prenzlauer Berg.

Berlin Lofts (☑0151 2121 9126; www.berlinlofts.com; Stephanstrasse 60 & Perleberger Strasse 16; studios from €44, apt from €127; @⚃; ⒮Westhafen, Birkenstrasse, ⒭Westhafen) Rents 14 lofts sleeping two to 14 in a handsomely converted old smithy and a bi-level horse barn. They're in two locations in Moabit, an up-and-coming neighbourhood northwest of the main train station. Public-transport connections are good. Trivia bonus: Kommune 1, Germany's first politically motivated student commune, formed in 1967, once hung out in one of the apartments.

is a flashpacker favourite. There's a bar for easing into the night and a tranquil courtyard to soothe that hangover. Spacious dorms have bunks, desks and lockers, while private rooms have TV and air-con. All have en suites. Optional breakfast is €6.

ODYSSEE GLOBETROTTER HOSTEL
HOSTEL €

Map p330 (☑030-2900 0081; www.globetrotterhostel.de; Grünberger Strasse 23; dm €15-21, d with shower €65; @⚃; Ⓢ Warschauer Strasse, ⒭M10 to Grünberger Strasse, ⒭Warschauer Strasse) Social types give high marks to this hostel that puts the 'fun' in funky and is a great launching pad for in-depth nightlife explorations. Clean rooms sport pine beds, lockers and artsy styling. Bathrooms are shared but there's plenty of them. Guest kitchen, backyard and on-site pub are all great socialising zones. Optional breakfast is €3.

APARTMENT HOSTEL SINGER 109
HOSTEL €

Map p330 (☑030-7477 5028; www.singer109.com; Singerstrasse 109; dm €21-25, s/d €58/78; Ⓢ Schillingstrasse, Strausberger Platz, ⒭Jannowitzbrücke) Close to sightseeing and nightlife, this attractive hostel in a historic brick building centres on a huge atrium with a lounge where cultural and language barriers melt quickly. A lift whisks you to shuteye zones in cheerfully painted and spacious dorm-style apartments, each with bathroom and lockers. Optional breakfast is €5.

★ MICHELBERGER HOTEL
HOTEL €€

Map p330 (☑030-2977 8590; www.michelbergerhotel.com; Warschauer Strasse 39; d €105-196; ⚃; Ⓢ Warschauer Strasse, ⒭Warschauer Strasse) The ultimate in creative crash pads, Michelsberger perfectly encapsulates Berlin's offbeat DIY spirit without being self-consciously cool. Rooms don't hide their factory pedigree, but are comfortable and come in sizes suitable for lovebirds, families or rock bands. Staff are friendly and clued-in, and there's a popular restaurant and live music in the lobby on some nights. Optional breakfast is €16.

NHOW HOTEL €€
Map p330 (☏030-290 2990; www.nhow-hotels.com/berlin; Stralauer Allee 3; d €115-295; P 🛜; Ⓢ Warschauer Strasse, 🚋 Warschauer Strasse) This riverside behemoth bills itself as a music and lifestyle hotel and underscores the point by having its own on-site recording studios. The look of the place is certainly dynamic, what with a sideways tower jutting out over the Spree and Karim Rashid's digi-pop design that would make Barbie proud. Worth a little extra: a room with a river view. Optional breakfast is €24.

ALMODÓVAR HOTEL HOTEL €€
Map p330 (☏030-692 097 080; www.almodovarhotel.de; Boxhagener Strasse 83; d €75-130; 🚲240, 🚋M13, 🚉Ostkreuz) Billing itself as Berlin's first 'biohotel', this is perfect for those wanting to keep their healthy ways while travelling. A yoga mat is a standard amenity in the 60 allergy-friendly rooms, while the locavore restaurant churns out vegan, raw food, lactose- and gluten-free dishes, and the spa offers ayurvedic treatments. Breakfast is €14.

HOTEL 26 HOTEL €€
Map p330 (☏030-297 7780; www.hotel26-berlin.de; Grünberger Strasse 26; d €70-130; P 🛜; Ⓢ Warschauer Strasse, 🚋M10 to Grünberger Strasse, 🚋 Warschauer Strasse) 🚲 Set back from the street and with a lovely garden out back, this architect-owned hotel in a revamped factory sparkles in happy-mood-inducing citrus colours. Clear lines and blond-wood furniture dominate both public areas and the rooms. Hotel 26 went green long before others jumped on the bandwagon: natural soaps, filtered water and a (mostly) organic cafe have been de rigeur since 2003.

UPSTALSBOOM HOTEL FRIEDRICHSHAIN HOTEL €€
Map p330 (☏030-293 750; www.upstalsboom.de; Gubener Strasse 42; d incl breakfast €100-130; P 🛜; Ⓢ Frankfurter Tor, Warschauer Strasse, 🚋 Warschauer Strasse) If this modern and well-kept hotel feels like a breath of fresh air, it may be because it's the Berlin branch of a small chain of German seaside resorts. Subtle maritime flair pervades the public areas, including the fish restaurant, while rooms have a clean, uncluttered look, pleasing colours and come in four sizes. Small spa and great views from the rooftop terrace. Enter via Kopernikusstrasse.

🛏 Prenzlauer Berg

★EASTSEVEN BERLIN HOSTEL HOSTEL €
Map p342 (☏030-9362 2240; www.eastseven.de; Schwedter Strasse 7; dm €18-22, d €52; @🛜; Ⓢ Senefelderplatz) Staff at this small and delightful hostel close to hip hang-outs and public transport go out of their way to make all feel welcome. It's easy to make new international friends at garden barbecues, spaghetti dinners or chilling in the lounge. Come bedtime, retreat to comfy pine beds in brightly painted dorms with lockers, or a private room. Breakfast is €3.

MEININGER HOTEL BERLIN PRENZLAUER BERG HOSTEL, HOTEL €
Map p342 (☏030-9832 1074; www.meininger-hotels.com; Schönhauser Allee 19; dm/d from €18/54; @🛜; Ⓢ Senefelderplatz) This popular hostel-hotel combo draws school groups, flashpackers and business types, which makes for an interesting guest mix. A lift whisks you to mod and spacious en-suite rooms and dorms with quality furnishings, flat-screen TVs and handy blackout blinds to combat jetlag (or hangovers). It's close to bars, markets and transport. Breakfast is €7.90. Check the website for other Meininger locations.

PFEFFERBETT HOSTEL €
Map p342 (☏030-9393 5858; www.pfefferbett.de; Christinenstrasse 18; dm €20-32, d €78; @🛜; Ⓢ Senefelderplatz) This convivial hostel has an edgy design nicely matching the industrial flair of its ex-brewery location. Dorms (some with bathroom) sleep four to eight and come with individual lockers. The women's dorm has thoughtful extras such as a hairdyer, cosmetic tissues and a make-up mirror. There are free concerts on Thursdays, a 24-hour bar and more liquid entertainment within stumbling distance. Optional breakfast is €6.50.

ACKSELHAUS & BLUE HOME BOUTIQUE HOTEL €€
Map p342 (☏030-4433 7633; www.ackselhaus.de; Belforter Strasse 21; ste/apt incl breakfast from €120/150; @🛜; Ⓢ Senefelderplatz, 🚋M10) At

this charismatic retreat in a 19th-century building you'll sleep in large, classily decorated themed rooms (eg Africa, Rome, Maritime), each with thoughtfully picked special features: a free-standing tub, perhaps, a four-poster bed or Chinese antiques. Many face the enchanting courtyard garden. Breakfast is served – beneath crystal chandeliers – until 11am (until 12.30pm at weekends).

LINNEN GUESTHOUSE €€
Map p342 (☎030-4737 2440; www.linnenberlin.com; Eberswalder Strasse 35; d €124-140; 📶; [S]Eberswalder Strasse) This little 'boutique inn' brims with charisma and character in each of its six rooms. No 4, for instance, gets forest-cabin flair from wooden walls decorated with bird feeders, while No 5 oozes vintage romance and comes with a soaking bath-tub. The on-site cafe serves an optional a la carte breakfast menu.

HOTEL KASTANIENHOF HOTEL €€
Map p342 (☎030-443 050; www.kastanienhof.biz; Kastanienallee 65; d €70-120; [P]@📶; [S]Rosenthaler Platz, 🚋M1 to Zionskirchstrasse, [S]Senefelderplatz) 🍃 Right on Kastanienallee with its plethora of cafes, restaurants and boutiques, this family-owned traditional charmer has staff that are polite and knowledgeable to a tee. The 35 good-sized rooms pair historical touches with flat-screen TVs, modern bathrooms and free wi-fi, making this an excellent value-for-money crash pad. Optional breakfast is €9.

MYER'S HOTEL BERLIN HOTEL €€
Map p342 (☎030-440 140; www.myershotel.de; Metzer Strasse 26; d incl breakfast €94-190; ❄📶; [S] Senefelder Platz) At this slightly aging 56-room boutique hotel, you'll sleep well in classically furnished rooms with stucco-ornamented ceilings, art and wooden floors. On a quiet side street, it has pleasant unwinding spots including a 24-hour lobby bar, a sauna and steam room, and a bucolic garden.

🛏 City West & Charlottenburg

25HOURS HOTEL BIKINI BERLIN HOTEL €€
Map p338 (☎030-120 2210; www.25hours-hotels.com; Budapester Strasse 40; r from €80; ❄@📶; [S] Zoologischer Garten, 🚆 Zoologischer Garten) The 'urban jungle' theme of this hip lifestyle outpost is a reflection of its location between the city's zoo and main shopping district. Rooms are stylish, if a tad compact, with the nicer ones facing the animal park. The hotel is part of the iconic Bikini Berlin redevelopment and popular with locals for its 10th-floor Monkey Bar and Neni restaurant. Optional breakfast is €18.

★HOTEL ASKANISCHER HOF HOTEL €€
Map p338 (☎030-881 8033; www.askanischer-hof.de; Kurfürstendamm 53; d incl breakfast €80-160; 📶; [S]Adenauerplatz) If you're after character and vintage flair, you'll find heaps of both at this 17-room jewel with a Roaring Twenties pedigree. An ornate oak door leads to a quiet oasis where no two rooms are alike, but all are filled with antiques, lace curtains, frilly chandeliers and time-worn oriental rugs. The quaint Old Berlin charms make a popular setting for fashion shoots.

HOTEL OTTO HOTEL €€
Map p338 (☎030-5471 0080; www.hotelotto.com; Knesebeckstrasse 10; d €125-150; [P]📶; [S]Ernst-Reuter-Platz) Otto would feel like 'just' a business hotel were it not for the helpful staff and cool perks like breakfast (€15) on the rooftop terrace, Aveda beauty products and complimentary coffee and cake in the afternoon. Rooms are fairly functional, but get character from bright colour accents and warm textures. 'Standard' rooms are pretty small.

H10 BERLIN KU'DAMM HOTEL €€
Map p338 (☎030-322 922 300; www.hotelh10berlinkudamm.com; Joachimstaler Strasse 31-32; r/loft from €100/170; [P]❄@📶; [S]Kurfürstendamm) Sheathed by an elegant brick facade, this effortlessly stylish city hotel incorporates some vintage features of a 150-year-old schoolhouse, but is largely characterised by a streamlined modern design, especially in the built-to-impress lobby. The light-drenched rooms pack plenty of style and amenities into a fairly compact frame. The lavish optional breakfast buffet is €16.

ELLINGTON HOTEL HOTEL €€
Map p338 (☎030-683 150; www.ellington-hotel.com; Nürnberger Strasse 50-55; d €115-270; [P]❄@; [S] Augsburger Strasse) Duke and Ella gave concerts in the jazz cellar and Bowie partied in the Dschungel nightclub, then the lights went out in the '90s. Now the handsome 1920s building has been resus-

citated as a high-concept jewel that wraps all that's great about Berlin – history, innovation, joie de vivre – into one attractive package. Rooms are stylishly minimalist. Optional breakfast is €20.

BLEIBTREU BERLIN BOUTIQUE HOTEL €€
Map p338 (☎030-884 740; www.bleibtreu.com; Bleibtreustrasse 31; d €100-150; @📶; 🚌 M29, M19, 109, [S]Uhlandstrasse) 🌿 On a leafy side street, the stylish Bleibtreu was a pioneer in sustainable lodging at its 1995 opening. The uncluttered rooms won't fit a ton of luggage, but feature untreated oak furniture, walls daubed in organic paint and a clever lighting system. New: Dudu 31, the second branch of the Asian crossover restaurant (and celebrity haunt) on Mitte's Torstrasse. Breakfast buffet is €19.

HOTEL-PENSION FUNK B&B €€
Map p338 (☎030-882 7193; www.hotel-pension-funk.de; Fasanenstrasse 69; d incl breakfast €82-129; 🚭📶; [S]Uhlandstrasse, Kurfürstendamm) This charismatic *Pension* in the home of silent-movie siren Asta Nielsen is a time-warp back to the Golden Twenties. Stuffed with art nouveau furniture and decor, it's perfect if you value old-fashioned charm over mod-cons. The 14 rooms vary quite significantly, so if size matters bring up the subject when booking. Cheaper ones have partial or shared facilities.

HOTEL ART NOUVEAU B&B €€
Map p338 (☎030-327 7440; www.hotelartnouveau.de; Leibnizstrasse 59; d €96-176; [P]@📶; [S]Adenauerplatz) A quaint birdcage lift drops you off with belle époque flourish at this arty B&B where rooms skimp neither on space nor charisma and offer a blend of youthful flair and tradition. The well-travelled owners are fluent English-speakers with a knack for creating a home-away-from-home ambience. Bonus points for the superb beds, the organic breakfast (€9) and the honour bar.

HOTEL SIR FK SAVIGNY HOTEL €€
Map p338 (☎030-323 015 600; www.hotel-sirsavigny.de; Kantstrasse 144; r from €110; 📶; 🚆Savignyplatz) Not only books but also hotels tell a story, and this is the one of Sir FK Savigny, a fictional character who welcomes guests to his cosmopolitan crash pad. The gracious public areas give way to smartly furnished rooms equipped with such lifestyle essentials as iPod docks and Nespresso machines, plus a minibar with free soft drinks. Breakfast is €18.

HOTEL Q! BOUTIQUE HOTEL €€
Map p338 (☎030-810 0660; www.hotel-q.com; Knesebeckstrasse 67; d €135-215; [P]❄📶; [S]Uhlandstrasse) Corners are eschewed at this snazzy boutique hotel with its retro-futuristic sculptural design, from the red-hot lobby to the sexy rooms, some with tubs right next to the bed. Note that the cheapest ones are tiny. Distinctive feature: the spa with indoor beach and on-site yoga and pilates classes. The optional breakfast is €20.

SANA BERLIN HOTEL HOTEL €€
(☎030-2005 1510; www.berlin.sanahotels.com; Nürnberger Strasse 33/34; r from €105; ❄@📶🏊; [S]Augsburger Strasse) The Berlin outpost of this happening Portuguese chain is a great fit for travellers with a penchant for streamlined design that carries through from the striking black-metallic lobby to the spacious rooms. Service is unpretentious and caring and the restaurant is a great place for indulging in Atlantic cuisine. The pool and gym are rather small, though. Breakfast is €18.

MITTENDRIN B&B €€
Map p338 (☎030-2362 8861; www.boutique-hotel-berlin.de; Nürnberger Strasse 16; d incl breakfast €100-200; 📶; [S] Augsburger Strasse, Wittenbergplatz) This sweet retreat close to primo shopping is a fantastic find for those who value individual service over fancy lobbies or rooftop bars. All four rooms bulge with character, hand-picked furnishings, tech touches like iPod docks and homey extras like fresh flowers. Breakfasts are gourmet affairs and, if desired, served in bed at no extra charge.

HOTEL-PENSION DITTBERNER B&B €€
Map p338 (☎030-881 6485; www.hotel-dittberner.de; Wielandstrasse 26; d €115-127; [P]@📶; [S]Adenauerplatz) This increasingly rare old-school B&B is a good choice if you like a personal ambience rather than high-tech touches and bundles of privacy. Travel back in time aboard an antique lift that deposits you at this charming property with a hospitality pedigree going back to the 1930s. It's a quiet place with retro furniture, plush rugs and armloads of artwork.

KU' DAMM 101 HOTEL €€

(☎030-520 0550; www.kudamm101.com; Kurfürstendamm 101; d from €90; [P] ❄ @ 📶; 🚌M19, 🚆 Halensee) This budget designer hotel sits on the far western end of Kurfurstendamm shopping strip, fairly close to the trade-fair grounds. Functional and mod rooms exude midcentury modern retro flair imbued with lots of geometric shapes (and a muted colour scheme). Breakfast (€15) is served in an airy 7th-floor lounge with a feast of views. The M19 bus down Kurfürstendamm stops 50m from the hotel and the Circle Line is a short walk away.

★HOTEL AM STEINPLATZ BOUTIQUE HOTEL €€€

Map p338 (☎030-554 4440; www.marriott.com; Steinplatz 4; r from €200; [P] ❄ @ 📶; [S]Ernst-Reuter-Platz) Vladimir Nabokov, Brigitte Bardot and Romy Schneider were among the guests of the original Hotel am Steinplatz, which got a second lease on life in 2013, a century after it first opened. Rooms in this art deco jewel reinterpret the 1920s in contemporary style with fantastic lamps and lighting, iPod docks and black-and-white bathrooms. Optional breakfast is €35.

LOUISA'S PLACE BOUTIQUE HOTEL €€€

Map p338 (☎030-631 030; www.louisas-place.de; Kurfürstendamm 160; ste from €155; [P] @ 📶 🏊; [S]Adenauerplatz) Louisa's is the kind of place that dazzles with class not glitz; it's an all-suite hideaway that puts great emphasis on customised guest services. Suites here are luxe and huge and have kitchens, the pool is small but refreshing, and the library palatial. A high-end restaurant shares the premises. Optional breakfast is €22.

WALDORF ASTORIA HOTEL €€€

Map p338 (☎030-8140 0000; www.waldorfastoria3.hilton.com; Hardenbergstrasse 28; r from €220; [P] ❄ @ 📶 🏊; [S]Zoologischer Garten, 🚆Zoologischer Garten) One of the newer hospitality temples in the City West, this skyline-altering tower hotel is the brand's first in Germany and predictably well suited for feeding luxury cravings. Pampering stations include the exquisite Guerlain spa with pool, the double-Michelin-starred restaurant and the sleek Lang Bar. Rooms on the higher floors boast sweeping views. Optional breakfast is €36.

SOFITEL BERLIN KURFÜRSTENDAMM HOTEL €€€

Map p338 (☎030-800 9990; www.sofitel.com; Augsburger Strasse 41; d €140-350; [P] ❄ @ 📶; [S]Kurfürstendamm) Renowned Berlin architect Jan Kleihues pulled out all the stops to create this award-winning alchemy of art, architecture and design. Supremely comfortable XL-sized rooms, a sophisticated but unfussy ambience, armloads of tasteful contemporary art and off-the-charts-friendly staff make this French-flavoured refuge a perfect launch pad for urban explorers. Optional breakfast is €28.

SAVOY HOTEL HOTEL €€€

Map p338 (☎030-311 030; www.hotel-savoy.com; Fasanenstrasse 9-10; d €150-280; @ 📶; [S]Zoologischer Garten, 🚆Zoologischer Garten) History streams through this intimate grand hotel as strongly as the Thames does through London. In business since 1929, there's something charmingly old school about this property, which has comfortably housed writer Thomas Mann and Talking Heads' David Byrne. The handsome rooms are classically furnished; some in the superior category have canopy beds and air-con. Optional breakfast is €19.

SWISSOTEL BERLIN HOTEL €€€

Map p338 (☎030-220 100; Augsburger Strasse 44; d from €160; [P] ❄ @ 📶; [S]Kurfürstendamm) In a grand curvaceous building by architects Gerkan, Marg & Partners, Swissotel scores high with both style-loving business and leisure travellers. You'll sleep well in modern rooms dressed in soothing earth tones and equipped with the gamut of mod-cons. Feast on Alpine classics at Restaurant 44, then assuage any pangs of guilt in the well-equipped 24-hour spa. Breakfast is €23.

Understand Berlin

Berlin Today

Berlin is a city that is truly 24/7, where creativity, sensory overload and hedonism roar with unapologetic abandon. Where New York might be the 'Big Apple', the German capital is the 'Big Appetite', and the hunger for experimentation and challenge is rarely sated. It's a city where you can fairly hear and feel the collision between past and future, what is possible and what is realistic, and the cultural hopes and the culture clashes between people who've joined together from around the globe in one big experiment.

Best on Film

Symphony of a City (1927) Fascinating silent documentary captures a day in the life of Berlin in the 1920s.

Downfall (2004) Chilling account of Hitler's last 12 days holed up in his Berlin bunker.

Good Bye, Lenin! (2003) Cult comedy tells the story of a young East Berliner who replicates East Germany (the GDR) for his ailing mother after the fall of the Wall.

The Lives of Others (2006) This Academy Award winner reveals the stranglehold the East German secret police had on innocent people.

Best in Print

Goodbye to Berlin (Christopher Isherwood; 1939) Brilliant semi-autobiographical account of early 1930s Berlin through the eyes of a gay Anglo-American journalist.

Berlin Alexanderplatz (Alfred Döblin; 1929) This stylised meander through the seamy 1920s is still an essential Berlin text.

Russian Disco (Wladimir Kaminer; 2000) Entertaining vignettes portraying postreunification Berlin.

Stasiland (Anna Funder; 2004) The Stasi's vast spying apparatus from the perspectives of both victims and perpetrators.

Economy on the Rise

It's a been a long road to recovery but Berlin is finally seeing slivers of sunlight on the horizon. Since 2005 its economy has consistently outpaced that of Germany as a whole, and the city is also leading the nation in new job creation. Although still 4.5% above the national average, unemployment dropped by two points to 11% in 2014.

It's Berlin's transformation from an industrial to a knowledge-based society that's at the root of this development. The growth of the digital economy especially has stimulated the job market. The city today attracts some of the world's brightest minds and invests heavily in such high-tech fields as biotechnology, communication and environmental technologies and transportation. In fact, the city now ranks among the top three innovative regions in the European Union.

Since 2006 Berlin has also positioned itself as Germany's start-up capital. Staffed by smart young professionals, these enterprises in turn feed talent into the research-and-development outfits of bigger companies. The 2014 opening in Prenzlauer Berg of The Factory, a Google-sponsored campus that brings together early-stage start-ups and established tech ventures such as Soundcloud and Mozilla, is a key indicator that Berlin-grown vision is ready for the big time.

Tourism continues to be another major driving force economically, with the number of annual overnight visitors breaking new records every year; in 2013 it soared to 11.3 million, five times as many as in 1993. And that's not even counting the roughly 100 million day trippers per year. The creative and cultural fields are booming as well, and their financial impact, though less tangible, cannot not be discounted either.

Still, the news is not all good. Berlin, which is one of 17 German federal states, has the highest number of welfare recipients among them. And although the city has reined in spending, keeping its books balanced remains tough with a debt legacy hovering around €60 billion.

Multiculturalism & Immigration

Berlin's multiculturalism is one of its greatest assets, even if successful social and economic integration remain major challenges. About 470,000 people of non-German nationality from around 190 countries live here today, accounting for about 13% of the total population. Turks constitute the largest community, a legacy of the worker migration of the 1960s and '70s to West Berlin. In East Berlin, contract labour came in smaller numbers from Vietnam, Cuba and Poland. Since the fall of the Berlin Wall, the united city has also absorbed about 100,000 people from the former Soviet republics. In recent years the global fiscal crisis and high youth unemployment have resulted in a wave of new arrivals from southern Europe, especially Spain and Italy. Over the same period the number of refugees and asylum seekers swelled by about 3000 to 9500.

Gentrification & the Housing Market

Try to put your finger on the pulse of Berlin and you'll find that, much like the mysterious movements on a Ouija board, the pulse is already moving on to another location. Today's downtrodden neighbourhood becomes tomorrow's dream of students and artists, young entrepreneurs and, eventually, developers. The city's famously low rents have become a thing of the past, office buildings have displaced beloved riverside party venues, and 'loft-living' is the new buzzword.

In other words, Berlin is fully in the grip of gentrification. And although this has resulted in cleaner streets, nicer flats and chic bars and restaurants, many locals don't like it one bit.

The main complaint is the lack of affordable housing, especially in the central districts where new residential construction is primarily aimed at cash-rich tenants. Of the 250 projects in development in 2014, one-fifth are in upmarket Mitte. A referendum in 2014 forced the city to roll back plans for thousands of fancy apartments around Tempelhofer Park, a beloved urban oasis on the site of a former airport.

The housing shortage and rising rents have been fuelled by migration to Berlin from other parts of Germany and abroad. Between June 2012 and June 2013 the population grew by 50,000 people.

The city government estimates that 137,000 new housing units will be needed by 2025 at an average of 10,000 per year. In the meantime, it wants to ban the unregulated short-term letting of an estimated 10,000 to 20,000 holiday flats. Controlling growth and keeping rents in check will be among the major challenges the government will have to face in years to come.

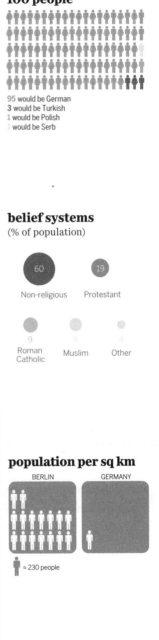

if Berlin were 100 people

95 would be German
3 would be Turkish
1 would be Polish
1 would be Serb

belief systems
(% of population)

60 Non-religious
19 Protestant
9 Roman Catholic
8 Muslim
4 Other

population per sq km

BERLIN   GERMANY

👤 ≈ 230 people

History

Berlin has long been in the cross-hairs of history: it staged a revolution, was head-quartered by fascists, bombed to bits, ripped in half and finally reunited – and that was just in the 20th century! Yet, Berlin is very much an accidental capital whose medieval birth was a mere blip on the map of history. It continued to exist in relative obscurity until becoming the royal capital of Prussia some 400 years later, but it wasn't until the 20th century that it significantly impacted on European – and indeed world – history.

Medieval Berlin

Berlin's medieval birthplace, around the Nikolaikirche, was devastated during WWII bombing raids. Today's 'Nikolaiviertel' is actually a replica of the quarter, dreamed up by the East German government in celebration of the city's 750th anniversary in 1987.

The recent discovery of an oak beam suggests that Berlin may have roots going back to 1183 but, for now, history records that the city was officially founded in 1237 by itinerant merchants as twin trading posts called Berlin and Cölln. The modest settlements flanked the Spree River in an area just southwest of today's Alexanderplatz. It was a profitable spot along a natural east–west trade route, about halfway between the fortified towns of Köpenick to the southeast and Spandau to the northwest whose origins can be traced to the 8th century. The tiny settlements grew in leaps and bounds and, in 1307, merged into a single town for power and protection. As the centre of the March (duchy) of Brandenburg, it continued to assert its political and economic independence and even became a player in the Hanseatic League in 1360.

Such confidence did not sit well with Sigismund, king of the Germans, who, in 1411, put one of his cronies, Friedrich von Hohenzollern, in charge of Brandenburg, thereby ushering in five centuries of uninterrupted rule by the House of Hohenzollern.

Reformation & the Thirty Years' War

The Reformation, kick-started in 1517 by Martin Luther in nearby Wittenberg, was slow to arrive in Berlin. Eventually, though, the wave of reform reached Brandenburg, leaving Elector Joachim II (r 1535–71) no

TIMELINE	1244	1307	1360
	Berlin is referenced in a document for the first time in recorded history, but the city's birthday is pegged to the first mention of its sister settlement Cölln seven years earlier in 1237.	Berlin and Cölln join forces by merging into a single town to assert their independence from local rulers.	The twin town of Berlin-Cölln joins the Hanseatic League but never plays a major role in the alliance and quits its membership in 1518.

choice but to subscribe to Protestantism. On 1 November 1539 the court celebrated the first Lutheran-style service in the Nikolaikirche in Spandau. The event is still celebrated as an official holiday (Reformationstag) in Brandenburg, the German federal state that surrounds Berlin, although not in the city state of Berlin itself.

Berlin prospered for the ensuing decades until drawn into the Thirty Years' War (1618–48), a conflict between Catholics and Protestants that left Europe's soil drenched with the blood of millions. Elector Georg Wilhelm (r 1620–40) tried to maintain a policy of neutrality, only to see his territory repeatedly pillaged and plundered by both sides. By the time the war ended, Berlin lay largely in shambles – broke, ruined and decimated by starvation, murder and disease.

Road to a Kingdom

Stability finally returned during the long reign of Georg Wilhelm's son, Friedrich Wilhelm (r 1640–88). Also known as the Great Elector, he took several steps that helped chart Brandenburg's rise to the status of a European powerhouse. His first order of business was to increase Berlin's safety by turning it into a garrison town encircled by fortifications with 13 bastions. He also levied a new sales tax, using the money to build three new neighbourhoods (Friedrichswerder, Dorotheenstadt and Friedrichstadt), a canal linking the Spree and the Oder Rivers (thereby cementing Berlin's position as a trading hub), as well as the Lustgarten and Unter den Linden.

But the Great Elector's most lasting legacy was replenishing Berlin's population by encouraging the settlement of refugees. In 1671, 50 Jewish families arrived from Vienna, followed by thousands of Protestant Huguenots – many of them highly skilled – who had been expelled from France by Louis XIV in 1685. The Französischer Dom (French Cathedral) on Gendarmenmarkt serves as a tangible reminder of Huguenot influence. Between 1680 and 1710, Berlin saw its population nearly triple to 56,000, making it one of the largest cities in the Holy Roman Empire.

The Great Elector's son, Friedrich III, was a man of great ambition, with a penchant for the arts and sciences. Together with his beloved wife, Sophie-Charlotte, he presided over a lively and intellectual court, founding the Academy of Arts in 1696 and the Academy of Sciences in 1700. One year later, he advanced his career by promoting himself to King Friedrich I (elector 1688–1701, king 1701–13) of Prussia, making Berlin a royal residence and the capital of the new state of Brandenburg-Prussia.

An 8m-long section is all that survives of Berlin's original city wall, built around 1250 from crude boulders and bricks and standing up to 2m tall. See it on Littenstrasse, near Alexanderplatz.

1411	1415	1443	1539
German King Sigismund puts Friedrich von Hohenzollern in charge as administrator of Brandenburg, marking the beginning of 500 years of Hohenzollern rule.	Friedrich von Hohenzollern's grip on power solidifies when Sigismund promotes him to elector and margrave of Brandenburg at the Council of Constance.	Construction of the Berliner Stadtschloss (City Palace) on the Spree island begins and becomes the electors' permanent residence in 1486.	Elector Joachim II celebrates the first Lutheran service and a year later passes a church ordinance making the new religion binding throughout Brandenburg.

The Age of Prussia

All cultural and intellectual life screeched to a halt under Friedrich's son, Friedrich Wilhelm I (r 1713–40), who laid the groundwork for Prussian military might. Soldiers were this king's main obsession and he dedicated much of his life to building an army of 80,000, partly by instituting the draft (highly unpopular even then, and eventually repealed) and by persuading his fellow rulers to trade him men for treasure. History quite appropriately knows him as the *Soldatenkönig* (soldier king).

Ironically these soldiers didn't see action until his son and successor Friedrich II (aka Frederick the Great; r 1740–86) came to power. Friedrich fought tooth and nail for two decades to wrest Silesia (in today's Poland) from Austria and Saxony. When not busy on the battlefield, 'Old Fritz', as he was also called, sought greatness through building. His Forum Fridericianum, a grand architectural master plan for Unter den Linden, although never completed, gave Berlin the Staatsoper Unter den Linden (State Opera House), Sankt-Hedwigs-Kathedrale, a former palace now housing the Humboldt Universität (Humboldt University) and other major attractions.

Frederick also embraced the ideas of the Enlightenment, abolishing torture, guaranteeing religious freedom and introducing legal reforms. With some of the leading thinkers in town (Moses Mendelssohn, Voltaire and Gotthold Ephraim Lessing among them), Berlin blossomed into a great cultural capital that came to be known as 'Athens on the Spree'.

Top Five Prussian Sites

Brandenburg Gate

Schloss and Park Sanssouci

Schloss Charlottenburg

Siegessäule

Reichstag

Napoleon & Reforms

Old Fritz's death sent Prussia into a downward spiral, culminating in a serious trouncing of its army by Napoleon at Jena-Auerstedt in 1806. The French marched triumphantly into Berlin on 27 October and left two years later, their coffers bursting with loot. Among the pint-sized conqueror's favourite souvenirs was the *Quadriga* sculpture from atop the Brandenburg Gate.

The post-Napoleonic period saw Berlin caught up in the reform movement sweeping through Europe. Public servants, academics and merchants now questioned the right of the nobility to rule. Friedrich Wilhelm III (r 1797–1840) instituted a few token reforms (easing guild regulations, abolishing bonded labour and granting Jews civic equality), but meaningful constitutional reform was not forthcoming. Power continued to be centred in the Prussian state.

The ensuing period of political stability was paired with an intellectual flourishing in Berlin's cafes and salons. The newly founded Universität zu Berlin (Humboldt Universität) was helmed by the philosopher Johann Gottlieb Fichte and, as it grew in status, attracted

One of the definitive histories on Prussia, Christopher Clark's *Iron Kingdom: The Rise and Downfall of Prussia* covers the period from 1600 to 1947 and shows the central role this powerhouse played in shaping modern Europe.

1618	1631	1640	1665
Religious conflict and territorial power struggles escalate into the bloody Thirty Years' War, devastating Berlin financially and halving its population, to a mere 6000 people.	An outbreak of the plague kills around 2000 Berliners, about a fifth of the population.	Friedrich Wilhelm, who will go down in history as the Great Elector, comes to power and restores a semblance of normality by building fortifications and infrastructure.	After major fires, a new law requires barns to move outside the city boundaries, thereby creating today's Scheunenviertel (Barn Quarter).

other leading thinkers of the day, including Hegel and Ranke. This was also the age of Karl Friedrich Schinkel, whose many projects – from the Neue Wache (New Guardhouse) to the Altes Museum (Old Museum) – still beautify Berlin.

Revolution(s)

The Industrial Revolution snuck up on Berliners in the second quarter of the 19th century, with companies like Siemens and Borsig vastly spurring the city's growth. In 1838 trains began chuffing between Berlin and Potsdam, giving birth to the Prussian railway system and spurring the founding of more than 1000 factories, including electrical giants AEG and Siemens. In 1841 August Borsig built the world's fastest locomotive, besting even the British in a race.

Tens of thousands of people now streamed into Berlin to work in the factories, swelling the population to more than 400,000 by 1847 and bringing the city's infrastructure close to collapse. A year later, due to social volatility and restricted freedoms, Berlin joined other German cities in a bourgeois democratic revolution. On 18 March two shots rang out during a demonstration, which then escalated into a full-fledged revolution. Barricades went up and a bloody fight ensued, leaving 183 revolutionaries and 18 soldiers dead by the time King Friedrich Wilhelm IV (r 1840–61) ordered his troops back. The dead revolutionaries are commemorated on Platz des 18 März immediately west of the Brandenburg Gate. In a complete turnabout, the king put himself at the head of the movement and ostensibly professed support for liberalism and nationalism. On 21 March, while riding to the funeral of the revolutionaries in the Volkspark Friedrichshain, he donned the red, black and gold tricolour of German unity. An elected Prussian national assembly met on 5 May.

However, disagreements between delegates from the different factions kept parliament weak and ineffective, making restoration of the monarchy child's play for General von Wrangel, who led 13,000 Prussian soldiers who had remained faithful to the king into the city in November 1848. Ever the opportunist, the king quickly switched sides again, dissolved the parliament and proposed his own constitution while insisting on maintaining supreme power. The revolution was dead. Many of its participants fled into exile.

The green octagonal public pissoirs scattered around Berlin are a legacy of the late 19th century when the municipal sanitation system could not keep up with the exploding population. About two dozen survive, including one on Chamissoplatz in Kreuzberg and another on Senefelderplatz in Prenzlauer Berg.

Bismarck & the Birth of an Empire

When Friedrich Wilhelm IV suffered a stroke in 1857, his brother Wilhelm became first regent and then, in 1861, King Wilhelm I (r 1861–88). Unlike his brother, Wilhelm had his finger on the pulse of the times and

1671	1685	1694	1701
Berlin's first Jewish community forms with just a few families arriving from Vienna at the invitation of the Great Elector. It grows to more than 1000 people by 1700.	Friedrich Wilhelm issues the Edict of Potsdam, allowing French Huguenot religious refugees to settle in Berlin, giving a 10-year tax break and granting them the right to hold services.	Elector Friedrich III founds the Akademie der Künste, Berlin oldest and most prestigious arts institution.	Brandenburg becomes a kingdom, with Berlin as its capital, when Elector Friedrich III has himself crowned King Friedrich I.

STATISTICS

was less averse to progress. One of his key moves was to appoint Otto von Bismarck as Prussian prime minister in 1862.

Bismarck's glorious ambition was the creation of a unified Germany with Prussia at the helm. An old-guard militarist, he used intricate diplomacy and a series of wars with neighbouring Denmark and Austria to achieve his aims. By 1871 Berlin stood as the proud capital of the German Reich (empire), a bicameral, constitutional monarchy. On 18 January the Prussian king was crowned Kaiser (emperor) at Versailles, with Bismarck as his 'Iron Chancellor'.

The early years of the German empire – a period called *Gründerzeit* (foundation years) – were marked by major economic growth, fuelled in part by a steady flow of French reparation payments. Hundreds of thousands of people poured into Berlin in search of work in the factories. Housing shortages were solved by building labyrinthine tenements (*Mietskasernen,* literally 'rental barracks'), where entire families subsisted in tiny and poorly ventilated flats without indoor plumbing.

New political parties gave a voice to the proletariat, foremost the Socialist Workers' Party (SAP), the forerunner of the Sozialdemokratische Partei Deutschlands (SPD; Social Democratic Party of Germany). Founded in 1875, the SAP captured 40% of the Berlin vote only two years later. Bismarck tried to make the party illegal but eventually, under pressure from the growing and increasingly antagonistic socialist movement, he enacted Germany's first modern social reforms, though this was not his true nature. When Wilhelm II (r 1888–1918) came to power, he wanted to extend social reform while Bismarck wanted stricter antisocialist laws. Finally, in March 1890, the Kaiser's scalpel excised his renegade chancellor from the political scene. After that, the legacy of Bismarck's diplomacy unravelled and a wealthy, unified and industrially powerful Germany paddled into the new century.

WWI & Revolution (Again)

The assassination of Archduke Franz Ferdinand, the heir to the Austrian throne, on 28 June 1914 triggered a series of diplomatic decisions that led to WWI, the bloodiest European conflict since the Thirty Years' War. In Berlin and elsewhere, initial euphoria and faith in a quick victory soon gave way to despair as casualties piled up in the battlefield trenches and stomachs grumbled on the home front. When peace came with defeat in 1918, it also ended domestic stability, ushering in a period of turmoil and violence.

On 9 November 1918, Kaiser Wilhelm II abdicated, bringing an inglorious end to the monarchy and 500 years of Hohenzollern rule. Power was transferred to the SPD, the largest party in the Reichstag, and its

Discover stat after stat on Berlin at the website of the Office of Statistics in Berlin (www. statistik-berlin-brandenburg.de).

1730	1740	1806	1810
The future king Frederick the Great is caught trying to desert to England along with a friend. Frederick's father orders the friend's execution and makes his son watch.	Frederick the Great, the philosopher king, turns Berlin into 'Athens on the Spree', a centre of the Enlightenment and an architectural showcase; French is the language of the elite.	After defeating Prussia, Napoleon leads his troops on a triumphant march through the Brandenburg Gate, marking the start of a two-year occupation of Berlin.	After the Napoleonic occupation ends, Berlin embarks on a period of reconstruction and reform that includes the creation of its first university by Wilhelm von Humboldt.

leader, Friedrich Ebert. Shortly after the Kaiser's exit, prominent SPD member Philipp Scheidemann stepped to a window of the Reichstag to announce the birth of the German Republic. Two hours later, Karl Liebknecht of the Spartakusbund (Spartacist League) proclaimed a socialist republic from a balcony of the royal palace on Unter den Linden. The struggle for power was on.

Founded by Liebknecht and Rosa Luxemburg, the Spartacist League sought to establish a left-wing, Marxist-style government; by year's end it had merged with other radical groups into the German Communist Party. The SPD's goal, meanwhile, was to establish a parliamentary democracy.

Supporters of the SPD and Spartacist League took their rivalry to the streets, culminating in the Spartacist Revolt in early January 1919. On the orders of Ebert, government forces quickly quashed the uprising. Liebknecht and Luxemburg were arrested and murdered en route to prison by Freikorps soldiers (right-leaning war volunteers); their bodies were dumped in the Landwehrkanal.

The Weimar Republic

In July 1919 the federalist constitution of the fledgling republic – Germany's first serious experiment with democracy – was adopted in the town of Weimar, where the constituent assembly had sought refuge from the chaos of Berlin. It gave women the vote and established basic human rights, but it also gave the chancellor the right to rule by decree – a concession that would later prove critical in Hitler's rise to power.

The so-called Weimar Republic (1920–33) was governed by a coalition of left and centre parties, headed by Friedrich Ebert and later Paul von Hindenburg – both of the SPD, which remained Germany's largest party until 1932. The republic, however, pleased neither communists nor monarchists. Trouble erupted as early as March 1920 when right-wing militants led by Wolfgang Kapp forcibly occupied the government quarter in Berlin. The government fled to Dresden, but in Berlin a general strike soon brought the 'Kapp Putsch' to a collapse.

The Golden Twenties

The giant metropolis of Berlin as we know it today was forged in 1920 from the region's many independent towns and villages (Charlottenburg, Schöneberg, Spandau etc), making Berlin one of the world's largest cities, with around 3.8 million inhabitants.

Otherwise, the 1920s began as anything but golden, marked by the humiliation of a lost war, social and political instability, hyperinflation, hunger and disease. Around 235,000 Berliners were unemployed,

HISTORY THE WEIMAR REPUBLIC

Historical Reads

....

Berlin Rising: Biography of a City (Anthony Read, David Fisher)

....

Berlin (David Clay Large)

....

Berlin Diary: Journal of a Foreign Correspondent 1934–41 (William Shirer)

....

The Candy Bombers (Andrei Cherny)

....

The Berlin Wall (Frederick Taylor)

1830	1837	1838	1848
The Altes Museum opens as the first of five institutions on Museumsinsel (Museum Island). The last (the Pergamonmuseum) opens exactly 100 years later.	The Industrial Age kicks into high gear with the founding of August Borsig's machine factory, which in 1840 builds Germany's first locomotive.	Berlin's first train embarks on its maiden voyage from Berlin to Potsdam, making the city the centre of an expanding rail network throughout Prussia.	Berlin is swept up in the popular revolutions for democratic reform and a united Germany but after a few months the Prussian army restores the old order.

and strikes, demonstrations and riots became nearly everyday occurrences. Economic stability gradually returned after a new currency, the *Rentenmark,* was introduced in 1923 and with the Dawes Plan in 1924, which limited the crippling reparation payments imposed on Germany after WWI.

Berliners responded like there was no tomorrow and made their city as much a den of decadence as it was a cauldron of creativity (not unlike today...). Cabaret, Dada and jazz flourished. Pleasure pits popped up everywhere, turning the city into a 'sextropolis' of Dionysian dimensions. Bursting with energy, it became a laboratory for anything new and modern, drawing giants of architecture (Bruno Taut, Martin Wagner, Hans Scharoun and Walter Gropius), fine arts (George Grosz, Max Beckmann and Lovis Corinth) and literature (Bertolt Brecht, Kurt Tucholsky, WH Auden and Christopher Isherwood).

The fun came to an instant end when the US stock market crashed in 1929, plunging the world into economic depression. Within weeks, half a million Berliners were jobless, and riots and demonstrations again ruled the streets. The volatile, increasingly polarised political climate led to clashes between communists and members of a party that had been patiently waiting in the wings – the Nationalsozialistische Deutsche Arbeiterpartei (National Socialist German Workers' Party, NSDAP, or Nazi Party), led by a failed Austrian artist and WWI corporal named Adolf Hitler. Soon jack boots, brown shirts, oppression and fear would dominate daily life in Germany.

Hitler's Rise to Power

The Siegessäule (Victory Column) in Tiergarten park has had starring roles in Wim Wenders' movie *Wings of Desire* and U2's 'Stay' music video. It also inspired Paul van Dyk's 1998 trance hit 'For an Angel' and the name of Berlin's leading gay magazine.

The Weimar government's inability to improve conditions during the Depression spurred the popularity of Hitler's NSDAP, which gained 18% of the national vote in the 1930 elections. In the 1932 presidential election, Hitler challenged Hindenburg and won 37% of the second-round vote. A year later, on 30 January 1933, faced with failed economic reforms and persuasive right-wing advisors, Hindenburg appointed Hitler chancellor. That evening, NSDAP celebrated its rise to power with a torchlit procession through the Brandenburg Gate. Not everyone cheered. Observing the scene from his Pariser Platz home, artist Max Liebermann famously commented: 'I couldn't possibly eat as much as I would like to puke'.

As chancellor, Hitler moved quickly to consolidate absolute power and to turn the nation's democracy into a one-party dictatorship. The Reichstag fire in March 1933 gave him the opportunity to request temporary emergency powers to arrest communists and liberal opponents and push through his proposed Enabling Law, allowing him to decree

1862	1871	1877	1891
Chief city planner James Hobrecht solves the housing shortage by constructing claustrophobic working-class ghettos of tenement blocks.	Employing an effective strategy of war and diplomacy, Prussian chancellor Otto von Bismarck forges a unified Germany with Prussia at its helm and Berlin as its capital.	Berlin's population reaches the one million mark, and this almost doubles by 1900.	Berlin engineer Otto Lilienthal, known as the 'Glider King', makes the world's first successful glider flight, over 25m. Five years later he dies in an air accident.

THE NIGHT OF THE LONG KNIVES

The brown-shirted Sturmabteilung (SA or Storm Troopers) was a Nazi organisation charged mainly with policing Nazi-party meetings and disrupting those convened by political opponents. Although it played an important role in Hitler's ascent to power, by 1934 it had become quite powerful in its own right thanks, in large part, to its leader Ernst Röhm. On 30 June of that year, feeling threatened, Hitler ordered the black-shirted Schutzstaffel (SS) to round up and kill the SA leadership (including Röhm and at least 75 others) to bring the organisation to heel.

Hitler hushed up what came to be known as the 'Night of the Long Knives' until 13 July, when he announced to the Reichstag that, from now on, the SA (which numbered two million, thus easily outnumbering the army) would serve under the command of the army which, in turn, would swear an oath of allegiance to Hitler. Justice would be executed by the SS under the leadership of former chicken farmer Heinrich Himmler, effectively giving the SS unchallenged power and making it Nazi Germany's most powerful – and feared – force.

laws and change the constitution without consulting parliament. When Hindenburg died a year later, Hitler fused the offices of president and chancellor to become Führer of the Third Reich.

Nazi Berlin

The rise of the Nazis had instant, far-reaching consequences for the entire population. Within three months of Hitler's power grab, all non-Nazi parties, organisations and labour unions ceased to exist. Political opponents, intellectuals and artists were rounded up and detained without trial; many went underground or into exile. There was a burgeoning culture of terror and denunciation, and the terrorisation of Jews started to escalate.

Hitler's brown-shirted Nazi state police, the Sturmabteilung, pursued opponents, arresting, torturing and murdering people in improvised concentration camps, such as the one in the Wasserturm in Prenzlauer Berg. North of Berlin, construction began on Sachsenhausen concentration camp. During the so-called Köpenicker Blutwoche (Bloody Week) in June 1933, around 90 people were murdered. On 10 May, right-wing students burned 'un-German' books on Bebelplatz, prompting countless intellectuals and artists to rush into exile.

Jewish Persecution

Jews were a Nazi target from the start. In April 1933, Joseph Goebbels, Gauleiter (district leader) of Berlin and head of the well-oiled Ministry of Propaganda, announced a boycott of Jewish businesses. Soon after,

1902	1918	1919	1920
After two decades of debate and eight years of construction, the first segment of the Berlin U-Bahn network is inaugurated, between Warschauer Strasse and Ernst-Reuter-Platz.	WWI ends on 11 November with Germany's capitulation, following the resignation of Kaiser Wilhelm II and his escape to Holland. The Prussian monarchy is dead.	The Spartacist Revolt led by Liebknecht, Luxemburg and Pieck is violently suppressed and ends with the murder of Liebknecht and Luxemburg by right-wing Freikorps troops.	On 1 October Berlin becomes Germany's largest city after seven independent towns, 59 villages and 27 estates are amalgamated into a single administrative unit. The population reaches 3.8 million.

OLYMPICS UNDER THE SWASTIKA

When the International Olympics Committee awarded the 1936 Games to Germany in 1931, the gesture was supposed to welcome the country back into the world community after its defeat in WWI and the tumultuous 1920s. No one could have known that only two years later, the fledgling democracy would be helmed by a dictator with an agenda to take over the world.

As Hitler opened the Games on 1 August in Berlin's Olympic Stadium, prisoners were putting the finishing touches on the first large-scale Nazi concentration camp at Sachsenhausen just north of town. As famous composer Richard Strauss conducted the Olympic hymn during the opening ceremony, fighter squadrons were headed to Spain in support of Franco's dictatorship. Only while the Olympic flame was flickering were political and racial persecution suspended and anti-Semitic signs taken down.

The Olympics were truly a perfect opportunity for the Nazi propaganda machine, which excelled at staging grand public spectacles and rallies, as was so powerfully captured by Leni Riefenstahl in her epic movie *Olympia*. Participants and spectators were impressed by the choreographed pageantry and warm German hospitality. The fact that these were the first Games to be broadcast internationally on radio did not fail to impress either.

From an athletic point of view, the Games were also a big success, with around 4000 participants from 49 countries competing in 129 events and setting numerous records. The biggest star was African American track-and-fieldster Jesse Owens, who was awarded four gold medals in the 100m, 200m, 4 x 100m relay and the long jump, winning the hearts of the German public and putting paid to Nazi beliefs in the physical superiority of the Aryan race. German Jews, meanwhile, were excluded from participating, with the one token exception being half-Jewish fencer Helene Mayer. She took home a silver medal.

Jews were expelled from public service and banned from many professions, trades and industries. The Nuremberg Laws of 1935 deprived 'non-Aryans' of German citizenship and forbade them to marry or have sexual relations with Aryans.

The international community, meanwhile, turned a blind eye to the situation in Germany, perhaps because many leaders were keen to see some order restored to the country after decades of political upheaval. Hitler's success at stabilising the shaky economy – largely by pumping public money into employment programs, many involving re-armament and heavy industry – was widely admired. The 1936 Olympic summer games in Berlin were a public-relations triumph, as Hitler launched a charm offensive, but terror and persecution resumed soon after the closing ceremony.

1920s	1921	1923	1923
Berlin evolves into a cultural metropolis, exerting a pull on leading artists, scientists and philosophers of the day, including Einstein, Brecht and Otto Dix.	The world's first highway – called AVUS – opens in the Grunewald after eight years of construction.	Berlin-Tempelhof Airport opens and soon becomes one of Europe's most important airports, along with Croydon in London and Le Bouget in Paris.	The Golden Twenties show their dark side when inflation reaches its peak and a loaf of bread costs 3.5 million marks – an entire wheelbarrow's worth.

For Jews, the horror escalated on 9 November 1938, with the Reichspogromnacht (often called Kristallnacht, or Night of Broken Glass). Using the assassination of a German consular official by a Polish Jew in Paris as a pretext, Nazi thugs desecrated, burned and demolished synagogues, Jewish cemeteries, property and businesses across the country. Jews had begun to emigrate after 1933, but this event set off a stampede.

The fate of those Jews who stayed behind deteriorated after the outbreak of WWII in 1939. At Hitler's request, a conference in January 1942 in Berlin's Wannsee came up with the Endlösung (Final Solution): the systematic, bureaucratic and meticulously documented annihilation of European Jews, carried out by around 100,000 Germans. Sinti and Roma (gypsies), political opponents, priests, gays and habitual criminals were targeted as well. Of the roughly seven million people who were sent to concentration camps, only 500,000 survived.

> Did you know that 9 November is Germany's 'destiny date'? It was the end of the monarchy in 1918, the day of the 1923 Hitler putsch in Munich, the Night of Broken Glass in 1938 and the day the Wall fell in 1989.

HISTORY RESISTANCE

Resistance

Resistance to Hitler was quashed early by the powerful Nazi machinery of terror, but it never vanished entirely, as is thoroughly documented in the excellent Topographie des Terrors (p89) exhibit. One of the best known acts of defiance was the 20 July 1944 assassination attempt on the Führer that was led by senior army officer Claus Graf Schenk von Stauffenberg. On that fateful day, Stauffenberg brought a briefcase packed with explosives to a meeting of the high command at the Wolfschanze (Wolf's Lair), Hitler's eastern-front military headquarters. He placed the briefcase under the conference table near Hitler's seat, then excused himself and heard the bomb detonate from a distance. What he didn't know was that Hitler had escaped with minor injuries thanks to the solid oak table which shielded him from the blast.

Stauffenberg and his co-conspirators were quickly identified and shot by firing squad at the army headquarters in the Bendlerblock in Berlin. The rooms where they hatched their plot now house the Gedenkstätte Deutscher Widerstand (p127), an exhibit about the efforts of the German Nazi resistance.

> **Top Five WWII Sites**
>
> Topographie des Terrors
>
> Haus der Wannsee Konferenz
>
> Holocaust Memorial
>
> Sachsenhausen concentration camp
>
> Gedenkstätte Deutscher Widerstand

WWII & the Battle of Berlin

WWII began on 1 September 1939 with the Nazi attack on Poland. Although France and Britain declared war on Germany two days later, this could not prevent the quick defeat of Poland, Belgium, the Netherlands and France. Other countries, including Denmark and Norway, were also soon brought into the Nazi fold.

1924	1929	1933	1935
Germany's first electric traffic light starts regulating the chaos around Potsdamer Platz.	The Great Depression hits Berlin, leaving half a million people unemployed. Thirteen members of the National Socialist German Workers Party are elected to city parliament.	Hitler is appointed chancellor; the Reichstag burns; construction starts on Sachsenhausen concentration camp; the National Socialist German Workers' Party rules Germany.	Germany's first public TV broadcast is made from Berlin on 22 March. It is shown three times weekly for 90 minutes. Most people can only watch it in so-called Fernsehstuben (TV parlours).

One of many fabulous films by Germany's best-known female director, Margarethe von Trotta, *Rosenstrasse* (2003) is a moving portrayal of a 1943 protest by a group of non-Jewish women trying to save their Jewish husbands from deportation.

In June 1941, Germany broke its nonaggression pact with Stalin by attacking the USSR. Though successful at first, Operation Barbarossa quickly ran into problems, culminating in the defeat at Stalingrad (today Volgograd) the following winter, forcing the Germans to retreat.

With the Normandy invasion of June 1944, Allied troops arrived in formidable force on the European mainland, supported by unrelenting air raids on Berlin and most other German cities. The final Battle of Berlin began in mid-April 1945. More than 1.5 million Soviet soldiers barrelled towards the capital from the east, reaching Berlin on 21 April and encircling it on 25 April. Two days later they were in the city centre, fighting running street battles with the remaining troops, many of them boys and elderly men. On 30 April the fighting reached the government quarter where Hitler was ensconced in his bunker behind the chancellery, with his long-time mistress Eva Braun, whom he'd married just a day earlier. Finally accepting the inevitability of defeat, Hitler shot himself that afternoon; his wife swallowed a cyanide pill. As their bodies were burned in the chancellery courtyard, Red Army soldiers raised the Soviet flag above the Reichstag.

Defeat & Aftermath

The Battle of Berlin ended on 2 May with the unconditional surrender by Helmuth Weidling, the commander of the Berlin Defence Area, to General Vasily Chuikov of the Soviet army. Peace was signed at the US military headquarters in Reims (France) and at the Soviet military headquarters in Berlin-Karlshorst, now a German-Soviet history museum (Deutsch-Russisches Museum Berlin-Karlshorst). On 8 May 1945, WWII in Europe officially came to an end.

The fighting had taken an enormous toll on Berlin and its people. Entire neighbourhoods lay in smouldering rubble and at least 125,000 Berliners had lost their lives. With around one million women and children evacuated, only 2.8 million people were left in the city in May 1945 (compared to 4.3 million in 1939), two-thirds of them women. It fell to them to start clearing up the 25 million tonnes of rubble, earning them the name *Trümmerfrauen* (rubble women). In fact, many of Berlin's modest hills are actually *Trümmerberge* (rubble mountains), piled from wartime debris and reborn as parks and recreational areas. The best known are the Teufelsberg in the Grunewald and Mont Klamott in the Volkspark Friedrichshain.

Some small triumphs came quickly: U-Bahn service resumed on 14 May 1945, newspaper printing presses began rolling again on 15 May, and the Berliner Philharmonie gave its first postwar concert on 26 May.

1936	1938	1942	1944
The 11th modern Olympic Games, held in Berlin in August, are a PR triumph for Hitler and a showcase of Nazi power. Anti-Jewish propaganda is suspended during the period.	On 9 November Nazis set fire to nine of Berlin's 12 synagogues, vandalise Jewish businesses and terrorise Jewish citizens during a night of pogroms called 'Kristallnacht'.	At the so-called Wannsee Conference, leading members of the SS decide on the systematic murder of European Jews, cynically called the 'Final Solution'.	On 20 July, senior army officers led by Claus Graf Schenk von Stauffenberg stage an assassination attempt on Hitler. Their failure costs their own and countless other lives.

Occupation

At the Yalta Conference in February 1945, Winston Churchill, Franklin D Roosevelt and Joseph Stalin had agreed to carve up Germany and Berlin into four zones of occupation controlled by Britain, the USA, the USSR and France. By July 1945, Stalin, Clement Attlee (who replaced Churchill after a surprise election win) and Roosevelt's successor, Harry S Truman, were at the table in Schloss Cecilienhof in Potsdam to hammer out the details.

Berlin was sliced up into 20 administrative areas. The British sector encompassed Charlottenburg, Tiergarten and Spandau; the French got Wedding and Reinickendorf; and the US was in charge of Zehlendorf, Steglitz, Wilmersdorf, Tempelhof, Kreuzberg and Neukölln. All these districts later formed West Berlin. The Soviets held on to eight districts in the east, including Mitte, Prenzlauer Berg, Friedrichshain, Treptow and Köpenick, which would later become East Berlin. The Soviets also occupied the land surrounding Berlin, leaving West Berlin completely encircled by territories under Soviet control.

The Big Chill

Friction between the Western Allies and the Soviets quickly emerged. For the Western Allies, a main priority was to help Germany get back on its feet by kick-starting the devastated economy. The Soviets, though, insisted on massive reparations and began brutalising and exploiting their own zone of occupation. Tens of thousands of able-bodied men and prisoners of war (POWs) ended up in labour camps deep in the Soviet Union. In the Allied zones, meanwhile, democracy was beginning to take root, and Germany elected state parliaments in 1946–47.

The showdown came in June 1948 when the Allies introduced the Deutschmark in their zones. The USSR regarded this as a breach of the Potsdam Agreement, under which the powers had agreed to treat Germany as one economic zone. The Soviets issued their own currency, the Ostmark, and promptly announced a full-scale economic blockade of West Berlin. The Allies responded with the remarkable Berlin Airlift.

Top Five Cold War Sites
....
Gedenkstätte Berliner Mauer
....
East Side Gallery
....
AlliiertenMuseum
....
Stasi Prison
....
DDR Museum

Two German States

In 1949 the division of Germany – and Berlin – was formalised. The western zones evolved into the Bundesrepublik Deutschland (BRD, Federal Republic of Germany or FRG) with Konrad Adenauer as its first chancellor and Bonn, on the Rhine River, as its capital. An economic aid package dubbed the Marshall Plan created the basis for West Germany's *Wirtschaftswunder* (economic miracle), which saw the economy

1945	1948	1949	1950
Soviet troops advance on Berlin in the final days of the war, devastating the city. Hitler commits suicide on 30 April, fighting stops on 2 May and the armistice is signed on 8 May.	After the Western Allies introduce the Deutschmark currency, the Soviets blockade West Berlin; in response the US and Britain launch the Berlin Airlift, ferrying necessities to the isolated city.	Two countries are born – the Bundesrepublik Deutschland (West Germany) and the Deutsche Demokratische Republik (East Germany).	GDR leaders raze the remains of the Prussian city palace for ideological reasons, despite worldwide protest.

grow at an average 8% per year between 1951 and 1961. The recovery was largely engineered by economics minister Ludwig Erhard, who dealt with an acute labour shortage by inviting about 2.3 million foreign workers, mainly from Turkey, Yugoslavia and Italy, to Germany, thereby laying the foundation for today's multicultural society.

The Soviet zone, meanwhile, grew into the Deutsche Demokratische Republik (German Democratic Republic or GDR), making East Berlin its capital and Wilhelm Pieck its president. From the outset, though, the Sozialistische Einheitspartei Deutschlands (SED, Socialist Unity Party of Germany), led by party boss Walter Ulbricht, dominated economic, judicial and security policy. In order to counter any opposition, the Ministerium für Staatssicherheit (Ministry for State Security, or Stasi) was established in 1950 and based its headquarters in Lichtenberg. Regime opponents were incarcerated at the super-secret Gedenkstätte Hohenschönhausen (Stasi Prison) nearby.

Economically, East Germany stagnated, in large part because of the Soviets' continued policy of asset stripping and reparation payments. Stalin's death in 1953 raised hopes for reform but only spurred the GDR government to raise production goals even higher. Smouldering discontent erupted in violence on 17 June 1953 when 10% of GDR workers took

Australian journalist Anna Funder documents the Stasi, East Germany's vast domestic spy apparatus, by letting both victims and perpetrators tell their stories in her 2004 book *Stasiland*.

THE BERLIN AIRLIFT

The Berlin Airlift was a triumph of determination and a glorious chapter in Berlin's post-WWII history. On 24 June 1948, the Soviets cut off all rail and road traffic into the city to force the Western Allies to give up their sectors and bring the entire city under their control.

Faced with such provocation, many in the Allied camp urged responses that would have been the opening barrages of WWIII. In the end wiser heads prevailed, and a mere day after the blockade began the US Air Force launched 'Operation Vittles'. The British followed suit on 28 June with 'Operation Plane Fare'.

For the next 11 months Allied planes flew in food, coal, machinery and other supplies to now-closed Tempelhof airport in the western city. By the time the Soviets backed down, the Allies had made 278,000 flights, logged a distance equivalent to 250 round trips to the moon and delivered 2.5 million tonnes of cargo. The Luftbrückendenkmal (Berlin Airlift Memorial; p155) outside the airport honours the effort and those who died carrying it out.

It was a monumental achievement that profoundly changed the relationship between Germany and the Western Allies, who were no longer regarded merely as occupational forces but as *Schutzmächte* (protective powers).

1950s	1951	1953	1957
Hundreds of thousands of East Germans move to West Berlin and western Germany, depleting the GDR's brain and brawn power.	Berlin enters the celluloid spotlight with the inaugural Berlin International Film Festival (Berlinale).	The uprising of construction workers on the Stalinallee (today's Karl-Marx-Allee) spreads across the GDR before being crushed by Soviet tanks, leaving several hundred dead and many more injured.	The first Trabant car rolls off the assembly line in East Germany. Production continues until 1990.

to the streets. Soviet troops quashed the uprising, with scores of deaths and the arrest of about 1200 people.

The Wall: What Goes Up...

Through the 1950s the economic gulf between the two Germanys widened, prompting hundreds of thousands of East Berliners to seek a future in the West. Eventually, the exodus of mostly young and well-educated East Germans strained the troubled GDR economy so much that – with Soviet consent – its government built a wall to keep them in. Construction of the Berlin Wall, the Cold War's most potent symbol, began on the night of 13 August 1961.

This stealthy act left Berliners stunned. Formal protests from the Western Allies, as well as massive demonstrations in West Berlin, were ignored. Tense times followed. In October 1961, US and Soviet tanks faced off at Checkpoint Charlie, pushing to the brink of war.

The appointment of Erich Honecker (1912–94) as leader of East Germany in 1971 opened the way for rapprochement with the West and enhanced international acceptance of the GDR. In September that year the Western Allies and the Soviet Union signed a new Four Power Accord in the *Kammergericht* (courthouse) in Schöneberg. It guaranteed access to West Berlin from West Germany and eased travel restrictions between East and West Berlin. The accord paved the way for the Basic Treaty, signed a year later, in which the two countries recognised each other's sovereignty and borders and committed to setting up 'permanent missions' in Bonn and East Berlin, respectively.

Life in the Divided City

For 45 years, Berlin was a political exclave in the cross-hairs of the Cold War. After the Berlin Wall was built in 1961, the city's halves developed as completely separate entities.

West Berlin

West Berlin could not have survived economically without heavy subsidies from the West German government in the form of corporate tax incentives and a so-called *Berlinzulage,* a monthly tax-free bonus of 8% on pretax income for every working Berliner. West Berliners had access to the same aspects of capitalism as all other West Germans with full access to a wide range of quality consumer goods, the latest technology and imported foods. Then as now, the main shopping spine was Kurfürstendamm and its extension, Tauentzienstrasse, the crown jewel of which, the KaDeWe department store, left no shopping desires unfulfilled.

HISTORY THE WALL: WHAT GOES UP...

Daring Young Men: the Heroism and Triumph of the Berlin Airlift, by Richard Reeves, examines this 'first battle of the Cold War' by telling the stories of the American and British pilots who risked their lives to save their former enemies.

1961	1963	1964	1967
Tragedy strikes just 11 days after the first stone of the Berlin Wall is laid. On 24 August, 24-year-old Günter Litfin is gunned down by border guards while attempting to swim across Humboldt Harbour.	US president John F Kennedy professes his solidarity with the people of Berlin when giving his famous 'Ich bin ein Berliner' speech at the town hall in West Berlin's Schöneberg on 26 June.	A master plan to turn Alexanderplatz, East Berlin's central square, into a socialist architectural showcase begins. The square's crowning glory, the TV Tower, opens in 1969.	The death of Benno Ohnesorg, an unarmed student who is shot by a police officer while demonstrating against the visit to West Berlin of the shah of Persia, draws attention to the student movement.

Since West Berlin was completely surrounded by East Berlin and East Germany, its residents liked to joke that no matter in which direction you travelled, you were always 'going east'. Still, West Berliners suffered no restrictions on travel and were free to leave and return as they pleased, as well as to choose their holiday destinations. Berlin was linked to West Germany by air, train and four transit roads, which were normal autobahns or highways also used by East Germans. Transit travellers were not allowed to leave the main road. Border checks were common and often involved harassment and time-consuming searches.

To alleviate acute housing shortages, three new satellite cities – Marzahn, Hohen-schönhausen and Hellersdorf – consisting of massive prefab housing blocks for 300,000 people were built in the 1970s and '80s on East Berlin's outskirts. Equipped with mod-cons like central heating and indoor plumbing, these apartments were much coveted.

East Berlin

From the outset, East Germany's economic, judicial and security policy was dominated by a single party, the SED. Among its prime objectives was the moulding of its citizens into loyal members of a new socialist society. Children as young as six years old were folded into a tight network of state-run mass organisations, and in the workplace the unions were in charge of ideological control and comformity. Officially, membership in any of these groups was voluntary, but refusing to join usually led to limits on access to higher education and career choices. It could also incite the suspicion of the much-feared Stasi.

In East Berlin, the standard of living was higher than in the rest of East Germany, with the Centrum Warenhaus on Alexanderplatz (today's Galeria Kaufhof) a flagship store. While basic foods (bread, milk, butter, some produce) were cheap and plentiful, fancier foods and high-quality goods were in short supply and could often only be obtained with connections and patience. Queues outside shops were a common sight and many items were only available as so-called *Bückware,* meaning that they were hidden from plain view and required the sales clerk to *bücken* (bend) to retrieve them from beneath the counter. Bartering for goods was also common practice. Western products could only be purchased in government-run retail stores called 'Intershops', and then only by the privileged few who had access to hard currency – the East German mark was not accepted.

Great Quotes

'Berlin is the testicle of the West. When I want the West to scream, I squeeze on Berlin.' – Nikita Krushchev, Soviet Communist Party Secretary, 1963

After the Wall went up in 1961, East Berliners, along with other East Germans, were only allowed to travel within the GDR and to other Eastern-bloc countries. Most holiday trips were state subsidised and union organised but who was allowed to go where, when and for how long depended on such factors as an individual's productivity and level of social and political engagement. Those who could afford it could book a package holiday abroad through the Reisebüro der DDR (GDR Travel Agency).

1971	1976	1987	1989
The four Allies sign the Four Power Accord, which confirms Berlin's independent status. East and West Germany recognise each other's sovereignty in the Basic Treaty.	The Palace of the Republic, which houses the GDR parliament and an entertainment centre, opens on 23 April, where the royal Hohenzollern palace had been demolished in 1950.	East and West Berlin celebrate the city's 750th birthday separately. On 12 June Ronald Reagan stands before the Brandenburg Gate to say 'Mr Gorbachev, tear down this Wall!'	On 9 October, East Germany celebrates the 40th anniversary of its founding as demonstrations in favour of reforms reverberate through East Berlin.

Women enjoyed greater equality in East Germany. An extensive government-run child-care system made it easier to combine motherhood and employment, and nearly 90% of all women were gainfully employed, many in such 'nontraditional' fields as engineering and construction. However, this gender equality did not necessarily translate into the private sphere, where women remained largely responsible for child-raising and domestic chores. Rising through the ranks at work or in organisations was also rare for women. In fact, the only female member of the Ministerrat (Council of Ministers) was Erich Honecker's wife, Margot Honecker.

The Wall:...Must Come Down

Hearts and minds in Eastern Europe had long been restless for change, but German reunification came as a surprise to the world and ushered in a new and exciting era. The so-called *Wende* (turning point, ie the fall of communism) came about as a gradual development that ended in a big bang – the collapse of the Berlin Wall on 9 November 1989 (see p37).

The Germany of today, with 16 unified states, was hammered out after a volatile political debate and a series of treaties to end post-WWII occupation zones. The newly united city of Berlin became a separate city-state. Economic union took force in mid-1990, and in August 1990 the Unification Treaty was signed in the Kronprinzenpalais on Unter den Linden. A common currency and economic union became realities in July 1990. In the same month, Pink Floyd played live their 1979 album *The Wall* to a crowd of 200,000 (and a TV audience of millions worldwide) on Potsdamer Platz.

In September 1990, representatives of East and West Germany, the USSR, France, the UK and the US met in Moscow to sign the Two-Plus-Four Treaty, ending postwar occupation zones and paving the way for formal German reunification. One month later, the East German state was dissolved; in December Germany held its first unified post-WWII elections. In 1991 a small majority (338 to 320) of members in the Bundestag (German parliament) voted in favour of moving the government to Berlin and of making Berlin the German capital once again. On 8 September 1994 the last Allied troops stationed in Berlin left the city after a festive ceremony.

The Postunification Years

With reunification, Berlin once again became the seat of government in 1999. Mega-sized construction projects such as Potsdamer Platz and the government quarter eradicated the physical scars of division but

The first Love Parade, a techno cavalcade that would draw millions of people to Berlin each summer between 1989 and 2006, actually kicked off modestly with just one truck and 150 ravers partying on West Berlin's Kurfürstendamm.

More Great Quotes

'I am gay and that's a good thing' – Berlin mayor Klaus Wowereit, 2001

'Berlin is poor but sexy' – Wowereit, 2004

'We want Berlin to become rich and stay sexy' – Wowereit, 2011

1989	1990	1990	1991
On 4 November, half a million Berliners in Alexanderplatz demand freedom of speech, press and assembly. The Berlin Wall opens on 9 November without a single bullet being fired.	'The Wall – Live in Berlin', starring Pink Floyd's Roger Waters, celebrates the Wall's demise on the former Potsdamer Platz death strip.	The official reunification of the two Germanys goes into effect on 3 October. The date becomes a national holiday.	Members of the Bundestag (German parliament) vote to reinstate Berlin as Germany's capital and to move the federal government here. Berliners elect the first joint city government.

did little to improve the city's balance sheet or unemployment statistics. It didn't help that Berlin lost the hefty federal subsidies it had received during the years of division. More than 250,000 manufacturing jobs were lost between 1991 and 2006, most of them through closures of unprofitable factories in East Berlin. Add to that the mismanagement, corruption and excessive spending led by governing mayor Eberhard Diepgen and it's no surprise that the city ran up a whopping debt of €60 million.

JEWISH BERLIN: MENDELSSOHN TO LIBESKIND

Since reunification, Berlin has had the fastest-growing Jewish community in the world. Their backgrounds are diverse: most are Russian Jewish immigrants but there are also Jews of German heritage, Israelis wishing to escape their war-torn homeland and American expats lured by Berlin's low-cost living and limitless creativity. Today there are about 13,000 active members of the Jewish community, including 1000 belonging to the Orthodox congregation Adass Yisroel. And since not all Jews choose to be affiliated with a synagogue, the actual population is estimated to be at least twice as high.

The community supports 10 synagogues, two *mikve* ritual baths, several schools, numerous cultural institutions and a handful of kosher restaurants and shops. The golden-domed Neue Synagoge (New Synagogue) on Oranienburger Strasse is the most visible beacon of Jewish revival, even though today it's not primarily a house of worship but a community and exhibition space. In Kreuzberg, the Jüdisches Museum (p153), a spectacular structure by Daniel Libeskind, tracks the ups and downs of Jewish life in Germany for almost 2000 years. Another key Jewish site is the Alter Jüdischer Friedhof, Berlin's oldest Jewish cemetery and final resting home of Enlightenment philosopher Moses Mendelssohn, who arrived in Berlin in 1743. His progressive thinking and lobbying paved the way for the Emancipation Edict of 1812, which made Jews full citizens of Prussia, with equal rights and duties.

By the end of the 19th century, many of Berlin's Jews, then numbering about 5% of the population, had become thoroughly German in speech and identity. When a wave of Hasidic Jews escaping the pogroms of Eastern Europe arrived around the same time, they found their way to today's Scheunenviertel, which at that time was an immigrant slum with cheap housing. By 1933 Berlin's Jewish population had grown to around 160,000 and constituted one-third of all Jews living in Germany. The well-known horrors of the Nazi years sent most into exile and left 55,000 dead. Only about 1000 to 2000 Jews are believed to have survived the war years in Berlin, often with the help of their non-Jewish neighbours. Many memorials throughout the city commemorate the Nazi's victims. The most prominent is, of course, the Holocaust Memorial (p85) near the Brandenburg Gate.

1994	1999	2001	2006
The last British, French, Russian and American troops withdraw from Berlin, ending nearly half a century of occupation and protection.	On 19 April the German parliament holds its first session in the historic Reichstag building, after complete restoration by Lord Norman Foster.	Openly gay politician Klaus Wowereit is elected governing mayor of Berlin.	Berlin's first central train station, the Hauptbahnhof, opens on 26 May. Two weeks later Germany kicks off the 2006 FIFA World Cup.

Elected in 2001, the new governing mayor Klaus Wowereit responded by making across-the-board spending cuts, but with a tax base eroded by high unemployment and ever-growing welfare payments, they did little initially to get Berlin out of the poorhouse. Eventually, though, the economic restructure away from a manufacturing base and towards the service sector began to bear fruit. Job creation in the capital has outpaced that of Germany in general for almost 10 years. No German city has a greater number of business start-ups. Its export quota has risen steadily, as has its population. The health, transport and green-technology industries are growing in leaps and bounds.

On the cultural front, Berlin exploded into a hive of cultural cool with unbridled nightlife, a vibrant art scene and booming fashion and design industries. In 2006 it became part of Unesco's Creative Cities Network. Some 170,000 people are employed in the cultural sector, which generates an annual turnover of around €13 billion. An especially important subsector is music, with nearly 10% of all related companies, including Universal and MTV, moving to Berlin over the past 20 years.

In June 2012, 486,709 (14.1%) of all people living in Berlin were foreigners. There are people from 185 nations, including 13,781 Americans, 10,911 Brits, 2541 Australians and 2171 Canadians. Berlin's Turkish community represents the single largest foreign population with 101,975 people.

2008	2009	2011	2013
The last flight takes off from Berlin-Tempelhof airport, which becomes an event space and public park.	Techno club Berghain is ranked number one on the Top 100 Clubs list by UK magazine *DJ Mag*.	Berlin's population passes the 3.5 million mark, growing 1.2%, the most within a single year since reunification in 1990. Most of the growth comes from people moving to Berlin.	Construction of the Berlin City Palace as the Humboldtforum intercultural centre commences on 21 June. Planned completion date is 2019.

Architecture

From the majestic dome atop the Reichstag to the cloud-piercing Fernsehturm (TV Tower), the jagged angles of the Jüdisches Museum (Jewish Museum) to the baroque splendour of Schloss Charlottenburg and the warped dynamism of the Berliner Philharmonie – Berlin boasts some mighty fine architecture. It's an eclectic mix, to be sure, shaped by the city's unique history, especially the destruction of WWII and the contrasting urban-planning visions during the years of division. Since reunification, though, Berlin has become a virtual laboratory for the world's elite architects, David Chipperfield, Norman Foster and Daniel Libeskind among them.

Modest Beginnings

Above: Nikolaikirche (p112)

Very few buildings from the Middle Ages until the 1700s have survived time, war and modernist town planning. Only two Gothic churches – the red-brick Nikolaikirche (1230) and Marienkirche (1294) – bear silent witness to the days when today's metropolis was just a small trading town. Nikolaikirche anchors the Nikolaiviertel, a mock-medieval quarter built on the site of the city's original settlement as East Germany's contribution to Berlin's 750th anniversary celebrations in 1987. It's a hodgepodge of genuine historic buildings like the Knoblochhaus and replicas of historic buildings such as the Gaststätte Zum Nussbaum.

A hint of residential medieval architecture also survives in the outer district of Spandau, both in the Gotisches Haus and the half-timbered houses of the Kolk quarter.

Traces of the Renaissance, which reached Berlin in the early 16th century, are rarer still, but notable survivors include the Jagdschloss Grunewald and the Zitadelle Spandau.

Going for Baroque

As the city grew, so did the representational needs of its rulers, especially in the 17th and 18th centuries. In Berlin, this role fell to Great Elector Friedrich Wilhelm, who systematically expanded the city by adding three residential quarters, a fortified town wall and a tree-lined boulevard known as Unter den Linden.

This was the age of baroque, a style merging architecture, sculpture, ornamentation and painting into a single *Gesamtkunstwerk* (complete work of art). In Berlin and northern Germany it retained a formal and precise bent, never quite reaching the exuberance favoured in regions further south.

The Great Elector may have laid the groundwork, but it was only under his son, Elector Friedrich III, that Berlin acquired the stature of an exalted residence, especially after he crowned himself *King* Friedrich I in 1701. Two major baroque buildings survive from his reign, both blueprinted by Johann Arnold Nering: Schloss Charlottenburg, which Johann Friedrich Eosander later expanded into a Versailles-inspired three-wing palace; and the Zeughaus (armoury; today's Deutsches Historisches Museum) on Unter den Linden. The museum's modern annex, named the IM Pei Bau (IM Pei Building) after its architect, was added in the 1990s. Fronted by a transparent, spiral staircase shaped like a snail shell, it's a harmonious interplay of glass, natural stone and light and an excellent example of Pei's muted postmodernist approach.

Meanwhile, back in the early 18th century, two formidable churches were taking shape on Gendarmenmarkt in the heart of the immigrant Huguenot community, which at the time accounted for about 25% of the population. These were the Deutscher Dom (German Cathedral) by Martin Grünberg, and the Französischer Dom (French Cathedral) by Louis Cayart.

No king had a greater impact on Berlin's physical layout than Frederick the Great. Together with his childhood friend, architect Georg Wenzeslaus von Knobelsdorff, he masterminded the Forum Fridericianum, a cultural quarter centred on today's Bebelplatz. It was built in a style called 'Frederician Rococo' that blended baroque

Built as a summer palace for King Friedrich I's wife Sophie-Charlotte, Schloss Charlottenburg was originally called Schloss Lietzenburg but was renamed after the popular queen's sudden death in 1705.

ARCHITECTURE GOING FOR BAROQUE

BERLIN & ITS WALLS

1250 The first defensive wall is built of boulders and stands 2m high.

1300s The wall is fortified with bricks and raised to a height of 5m.

1648–1734 The medieval wall is replaced by elaborate fortifications.

1734–1866 A customs wall with 18 city gates replaces the bastion.

1961–1989 The Berlin Wall divides the city.

Schloss Charlottenburg (p201)

and neoclassical elements. Since the king's war exploits had emptied his coffers, he could only afford to partially realise his vision by building the neoclassical Staatsoper Unter den Linden (State Opera House); the St-Hedwigs-Kathedrale (St Hedwig Cathedral), inspired by Rome's Pantheon; the playful Alte Königliche Bibliothek (Old Royal Library); and the Humboldt Universität (Humboldt University), originally a palace for the king's brother Heinrich. Knobelsdorff also designed the Neuer Flügel (New Wing) expansion of Schloss Charlottenburg. His crowning achievement, though, was Schloss Sanssouci (Sanssouci Palace) in Potsdam.

After Knobelsdorff's death in 1753, two architects continued in his tradition: Philipp Daniel Boumann – who designed Schloss Bellevue (Bellevue Palace) for Frederick's youngest brother, August Ferdinand – and Carl von Gontard, who added the domed towers to the Deutscher Dom and Französischer Dom on Gendarmenmarkt.

The Schinkel Touch

The architectural style that most shaped Berlin was neoclassicism, thanks in large part to one man: Karl Friedrich Schinkel, arguably Prussia's most prominent architect (see p270). Turning away from baroque flourishes, neoclassicism drew upon columns, pediments, domes and other design elements that had been popular throughout antiquity.

Schinkel assisted with the design of Queen Luise's mausoleum in Schloss Charlottenburg's park in 1810, but didn't truly make his mark until his first major solo commission, the Neue Wache (New Guardhouse) on Unter den Linden, was completed in 1818. Originally an army guardhouse, it is now an antiwar memorial accented with a haunting sculpture by Käthe Kollwitz.

Top Four Prussian Palaces

Schloss Sanssouci, Potsdam

Schloss Charlottenburg, Berlin

Neues Palais, Potsdam

Schlösschen auf der Pfaueninsel, Wannsee

Reiterdenkmal Friedrich der Grosse monument (p90) on Unter den Linden

The nearby Altes Museum (Old Museum) on Museumsinsel (Museum Island), with its colonnaded front, is considered Schinkel's most mature work. Other neoclassical masterpieces include the Schauspielhaus (now the Konzerthaus Berlin) on Gendarmenmarkt and the Neue Pavillon (New Pavilion) in Schlossgarten Charlottenburg. Schinkel's most significant departure from neoclassicism, the turreted Friedrichswerdersche Kirche, was inspired by a Gothic revival in early-19th-century England.

After Schinkel's death in 1841, several of his disciples kept his legacy alive, notably Friedrich August Stüler, who built the original Neues Museum (New Museum) and the Alte Nationalgalerie (Old National Gallery), both on Museumsinsel, as well as the Matthäuskirche (Church of St Matthew) in today's Kulturforum.

Housing for the Masses

In his 1930 book *Das Steinerne Berlin* (Stony Berlin), Werner Hegemann fittingly refers to Berlin as 'the largest tenement city in the world.' The onset of industrialisation in the middle of the 19th century lured hundreds of thousands to the capital who dreamed of improving their lot in the factories. Something had to be done to beef up the city's infrastructure and provide cheap housing for the masses, and quick. A plan drawn up in 1862 under chief city planner James Hobrecht called for a city expansion along two circular ring roads bisected by diagonal roads radiating in all directions from the centre – much like the spokes of a wheel. The land in between was divided into large lots and sold to speculators and developers. Building codes were limited to a maximum building height of 22m (equivalent to five stories) and a minimum courtyard size of 5.34m by 5.34m, just large enough for fire-fighting equipment to operate in.

Berlin's architectural growth was notably influenced by advancements in transportation. The first train chugged from Berlin to Potsdam in 1838, the first S-Bahn rumbled along in 1882 and the U-Bahn kicked into service in 1902.

Such lax regulations led to the uncontrolled spread of sprawling working-class tenements called *Mietskasernen* (literally 'rental barracks') in newly created peripheral districts such as Prenzlauer Berg, Kreuzberg, Wedding and Friedrichshain. Each was designed to squeeze the maximum number of people into the smallest possible space. Entire families crammed into tiny, lightless flats reached via internal staircases that also provided access to shared toilets. Many flats doubled as workshops or sewing studios. Only those facing the street offered light, space and balconies – and they were reserved for the bourgeoisie.

Walking around Berlin, it's hard to visualise what the city looked like before WWII. Nick Gay's book *Berlin Then and Now* handily juxtaposes historical and recent images of major landmarks, streets and squares.

The Empire Years

The architecture in vogue after the creation of the German Empire in 1871 reflects the representational needs of the united Germany and tends towards the pompous. No new style, as such, emerged as architects essentially recycled earlier ones (eg Romanesque, Renaissance and baroque, sometimes weaving them all together) in an approach called Historismus (Historicism) or Wilhelmismus, after Emperor Wilhelm I.

As a result, many buildings in Berlin look much older than they actually are. Prominent examples include the Reichstag by Paul Wallot and the Berliner Dom (Berlin Cathedral) by Julius Raschdorff, both in neo-Renaissance style. Franz Schwechten's Anhalter Bahnhof and the Kaiser-Wilhelm-Gedächtniskirche (Memorial Church), both in ruins, reflect the neo-Romanesque, while the Bodemuseum by Ernst von Ihne is a neo-baroque confection.

While squalid working-class neighbourhoods hemmed in the north, east and south of the city centre, western Berlin (Charlottenburg, Wilmersdorf) was being developed for the middle and upper classes under none other than the 'Iron Chancellor' Otto von Bismarck himself. He widened the Kurfürstendamm, lining it and its side streets with attractive town houses. Those with serious money and status moved even further west, away from the claustrophobic centre. The villa colonies in leafy Grunewald and Dahlem are another Bismarck legacy and remain among the ritziest residential areas today.

PRUSSIA'S BUILDING MASTER: KARL FRIEDRICH SCHINKEL

Few architects have shaped the Berlin cityscape as much as Karl Friedrich Schinkel (1781–1841). After studying under David Gilly at the Prussian Building Academy in Berlin, he decamped to Italy for a couple of years to examine classical architecture in situ. He returned to a Prussia hamstrung by Napoleonic occupation and was forced to scrape by as a romantic painter and furniture and set designer.

Things improved dramatically as soon as the French left Berlin in 1808, allowing Schinkel to quickly climb the career ladder within the Prussian civil service and eventually to become chief building director for the entire kingdom. He travelled tirelessly throughout the land, designing buildings, supervising construction and even developing principles for the protection of historic monuments.

Drawing inspiration from classical Greek architecture, Schinkel very much defined Prussian architecture between 1810 and 1840. His designs strive for the perfect balance between functionality and beauty, achieved through clear lines, symmetry and an impeccable sense for aesthetics. Berlin, which came to be known as 'Athens on the Spree', is littered with his buildings.

Schinkel fell into a coma in 1840 and died one year later in Berlin. He's buried on the Dorotheenstädtischer Friedhof in Mitte.

Berliner Dom (p115)

The Birth of Modernism

While most late-19th-century architects were looking to the past, a few progressive minds managed to make their mark, mostly in industrial and commercial design. Sometimes called the 'father of modern architecture', Peter Behrens (1868–1940) taught later modernist luminaries such as Le Corbusier, Walter Gropius and Ludwig Mies van der Rohe. One of his earliest works, the 1909 AEG Turbinenhalle at Huttenstrasse 12-14 in Moabit, is considered an icon of early industrial architecture.

After WWI the 1920s spirit of innovation lured some of the finest avant-garde architects to Berlin, including Bruno and Max Taut, Le Corbusier, Mies van der Rohe, Erich Mendelsohn, Hans Poelzig and Hans Scharoun. In 1924 they formed an architectural collective called Der Ring (The Ring) whose members were united by the desire to break with traditional aesthetics (especially the derivative Historicism) and to promote a modern, affordable and socially responsible approach to building.

Their theories were put into practice as Berlin entered another housing shortage. Led by chief city planner Martin Wagner, Ring members devised a new form of social housing called *Siedlungen* (housing estates). It opened up living space and incorporated gardens, schools, shops and other communal areas that facilitated social interaction. Together with Bruno Taut, Wagner himself designed the Hufeisensiedlung (Horseshoe Colony) in Neukölln which, in 2008, became one of six Berlin housing estates recognised as a Unesco World Heritage site (see p273).

In nonresidential architecture, expressionism flourished with Erich Mendelsohn as its leading exponent. This organic, sculptural approach is nicely exemplified by the Universum Kino (Universum Cinema; 1926), which is today's Schaubühne theatre at Lehniner Platz; it greatly

In the 1920s Adolf Hitler's stepbrother Alois was a waiter at Weinhaus Huth, the only complete building on Potsdamer Platz to survive WWII intact. During the Cold War, it stood forlorn in the middle of the death strip for decades.

JOHN FREEMAN/GETTY IMAGES ©

German Democratic Republic–era building on Karl-Marx-Allee (p174)

influenced the Streamline Moderne movie palaces of the 1930s. Emil Fahrenkamp's 1931 Shell-Haus at Reichspietschufer 60 follows similar design principles. Reminiscent of a giant upright staircase, it was one of Berlin's earliest steel-frame structures concealed beneath a skin of travertine. Its extravagant silhouette is best appreciated from the southern bank of the Landwehrkanal.

Nazi Monumentalism

Modernist architecture had its legs cut out from under it as soon as Hitler came to power in 1933. The new regime immediately shut down the Bauhaus School, one of the most influential forces in 20th-century building and design. Founded by Walter Gropius in 1919, it had moved to Berlin from Dessau only in 1932. Many of its visionary teachers, including Gropius, Mies van der Rohe, Wagner and Mendelsohn, went into exile in the USA.

Back in Berlin, Hitler, who was a big fan of architectural monumentalism, put Albert Speer in charge of turning Berlin into the 'Welthauptstadt Germania', the future capital of the Reich. Today, only a few buildings offer a hint of what Berlin might have looked like had history taken a different turn. These include the coliseum-like Olympiastadion, Tempelhof Airport and the former air force ministry that now houses Germany's Federal Finance Ministry.

A Tale of Two Cities

Even before the Wall was built in 1961, the clash of ideologies and economic systems between East and West also found expression in the architectural arena.

East Berlin

East Germans looked to Moscow, where Stalin favoured a style that was essentially a socialist reinterpretation of good old-fashioned neoclassicism. The most prominent East German architect was Hermann Henselmann, the brains behind the Karl-Marx-Allee (called Stalinallee until 1961) in Friedrichshain. Built between 1952 and 1965, it was East Berlin's showcase 'socialist boulevard' and, with its Moscow-style 'wedding-cake buildings', the epitome of Stalin-era pomposity. It culminates at Alexanderplatz, the central square that got a distinctly socialist makeover in the 1960s.

While Alexanderplatz and the Karl-Marx-Allee were prestige projects, they did not solve the need for affordable modern housing. The government responded by building three massive satellite cities on the periphery – Marzahn, Hohenschönhausen and Hellersdorf – that leapt off the drawing board in the 1970s and '80s. Like a virtual Legoland for giants, these huge housing developments largely consist of row

UNCOMMON ENVIRONS FOR THE COMMON MAN

Architecturally speaking, Museumsinsel, Schloss Sanssouci and the Hufeisensiedlung in Neukölln could not be more different. Yet all have one thing in common: they are Unesco World Heritage sites. Along with five other working-class housing estates throughout Berlin, the Hufeisensiedlung was inducted onto this illustrious list in July 2008.

Created between 1910 and 1933 by such leading architects of the day as Bruno Taut and Martin Wagner, these icons of modernism are the earliest examples of innovative, streamlined and functional – yet human-scale – mass housing and stand in stark contrast to the slum-like, crowded tenements of the late 19th century. The flats, though modest, were functionally laid out and had kitchens, private baths and balconies that let in light and fresh air. For further details, see http://whc.unesco.org.

Hufeisensiedlung/Neukölln (Lowise-Reuter-Ring; [S]Parchimer Allee) Taut and Wagner dreamed up the 3-storey-high horseshoe-shaped colony (1933–35) with 1000 balconied flats wrapping around a central park. From the station follow Fritz-Reuter-Allee north.

Gartenstadt Falkenberg/Köpenick (Akazienhof, Am Falkenberg & Gartenstadtweg; [R]Grünau) Built by Taut between 1910 and 1913, the oldest of the six Unesco-honoured estates is a cheerful jumble of colourfully painted cottages. Approach from Am Falkenberg.

Siemensstadt/Spandau (Geisslerpfad, Goebelstrasse, Heckerdamm, Jungfernheideweg, Mäckeritzstrasse; [S]Siemensdamm) This huge development (1929–31) combines Walter Gropius' minimalism, Hugo Häring's organic approach and Hans Scharoun's ship-inspired designs. Best approach is via Jungfernheideweg.

Schillerpark Siedlung/Wedding (Barfussstrasse, Bristolstrasse, Corker Strasse, Dubliner Strasse, Oxforder Strasse, Windsorer Strasse, Wedding; [S]Rehberge) Inspired by Dutch architecture, this large colony (1924–30) was masterminded by Taut and sports a dynamic red-and-white-brick facade. Best approach is via Barfussstrasse.

Weisse Stadt/Reinickendorf (Aroser Allee, Baseler Strasse, Bieler Strasse, Emmentaler Strasse, Genfer Strasse, Gotthardstrasse, Romanshorner Weg, Schillerring, Sankt-Galler-Strasse; [S]Residenzstrasse) Martin Wagner's 'White City' (1929–31) includes shops, a kindergarten, cafe, central laundry and other communal facilities. Best approach is via Aroser Allee.

Wohnstadt Carl Legien/Prenzlauer Berg (Erich-Weinert-Strasse; [R]Prenzlauer Allee) For this development (1928–30) in Prenzlauer Berg, Taut arranged rows of 4-to-5-storey-high houses and garden areas in a semi-open space. Approach via Erich-Weinert-Strasse.

Apartment buildings in the Hansaviertel

upon row of rectangular high-rise *Plattenbauten,* ie buildings made from large, precast concrete slabs. Marzahn alone could accommodate 165,000 people in 62,000 flats. Since they offered such mod cons as private baths and lifts, this type of housing was very popular among East Germans, despite the monotony of the design.

The only remaining prewar buildings in what was East Berlin are Peter Behrens' Berolinahaus (1930) and Alexanderhaus (1932).

West Berlin

In West Berlin, urban planners sought to eradicate any hint of monumentalism and to rebuild the city in a modernist fashion. Their equivalent of the Karl-Marx-Allee became the Hansaviertel, a loosely structured leafy neighbourhood of mid-rise apartment buildings and single-family homes, northwest of Tiergarten. Built from 1954 to 1957, it drew the world's top architects, including Gropius, Alvar Aalto and Le Corbusier and was intended to be a model for other residential quarters.

The 1960s saw the birth of a large-scale public building project, the Kulturforum, a museum and concert-hall complex conceptualised by Hans Scharoun. His Berliner Philharmonie, the first building in the complex to be completed (1963), is considered a masterpiece of sculptural modernism. Among the museums, Mies van der Rohe's temple-like Neue Nationalgalerie (New National Gallery) is a stand out. A massive glass-and-steel cube, it perches on a raised granite podium and is lidded by a coffered, steel-ribbed roof that seems to defy gravity.

The West also struggled with a housing shortage and built its own versions of mass-scale housing projects, including Gropiusstadt in southern Neukölln and the Märkisches Viertel in Reinickendorf, in northwest Berlin.

ARCHITECT HANS SCHAROUN. IMAGE DAVID BANK/GETTY IMAGES ©

Berliner Philharmonie (p126)

Interbau 1987

While mass housing mushroomed on the peripheries, the inner city suffered from decay and neglect on both sides of the Wall. In West Berlin, an international architectural exposition called Interbau (IBA) 1987 was to set new initiatives in urban renewal by blending two architectural principles: 'Careful Urban Renewal' would focus on rehabilitating existing buildings; and 'Critical Reconstruction' would require any new buildings to fit in with the existing urban fabric.

Planning director Josef Paul Kleihues invited the royalty of international architecture to take up the challenges of Interbau, among them Rob Krier, Peter Eisenman, James Stirling, Aldo Rossi, Arata Isozaki and OM Ungers. Eastern Kreuzberg and the area south of the Tiergarten received the most attention. Good places to study the legacy of Interbau 1987 are on a stroll along the Fraenkelufer in Kreuzberg and along the streets surrounding the Jüdisches Museum such as Lindenstrasse, Ritterstrasse and Alte Jakobstrasse.

The New Berlin

Reunification presented Berlin with both the challenge and the opportunity to redefine itself architecturally. With the Wall gone, the two city halves had to be physically rejoined across huge gashes of empty space. Critical Reconstruction continued to be the guiding vision under city planning director Hans Stimmann. Architects had to follow a long catalogue of parameters with regard to building heights, facade materials and other criteria with the goal of rebuilding Berlin within its historic forms rather than creating a modern, vertical city.

Top Five Buildings since 1990

....

Jüdisches Museum (Daniel Libeskind)

....

Reichstag Dome (Norman Foster)

....

Sony Center (Helmut Jahn)

....

Neues Museum (David Chipperfield)

....

Hauptbahnhof (central train station; Gerkan, Marg und Partner)

Potsdamer Platz

The biggest and grandest of the post-1990 Berlin developments, Potsdamer Platz is a modern reinterpretation of the historic square that was Berlin's bustling heart until WWII. On terrain once divided by the Berlin Wall has sprung an urban quarter laid out along a dense, irregular street grid reminiscent of a 'European city'. Led by Renzo Piano, it's a collaboration of an international roster of renowned architects, including Helmut Jahn, Richard Rogers and Rafael Moneo. Structures are of medium height, except for three gateway high-rises overlooking the intersection of Potsdamer Strasse and Ebertstrasse.

If you want to learn more about Berlin's contemporary architecture, sign up for a tour (also in English) with Ticket B (www. ticket-b.de), an architect-run guide company.

Pariser Platz

Pariser Platz was also reconstructed from the ground up. It's a formal, introspective square framed by banks, embassies and the Hotel Adlon that, in keeping with Critical Reconstruction, had to have natural stone facades. The one exception is the glass-fronted Akademie der Künste (Academy of Arts). Its architect, Günter Behnisch, had to fight tooth and nail for this facade, arguing that the square's only public building should feel open, inviting and transparent. The Adlon, meanwhile, is an almost exact replica of the 1907 original.

Diplomatenviertel

Some of Berlin's most exciting new architecture is clustered in the revitalised Diplomatenviertel (Diplomatic Quarter) on the southern edge of Tiergarten, where many countries rebuilt their embassies on their historic pre-WWII sites.

Government Quarter

The 1991 decision to move the federal government back to Berlin resulted in a flurry of building activity in the empty space between the Reichstag and the Spree River. Designed by Axel Schultes and Charlotte Frank, and arranged in linear east–west fashion, are the Federal Chancellery, the Paul-Löbe-Haus and the Marie-Elisabeth-Lüders-Haus. Together they form the Band des Bundes (Band of Federal Buildings) in a symbolic linking of the formerly divided city halves across the Spree.

The opening of Berlin's Brandenburg Airport in Schönefeld has been delayed indefinitely. A referendum in May 2014, however, prevented the city from partly developing Tempelhof Airport, which closed in 2008. Much to the delight of Berliners, it will remain a public park.

Overlooking all these shiny new structures is the Reichstag, home of the Bundestag (German parliament), the glass cupola of which is the most visible element of the building's total makeover, masterminded by Norman Foster.

The glass-and-steel 'spaceship' on the northern riverbank is Berlin's first-ever central train station, the sparkling Hauptbahnhof designed by the Hamburg firm of Gerkan, Marg und Partner and completed in 2006.

More Architectural Trophies

In Kreuzberg, Daniel Libeskind's deconstructivist Jüdisches Museum (1999) is among the most daring and provocative structures in the new Berlin. With its irregular, zigzagging floor plan and shiny zinc skin pierced by gash-like windows, it is not merely a museum but a powerful metaphor for the troubled history of the Jewish people. Libeskind also designed the museum's extension, which opened in a nearby converted flower market in June 2013.

Near Gendarmenmarkt, along Friedrichstrasse, the Friedrichstadtpassagen (1996) is a trio of luxurious shopping complexes, including the glamorous Galeries Lafayette, that hide their jewel-like interiors behind postmodern facades.

Across town, in the City West, several new structures have added some spice to the rather drab postwar architecture around Kurfürstendamm. The Ludwig-Erhard-Haus (1997), home of the Berlin stock market, is a great example of the organic architecture of the UK's Nicholas Grimshaw. Nearby, Kleihues' Kantdreieck (1995) establishes a visual accent on Kantstrasse by virtue of its rooftop metal 'sail'. Noteworthy buildings along Ku'damm itself are Helmut Jahn's Neues Kranzler Eck (2000) and the Neues Ku-Damm-Eck (2001), a corner building with a gradated and rounded facade, designed by Gerkan, Marg und Partner and festooned with sculptures by Markus Lüpertz.

Another highlight is David Chipperfield's reconstruction of the Neues Museum (2009) on Museumsinsel. Like a giant jigsaw puzzle, it beautifully blends fragments from the original structure, which was destroyed in WWII, with modern elements. The result is so harmonious and impressive, it immediately racked up accolades, including the prestigious award from the Royal Institute of British Architects (RIBA) in 2010.

Recent Developments & the Future

You'd think that the ballet of cranes would finally have disappeared more than 25 years after reunification, but there are still plenty of large-scale projects on the drawing board or under construction. In 2014 the first spies started moving into the new Berlin home of the Bundesnachrichtendienst (BND; Germany's foreign intelligence agency) on Chausseestrasse, just north of the Scheunenviertel. Designed by Kleihues + Kleihues, the giant compound sits on a lot once occupied by the GDR-era Stadium of the World Youth.

The City West has also garnered several high-profile additions including the towering Waldorf Astoria Hotel and the reborn Bikini Berlin. For decades regarded as a 1950s architectural icon of the city's post-WWII revival, the latter reopened as a chic shopping mall in late April 2014 in a spectacularly rehabilitated building. The curious name was inspired by its design: two 200m-long upper and lower sections are separated by an open floor supported by a curtain of columns. Today the middle section is chastely covered by a glass facade.

The current reconstruction of the Berliner Stadtschloss, the former Prussian city palace, on Schlossplatz, across from Museumsinsel, is to be known as Humboldt-Forum; it will only resemble its historic predecessor from the outside, with the modern interior housing museums and cultural institutions.

With its cool and calm facade, the DZ Bank on Pariser Platz seems untypical for its exuberant architect, Frank Gehry. The surprise, though, lurks beyond the foyer leading to a light-flooded atrium anchored by an enormous sci-fi-esque stainless-steel sculpture used as a conference room.

Painting & Visual Arts

The arts are fundamental to everything Berlin holds dear, and the sheer scope of creative activity in the city is astounding. Half the reason Berliners are always so busy is because of the efforts required to keep up with the ever-changing cultural kaleidoscope of trends and events. And with a history of international excellence in most fields, expectations and standards are always set high. The city itself provides an iconic setting for a spectrum of visual arts, its unmistakable presence influencing artists and residents just as it does those canny visitors who take the time to dive in.

The coppersmith Emanuel Jury, who cast the *Quadriga* sculpture atop the Brandenburg Gate, used his niece as a model for the Goddess Victoria, pilot of the chariot.

Early Beginnings

Fine art only began to flourish in Berlin in the late 17th century, when self-crowned King Friedrich I founded the Akademie der Künste (Academy of Arts) in 1696, egged on by court sculptor Andreas Schlüter. Schlüter repaid the favour with outstanding sculptures, including the *Great Elector on Horseback,* now in front of Schloss Charlottenburg, and the haunting masks of dying warriors in the courtyard of today's Deutsches Historisches Museum (German Historical Museum). Artistic accents in painting were set by Frenchman Antoine Pesne, who became Friedrich I's court painter in 1710. His main legacy is his elaborate portraits of the royal family members.

The arts also reached a heyday under Friedrich I's grandson, Friedrich II (Frederick the Great), who became king in 1740. Friedrich drew heavily on the artistic expertise of his friend Georg Wenzeslaus von Knobelsdorff, a student of Pesne, and also amassed a sizeable collection of works by such French artists as Jean Antoine Watteau.

The 19th Century

Neoclassicism emerged as a dominant sculptural style in the 19th century. Johann Gottfried Schadow's *Quadriga* – the horse-drawn chariot atop the Brandenburg Gate – epitomises the period. Schadow's student Christian Daniel Rauch had a special knack for representing idealised, classical beauty in a realistic fashion. His most famous work is the 1851 monument of Frederick the Great on horseback on Unter den Linden.

In painting, heart-on-your-sleeve romanticism that drew heavily on emotion and a dreamy idealism dominated the 19th century. A reason for this development was the awakening of a nationalist spirit in Germany, spurred by the Napoleonic Wars. Top dog of the era was Caspar David Friedrich, best known for his moody, allegorical landscapes. Although more famous as an architect, Karl Friedrich Schinkel also created some fanciful canvases. Eduard Gärtner's paintings documenting Berlin's evolving cityscape found special appeal among the middle classes.

Into the 20th Century

Berliner Secession

The Berliner Secession was formed in 1898 by a group of progressive-minded artists who rejected the traditional teachings of the arts academies that stifled any new forms of expression. The schism was triggered in 1891, when the established Verein Berliner Künstler (Berlin Artist Association) refused to show paintings by Edvard Munch at its annual salon, and reached its apex in 1898 when the salon jury rejected a landscape painting by Walter Leistikow. Consequently, 65 artists banded together under leadership of Leistikow and Max Liebermann and seceded from the Verein. Other famous Berliner Secession members included Lovis Corinth, Max Slevogt, Ernst Ludwig Kirchner, Max Beckmann and Käthe Kollwitz.

Expressionism

In 1905, Kirchner, along with Erich Heckel and Karl Schmidt-Rottluff, founded the artist group Die Brücke (The Bridge) in Dresden. It turned the art world on its head with ground-breaking visions that paved the way for German expressionism. Shapes and figures that teeter on the abstract – without ever quite getting there – drenched with bright, emotional colours, characterise the aesthetic of Die Brücke. It moved to Berlin in 1911 and disbanded in 1913. The small Brücke Museum in the Grunewald has a fantastic collection of these influential canvases.

Ironically, it was the expressionists that splintered off from the Berliner Secession in 1910 after their work had been rejected by the Secession jury. With Max Pechstein at the helm, they formed the Neue Secession. The original group continued but saw its influence waning, especially after the Nazi power grab in 1933.

The Bauhaus

The year 1919 saw the founding of the Bauhaus movement and school in Weimar. It was was based on practical anti-elitist principles bringing form and function together, and had a profound effect on all modern design – visit the Bauhaus Archiv for ample examples. Although the school moved to Dessau in 1925 and only to Berlin in 1932, many of its most influential figures worked in Berlin. It was forced by the Nazis to close down in 1933.

After the Nazi takeover many artists left the country and others ended up in prison or concentration camps, their works confiscated or destroyed. The art promoted instead was often terrible, favouring straightforward 'Aryan' forms and epic styles. Propaganda artist Mjölnir defined the typical look of the time with block Gothic scripts and idealised figures.

A student of Rauch, the sculptor Reinhold Begas developed a neo-baroque, theatrical style that met with a fair amount of controversy in his lifetime. Major works include the Neptune fountain next to the Marienkirche below the TV Tower, and the Schiller memorial on Gendarmenmarkt.

PAINTING & VISUAL ARTS INTO THE 20TH CENTURY

ZILLE SEASON

Born in Dresden in 1858, Heinrich Zille moved to Berlin with his family when he was a child. A lithographer by trade, he became the first prominent artist to evoke the social development of the city as the tendrils of modernity reached Berlin. His instantly recognisable style depicted everyday life and real people, often featuring the bleak *Hinterhöfe* (back courtyards) around which so much of their lives revolved. Even during his lifetime Zille was acknowledged as one of the definitive documenters of his time, and since his death in 1929 his prolific photographic work has also come to be seen as a valuable historical record.

In 1903 Zille was accepted into the Berliner Secession, although he didn't really regard himself as an 'artist' as such, but more as a hard-working illustrator. When he died, thousands of Berliners turned out to pay their respects to the man whose pictures chronicled their daily lives with sharp humour and unsentimental honesty. There's a Zille Museum in the Nikolaiviertel dedicated to his life and work.

Berlin Dada

Dada was an avant-garde art movement formed in Zurich in 1916 in reaction to the horrors of WWI. It spread to Berlin in 1918 with the help of Richard Huelsenbeck, who held the first Dada event in a gallery in February that year and later produced the *First German Dada Manifesto*. Founding members included George Grosz, photomontage inventor John Heartfield and Hannah Höch, but Marcel Duchamp, Kurt Schwitters and Hans Arp were also among the many others who dabbled in Dada.

Uncompromisingly turning away from convention, Dada took an irrational, satirical and often absurdist approach that found expression not only in the visual arts but also in theatre, dance and literature. Dadaists embraced collage and montage and considered chance and spontaneity integral parts of the artistic process. In Berlin especially, there was often a political undercurrent and a tendency to shock and provoke. The First International Dada Fair in 1920, for instance, took place beneath a suspended German officer dummy with a pig's head.

Art-world honchos descend upon Berlin in late April for the annual Gallery Weekend when you can hopscotch around 40 galleries, and the Berlin Biennale, a curated forum for contemporary art held over two months in spring every other year.

Post WWII

After WWII, Berlin's art scene was as fragmented as the city itself. In the east, artists were forced to toe the 'socialist-realist' line, at least until the late 1960s when artists of the so-called Berliner Schule, including Manfred Böttcher and Harald Metzkes, sought to embrace a more interpretative and emotional form of expression inspired by the colours and aesthetic of Beckmann, Matisse, Picasso and other classical modernists. In the '70s, when conflicts of the individual in society became a prominent theme, underground galleries flourished in Prenzlauer Berg and art became a collective endeavour.

In postwar West Berlin, artists eagerly embraced abstract art. Pioneers included Zone 5, which revolved around Hans Thiemann, and surrealists Heinz Trökes and Mac Zimmermann. In the 1960s politics was a primary concern and a new style called 'critical realism' emerged, propagated by artists like Ulrich Baehr, Hans-Jürgen Diehl and Wolfgang Petrick. The 1973 movement Schule der Neuen Prächtigkeit (School of New Magnificence) had a similar approach. In the late 1970s and early 1980s, expressionism found its way back onto the canvasses of Salomé, Helmut Middendorf and Rainer Fetting, a group known as the Junge Wilde (Young Wild Ones). One of the best-known German neo-expressionist painters is Georg Baselitz, who lives in Berlin and who became internationally famous in the 1970s with his 'upside-down' works.

To keep a tab on the contemporary art scene, check out the latest shows at the city's many high-calibre galleries such as Galerie Eigen+Art or Contemporary Fine Arts and visit the collections at Hamburger Bahnhof and the Sammlung Boros.

The Present

Art aficionados will find their compass on perpetual spin in Berlin, which has developed one of the most exciting and dynamic arts scenes in Europe. With an active community of some 10,000 artists, there have been notable successes, most famously perhaps Danish-Icelandic artist Olafur Eliasson. Other major leaguers like Thomas Demand, Jonathan Meese, Via Lewandowsky, Isa Genzken, Tino Seghal, Esra Ersen, John Bock and the artist duo Ingar Dragset and Michael Elmgreen all live and work in Berlin, or at least have a second residence here.

Berlin has also emerged as a European street-art capital with some major international artists like Blu, JR and Os Gemeos leaving their mark on the city. Local top talent includes Alias and El Bocho. Street art is especially prevalent in eastern Kreuzberg (especially around the U-Bahn station Schlesisches Tor) as well as in Mitte (Haus Schwarzenberg) and at the Urban Spree gallery in Friedrichshain.

Literature & Film

Since its beginnings, Berlin's literary scene has reflected a peculiar blend of provincialism and worldliness, though Berlin didn't emerge as a centre of literature until relatively late and took until the dynamic 1920s to peak. In contrast, Berlin's pioneering role in movie history is undeniable: in 1895 Max Skladanowsky screened early films on a bioscope, in 1912 one of the world's first film studios was established in Potsdam and since 1951 Berlin has hosted a leading international film festival.

Literature

First Words

Berlin's literary history began during the 18th-century Enlightenment, an epoch dominated by humanistic ideals. A major author from this time was Gotthold Ephraim Lessing, noted for his critical works, fables and tragedies, who wrote the play *Minna von Barnhelm* (1763) in Berlin. During the Romantic period, an outgrowth of the Enlightenment, it was the poets who stood out, including Achim von Arnim, Clemens Brentano, and Heinrich von Kleist who committed suicide at Wannsee lake in 1811.

In the mid-19th century, realist literature captured the imagination of the newly emerging middle class. Theodor Fontane raised the Berlin society novel to an art form by showing both the aristocracy and the middle class mired in their societal confinements. His 1894 novel, *Effi Briest,* is among his best-known works. Naturalism, a spin-off of realism, painstakingly re-created the milieus of entire social classes. Gerhard Hauptmann's portrayal of social injustice and the harsh life of the working class won him the Nobel Prize for Literature in 1912.

Modernism & Modernity

In the 1920s Berlin became a literary hotbed, drawing writers like Alfred Döblin whose definitive *Berlin Alexanderplatz* is a stylised meander through the seamy 1920s, and Anglo-American import Christopher Isherwood whose brilliant semi-autobiographical *Berlin Stories* formed the basis of the musical and film *Cabaret.* Other notables include the political satirists Kurt Tucholsky and Erich Kästner. Many artists left Germany after the Nazis came to power, and those who stayed often kept their mouths shut and worked underground, if at all.

In West Berlin, the postwar literary revival was led by *The Tin Drum* (1958), by Nobel Prize–winner Günter Grass, which traces recent German history through the eyes of a child who refuses to grow. In the mid-1970s, a segment of the East Berlin literary scene began to detach itself slowly from the socialist party grip. Christa Wolf is one of the best and most controversial East German writers, while Heiner Müller had the distinction of being unpalatable in both Germanys. His dense, difficult works include *The Man Who Kept Down Wages* and the *Germania* trilogy of plays.

Berlin Cult Novels

....

Berlin Alexanderplatz, *Alfred Döblin (1929)*

....

Goodbye to Berlin, *Christopher Isherwood (1939)*

....

Alone in Berlin, *Hans Fallada (1947)*

....

Wall Jumper, *Peter Schneider (1983)*

....

Berlin Blues, *Sven Regener (2001)*

Recent Trends

In the 1990s, a slew of novels dealt with German reunification. Many of them are set in Berlin, including Thomas Brussig's tongue-in-cheek *Helden wie Wir* (Heroes Like Us, 1998) and Jana Hensel's *Zonenkinder* (2002), which reflects upon the loss of identity and the challenge of adapting to a new society.

Sven Regener, the frontman of the Berlin band Element of Crime, penned the hugely successful *Berlin Blues* (2001), a boozy trawl through Kreuzberg nights at the time of the fall of the Wall. The runaway success story, however, has been Russian-born author Wladimir Kaminer, whose amusing, stranger-than-fiction vignettes in *Russendisko* (Russian Disco, 2000) established both the author and his Russian disco parties firmly on the Berlin scene. Both *Berlin Blues* and *Russendisko* were made into feature films. Foreign authors too continue to be inspired by Berlin. Ian McEwan's *The Innocent* (1990) is an old-fashioned spy story set in the 1950s. The *Berlin Noir* trilogy (1989–91), by British author Philip Kerr, features a private detective solving crimes in Nazi Germany. Berlin history unfolds in a dream-like sequence in *Book of Clouds* (2009) by Chloe Aridjis. To see who gets our vote for top reads set in Berlin, see p246.

Cool places to plug into German movie history are the Museum für Film und Fernsehen at Potsdamer Platz, the Filmmuseum Potsdam and the Filmpark Babelsberg.

Film

Before 1945

The legendary UFA (Universum Film AG), one of the world's first film studios, began shooting in Potsdam, near Berlin, in 1912 and continues to churn out both German and international blockbusters in its modern incarnation as the Filmstudios Babelsberg. The 1920s and early '30s were a boom time for Berlin cinema, with the mighty UFA emerging as Germany's flagship dream factory and Marlene Dietrich's bone structure and distinctive voice seducing the world. As early as 1919, Ernst Lubitsch produced historical films and comedies such as *Madame Dubarry*, starring Pola Negri and Emil Jannings; the latter went on to win the Best Actor Award at the very first Academy Awards ceremony in 1927.

Other 1920s movies were heavily expressionistic, using stark contrast, sharp angles, heavy shadows and other distorting elements. Well-known flicks employing these techniques include *Nosferatu*, a 1922 Dracula adaptation by FW Murnau, and the ground-breaking *Metropolis* (1927), by Fritz Lang. One of the earliest seminal talkies was Josef von Sternberg's *Der Blaue Engel* (1930) starring Dietrich. After 1933, though,

---

FAMOUS FILM LOCATIONS
....

Wings of Desire (1987) The top of the Siegessäule (Victory Column) in Tiergarten is a place where angels congregate and listen to people's thoughts.

Bourne Supremacy (2004) The epic car chase where Bourne (Matt Damon) forces Russian assassin Kirill (Karl Urban) to crash his car into a concrete divider in a tunnel was filmed in the Tiergartentunnel a year and a half before its official opening in 2006.

Good Bye, Lenin! (2003) The flat where Alexander Kerner (Daniel Brühl) recreates life in East Berlin for his ailing mother is in a modern high-rise at Berolinastrasse 21.

The Lives of Others (2006) The apartment where two of the main characters, the playwright Georg Dreymann (Sebastian Koch) and his actor wife Christa-Maria Sieland (Martina Gedeck), make their home is at Wedekindstrasse 21 in Friedrichshain.

The Hunger Games: Mockingjay part 2 (2015) Scenes from the third instalment in this successful series were filmed at Tempelhof Airport.

MARLENE DIETRICH

Marlene Dietrich (1901–92) was born Marie Magdalena von Losch into a middle-class Berlin family. After acting school, she first captivated audiences as a hard-living, libertine flapper in 1920s silent movies, but quickly carved a niche as the dangerously seductive femme fatale. The 1930 talkie *Der Blaue Engel* (The Blue Angel) turned her into a Hollywood star and launched a five-year collaboration with director Josef von Sternberg.

Dietrich stayed in Hollywood after the Nazi rise to power, though Hitler reportedly promised perks and the red-carpet treatment if she moved back to Germany. She responded with an empty offer to return if she could bring along Sternberg – a Jew and no Nazi favourite. She took US citizenship in 1937 and entertained Allied soldiers on the front.

After the war, Dietrich retreated slowly from the public eye, making occasional appearances in films but mostly cutting records and performing live cabaret. Her final years were spent in Paris, bedridden and accepting few visitors, immortal in spirit as mortality caught up with her.

film-makers found their artistic freedom increasingly curtailed, and by 1939 practically the entire industry had fled to Hollywood.

Films made during the Nazi period were mostly of the propaganda variety, with brilliant if controversial Berlin-born director Leni Riefenstahl (1902–2003) greatly pushing the genre's creative envelope. Her most famous film, *Triumph of the Will,* documents the 1934 Nuremberg Nazi party rally. *Olympia,* which chronicles the 1936 Berlin Olympic Games, was another seminal work.

After 1945

Like most of the arts, film-making has generally been well funded in Berlin since 1945. During the 1970s in particular, large subsidies lured directors back to the city, including such New German Film luminaries as Rainer Werner Fassbinder, Volker Schlöndorf, Wim Wenders and Werner Herzog. It was Wenders who made the highly acclaimed *Wings of Desire* (1987), an angelic love story swooping around the old, bare noman's-land of Potsdamer Platz.

Some of the best films about the Nazi era include Wolfgang Staudte's *Die Mörder sind unter uns* (Murderers Among Us, 1946); Fassbinder's *Die Ehe der Maria Braun* (The Marriage of Maria Braun, 1979); Margarethe von Trotta's *Rosenstrasse* (2003), and Oliver Hierschbiegel's extraordinary *Der Untergang* (Downfall, 2004), depicting Hitler's final days.

The first round of postreunification flicks were light-hearted comedy dramas. A standout is the cult classic *Good Bye, Lenin!* (2003), Wolfgang Becker's witty and heart-warming tale of a son trying to re-create life in the GDR to save his sick mother. It was Florian von Donnersmarck who first trained the filmic spotlight on the darker side of East Germany, with *The Lives of Others* (2006), an Academy Award–winner that reveals the stranglehold the East German secret police (Stasi) had on ordinary people.

Today

These days, 'Germany's Hollywood' is no longer in Munich or Hamburg but in Berlin, with an average of 300 German and international productions being filmed on location and at the Filmstudios Babelsberg each year. Well-trained crews, modern studio and postproduction facilities, government subsidies and authentic 'old world' locations regularly attract such Hollywood royalty as Quentin Tarantino (*Inglorious Basterds,* 2009) and George Clooney (*Monuments Men,* 2014). Big productions filmed in 2014 included parts 3 and 4 of *The Hunger Games* and Tom Hanks' *Hologram for a King*. For our top four Berlin flicks, see p246.

Berlin's film-fan tourism generates over €330 million in annual revenue. To visit famous film locations, sign up for the multimedia 'Filmstadt Berlin' tour by video Bustour (www. videobustour.de). Sta Tours (www. sta-tours.de) take you to the homes of film legends.

Aside from the headline-grabbing Berlinale, dozens of other film festivals are held throughout the year, including the Israel Film Festival and the Too Drunk to Watch Punk festival. See http://berliner-filmfestivals.de for the schedule.

Music

Just like the city itself, Berlin's music scene is a shape-shifter, fed by the city's appetite for diversity and change. With at least 2000 active bands and dozens of indie labels, the city is Germany's undisputed music capital. About 60% of the country's music revenue is generated here, and it's where Universal Music and MTV have their European headquarters. Every September, Berlin Music Week brings together labels, agents, performers, DJs, club owners and fans for seven days of musical immersion.

The Beauty of Transgression: a Berlin Memoir, by US-born artist Danielle de Picciotto (partner of Einstürzende Neubauten bassist Andreas Hacke) beautifully captures the atmosphere and history of Berlin's creative underground from the 1980s to today.

Beginnings

For centuries Berlin was largely eclipsed by Vienna, Leipzig and other European cities when it came to music. Notable exceptions include Carl Maria von Weber's Der Freischütz (The Marksman), which premiered in 1821 at today's Konzerthaus on Gendarmenmarkt in 1821 and is considered the first important German Romantic opera. Weber's music also influenced Berlin-born Felix Mendelssohn-Bartholdy's A Midsummer Night's Dream from 1843. The same year fellow composer Giacomo Meyerbeer became Prussian General Music Director.

The Berliner Philharmoniker was established in 1882 and quickly gained international stature under Hans von Bülow and, after 1923, Wilhelm Furtwängler. After WWII, Herbert von Karajan took over the baton. In East Germany, a key figure was Hanns Eisler, composer of the country's national anthem.

The 1920s

Cabaret may have been born in 1880s Paris, but it became a wild and libidinous grown-up in 1920s Berlin with jazz the dominant sound, especially after American performer Josephine Baker's headline-grabbing performances at the Theater des Westens dressed in nothing but a banana skirt. More home-grown cabaret music came in the form of the Berlin Schlager – light-hearted songs with titles like 'Mein Papagei frisst keine harten Eier' ('My Parakeet Doesn't Eat Hard-Boiled Eggs'), which teetered on the silly and surreal. The most successful Schlager singing group was the a cappella Comedian Harmonists, who were famous for their perfect harmonies of voices that sounded like musical instruments.

Another runaway hit was *The Threepenny Opera,* written by Bertolt Brecht with music by Kurt Weill. It premiered in 1928 with such famous songs as 'Mack the Knife'. Friedrich Hollaender was another key composer in the cabaret scene. Among his most famous songs is 'Falling in Love Again', sung by Marlene Dietrich in *Der Blaue Engel.* Like so many other talents (including Weill and Brecht), Hollaender left Germany when the Nazis brought down the curtain, and continued his career in Hollywood.

The pulsating 1920s drew numerous classical musicians to Berlin, including Arnold Schönberg and Paul Hindemith, who taught at the Akademie der Künste and the Berliner Hochschule, respectively. Schönberg's atonal compositions found a following here, as did his experimentation with noise and sound effects. Hindemith explored the new medium of radio and taught a seminar on film music.

Pop, Punk & Rock before 1990

Since the end of WWII, Berlin has spearheaded many of Germany's popular music innovations. Riding the New Age wave of the late 1960s, Tangerine Dream helped to propagate the psychedelic sound, while a decade later Kreuzberg's subculture launched the punk movement at SO36 and other famous clubs. Regulars included David Bowie and Iggy Pop, who were Berlin flat buddies on Hauptstrasse in Schöneberg in the 1970s. Trying to kick a drug addiction and greatly inspired by Berlin's brooding mood, Bowie partly wrote and recorded his Berlin Trilogy (*Low, Heroes, Lodger*) at the famous Hansa Studios (p132). Check out Thomas Jerome Seabrook's *Bowie in Berlin: a New Career in a New Town* (2008) for a cool insight into those heady days.

In East Germany, access to Western rock and other popular music was restricted and few Western stars were invited to perform live. Eastern artists' own artistic freedom was greatly compromised as all lyrics had to be approved and performances were routinely monitored. Nevertheless, a slew of home-grown *Ostrock* (eastern rock) bands emerged. Some major ones like The Puhdys, Karat, Silly and City managed to get around the censors by disguising criticism in seemingly innocuous metaphors or by deliberately inserting provocative lyrics they fully expected to be deleted. All built up huge followings on both sides of the Wall.

Many nonconformists were placed under an occupational ban and prohibited from performing. Singer-songwriter Wolf Biermann became a cause célèbre when, in 1976, he was not allowed to return to the GDR from a concert series in the West despite being an avid – albeit regime-critical – socialist. When other artists rallied to his support, they too were expatriated, including Biermann's stepdaughter Nina Hagen, an East Berlin pop singer who later became a West Berlin punk pioneer. The small but vital East Berlin punk scene produced Sandow and Feeling B, members of whom went on to form the industrial metal band Rammstein in 1994, still Germany's top musical export.

Once in West Berlin, Hagen helped chart the course for Neue Deutsche Welle (German New Wave). This early '80s sound produced such Berlin bands as D.A.F, Trio, Neonbabies, Ideal and UKW, as well as Rockhaus in East Berlin. The '80s also saw the birth of Die Ärzte, whose last (and 26th) album, *auch,* was released in 2012. Einstürzende Neubauten pioneered a proto-industrial sound that transformed oil drums, electric drills and chainsaws into musical instruments. Its founder Blixa Bargeld joined Bad Seeds, helmed by Nick Cave, who spent some heroin-addled time in Berlin in the early 1980s.

Pop, Rock & Hip-Hop after 1990

Since reunification, hundreds of indie, punk, alternative and goth bands have gigged to appreciative Berlin audiences. The still active Die Ärzte, Element of Crime

---

BERLIN TRACKS

1973
Berlin (Lou Reed) Dark song about the tragedy of two star-crossed junkies.

1977
Heroes (David Bowie) Two lovers in the shadow of the 'Wall of Shame'.

1991
Zoo Station (U2) Bono embarks on a surreal journey inspired by a Berlin train station.

1995
Born to Die in Berlin (The Ramones) Drug-addled musings revealing Berlin's dark side.

2000
Dickes B (Seeed) Reggae ode to the 'Big B' (ie Berlin).

2003
Berlin Du Bist So Wunderbar (Kaiserbase) The beer commercial turned chart buster.

2007
Kreuzberg (Bloc Party) Looking for true love...

2008
Schwarz zu Blau (Peter Fox) Perfect portrait of Kottbusser Tor grit and grunge.

2013
Where are We Now? (David Bowie) Melancholic reminiscence of Bowie's time in 1970s Berlin.

and Einstürzende Neubauten were joined by other successful exports, such as alternative punk rockers Beatsteaks, and the pop-rock band Wir sind Helden, helmed by the charismatic Judith Holofernes, who released her first solo album in 2014. The Beatsteaks made headlines the same year with their latest (and seventh) studio album.

Other fine Berlin music originates from a jazz/breaks angle (electro-jazz and breakbeats, favouring lush grooves, obscure samples and chilled rhythms). Remix masters Jazzanova are top dogs of the downtempo scene. Their Sonar Kollektiv label also champions similar artists, including Micatone. Reggae-dancehall has been huge in Berlin ever since Seeed was founded in 1998. Its frontperson Peter Fox's solo album *Stadtaffe* (2008) was one of the best-selling albums in Germany and also won the 2010 Album of the Year Echo Award (the 'German Grammy'). Also commercially successful is Culcha Candela, who have essentially popified the Seeed sound and released their fifth studio album, *Flätrate,* in 2011.

Home-grown rap and hip-hop has a huge following, thanks to Sido, Fler, Bushido and Kool Savas, who co-founded Masters of Rap (MOR) in 1996. Also hugely successful are Berlin-based Casper and Marteria. K.I.Z., meanwhile, are more of a gangsta rap parody. Other famous Berlin-based artists include eccentric Canadian transplant King Khan, who fuelled the garage rock revival; the country and western band Boss Hoss, the electro-folky singer-songwriter Clara Hill, the indie rock band Gods of Blitz and the uncategorisable 17 Hippies.

Resources

Groove
(www.groove.de)

de:bug (www.
de-bug.de)

Spex (www
.spex.de)

Resident Advisor
(www.resident
advisor.net)

Techno Town

Call it techno, electro, house, minimal – electronic music is the sound of Berlin and its near-mythical club culture has defined the capital's cool factor and put it on the map of global hedonists. The sound may have been born in Detroit but it came of age in Berlin.

The seed was sown in dark and dank cellar club UFO on Köpenicker Strasse in 1988. The 'godfathers' of the Berlin sound, Dr Motte, Westbam and Kid Paul, played their first gigs here, mostly sweat-driven acid house all-night raves. It was Motte who came up with the idea to take the party to the street with a truck, loud beats and a bunch of friends dancing behind it – and the Love Parade was born (it peaked in 1999 with 1.5 million people swarming Berlin's streets).

The Berlin Wall's demise, and the vacuum of artistic freedom it created, catapulted techno out of the underground. The associated euphoria, sudden access to derelict and abandoned spaces in eastern Berlin and lack of control by the authorities were all defining factors in making Berlin a techno mecca. In 1991 the techno-sonic gang followed UFO founder Dimitri Hegemann to Tresor, which launched camouflage-sporting DJ Tanith along with trance pioneer Paul van Dyk. Today, the Tresor label is still a seminal brand representing Jeff Mills, Blake Baxter and Cristian Vogel, among many others.

Paul Kalkbrenner's 2008 semi-autobiographical *Berlin Calling* was the first mature film about the techno scene in Berlin.

Key label BPitch Control, founded by Ellen Allien in 1999, launched the careers of Modeselektor, Apparat, Sascha Funke and Paul Kalkbrenner. Another heavyweight is the collective Get Physical, which includes the dynamic duo M.A.N.D.Y. who fuse house and electro with minimal and funk to create a highly danceable sound. The charmingly named Shitkatapult, founded in 1997 by Marco Haas (aka T.Raumschmiere), is focused on minimalist styles and counts Apparat and Daniel Meteo among its artists.

Foreign artists too have influenced the Berlin scene, including the provocative Canadian songster and performance artist Peaches, UK–Canadian techno innovator Richie Hawtin and Chilean minimalist master Ricardo Villalobos.

Survival Guide

Transport

ARRIVING IN BERLIN

Most visitors arrive in Berlin by air. Since the opening of the new Berlin Brandenburg Airport has been delayed indefinitely, flights continue to land at the city's Tegel and Schönefeld airports.

Lufthansa and practically all other major European airlines and low-cost carriers (including easyJet, Ryanair and Germanwings) operate direct flights to Berlin from throughout Europe. There are a few direct flights from US gateway cities such as Miami and New York, but normally travel from outside Europe involves a change of planes in another European city such as Frankfurt or Amsterdam.

Depending on your departure point, travel to Berlin by train or bus is a viable alternative. Coming from London, for instance, you could be in Berlin in as little as nine hours by taking a combination of the Eurostar and German high-speed trains.

Flights, cars and tours can be booked online at lonelyplanet.com.

Tegel Airport

Tegel Airport (TXL; ☑030-6091 1150; www.berlin-airport.de) is in the northwestern suburb of Tegel, about 8km northwest of Bahnhof Zoo and 13km northwest of Alexanderplatz. It is only served directly by bus. Buy tickets from official transport staff, vending machines at the bus stop or directly from the bus driver (change given).

Bus

➠ The TXL express bus connects Tegel to Alexanderplatz (€2.60, Tariff AB; 40 minutes) via Hauptbahnhof (central train station) and Unter den Linden every 10 minutes.

➠ For the City West around Bahnhof Zoologischer Garten take bus X9 (€2.60, Tariff AB; 20 minutes), which also runs at 10-minute intervals.

➠ Bus 109 heads to U-/S-Bahn station Zoologischer Garten and is slower and useful only if you're headed somewhere along Kurfürstendamm (€2.60, Tariff AB; 20 to 30 minutes).

U-Bahn

➠ The U-Bahn station closest to the airport is Jakob-Kaiser-Platz, which is served by bus 109 and X9. From here, the U7 takes you directly to Schöneberg and Kreuzberg.

➠ Trips cost €2.60 (Tariff AB).

S-Bahn

The closest S-Bahn station is Jungfernheide, which is a stop on the S41/S42 (the Ringbahn, or circle line). It is linked to the airport by bus X9. Another Ringbahn station, Beusselstrasse, is also a stop on the TXL bus route.

CLIMATE CHANGE & TRAVEL

Every form of transport that relies on carbon-based fuel generates CO_2, the main cause of human-induced climate change. Modern travel is dependent on aeroplanes, which might use less fuel per kilometre per person than most cars but travel much greater distances. The altitude at which aircraft emit gases (including CO_2) and particles also contributes to their climate change impact. Many websites offer 'carbon calculators' that allow people to estimate the carbon emissions generated by their journey and, for those who wish to do so, to offset the impact of the greenhouse gases emitted with contributions to portfolios of climate-friendly initiatives throughout the world. Lonely Planet offsets the carbon footprint of all staff and author travel.

Taxi

Taxi rides cost about €20 to Zoologischer Garten and €25 to Alexanderplatz and take 30 to 45 minutes. There's a €0.50 surcharge for trips originating at Tegel airport.

Schönefeld Airport

Schönefeld Airport (SXF; ☎030-6091 1150; www.berlin-airport.de) is located about 22km southeast of Alexanderplatz and directly served by S-Bahn and regional trains. Travel to the city center requires a transport ticket covering zones ABC (€3.20) available from vending machines at the station (cash and debit cards, change given). Tickets must be validated before boarding.

S-Bahn & Regional Trains

➡ The airport train station is 400m from the terminals. Free shuttle buses run every 10 minutes; walking takes five to 10 minutes.

➡ Airport-Express trains go to central Berlin twice hourly. Note: these are regular Deutsche Bahn regional trains denoted as RE7 and RB14 in timetables. The journey takes 20 minutes to Alexanderplatz and 30 minutes to Zoologischer Garten.

➡ The S-Bahn S9 runs every 20 minutes and is slower, but useful if you're headed to Friedrichshain (eg Ostkreuz, 30 minutes) or Prenzlauer Berg (eg Schönhauser Allee, 45 minutes).

➡ For the Messe (trade fair grounds), take the S45 to Südkreuz and change to the S41 to Messe Nord/ICC. Trains run every 20 minutes and the journey takes 55 minutes.

U-Bahn

Schönefeld is not served by the U-Bahn. The nearest station, Rudow, is about a 10-minute ride on bus X7

or bus 171 from the airport. From Rudow, the U7 takes you straight into town. This connection is useful if you're headed for Neukölln or Kreuzberg. You will need an ABC transport ticket (€3.20).

Taxi

A cab ride to central Berlin averages €40 and takes 40 minutes to an hour.

Berlin Brandenburg Airport

The opening of Berlin's new central airport, located about 24km southeast of the city center, next to Schönefeld airport, has been delayed indefinitely. Check www.berlin-airport.de for the latest.

Hauptbahnhof (Central Train Station)

Berlin's **Hauptbahnhof** (www.berlin-hauptbahnhof.de; Europaplatz, Washingtonplatz; S Hauptbahnhof, R Hauptbahnhof) is in the heart of the city, just north of the Government Quarter and within walking distance of major sights and hotels. From here, the U-Bahn, S-Bahn, trams and buses provide links to all parts of town. Taxi ranks are located outside the north exit (Europaplatz) and the south exit (Washingtonplatz).

➡ Buy tickets in the Reisezentrum (travel center) located between tracks 14 and 15 on the first upper level (OG1), online at www.bahn.de and, for shorter distances, at station vending machines.

➡ The left-luggage office (€5 per piece, per 24 hours) is behind the Reisebank currency exchange on level OG1, opposite the Reisezentrum.

Zentraler Omnibusbahnhof (Central Coach Station)

Most long-haul buses arrive at the **Zentraler Omnibusbahnhof** (ZOB; ☎030-302 5361; www.iob-berlin.de; Masurenallee 4-6; S Kaiserdamm) near the trade fair grounds on the western city edge.

➡ Eurolines is the umbrella organisation of dozens of long-haul operators connecting 500 destinations across Europe.

➡ The closest U-Bahn station is Kaiserdamm, about 400m north and served by the U2 line, which takes you to Bahnhof Zoologischer Garten in about 8 minutes and to Alexanderplatz in 28 minutes. Tickets cost €2.60.

➡ The nearest S-Bahn station is Messe Süd/ICC about 200m east of ZOB. It is served by the Ringbahn (circle line) S41/42, which is handy if you're headed for such districts as Prenzlauer

Berg, Friedrichshain or Neukölln. You need an AB ticket (€2.60).

➡ Budget about €14 for a taxi to the western city centre and €22 to the eastern city centre.

GETTING AROUND BERLIN

Berlin's extensive and efficient public transport system is operated by **BVG** (✆030-194 49; www.bvg.de) and consists of U-Bahn (underground, or subway), S-Bahn (light rail), buses and trams. For trip planning and general information, call the 24-hour hotline or check the website.

The U-Bahn is usually the most efficient way of getting around town, but the S-Bahn comes in handy for covering longer distances, while buses, trams and bicycles are useful for shorter journeys.

U-Bahn

➡ The U-Bahn is the quickest way of getting around Berlin. Lines (referred to as U1, U2 etc in this book) operate from 4am until about 12.30am and throughout the night on Friday, Saturday and public holidays (all lines except the U4 and U55). From Sunday to Thursday, night buses take over in the interim.

➡ Individual reviews indicate the closest station.

S-Bahn & Regional Trains

➡ S-Bahn trains (S1, S2 etc) don't run as frequently as the U-Bahn, but make fewer stops and thus are useful for covering longer distances. Trains operate from 4am to 12.30am and all night on Friday, Saturday and public holidays.

➡ Individual reviews indicate the closest station.

➡ Destinations further afield are served by RB and RE trains. You'll need an ABC or **Deutsche Bahn** (✆01806 99 66 33; www.bahn.de) ticket to use these trains.

Bus

➡ Buses are slow but useful for sightseeing on the cheap (especially routes 100 and 200). They run frequently between 4.30am and 12.30am. Night buses (N19, N23, etc) take over after 12.30am.

➡ MetroBuses, designated M19, M41 etc, operate 24/7.

Tram

Trams (*Strassenbahn*) operate almost exclusively in the eastern districts. Those designated M1, M2 etc, run 24/7. A useful line is the

TICKETS & PASSES

➡ The transport network is divided into fare zones A, B and C with tickets available for zones AB, BC or ABC. One ticket is valid for travel on all forms of public transportation.

➡ Most trips within Berlin require an AB ticket, which is valid for two hours (interruptions and transfers allowed, but not round-trips). Notable exceptions include trips to Potsdam and Schönefeld Airport, where the ABC tariff applies.

➡ Children aged six to 14 qualify for reduced (*ermässigt*) rates; kids under six travel free.

➡ Tickets are available from bus drivers, vending machines at U- or S-Bahn stations (English instructions available), vending machines aboard trams and from station offices and news kiosks sporting the yellow BVG logo. Some vending machines accept debit cards. Bus drivers and tram vending machines only take cash.

➡ Single tickets, except those bought from bus drivers and in trams, must be validated (stamped) at station platform entrances. Anyone caught without a valid ticket must pay a €40 on-the-spot fine.

➡ If you're taking more than two trips in a day, a day pass (*Tageskarte*) will save you money. It's valid for unlimited rides on all forms of public transport until 3am the following day. The group day pass (*Kleingruppen-Tageskarte*) is valid for up to five people traveling together.

➡ For short trips, buy the *Kurzstreckenticket,* which is good for three stops on the U-Bahn and S-Bahn or six on any bus or tram; no changes allowed.

➡ For longer stays, consider the seven-day pass (*Wochenkarte*), which is transferable and lets you take along another adult and up to three children aged six to 14 for free after 8pm Monday to Friday and all day on Saturday, Sunday and holidays.

M1, which links Prenzlauer Berg with Museum Island via Hackescher Markt. Each review mentions the nearest stop.

Taxi

➡ You can order a **taxi** (☎030-20 20 20, 030-44 33 11) by phone, flag one down or pick one up at a rank. At night, cars often line up outside theatres, clubs and other venues.

➡ Flag fall is €3.40, then it's €1.79 per kilometre up to 7km and €1.28 for each additional kilometre. There's a surcharge of €1.50 if paying by credit or debit card, but none for night trips. Bulky luggage that does not fit into the trunk is charged at €1 per piece.

➡ Tip about 10%.

➡ Sample fares: Alexanderplatz to Zoologischer Garten is €18; Kollwitzplatz to Gendarmenmarkt is €11; East Side Gallery to Brandenburger Tor is €16; and the Jewish Museum to Hackescher Markt is €11.

A great way to cover short distances quickly is the *Kurzstreckentarif* (short-trip rate), which lets up to four people ride in a cab for up to 2km for a mere €4. This only works if you flag down a moving taxi and tell the driver you want a *'Kurzstrecke'* before he or she has activated the regular metre. If you want to continue past 2km, regular rates apply to the entire trip. Passengers love it, but cabbies don't, and there's been talk about tossing the tariff altogether.

Bicycle

Bicycles are handy both for in-depth explorations of local neighbourhoods and for getting across town. More than 650km of dedicated bike paths make getting around less intimidating even for riders who are not experienced or confident. Do watch out for tram tracks, though.

Bicycles may be taken aboard designated U-Bahn and S-Bahn carriages (usually the last ones; look for the bicycle logo) as well as on night buses (Sunday to Thursday only) and trams. You need a separate bicycle ticket called a *Fahrradkarte* (€1.70). Taking a bike on regional trains (RE, RB) costs €3.20 per trip or €6 per day.

The websites www.bbbike.de and www.vmz-info.de are handy for route planning.

TRAVEL FARES

TICKET TYPE	AB (€)	BC (€)	ABC (€)
Einzelfahrschein (single)	2.60	2.90	3.20
Ermässigt (reduced single)	1.60	2	2.30
Tageskarte (day pass)	6.70	7	7.20
Kleingruppen-Tageskarte (group day pass)	16.20	16.50	16.70
Wochenkarte (7-day pass)	28.80	29.70	35.60

Hire

Many hostels and hotels have guest bicycles, often for free or a nominal fee. If not, rental stations are practically at every corner. These include not only the expected (bike shops, gas stations) but also convenience stores, cafes and even clothing boutiques.

Prices start at €6 per day, although the definition of 'day' can mean anything from eight hours to 24 hours. A cash or credit-card deposit and/or photo ID is usually required.

The following outfits are recommended. Call or check the website for branches and be sure to book ahead, especially in summer.

Fahrradstation (☎0180 510 8000; www.fahrradstation.com) Large fleet of quality bikes, English-speaking staff and seven branches in Mitte, Kreuzberg, Charlottenburg, Prenzlauer Berg and Potsdam. Bike rentals start at €15 per day or €50 per week. The Friedrichstrasse branch rents e-bikes. Offers online bookings.

Prenzlberger Orange Bikes (Map p342; ☎030-4435 6852; www.orange-bikes.de; Kollwitzstrasse 37, Prenzlauer Berg; per 24hr €7; 🕐noon-6pm Apr-Nov; [S]Senefelderplatz) The cheapest bike rentals in town with proceeds going to social projects for kids and youth.

Lila Bike (Map p342; ☎0176 9957 9089; www.berlin-citytours-by-bike.de; Schönhauser Allee 41; first 24hr €8, additional 24hr €5; 🕐10am-8pm Mon-Sat, 1-8pm Sun, closed 3-4pm; [S] Eberswalder Strasse) Small outfit in Prenzlauer Berg; great prices.

Car & Motorcycle

Driving in Berlin is more hassle than it's worth, especially since parking is expensive and hard to find. If you're bringing in your own car, be aware that central Berlin (defined as the area bounded by the S-Bahn circle line) is a restricted low-emission zone, meaning that all cars entering (yes, even foreign ones) must display a special sticker called *Umweltplakette* . Drivers caught without one will be fined €40. Buy one at www.umwelt-plakette.de.

Hire

All the big internationals maintain branches at the airports, major train stations

CALL A BIKE

Call a Bike (☑ 069-4272 7722; www.callabike.de) is an automated cycle-hire scheme offered by Deutsche Bahn (German Rail). In order to use it, you need a credit card to pre-register for free online or at one of the dozens of docking stations scattered around the central districts. The website has a map but, alas, it is in German only at this point. Machines at the docking stations, though, have English instructions.

Once you're set up, select a bike and call the phone number marked on it in order to release the lock. When you're done, you must drop it at another docking station. The base fee for renting a bike is €0.08 per minute up to a maximum of €15 per 24 hours. Fees are charged to your credit card.

Hiring a Bike

Once you've signed up, picking up a bike is actually pretty straightforward.

Unlocking a bike at a terminal Touch the screen and identify yourself with your credit, debit or customer card. Select the number of bicycles (maximum of two per customer). Go to the assigned bicycle and tap on the lock display to open the lock.

Unlocking a bike by phone Select a bike and call the red-rimmed phone number on the lock. Confirm your request. Tap on the lock display to open the lock.

Interrupting your trip Lock the bike. To unlock it, you need your personal ID code, which you'll be given after registering. It also displays briefly on your lock when locking the bike.

Returning the bike Return the bike at any rental station. Lock the rear wheel and push the button on the right side of the lock. Wait for confirmation.

and throughout town. Book in advance for the best rates.

Taking your rental vehicle into an Eastern European country, such as the Czech Republic or Poland, is often a no-no; check in advance if you're planning a side-trip from Berlin.

TOURS

Walking Tours

Several English-language walking-tour companies run introductory spins that take in both blockbuster and offbeat sights, plus themed tours (eg Third Reich, Cold War, Sachsenhausen, Potsdam). Tours don't require reservations – just show up at one of the meeting points. Since these change quite frequently, keep an eye out for flyers in hotel or hostel lobbies or at tourist offices; alternatively, contact the companies directly.

Alternative Berlin Tours (☑0162 819 8264; www.alternativeberlin.com) Pay-

what-you-want twice-daily subculture tours that get beneath the skin of the city, plus a street-art workshop, an alternative pub crawl and the hardcore 'Twilight Tour'.

Berlin Walks (☑030-301 9194; www.berlinwalks.de; adult €12-15, concession €10-12) Berlin's longest-running English-language walking tour company also does tours of Sachsenhausen Concentration Camp and Potsdam.

Brewer's Berlin Tours (☑0177 388 1537; www.brewersberlintours.com; adult/concession €15/12) Local experts run an epic all-day Best of Berlin tour and a shorter donation-based Berlin Express tour.

Insider Tour Berlin (☑030-692 3149; www.insidertour.com; tours €12-15, concession €10-12) Insightful general and themed tours of Berlin, plus day trips to Dresden and Potsdam, and a pub crawl.

New Berlin Tours (www.newberlintours.com; adult €12-14, concession €10-13)

Entertaining and informative city spins by the pioneers of the donation-based 'free tour' and the pub crawl.

Bicycle Tours

The companies listed below both get top marks for their various English-language tours. Reservations are recommended.

Berlin on Bike (Map p342; ☑030-4373 9999; www.berlinonbike.de; Knaackstrasse 97; tours incl bike adult/concession €19/17; ⊗ English tours 11am Mar-Oct; Ⓢ Eberswalder Strasse) This company offers a general city tour (Berlin's Best) and a Berlin Wall tour, as well as half a dozen themed tours (eg Kreuzberg, Berlin by Night, Future Berlin) available on request. Reservations recommended.

Fat Tire Bike Tours (Map p320; ☑030-2404 7991; www.fattirebiketours.com/berlin; Panoramastrasse 1a; adult/concession €24/22;

Ⓢ Alexanderplatz, Ⓡ Alexanderplatz) Has classic city, Nazi-era and Berlin Wall tours as well as a 'Raw: Berlin Exposed' tour that gets under the city's urban, subcultural skin. Tours leave from the TV Tower main entrance. E-bike tours available. Reservations recommended (and for some tours required).

Boat Tours

Tours range from one-hour spins around Museumsinsel (from €12) to longer trips to Schloss Charlottenburg and beyond (from €15). Young children usually travel for free; those under 14 and seniors get 50% off. Most tours offer live commentary in English and German. **Stern und Kreisschiffahrt** (☏ 030-536 3600; www.sternundkreis.de; Ⓡ Treptower Park) is one of the major operators. The main season runs from April to mid-October with a limited schedule in winter.

Bus Tours

Colourful buses tick off the key sights on two-hour loops with basic taped commentary in eight languages. During the day, you're free to get off and back on at any of the stops, paying only once. Buses depart roughly every 15 or 30 minutes between 10am and 5pm or 6pm daily; tickets can be purchased on board and cost from €10 to €20 (half-price for teens, free for children). Traditional tours where you don't get off the bus, combination boat and bus tours as well as trips to Potsdam and the Spreewald are also available. Look for flyers in the hotel lobby or at tourist offices.

Speciality Tours

Berlin Music Tours (☏ 030-3087 5633; www.musictours-berlin.com; bus/walking tours in German €29/12; ☺ bus tour 12.30pm Sat, walking tour 2pm Sun) BMT's bus tour gives you the lowdown on the last 40 years of Berlin's music history – from Iggy and Bowie to U2 and Rammstein, cult clubs to the Love Parade – along with the scoop on who's rocking the city right now. Also available: walking tours, private minibus tours and Hansa Studios tours. English tours on request (price depends on group size). Reservations essential.

Berlinagenten (☏ 030-4372 0701; www.berlinagenten.com) Get a handle on all facets of Berlin's urban lifestyle with an insider private guide who opens doors to hot and/or secret bars, boutiques, restaurants, clubs, private homes and sights. Dozens of culinary, cultural and lifestyle tours on offer, including the bestselling 'Gastro Rallye' for the ultimate foodie. Prices depend on group size.

Berliner Unterwelten (☏ 030-4991 0517; www.berliner-unterwelten.de; adult/concession €10/8; ☺ English tours 1pm Mon & 11am Thu-Mon year-round, 11am Wed Mar-Nov, 1pm Wed-Sun Apr-Oct; Ⓢ Gesundbrunnen, Ⓡ Gesundbrunnen) Pick your way past heavy steel doors, hospital beds and filter systems on a tour of a WWII underground bunker. Buy tickets at the kiosk next to the south exit of the Gesundbrunnen U-Bahn station.

Sta Tours Berlin (☏ 030-3010 5151; www.sta-tours.de; for groups of up to 6, per person €35; ☺ by appointment) If you're a German-film buff, first visit the **Museum für Film**

und Fernsehen (☏ 030-300 9030; www.deutsche-kinemathek.de; Potsdamer Strasse 2; adult/concession €7/4.50; ☺ 10am-6pm Tue, Wed & Fri-Sun, to 8pm Thu; ▣ 200, Ⓢ Potsdamer Platz, Ⓡ Potsdamer Platz), then let celluloid expert Birgit Wetzig-Zalkind take you on two-hour van tours of the places where Billy Wilder, Leni Riefenstahl, Marlene Dietrich and other legends lived and played.

Trabi Safari (Map p322; ☏ 030-2759 2273; www.trabi-safari.de; Zimmerstrasse 97; per person €34-60, Wall Ride €79-89; Ⓢ Kochstrasse) Catch the *Good Bye, Lenin!* vibe on tours of Berlin's classic sights or the 'Wild East' as you drive or ride as a passenger in a convoy of GDR-made Trabant cars (Trabi) with live commentary (in English by prior arrangement) piped into your vehicle. The two-hour Wall Ride has you steering towards Berlin Wall–related stops, or jump aboard Mustang Safaris around the former American sector in West Berlin in a classic Mustang. Drivers need to bring their licence.

videoBustour (Map p322; ☏ 030-4402 4450; www.videobustour.de; Unter den Linden 40; adult/concession €19.50/16.50; ☺ Berlin Past and Present 11am Sat, themed tours 1.30pm Sat; ▣ 100, 200, Ⓢ Friedrichstrasse) The past moves into the present as you're shown historical footage and photographs on a TV screen while passing Berlin's famous landmarks in a bus. Four themed tours – Movie City Berlin, the Golden Twenties, Famous Crime Scenes and Hitler's Berlin – run on alternating Saturdays. English tours upon request.

Directory A–Z

Customs Regulations

➜ Goods brought in and out of countries within the EU incur no additional taxes provided duty has been paid somewhere within the EU and the goods are only for personal use.

➜ Duty-free shopping is only available if you're leaving the EU.

Discount Cards

Berlin Welcome Card (www.berlin-welcomecard.de; travel in AB zones 48/72hr €18.50/25.50, 48hr incl Potsdam & up to 3 children under 15yr €20.50, 72hr incl Museum Island €40.50) Entitles you to unlimited public transport and up to 50% discount to 200 sights, attractions and tours for periods of two, three or five days. Sold online, at tourist offices, at U-Bahn and S-Bahn vending machines, on buses, and at BVG offices.

CityTourCard (☑030-2500 2379; www.citytourcard.com; travel in AB zone 48hr/72hr/5 days €16.90/23.90/30.90) This card provides unlimited public transport and a minimum 15% discount at 40 partner sights, attractions and tours, for two, three or five days. Available online, at BVG offices, and at U-Bahn and S-Bahn vending machines.

Museumspass Berlin (www.visitberlin.de; adult/concession €24/12) Buys admission to the permanent exhibits of about 50 museums for three consecutive days, including big draws like the Pergamonmuseum. Sold at tourist offices and participating museums.

Electricity

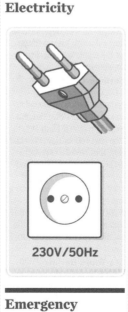

230V/50Hz

Emergency

➜ **Ambulance** (☑112)
➜ **Fire Department** (☑112)
➜ **Police** (☑110)

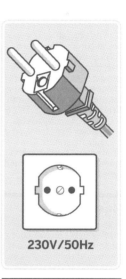

230V/50Hz

Internet Access

➜ Many hotels, hostels and *pensions* (B&Bs) have wireless internet access (called W-LAN; pronounced vay-lan), DSL or an internet corner for their guests, often at no charge. If they don't, ask staff to direct you to the nearest internet cafe.

➜ At some hotels or hostels wi-fi may be limited to some rooms and/or public areas. Some hotels (usually top-end and business hotels) charge as much as €25 per day for wi-fi access.

➜ There are now around 100 public hotspots for free 30-minute access scattered around the city. For locations, check www.publicwifi.de. To pin down private ones, try www.hotspot-locations.com.

➡ Numerous cafes and bars tout free wi-fi hotspots. If necessary, you'll be given a password when placing your order.

➡ Internet cafes tend to have the lifespan of a fruit fly, so we have not listed any. If you need one, ask at your hotel.

Legal Matters

➡ By law you must possess some form of photographic identification, such as your passport, national identity card or driver's licence.

➡ The permissible blood-alcohol limit is 0.05% for drivers and 0.16% for bicyclists. Anyone caught exceeding this amount is subject to stiff fines, a confiscated licence or even jail time. Drinking in public is not illegal, but be discreet about it.

➡ Cannabis possession is a criminal offence and punishable with fines and jail time. However, possession of small amounts of marijuana is rarely punished. Those caught with larger amounts or any amount of 'harder' recreational drugs like heroin or cocaine are less likely to avoid legal consequences. Searches upon entering clubs are common.

➡ If arrested, you have the right to make a phone call and are presumed innocent until proven guilty, although you may be held in custody until trial. If you don't know a lawyer, contact your embassy.

Medical Services

➡ The standard of healthcare is high and there are many English-speaking doctors in Berlin. **Call-a-Doc** (☎01805 321 303; www.calladoc.com; 🕑24hr) can make free nonemergency physician referrals in English.

➡ The most central hospital with a 24-hour emergency room is the renowned **Charité Mitte** (☎030-450 50; www.charite.de; Charitéplatz 1; 🕑24hr; 🚌147, [S]Oranienburger Tor).

➡ If you are a citizen of the EU, the European Health Insurance Card (EHIC) entitles you to reduced-cost or free medical treatment for illness or injury, but not emergency repatriation home. Check with your local health authorities for information on how to obtain an EHIC. Non-EU citizens should check if a similar reciprocal agreement exists between their country and Germany, or if their policy at home provides worldwide healthcare coverage.

➡ If you need to buy travel health insurance, be sure to get a policy that also covers emergency repatriation. While some plans pay doctors or hospitals directly, note that many healthcare providers may still demand immediate payment from nonlocals. Most do not accept credit cards.

➡ There are no vaccinations required to visit Germany.

Pharmacies

➡ German chemists (drugstores, *Drogerien*) do not sell any kind of medication, not even aspirin. Even over-the-counter *(rezeptfrei)* medications for minor health concerns, such as a cold or upset stomach, are only available at a pharmacy *(Apotheke)*. For more serious conditions, you will need to produce a prescription *(Rezept)* from a licensed physician. If you take regular medication, be sure to bring a full supply for your entire trip, as the same brand may not be available in Germany.

➡ The names and addresses of pharmacies open after hours (these rotate) are posted in every pharmacy window, or call ☎011 41 for a recorded message of after-hour pharmacies.

Money

ATMs & Debit Cards

➡ The easiest way to obtain cash is by using your debit (bank) card at an ATM (*Geldautomat*) linked to international networks such as Cirrus, Plus, Star and Maestro. ATMs are ubiquitous and accessible 24/7.

➡ Many ATM cards double as debit cards and many shops, hotels, restaurants and other businesses accept them as payment. Most places use the 'chip and pin' system: instead

IMPORT RESTRICTIONS

ITEM	DUTY-FREE	TAX & DUTY PAID WITHIN EU
Tobacco	200 cigarettes or 100 cigarillos or 50 cigars or 250g tobacco	800 cigarettes or 200 cigars or 400 cigarillos or 1kg tobacco
Spirits & liqueurs	1L spirits or 2L fortified wine	10L spirits or 20L fortified wine
Beer & wine	16L beer, 4L wine	110L beer, 90L wine (with no more than 60L sparkling wine)
Other goods	Up to a value of €300 if arriving by land or €430 if arriving by sea or air (€175 for under 15yr)	n/a

PRACTICALITIES

➜ **Currency** Euro (€)

➜ **Clothing** For women's clothing sizes, a German size 36 equals a size 6 in the US and a size 10 in the UK, then increases in increments of two, making size 38 a US 8 and UK 12, and so on.

➜ **DVD** Germany is in region code 2.

➜ **Laundry** There are dry cleaners (*Reinigung*) and self-service laundrettes (*Waschsalon*) scattered all over Berlin. Most hostels have washing machines for guest use, while many hotels offer a cleaning service, although this can be pricey.

➜ **Newspapers & Magazines** Widely read local dailies are *Tagesspiegel, Berliner Zeitung, Berliner Morgenpost* and *taz*.

➜ **Weights & Measures** Metric system.

of signing, you enter your PIN. If your card isn't chip-and-pin enabled, you may be able to sign the receipt – ask first.

Cash

Cash is king in Germany, so always carry some with you and plan to pay with cash in most places.

Changing Money

➜ Currency exchange offices (*Wechselstuben*) can be found at airports and major train stations.

➜ **Reisebank** (www.reisebank.de) Zoologischer Garten, Hauptbahnhof, Ostbahnhof and Bahnhof Friedrichstrasse.

➜ **Euro-Change** (www.euro-change.de) Zoologischer Garten and Alexanderplatz stations; Friedrichstrasse 80.

➜ Reisebank keeps slightly longer hours (at least until 8pm); on Sundays, the airports are your only option.

Credit Cards

➜ Credit cards are becoming more widely accepted (especially in hotels and upmarket shops and restaurants), but it's best not to assume that you'll be able to use one – enquire first.

➜ Visa and MasterCard are more commonly accepted than American Express.

➜ Some places require a minimum purchase with credit card use.

Tipping

➜ Restaurant bills always include a *Bedienung* (service charge), but most people add 5% or 10% unless the service was truly abhorrent. The same tip applies for bar tabs.

➜ It's considered rude to leave the tip on the table. Instead, tell the server the total amount you want to pay (for instance, if the bill is €28, say €30). If you don't want change back, say '*Stimmt so*' (that's fine).

➜ Tip hotel cleaning staff €1 to €2 per day, and porters the same amount per bag. Toilet attendants expect €0.20 to €0.50.

➜ Tip taxi drivers 10%, always rounding off to a full euro.

Opening Hours

Standard opening hours:

Banks 9.30am-6pm Mon-Fri, some to 1pm Sat

Bars 6pm-1am or later

Boutiques 11am-7pm Mon-Fri, to 4pm Sat

Cafes 8am-8pm

Clubs 11pm-5am or later

Post Offices 9am-6pm Mon-Fri, to 1pm Sat

Shops 10am-8pm Mon-Sat

Restaurants 11am-11pm

Supermarkets 8am-8pm or later, some 24hr

Post

➜ You can buy stamps at post offices and at convenience stores offering postal services. The rate for standard-sized letters up to 20g is €0.60 to destinations within Germany and €0.75 elsewhere in the world. For other rates, see www.deutschepost.de.

➜ Mail takes a day or two within Germany, three to five days to the USA and European destinations, and five to seven to Australasia.

Central post office branches with late hours:

Charlottenburg (Map p338; Europa Presse Center, Tauentzienstrasse 9; ⏰7.30am-10.30pm; Ⓢ Zoologischer Garten, Ⓡ Zoologischer Garten)

Mitte (Map p320; Grunerstrasse 20; ⏰8am-9pm Mon-Sat; Ⓢ Alexanderplatz, Ⓡ Alexanderplatz)

Public Holidays

Shops, banks and public and private offices are closed on the following *gesetzliche Feiertage* (public holidays):

Neujahrstag (New Year's Day) 1 January

Ostern (Easter) March/April; Good Friday, Easter Sunday and Easter Monday

Christi Himmelfahrt (Ascension Day) Forty days after Easter, always on a Thursday

Maifeiertag (Labour Day) 1 May

Pfingsten (Whitsun/Pentecost Sunday and Monday) May/June

Tag der Deutschen Einheit (Day of German Unity) 3 October

Reformationstag (Reformation Day; Brandenburg state only) 31 October

Weihnachtstag (Christmas Day) 25 December

Zweiter Weihnachtstag (Boxing Day) 26 December

Safe Travel

➡ Travellers will rarely get tricked, cheated or conned simply because they're tourists. Berlin is one of the safest and most tolerant of European cities. Walking about at night, even for a woman alone, is not usually dangerous. Of course, you should keep your wits about you, just as you would at home. Always carry enough cash for a cab ride back to wherever you're staying.

➡ If people on the street approach you for cash, they are generally not dangerous – just ignore them. The same goes for the hard-up types standing near U-Bahn entrances trying to sell you used tickets for a few cents. Don't fall for it – it's illegal and most likely the ticket is no longer valid.

➡ On the U-Bahn or S-Bahn, you'll encounter homeless folks selling street newspapers (called *Motz* or *Strassenfeger*) or asking for a small donation. Buskers are also quite common. You're free to give or not to give.

Taxes & Refunds

Prices for goods and services include a value-added tax (VAT; *Mehrwertsteuer*), which is 19% for regular goods and 7% for food and books. If your permanent residence is outside the EU, you can have a large portion of the VAT refunded, provided you shop at a store displaying the 'Tax-free for tourists' sign and obtain a tax-free form for your purchase from the sales clerk. At the airport, show this form, your unused goods and the receipt to a customs official before checking your luggage. The customs official will stamp the form, which you can then take straight to the cash refund office at the airport

Telephone

Mobile Phones

➡ Mobile phones (*Handys*) work on GSM900/1800. If your home country uses a different standard, you'll need a multiband GSM phone in Germany. Check your contract for exorbitant roaming charges.

➡ If you have an unlocked phone that works in Germany, you may be able to cut down on roaming charges by buying a prepaid, rechargeable local SIM card. The cheapest and least complicated of these are sold at discount supermarkets such as Aldi and Lidl. Top-up cards are also available at these stores as well as at convenience stores.

➡ Calls made from landlines to German mobile phone numbers are charged at higher rates than those to other landlines. Incoming calls on mobile numbers are free.

Phone Codes

German phone numbers consist of an area code, which starts with 0, and the local number. The area code for Berlin is ☑030. If dialling a Berlin number from a Berlin-based landline, you don't need to dial the area code.

If you're using a landline outside Berlin, or a mobile phone, you must dial it.

Calling Berlin from abroad Dial your country's international access code, then ☑49 (Germany's country code), then the area code (dropping the initial 0, so just ☑30) and the local number.

Calling internationally from Berlin Dial ☑00 (the international access code), then the country code, then the area code (without the zero if there is one) and the local number.

Phonecards

➡ Most public payphones only work with Deutsche Telecom (DT) phonecards, available in denominations of €5, €10 and €20 from DT stores, post offices, newsagents and tourist offices.

➡ For long-distance and international calls, prepaid calling cards issued by other providers tend to offer better rates. Those sold at Reisebank (www. reisebank.de) branches are reliable and offer fairly competitive rates. Landline calls within Germany and to the UK, for instance, are charged at €0.05 per minute. Calls made from mobile phones or phone booths cost an extra €0.23 per minute.

Time

Clocks in Germany are set to central European time (GMT/UTC plus one hour).

SMOKING REGULATIONS

➡ Except in designated areas, smoking is not allowed in public buildings or at airports and train stations.

➡ Smoking is not allowed in restaurants and clubs unless there is a completely separate and enclosed room set aside for smokers.

➡ Owners of single-room bars and pubs smaller than 75 sq metres, who don't serve anything to eat and keep out customers under 18 years of age, may choose to be a '*Raucherbar*', ie allow smoking. The venue must be clearly designated as such.

Daylight-savings time kicks in on the last Sunday in March and ends on the last Sunday in October. The use of the 24-hour clock is common. As daylight-savings time differs across regions, the following times are indicative only:

CITY	NOON IN BERLIN
Auckland	11pm
Cape Town	1pm
London	11am
New York	6am
San Francisco	3am
Sydney	9pm
Tokyo	8pm

Toilets

➡ German toilets are sit-down affairs. Men generally sit down when peeing.

➡ Free-standing, 24-hour public toilet pods have become quite commonplace. The cost is €0.50 and you have 15 minutes. Most are wheelchair-accessible.

➡ Toilets in malls, clubs, beer gardens etc often have an attendant who expects a tip of between €0.20 and €0.50.

Tourist Information

Visit Berlin (Map p322; www.visitberlin.de; Brandenburger Tor, Pariser Platz), the Berlin tourist board, operates four walk-in offices, info desks at the airports, and a **call centre** (☑030-2500 2333; ⏰9am-7pm Mon-Fri, 10am-6pm Sat, 10am-2pm Sun) whose multilingual staff field general questions and make hotel and ticket bookings.

Brandenburger Tor (Map p322; Pariser Platz; ⏰9.30am-7pm Apr-Oct, to 6pm Nov-Mar; ⓢBrandenburger Tor, ⓇBrandenburger Tor)

Hauptbahnhof (Hauptbahnhof, Europaplatz entrance, ground fl; ⏰8am-10pm; ⓢHauptbahnhof, ⓇHauptbahnhof)

Neues Kranzler Eck (Map p338; Kurfürstendamm 22, Neues Kranzler Eck; ⏰9.30am-8pm Mon-Sat; ⓢKurfürstendamm)

TV Tower (Map p320; ground fl; ⏰10am-6pm Apr-Oct, to 4pm Nov-Mar; ⍰100, 200, ⓢAlexanderplatz, ⓇAlexanderplatz)

Travellers with Disabilities

➡ Access ramps and/or lifts are available in many public buildings, including train stations, museums, concert halls and cinemas. Newer hotels have lifts and rooms with extra-wide doors and spacious bathrooms. For a data bank assessing the accessibility of cafes, restaurants, hotels, theatres and other public spaces (in German), check with **Mobidat** (☑030-7477 7115; www.mobidat.de).

➡ Most buses and trams are wheelchair-accessible and many U-Bahn and S-Bahn stations are equipped with ramps or lifts. For trip-planning assistance, contact the **BVG** (☑030-194 49; www.bvg.de). Many stations also have grooved platforms to assist blind and vision-impaired passengers. Seeing-eye dogs are allowed everywhere. Hearing-impaired passengers can check upcoming station names on displays installed in all forms of public transport.

➡ **Rollstuhlpannendienst** (☑0177 833 5773; www.roll-stuhlpannendienst.de) provides 24-hour wheelchair repairs. The same company also offers wheelchair rentals.

Visas

➡ EU nationals only need their national identity card or passport to enter Germany. If you intend to stay for an extended period, you must register with the authorities (*Bürgeramt*, or Citizens' Office) within two weeks of arrival.

➡ Citizens of Australia, Canada, Israel, Japan, New Zealand, Switzerland and the US, among others, only need a valid passport (no visa) if entering as tourists for a stay of up to three months within a six-month period. Passports must be valid for at least another four months beyond the planned departure date.

➡ Nationals from other countries need a Schengen Visa. Applications for a Schengen Visa must be filed with the embassy or consulate of the country that is your primary destination. It is valid for stays of up to 90 days. Legal permanent residency in any Schengen country makes a visa unnecessary, regardless of your nationality.

➡ For full details and current regulations, see www.auswaertiges-amt.de or check with a German consulate in your country.

Women Travellers

➡ Berlin is remarkably safe for women to explore, even solo. Simply use the same common sense you would at home.

➡ Going alone to cafes and restaurants is perfectly acceptable, even at night.

➡ In bars and nightclubs, solo women are likely to attract some attention, but if you don't want company, most men will respect a firm 'no, thank you'. Drinks spiked with rohypnol or other drugs are a potential problem in some places – don't leave your drink unattended!

➡ If assaulted, call the **police** (☑110). For help in dealing with the emotional and physical trauma associated with an attack, contact the **Women's Crisis Hotline** (☑030-251 2828, 030-216 8888, 030-615 4243). The hotlines are, however, not staffed around the clock.

Language

German belongs to the West Germanic language family and has around 100 million speakers. It is commonly divided into Low German (*Plattdeutsch*) and High German (*Hochdeutsch*). Low German is an umbrella term used for the dialects spoken in Northern Germany. High German is the standard form; it's also used in this chapter.

German is easy for English speakers to pronounce because almost all of its sounds are also found in English. If you read our coloured pronunciation guides as if they were English, you should be understood just fine. Note that kh sounds like the 'ch' in 'Bach' or in the Scottish 'loch' (pronounced at the back of the throat), r is also pronounced at the back of the throat, zh is pronounced as the 's' in 'measure', and ü as the 'ee' in 'see' but with rounded lips. The stressed syllables are indicated with italics in our pronunciation guides. The markers (pol) and (inf) indicate polite and informal forms.

BASICS

Hello.	*Guten Tag.*	*goo·*ten tahk
Goodbye.	*Auf Wiedersehen.*	owf vee·der·*zay·*en
Yes./No.	*Ja./Nein.*	yah/nain
Please.	*Bitte.*	*bi·*te
Thank you.	*Danke.*	*dang·*ke
You're welcome.	*Bitte.*	*bi·*te
Excuse me.	*Entschuldigung.*	ent·*shul·*di·gung
Sorry.	*Entschuldigung.*	ent·*shul·*di·gung

> ### WANT MORE?
>
> For in-depth language information and handy phrases, check out Lonely Planet's *German Phrasebook*. You'll find it at **shop.lonelyplanet.com**, or you can buy Lonely Planet's iPhone phrasebooks at the Apple App Store.

How are you?
Wie geht es Ihnen/dir? (pol/inf) — vee gayt es ee·nen/deer

Fine. And you?
Danke, gut. Und Ihnen/dir? (pol/inf) — dang·ke goot unt ee·nen/deer

What's your name?
Wie ist Ihr Name? (pol) — vee ist eer *nah·*me
Wie heißt du? (inf) — vee haist doo

My name is ...
Mein Name ist ... (pol) — main *nah·*me ist ...
Ich heiße ... (inf) — ikh *hai·*se ...

Do you speak English?
Sprechen Sie Englisch? (pol) — shpre·khen zee *eng·*lish
Sprichst du Englisch? (inf) — shprikhst doo *eng·*lish

I don't understand.
Ich verstehe nicht. — ikh fer·*shtay·*e nikht

ACCOMMODATION

guesthouse	*Pension*	pahng·*zyawn*
hotel	*Hotel*	ho·*tel*
inn	*Gasthof*	*gast·*hawf
youth hostel	*Jugendherberge*	*yoo·*gent·her·ber·ge
Do you have a ... room?	*Haben Sie ein ...?*	*hah·*ben zee ain ...
double	*Doppelzimmer*	do·pel·tsi·mer
single	*Einzelzimmer*	ain·tsel·tsi·mer
How much is it per ...?	*Wie viel kostet es pro ...?*	vee feel *kos·*tet es praw ...
night	*Nacht*	nakht
person	*Person*	per·*zawn*

Is breakfast included?
Ist das Frühstück inklusive? — ist das *frü·*shtük in·kloo·*zee·*ve

DIRECTIONS

Where's ...?
Wo ist ...? — vaw ist ...

What's the address?
Wie ist die Adresse? — vee ist dee a-*dre*-se

How far is it?
Wie weit ist es? — vee vait ist es

Can you show me (on the map)?
Können Sie es mir — *ker*-nen zee es meer
(auf der Karte) zeigen? — (owf dair *kar*-te) *tsai*-gen

How can I get there?
Wie kann ich da — vee kan ikh dah
hinkommen? — *hin*-ko-men

Turn ...	*Biegen Sie ... ab.*	bee-gen zee ... ab
at the corner	*an der Ecke*	an dair *e*-ke
at the traffic lights	*bei der Ampel*	bai dair *am*-pel
left	*links*	lingks
right	*rechts*	rekhts

EATING & DRINKING

I'd like to reserve a table for ...	*Ich möchte einen Tisch für ... reservieren.*	ikh *merkh*-te *ai*-nen tish für ... re-zer-*vee*-ren
(eight) o'clock	*(acht) Uhr*	(akht) oor
(two) people	*(zwei) Personen*	(tsvai) per-*zaw*-nen

I'd like the menu, please.
Ich hätte gern die — ikh *he*-te gern dee
Speisekarte, bitte. — *shpai*-ze-kar-te *bi*-te

What would you recommend?
Was empfehlen Sie? — vas emp-*fay*-len zee

What's in that dish?
Was ist in diesem — vas ist in *dee*-zem
Gericht? — ge-*rikht*

I'm a vegetarian.
Ich bin Vegetarier/ — ikh bin ve-ge-*tah*-ri-er/
Vegetarierin. (m/f) — ve-ge-*tah*-ri-e-rin

That was delicious.
Das hat hervorragend — das hat her-*fawr*-rah-gent
geschmeckt. — ge-*shmekt*

Cheers!
Prost! — prawst

Please bring the bill.
Bitte bringen Sie — *bi*-te bring-en zee
die Rechnung. — dee *rekh*-nung

Key Words

| **bar (pub)** | *Kneipe* | *knai*-pe |
| **bottle** | *Flasche* | *fla*-she |

To get by in German, mix and match these simple patterns with words of your choice:

When's (the next flight)?
Wann ist (der — van ist (dair
nächste Flug)? — *naykhs*-te flook)

Where's (the station)?
Wo ist (der Bahnhof)? — vaw ist (dair *bahn*-hawf)

Where can I (buy a ticket)?
Wo kann ich (eine — vaw kan ikh (*ai*-ne
Fahrkarte kaufen)? — *fahr*-kar-te kow-fen)

Do you have (a map)?
Haben Sie — *hah*-ben zee
(eine Karte)? — (*ai*-ne *kar*-te)

Is there (a toilet)?
Gibt es (eine Toilette)? — gipt es (*ai*-ne to-a-*le*-te)

I'd like (a coffee).
Ich möchte — ikh *merkh*-te
(einen Kaffee). — (*ai*-nen ka-*fay*)

I'd like (to hire a car).
Ich möchte — ikh *merkh*-te
(ein Auto mieten). — (ain *ow*-to mee-ten)

Can I (enter)?
Darf ich — darf ikh
(hereinkommen)? — (her-*ein*-ko-men)

Could you please (help me)?
Könnten Sie — *kern*-ten zee
(mir helfen)? — (meer *hel*-fen)

Do I have to (book a seat)?
Muss ich (einen Platz — mus ikh (*ai*-nen plats
reservieren lassen)? — re-zer-*vee*-ren *la*-sen)

bowl	*Schüssel*	*shü*-sel
breakfast	*Frühstück*	*frü*-shtük
cold	*kalt*	kalt
cup	*Tasse*	*ta*-se
daily special	*Gericht des Tages*	ge-*rikht* des *tah*-ges
delicatessen	*Feinkostgeschäft*	*fain*-kost-ge-sheft
desserts	*Nachspeisen*	*nahkh*-shpai-zen
dinner	*Abendessen*	*ah*-bent-e-sen
drink list	*Getränkekarte*	ge-*treng*-ke-kar-te
fork	*Gabel*	*gah*-bel
glass	*Glas*	glahs
grocery store	*Lebensmittelladen*	*lay*-bens-mi-tel-lah-den
hot (warm)	*warm*	warm
knife	*Messer*	*me*-ser
lunch	*Mittagessen*	*mi*-tahk-e-sen

arket	Markt	markt
plate	Teller	te·ler
restaurant	Restaurant	res·to·rahng
set menu	Menü	may·nü
spicy	würzig	vür·tsikh
spoon	Löffel	ler·fel
with/without	mit/ohne	mit/aw·ne

Meat & Fish

beef	Rindfleisch	rint·flaish
carp	Karpfen	karp·fen
fish	Fisch	fish
herring	Hering	hay·ring
lamb	Lammfleisch	lam·flaish
meat	Fleisch	flaish
pork	Schweinefleisch	shvai·ne·flaish
poultry	Geflügelfleisch	ge·flü·gel·flaish
salmon	Lachs	laks
sausage	Wurst	vurst
seafood	Meeresfrüchte	mair·res·frükh·te
shellfish	Schaltiere	shahl·tee·re
trout	Forelle	fo·re·le
veal	Kalbfleisch	kalp·flaish

Fruit & Vegetables

apple	Apfel	ap·fel
banana	Banane	ba·nah·ne
bean	Bohne	baw·ne
cabbage	Kraut	krowt
capsicum	Paprika	pap·ri·kah
carrot	Mohrrübe	mawr·rü·be
cucumber	Gurke	gur·ke
fruit	Frucht/Obst	frukht/awpst
grapes	Weintrauben	vain·trow·ben
lemon	Zitrone	tsi·traw·ne
lentil	Linse	lin·ze
lettuce	Kopfsalat	kopf·za·laht
mushroom	Pilz	pilts
nuts	Nüsse	nü·se
onion	Zwiebel	tsvee·bel
orange	Orange	o·rahng·zhe
pea	Erbse	erp·se
plum	Pflaume	pflow·me
potato	Kartoffel	kar·to·fel
spinach	Spinat	shpi·naht
strawberry	Erdbeere	ert·bair·re

tomato	Tomate	to·mah·te
vegetable	Gemüse	ge·mü·ze
watermelon	Wassermelone	va·ser·me·law·ne

Other

bread	Brot	brawt
butter	Butter	bu·ter
cheese	Käse	kay·ze
egg/eggs	Ei/Eier	ai/ai·er
honey	Honig	haw·nikh
jam	Marmelade	mar·me·lah·de
pasta	Nudeln	noo·deln
pepper	Pfeffer	pfe·fer
rice	Reis	rais
salt	Salz	zalts
soup	Suppe	zu·pe
sugar	Zucker	tsu·ker

Drinks

beer	Bier	beer
coffee	Kaffee	ka·fay
juice	Saft	zaft
milk	Milch	milkh
orange juice	Orangensaft	o·rang·zhen·zaft
red wine	Rotwein	rawt·vain
sparkling wine	Sekt	zekt
tea	Tee	tay
water	Wasser	va·ser
white wine	Weißwein	vais·vain

EMERGENCIES

Help!	Hilfe!	hil·fe
Go away!	Gehen Sie weg!	gay·en zee vek

Signs	
Ausgang	Exit
Damen	Women
Eingang	Entrance
Geschlossen	Closed
Herren	Men
Toiletten (WC)	Toilets
Offen	Open
Verboten	Prohibited

I the police!
Rufen Sie die Polizei!   roo·fen zee dee po·li·tsai

Call a doctor!
Rufen Sie einen Arzt!   roo·fen zee ai·nen artst

Where are the toilets?
Wo ist die Toilette?   vo ist dee to·a·le·te

I'm lost.
Ich habe mich verirrt.   ikh hah·be mikh fer·irt

I'm sick.
Ich bin krank.   ikh bin krangk

It hurts here.
Es tut hier weh.   es toot heer vay

I'm allergic to ...
Ich bin allergisch   ikh bin a·lair·gish
gegen ...   gay·gen ...

SHOPPING & SERVICES

I'd like to buy ...
Ich möchte ... kaufen.   ikh merkh·te ... kow·fen

I'm just looking.
Ich schaue mich nur um.   ikh show·e mikh noor um

Can I look at it?
Können Sie es mir   ker·nen zee es meer
zeigen?   tsai·gen

How much is this?
Wie viel kostet das?   vee feel kos·tet das

That's too expensive.
Das ist zu teuer.   das ist tsoo toy·er

Can you lower the price?
Können Sie mit dem   ker·nen zee mit dem
Preis heruntergehen?   prais he·run·ter·gay·en

There's a mistake in the bill.
Da ist ein Fehler   dah ist ain fay·ler
in der Rechnung.   in dair rekh·nung

ATM	*Geldautomat*	gelt·ow·to·maht
post office	*Postamt*	post·amt
tourist office	*Fremden-*	frem·den-
	verkehrsbüro	fer·kairs·bü·raw

TIME & DATES

What time is it?
Wie spät ist es?   vee shpayt ist es

It's (10) o'clock.
Es ist (zehn) Uhr.   es ist (tsayn) oor

Question Words

What?	*Was?*	vas
When?	*Wann?*	van
Where?	*Wo?*	vaw
Who?	*Wer?*	vair
Why?	*Warum?*	va·rum

At what time?
Um wie viel Uhr?   um vee feel oor

At ...
Um ...   um ...

morning	*Morgen*	mor·gen
afternoon	*Nachmittag*	nahkh·mi·tahk
evening	*Abend*	ah·bent
yesterday	*gestern*	ges·tern
today	*heute*	hoy·te
tomorrow	*morgen*	mor·gen
Monday	*Montag*	mawn·tahk
Tuesday	*Dienstag*	deens·tahk
Wednesday	*Mittwoch*	mit·vokh
Thursday	*Donnerstag*	do·ners·tahk
Friday	*Freitag*	frai·tahk
Saturday	*Samstag*	zams·tahk
Sunday	*Sonntag*	zon·tahk
January	*Januar*	yan·u·ahr
February	*Februar*	fay·bru·ahr
March	*März*	merts
April	*April*	a·pril
May	*Mai*	mai
June	*Juni*	yoo·ni
July	*Juli*	yoo·li
August	*August*	ow·gust
September	*September*	zep·tem·ber
October	*Oktober*	ok·taw·ber
November	*November*	no·vem·ber
December	*Dezember*	de·tsem·ber

TRANSPORT

Public Transport

boat	*Boot*	bawt
bus	*Bus*	bus
metro	*U-Bahn*	oo·bahn
plane	*Flugzeug*	flook·tsoyk
train	*Zug*	tsook
At what time's the ... bus?	*Wann fährt der ... Bus?*	van fairt dair... bus
first	*erste*	ers·te
last	*letzte*	lets·te
next	*nächste*	naykhs·te

Numbers

1	eins	ains
2	zwei	tsvai
3	drei	drai
4	vier	feer
5	fünf	fünf
6	sechs	zeks
7	sieben	zee·ben
8	acht	akht
9	neun	noyn
10	zehn	tsayn
20	zwanzig	tsvan·tsikh
30	dreißig	drai·tsikh
40	vierzig	feer·tsikh
50	fünfzig	fünf·tsikh
60	sechzig	zekh·tsikh
70	siebzig	zeep·tsikh
80	achtzig	akht·tsikh
90	neunzig	noyn·tsikh
100	hundert	hun·dert
1000	tausend	tow·sent

A ... to (Cologne).	Eine ... nach (Köln).	ai·ne ... nahkh (kerln)
1st-/2nd-class ticket	Fahrkarte erster/zweiter Klasse	fahr·kar·te ers·ter/tsvai·ter kla·se
one-way ticket	einfache Fahrkarte	ain·fa·khe fahr·kar·te
return ticket	Rückfahrkarte	rük·fahr·kar·te

At what time does it arrive?
Wann kommt es an?   van komt es an

Is it a direct route?
Ist es eine direkte   ist es ai·ne di·rek·te
Verbindung?   fer·bin·dung

Does it stop at ...?
Hält es in ...?   helt es in ...

What station is this?
Welcher Bahnhof   vel·kher bahn·hawf
ist das?   ist das

What's the next stop?
Welches ist der   vel·khes ist dair
nächste Halt?   naykh·ste halt

I want to get off here.
Ich möchte hier   ikh merkh·te heer
aussteigen.   ows·shtai·gen

Please tell me when we get to ....
Könnten Sie mir bitte   kern·ten zee meer bi·te
sagen, wann wir in   zah·gen van veer in
... ankommen?   ... an·ko·men

Please take me to (this address).
Bitte bringen Sie mich   bi·te bring·en zee mikh
zu (dieser Adresse).   tsoo (dee·zer a·dre·se)

platform	Bahnsteig	bahn·shtaik
ticket office	Fahrkarten-verkauf	fahr·kar·ten·fer·kowf
timetable	Fahrplan	fahr·plan

Driving & Cycling

I'd like to hire a ...	Ich möchte ein ... mieten.	ikh merkh·te ain ... mee·ten
4WD	Allrad-fahrzeug	al·raht·fahr·tsoyk
bicycle	Fahrrad	fahr·raht
car	Auto	ow·to
motorbike	Motorrad	maw·tor·raht

How much is it per ...?	Wie viel kostet es pro ...?	vee feel kos·tet es praw ...
day	Tag	tahk
week	Woche	vo·khe

bicycle pump	Fahrradpumpe	fahr·raht·pum·pe
child seat	Kindersitz	kin·der·zits
helmet	Helm	helm
petrol	Benzin	ben·tseen

Does this road go to ...?
Führt diese Straße   fürt dee·ze shtrah·se
nach ...?   nahkh ...

(How long) Can I park here?
(Wie lange) Kann ich   (vee lang·e) kan ikh
hier parken?   heer par·ken

Where's a petrol station?
Wo ist eine Tankstelle?   vaw ist ai·ne tangk·shte·le

I need a mechanic.
Ich brauche einen   ikh brow·khe ai·nen
Mechaniker.   me·khah·ni·ker

My car/motorbike has broken down (at ...).
Ich habe (in ...) eine   ikh hah·be (in ...) ai·ne
Panne mit meinem   pa·ne mit mai·nem
Auto/Motorrad.   ow·to/maw·tor·raht

I've run out of petrol.
Ich habe kein   ikh hah·be kain
Benzin mehr.   ben·tseen mair

I have a flat tyre.
Ich habe eine   ikh hah·be ai·ne
Reifenpanne.   rai·fen·pa·ne

Are there cycling paths?
Gibt es Fahrradwege?   geept es fahr·raht·vay·ge

Is there bicycle parking?
Gibt es Fahrrad-   geept es fahr·raht·
Parkplätze?   park·ple·tse

GLOSSARY

You may encounter the following terms and abbreviations while in Berlin.

Bahnhof (Bf) – train station
Berg – mountain
Bibliothek – library
BRD – Bundesrepublik Deutschland (abbreviated in English as FRG – Federal Republic of Germany); see also *DDR*
Brücke – bridge
Brunnen – fountain or well
Bundestag – German parliament

CDU – Christliche Demokratische Union (Christian Democratic Union), centre-right party

DDR – Deutsche Demokratische Republik (abbreviated in English as GDR – German Democratic Republic); the name for the former East Germany; see also *BRD*
Denkmal – memorial, monument
Dom – cathedral

ermässigt – reduced (eg admission fee)

Fahrrad – bicycle
Flohmarkt – flea market
Flughafen – airport
FRG – Federal Republic of Germany; see also *BRD*

Gasse – lane or alley
Gästehaus, Gasthaus – guesthouse
GDR – German Democratic Republic (the former East Germany); see also *DDR*
Gedenkstätte – memorial site
Gestapo – Geheime Staatspolizei (Nazi secret police)

Gründerzeit – literally 'foundation time'; early years of German empire, roughly 1871–90

Hafen – harbour, port
Hauptbahnhof (Hbf) – main train station
Hof (Höfe) – courtyard(s)

Imbiss – snack bar, takeaway stand
Insel – island

Kaiser – emperor; derived from 'Caesar'
Kapelle – chapel
Karte – ticket
Kiez(e) – neighbourhood(s)
Kino – cinema
König – king
Konzentrationslager (KZ) – concentration camp
Kristallnacht – literally 'Night of Broken Glass'; Nazi pogrom against Jewish businesses and institutions on 9 November 1938
Kunst – art
Kunsthotels – hotels either designed by artists or liberally furnished with art

Mietskaserne(n) – tenement(s) built around successive courtyards

Ostalgie – fusion of the words Ost and Nostalgie, meaning nostalgia for East Germany

Palais – small palace
Palast – palace
Passage – shopping arcade
Platz – square

Rathaus – town hall
Reich – empire
Reisezentrum – travel centre in train or bus stations

Saal (Säle) – hall(s), large room(s)
Sammlung – collection
S-Bahn – metro/regional rail service with fewer stops than the U-Bahn
Schiff – ship
Schloss – palace
See – lake
SPD – Sozialdemokratische Partei Deutschlands (Social Democratic Party of Germany)
SS – Schutzstaffel; organisation within the Nazi Party that supplied Hitler's bodyguards, as well as concentration camp guards and the Waffen-SS troops in WWII
Stasi – GDR secret police (from Ministerium für Staatssicherheit, or Ministry of State Security)
Strasse (Str) – street

Tageskarte – daily menu; day ticket on public transport
Tor – gate
Trabant – GDR-era car boasting a two-stroke engine
Turm – tower
Trümmerberge – rubble mountains

U-Bahn – rapid transit railway, mostly underground; best choice for metro trips
Ufer – bank

Viertel – quarter, neighbourhood

Wald – forest
Weg – way, path
Weihnachtsmarkt – Christmas market
Wende – 'change' or 'turning point' of 1989, ie the collapse of the GDR and the resulting German reunification

Behind the Scenes

SEND US YOUR FEEDBACK

We love to hear from travellers – your comments keep us on our toes and help make our books better. Our well-travelled team reads every word on what you loved or loathed about this book. Although we cannot reply individually to postal submissions, we always guarantee that your feedback goes straight to the appropriate authors, in time for the next edition. Each person who sends us information is thanked in the next edition – and the most useful submissions are rewarded with a selection of digital PDF chapters.

Visit **lonelyplanet.com/contact** to submit your updates and suggestions or to ask for help. Our award-winning website also features inspirational travel stories, news and discussions.

Note: We may edit, reproduce and incorporate your comments in Lonely Planet products such as guidebooks, websites and digital products, so let us know if you don't want your comments reproduced or your name acknowledged. For a copy of our privacy policy visit lonelyplanet.com/privacy.

OUR READERS

Many thanks to the travellers who used the last edition and wrote to us with helpful hints, useful advice and interesting anecdotes: Annette Castro, Tom Drinkwater, Patrick Frew, Moran Gur, John Ingman, Anders Jeppsson, Olli Löfberg, Torben Retboll, Lis Robinson, Sylvia Suvaal, Ann Wallace Paterson, Miriam Bers, Claudia Scheffler, Regine Schneider, Ubin Eoh, Frank Engster, Heiner and Claudia Schuster, Renate Freiling, Silke Neumann, Kirsten Schmidt, Christian Tänzler, Julia Ana Herchenbach, Johann Scharfe, Shachar and Doreen Elkanati, Ariela Abramovici-Dähne, Craig Robinson, Mike Meinke, Virginia Shmuel, Jan Czyszke and, of course, David Peevers.

AUTHOR THANKS

Andrea Schulte-Peevers

Big, heartfelt thanks to all of these wonderful people who plied me with tips, insights, information, ideas and encouragement (in no particular order): Henrik Tidefjärd, Susan

ACKNOWLEDGMENTS

Berlin S+U-Bahn Map © 2014 Kartographie Berliner Verkehrsbetrieben (BVG).

Cover photograph: Berliner Dom with the Fernsehturm in the background, Miles Ertman/Robert Harding World Imagery/Corbis.

BEHIND THE SCENES

THIS BOOK

This 9th edition of Lonely Planet's *Berlin* guidebook was researched and written by Andrea Schulte-Peevers. The previous two editions were also written by Andrea. This guidebook was commissioned in Lonely Planet's London office, and produced by the following:

Destination Editors Gemma Graham, Anna Tyler

Product Editor Carolyn Boicos

Senior Cartographer Valentina Kremenchutskaya

Book Designer Clara Monitto

Assisting Editors Kate Mathews, Anne Mulvaney, Charlotte Orr, Kirsten Rawlings, Sally Schafer, Saralinda Turner

Assisting Cartographer Corey Hutchison

Cover Researcher Naomi Parker

Assisting Book Designers Wibowo Rusli, Wendy Wright

Thanks to Sasha Baskett, Elin Berglund, Ryan Evans, Larissa Frost, Jouve India, Wayne Murphy, Claire Naylor, Karyn Noble, Lauren Wellicome

See also separate subindexes for:

✕ **EATING P311**

🍷 **DRINKING & NIGHTLIFE P312**

☆ **ENTERTAINMENT P313**

🛍 **SHOPPING P313**

🛏 **SLEEPING P314**

Index

Sights 000
Map Pages **000**
Photo Pages **000**

Berlin Maps

Sights

- Beach
- Bird Sanctuary
- Buddhist
- Castle/Palace
- Christian
- Confucian
- Hindu
- Islamic
- Jain
- Jewish
- Monument
- Museum/Gallery/Historic Building
- Ruin
- Sento Hot Baths/Onsen
- Shinto
- Sikh
- Taoist
- Winery/Vineyard
- Zoo/Wildlife Sanctuary
- Other Sight

Activities, Courses & Tours

- Bodysurfing
- Diving
- Canoeing/Kayaking
- Course/Tour
- Skiing
- Snorkelling
- Surfing
- Swimming/Pool
- Walking
- Windsurfing
- Other Activity

Sleeping

- Sleeping
- Camping

Eating

- Eating

Drinking & Nightlife

- Drinking & Nightlife
- Cafe

Entertainment

- Entertainment

Shopping

- Shopping

Information

- Bank
- Embassy/Consulate
- Hospital/Medical
- Internet
- Police
- Post Office
- Telephone
- Toilet
- Tourist Information
- Other Information

Geographic

- Beach
- Hut/Shelter
- Lighthouse
- Lookout
- Mountain/Volcano
- Oasis
- Park
- Pass
- Picnic Area
- Waterfall

Population

- Capital (National)
- Capital (State/Province)
- City/Large Town
- Town/Village

Transport

- Airport
- Border crossing
- Bus
- Cable car/Funicular
- Cycling
- Ferry
- Metro station
- Monorail
- Parking
- Petrol station
- S-Bahn/Subway station
- Taxi
- T-bane/Tunnelbana station
- Train station/Railway
- Tram
- Tube station
- U-Bahn/Underground station
- Other Transport

Note: Not all symbols displayed above appear on the maps in this book

Routes

- Tollway
- Freeway
- Primary
- Secondary
- Tertiary
- Lane
- Unsealed road
- Road under construction
- Plaza/Mall
- Steps
- Tunnel
- Pedestrian overpass
- Walking Tour
- Walking Tour detour
- Path/Walking Trail

Boundaries

- International
- State/Province
- Disputed
- Regional/Suburb
- Marine Park
- Cliff
- Wall

Hydrography

- River, Creek
- Intermittent River
- Canal
- Water
- Dry/Salt/Intermittent Lake
- Reef

Areas

- Airport/Runway
- Beach/Desert
- Cemetery (Christian)
- Cemetery (Other)
- Glacier
- Mudflat
- Park/Forest
- Sight (Building)
- Sportsground
- Swamp/Mangrove

MAP INDEX

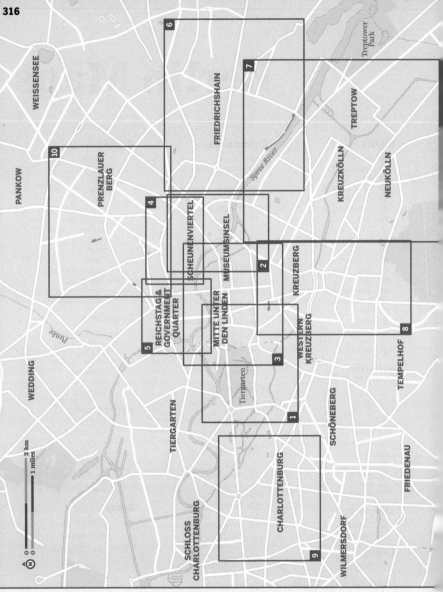

POTSDAMER PLATZ & TIERGARTEN *Map on p318*

POTSDAMER PLATZ & TIERGARTEN

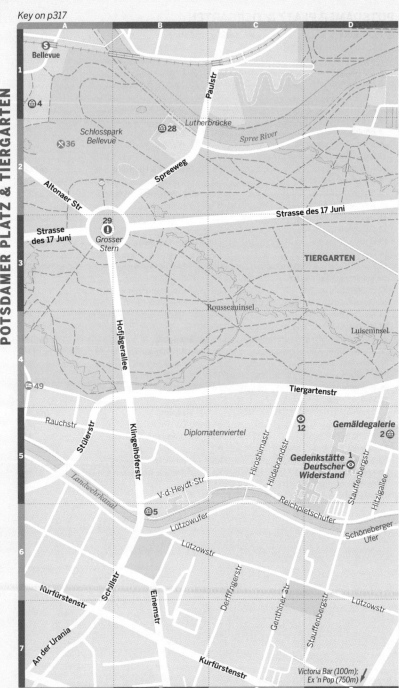

Bellevue

Schlosspark Bellevue

Paulstr

Lutherbrücke

Spree River

28

36

Spreeweg

Altonaer Str

Strasse des 17 Juni

TIERGARTEN

Strasse des 17 Juni

29 Grosser Stern

Hofjägerallee

Rousseauinsel

Luiseninsel

49

Tiergartenstr

Rauchstr

Stülerstr

Klingelhöferstr

Diplomatenviertel

Hiroshimastr

Hildebrandstr

12

Gemäldegalerie 2

Gedenkstätte Deutscher Widerstand 1

Stauffenbergstr

Hitzigallee

Landwehrkanal

V-d-Heydt-Str

5

Reichpietschufer

Lützowufer

Schöneberger Ufer

Lützowstr

Kurfürstenstr

Schillstr

Einemstr

Derfflingerstr

Genthiner Str

Stauffenbergstr

Lützowstr

An der Urania

Kurfürstenstr

Victoria Bar (100m); Ex 'n Pop (750m)

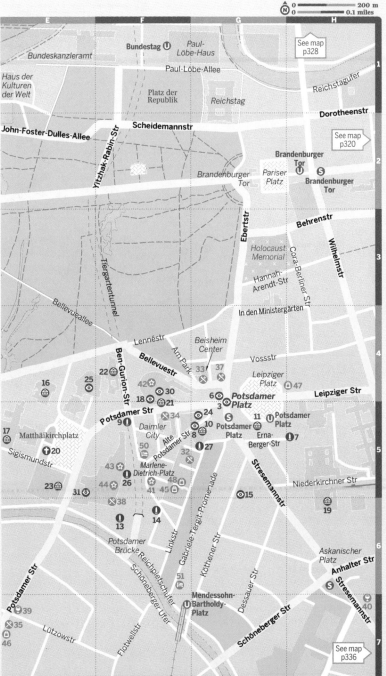

N 0 —————————— 200 m
0 —————————— 0.1 miles

See map p328

See map p320

See map p336

Bundeskanzleramt

Bundestag

Paul-Löbe-Haus

Paul-Löbe-Allee

Haus der Kulturen der Welt

Platz der Republik

Reichstag

Reichstagufer

Dorotheenstr

John-Foster-Dulles-Allee

Scheidemannstr

Brandenburger Tor

Pariser Platz

Brandenburger Tor

Behrenstr

Yitzhak-Rabin-Str

Ebertstr

Wilhelmstr

Holocaust Memorial

Hannah-Arendt-Str

Cora-Berliner-Str

Tiergartentunnel

Bellevueallee

In den Ministergärten

Lennéstr

Beisheim Center

Vossstr

Bellevuestr

Am Park

33 37

Leipziger Platz

47

Leipziger Str

Ben-Gurion-Str

22

42 30

Potsdamer Platz

16

25

18 21

6 3 S

17 Matthäikirchplatz

Potsdamer Str

9

Daimler City

34 24 11 Potsdamer Platz

10 Potsdamer Platz

8 Erna-Berger-Str 7

20

50 Alte Potsdamer Str

27

Sigismundstr

43 Marlene-Dietrich-Platz

32

23 31 44 26

48

Streesemannstr

Niederkirchner Str

41 45

15

19

38

Lintkstr

Gabriele-Tezit-Promenade

14

Köthener Str

Dessauer Str

13

Potsdamer Brücke

Reichpietschufer

Askanischer Platz

Anhalter Str

51

Schöneberger Ufer

Mendessohn-Bartholdy-Platz

Stresemannstr

S

40

39

Lützowstr

Flotwellstr

Schöneberger Str

35

46

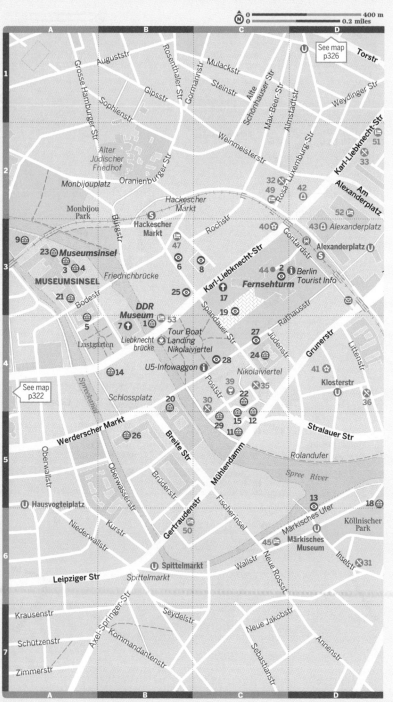

0   400 m
0   0.2 miles

See map p326

Torstr

A

B

C

D

Grosse Hamburger Str

Auguststr

Rosenthaler Str

Gormannstr

Mulackstr

Steinstr

Alte Schönhauser Str

Max-Beer-Str

Almstadtstr

Weydinger Str

Karl-Liebknecht-Str

Gipsstr

Sophienstr

Weinmeisterstr

Rosa-Luxemburg-Str

1

Alter Jüdischer Friedhof

Oranienburger Str

32
49
42

51
33

Am Alexanderplatz

2

Monbijouplatz

Hackescher Markt

52

Monbijou Park

Burgstr

Rochstr

Rostr

40

Gontardstr

43 Alexanderplatz

Alexanderplatz

9

Hackescher Markt

47

44 2
Berlin Tourist Info

3

23 Museumsinsel

3 4

Friedrichbrücke

6

8

25

Karl-Liebknecht-Str

Fernsehturm

17

MUSEUMSINSEL

21

Bodestr

DDR Museum

5

7 1 53

19

Spandauer Str

Rathausstr

Grunerstr

Littenstr

Lustgarten

Liebknecht brücke

Tour Boat Landing
Nikolaiviertel

27

Judenstr

24

41

Klosterstr

36

4

14

U5-Infowaggon

28

Nikolaiviertel

35

39

Schlossplatz

20

30

Poststr

22

Stralauer Str

29

15 12

11

5

26

Werderscher Markt

Breite Str

Mühlendamm

Rolandufer

Spree River

13

18

Oberwallstr

Oberwasserstr

Brüderstr

Fischerinsel

Märkisches Ufer

Köllnischer Park

Inselstr

31

Hausvogteiplatz

Niederwallstr

Kurstr

Gertraudenstr

50

Wallstr

Neue Rossstr

45 Märkisches Museum

6

Leipziger Str

Spittelmarkt

Spittelmarkt

7

Krausenstr

Schützenstr

Zimmerstr

Axel-Springer-Str

Kommandantenstr

Seydelstr

Neue Jakobstr

Sebastianstr

Annenstr

See map p322

Spreekanal

A

B

C

D

HISTORIC MITTE

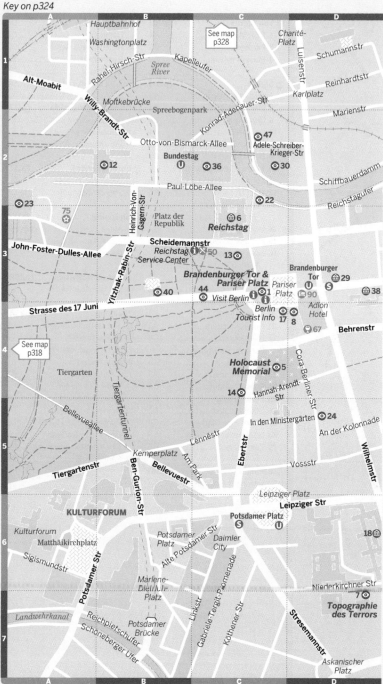

Key on p324

See map p328

Hauptbahnhof
Washingtonplatz
Charité-Platz
Schumannstr
Rahel-Hirsch-Str
Kapelleufer
Luisenstr
Reinhardtstr
Alt-Moabit
Spree River
Karlplatz
Moftkebrücke
Marienstr
Willy-Brandt-Str
Spreebogenpark
Konrad-Adenauer-Str
Schiffbauerdamm
Otto-von-Bismarck-Allee
47
Adele-Schreiber-Krieger-Str
12
Bundestag
36
30
Paul-Löbe-Allee
22
Reichstagufer
23
75
Platz der Republik
6
Reichstag
Heinrich-Von-Gagern-Str
John-Foster-Dulles-Allee
Scheidemannstr
Reichstag Service Center
50
13
Brandenburger Tor
29
38
Yitzhak-Rabin-Str
Brandenburger Tor & Pariser Platz
Pariser Platz
90
Adlon Hotel
40
44
1
Strasse des 17 Juni
Visit Berlin
Berlin Tourist Info
17
8
67
Behrenstr
See map p318
Tiergarten
Holocaust Memorial
5
Cora-Berliner-Str
14
Hannah-Arendt-Str
Tiergartentunnel
Bellevueallee
In den Ministergärten
24
An der Kolonnade
Lennéstr
Am Park
Ebertstr
Vossstr
Wilhelmstr
Tiergartenstr
Kemperplatz
Bellevuestr
Leipziger Platz
Leipziger Str
Ben-Gurion-Str
Potsdamer Platz
KULTURFORUM
Kulturforum
Matthäikirchplatz
Potsdamer Platz
Alte Potsdamer Str
Daimler City
18
Sigismundstr
Potsdamer Str
Marlene-Dietrich-Platz
Linkstr
Gabriele-Tergit-Promenade
Köthener Str
Niederkirchner Str
7
Topographie des Terrors
Landwehrkanal
Reichpietschufer
Schöneberger Ufer
Potsdamer Brücke
Stresemannstr
Askanischer Platz

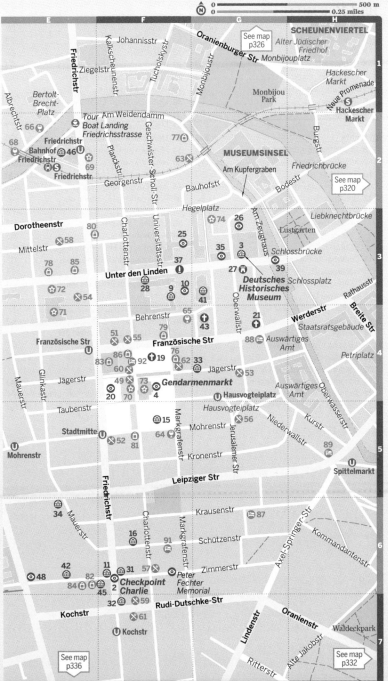

0 — 500 m
0 — 0.25 miles

SCHEUNENVIERTEL

See map p326

Alter Jüdischer Friedhof
Monbijouplatz

Johannisstr
Kalkscheunenstr
Tucholskystr
Oranienburger Str
Monbijoustr

Hackescher Markt
Neue Promenade

Friedrichstr
Ziegelstr

Bertolt-Brecht-Platz

Monbijou Park

Hackescher Markt

Albrechtstr

66

Am Weidendamm
Tour Boat Landing Friedrichstrasse

77

Geschwister-Scholl-Str

MUSEUMSINSEL

Burgstr

68

Friedrichstr
Bahnhof 46

69

63

Am Kupfergraben

Friedrichbrücke

See map p320

Friedrichstr

Georgenstr

Bodestr

Plandstr

Bauhofstr

Dorotheenstr

80

Charlottenstr
Universitätsstr

Hegelplatz

74

26

Liebknechtbrücke
Lustgarten

58

Mittelstr

25

35

3

Schlossbrücke

78 85

37

27

39

Schlossplatz

Rathausstr

Unter den Linden

28

Deutsches Historisches Museum

Schlossplatz

Breite Str

72

9 10

41

Oberwallstr

Werderstr

54

71

Behrenstr

65

21

43

Staatsratsgebäude

Am Zeughaus

51 55

79

Französische Str

88 Auswärtiges Amt

Petriplatz

Französische Str

Französische Str

86

76

Mauerstr
Glinkastr

83

92 19

60

62 33

Jägerstr

53

Jägerstr

49 73

Gendarmenmarkt

Auswärtiges Amt

Oberwasserstr

20 70

4

Hausvogteiplatz

Kurstr

Taubenstr

15

Hausvogteiplatz

56

Niederwallstr

89

Stadtmitte

52 81

64

Mohrenstr

Jerusalemer Str

Spittelmarkt

Mohrenstr

Kronenstr

Leipziger Str

Friedrichstr

34

Mauerstr

Krausenstr

87

Axel-Springer-Str

Kommandantenstr

16

Charlottenstr

91

Schützenstr

42

Markgrafenstr

Zimmerstr

48

11 31 57

82

84

2

45

Checkpoint Charlie

Peter Fechter Memorial

32 59

Rudi-Dutschke-Str

Kochstr

61

Lindenstr

Oranienstr

Waldeckpark

Kochstr

See map p336

Alte Jakobstr

Ritterstr

See map p332

HISTORIC MITTE

HISTORIC MITTE

SCHEUNENVIERTEL

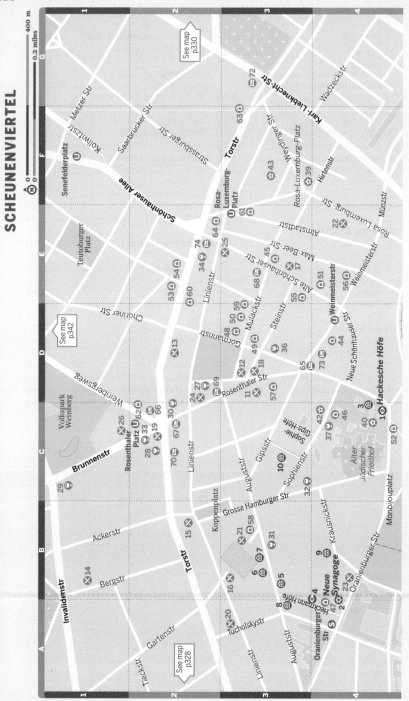

See map p330

See map p342

See map p328

Volkspark
Weinberg

Teutoburger
Platz

Senefelderplatz

Metzer Str

Kollwitzstr

Saarbrucker Str

Strassburger Str

Schönhauser Allee

Choriner Str

Weinbergsweg

Brunnenstr

Rosenthaler
Platz

Torstr

Ackerstr

Bergstr

Invalidenstr

Gartenstr

Tieckstr

Linienstr

Tucholskystr

Auguststr

Koppenplatz

Linienstr

Grosse Hamburger Str

Gipsstr

Sophie-Gips-Höfe

Sophienstr

Auguststr

Krausnickstr

Oranienburger Str

Monbijouplatz

Alter
Jüdischer
Friedhof

Hackesche Höfe

Neue Schönhauser Str

Weinmeisterstr

Münzstr

Rosa-Luxemburg-Str

Almstadtstr

Max-Beer-Str

Alte Schönhauser Str

Mulackstr

Gormannstr

Steinstr

Rosenthaler Str

Linienstr

Torstr

Rosa-
Luxemburg-
Platz

Weydingerstr

Rosa-Luxemburg-Platz

Hirtenstr

Karl-Liebknecht-Str

Wadzeckstr

Neue
Synagoge

Heckmann Höfe

Oranienburger
Str

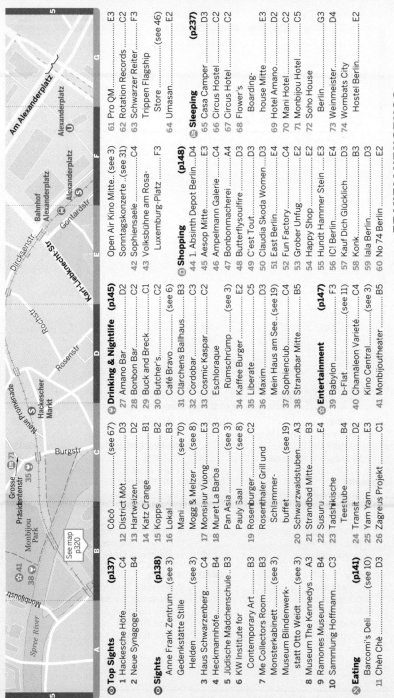

SCHEUNENVIERTEL

327

◎ Top Sights (p137)
1 Hackesche Höfe	C4
2 Neue Synagoge	B4

◎ Sights (p138)
Anne Frank Zentrum	(see 3)
Gedenkstätte Stille Helden	(see 3)
3 Haus Schwarzenberg	C4
4 Heckmannhöfe	B4
5 Jüdische Mädchenschule	B3
6 KW Institute for Contemporary Art	B3
7 Me Collectors Room	B3
Monsterkabinett	(see 3)
Museum Blindenwerk- statt Otto Weidt	(see 3)
8 Museum The Kennedys	A3
9 Ramones Museum	B4
10 Sammlung Hoffmann	C3

✕ Eating (p141)
Barcomi's Deli	(see 10)
11 Chén Chè	D3
Côcô	(see 67)
12 District Môt	D3
13 Hartweizen	D2
14 Katz Crange	B1
15 Kopps	B2
16 Lokal	B3
Mani	(see 70)
Mogg & Melzer	(see 8)
17 Monsiaur Vuong	E3
18 Muret La Barba	B4
Pan Asia	(see 3)
Pauly Saal	(see 8)
19 Rosenburger	C2
Rosenthaler Grill und Schlemmer- buffet	(see 19)
20 Schwarzwaldstuben	A3
21 Strandbad Mitte	B3
22 Susuru	E4
23 Tadshikische Teestube	B4
24 Transit	D2
25 Yam Yam	E3
26 Zagreus Projekt	C1

◎ Drinking & Nightlife (p145)
27 Amano Bar	D2
28 Bonbon Bar	C2
29 Buck and Breck	C1
30 Butcher's	C2
Café Bravo	(see 6)
31 Clärchens Ballhaus	B3
32 Cordobar	C3
33 Cosmic Kaspar Eschloraque	C2
Rümschrümp	(see 3)
34 Kaffee Burger	E2
35 Liberate	C5
36 Maxim	D3
Mein Haus am See	(see 19)
37 Sophienclub	C4
38 Strandbar Mitte	B5

◎ Entertainment (p147)
39 Babylon	F3
b-Flat	(see 11)
40 Chamäleon Varieté	C4
Kino Central	(see 3)
41 Monbijoutheater	C1
Open Air Kino Mitte	(see 3)
Sonntagskonzerte	(see 31)
42 Sophiensaele	C4
43 Volksbühne am Rosa- Luxemburg-Platz	F3

◎ Shopping (p148)
44 1 Absinth Depot Berlin	D4
45 Aesop Mitte	E3
46 Ampelmann Galerie	C4
47 Bonbonmacherei	A4
48 Butterflysoulfire	D3
49 C'est Tout	D3
50 Claudia Skoda Women	D3
51 East Berlin	E4
52 Fun Factory	C4
53 Grober Unfug	E2
54 Happy Shop	E2
55 Hundt Hammer Stein	E3
56 ICI Berlin	E4
57 Kauf Dich Glücklich	D3
58 Konk	B3
59 lala Berlin	D3
60 No 74 Berlin	E2
61 Pro QM	E3
62 Rotation Records	C2
63 Schwarzer Reiter	F3
Trippen Flagship Store	(see 46)
64 Umasan	E2

◎ Sleeping (p237)
65 Casa Camper	D3
66 Circus Hostel	C2
67 Circus Hotel	C2
68 Flower's Boarding- house Mitte	E3
69 Hotel Amano	D2
70 Mani Hotel	C2
71 Monbijou Hotel	C5
72 Soho House Berlin	G3
73 Weinmeister	D4
74 Wombats City Hostel Berlin	E2

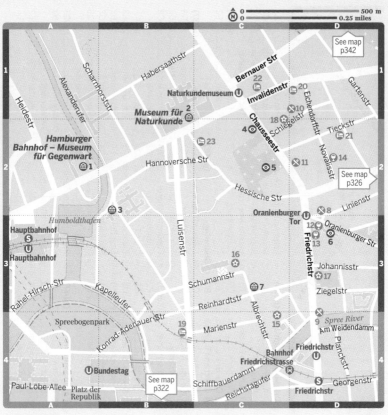

FRIEDRICHSHAIN *Map on p330*

Key on p329

FRIEDRICHSHAIN

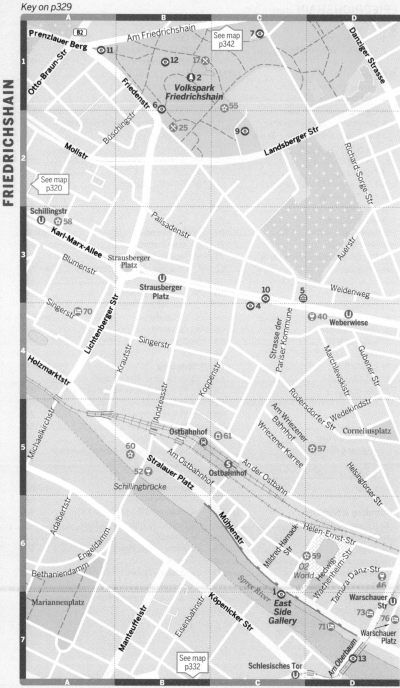

Prenzlauer Berg

Am Friedrichshain

Danziger Strasse

Otto-Braun-Str

⊙ 11

⊙ 12

17 ⊗

7 ⊙

See map
p342

Friedenstr

⚓ 2

⊙ 6

*Volkspark
Friedrichshain*

✪ 55

⚓ 25

9 ⊙

Landsberger Str

Mollstr

Büschingstr

See map
p320

Richard-Sorge-Str

Schillingstr

Ⓤ ✪ 58

Palisadenstr

Auerstr

Karl-Marx-Allee

Blumenstr

Strausberger
Platz

Ⓤ

Strausberger
Platz

10 ⊙

5 🏛

Weidenweg

Singerstr

🍴 70

⊙ 4

⊙ 40

Ⓤ

Weberwiese

Lichtenberger Str

Singerstr

Krautstr

Koppenstr

Strasse der Pariser Kommune

Marchlewskistr

Gubener Str

Holzmarktstr

Michaelkirchstr

Andreasstr

Rudersdorfer Str

Wedekindstr

Corneliusplatz

Am Wriezener
Bahnhof

Wriezener Karree

Ostbahnhof

📷 61

An der Ostbahn

✪ 57

Helsingforser Str

60 ✪

Stralauer Platz

Am Ostbahnhof

🚇 Ostbahnhof

52 🏨

Schillingbrücke

Mühlenstr

Helen-Ernst-Str

Mildred-Harnack-Str

✪ 59

Hedwig-Wachenheim-Str

Tamara-Danz-Str

Adalbertstr

Engeldamm

O2
World

46

Bethaniendamm

Spree River

Warschauer
Str

Ⓤ

Mariannenplatz

1 ⊙

73 🏨

76 🏨

Köpenicker Str

*East
Side
Gallery*

71 🏨

Warschauer
Platz

Manteuffelstr

Eisenbahnstr

See map
p332

Schlesisches Tor

Am Oberbaum

⊙ 13

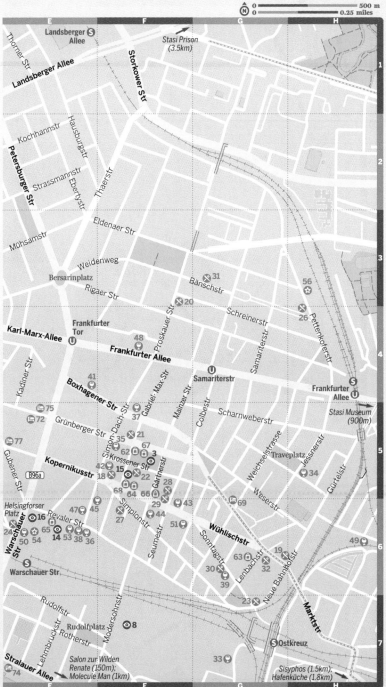

EASTERN KREUZBERG & NEUKÖLLN

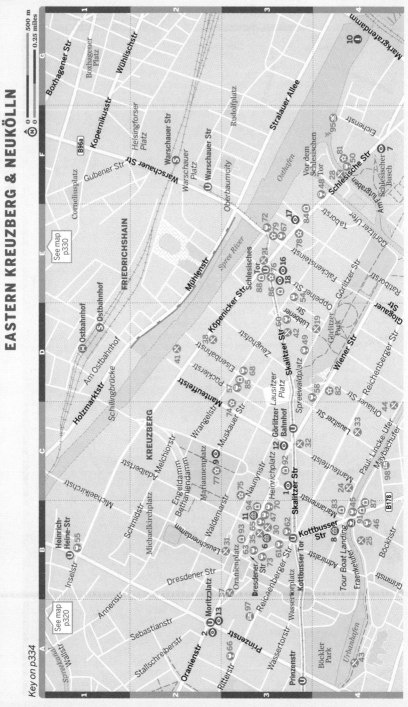

See map p330

See map p320

Key on p334

500 m
0.25 miles

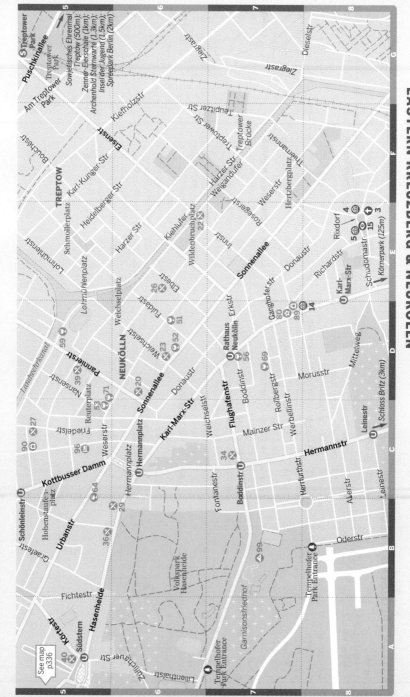

EASTERN KREUZBERG & NEUKÖLLN

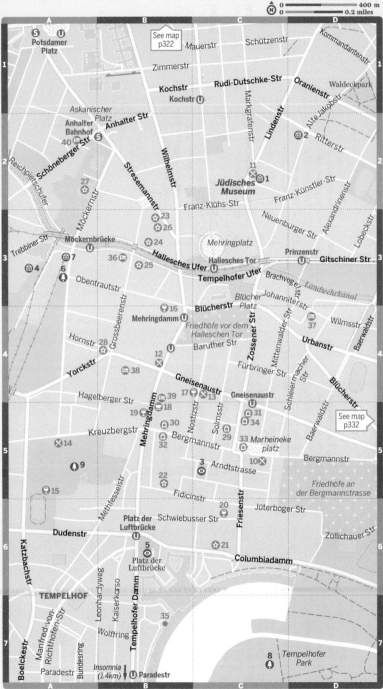

See map p322

400 m
0.2 miles

Potsdamer Platz

Mauerstr
Schützenstr
Kommandantenstr

Zimmerstr

Kochstr
Rudi-Dutschke-Str
Oranienstr
Waldeckpark

Kochstr

Markgrafenstr

Lindenstr

Alte Jakobstr

Ritterstr

Askanischer Platz

Anhalter Str

Anhalter Bahnhof
40

Schöneberger Str

Wilhelmstr

Stresemannstr

Reichpietschufer

Franz-Künstler-Str

Franz-Klühs-Str

Jüdisches Museum

11

27

Möckernstr

23
26

24

Mehringplatz

Neuenburger Str

Alexandrinenstr

Lobeckstr

Trebbiner Str

Möckernbrücke

36

25

Halleches Ufer

Halleches Tor

Tempelhofer Ufer

Prinzenstr

Gitschiner Str

Obentrautstr

Brachvogelstr

Johanniterstr

Landwehrkanal

4

7

6

Blücher Platz

Grossbeerenstr

16

Mehringdamm

Blücherstr

Friedhöfe vor dem Hallechen Tor

Baruther Str

Zossener Str

Mittenwalder Str

Schleiermacher Str

Urbanstr

Wilmsstr

Baerwaldstr

Hornstr

28

Yorckstr

12

Fürbringer Str

Blücherstr

38

Gneisenaustr

13

Gneisenaustr

See map p332

Hagelberger Str

17

39

18

Nostizstr

Solmsstr

31

34

Baerwaldstr

19

Mehringdamm

30

32

Bergmannstr

29

33

Marheineke platz

14

Kreuzbergstr

10

Bergmannstr

9

3

Arndtstrasse

Friedhöfe an der Bergmannstrasse

15

22

Fidicinstr

20

Jüterboger Str

Platz der Luftbrücke

Schwiebusser Str

Friesenstr

Züllichauer Str

Dudenstr

5

Platz der Luftbrücke

21

Columbiadamm

TEMPELHOF

Katzbachstr

Manfred-von-Richthofen-Str

Leonhardyweg

Kaiserkorso

Tempelhofer Damm

35

Boelckestr

Bundesring

Wolffring

Paradestr

Insomnia (1.4km)

Paradestr

8

Tempelhofer Park

WESTERN KREUZBERG

WESTERN KREUZBERG

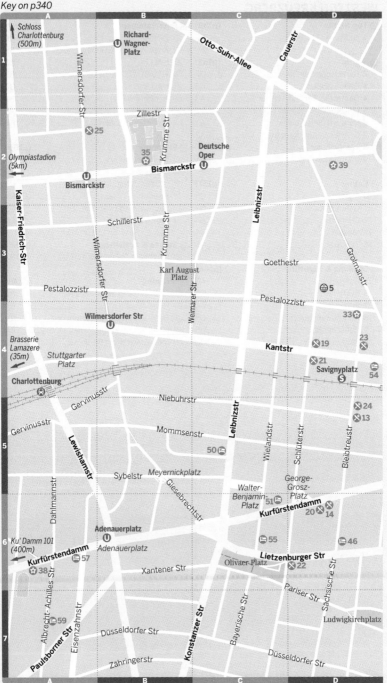

Key on p340

CITY WEST & CHARLOTTENBURG

Schloss
Charlottenburg
(500m)

Richard-
Wagner-
Platz

Otto-Suhr-Allee

Cauerstr

Wilmersdorfer Str

Zillestr

Krumme Str

Deutsche
Oper

25

35

Bismarckstr

39

Olympiastadion
(5km)

Bismarckstr

Kaiser-Friedrich-Str

Schillerstr

Krumme Str

Leibnizstr

Karl August
Platz

Weimarer Str

Goethestr

Grolmanstr

Wilmersdorfer Str

Pestalozzistr

Pestalozzistr

5

33

Wilmersdorfer Str

Kantstr

19

23

Brasserie
Lamazere
(35m)

Stuttgarter
Platz

Savignyplatz

21

54

Charlottenburg

Gervinusstr

Niebuhrstr

Leibnizstr

Wielandstr

Schlüterstr

Bleibtreustr

24

13

Gervinusstr

Lewishamstr

Mommsenstr

50

Dahlmannstr

Sybelstr

Meyernickplatz

Giesebrechtstr

Walter-
Benjamin-
Platz

George-
Grosz-
Platz

Kurfürstendamm

51

20

14

Ku' Damm 101
(400m)

Adenauerplatz

Adenauerplatz

55

Lietzenburger Str

46

Kurfürstendamm

57

Olivaer Platz

22

38

Xantener Str

Sächsische Str

Albrecht-Achilles-Str

Eisenzahnstr

Konstanzer Str

Bayerische Str

Pariser Str

Ludwigkirchplatz

59

Paulsborner Str

Düsseldorfer Str

Zähringerstr

Düsseldorfer Str

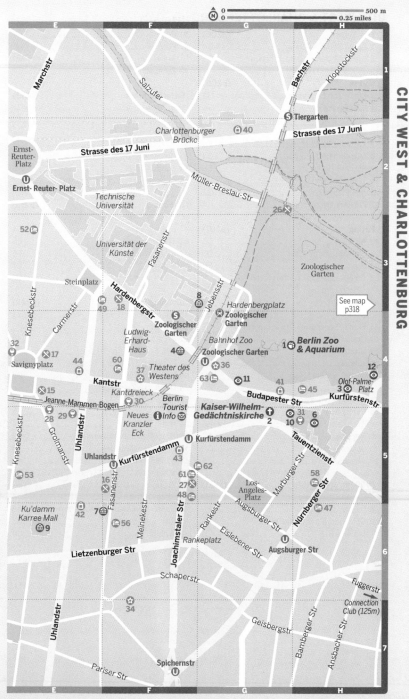

CITY WEST & CHARLOTTENBURG *Map on p338*

PRENZLAUER BERG *Map on p342*

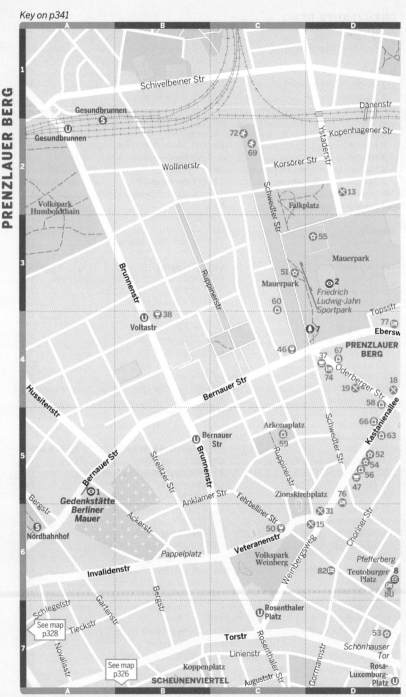

PRENZLAUER BERG

Schivelbeiner Str

Gesundbrunnen

Dänenstr

Gesundbrunnen

72

Kopenhagener Str

Wollinerstr

69

Korsörer Str

Ystaderstr

Schwedter Str

13

Volkspark
Humboldthain

Falkplatz

Brunnenstr

Ruppinerstr

55

Mauerpark

51

Mauerpark

2

Friedrich
Ludwig-Jahn
Sportpark

38

60

Topsstr

Voltastr

77

Ebersw

7

46

PRENZLAUER
BERG

37 67

Hussitenstr

74

Oderberger Str

18

19

Kastanienallee

58

Bernauer Str

66

63

Arkonaplatz

52

59

54

Bernauer
Str

Brunnenstr

Ruppinerstr

Schwedter Str

56

47

Bernauer Str

Strelitzer Str

Zionskirchplatz

76

Gedenkstätte
Berliner
Mauer

1

Anklamer Str

Fehrbelliner Str

31

Bergstr

Ackerstr

50

15

Chorinerstr

Nordbahnhof

Pappelplatz

Veteranenstr

Volkspark
Weinberg

Weinbergsweg

Pfefferberg

Invalidenstr

82

Teutoburger
Platz

8

Schlegelstr

Gartenstr

Bergstr

See map
p328

Tieckstr

Rosenthaler
Platz

Novalisstr

See map
p326

Torstr

53

Schönhauser
Tor

Linienstr

Rosenthaler Str

Gormannstr

Koppenplatz

Rosa-
Luxemburg-
Platz

SCHEUNENVIERTEL

Auguststr

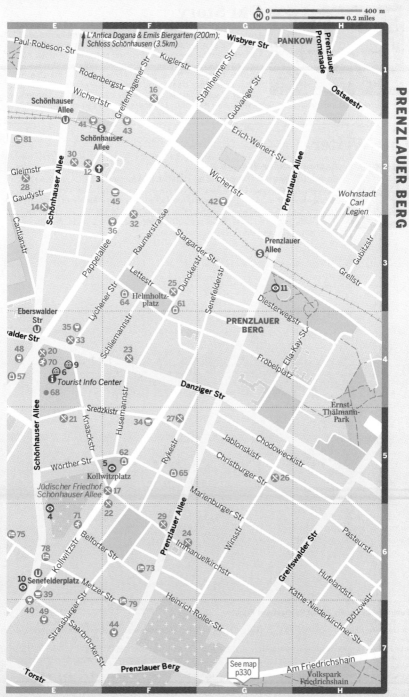

0 — 400 m
0 — 0.2 miles

PRENZLAUER BERG

Paul-Robeson-Str

L'Antica Dogana & Emils Biergarten (200m);
Schloss Schönhausen (3.5km)

Wisbyer Str   PANKOW

Prenzlauer Promenade

Ostseestr

Rodenbergstr   Kuglerstr

Wichertstr   Grefswhagener Str   16

Stahlheimer Str   Gudvanger Str

Schönhauser Allee   41   43   Erich-Weinert-Str

Prenzlauer Allee

81   Schönhauser Allee

30   12   3

Gleimstr   28   Wichertstr

Gaudystr   14   42   Wohnstadt Carl Legien

Cantianstr   45   Prenzlauer Allee   Gubitzstr

36   32   Grellstr

Pappelallee   Raumerstrasse   Stargarder Str

Lettestr   Dunckerstr   Senefelderstr   11   Diesterwegstr

Lychener Str   25   64   Helmholtzplatz   61

Eberswalder Str   35   PRENZLAUER BERG   Ella-Kay-Str

walder Str   33   Schliemannstr   23   Fröbelplatz

48   20   70   6   9   Danziger Str   Ernst-Thälmann-Park

57   Tourist Info Center   68

Schönhauser Allee   21   Knaackstr   Husemannstr   34   27   Jablonskistr   Chodowieckistr

Wörther Str   62   Rykestr   Christburger Str   26

5   65

Kollwitzplatz   Marienburger Str   Pasteurstr

Jüdischer Friedhof Schönhauser Allee   17   22   29   Winsstr   Greifswalder Str   Hufelandstr

4   71   24   Immanuelkirchstr   Käthe-Niederkirchner-Str

75   78   73   Bötzowstr

10   Senefelderplatz   Metzer Str   79

39   Prenzlauer Allee   Heinrich-Roller-Str

40   49   Strassburger Str   Saarbrücker Str   44

Torstr   Prenzlauer Berg   See map p330   Am Friedrichshain   Volkspark Friedrichshain

Our Story

A beat-up old car, a few dollars in the pocket and a sense of adventure. In 1972 that's all Tony and Maureen Wheeler needed for the trip of a lifetime – across Europe and Asia overland to Australia. It took several months, and at the end – broke but inspired – they sat at their kitchen table writing and stapling together their first travel guide, *Across Asia on the Cheap*. Within a week they'd sold 1500 copies. Lonely Planet was born.

Today, Lonely Planet has offices in Franklin, London, Melbourne, Oakland, Beijing and Delhi, with more than 600 staff and writers. We share Tony's belief that 'a great guidebook should do three things: inform, educate and amuse'.

Our Writer

Andrea Schulte-Peevers

Born and raised in Germany and educated in London and at UCLA, Andrea has travelled the distance to the moon and back in her visits to some 75 countries, but her favourite place in the world is still Berlin. She's written about her native country for two decades and authored or contributed to some 80 Lonely Planet titles, including all editions of this guide, the *Germany* country guide, the *Discover Germany* guide and the *Pocket Berlin* guide.

Published by Lonely Planet Publications Pty Ltd
ABN 36 005 607 983
9th edition – Feb 2015
ISBN 978 1 74321 392 6
© Lonely Planet 2015   Photographs © as indicated 2015
10 9 8 7 6 5 4 3 2 1
Printed in China